The
Sociology of Law:
A
Conflict Perspective

Charles E. Reasons
The University of Calgary
Calgary, Alberta

Robert M. Rich
Consulting Criminologist
Alexandria, Virginia

Butterworths
Toronto

CANADA:
  BUTTERWORTH & CO. (CANADA) LTD.
    TORONTO: 2265 MIDLAND AVENUE, SCARBOROUGH, M1P 4S1

UNITED KINGDOM:
  BUTTERWORTH & CO. (PUBLISHERS) LTD.
    LONDON: 88 KINGSWAY, WC2B 6AB

AUSTRALIA:
  BUTTERWORTH PTY. LTD.
    SYDNEY: 586 PACIFIC HIGHWAY, CHATSWOOD, NSW 2067
    MELBOURNE: 343 LITTLE COLLINS STREET, 3000
    BRISBANE: 240 QUEEN STREET, 4000

NEW ZEALAND:
  BUTTERWORTHS OF NEW ZEALAND LTD.
    WELLINGTON: 77-85 CUSTOM HOUSE QUAY, 1

SOUTH AFRICA:
  BUTTERWORTH & CO. (SOUTH AFRICA) (PTY.) LTD.
    DURBAN: 152/154 GALE STREET

Canadian Cataloguing in Publication Data

  Reasons, Charles E., 1945-
    The sociology of law

  ISBN 0-409-86180-4 pa.

  1. Sociological jurisprudence - Addresses,
  essays, lectures.   I. Rich, Robert M.   II. Title.

K376.R42   340.1'15   C78-001180-5

To Pam and Trent

Preface

Our major purpose in doing this book is to provide a much
needed alternative to current sociology of law books. Most books
in the sociology of law either take a functionalist approach toward
the study of law or fail to present an explicit theoretical perspective. Furthermore, they largely fail to address the role of ideology,
politics and the state in the analysis of law. We present the major
paradigms in the sociology of law, with particular emphasis upon
conflict and Marxist approaches. Also, we provide cross-national
analysis of the socio-political basis of law in various ideological
settings. Finally, the often neglected issue of praxis is addressed
for those concerned with the relationship between thinking and
doing. Generally, we hope that this work will act as a catalyst for
those concerned with the law and legal institutions.

Part One provides a number of different meanings of law.
While the meaning of law is often assumed to be self evident, the
articles in this section point out a wide variety of meanings. From
traditional perspectives to Marxist analysis, the meaning one gives
to law is very much ideologically based.

The relationship between jurisprudence and sociology is
discussed in the second part. Two opposing approaches are
presented which identify differing ideological basis for the study
of law and for the role of such study in society. These articles
highlight contemporary debates concerning the role of science in
social policy analysis and social change.

An increasingly significant issue in the study of society and
human behaviour is the basic way social scientists approach their
subject matter. Such differences in paradigms are the topic for
Part III. The two major paradigms are analyzed with particular
attention given to the emerging conflict paradigm.

In Part IV law and socio-political structure are addressed.
Through an analysis of the emergence of the nation state and its
subsequent ideological variations the import of socio-political
structure upon legal form and content is dramatically evident.
Emphasis is particularly focused upon non-Western legal forms
and their basis in differing social, cultural and political settings.

Both the use of law for social change and the impact of social
change upon the law are the subject of Part V. While law is often
viewed as a mechanism for social change, one must analyze the
social, cultural and political context in which such efforts are
taken. Furthermore, the fact that legal institutions are often more a
reflection of society than a creator of it becomes evident in
analysis of nation-states which undergo dramatic changes.

The final section discusses the relationship between one's
theory of law and one's involvement in social change. How does
the student of law and society approach the world about him? The

articles in this section provide some suggestions for those
concerned with both ideas and action.

Charles E. Reasons
Robert M. Rich

Acknowledgments

We would like to acknowledge the help of two secretaries (who wish to remain anonymous) for their help in completing this manuscript. Also, our two undergraduate reviewers—Trudie Smith and Linda Charmaine Spencer—provided cogent commenting plus help in the tedious aspects of preparation of the manuscript. Finally, we would like to thank those whose contributions are included in the book.

Table of Contents

PART ONE

THE MEANING OF LAW

Law Definitions

The search for *the* meaning of law has long been a concern for the sociology of law whether from a civil or criminal law, jurisprudential, or anthropological perspective. Reviews of the literature by Akers and Hawkins, and Rich indicate that there are almost as many definitions of law as there are theorists.[1]

Selznick in an article in *The International Encyclopedia of the Social Sciences*, Gould and Kolb in *A Dictionary of the Social Sciences*, and *Black's Law Dictionary* all give definitions of law which are quite specific.[2] For example Black defines law as

> . . . that which is laid down, ordained, or established. A rule or method according to which phenomenon or actions co-exist or follow each other. That which must be obeyed and followed by citizens, subject to sanctions or legal consequences.[3]

Pennock in *A Dictionary of the Social Sciences* defines law

> . . . as a rule of human conduct that the bulk of the members of a given political community recognize as binding upon all its members —this recognition being induced by certain factors such as general obedience to the rule, the organization of sanctions for its enforcement and of procedures for its interpretation and application, and a general conviction of the rightness of the rule especially when this conviction is reinforced by the knowledge that others believe it right or at least act in accordance with it.[4]

Feeley

In the first article, Feeley notes that the most important feature of these definitions and literature surveys is a common understanding of the law concept. He states that most theorists define law as a command or order to do or refrain from doing some specified act or acts and is distinguished from other norms by the threat of physical coercion attached to the order.

Feeley's major premise is that current research in sociology of law is misguided and suffers from several shortcomings. In particular he challenges the command definition of law and the function of sanction within this coercive legal definition. Further more, the inadequate use of the legal concept leads researchers to vague and more or less useless statements about law and society.

The first shortcoming is the problem of goal identification. Feeley states that the "legal effectiveness" approach posits the ideal or goal of a law as a benchmark and then measures the extent to which it is or is not being met. Research characterized in terms of the examination of the gap between "law-in-theory" and the "law-in-action" is a normative endeavor which is value-biased. Thus, there is a problem in comprehension of legal

language so the researcher does not clearly know how to measure
the effects of an ambiguous law. Secondly, the researcher may
misinterpret or impose his own interpretation of the law in terms
of its stated goal and reach a biased conclusion regarding the
research on the statute. This may be more a quality of the civil
law but it certainly is not of the criminal law. The latter must be
quite specific as to purpose and goal attainment so that Feeley is
only partially correct in his criticism of the "legal effectiveness
approach".

Another problem is whether law is so distinctive a social
phenomena that it can serve as a core concept in the development
of general social theory. Feeley states that law does not perform a
unique social function, nor is it a singular form of social control.
Law does not appear to be a fundamental phenomenon. It is not
ubiquitous, and its nature varies. Thus, a basic social theory is
not likely to be formed around the law concept. Feeley does not
think it useful to search for a general theory of law since he
considers the concept as not universal. He believes there is a
distinction between law and authority which is blurred by
theorists who feel that law is generic. This interpretation would
depend on one's analysis of data gathered from traditional as well
as industrial societies' socio-legal structures. Further, one would
also have to examine the evaluation of both civil and criminal law
in a given society to determine whether law is generic.

The last problem of most research is its unwillingness to
consider a new definition of the legal concept since most theorists
accept the definition that law is a direct command supported by
the threat of sanctions. Feeley thinks the concept of law as
command is overly static (i.e., as direct commands requiring
particular responses). This view ignores laws that do not define
and mandate specific behaviour (i.e., laws which define and give
legitimacy to official public positions and grant some degree of
open-ended discretion).

Secondly, the command concept of law ignores other forms of
law and is only appropriate for the criminal law. Feeley describes
three other forms of law other than the usual command form.
Laws are also status conferring (i.e., selectively extend or withhold officially recognized status to certain classes of people).
Similar to status conferring laws are laws which define individual
rights as against the government. The last form of law is based on
selective incentives which distribute rewards rather than punish.

These other forms of law, in contrast to the law as command,
are predominantly found in the civil law, especially the laws of
contract and equity. Feeley appears to be concerned over lack of
research into civil law and too much emphasis on criminal law
studies. Thus, he is suggesting that theorists develop a broader
concept of the law. He also feels that the legal concept should be
reformulated in terms of its functions and its forms.

Theorists are preoccupied with the law as command concept

according to Feeley and are not concerned with either the law of tort or the manifest and latent functions of law. There is also little concern with research on the multiplicity of functions of laws. He believes policy making decisions of national scope preoccupy the theorist's research endeavors. The forms of law can be likened to a continuum with commands and field controls of aggregates as the polar extremities. Command law is direct and applies to all members of a class while laws designed to manipulate fields apply to a part of a class and aim at indirectly controlling peoples' behaviour. Feeley perceives the law as both an instrument of social control and change that can be used in both direct and indirect ways to alter public policy as well as private behavior.

Finally, Feeley's research concerns the focus of an enlarged analysis of the sociology of law. He examines a number of concepts such as Black's process of legal mobilization, the general preventive effects of law, and law as a pricing mechanism.

Feeley contends that the mechanics of dispute processing or mobilization have several weaknesses as a concept, such as: a failure to identify the nature of legal agencies and the scope and boundaries of the mobilization process; downplaying the power of law to resolve issues through anticipatory reaction and informal application; and concentrating on the analysis of specific orders emanating from trouble cases that have reached the court. The mobilization concept does not recognize the fact that law may be used to control people in a variety of ways (i.e., the law is often set in motion by individuals who apply it to themselves and others without the utilization of legal institutions).

The general preventive effects of law approach is not as narrow as the concern with mobilization and trouble cases in formal governmental settings but is limited in the same way as the command concept of law. Feeley modifies the approach by altering the concepts of general and specific prevention to general and specific effects. General effects refer to the public results of a particular law or laws including those indirect effects not necessarily perceived by those whose activity is being regulated. Specific effects refer to the processes and effects of laws which require active participation by people in organizing the law to resolve a dispute or claim.

Law as a pricing mechanism examines the ways in which legal changes affect the costs of engaging in an activity. This conception sees laws as a subtle pricing mechanism which attempts to stimulate or slow public or private processes by varying the costs of participation. By adjusting the costs of an activity, both individuals and organizations must change their form of interaction. Thus this approach to law does not examine only prohibitions or requirements but deals with adjustments that have general effects on the rate and duration of an activity (i.e., control activities through environment manipulating devices producing indirect effects on persons and organizations).

Feeley's attempt to broaden the law concept and to examine legal functions and forms has not lead to a crystallization of thought on the subject but, as Feeley himself states, to a rationale for the elimination of a distinct theory of the sociology of law. Furthermore, his claim that his own research clearly shows that the law is a result of the practice of political power is only indirectly demonstrated.

Feeley demonstrates from the data presented that he is a structural-functionalist, not a conflict theorist. His conceptual framework is concerned with an analysis of existing theoretical views of law and society and their limitations. His reformulation of the legal concept in terms of the *functions and forms* of law is also structural-functionalist as is his so-called "expanded view" of the law and society field. There is no attempt to examine the sociology of law field from a radical perspective (*i.e.*, Marxian or conflict theory) or is there an attempt to view the field from a social action or social interactionist perspective. Therefore, Feeley's critique of the legal concept and of the law and society field is one of applying formal organizational and economic theories to the analysis of the legal institution. His approach is to replace one form of institutional analysis (*i.e.*, criminal justice) with another (*i.e.*, commerce and industry). Thus criminal law as command is replaced by civil law (*i.e.*, law merchant and equity law).

Quinney

A radical approach to the Western concept of law is proposed by Quinney who is convinced that our traditional view of the inevitability of law is a myth which is perpetuated by those in power.[5] A radical social theory of law will aid in the revision of our notions concerning law and order, natural law, civil liberties, civil disobedience, and morality.

The actual role of law in society is quite different from what we have been traditionally told. The structural-functional or consensus model perceives law as a special form of social control that exerts pressure upon each person so as to make him be a model citizen whose conduct conforms to societal norms. Therefore, law can be assumed to possess several characteristics. It is a societal product that reflects societal consciousness. It reflects the needs of society. It serves those interests that are for societal good, and it orders individual and group disputes in the name of social order. This mythical view of law regards it as an instrument of society that controls diversity and change in the name of social order and consistency. Thus, law is used for the good of the whole society.

Social theorists have traditionally believed that laws protect

all citizens and bring order, progress, and civilization to humanity. This idea of law is based on the traditional (*i.e.*, structural-
functional) assumption that humanity must be controlled and
regulated for the good of both the individual and the society.
Quinney believes that traditional structural-functional theorists
(*i.e.*, consensus) perpetuate the myth of law and order through use
of the concept of the rule of law (*i.e.*, to obey the law is a good, a
moral absolute). This conception of law as a tool for the maintenance of the status-quo is abhorrent to Quinney since this is an
ideological weapon used to maintain the dominance of the upper
classes over the rest of society. In reality, the law of the people is
the law of the elite used to promote and protect its own interests.

The concept of natural law plays an important role in
Quinney's radical view of law. Radical theory perceives natural
law as a tool protecting the rights of each member of society as
well as the rights of social groups within society. Only man and
collectivities of men have rights as society and its institutions do
not possess these inalienable rights. Government is only a tool of
the people and can be valued only as long as it serves the people.
It has no moral value if it serves only the elite and their representatives. Legal positivism and its structural-functional adherents
hold a view of natural law which Quinney opposes since it
minimizes individual freedom and the right of revolution (*i.e.*, the
good of society rather than the good of the individual is stressed
so that societal demands rather than individual rights are met).

Individual freedom is a right guaranteed by the concept of
natural law but is more a theoretical concept than a practical
application according to Quinney. Civil liberties are abstractly
guaranteed and are the province of the ruling class which controls
the government and economy. Only when the goverment is controlled by the people can civil liberties and the greater issue of
human rights be secured.

The related concept of civil disobedience faces the same
problem in application as the concept of individual freedom (*i.e.*, it
is more for the protection of the elite and their authority structure
than for the right of citizens to express their dissatisfaction with
the functioning of contemporary government). Civil disobedience
does not coincide with the elitist position that it is more important
to preserve law and order than it is to allow a fair and equitable
life for the average member of society. Civil disobedience may be
a moral right but the legal system of society must be obeyed no
matter how unjust it is in reality. Verbal expression of opinion
differences may be tolerated but refusal to obey governmental
commands cannot be tolerated unless the majority of the people
challenge the government.

From the conflict perspective of Quinney, the structural-
functionalist interpretation of the role of civil disobedience in
society is false. The individual who breaks the law in the name of
civil disobedience is not bound by the rules of the system since to

obey the system is to preserve it. According to Quinney, if the law is immoral, then violation of it is not to be considered immoral. Thus, violations of laws which reflect an oppressive government or governmental policy are justified in the name of human rights.

Civil disobedience can never succeed in society since the elite control public opinion, the government, and the law. The true will of the majority can never be expressed unless the law is changed. However, the legal system of society is controlled by the government which is under the grip of the elite. This aspect of Quinney's argument appears inconsistent since only an overthrow of the elite will bring about the ultimate changes required to create a new society and legal system.

    To have a legal system or not is a debatable point to Quinney. Many theorists assume that a legal system stripped of its moralistic overtones would be a more just system. For instance, the criminal law could abolish all crimes without victims (i.e., drunkenness, prostitution, gambling, etc.) and thus eliminate moral bias. Quinney believes that the criminal law is inherently moralistic. Thus, legal reform or revolution cannot be accomplished by eliminating morality from the law since one form of morality or another determines the form and function of criminal law (i.e., egalitarian, totalitarian, etc).

    Quinney's solution to the problem of bringing about change in the legal system is a faith in a natural law of human rights. One must be educated to the fact that the law exists to protect the status quo and is utilized to prevent the changes that will make all citizens free. The law and order doctrine as a positive absolute value is spread by the elite in order to control the masses and stifle dissent. The elitist authority structure uses the law not only to control the masses but to further its own purposes.

    Specific alternative solutions to the problem of an elitist criminal law system are advocated by Quinney. The criminal law could be abolished since it does not prevent or control crime anyway. Secondly, the criminal law statutes could be kept as symbols of how people should behave but never be enforced. A more realistic solution to the law problem is to decentralize it since one criminal code can not deal with the realities of a pluralistic society. Quinney believes that the problem with the criminal law has been acceptance of a centralized system of control. He feels that a decentralized government would provide the basis for a democratic criminal law which would stress subcultural differences rather than legal substance. Law outside the culture area (i.e., regional, rural-urban) would only provide for the regulation of needed services such as health, transportation, and welfare. This decentralized legal system would ultimately create a life for all free of oppression and allow people to become truly liberated. This solution of decentralization of the criminal law may be no solution at all since, in the United States, the fifty sovereign states were set up originally to cater to subcultural needs. This state autonomy has worked to the detriment of human rights in several areas which is why in the late 1950's the Supreme Court and Congress began centralizing the criminal codes to make them all begin to conform to offer more basic rights to all citizens. Thus, it appears Quinney would have us go backward to a utopian idea founded in a gemeinschaft social order which increasingly has failed in our gesselschaft reality.

The radical approach employed by Quinney is self-evident from his attack upon what he calls the liberal consensus theorists. The argument he puts forward concerning elite control of the state and its political and legal systems is a clear example of exposing the myths of contemporary society. Quinney's analysis of the shortcomings of the legal system points up his theoretical shifts as a theorist since 1969 when he began to seriously question the structural-functional approach.[6] In 1970 he presented a conflict perspective which is evidenced by his concern with exposing the myths of a criminal justice system and his theoretical attempt to find a better legal system for society. By 1977 Quinney's intellectual position shifted from a non-Marxian conflict perspective to a Marxian perspective. His search for a theory proposing a legal system free from control by elites utilizing a non-Marxian approach had obviously failed him intellectually. Thus, in *Class, State, and Crime* he proposes a socialist theory of law and criminal justice.

Balbus

Balbus outlines the essentials of a Marxian theory of law in the last article of this section.[7] He rejects both the formalist and instrumentalist approaches to law, emphasizing the notion that law must be explained by the systemic requirements of capitalism. Thus, while the law is relatively autonomous from the will of social actors, it derives its essential meaning and direction from the commodity form of capitalist society.

After reviewing the logic of the commodity form, he discusses the logic of the legal form. Individuals become commodities which are viewed legally as equal, although qualitatively different. The notion of one man one vote is the universal political equivalent commodity form which makes an abstraction of real men. The law as a universal political equivalent precludes qualitatively different interests and social origins of individuals from entering into the calculus of political exchange. Therefore, the legal form eliminates distinct interests and social origins out of existence with such abstractions as "will" and "rights" replacing the actual needs of socially differentiated individuals.

The emphasis upon individual equality in capitalist society

ignores class differences and social inequalities. Such an emphasis reinforces systemic inequalities by detracting from the formation of needed class consciousness for substantive equality. Individualism is an alienated form of individuality and the legal form is in essence a religious form. By appealing to "common interest" or "public interest", the recognition of class interests is thwarted.

Legal obligations are wed to the concrete particularisms of capitalist society. A socialist society would transcend alienated self-interest and abstract universalism of legal obligation, with individuals acting as social individuals bound by the concrete universal of social need. Delegitimation requires a break from the logic of equality such that a rich person would pay more for an offense than a poor person, *i.e.*, class justice. Our fetishism of laws is evident when we view it as autonomous (as if we owe our existence to it), rather than law being a product of our efforts.

While the law serves the interests of capital as a class (not necessarily individual capitalists), the form of capitalism is changing. The transformation from competitive capitalism-legalism to monopoly capitalism-technocracy suggests a decline in the commodity form.

Conclusion

A comparison of the three theoretical postions presented (*i.e.*, Feeley, Quinney, and Balbus) shows a common dissatisfaction with traditional definitions of the law although different solutions are presented to this dissatisfaction. Feeley takes the structural-functional view with only a vague awareness of conflict theory, let alone other theoretical perspectives. On the other hand, Quinney takes a radical view of sociology of law, with Balbus presenting a Marxist theory of law.

It should be noted that the three theorists basically are concerned with the failure of traditional (*i.e.*, structural-functional) theory to define and explain crime and criminal behavior in the post-industrial American society. Feeley wants to borrow intellectually from other disciplines rather than radically depart from traditional theory while Quinney has totally abandoned structural-functionalism and is seeking radical theories to explain the evolution of law and criminality within industrial society. Balbus places law and the legal form within the context of capitalism in his Marxist analysis. It should now be evident that the kind of research and the social change implications vary for each approach presented above.

NOTES

1.   Ronald Akers and Richard Hawkins, *Law and Control in Society*. New Jersey: Prentice-Hall, 1975, pp. 5-15; Robert Rich, *The Sociology of Law: An Introduction to its Theorists and Theories*. Washington, D.C.: University Press of America, 1977.

2.   Phillip Selznick, "The Sociology of Law", in *The International Encyclopedia of the Social Sciences*. New York: Free Press, 1968, pp. 50-58: Julius Gould and William Kolb, *A Dictionary of the Social Sciences*. New York: Free Press, 1964, pp. 378-380; and Henry Black, *Black's Law Dictionary*. St. Paul: West Publishing Company, 1968, pp. 1028-1029.

3.   Henry Black, *op. cit.*, 1028.

4.   Gould and Kolb, *op. cit.*, 378

5.   For a radical definition of crime see Herman Schwendinger and Julia Schwendinger, "Defenders of Order or Guardians of Human Rights?" *Issues in Criminology* 5 (Summer, 1970): 123-157, and Herman Schwendinger and Julia Schwendinger, "Social Class and the Definition of Crime," *Crime and Social Justice* 7 (Spring-Summer, 1977): 4-14.

6.   Richard Quinney, *Crime and Justice in Society*. Boston: Little, Brown and Company, 1969, pp. 1-20; Quinney, *Social Reality of Crime*. Boston: Little, Brown and Company, 1970; Quinney, *Class, State, and Crime: On the Theory and Practice of Criminal Justice*. New York: David McKay Company, 1977.

7.   For discussions of this approach see Taylor, Walton, and Young, *The New Criminology*. New York: Harper and Row, 1973, pp. 252-267; Piers Beirne, "Marxism and the Sociology of Law: Theory or Practice", *British Journal of Law and Society* 2 (Summer, 1975): 78-81; Jay Weinrotn, "A Marxian View of Crime", *Philosophy in Context* 2 (1973): 33-40; Paul Q. Herst, "Marx and Engels on Law, Crime and Morality", *Economy and Society* 1 (February, 1972): 28-56; Stephen K. Mugford, "Marxism and Criminology", *The Sociological Quarterly* 15 (Autumn, 1974): 591-96.

Chapter 1

The Concept of Laws in Social Science:
A Critique and Notes on
an Expanded View*

Malcolm M. Feeley†

I. Introduction

During the past decade there has been a resurgence of interest
in the problem of law and social control. Indicative of this
interest, a rekindling of an earlier tradition, is the founding of the
Law and Society Association and its journal the *Law & Society
Review*, the growth of course offerings both in law schools and
social science departments, and the emergence of a rapidly growing body of literature. Research interests in this area, often
captured by such terms as impact, compliance, legal effectiveness,
and law and social change, have diverged from the traditional
preoccupation with the development and meaning of formal legal
doctrine and from the more recent behavioral concerns with
judicial decisionmaking, to address the broader questions of the
effects of law on society at large.[1] While varying in breadth,
depth, and precise focus, most of this research treats law as an
independent variable and its consequences as the dependent
variables, the events *caused* by the law. In the language of

* Malcolm M. Feeley, "The Concept of Laws in Social Science: A Critique and
  Notes on an Expanded View," *Law & Society Review*, Vol. 10 (1976): 497-523.
  Reprinted by permission of the Law and Society Association.
  An earlier version of this paper was presented at the 1974 annual meetings of
  The American Political Science Association.
† Professor, Yale University.

systems theory, the formal legal rules are the "policy outputs" while changes—of whatever scope—are the "policy outcomes." Although these studies vary from one-shot case histories to projects involving multiple controls and multiple time series analyses, they all tend to conform to this general design.

Another distinguishing feature of this body of work is that it attempts to measure the *effectiveness* of laws. This problem is typically characterized as the examination of the "gap" between the *ideal* of the law and the *actual* practices flowing from it, and has led to searches for the characteristics that laws must possess and the social conditions that must be present if a law is to accomplish its stated goals. This concern is often accompanied by other questions as well. Under what conditions can law bring about *social* change or *attitude* change? Under what circumstances will law be obeyed? How efficacious is the deterrent function of the law? How important is law in maintaining social control?

The common basis of this research goes beyond a shared methodological perspective. The most important shared feature of this research is a common understanding of the concept of law and of its functions. Although most scholars do not explicitly define the concept of law, most contemporary social scientists hold an Austinian concept, and would probably agree in large measure with the following definition by Hoebel (1954:28):

> . . . for working purposes law may be defined in the terms: A social norm is legal if its neglect or infraction is regularly met, in threat or in fact, by the application of physical force by an individual or group possessing the socially recognized privilege of so acting.

That is, law is viewed as a command or order to do or refrain from doing some specified act(s), and is distinguished from other norms by the threat of physical coercion attached to the order.[2]

In sum, despite many important differences, two main features characterize the approaches of most of the current social science research on law and society: 1) the basic research problem is regarded as the investigation of the "gap" between the legal ideal and actual practices, and 2) law is understood as a command supported by sanction. It is my contention that both these views are inadequate and misleading. The characterization of the research problem as the examination of the "gap" between the "ideal" and "real" is theoretically indefensible, and the characterization of law as command is much too narrow. The result is that little theoretically useful work is being pursued, and that generalizations about the functioning of law are based on too narrow a notion of law. In the following sections I shall examine both these assertions, propose some alternatives, and then move toward development of a more inclusive framework.

II. Shortcomings of Current Approaches

A. Problems of Goal Identification

A standard feature of the legal effectiveness approach is to posit the *ideal* or *goal* of a law as a benchmark and then measure the extent to which it is or is not being met. Thus, for instance, it has been argued (e.g., by Wasby, 170: 247ff) that the Supreme Court's reapportionment decisions were relatively successful in securing their intended consequences while the school desegregation decisions were not. Implicit in such an approach is the assumption that it is possible to identify, operationalize, and measure the goals of the law. Goals may be drawn from the explicit language of the law or discerned as implicit in the law. Others may cast their nets more broadly, contrasting actual practices with a generalized ideal or set of standards regarded as implicit in the *spirit* of the law.[3]

Interestingly, the specification of such goals—the law-in-theory—is rarely regarded as problematic by the researchers who follow this approach.[4] Typically legal goals tend to be viewed as self-evident or easily identified and are posited without much ado. Frequently they are not even restated by the researchers with much precision or explicitness.[5] Thus the basis of comparision—the *standard* against which reality is measured—is rarely clearly identified and operationalized.[6] This is a common feature of both narrowly drawn studies and more ambitious ones. One indication of their vagueness is that these posited ideals can often be countered with distinctly different views that others have derived from the same body of laws.[7]

An approach which characterizes a research problem in terms of the examination of the gap between the law-in-theory and the law-in-action is essentially a normative not a scientific endeavor.[8] Ironically, the very feature that may make it appear to be "objective" is the very cause of its value biases. There are two dimensions to this problem.

First, the language of the law is frequently so vague that the specific behavior it "commands" is not unambiguous or clearly derivable from it. The nature of the judicial and legislative process tends to institutionalize this ambiguity. Appellate judges frequently make new laws by haltingly moving away from an unsatisfactory position rather than precisely stating a new goal, and legislators frequently can agree only by increasing the ambiguity of statutory language. The task of goal specification becomes even more complicated as one moves away from the examination of a narrow and relatively specific rule to a complex of interrelated court rulings, legislative actions, and administrative directives. Here the task of specifying precise goals frequently gives way to the elaboration of a more generalized set of expectations (*i.e.*, the "spirit" of the laws) which cannot meaningfully be broken down into constituent elements whose effects can be independently measured.

There is a second and much more serious obstacle to this "effectiveness" approach. By focusing on a single goal or set of goals—the formally stated purpose—a serious distortion is introduced into the analysis. What is posited in the name of detached objectivity as "the" goals or purposes of the law can in fact be a substitution of the researcher's own—or someone else's—goals and values for those held either by the promulgators or the "recipients" of the law. For example, in studying the implementation of provisions of the Safe Streets Act of 1968 which mandate the development of statewide criminal justice plans, I met with responses varying from a belief that the provisions ultimately envision a single state criminal justice budget to a belief that they may be virtually ignored since the "real" purpose of the Act was purely symbolic. Thus by adopting as a standard or benchmark the literal (or implied) *formal* goals of the law, considerable ambiguity and unsuspected bias may creep into the analysis. Social scientists tend to be suspicious of formal declarations of the goals of formal organizations (Etzioni, 1960; Mohr, 1973). The law seems especially worthy of this same skepticism.

B.   Is Law Generic?

So far my criticism of the legal effectiveness approach has been methodological, focusing on the problems of identifying the goals of laws. Another problem that can appropriately be raised here is whether law is so distinctive a social phenomena that it can serve as a *core* concept in the development of general social theory. My answer is that it *probably* is not: law does not perform a unique social function, nor is it a singular form of social control. Hence it need not be singled out for separate theoretical concern. Legal rules are only one of a number of systems of rules, often overlapping and entwined, which shape people's aspirations and actions, and by which they are judged and resolve their troubles. In different cultures and at different times, law performs different functions and is entwined in different ways with other forms of social control and methods of dispute settlement. What may be regulated by law at one time or in one setting may very well be controlled by informal peer group pressure, self-help, or other authoritative institutions in another.[9] Law, unlike kinship, language, or power, does not seem to be a fundamental phenomenon. Unlike these other phenomena law is not ubiquitous, and its nature varies; hence it does not capture a constant, identifiable activity, process, or set of relationships around which basic social theory is likely to be formed.

My argument here is in contrast to Selznick (1969), who takes the position that law is a fundamental social process, and who explicitly seeks a theory of the distinctively legal. Interested as he is, in private institutions and justice, Selznick (1969:4) argues that:

> If we are to study justice in industry, or in any other specialized institution, we must first be clear that law is found in many settings; it is not uniquely associated with the state. We need a concept of law that is sufficiently general to embrace legal experience within "private" associations, but not so general as to make law lose its distinctive character or become equivalent to social control.

When an institution possesses authority and issues rules, it is, according to this formulation, a legal order. Selznick writes (1969:5,7): "A legal order is known by the existence of authoritative rules," and "We should see law as endemic in all institutions that rely for social control on formal authority and rule-making." The argument that law is generic appears convincing, but only because "the view of law sketched here assimilates the theory of law to the theory of authority" (1969:7). The two concepts are joined into one; they incorporate each other.

But this may be forcing uniformity at the expense of great distortion. To equate the two concepts in the search for a sufficiently general phenomenon may point to the ubiquity of rule-governed behavior, and may lead to a useful understanding of the normative order, but it seems also to lose sight of important distinctive features of what are commonly considered *legal* rules. To equate the law of the state with the "law" of the internal operations of the corporation, the "law" of the monastery, and perhaps the rules of grammar, is I think to obscure important differences, differences that other readers of jurisprudence would not so readily abandon, and differences which are rooted in the traditional concerns of social scientists, who grant coercion a greater function in the legal order than does Selznick. To assimilate the two concepts may lead to the blurring over of the very distinction and question that is central to much sociolegal research: under what conditions does law supplant other forms of authority?

To suggest that coercion occupies a more distinctive element in the concept of law than Selznick appears to give it, is not however, to argue that law is nothing other than an arrangement of static commands to be followed upon fear of pain and suffering. As I argue below, such a narrow concept of law has already impoverished too much social science research on legal phenomena. But virtually to abandon coercion as a *necessary* element in the concept is, I think, to err in the opposite direction, and Selznick, although he attempts to, provides no convincing reason for doing so. He writes (1969:8):

> To equate law and the state impoverishes sociological analysis, because the concept of law should be available for study of any setting in which human conduct is subject to explicit rule-making; and when we deny the place of law in specialized institutions we withhold from

the private setting the funded experience of the political community in matters of governance.

This appeal is not convincing. It fails because it confuses similarity with identity. That there are similarities among various types of authoritative systems of rules no one would deny. That insights can be shared and generalized no one would deny. Even to grant the "funded experience of the political community in matters of governance" to the "private setting" does not require that the two be totally equated. Similarities, even great similarities, need not be taken for identities, especially when the distinctions serve useful purposes.

If law is in fact distinct in certain ways from other types of authoritative systems of rules, then it may not provide a useful focus for development of general social theory. What is distinctively legal in one culture may not be so in another. A dispute which in one society might be resolved by legal institutions may in another be pursued by self-help. If this is the case, dispute processing, not law, seems to be the more general social process around which social theory might be constructed. Law is only one possible component of the process, and clearly an exclusive focus on law would provide an incomplete understanding of dispute processing. In this perspective, there is no need—indeed it would be incorrect—to attempt to factor out and treat separately that which is distinctively legal.

However, law obviously does deserve particularly careful attention from social scientists. Although its range and method vary across cultures and time, law permeates many walks of life, provides insights into many types of social processes, and in modern societies has assumed ever-increasing importance as a means of social control. These are reasons enough for considerable attention. My argument here is intended to cast doubt only on the wisdom of searching for a general theory of the *distinctively* legal.[10]

C.   Deficiencies of the Received Concept of Law

Most contemporary research on law and society suffers from its unwillingness to even consider a definition of the concept of law and hence the boundaries of investigation. This reluctance is perhaps the most widely shared feature of social scientists interested in law.[11] While it is dangerous to generalize about such an open-ended body of literature, my point is supported, I think, by the paucity of conceptual analysis of the central term—law—in most of the articles reprinted in six widely circulated law and society readers.[12] With but a few exceptions the authors of these articles accept uncritically and without comment a view of law as direct command supported in varying degrees by the threat of sanctions. Indeed, most of the pieces reprinted in these volumes deal with the criminal law, and even when they do not, the criminal law-command paradigm is often maintained in discussions of regulatory activities.

There are a number of weaknesses in this conception of law as command. Two in particular seem to have adversely affected social science research: 1) the conception of law as command is overly static, and 2) it is so preoccupied with a criminal law model that it ignores other forms of laws.

By overly static I mean that law tends to be characterized as a set of do's and don't's, as direct commands requiring specifiable, particular responses. Such a view ignores laws that do not define and mandate specific behavior. Kelsen and many others have argued that systems of laws are composed of a mixture of both static and dynamic norms and have criticized Austin's conception of law for being exclusively preoccupied with only some types of static norms. This seems to be a needed corrective to most current social science conceptions of law as well. Following Kelsen's terminology, static norms are provisions which require specific behavior or define specific actions. While broader than commands, they would include the stark do's and don't's issued by Austin's sovereign. On the other hand, dynamic norms are laws about laws; they define offices and grant authority to designated persons or offices. They may specify the ways in which additional norms are to be enacted, outline the boundaries of official discretion, and prescribe procedures for the exercise of power. They define, for instance, who is a public official. Further, actions by public officials derive from such laws and many important public policies may be traced to them. Thus, for example, specific, non-generalized decisions to send troops to Little Rock, or alter the prime interest rate, or redraw school district boundaries—all of which are lawful orders—all stem from open-ended dynamic norms, rather than from static laws mandating specific behavior. Most public policy-making is of this sort—filling out specifics or acting within a broadly drawn plan—as is obvious when the great variety of government administrative behavior is considered. Thus the laws which define and give legitimacy to official public positions and grant some degree of open-ended discretion are important aspects of legal behavior. They seem to me to be of particular concern precisely because they grant authority to engage in actions of great importance but also of extremely low visibility.

The second weakness involves the limited perspectives of the command model of law. This model, most appropriate for the substantive criminal law, ignores a variety of other important forms of law, such as laws which simply define, laws which confer rights, and laws which provide selective incentives rather than negative sanctions. Although these are all important means of shaping public policies, none of them can easily be characterized as a command and it is probably for this reason that they are generally ignored in most discussions of law and social control.

Laws of *definition* simply define, they do not command. Nor are sanctions necessarily directly attached to them. For instance, in order to obtain a valid driver's license a person must be over eighteen, have good eyesight, and pass a driving test. Legal rules spell out these conditions. If one wants a license they must be followed; if they are not, no valid license is forthcoming. If a couple wants to be married, certain provisions must be met; if they are not, there is no valid marriage. If businessmen want a contract, they must follow certain procedures. If one wants an entitlement to property, certain conditions must be met.

To say that it is not particularly meaningful to speak of commands or compliance or noncompliance to these norms does not mean that they have no impact or significant effect on society or are not viewed instrumentally by public officials as means by which to pursue desired social change or control. Their impact is, however, likely to be in combination with other laws and actions and their effects indirect, in contrast to the command type of laws. The possession of a valid driver's license, marriage certificate, school diploma or piece of land are necessary for a host of subsequent opportunities, both public and private, and the control of recruitment and access to such opportunities is in part accomplished by variously defining eligibility requirements and opportunity costs. This manipulation can in turn be used as a conscious instrument of social control and change.

Laws may also be *status* conferring rules. Such laws selectively extend or withhold officially recognized status to designated classes of people. Perhaps most obviously they identify and create public officials themselves. These status-conferring laws are important in allocating public benefits and deprivations. Perhaps even more important is their effect on benefits flowing from private sources. Public certification of educational achievement, property ownership or tax payment are not only important with respect to voting, holding public office or receiving government benefits, but also with respect to opportunities they facilitate (or impede) within the private sphere. Such status-conferring norms, while appearing on the surface to be neutral laws, can have a variety of decidedly non-neutral consequences. This fact has often been recognized and exploited by social planners.

Similar to status-conferring norms are laws which define individual rights as against the government. Their impact too cannot properly be understood in terms of the command model, although they may even take the form of commands. This is because one of their major functions may be to *facilitate* purely private activity. For instance, Arnold Rose (1954) compared voluntary associations in the United States and France. Noting their great variety and proliferation in the United States, in sharp contrast to their scarcity in France, Rose traced these differences to the variations in the laws of the two countries. He argues that American law (such as the First Amendment) performs an important facilitative function and tends to encourage and foster the growth of private voluntary organizations, while French law is restrictive and has a dampening effect. These laws, he concludes, have had profound consequences for mass political participation and the development of democratic institutions in the two countries. Most important for our present purpose, Rose asserts that these consequences are in part planned, conscious policies, not unanticipated by-products of other actions.

A more contemporary and perhaps more obvious example of the facilitative function of rights-laws is seen in the recent Supreme Court ruling on abortion. The full impact of this decision cannot meaningfully be captured by conventional impact analysis, which would characterize the ruling in terms of a command and would focus on how doctors, hospitals and legislatures responded to the decision. Rather, its most significant impact may be its symbolic legitimization of biological manipulation or its fostering a new definition of life and death. Other more immediate effects might be the altered number of women in the labor market, changes in size and composition of families, reductions in population growth, and changes in the class and ethnic composition of society. By varying the availability of abortion and contraception, Eastern European countries so I am told, have for a number of years attempted to affect the size of the labor force and the rate of population growth.

Provisions which selectively and strategically distribute incentives are another kind of law which is often ignored in the command view of law. Clearly the use of incentives is an important feature of legal policymaking, especially in a market economy and contract-oriented society where so much of government action takes the form of exerting marginal influence and control over activities nominally within the "private" sector. Perhaps the most obvious types of incentives are taxes, subsidies, and outright grants. Surprisingly, sociologists and political scientists have almost completely ignored these forms of law as instruments of calculated social control, leaving them to be considered by lawyers and economists. Although acknowledging that the power to tax is the power to destroy, political scientists have put little effort into the examination of the ways in which tax rates and coverage have been used to stimulate desired social ends or impede undesired activities (e.g., oil depletion allowances, capital gains tax rates, exemptions for certain organizations).[13] Sanctioning is a double-edged sword; not only can law shape conduct by the threat or application of negative sanctions, it can also pursue goals by selectively awarding benefits. Perhaps the most dramatic instance of such incentives is the Homestead Act of 1862, which provided free land and significantly affected the growth of the American West. Other examples of instrumental use of subsidies include tax breaks for home-owners, condemnation rights, cheap or free land to railroads, and lower than cost services to stimulate certain "private" activities and retard others.

Perhaps some societies have systems of legal rules comprised primarily of stark do's and don't's, but it is likely that most societies rely extensively on other forms of laws as well. These other forms provide especially subtle means of legal control, in part because they effectively render the influence of the state invisible, concealing the political character of social conflict and resource allocation. They facilitate and guide the development of private law-making (e.g., contracts), provide a means of effecting marginal adjustments in purely private processes, and generally provide for a far greater variety of alternatives than those available in a system of static rules in the form of stark commands.

Each of these several types of laws—definitions, status and right conferring, and selective incentives—are distinguishable from command laws in a number of ways. Usually their form is different. This no doubt has contributed to their being more or less ignored in social scientists' discussions of law and social control. Their impact too tends to follow a different path. Changes brought about by such laws are not likely to be formally stated, clearly identified or even widely acknowledged. Neither are they likely to be immediately obvious to the outside observer and at times even to *all* their sponsors. Further, in contrast to the bluntness of most command-type laws, these facilitative types of law are likely to pursue their ends by altering the *rates* of an activity rather than flatly prohibiting or requiring a prescribed pattern of behavior. In relatively stable complex societies and particularly in market-oriented societies, the various kinds of facilitative laws taken together are probably more important as instruments of change and control than are the blunt command-type laws.

III. A Reformulation of the Central Concept

A careful analysis of the nature and scope of law is required before empirical generalizations about its functioning can assume theoretical intelligibility. I have argued that the dominant Austinian conception of law pervading most of the social sciences is too narrow, and have identified several important forms of law which it tends to omit. This narrowness of concept, I have argued, has its parallel in the narrowness of empirical investigation and generalization. These observations in turn have prompted a brief examination of the functioning of other forms of law.

Although most sociologists and political scientists have steered away from such conceptual analysis, such concerns are central to the province of legal philosophy. Indeed analytic jurisprudence since Austin has been preoccupied with identifying the nature and scope of law and locating the role of coercive sanctions in the law. Both Kelsen (1961) and Hart (1961) have criticized the Austinian command model for its failure to include much that is commonly understood to be law.

To challenge the command model and its conception of the function of sanctions, one need not propose a definition of law altogether devoid of a coercive element.[14] Indeed even the harshest critics of the Austinian school have not abolished sanctions as a necessary element in the concept of law, but have sought to give them a more subtle and indirect function. For instance, I argued earlier that some laws are purely definitional, and have no sanctions attached to them. This does not mean, however, that coercion is not intimately entwined with such laws as they connect with other laws and practices. Obviously sanctions are associated with marriage laws, as any unmarried taxpayer can attest. I am not proposing here to make a substantive contribution to the continuing philosophical debate. Nor do I want to undertake an extended analysis of all the problems raised by such an inquiry. Rather I want to draw on the distilled wisdom of these discussions in order to enlarge the conceptual basis for orienting empirical investigation and developing social theory. My point is merely to emphasize that social scientists have not drawn on a concept of law that adequately addresses forms of law other than commands, a conceptual failure that has led to improperly drawn boundaries of investigation. More importantly, empirical investigations premised upon this initial failure have led to generalizations about law and society that are of questionable usefulness.

Having done little more than point to the need for development of a richer concept of law, I will here only suggest that a reformulated understanding must comprehend at least two features of the law: the variety of its *functions* and the variety of its *forms*.

A.   The Functions of Law

Are the purposes of laws stated directly, generally acknowledged by their framers, and obvious to the target population? While typically there may be a public consensus as to the literal intent and purpose of some criminal laws (even if the purposes are not always agreed with), there may be other less obvious functions of these laws as well. For other laws there may be little or no consensus on purpose at all. Not only do the manifest functions of laws require identification, so too do the variety of latent and indirect functions, for it is these "by-products" that may in fact have given rise to the law's passage. For instance, while tax laws are universally regarded as means of raising revenue, the variety of other purposes pursued through such laws may be less obvious to those affected by them, although clearly intended by the sponsors of the laws. Their importance as mechanisms of social control—apart from revenue raising and spending—must clearly be acknowledged.

Tort law provides another interesting example of the indirect social control functions of law. Tort law has evolved into a multi-faceted instrument capable of pursuing simultaneously a variety of important although not immediately obvious social control goals. If early theorists of tort law did not discuss them, such social control functions of tort law are not viewed as unanticipated consequences of the purely private law of torts, but rather are considered a vital component of the conscious (although not publicly visible) development of the law itself. Such diverse governmental policies as crime control and workman's compensation have all had their roots in the "private law" field of torts; and such questions as general deterrence, income distribution, and industrial growth are now included in theoretical discussions of the "private" law of torts.[15]

These features of tax and tort law are not, however, generally thought of by social scientists in terms of social control. Taxes by and large are viewed as devices to raise revenue, and tort law, if thought of at all, is viewed as a means by which private individuals can recover damages done them by others. Nevertheless, as my brief discussion suggests, important and wide-ranging public purposes are consciously pursued as seemingly by-products of the publicly announced purposes of these laws. But what may be regarded as a latent and inconsequential function for some may be manifest to others, and in modern societies complex laws are likely to be adopted and supported precisely because they are capable of pursuing a variety of diverse purposes simultaneously. Because they are preoccupied with laws as commands, socio-legal scholars frequently do not cast their nets wide enough to identify these other kinds of laws or the multiplicity of functions of laws, and as a consequence they often understate and ignore important efforts at social control, efforts which are all the more important because they go unrecognized by a broader public, are frequently of low visibility, and are effectively depoliticized, matters for "specialists" and not for widespread "public debate."

Social scientists naturally tend to focus on celebrated commands and direct orders of the highly visible policy-makers who are wrestling with the glamorous issues of the day. However, much governmental policymaking is institutionalized in positions of low visibility with partial and fragmented responsibilities (cf. Shapiro [1970]). This observation, which has repeatedly been made with respect to the importance of bureaucracies in modern societies, is particularly applicable to courts in common law countries, where important policies are not only developed in a fragmented incremental way but are also effectively "depoliticized."

B. Forms of Law

Efforts at social control through law can range from explicit commands to the manipulation of field controls of entire populations.[16] The command approach envisions an ideal pattern of behavior for every individual within a clearly designated class. Field controls, on the other hand, are designed to affect the behavior of only a (usually small) portion within a target group by altering its field or environment so that some individuals' choices and behavior will be altered. Such manipulation of the environment is analogous to raising and lowering prices to affect demand, consumption, and substitution. This form of legal control is aimed at conditions and aggregates rather than specific individuals.

In contrast to the bluntness and directness of laws in the form of commands, laws designed to manipulate fields are likely to approach their goals indirectly. They are not intended to command each individual to follow a precisely prescribed path, but rather aim at an aggregate or systemic response. They are designed to control the rate of an activity by altering the costs of engaging in it. Presumably increasing the cost of participation will decrease the demand for the activity and redirect interests elsewhere. For example, rather than rationing gasoline or flatly prohibiting automobiles with large engines, the same goal—reducing fuel consumption—might be pursued by placing progressive taxes on automobiles according to their fuel consumption. Or in order to reduce the number of traffic fatalities due to defective automobiles, owners might be commanded to periodically have their automobiles inspected. Or the same goal might be pursued indirectly. Mandatory insurance laws have the effect of discouraging the use of old (and increasingly unsafe in the aggregate) automobiles. Drivers, unwilling to invest the high costs of insurance in low value automobiles, as a consequence may not drive them. Likewise innovation and economic growth can be stimulated by the selective use of tax credits. The possible advantages of this indirect approach are obvious. It is largely "self-enforcing," and provides greater flexibility than would all-or-nothing commands.[17]

Obviously commands and field controls of aggregates are two extremes along an ill-defined continuum and are subject to a variety of ambiguities, especially since the same law (or set of laws) may frequently contain both types of controls.[18] Nevertheless, the distinction is useful to characterize and emphasize the range of forms that legal control may take. Command-like laws are likely to be more direct and more visible to the affected individuals, than are field controls. The latter are, I suspect, more characteristic of efforts at planned social control and change in complex societies.

Reflection on this variety of forms of legal control suggests that the conditions for the efficacy of law traditionally offered by public law scholars and sociologists may be misleading, too narrow, or wrong. For instance, one scholar (Rogers, 1971: 646) has

. . . hypothesized that congruence between policy outputs and policy outcomes will be greatest when four measurable conditions prevail:

1) When the regulated agree both that a legal standard has been established by a legitimate source and that the standard requires compliance . . . 2) When the law clearly and carefully defines both who is responsible for seeing that a law is obeyed and the type and amount of compliance required . . . 3) When the regulated perceive that certain and severe sanctions will result from noncompliance . . . 4) When those who are to receive the benefits of the law are cohesive and take strong actions to achieve their rights.

These observations may be almost wholly irrelevant when applied to facilitative laws, the efficacy of which rests on their ability to shape consumer choices. In fact, something like the opposite may obtain. The more complex, multipurposed, and indirect the laws aimed at marginally affecting the rate of some activity, the less likely that the policy implications and the path between cause and effect may even be detected by the affected population. Law, then, can be a powerful tool of social control and change precisely because it can adjust for intensity of preference and can be exercized without always having recourse to direct clearly announced commands, clarity of purpose, or understanding by the affected population.[19] Not only can law powerfully influence behavior while those affected by a policy remain entirely unaware of it, but it may effectively depoliticize the policymaking process.

IV. Toward an Expanded View

In the preceding sections I pointed to the need both to broaden the concept of law and to enlarge the understanding of its functions and forms, and called into question some received generalizations about the law and social control.[20] In light of this two central questions emerge: What is the scope and nature of activity to be included within the study of law and social control? What is an appropriate theoretical perspective?

Much of the literature on impact and compliance to law, concerned as it often is with blunt commands, has tended to focus on the pronouncements of and responses to court decisions. This is clearly too narrow a focus. Courts as we know them do not exist in some societies, nor in most societies are they major sources or interpreters of law. Legislatures and administrative bodies probably far outweigh them in both volume and importance as sources of commands. Clearly, then, an exclusive focus on court decision-making and the consequences of these decisions is too narrow and ignores too much of what is commonly considered legal activity.[21]

What, then, would be the proper focus of an expanded study of law and social control?[22] Black (1972b: 126) has suggested that a major focus should be on the process of legal mobilization since:

The day-to-day entry of cases into any legal system cannot be taken for granted. Cases of alleged illegality and disputes do not move automatically to legal agencies for disposition or settlement. Without mobilization of the law, a legal control system lies out of touch with the human problems it is designed to oversee. Mobilization is the link between the law and the people served or controlled by the law.

This focus seems desirable because it moves beyond a narrow concern with courts to include all "legal agencies." But it also raises the question of what precisely is a *legal agency?* Obviously courts are and administrative agencies are, but what about arbitration panels? Any institution that "settles" disputes by means of applying "legal" rules? Attorneys in their offices making appeals to a hypothetical neutral tribunal as they negotiate with each other for their clients? Certainly mobilization is a "link between the law and the people served or controlled," but it is difficult to say much about this link until its nature and scope are clearly specified. Thus, for instance, it would be of questionable value to consider the mobilization of commercial law complaints in the courts without simultaneously understanding the mobilization of commercial law complaints in arbitration, an institution that the above quote may or may not envision as a "legal agency." One cannot say how a single element contributes to the whole until that whole is first identified. In this instance a failure to identify the nature of the legal agencies and the scope and boundaries of the mobilization process makes it difficult to say much about the frequency and consequences of mobilization, or to compare the process of mobilization in different areas of the law.

The focus on mobilization is bothersome for another and more important reason. Even when acknowledging that mobilization "mediates between the prescriptions of law and the disposition of cases" (Black, 1972b: 127) the focus is nevertheless incomplete and misses perhaps the most important way in which law intrudes into people's lives. *The genius and the power and the importance of legal authority is precisely because it is self-applying and self-mobilizing.* By this I do not mean only that disputes can be brought into court by private citizens as well as public officials. I mean that the locus of the primary social control function of law is not found in the specific orders emanating from the occasional "trouble cases" which have for one reason or another necessitated mobilization of formal legal machinery. Indeed these cases, an undetermined and highly unrepresentative small set of situations, probably represent an extreme "last resort" in the process of control. *Rather the law is most often set in motion by people who apply it to themselves and to each other without benefit of explicit mobilization of legal institutions.* The basic aspect of law and social control is found in the unheralded response and anticipation to abstract sets of rules which intrude in the lives of people and get them to do things they would otherwise not do. The mobilized cases, in a sense, may represent little more than the occasional failure or rupture in an otherwise largely invisible or at least self-applying system of control.

The problem of how to treat rules has always puzzled social

scientists. Rules are abstractions, impossible to "observe" and difficult to assign cause to. Thus it is understandable that in an effort to come to grips with the control functions of law so many would want to latch onto the easily observed "behavior" of officials, receiving complaints, making legal rules, and applying them. But to focus on the courts or the mobilization of cases is to miss the most essential and most powerful features of social control through law. In a host of both blunt and subtle ways law creates a set of categories through which people must filter their thinking and organize their lives. It is a complex pricing system which not only puts a value on the wants people may be inclined to pursue, but also affects them indirectly in that people must also adjust their wants to the behavior of others whose preferences are in turn shaped by the law. Thus law may be used to control people in a variety of ways that cannot be understood from the mobilization perspective.

An emphasis on judicial activity and mobilization overlooks the power of law to "resolve" issues through anticipatory reaction, and informal application.[23] For instance, disputes in "private law" fields are usually settled by the parties themselves as they invoke "the law" to support their positions. Petty crimes are often "settled" by means of restitution after the victim threatens to call the police, and individuals often apply the law to themselves and adjust their behavior accordingly in order to avoid these possibilities altogether. In each case a law, a legal forum or an agency may be invoked but not directly activated.

To test the shortcomings of the mobilization focus, one can, without too much suspension of disbelief, conceive of a legal system or at least areas of law in which there are no conflicts and thus no disputes to settle and no cases to mobilize. It would, however, be erroneous to conclude from this absence of activity that the law was having no effect at all. Quite the contrary, it might be argued that the law was operating with perfect efficiency since would-be disputants always anticipated the likely consequences of their proposed actions and declined to pursue them. It is one of the tasks of the empirical study of law to sort out the various explanations for such behavior in this and less extreme situations. Such a concern turns the primary focus away from the courts, police, and other "legal actors" and away from mobilization or "trouble cases" to focus on the public at large, including those who are *not* drawn into the formal mechanics of dispute processing or mobilization.[24]

An increasing number of socio-legal scholars are beginning to react against the narrow focus imposed by the concern with mobilization and "trouble cases" in formal governmental forums. Within recent years there has been a growing recognition among criminologists that the central questions of law and social control may not deal with characteristics of criminals, the activities of police, or how cases get or do not get to court, but rather with the

general preventive effects of law. While many people break the
law, some of them are discovered, and a few of them are apprehended, why do others comply with the law? How many of them
decline to engage in an activity because it is prohibited by law?
Which is more important, the magnitude of the criminal sanction
or the likelihood of apprehension? How does criminal law function
as a moralizing and threatening instrument? These are but a few
of the questions raised by this perspective.

This perspective was given impetus by Andenaes' influential
article (1966), and since then has received considerable attention
from other social scientists (Gibbs, 1975, Zimring and Hawkins,
1973, Tittle and Logan, 1973, Ehrlich, 1972). Andenaes speaks of
general preventive effects of punishment (the "effects of punishment upon members of society in general") and specific prevention
(the effect "on the many being punished"). He argues convincingly
(1966: 950) that the major focus for students of the criminal law
should be on general prevention, despite the fact that " . . . general
prevention is more concerned with the psychology of those obedient to the law than with the psychology of criminals." In essence,
he concludes, the primary focus of attention should be on those
people whom the law deters and who, therefore, are never brought
within the grasp of the formal legal machinery or officials. The
importance and implications of this point are elaborated with
great clarity in Jack Gibbs' (1975) thoughtful book which systematically catalogues a number of properties of punishments of
crimes which are likely to be relevant in developing a theory of
deterrence.[25]

The focus on the general preventive effects of law is quite
appropriate for criminal law, and the same set of questions can
easily be generalized to other forms of "command" as well. However, this focus suffers from all the limitations of the command
conception of law in general, and requires modification before it
can assume a form generalizable for all laws and serve as the
basis for focusing inquiry on law and social control. Rather than
referring to general and specific prevention or deterrence, it is
possible to speak of general and specific *effects*. General effects
refer to the larger public consequences of a particular law or
system of laws, including those indirect effects not necessarily
perceived by the persons whose activity is being regulated. On the
other hand, specific effects refer to the processes and consequences of laws which require conscious participation by individuals
in mobilizing the machinery of law to process a dispute or pursue
a claim.

For example, the general effect of automobile accident law
may involve such things as the conditions insurance companies
place on their policy holders, which in turn have consequences for
the frequency, seriousness, and cost of accidents, while the
specific effects have to do with the immediate behavior of those
individuals involved in an accident or otherwise brought into the

mobilized machinery of the law. To take another example, increasing the liability of a manufacturer for the safety of its products may produce a rash of law suits and facilitate the claims of injured consumers, but the general effects may be to alter the price of the goods, to stimulate the use of substitutes, to improve quality control in the industry, and perhaps even to cause the collapse of the industry. Changes in laws affect in a variety of anticipated and unanticipated ways the costs of engaging in an activity. Specific effects of laws concern the immediate response and reaction to the law; general effects involve an examination of how individuals and organizations adjust to and cope with increased or decreased costs of pursuing their own interests (whether purely private or public).

In this view law can be conceived of as an elaborate and subtle pricing mechanism which cannot only flatly prohibit or expressly require, but can also supplement and shape natural systems of exchange and interaction by slightly adjusting the costs of an activity. Thus it must be understood as only one of a number of interrelated factors in complicated systems of interaction.[26] Varying the nature and content of the law, whether it is the substantive or procedural criminal law, rules of standing, or any type of public or private law, can affect ongoing systems in a variety of ways by altering supply, demand, opportunity, alternatives, transaction costs, etc. of those participating in the system. All this can ultimately be translated into general effects on the rate and duration of an activity.[27] Its main control effects are not limited to the occasional instance when someone challenges the propriety and ambiguity of the pricing system, but rather the great bulk of the instances when people accept it and alter their behavior accordingly.

While some activities are likely to be controlled or affected by direct commands, control through devices manipulating environments and producing indirect effects is probably a more typical feature of control in complex societies. The law is a much more subtle and finely tuned instrument for expressing and controlling the distribution of values than those preoccupied with the blunt command model of law usually envision. It includes a great variety of techniques and forms, can operate in an indirect and almost imperceptible way, and can unobtrusively enter into all walks of life. In common law countries all this is reinforced by the decentralized, incremental and depoliticized nature of the judicial policy-making process. This may be further reinforced by the growth of large private organizations—insurance companies, banks, corporations, unions, universities, etc.—that engage in extensive planning in anticipation of *possible* legal effects and as a means of avoiding trouble cases. Thus procedures for avoiding legal trouble are built into their own "private" control systems.

The perspective outlined here may appear foreign to many social scientists, but is familiar to economists. While sociologists and political scientists, for instance, are prone to look for commands or command-like statements of regulation when considering forms of legal control, economists are more likely to see social life in terms of on-going systems of private exchange, and to approach the analysis of legal control by searching for factors that indirectly affect these systems. The differences, however, go deeper and also involve the ways problems are characterized and theories constructed.

Some of these differences may be illustrated by examining how the two approaches might characterize a research problem. The more empirically oriented social scientist might focus on the law as an independent variable and then trace its consequences— the dependent variables—with either a comparative or before/after research design. This is typical of many compliance and impact studies. On the other hand, the economist is more likely to first identify the elements and dynamics of a process of social choice, generate a theory about the calculus of choice and then examine the system as a whole, with perhaps a special emphasis on the functions of the law. The single independent variable (the law) and the causal language of the former are in sharp contrast to the latter, which would speak of a process of interaction, in which "the law" would be only one of a number of factors.[28]

If theoretically inclined at all, the "empirical" approach would lead to construction of a "theory of impact" or effectiveness. On the other hand, the economic approach would generate a theory of decision-making under a specified set of conditions. If it were a decision which was directly or indirectly affected by the law (e.g., a command flatly prohibiting an action or a provision indirectly affecting the cost of an activity), then one of the elements in the calculus of choice would be "the law." This conception views law as a subtle pricing mechanism which seeks to stimulate or retard processes—whether public or private—by varying the costs of participation in them. This approach, however, does not lead to a distinctive focus on law itself, since law is simply one of a number of elements in the decision. As a part, it can only be understood in the light of the whole.

The broader conception of the functions of law ought also be congenial to Marxists, whose conceptions of the state are broad enough to include both public and private law of Anglo-American political and legal theory. Marx, for instance, could examine the origins of the family and private property in his discussion of the state. Indeed the modern state, in his conception, is little more than the superstructure of laws and institutions assuring the privilege of the dominant classes by guaranteeing their existence and facilitating their "private" activities and relationships. "The modern state," Marx cogently asserted in the Manifesto, "is merely a committee which manages the common business of the bourgeoisie." Clearly such a view not only obliterates the importance of the distinction between public law and private law but also the distinction between command-like and facilitative laws.

This paper is not intended to develop a comprehensive theory of law or to urge agreement on the domain of the field of law or on a single preferred theoretical approach. The major thrust of my comments has been to direct the attention and interests of those engaged in legal studies to a broader conception of law and to a greater variety of functions and forms of law. More particularly this paper appeals to social scientists to recognize that all law-making and law-application is the exercise of political power and to focus attention on a greater variety of laws and problems than heretofore. Ironically, however, my position, if followed, seems to lead to the abolition of a rationale for a distinctive discipline of legal studies or a separate theory of law and society.

NOTES

1.   A list of published works in this area is too long to include here. There are, however, a number of widely read collections which contain representative samples of some of the best work in this area. See Simon (1968), Friedman and Macaulay (1969), Schwartz and Skolnick (1970), Grossman and Grossman (1971), Becker and Feeley (1972), Krislov et al. (1972), Black and Mileski (1973), and Akers and Hawkins (1975). In addition see Wasby (1970).

2.   Compare this definition with Austin's discussion (1955: 14 et seq.).

3.   The several studies (such as Yale Law Journal, 1967) of compliance with the Supreme Court's Miranda decision are apt examples of the first approach, while various studies (such as Crain, et al. [1969]) of reactions to the federal courts' rulings on school desegregation exemplify the second. Skolnick's (1966) and Blumberg's (1970) studies of criminal justice practices are examples of the third.

4.   On this point, see Black (1972a) and Abel (1973). As the problem appears in the research on criminal justice see Feeley (1973).

5.   Skolnick's (1966) study of the police, for example, regularly compares observed practices with an unarticulated ideal of due process and the standard of a policeman's role in a democratic society. Blumberg (1970) holds up a particular adversarial ideal which he assumes is required by the law and against which he contrasts the "divergences" of observed practices, but this ideal is not specified with any precision nor is it specifically and unambiguously derivable from provisions in the law. Even Sudnow (1965) in his discussion of public defenders and "normal crimes" seems to have an implicit private practitioner standard against which he contrasts the behavior of public defenders.

6.   Standard procedures in evaluation research, on the other hand, call for relative comparisons of possible alternatives. The basis for comparison and evaluation is neither an ill-defined ideal nor an absolute goal, but rather is a set of other possible alternatives (Suchman, 1967). While this strategy for comparison seems desirable for impact studies, unfortunately it will probably not be followed since it is a clear acknowledgment that the research is applied research, not "theoretical social science."

7.   See, for example, the various views on the constitutionality of preventive detention. Contrast Dershowitz (1973), with Mitchell (1969). On prohibition, see Gusfield (1963).

8.   For a more detailed statement on this point see Black (1972a).

9.   See, for example, the discussion of the varying scope of law in Hoebel (1954).

10.   In addition to Selznick, also see Auerbach (1966) and Skolnick (1966b).

11.   There are at least two partial exceptions to this assertion. Both Hoebel (1954) and Barkun (1966) have prefaced their important works with such an attempt at conceptual clarification. They are, however, in my opinion both failures. In each instance the works of Kelsen, Hart, Fuller, and other important legal theorists have either been ignored completely or dismissed without any serious examination. In contrast, see Gibb's (1968) insightful but unfortunately neglected article in which he carefully examines various definitions of law and shows their importance in empirical research and in forming generalizations.

12.   They are: Simon (1968), Friedman and Macaulay (1969), Schwartz and Skolnick (1970), Grossman and Grossman (1971), Black and Mileski (1973), and Akers and Hawkins (1975).

13.   For analysis of the various functions and consequences of tax laws see Bittker et al. (1968) and Surrey (1973).

14.   Some social scientists have, however, mistakenly engaged in such an attempt. See Barkun (1966).

15.   The public policy perspective and the acknowledgment of multiple functions of tort law is by now more or less the orthodox position. See Calabresi (1970) and Posner (1973).

16.   This distinction is adapted from the discussion by Dahl and Lindblom (1953: 93-128).

17.   For an interesting analysis contrasting the failures of subsidized housing programs with the successes of promoting homeownership by tax deductions for mortgage interest see Baer (1975).

18.   Command-type controls resemble field controls insofar as total compliance of all individuals is rarely expected or obtained. At some point the costs of increased enforcement outweigh the costs of noncompliance so that some crime becomes socially efficient. The differences in the form of control, however, are still important.

19.   Curiously critics of pluralist theories of American politics have failed to examine the functions of law in structuring inequalities. Their criticisms of law tend to sound much like those of their pluralist opponents; both focus on the degree of differential access to the resources of law or on a few "big decisions" rather than examine the structural features of the legal system itself. For a brilliant corrective to this shortcoming see Pashukanis (1951).

20.   One rather obvious conclusion is that the distinction between private and public law is of dubious value for analytic purposes and for drawing the boundaries of the field. In a recent article Shapiro (1972) has gone a long way toward abolishing this distinction for political scientists, but his argument seems to fall one small step short. His basic contention is that the categories are often not useful since many so-called private laws (e.g., torts) are easily shown to be infused with explicit considerations of public policy and hence are political. I am in total agreement but

would urge the point even more strongly. All laws are by definition political; they allocate values, are authoritative, and hence are policy. Thus all law-making from whatever source is political policy-making. This is not to obliterate the important, if complex, distinction between rule-enforcement and rule-making. While there may be "neutral" norm application, there are no value neutral norms.

21.   This focus on courts and judges may be the residual legacy of the legal realists' influence. *Cf.* Fuller's (1940: 53) response to their position that the law is what the judges in fact do:

> . . . why should we stop with judges and exclude commissioners? And for that matter, what of officials whose duties are even further removed from those of a judge, like a sheriff and the sanitary inspector? They too "behave" in ways that are important to the rest of us, and they too have their rules that they can talk about and their rules they act on.

22.   For a deliberate choice of dispute processing as a focus, see Abel (1974). After wrestling with how law and legal disputes might be isolated for analysis, Abel, a lawyer-anthropologist, concludes that the task is not particularly fruitful. He then proceeds to develop a theory of not just legal dispute processing, but all dispute processing, which he argues is the more general phenomena, the more theoretically justifiable, and more applicable to cultures whose notions of disputes, rules, and law differ markedly from those in the West.

23.   For an examination of the problem of anticipated reactions in relation to the study of Supreme Court decisions, see Feeley (1972).

24.   Gerstein's (1970) discussion of "The Practice of Fidelity to Law" also seems to reach this conclusion.

25.   The several properties of punishments which Gibbs (1975: 144) identifies as likely to have a bearing on general deterrence are: 1) objective certainty, 2) perceived certainty, 3) perceived severity of prescribed punishments, 4) perceived severity of actual punishments, 5) presumptive severity of actual punishments, 6) objective celerity, 7) perceived celerity, 8) presumptive severity of prescribed punishments, and 9) knowledge of prescribed punishments. He observes:

> Needless to say, the prospect of treating all nine properties in a deterrence theory is foreboding; hence it would be desirable to dismiss some of the properties as irrelevant. But such selectivity cannot be justified at this stage. . . . All of the foregoing should make it clear that the methodology of deterrence research cannot be simple unless one is willing to tolerate oversimplified, incomplete, and crude investigations.

Many of these same properties and this observation have a direct application for those interested in pursuing the more general inquiry into law and social control as well.

26.   *Cf.* my attempt (Feeley, 1970: 407) at a general explanation for the adoption of criminal laws in all societies.

27.   The single best introduction to this perspective is Posner (1974). For some critical appraisals of this book, see Leff (1974), and Buchanan (1974).

28.   Compare, for example, a sociologist's approach with an economist's approach to the analysis of criminal sanctions. Using a standard research design, Schwartz and Orleans (1967) in a study entitled "On Legal Sanctions," identify the legal threat of criminal sanctions as one independent variable, try to control for all other possible sources of change, and then compare sanctions with other treatments to ascertain resulting behavioral changes (in this case increased tax payment). They then offer some concluding generalizations about the efficacy of legal sanctions compared to other treatments. On the other hand, Ehrlich (1972), an economist, constructs a model of individual choice under various conditions, including the possibility of the application of criminal sanctions. In constructing a general model of individual choice, he identifies a variety of elements entering into a decision, only one of which is the likelihood of sanctions being applied. He proceeds to examine how individuals make decisions when one of the elements of consideration is the possibility of sanctions being applied, and then tests his deduced propositions against data on crime and arrest rates.

REFERENCES

Abel, Richard, "Law Books and Books About Law," Stanford Law Review 26 (1973): 175.

————, "A Comparative Theory of Dispute Institutions in Society," Law & Society Review 8 (1974): 217.

Akers, Ronald and Hawkins, Richard, Law and Control in Society. Englewood Cliffs: Prentice-Hall, 1975.

Andenaes, Johannes, "General Preventive Effects of Punishment," University of Pennsylvania Law Review 114 (1966): 949.

Auerbach, Carl A. "Legal Tasks for the Sociologist," Law & Society Review 1 (1966): 91.

Austin, John, The Province of Jurisprudence Determined. London: Weidfield and Nicholson, 1955 [1832].

Baer, William C., "On the Making of Perfect and Beautiful Social Programs," The Public Interest 39 (1975): 80.

Barkun, Michael, Law Without Sanctions. New Haven: Yale University Press, 1966.

Becker, Theodore and Feeley, Malcolm (eds.), The Impact of Supreme Court Decisions (2nd ed.). New York: Oxford University Press, 1972.

Bittker, Borris I., Galvin, Charles O., Musgrave, R.A., and Pechman, Joseph A., A Comprehensive Income Tax Base? A Debate. Branford: Federal Tax Press, 1968 [Reprinted in part from Harvard Law Review 80 and 81 (1967-1968)].

Black, Donald, "The Boundaries of Legal Sociology," Yale Law Review 81 (1972a): 1086.

————, "The Mobilization of Law, "Journal of Legal Studies 2 (1972b): 125.

_____, and Mileski, Maureen (eds.), *The Social Organization of Law*. New York: Academic Press, 1973.

Blumberg, Abraham, *Criminal Justice*. Chicago: Quadrangle Books, 1970.

Buchanan, James, "Good Economics—Bad Law, "*Virginia Law Review* 60 (1974): 451.

Calabresi, Guido, *The Costs of Accidents*. New Haven: Yale University Press, 1970.

Crain, Robert with the assistance of Inger, Morton, McWorter, Gerald A., and Vanecko, James J., *The Politics of School Desegregation*. New York: Doubleday, 1969.

Dahl, Rovert and Lindblom, Charles E., *Politics, Economics, and Welfare*. New York: Harper and Row, 1954.

Dershowitz, Alan, "Preventive Confinement: A Suggested Framework for Constitutional Analysis," *Texas Law Review* 51 (1973): 1277.

Edelman, Murray, *The Symbolic Uses of Politics*. Urbana: University of Illinois Press, 1964.

Ehrlich, Isaac, "The Deterrent Effect of Criminal Law Enforcement," *Journal of Legal Studies* 1 (1972): 259.

Etzioni, Amitai, "Two Approaches to Organizational Analysis: A Critique and A Suggestion," *Administrative Science* Quarterly 5 (1960): 257.

Feeley, Malcolm, "Coercion and Compliance," *Law & Society Review* 4 (1970): 407

_____, "Power, Impact and the Supreme Court," in T. Becker and M. Feeley (eds.), *The Impact of Supreme Court Decisions* (2nd ed.). New York: Oxford University Press, 1972.

_____, "Two Models of the Criminal Justice System: An Organizational Perspective," *Law & Society Review* 7 (1973): 407.

Friedman, Lawrence and Macaulay, Stewart (eds.), *Law and the Behavioral Sciences*. Indianapolis: Bobbs-Merrill, 1969.

Fuller, Lon, *The Law in Quest of Itself*. Boston: Beacon Press, 1940.

Gerstein Robert, "The Practice of Fidelity to Law," *Law & Society Review* 4 (1970): 259.

Gibbs, Jack, "Definitions of Law and Empirical Questions," *Law & Society Review* 2 (1968): 429.

_____, *Crime, Punishment and Deterrence*. New York: Elsevier, 1975.

Grossman, Joel and Grossman, Mary (eds.), *Law and Change in Modern America*. Pacific Palisades: Goodyear Publishing Co., 1971.

Gusfield, Joseph R., *Symbolic Crusade*. Urbana: University of Illinois Press, 1963.

Hart, H.L.A., *The Concept of Law*. Oxford: Clarendon Press, 1961.

Hoebel, E.A., *The Law of Primitive Man*. Cambridge: Harvard University Press, 1954.

Kelsen, Hans, *General Theory of Law and State*. New York: Russell and Russell, 1961.

Krislov, Samuel, Boyum, Keith O., Clark, Jerry N., Shaffer, Roger C., and White, Susan O., *Compliance and the Law.* Beverly Hills: Sage Publications, 1972 [Originally published as *Law & Society Review* 4 (4) and 5 (1) (1970)].

Lasswell, Harold, *Politics: Who Gets What, When, How.* New York: P. Smith, 1950.

Leff, Arthur, "Economic Analysis of Law: Some Realism about Nominalism," *Virginia Law Review* 60 (1974): 451.

Mitchell, John, "Bail Reform and the Constitutionality of Pre-trial Detention," *Virginia Law Review* 55 (1969): 1223.

Mohr, Lawrence, "The Concept of Organizational Goal," *American Political Science Review* 67 (1973): 470.

Pashukanis, E. B., "The General Theory of Law and Marxism," in H. Babb (trans.), *Soviet Legal Philosophy.* Cambridge: Harvard University Press, 1951.

Posner, Richard, *Economic Analysis of Law.* Boston: Little Brown and Co., 1974.

Rogers, Harrell, "Law as an Instrument of Public Policy," *American Journal of Political Science* 14 (1971): 638.

Rose, Arnold, "Voluntary Associations in France," in Arnold Rose (ed.), *Theory and Method in The Social Sciences.* Minneapolis: University of Minnesota Press, 1954.

Schwartz, Richard and Orleans, Sonya, "On Legal Sanctions," *University of Chicago Law Review* 34 (1967): 275.

Schwartz, Richard and Skolnick, Jerome (eds.), *Society and the Legal Order.* New York: The Free Press, 1970.

Selznick, Philip, "Sociology and Natural Law," *Natural Law Forum* 6 (1961): 84.

————, *Law, Society and Industrial Justice.* New York: Russell Sage Foundation, 1969.

Shapiro, Martin, "Decentralized Decision-Making in the Law of Torts," in *Political Decision-Making.* S.S. Ulmer (ed.). New York: Van Nostrand, 1970.

————, "From Public Law to Public Policy or the Public in 'Public Law'," *PS* 5 (1972): 410.

Simon, Rita James, *The Sociology of Law.* San Francisco: Chandler Publishing Company, 1968.

Skolnick, Jerome, *Justice Without Trial.* New York: John Wiley and Sons, 1966a.

————, "Social Research on Legality: A Reply to Aeurbach," *Law & Society Review* 1 (1966b): 105.

Suchman, Edward A. *Evaluative Research.* New York: Russell Sage Foundation, 1967.

Sudnow, David, "Normal Crimes: Sociological Features of the Penal Code in a Public Defender's Office," *Social Problems* 12 (1965): 272.

Surrey, Stanley S. *Pathways to Tax Reform.* Cambridge: Harvard University Press, 1973.

Tittle, Charles, and Logan, Charles, "Sanctions and Deviance: Evidence and Remaining Questions," *Law & Society Review* 7 (1973): 371.

Wasby, Stephen, *The Impact of the United States Supreme Court.* Chicago: Dorsey, 1970.

Yale Law Journal, "Project: Interrogations in New Haven: The Impact of Miranda," *Yale Law Journal* 76 (1967): 1519.

Zimring, Franklin, and Hawkins, Gordon, *Deterrence: The Legal Threat in Crime Control.* Chicago: University of Chicago Press, 1973.

Chapter 2

The Ideology of Law: Notes for a
Radical Alternative to Legal Oppression*

Richard Quinney†

Can you imagine a world that was not regulated by law? A world that was not ordered, by either man-made law or the laws of nature. Few people of Western civilization have been able to. Such ideas are unthinkable; our tenuous existence would likely fall apart if we admitted the possibility of a lawless reality. Yet the reverse of these ideas is a distinct possibility. After all, in the East the notion of fixed laws is absent. The Chinese never developed the Western belief in the necessity of law.

Belief in law has a firm grounding in Western philosophy. Developing in the Judaeo-Christian religions was the idea of divine purpose or pattern that gradually unfolds in human history. This encouraged the idea of a natural order of things according to physical laws. Greek rationalism contributed to the idea that the universe is governed by intelligible laws, laws that are capable of being grasped by the human mind. The emergence of science was a culmination of these notions. Moreover, religion gave support to the discovery of God's handiwork. Thus we carry to this day the unquestioned belief that we live in an ordered universe that is

* Richard Quinney, "The Ideology of Law: Notes for a Radical Alternative to Legal Oppression," *Issues in Criminology* 7 (1) (1972): 1-35. Reprinted by permission of *Crime and Social Justice.*

† Richard Quinney received his B.S. from Carroll College in 1956, his M.A. from Northwestern University in 1957 and his Ph.D. from the University of Wisconsin in 1962. He is presently a Professor in the Department of Sociology at New York University.

subject to human understanding. Any other belief is anti-Western and (at first glance) atheistic, certainly unscientific.

The popular concern today with *law and order* is entirely consistent with our intellectual history. And the use of law to repress threatening elements is similarly consistent with the history of our social practices. In other words, what we are experiencing today is not a break with our past, but is a logical extension of Western history.

I am contending here that only with a revision in our Western social theory can we create a world that frees us from the dead hand of the legalistic mentality. Another reality is possible. One that liberates us. A radical social theory thus confronts the foundations of Western philosophy: the assumption of the inevitability of law. Radical social theory revises our notions about the related ideas of law and order, natural law, civil liberties, civil disobedience, and morality. In the course of the revision we are developing a new understanding about the role of law in society. And we come to realize that the ideal of law is a myth that has been perpetuated by a narrow Western intelligence.

I.

The role of law in society is vastly different from what we have been led to believe in our mythology. The image of law has been remarkably consistent, whether in the popular mind or in academic discipline. That image is perhaps best expressed in sociological jurisprudence, a school of legal philosophy which drew its inspiration from early sociology. Its leading figure, Roscoe Pound, saw law as a specialized form of social control which brings pressure to bear upon each man "in order to constrain him to do his part in upholding civilized society and to deter him from anti-social conduct, that is, conduct at variance with the postulates of social order" (1942:18).

In jurisprudence, law as a product of society is conceived of as a law that reflects the consciousness of the total society. This consensus model of law, regarding criminal law in particular, is described like this (Friedmann, 1964:143): "The state of criminal law continues to be—as it should—a decisive reflection of the social consciousness of a society. What kind of conduct an organized community considers, at a given time, sufficiently condemnable to impose official sanctions, impairing the life, liberty, or property of the offender, is a barometer of the moral and social thinking of a community." Similarly, Pound, in formulating his theory of interests, looked upon law as reflecting the needs of the well-ordered society. In fact, the law was a form of "social engineering" in a civilized society.

For the purpose of understanding the law of today I am content to think of law as a social institution to satisfy social wants—the claims and demands involved in the existence of civilized society—by giving effect to as much as we may with the least sacrifice, so far as such wants may be satisfied or such claims given effect by an ordering of human conduct through politically organized society. For present purposes I am content to see in legal history the record of a continually wider recognizing and satisfying of human wants or claims or desires through social control; a more embracing and more effective securing of social interests; a continually more complete and effective elimination of waste and precluding of friction in human enjoyment of the goods of existence—in short, a continually more efficacious social engineering (1922:98-99).

Thus, according to Pound's theory, law serves those interests that are for the good of the whole society. Only the right law could emerge in a civilized society.

Furthermore, a *pluralistic* model dominates most of legal philosophy. Law, supposedly, orders human relations by restraining individual actions and by settling disputes between competing groups. Again Pound:

Looked at functionally, the law is an attempt to satisfy, to reconcile, to harmonize, to adjust these overlapping and often conflicting claims and demands, either through securing them directly and immediately, or through securing certain individual interests, or through delimitations or compromises of individual interests, so as to give effect to the greatest total of interests or to the interests that weigh most in our civilization, with the least sacrifice of the scheme of interests as a whole (1943:39).

In sociological jurisprudence, then, law is regarded as an instrument which naturally controls private interests according to the requirements of social order.

In the legal thinking that dominates our image of law, therefore, society is regarded as being relatively homogeneous and static, rather than being characterized by diversity, coercion, and change. Moreover, rather than viewing law as the *result* of the operation of private interest, law is seen as something that operates *outside* of particular interests for the good of the whole society. At best, this is a naive conception of law. But it is also dangerous, in that it would have us live according to a myth.

In contrast to the dominant image of law, I suggest that the following description is closer to the truth (Quinney, 1969:25): "Law incorporates the interests of specific persons and groups in society. Seldom is law the product of the whole society. Rather than representing the interests of all members of society, law consists of the interests of only specific segments of the population. Law is made by men, particular men representing special interests, who have the power to translate their interests into public policy. In opposition to the pluralistic conception of politics, law does not represent the compromise of the diverse interests in society, but supports some interests at the expense of others." Yet, in spite of this reality, we are all supposed to be bound by the same law. Traditional legal theory attempts to intimidate us—to make slaves of us—on the basis of a myth.

While law is to protect all citizens, it starts as a tool of the dominant class and ends by maintaining the dominance of that class. Law serves the powerful over the weak; it promotes the war of the powerful against the powerless. Moreover, law is used by the state (and its elitist government) to promote and protect itself. We are all bound by that law. We are indoctrinated with the ideology that it is *our* law, to be obeyed because we are all citizens of a single nation. Until law is the law of the people, law can be nothing other than official oppression.

II.

The search for order has been the principal concern of the social theorist. Confused by the disorder about him, the social theorist has advanced theories that not only provide a particular view of reality, but serve as a rationale for controlling the people. Stability has been sought—theoretically and practically—at the expense of significant social change and the realization of human potential. The arguments for social order, whether advanced by conservatives or liberals, men of knowledge or men of the world, have been made by those who have too much to lose by admitting change into their schemes. A crisis in social order has existed only when the positions of those who hold power or benefit from current power arrangements are threatened. Then the social order theories and the demands for order are written and proclaimed.

A preoccupation with order has not only been the driving force in social theory, but the same concern accounts for the very existence of law. The creation of law is merely an application of Western man's belief that all things are caused and ordered. Just as law is to be found in nature, law is found in society. The laws of nature are to become embodied in the law that man makes. Thus, man-made law serves to maintain the natural laws of social order. Man on earth, so the doctrine goes, must regulate himself, as the world of nature is ordered. God is in his heaven and all is well on earth.

The debate on the necessity of man-made law is an old one. Whether or not one argues for or against the inevitability of law depends on his conception of man. For those who argue that law is necessary, there is the belief that man's nature is basically evil, or at least that he has forces within him which require restraint through penal law. On the other hand, those who argue that law is unnecessary believe in the inherent goodness of man. For them any negative conditions are to be found in the social environment, possibly in the government or in the legal system itself. Legal scholars, while recognizing these contrasting possibilities, inevitably side with the first argument, suggesting that law is the great civilizer and source of progress:

> Leading philosophers, from Plato to Marx, may have urged that law is an evil thing of which mankind would do well to rid itself. Yet, for all the philosophic doubts, experience has shown that law is one of the great civilizing forces in human society, and that the growth of civilization has generally been linked with the gradual development of a system of legal rules, together with machinery for their regular and effective enforcement (Lloyd, 1964: 7).

I suspect that the reason the existence of law is not questioned rests on the naive assumption that order can be achieved and maintained only through law. A case in point (Lloyd, 1964:24): "The idea that human society, on whatever level, could ever conceivably exist on the basis that each man should simply do whatever he thinks right in the particular circumstances is too fanciful to deserve serious consideration." The fear is taken to the point that such a society would not merely be a "society without order," but would be the very negation of society. The radical proposal that law be eliminated seldom receives a welcome reception.

The traditional idea of law is bound by the assumption that man must be regulated. Man must be controlled, so the idea continues, for his own good and certainly for the good of social order. Emile Durkheim set the pace for modern times by suggesting that man must be restrained because of his insatiable passions:

> Imagine a being liberated from all external restraint, a despot still more absolute than those of which history tells us, a despot that no external power can restrain or influence. By definition, the desires of such a being are irresistible. Shall we say, then, that he is all-powerful? Certainly not, since he himself cannot resist his desires. They are masters of him, as of everything else. He submits to them; he does not dominate them (1961:44).

More recently George Kennan, former member of the U.S. Foreign Service and Princeton's Institute for Advanced Studies, came out against the "permissiveness" in our society. In an attitude typical of authoritarians, he criticized the way the younger generation is living nowadays. Referring especially to "hippies", Kennan wrote:

> They are misjudging, here, the innermost nature of man's estate. There is not, and cannot be, such a thing as total freedom. The normal needs of frailties of the body, not to mention the elementary demands of the soul itself, would rule that out if nothing else did. But beyond that, any freedom *from* something implies a freedom *to* something. And because our reality is a complex one, in which conflicts of values are never absent, there can be no advance toward any particular objective, not even the pursuit of pleasure, that does not imply the sacrifice of other possible objectives. Freedom, for this

reason, is definable only in terms of the obligations and restraints and sacrifices it accepts. It exists, as a concept, only in relationship to something else which is by definition its opposite; and that means commitment, duty, self-restraint (1968:10-11).

Man must be restrained, the argument goes, in order to make him free. For the legalist, law provides that restraint. Instant, external, and official repression.

The legal mentality is an integral part of today's demand for law and order. Man, even in the best of times, must be restrained. But given what seems to be a time of chaos and disorder, even more drastic measures are justified. Liberals today are among the first to support the assumptions of law and order, although their rhetoric may be prettier than that of the right. Staughton Lynd (1970:31), in an article that touches on the demand for law and order, comments exactly on this repressive legal mentality of modern liberals:

> Rather than moving with life, like a gardener or a teacher, our society rigidly confronts life like a policeman. Repression and authoritarianism are on the rise in America because at its highest levels the society believes it is better (for other people) to be dead than different. And so in every institution, at every age, in every meeting of those with more power and those with less, there is indeed a crisis of law and order. The people who talk most about it are those who have the power, hence the law and order, and feel no need for change. They—and I am talking not of George Wallace but of the Ivy League graduates in Wall Street and government—are apparently prepared to destroy the world rather than let it become something which they don't run.

The liberal terminology for what passes as law and order in everyday parlance is the *rule of law*. That rule has been raised to a kind of moral absolute. To obey the law becomes a good in its own right, beyond the goals that underlie each law. And while such ideas as "due process" are appealing, they become in their administration devices that further a particular authority structure. Supposedly the law protects the rights of each of us, but this ideal is negated by the fact that the entire legal system is played according to rules formulated and enforced by a legal establishment that is part of the authority structure. Meanwhile, we are all to feel bound by the law, no matter what it is. The legalist—with only minor variations on occasion—tells us this.

One of the most telling comments on the rule of law is found in a statement made in 1969 by William T. Gossett, then President of the American Bar Association. Applying the rule of law to "unrest in our colleges and universities," he raises several issues regarding the rule of law. The entire statement bears reading:

> The American Bar Association views with profound disquiet the current tendency among groups of our citizens, and especially among many young people, to disregard the rule of the law upon which a democratic society must depend for its viability and progress. Those

who elect to defy a law because of some dictate of conscience or the intensity of their cause must be prepared to accept the normal penalties of non-compliance, subject of course to the requirements of due process. They cannot expect to escape those penalties by questioning the legitimacy or the moral validity of the law; for the consequences of allowing such conduct to occur with impunity would be anarchy, not order, and an anarchic society is a lawless society. The ancient maxim that liberty is derived through restraint, that freedom comes through order, is no less true today than in past times in our history.

These considerations apply with special force to the current state of unrest in our colleges and universities, where groups of students, aided in some cases by faculty members, have defied the legitimate authority of the institutions and have sought by recourse to intimidation and violence to disrupt normal academic operations. Whatever may be the virtue of the ends desired, there can be no justification in law or morality for this flagrant denial by a minority of the overriding right of the majority of students and faculty. In these days, institutions of higher education are at the core of our society. If they are prevented, through violence, from discharging their duties, our entire society will be placed in jeopardy.

The right to dissent and protest is an indispensable part of democracy, and our institutions must respond appropriately to just grievances and reasonable demands for change. Thus, orderly change effected by peaceful procedures is at the heart of the democratic process. Because such peaceful procedures do exist in the institutions of American society, there can be no justification for recourse to violence; and our society is threatened not only by those who resort to violence, but also by the unduly repressive measures that are being adopted in response to violence. Therefore, the current tendency to reject peaceful procedures and to impose the will of a minority must be opposed with all appropriate means by those who believe in liberty and justice (1969:3).

This statement by a President of the American Bar Association embodies the complex of ideas that make up the rule of law. The questions raised and the answers proposed can be challenged at every point by an alternative perspective, the radical perspective. The ideology can be exposed and a new reality can be constructed.

III.

Any conception of law carries with it certain assumptions about *natural law*. For those who emphasize order, there is the belief that a natural law protects society against threats from the individual. On the other hand, when social order is seen for what it really is, a rationale for existing authority, natural law is a body of thought that provides man with certain inalienable rights. According to the radical image of natural law, then, man has rights and "society" does not. Government is an artificial scheme that is constructed to serve the people. Therefore, it is to be valued only as long as it continues to serve the people.

But whatever the specific content of natural law, the underlying problem is the relation of the law man makes ("positive law") to some higher ideal. Several questions then arise: Should man-made law enforce morals? Can there be a positive law devoid of morals? Must the individual always obey positive law? When are morals more binding than law? The answers today, as in the past, vary considerably, depending to a great extent on one's conception of man and society.

The Hebraic and Greek conceptions of law recognized the contrast between positive law and moral law. In the Hebraic conception any human law that was contrary to divine law lacked validity and was to be ignored; man-made sanctions could not prevail against God's law. According to the Greek view, however, there was the moral obligation to obey the law of the state even when that law seemed to be immoral; the individual must abide by the state's punishment for violating the positive law. Precisely stated (Lloyd, 1964:55), "The Hebrew view then insists that human law is to be obeyed only when it corresponds with divine law; the Greek view, on the other hand, is that human law may conflict with moral law but the citizen must still obey the law of his state though he may and indeed should labour to persuade the state to change its law to conform with morality."

The prevailing view of the modern world toward law obviously comes close to the Greek conception. In fact, this view has tended to dominate most stances toward law and order since Greek times, although there have been some important and far-reaching exceptions. Gradually, out of stoic philosophy arose the notion that law necessarily varies from one state to another, but with some natural principles applies to all mankind. An important feature of this idea was the emphasis on rational determination of justice. Added to this was the medieval scholastic distinction between divine law, known only by revelation, and natural law, which was rational and known through human reason. Natural law did not cover all human affairs, there being many matters which needed regulation by man-made law. Human law, then, was entitled to play a major role in human government. Nevertheless, exponents of this doctrine remained ambiguous on how the individual was to act when the state imposed sanctions on him contrary to natural law. In the end Aquinas thought that obedience would have to be rendered unto the state so as to avoid the breakdown of law and order. God would have to resolve the matter in his own way.

The Christian notion that moral law dictates the content of human law, and therefore that law and morals must necessarily coincide, found its test in the Reformation. While the Catholic Church adhered to the scholastic philosophy, the theology of the Reformation came to grips with the application of the Christian doctrine in the secular world. The results were not always neatly consistent.

Martin Luther showed the difficulty when he was faced with the German peasants' rebellion. Luther had expounded on the liberty of the Christian man. The German peasants, confronted with certain grievances, including a heavy tax burden imposed by the lords, interpreted Luther to mean social and political freedoms as well. Luther responded by denunciating the peasants' cause:

> No one should willfully resist authority, as St. Paul says—"Let every soul be subject unto the higher powers with fear and awe" . . . You say that the government is wicked and unbearable and destroys us body and soul. My answer is that even if princes are wicked and unjust it does not excuse rebellion . . . Be obedient not only to good rules but to wicked ones. For well or for woe, you must bear your lot in patience, for God is just and will not let you suffer long. Take care that you do not jump from the frying pan into the fire; that in trying to get bodily freedom you do not lose forever your lives, property and souls (Quoted in Schapiro, 1909:81-86).

Luther then advised the German princes to mercilessly slay the peasant rebels. He deeply feared that his real message—salvation in another world dependent on faith in God's love and mercy— would be perverted to temporal ends. Is there any doubt now that Luther wasn't chronically constipated?

John Calvin had his own problems. The state as a law-making and law-enforcing body—was a necessary entity for Calvin. It was ultimately a theological creation. If man had not brought the Fall upon himself, a legal order would not be necessary. But man failed to remain in the integrity of his original nature.

> Let us realize, then, that not without reason has God established the order of earthly justice; but because He considered the corruption that is within us. We are well warned by that as I have already said, to humble ourselves seeing that our vices require such a remedy. All the more we must extoll the goodness of God because He decided to assure that harmony would prevail and that we should not despair: which would come about if there were no law in the world (Quoted in Little, 1969:41).

Because of man's inordinate disobedience, the temporal state must exist and secure its power if for no other reason than to protect the sovereignty of God's order. This is the conservative bias in Calvin's political thought. He is hesitant to recommend any sort of justifiable revolutionary action.

But then Calvin creates a dilemma in his thought: How to adapt earthly power to God's Kingdom? While Calvin's passion for order on earth is strong, his belief in the progressive character of the Kingdom of God is overwhelming. Ultimately the Kingdom of God cannot exist with the state. For Calvin the movement of history is from political-legal regulation to the self-determining freedom of the conscience. The coercive element of the state cannot finally be adapted to the free-willing potential of the Christian life. The old order must eventually give way to the new.

The practical tension between positive law and natural law, however, was not reconciled. The Anglican churchman tended to opt for the conservative aspect of Calvinism. The citizen was simply to conform to the existing political order. The Puritans in the American colonies likewise were not particularly bold in establishing the rights of man. The Massachusetts Bay Colony, as a "City upon a Hill," an example of godliness to the world, was based on the belief that government exists to regulate imperfect man and that political commands must be obeyed. Out of such ideas the Puritans developed a conception of the covenant. Under this conception government was viewed as originating in a compact among the people. But more than this, the power of the state was viewed as legitimate because it was a government conforming to what God had decreed. Today we call this "the rule of law."

The Puritans regarded themselves as an elite chosen by God to represent Him on earth. They also held that the positions of their elected leaders were ordained by God. Once elected, the governor and the magistrates were granted power through divine authority. As "Gods upon earth," the leaders must be obeyed in order that the covenant be kept. This idea was forcefully expressed to the Puritans by Governor John Winthrop when he declared that "the determination of law belongs properly to God: He is the only lawgiver, but He hath given power and gifts to man to interpret commonwealth, and subordinately to other magistrates and judges according to their several places" (Quoted in Morris, 1959:35). The logical conclusion of the covenant was rule by a few (Haskins, 1960:44-45): "The government of Massachusetts was thus a dictatorship of a small minority who were unhesitantly prepared to coerce the unwilling to serve the purposes of society as they conceived it."

Meanwhile, during the emergence of a new humanism in the fifteenth century, the notion of a *secular* natural law was developing. Enduring to the end of the eighteenth century was a Golden Age of natural law. Man-made, law, accordingly, contained precepts of a higher order, ordained by the rational order of human affairs rather than by God. The notion gradually held that man possesses certain *fundamental rights*. These "natural rights" of man could be rationally constructed and would achieve a universal system of justice. The consequence of this idea of natural law was a declaration of man's fundamental democratic rights, restricting the authority of rules and ensuring the rights of the people. This declaration contained within it revolutionary implications that soon found expression in the United States and France.

For a good part of the eighteenth century numerous English

and American writers laid the foundations for the natural law idea of human rights. They established the radical idea that moral truths are self-evident to the common man and that in forming a government men do not give up any of their inalienable natural rights.

The *right of revolution* itself is a natural law in the radical tradition. Not only was the American Revolution founded on this right, but the documents of that revolution and the subsequent constitution guaranteed the natural rights of the people. Government is for and by the people, and when it ceases to be that way the people have the right and duty to change it through revolution if necessary. The Declaration of Independence eloquently presents the position:

> We hold these truths to be self-evident, that all men are created
> equal; that they are endowed by their Creator with unalienable rights;
> that among these, are life, liberty and the pursuit of happiness. That
> to secure these rights governments are instituted among men,
> deriving their just powers from/the consent of the governed; that,
> whenever any form of government becomes destructive of these ends,
> it is the right of the people to alter or to abolish it, and to institute a
> new government . . .

Even with the American Revolution, natural law ideas were beginning to wane. The Founding Fathers themselves were less than wholehearted in suggesting revolution by the people once the new nation was established. Notions soon arose which gave support to maintaining temporal governments, usually at the expense of denying individual freedoms. If any morality existed, it meant nothing more than the duty to obey established governments and their laws. What was happening in political philosophy was that the rights of man were being replaced by a notion about the rights of society. Hegel's philosophy of the moral superiority of the state over the individual gave support to a doctrine that the individual's highest right was to obey the law of the state, a doctrine which found its fulfillment in Nazi Germany. Finally, the value-free commitment of science, the legal positivism of legal philosophy, and consensus liberalism played their parts in the movement away from a natural law that assures individual freedom.

But the times are changing. There is currently emerging a renewed sense of human rights. One sign is the renewed interest in natural law among legal scholars. Some of the conceptions, however, pertain only to a minor aspect of the relation between morality and law, being concerned primarily with the law that regulates sexual morality. Most of these writings have been stimulated by the Wolfenden Report on homosexuality and prostitution. Lord Devlin (1965), for example, suggests that in this realm at least society is justified in taking legal steps to preserve its moral code. H.L.A. Hart (1961; 1963) responds to Devlin by suggesting that the laws based on such moral codes are certainly legal, but that the regulation of private morality is not the business of law. Lon Fuller (1964) replies, moving beyond sexual morality, that law which itself is immoral is not really law.

Both Hart and Fuller then present what they call "the minimum content of natural law." For Hart this minimum is directed toward the single objective of "human survival." For Fuller the minimum content of natural law is the preservation of the "channels of communication." As I read both of these writers the minimums they prescribe are achieved through the preservation of society. That is, the emphasis in both conceptions of natural law is on *societal demands* rather than on *individual rights*. To be certain, both writers have the individual in mind, but for the good of the individual society must make demands and assert its right to exist. In the meantime libertarian rights may be either ignored or forfeited. This is not my idea of natural law.

But while there is a demand for social order, for law and order, there is a renewed belief in the natural rights of man, including once again the right of revolution. Man, accordingly, determines the rightness of government, his government, rather than government determining the rightfulness of man's actions. In *Intellectual Origins of American Radicalism*, Staughton Lynd affirms this natural law belief for our time:

> That the proper foundation for government is a universal law of right and wrong self-evident to the intuitive common sense of every man; that freedom is a power of personal self-direction which no man can delegate to another; that the purpose of society is not the protection of property but fulfillment of the needs of living human beings; that good citizens have the right and duty, not only to overthrow incurably oppressive governments, but before that point is reached to break particular oppressive laws; and that we owe our ultimate allegiance, not to this or that nation, but to the whole family of man (1968:vi).

Natural law in a radical theory thus protects the rights of each person. Modern natural law also protects the rights of any self-determined collective of people. On the societal level, and within communities, revolution is not only our right but our moral duty when governments are no longer the governments of the people. Such was the original meaning of natural law. And such is the meaning of natural law in radical social theory.

IV.

The guarantee of individual freedom, while basic to radical theory has to be viewed in larger perspective. The idea of individual freedom certainly must be preserved—even those freedoms that liberals restrict us to and fondly refer to as "civil liberties." But the danger with a sole interest in such liberties is that we may too easily ignore the context within which they operate. In other words, in thinking we have individual freedom, we overlook the fact that individual freedom is an ideal that is administered according to specific rules by those who have authority in the society. When liberties are not in the hands of the people, but in the hands of the ruling elite, then we do not actually have our rights in practice.

Thomas Jefferson, who we can easily credit with preserving the natural law idea of individual freedoms on American soil, himself limited the application of human rights. To be sure, the Bill of Rights guaranteed such rights as freedom of the press, freedom of speech, of religion, of assembly, due process and the like. But all these liberties, make no mistake, were to be strictly regulated. And there was a point at which the government itself could not be jeopardized at the expense of individual freedoms.

Jefferson's basic attitude toward democracy and individual freedoms became obvious after the American Revolution, while he was Minister to France. The French Revolution was underway, receiving considerable inspiration from the American experience. Throughout the revolution in France, Jefferson maintained a moderate stance. At each point in the revolution he expected the movement to come to an end. His advice and observations were always in respect to yesterday's progress toward democratization. Jefferson's opinions always had to catch up with what the French patriots had already accomplished. Essentially he believed that the nation could not go from absolute monarchy to democracy all at once. He hoped at best for a constitutional monarchy that would guarantee individual freedoms and the beginnings of representative government "a moderate government, in which the people will have a good share." (There could be individual freedoms without complete democracy.) Jefferson thought that the people should ask for no more than the monarchy was ready to grant and the aristocracy was willing to tolerate, "lest they should shock the dispositions of the courts, and even alarm the public mind, which must be left to open itself to successive improvements."

Jefferson had it in his mind to balance a degree of popular government with social order. He always chose the moderate path. He was wrong. "For the Revolution proved to be a good deal more than Jefferson's idea of it. Not merely a constitutional reformation but a vast social upheaval, it could not be accomplished in the amible spirit Jefferson advocated" (Peterson, 1970:374).

The modern liberal's position regarding individual rights, narrowly construed as civil liberties, has not moved beyond Jefferson's moderate position. Lipset (1963:90), for example, talks about civil liberties once he is assured that the nation has obtained legitimacy:

All states that have recently gained independence are faced with two interrelated problems; legitimating the use of political power and establishing national identity. And if it is a democratic policy they seek to establish, they must develop institutional and normative constraints upon efforts to inhibit organized opposition or to deny civil liberties to individual critics of those in power.

Furthermore, in his concept of stable democracy, Lipset gives much attention to protecting the rights of the minorities. The problem in this theory is that what he primarily fears is the denial of rights to a minority by a populist group. The same fears are not extended to the denial of rights by the *ruling minority* that controls the total population. Once the ruling minority secures legitimacy, it can establish its own rules for playing the game of civil liberties. The people may be protected from one another, but they are not necessarily protected from the ruling minority.

The actual lack of civil liberties is obvious in liberal democracy, contrary to all the rhetoric and the pleas for protecting civil liberties. Such advocates would be (and are) the first to restrict civil liberties when their government is threatened to the point of becoming unstable. Although the people have the right to resist oppressive government, even to overthrow it, the guarantees can be suddenly withdrawn or reinterpreted. Tom Hayden (1970:44-45), in a chapter titled "A Note to Liberals," describes this situation:

> We are in a condition in which the First Amendment freedoms do not work effectively. Citizens have the right to speak, assemble, and protest freely until their actions begin to have a subversive effect on unresponsive authorities. It can be expressed as an axiom: at the point at which protest becomes effective, the state becomes repressive. Constitutional rights become primarily rhetorical. They are not extended to those who might use them to make basic structural change, to those who represent the beginning of a new society.

Thus, abstract freedoms may flourish with ease. And we have these freedoms as long as our protests and actions are ineffectual and as long as we behave according to the rules that are administered by the governing class. However, when the authority of that class is threatened, a host of laws can be evoked. Not only may civil liberties be abridged, but repressive laws may be used to suppress potentially effective action. "Hence the dissenter has the freedom to become a victim in the social process and history, and a battery of sedition, espionage, criminal anarchy, or labor laws exist in readiness for the appropriate moment of social tension and the breakdown in the social and ideological consensus which exists during periods of peace and stability. The celebrants of American freedom rarely confront the concepts of order that underlie the large body of law for suppression that always exists in reserve" (Kolko, 1969:8).

The conclusion to be drawn is that, first, civil liberties are a tenuous and incomplete safeguard of human rights. Second, those liberties that are abstractly guaranteed are the province of the ruling class. That is, those from whom we are to be protected dispense our civil liberties. There is a one-way allocation of civil liberties, from the top down, from those with power to those without. Civil liberties are thus parcelled out to us at the discretion of the authority that we wish to dissent from, alter, or destroy. All is on their terms according to their rules and their application of the rules. That we should get a fair hearing is stretching even the best of liberal imagination.

Third, even the opportunity to use our civil liberties is severely limited in a liberal, ruling class democracy. The positions of power, the economic resources and the means of communication are possessed by the ruling class. By such an arrangement the chances are slight that the opposition can ever get into a position to effectively protest or threaten an oppressive government. Only by the most extreme, and almost by definition, the most illegal of means can the opposition be assured of a voice and possibly effective action. I am afraid than an opposition can expect little more from civil liberties than a device that gives the air of legitimacy to existing authority.

Finally, however precious the operation of civil liberties, the idea is not likely to be discarded. But we must be aware that the idea usually holds out false hope and grants legitimacy to that which needs to be changed. Also, we must not be so misled by the ideal that we fail to see what actually happens when civil liberties are dispensed.

From all this one can only conclude that civil liberties are not enough. There is a higher good. Civil liberties are only a small part of the greater liberties we know as human rights. We all have the right to live, to develop to the fullest of our human potential (individually and collectively), and to eliminate governments that deny these rights. What we know narrowly as civil liberties does little more than secure existing power arrangements and avoid the greater human rights. Our liberal democracies today, almost by definition, are not able to guarantee and promote these rights. Only when governments belong to the people can these human rights be achieved. And they need not necessarily be secured by means of a legal system.

V.

The same problems are found regarding *civil disobedience*. Civil disobedience—a long-recognized concept—must be understood in context. While the concept is inextricably linked to the issues of democratic government, morality, and social change, it cannot be understood without realizing how it is interpreted and qualified in practice. As with all our rights, civil disobedience is regulated by the ruling class. And so many of the theories of civil disobedience have been formulated with the interest of structured authority and stability in mind. The idea of civil disobedience, as propounded by many social theorists, is more for the protection of existing authority than it is for the right of the citizen to express his morality and to bring about necessary changes in government.

The idea of civil disobedience presupposes the concept of legality. Only a legalistic mind could raise the issue of civil disobedience; only within a concrete system of law would civil disobedience be raised as a problem. Even the progressive discussions of civil disobedience begin by assuming the presence of a legal system, taking the legalists on their own terms. Civil disobedience is a part of the assumption that law is necessary— that social order is to be maintained by a legal system. The liberal theorists, in particular, conceive of civil disobedience within the confines of law and order.

The legalists—liberals and conservatives alike—begin by suggesting that disobedience to law may be a *moral* right, but that disobedience cannot be *legally* justified. This is a serious distinction. For it carries with it the clear warning that a system of law is to be honored no matter how unjust it or any part of it is. We are asked to obey the law without any questions of justice. Justice, on the contrary, if it is recognized at all, is only to be considered outside of the law. The immorality of this law and order approach is illustrated in George Kennan's revealing conclusion to the question of civil disobedience:

> In the final analysis, the question of civil disobedience is, I am sure, a matter of temperment. Humanity divides, it has been said, between those who, in their political philosophy, place the emphasis on order and those who place it on justice. I belong in the first of these categories. Human justice is always imperfect. The laws on which it bases itself are always to some extent unjust. These laws have therefore only a relative value; and it is only relative benefits that can be expected from the effort to improve them. But the good order of society is something tangible and solid. There is little that can be done about men's motives; but if men can be restrained in their behavior, something is accomplished (1968:149-50).

As one of our leading liberal spokesmen, Kennan adds: "The benefit of the doubt should lie, therefore, with the forces of order, not with the world-improvers."

The legalist position is quite clear: to preserve law and order at the expense of morality and a just human existence. Nevertheless, the legalists continue to provide us with their wordy defences of civil disobedience. But the irony is that by the time they complete their analysis, there is little left to the idea of civil disobedience. Other than the right for the existing government to protect itself.

Thus, the qualifications are many and significant. We only have to begin with Thoreau's classic discussion (1963) to find that civil disobedience is little more than a "no" vote made by a single person. Thoreau said: "Let your life be a counter-friction to stop the machine. What I have to do is to see, at any rate, that I do not lend myself to the wrong which I condemn." So he spent the night in a Massachusetts jail. Civil disobedience was not a positive, and possibly collective, action that would attempt to remove an unjust condition. It was merely a personal refusal to lend support to actions by the government, a token of one's morality.

The legalist likes to distinguish between types of civil disobedience or to compare civil disobedience to other activities. While all forms of civil disobedience are regarded as illegal, some are more serious than others. Thus we are provided with the definitional distinction between "dissent" and "civil disobedience." Dissent is to refer to the verbal expression of a difference of opinion while civil disobedience is a refusal to obey the commands of government, supposedly by an opposing physical action or by the lack of any action at all. Then we are told by Sidney Hook (1967:27) that while the right of dissent is "integral to free society," "there must be limits to dissent when it takes the form of action, otherwise the result is anarchy." In the same response, Hook notes: "The limits of civil disobedience in a democracy begin when it becomes universal, when resistance to law, passive or active, takes the form of violence or has consequences leading to social chaos." Civility! Civil disobedience is good etiquette (but illegal) until it becomes effective. Disobedience is all right as long as it is civil.

The argument, that "democratic" government cannot be threatened, is advanced by the recent National Commission of the Cause and Prevention of Violence (the Milton Eisenhower Commission). In its final report (1970:86-87), in a chapter prepared by several liberal law professors, we are warned of the "contagion" effect of civil disobedience. We are informed:

> There is every reason to believe that the lesson taught by much of the current disobedience to law is disastrous from the standpoint of the maintenance of a democratic society . . . The experience of India seems to indicate that civil disobedience has a strong tendency to become a pattern of conduct which soon replaces normal legal processes as the usual way in which society functions. Put in American terms, this would mean, once the pattern is established, that the accepted method of getting a new traffic light might be to disrupt traffic by blocking intersections, that complaints against businessmen might result in massive sit-ins, that improper garbage service might result in a campaign of simply dumping garbage into the street, and so on . . . The adverse effect upon normal democratic processes is obvious. Though not intended to destroy democratic processes, civil disobedience tends plainly to impair their operation. This is a fact to which those who engage in civil disobedience should give consideration lest, in seeking to improve society, they may well seriously injure it.

We are asked by the National Commission to suspend any action that might effectively change oppressive situations, for the good of simply protecting the existing government.

It becomes clear that the legal system really has no place for civil disobedience, other than to assure that the offender is punished. Punishment—that is the legalist's most emphatic argument. Uncritically we are told to look to Socrates who insisted that he would accept the death penalty for an act he thought was morally right. "In war, and in the court of justice, and everywhere, you must do whatever your state and your country tell you to do, or you must persuade them that their commands are unjust." In the meantime you die.

This is the argument that centuries later goes unquestioned. Former Supreme Court justice, Abe Fortas (1968:124), in his book on civil disobedience, confirms the doctrine: "Civil disobedience is violation of the law. Any violation of law must be punished, whatever its purpose, as the theory of civil disobedience recognizes." Law and order are the paramount values: "For after all, each of us is a member of an organized society. Each of us benefits from its existence and its order. And each of us must be ready, like Socrates, to accept the verdict of its institutions if we violate their mandate and our challenge is not vindicated."

George Kennan goes further. While some legalists would accept the right of civil disobedience *if* the punishment is accepted, Kennan maintains, after discussing actions of the student left, that acceptance of the punishment does not in anyway excuse civil disobedience. He would, in fact, rule out all civil disobedience.

> These observations reflect a serious doubt whether civil disobedience has any place in a democratic society. But this is one objection I know will be offered to this view. Some people, who accept our political system believe that they have a right to disregard it and to violate the laws that have flowed from it so long as they are prepared, as a matter of conscience, to accept the penalities established for such behavior.
>
> I am sorry; I cannot agree. The violation of law is not, in the moral and philosophic sense, a privilege that lies offered for sale with a given price tag, like an object in a supermarket, available to anyone who has the price and is willing to pay for it. It is not like the privilege of breaking crockery in a tent at the country fair for a quarter a shot. Respect for the law is not an obligation which is exhausted or obliterated by willingness to accept the penalty for breaking it (1968:15-16).

But more liberal legalists would permit civil disobedience as long as the violator accepts the penalty. And some would qualify this by arguing that the necessity of accepting the punishment depends on the *kind* of law that is broken. (The problem here, of course, is that it is the state that decides *what* law it wants to invoke in order to prosecute and punish the person.) Philosopher

Carl Cohen thus differentiates between "direct disobedience" and "indirect disobedience" in relation to accepting the penalty.

> Should he accept his punishment, then, as right? That depends on what he did, on what kind of law he broke. If he deliberately *disobeyed a law he thought immoral in itself* he is justified, of course, in fighting punishment in every reasonable way at his command, chiefly through the courts. He will seek to have the bad law struck down, or at least to have it declared inapplicable in his case. If he loses in the end, he is likely, as a citizen who is generally law-abiding, to accept the punishment, not as right but as a painful price he helps to pay for a law-governed community. If the law he broke was really in itself immoral (and we may be in some doubt about that), the legal system will have done an injustice; but we cannot allow every man to sit as the judge in his own case. Of course justice is not always done, and the fight against bad laws must never stop, but miscarriages of justice do not, in themselves, justify the abandonment of a legal system.
>
> If, on the other hand, the disobedient has deliberately broken what he knows to be itself a good law (a traffic or trespass law, or the like) to protest some other evil, say, the war in Vietnam, or oppression in the cities, it is right for him to be punished, not because he is a bad man but because punishment in such cases of indirect disobedience is a part—an essential part—of the act of protest itself (1968:599).

From the radical perspective, however, the problem with any of these discussions on punishment and civil disobedience is that they all assume that the individual must be bound by the rules of the system. This is understandable since those who make the arguments are trying to preserve that system. But if we are ever to be liberated, we cannot take the system on its own terms. If the law is an immoral one, then it must be violated *and* the violator *should not* accept the punishment. By accepting the punishment we allow the sytem to continue operating immorally. We also commit an immoral act by accepting the punishment. And when other laws are violated in the course of acting against an oppressive governmental policy (or against the existence of government itself), that punishment should not be accepted either. To accept the punishment is again to restrict oneself to the rules of the game established by the oppressive government. The person who protests or who attempts more directly to bring about necessary changes has to use all the devices at his disposal. To accept the punishment under any circumstance is as immoral as it is cowardly.

The final legalist argument qualifies civil disobedience to the point that civil disobedience has no potential as moral force and as a method of eliminating oppressive conditions: the majoritarian argument. Following the eighteenth century liberal, John Locke, it is maintained that governments can only be legitimately challenged by the will of the majority. As Staughton Lynd has noted, however, this is the reason that a bourgeois gentleman like Locke could justify revolution with such confidence. The chances that a majority of people would advocate revolution in a country dominated by a ruling elite that controls public opinion, while at the same time claiming to be the people's government, is slight. And civil disobedience has about the same chance of being the mode of behavior for the majority of the population.

But the majoritarian argument is still advanced by liberal theorists. It serves the purpose of those who cannot understand what is happening in the world today. Kennan (1968:13), again writing about the actions of the student left and "those young people in all the glory of their defiant rags and hairdos," informs us:

> If you accept a democratic system, this means that you are prepared to put up with those of its workings, legislative or administrative, with which you do not agree as well as with those that meet with your concurrence. This willingness to accept, in principle, the workings of a system based on the will of the majority, even when you yourself are in the minority, is simply the essence of democracy. Without it there could be no system of representative self-government at all.

Kennan clearly has a narrow image of self-government.

But there is more, as he continues:

> When you attempt to alter the workings of the system by means of violence of civil disobedience, this, it seems to me, can have only one of two implications: either you do not believe in democracy at all and consider that society ought to be governed by enlightened minorities such as the one to which you, of course, belong; or you consider that the present system is so imperfect that it is not truly representative, that it no longer serves adequately as a vehicle for the will of the majority, and that this leaves to the unsatisfied no adequate means of self-expression other than the primitive one of calling demonstrations and mass defiance of established authority (1968:13).

Kennan not only misunderstands how majorities are formed in his elitist democracy, but he also fails to realize that those who do not have the power have no other way to act democratically than by acts of civil disobedience.

In response to the majoritarian theory, H. Rap Brown has presented the appropriate argument for our times. He contends that men cannot be bound by laws to which they have not given their consent. This means, correctly, that most blacks are not bound by most laws in the United States. Even in terms of the liberal idea of representation, blacks have not been represented in making the laws. Yet they, according to the legalist theory, are supposed to be bound by these laws. And are not those who exclude others from the decisions that affect their lives the offenders? H. Rap Brown writes:

> Who are the real outlaws in this country? They say I am an outlaw. I am charged with inciting Black people to "riot." It is against the "law" to riot. But did you or I have any say in passing this law? Do we have much of a say in any of the laws passed in this country? I

consider myself neither morally nor legally bound to obey laws which were made by a group of white "law-makers" who did not let my people be represented in making those laws (1969:105).

He adds, "That government which makes laws that you and I are supposed to obey, without letting us be a part of that government is an illegal government."

The majoritarian idea can no longer intimidate us. For other segments of the population, as well as blacks, law-making is not a representative matter. The laws have been made by a ruling elite. Only when laws belong to all the people can a majoritarian argument apply to any of our actions, civil disobedient or otherwise.

Which brings me to the conclusion that all the liberal arguments (and qualifications) for civil disobedience are faulty and inadequate. The liberal's view of civil disobedience will only intensify the problems we now have in American society. This is the point made over and over again in Howard Zinn's critique of Fortas's theory of civil disobedience. At one place in his book, Zinn suggests speaking about that theory (1968:37): "If followed, it guarantees that the most fundamental ills of American society will remain unassailable by civil disobedience, and thus left to the ordinary weak ministrations of free speech and the electoral system, which have hardly been able to budge these problems. Our most deep-rooted troubles are not represented by specific laws, but are so woven into American society that the only way to get at them is to attack the fabric at any vulnerable point." Only a new approach to law (and civil disobedience) will allow us to attack the problems of our age.

This means that the present legal system—with most of its assumptions—must be changed. The old legal system will not work in a new society. And a new society cannot be achieved without first making changes in the old legal system. The old (that is, the existing) legal system attempts to preserve current conditions. Any protest or effective action is legally denied under the present system. Who are the ones defined as being disobedient, as being criminals? Those who attempt to bring about a just society. The ruling class—no matter what laws they violate— never define themselves as disobedient or criminal. Their system must be removed before a just existence can be achieved. It is *conscience*, not the existing law, that guides our actions. The only valid law today is the one that appeals to the conscience of men.

VI.

Can law be changed to meet the needs of a new society? Is a legal system really necessary? If there are to be laws, how should they relate to morals? Most legal scholars begin by assuming that some kind of legal system is necessary. This is, however, from the radical perspective, still a problematic assumption. Certainly if a legal system is to exist, it will have to be markedly different from the one we have today.

The legal scholars who are considering the problem of changing the legal system begin, rightly, by asking what goals the legal enterprise serves (or should serve) and what laws achieve these goals. The common conclusion seems to be that much of our law—criminal law in particular—is serving moralistic interests. These writers then suggest that the legal system should be stripped of these moralistic interests. The following is characteristic of the discussions and conclusions that are being offered:

> The first principle of our cure for crime is this: we must strip off the moralistic excrescences on our criminal justice system so that it may concentrate on the essential. The prime function of the criminal law is to protect our persons and our property; these purposes are now engulfed in a mass of other distracting, inefficiently performed, legislative duties. When the criminal law invades the spheres of private morality and social welfare, it exceeds its proper limits at the cost of neglecting its primary tasks. The unwarranted extension is expensive, ineffective, and criminogenic (Morris and Hawkins, 1970:2).

The more specific proposals that subsequently follow include the partial or complete repeal of those criminal laws that regulate drunkenness, drug use, gambling, disorderly conduct, vagrancy, abortion, adultry, prostitution, and homosexuality.

As to the proper sphere of law, these writers usually subscribe to John Stuart Mill's principle from his essay On Liberty:

> That principle is, that the sole end for which mankind are warranted, individually or collectively, in interfering with the liberty of action of any of their members is self-protection. That the only purpose for which power can be rightfully exercised over any member of a civilized community against his will, is to prevent harm to others. His own good, either physical or moral, is not a sufficient warrant, he cannot rightfully be compelled to do or forbear because it would be better for him to do so, because it will make him happier, because, in the opinion of others, to do so would be wise or even right (1947:9).

No matter what one's political persuasion, this statement of human freedom at first glance seems sufficient.

However, at a closer look, and with further reading of Mill, our liberties become qualified and restricted. For instance, if one's opponent can be declared to be a member of the "uncivilized," any and all freedoms can be denied. The same holds for minors and those who have allegedly lost control over their senses. And even more insidious, the doctrine that power can be exercised against one's will "to prevent harm to others" is open to some interpretation; and also considerable misinterpretation. If, for example, those in power have decided that anyone or any particular activity presents a possible harm to others, the right exists to limit freedom. A government can declare as criminal almost anything that can arbitrarily be defined as a harm to others. Disrupting the government could be (and is) easily defined as criminal because it is regarded as a harm to others, especially a harm to the existing society and government.

Likewise, the followers of Mill—and would-be reformers of the criminal law—include within the function of the criminal law not only the protection of the lives and property of citizens, but "the preservation of public order and decency" (Morris and Hawkins, 1970:26). Once you include such nebulous things as public order and decency, almost everything and everybody can be restricted by the criminal law.

And furthermore, I find it difficult to support the position that criminal law can be stripped of its moral judgments. To the contrary, the very stuff of criminal law is moral. The criminal law is moralistic if for no other reason than it takes the position that *any* human actions should be limited. The assumption that either the society or the individual should be regulated is a moral one. And certainly the decision to regulate specific substantive actions is moralistic. A moral decision is taken when it is decided to protect others by means of the criminal law. No legal reform, or even legal revolution, cannot be achieved by taking morality out of the law.

But what then is the answer, if the question is the proper nature of criminal law in our age? When the game of limiting criminal law in terms of morals is played, the problem becomes that of whose morality is to be included and whose morality is to be excluded. The arbitrariness of this approach seems to preclude its possibility as an answer to the question of law. Besides, does the state have the right to restrict the freedoms of some persons and not those of others? A belief in a natural law of human rights prevents this kind of solution.

I can conceive of three alternatives. First, quite simply, criminal law could be *eliminated* completely. Perhaps it is too much of a burden on the law to expect it to keep people good. Let us assume, rather, that people are good and that morals do not need the law to assure their effectiveness. There seems to be no research to support the claim that law is needed to enforce morality, whatever that morality may be. For example, I am fairly certain that the amount of murder would not be changed by repealing all of the homicide laws.

The second alternative to existing laws, which is actually a variation of the first, would be to retain our criminal laws, and even enact more, as a *symbolic* gesture of what we regard as good in man. Of course, as symbols of goodness, the laws would then *never* be enforced. This proposal is intolerable to the legal scholars who make force and coercion central to their theories. John Austin (1885) and Hans Kelsen (1949), for example, have held that a legal system is made valid through the enforcement of prescribed penalties. Without coercion the legal system would not be effective, the argument goes, and the system of rules would not qualify as a legal system at all. But I am arguing that not only is such a conception of law repressive, but it is also useless as a positive force in human social existence. Outside of providing for revenge and retribution, I doubt if existing criminal law serves any other useful function. If some men feel compulsive about making laws, why not just regard the laws as symbolic?

The third alternative is much more complex. The basic premise is that of a *decentralized* law. It is based on the belief that a monolithic substantive criminal law cannot serve the needs of a heterogeneous society. No longer can we expect such laws to be binding on all persons, in similar realms of conduct, throughout an extensive geographical jurisdiction. Such law is doomed to failure just as it is a violation of basic human rights.

The problem with criminal law has always been the doctrine of monolithic control combined with the myth of cultural consensus in society. This doctrine, if ever valid, cannot be applied to modern society. Consensus does not (and cannot) exist on a large scale, and monolithic control is an impossibility as well as being a dictatorial concept of government. Any amount of homogeneity can only be achieved on a local level. And any amount of democratic government can exist only on a local basis. Decentralized government would thus provide the basis for a criminal law that would be both democratic and possible. Such criminal law is more a matter of *territoriality* than a question of substantive coverage.

Rather than talking simply about the reduction of criminal law, therefore, we may redefine the problem. And it becomes a matter of changing the concept and scope of the law. Each community, accordingly, would enact its own laws in terms of democratic procedures. Some communities might decide not to enact laws at all. This idea of law supports the belief in self-determination of separate groups. Not only would law then be meaningful to the people involved, but it would allow the members of the community to shape their own lives, to determine their own destinies.

Support for this third alternative is found in a recent book on the tribal rights of the American Indians, We Talk, You Listen, by Vine Deloria, Jr. (1970). The author offers a new America that finds precedent in the customs of the native Americans. He suggests the need for a Constitution that guarantees "group rights." The present Constitution is not concerned with tribal self-expression, but only with individual rights that guarantee protection against tyranny by the state, by other individuals, and by groups against the individual. With the recognition of tribal or group rights, individuals will enjoy both individual rights and group rights. And according to the Indian concept, property could be held in common by the tribe or community. This practice is being worked out today in hippie communes. What may be emerging is a "new individualism" within the group, tribe, commune, or community. It would be a right secured by the Constitution.

Communities would then be free to develop their own systems of regulation, if such systems are at all necessary. An experience that gives support to this possibility is that of the popular tribunal in Cuba (see Berman, 1969). Neighborhoods have their own courts, staffed by judges and other personnel elected democratically from within the community. Little emphasis is placed on sanctions of any kind. Rather, violators continue to be integrated into activities within the community. Law thus plays an educative role in the community, rather than a punitive one. What is important is maintaining peace and understanding in the community rather than enforcement of the law for the sake of enforcement.

Similar proposals are being suggested in the United States. Radical groups such as the Black Panthers are proposing, for instance, community control of the police. There is no doubt that not only are these proposals the correct ones for our age, they will become realities in our time. What we are moving toward is domestic sovereignty within the framework of intranational and international relationships.

Any law outside of the community, then, will be either of a constitutional or an instrumental nature. Constitutionally we will all—as individuals, as groups, and as individuals within groups—be protected from all possible forms of oppression. Any other law on the national level will pertain solely to the regulation of services for the people. These regulations will provide for such instrumental services as health, public transportation, the environment, and a guaranteed income. These provisions will assure individual and group rights rather than engaging in the enterprise of substantive criminal law.

The end product will be a life released from the repressions of today. If a legal system is to exist, its purpose must be to assure a liberated life. Whether man needs law to provide this is still an open question. What is certain is that any law in the future will be drastically different from the law of today. Ultimately it is not law that makes man good. Man is basically good. It is the institutions which oppress him that make for any shortcomings in man. Let man be free. Let him control his own institutions rather than be controlled by them. And he will be the good man that he is by the nature of his being.

VII.

Meanwhile: existing law is being used to prevent the changes that would make men free. How could anything else be expected?

Law today exists to protect the status quo. Liberals tell us not to ask for more than the system is willing to grant.

Thus legal repression grows stronger each day. There is no sign that either the actions that inspire this repression or the repression itself will subside in the near future. A dialectic that is more than words is shaping the future for all of us. To argue that the radical actions must stop is to submit to the tyranny of oppression. But since the oppressor has the power, he is able to officially place the blame on those who would remove the oppression. If there is any cause for today's unrest, it is the unwillingness of those in power to listen and act in a way that would solve the just grievances. But the irony is that what might have been solved within the framework of the existing system is now beyond that point. We now know that a system which makes the lives of so many unbearable is a system that cannot correct itself. That is why our actions no longer take place within that system. And that is why the system is using everything at its disposal to repress our actions.

The repression we experience today is not a new phenomenon in American life, not a new form of conservatism, not primarily a "right wing" reaction. What we experience is a characteristic that runs through the American conception of liberal democracy. We have been led to believe for ages that the population is to submit to the sovereignty of the nation. We were told that only a few people were capable of leading the rest. And that our leaders were to be trusted, that we were to turn our fates over to those in authority, merely because they were in authority.

In the same way, we have taken at face value the belief that law is an absolute good in itself. Order, as well, has become an absolute value, a value that actually benefits those who rule at the expense of those who are ruled. Because of this indoctrination, many citizens today are willing to take up the law and order challenge that is being perpetuated by the power structure. Those not falling for this devious scheme are the ones who are feeling the actual pains of repression. They are the ones—in all their suffering—who will take us out of the theory and practice of repression.

The law is the first and last weapon of repression. As a last resort it is being used today to preserve the old order. Thus, legal repression is all around us. One has only to look at the recent enactment of new laws. (Even the old laws were not repressive enough to fight the forces of change.)

To begin with, the war on crime, that started in the 1960's, has resulted in legislation that is constitutionally questionable as well as being blatantly repressive. The ostensible objective of the crime bill was to assist state and local governments in reducing the incidence of crime by increasing the effectiveness of law enforcement and criminal administration. By the time the legislation was completed, amendments were added which were strictly concerned with law and order. One amendment (Title II) was a deliberate attempt to overturn previous Supreme Court decisions that supposedly were responsible for "coddling criminals" and "handcuffing the police." In the bill that was enacted, all voluntary confessions and eyewitness identifications—regardless of whether a defendant is informed of his rights of counsel—could be admitted in federal courts. In another provision (Title III) state and local police were given broad license to tap telephones and engage in other forms of eavesdropping. Law enforcement officials were permitted to engage in these practices for brief periods without even a court order. Another provision provided that any persons convicted of "inciting a riot or civil disorder," "organizing, promoting, encouraging, or participating in a riot or civil disorder," or "aiding and abetting" any person in committing such offenses shall be disqualified for employment by the federal government for five years. The legislation was an outright attempt to control by means of law any behavior that would threaten the established social and political order.

Other cases of legal repression have followed. The so-called "Organized Crime Control Act of 1969" raises basic constitutional questions about such matters as grand jury powers, illegally obtained evidence, long-term sentencing, self-incrimination, and due process of law. The legislation also has a provision allowing imprisonment of "dangerous special offenders" for up to thirty years. And since the bill states that "no limitations shall be placed on the information," a person may be sentenced on rumor and hearsay. This law has more to do with *anyone* that the authorities want removed than it does with organized crime in particular.

After several years of controversy, a crime bill has been enacted for the District of Columbia. The law is a victory for Attorney General John Mitchell, who has turned the Department of Justice into a department of legal repression (see Harris, 1970). While the law is for the District of Columbia, Mitchell and Nixon have made it quite clear that the bill is to be a "model" for the codes that likely will be enacted in other states. The law, among other things, authorizes "no-knock" (or what Mitchell calls "quick entry") searches, under which the police could force their way into a building without announcing their presence or identifying themselves if they believed that evidence inside would otherwise be destroyed. There is the "preventive detention" clause under which a defendant could be jailed without bail for up to 60 days if it is felt that he might commit further crimes if he were released. There is authorization for wiretaps by the police and establishment of a mandatory five-year sentence upon a second conviction for a crime of violence in which the defendant was carrying a gun. Again, legal repression rather than the removal of oppressive social conditions is used when the authority structure is threatened.

In addition to legal repression on the national level, there have been numerous laws enacted on the state and local level with the objective of establishing order. There are the laws that make "rioting" a crime, laws that make criminal political activities on the university campus, laws that make the crossing of state lines for political purposes illegal, laws that make communication among a number of people a "conspiracy." These and others represent the last attempt by an old society to prevent the coming of the new.

The repression is being made real through the strict enforcement and administration of these laws. Specific groups are being singled out of the population as threats to the establishment, the Black Panthers in particular. Over 400 Panthers were arrested in the first year of Nixon's administration. Since the Black Panther party was founded, nearly thirty members have been killed by the police. Offices of the party have been raided by the police in Chicago, Des Moines, Oakland, Los Angeles, and in several other cities. Most of the Panther leaders have been either killed, jailed, or forced into exile. Other members are currently being investigated by congressional committees and grand juries. The FBI regards the Panthers as the greatest single threat to national security. All of this may be going even beyond repression. As Tom Hayden (1970:118) observes: "The Panthers are the target not of repression but of an undeclared war. Under a state of repression, the heretic at least is accorded bail, trial, and appeal. In a state of war, victims are killed or rounded up without serious regard for legal 'niceties.' The Panthers held in jails across America today are no different from prisoners held in Santo Domingo, Saigon, or any other center of the American empire."

And there are the continual political trials: Captain Levy, the Presidio mutiny case, the Oakland Seven, the Baltimore Four, the Boston Five, the Chicago Seven, and the Catonsville Nine to name only a few of the most publicized cases. In these cases, the most dubious of charges have been made, the shabbiest being the "conspiracy" charge. As a political weapon, the conspiracy charge requires that the prosecution show merely that the defendants conspired, or rather, communicated in some way regarding a demonstration, draft resistance, or whatever. The prosecution need not show that the defendents actually engaged in particular overt acts, but merely that they said something. Among other things, the conspiracy charge is an effective form of political harrassment whereby those who threaten the system can be detained for long periods of time at great personal expense.

The established authority is thus able to use the law, its law, in the attempt to maintain control over the people. Furthermore, those in power are able to justify their actions through law. And most critically, they can pursue *their own* criminal activities without being defined as criminal. The police are seldom charged and convicted of crimes when they murder, violate constitutional

rights, assault, and so on. The government itself when engaging in
an illegal policy is not prosecuted as a criminal. All of this is
understandable, no matter how immoral or how criminal, since
those in power, those who control the legal system, are not likely
to prosecute themselves and define their official policies as
criminal.

War crimes. We sometimes hear about them, without the
mention of a war criminal. If a criminal is mentioned, it is not our
government who is pursuing an illegal war but combatants who
are indicted for killing beyond the call of duty. As a result of the
My Lai massacre, for example, several officers and enlisted men
have been prosecuted. But what obviously is not being asked is
that the makers of American war policy be prosecuted for the
crimes. That the government itself is criminal in southeast Asia is
beyond legal consideration.

But in terms of a superior (legal as well as moral) law, the
federal government is waging an illegal war in Southeast Asia.
The war is illegal in terms of the United Nations Charter, the
Hague Convention, the Geneva Accords, and likely the Constitution of the United States. Even the officers who administer
military orders are subject to the higher law as developed at
Nurenburg. But, again, because the rulers control and manipulate
the legal system to their own advantage, neither the nation nor its
leaders are prosecuted as criminals.

Even when the constitutionality of the war is questioned, as it
has been several times in the last two or three years, a legal
counterargument is conveniently advanced and upheld by the
government's courts. Under the so-called "political question"
doctrine, the courts claim that they have no jurisdiction over the
matter. The federal court in Boston that tried the Spock case (the
Boston Five), for example, declared on the basis of this doctrine
that it would not hear any arguments about the constitutionality
of the war.

Similarly, in a recent case that explicitly attempts to deal
with the unconstitutionality of the war, *Massachusetts vs. Laird*,
the government submitted a brief which declared:

> In sum, we submit that the Constitutionality of the American military
> presence in Vietnam is a non-justiciable issue that cannot be decided
> by this court. This conclusion follows from each one of the six tests
> of whether an issue presents a non-justiciable political question, and
> from the general test of justiciability. This in no way means,
> however, as Massachusetts would have this Court believe, that the
> grant of power to Congress in Article I, Sec. 8 "to declare war" is
> thereby rendered meaningless. As this Court has recognized, there are
> certain provisions of the Constitution which are to be enforced
> exclusively by the political departments of the Government. This
> does not mean that they are unenforceable; simply that they are
> unenforceable through judicial means (Quoted in *The New York
> Times*, September 25, 1970:43).

The courts deal with "political" matters only when these matters belong to the government. The political concerns of the people are fair game for the courts. Why not? The courts and the government are an integral part of the system, though they sometimes argue separation of powers. The argument separates the problem and consolidates the power. Legal repression operates only one way—for the benefit of the government.

VIII.

In a radical social theory our commitment is to justice. Laws are not taken necessarily as the measure of that justice. Indeed, the legal system often is the very negation of justice. Our allegiance is to a vision beyond the boundaries of the state. The old law simultaneously represses those who would allow their ideals to determine their actions while the government itself ignores the law. Thus, an attack on the old laws as well as the old institutions is a vital part of our radical age. We will experience a confrontation of old law and new conscience for some time to come.

The liberal response to today's conscience and action is as inadequate as it is immoral. We are told to conform to the law for the sake of the law itself. We are told to uphold order for the sake of order. We are told to be tolerant—while the government carries on an illegal and immoral war and is intolerant of dissent that might be effective.

Those in power can well advise us to be tolerant when they control how and when they will be tolerant or intolerant. Then we are told (Fortas, 1968:126) how well the present system is working with all its guarantees: "For the citizen, the guarantee of freedom of speech, of press, of peaceable assembly, of protest, or organization and dissent provides powerful instruments for effecting change. And ultimately, the all-important power of the vote—access to the ballot box—furnishes the most effective weapon in the citizen's arsenal." Finally:

> In short, we have known that our democratic processes do indeed function, and that they can bring about fundamental response to fundamental demands, and can do this without revolution, and despite the occasional violence of those who either reject or have not attained the maturity and restraint to use, and not to abuse, their freedom. This is an extraordinary tribute to our institutions (1968: 126).

If our institutions are functioning so well, why do so many demand such far-reaching changes, and why is repression the only response of the old institutions?

> The system no longer even provides us with a basic element of our so-called legal guarantees: the fair trail. The courts, just like the law in general, are a myth.

The court in American society is something like the church. There is a widespread conspiracy to hold the court holy, above the world of sin and deals with power. It is to be treated with a special respect; quiet is to be observed by those who enter, and speech is only to follow formal procedure. The judge is a high priest possessed of a wisdom that mere citizens do not have. He wears robes, makes interpretations of obscure scriptures, and holds a gavel (like a cross) representing authority. He is referred to as "Your Honor" or "If the Court please . . . ," much as the Pope is "His Holiness." Perhaps more than any other public institution in America, the court system demands an absolute conformity to its rules and its atmosphere. If citizens will only respect this institution, then all their conflicts can be sifted, negotiated, and resolved.

At the same time, everyone knows that this concept of the courts is a myth. The court is political; the judges are elected or (in most cases) appointed by politicians. Behind those robes are men of political motivation: landlords, underworld figures, partisan manipulators. Nearly all of them are white, middle-class, middle-aged, conservative males. The laws they administer favor rich against poor, white against black, respectable against nonconformist (Hayden, 1970:97-98). The courts will never operate for the people under the old legal system.

Those who govern, are responsible for the problems (and the "disorder") today. Following an obsolete theory of government, law, and society, they are unable to respond in a way that would even begin to solve our problems. Their only reaction is one of further repression. Only if we start anew, with entirely different assumptions, can social and political life be put back together again.

The old system has shown that it cannot be reformed. The ideals of liberalism were corrupted by practices that may or may not have been inspired by those ideals. Whatever the problem, both ideal and practice fail us today: The repressive legal system of liberal practice is the last attempt to preserve a system that has outlived its time. Law as we experience it today is oppressive. Like all forms of oppression, the existing legal system must be removed. Then we can live again—according to the radical image of man and society.

REFERENCES

Austin, John, Lectures on Jurisprudence or the Philosophy of Positive Law. London: J. Murray, 1885.

Berman, Jesse, "The Cuban Popular Tribunals." Columbia Law Review. 69 (1969): 1317-1354.

Brown, H. Rap, Die Nigger Die! New York: Dial Press, 1969.

Cohen, Carl, "Civil Disobedience: Moral or Not?" The Nation. December 2 (1968): 597-600.

Delona, Vine, Jr., We Talk, You Listen. New York: Macmillan, 1970.

Devlin, Patrick, *The Enforcement of Morals*. London: Oxford University Press, 1965.

Durkheim, Emile, *Moral Education. A Study in the Theory and Application of the Sociology of Education*. Trans. Everett K. Wilson and Herman Schnurer. New York: The Free Press, 1961.

Friedmann, Wolfgang, *Law in a Changing Society*. Harmondsworth, England: Penguin Books, 1964.

Fuller, Lon, *The Morality of Law*. New Haven: Yale University Press, 1964.

Gossett, William T., *American Bar News*. 14 (1969): 3.

Harris, Richard, *Justice*. New York: Dutton, 1970.

Hart, H.L.A., *The Concept of Law*. London: Oxford University Press, 1961.

———, *Law, Liberty and Morality*. Stanford University Press, 1963.

Haskins, George Lee, *Law and Authority in Early Massachusetts*. New York: Macmillan, 1960.

Hayden, Tom, *Trial*. New York: Holt, Rinehart and Winston, 1970.

Hook, Sidney, "On Civil Disobedience, 1967." *The New York Times Magazine*. November 26, 1967: 124-126.

Kelsen, Hans, *General Theory of Law and State*. Trans. by Anders Wedberg. Cambridge, Mass.: Harvard University Press, 1949.

Kennan, George F., *Democracy and the Student Left*. New York: Bantam Books, 1968.

Kolko, Gabriel, *The Roots of American Foreign Policy*. Boston: Beacon Press, 1969.

Lipset, Seymour Martin, *The First New Nation*. New York: Basic Books, 1963.

Little, David, *Religion, Order, and Law: A Study in Pre-Revolutionary England*. New York: Harper & Row, 1969.

Lloyd, Dennis, *The Idea of Law*. Harmondsworth, England: Penguin Books, 1964.

Lynd, Staughton, *Intellectual Origins of American Radicalism*. New York: Pantheon, 1968.

———, "Again—Don't Tread on Me." *Newsweek*, July 6, 1970: 31.

Mill, John Stuart, *On Liberty*. Alburey Castell ed. New York: Appleton-Century-Crofts, 1947.

Morris, Norval and Hawkins, Gordon, *The Honest Politicians Guide to Crime Control*. Chicago: University of Chicago Press, 1970.

Morris, Richard, *Studies in the History of American Law*. 2nd ed. New York: John M. Mitchell, 1959.

National Commission on the Causes and Prevention of Violence, *To Establish Justice, To Insure Domestic Tranquility*. New York: Bantam Books, 1970.

The New York Times, Massachusetts v. Laird. September 25, 1970: 43.

Peterson, Merrill D., *Thomas Jefferson and the New Nation*. New York: Oxford University Press, 1970.

Pound, Roscoe, *An Introduction to Legal Philosophy*. New Haven: Yale University Press, 1922.

————, *Social Control Through Law*. New Haven: Yale University Press, 1942.

————, "A Survey of Social Interest." *Harvard Law Review*. 57(1943): 1-39.

Quinney, Richard, "Toward a Sociology of Criminal Law." in Richard Quinney (ed.) *Crime and Justice in Society*. Boston: Little Brown, 1969: 1-30.

Schapiro, J.S., *Social Reform and the Reformation*. New York: Columbia University Press, 1909.

Thoreau, Henry David, *Thoreau: People, Principles and Politics*. Milton Meltzer ed. New York: Hill and Wang, 1963.

Zinn, Howard, *Disobedience and Democracy*. New York: Vintage Books, 1968.

Chapter 3

Commodity Form and Legal Form;
an essay on the "Relative
Autonomy" of the Law*

Isaac D. Balbus

Prefatory Note

After a good deal of thought I have decided not to respond directly to
Professor Trubek's exhaustive review of *The Dialectics of Legal Repression*,
but will rather leave it to readers of my book to determine for themselves the
adequacy of his description, analysis, and evaluation of the material contained
therein. However, insofar as Professor Trubek also refers briefly in his essay
to my "more recent," and until now unpublished work, it seems appropriate to
present a sample of this work, especially since Trubek himself argues that it
entails a "major refinement" which "allows Balbus to explain what remains
unexplained in *The Dialectics*." Indeed, *in certain respects* the following essay
constitutes an autocritique of the theoretical analysis in my book, and a
comparison of the two will thus permit the reader to assess indirectly the
extent of my agreement with Trubek's critique. At the same time, what follows
also constitutes an implicit and, at times explicit, critique of Trubek's own
effort to elaborate and apply an alternative to my position, the effort he calls
"critical social thought about law."

I. Introduction

In this essay I attempt to outline the essentials of a Marxian
theory of law. This theory, as we shall see, entails a simultaneous

---

* Isaac D. Balbus, "Commodity Form and Legal Form: An Essay on the 'Relative
Autonomy' of The Law," *Law & Society Review*, Vol. II (1977): 571-588. Reprinted
by permission of The Law and Society Association.

rejection of both an *instrumentalist* or reductionist approach,
which denies that the legal order possesses any autonomy from
the demands imposed on it by actors of the capitalist society in
which it is embedded, and a *formalist* approach, which asserts an
absolute, unqualified autonomy of the legal order from this
society. The instrumentalist approach—whether pluralist or crude
Marxist—conceives of the law as a mere instrument or tool of the
will of dominant social actors and thus fails even to pose the
problem of the specific *form* of the law and the way in which this
form articulates with the overall requirements of the capitalist
system in which these social actors function.[1] The formalist
approach, on the other hand, locates and describes the specificity
of the legal form but, insofar as it treats this form as a closed,
autonomous system whose development is to be understood
exclusively in terms of its own "internal dynamics," is likewise
unable even to conceptualize the relationship between the legal
form and the specifically capitalist whole of which it is a part.[2] In
short, neither approach is capable of explaining why a specifically
legal form of the exchange of people is inextricably intertwined
with a specifically capitalist form of the exchange of products. It
is precisely that problem to which this essay is addressed.

The debate between the instrumentalists and the formalists—
which has dominated legal theory for at least two hundred years
and continues to flourish today—has always been extraordinarily
misleading. It is characterized by a false dichotomy which arises
from an inadequate starting point shared by *both* approaches, *i.e.,*
the assumption that the law must be judged "autonomous" to the
extent that it functions and develops independently of the *will* of
extralegal social actors. Given this common conceptual terrain,
their dispute is necessarily and merely a dispute over the "facts;"
formalists "discover" that the law is independent of the will of
social actors, and thus conclude that it is "autonomous," whereas
instrumentalists "find," to the contrary, that the law is directly
responsive to the will of these actors and thus conclude that the
law is "not autonomous." Neither understands that the answer to
the question whether the law is independent of the will of social
actors *in no way* disposes of the question whether the law is
autonomous from the capitalist *system* of which these actors are
the agents. Even more: the formulation that *to the degree that the
law does not respond directly to the demands of powerful social
actors it is autonomous, in the sense that it functions and develops
according to its own internal dynamics* omits the possibility that
the law is not autonomous from, but rather articulates with and
must be explained by, the systemic requirements of capitalism
precisely because it does not respond directly to the demands of
these actors. In other words, it is one thing to argue that the legal
order is autonomous from the preferences of actors outside this
order, but quite another to argue that is autonomous from the
capitalist system (unless one were to commit the "voluntarist"

error of equating the preferences of actors with those activities
that must be performed if the system in which they function is to
survive). Indeed, I will try to demonstrate that it is precisely
because the law *is* autonomous in the first sense that it is *not*
autonomous in the second or, to put it another way that the
relative autonomy of the legal form from the will of social actors
entails at the same time an essential *identity* or homology between
the legal form and the very "cell" of capitalist society, the
commodity form. Thus the Marxian theory of the "relative
autonomy" of the law, which I am proposing, cannot be understood
as a *compromise* between the instrumentalist and formalist
positions; rather it purports to *transcend* the opposition between
these positions by rejecting the common conceptual terrain on
which they are based and elaborating a wholly different
theoretical terrain. This requires a brief summary of Marx's
analysis of the logic of the commodity form.

II. The Logic of the Commodity Form

This logic, Marx tells us in the first chapter of Volume I of
Capital, is that of a "mysterious," twofold and, in fact, contradictory reality. A commodity, to begin with, is a use-value: it is a
qualitatively distinct object which exists to fulfill a qualitatively
distinct, concrete human need and has been brought into existence
by a qualitatively distinct form of labor, which Marx calls
"concrete labor." In their role as use-values different commodities
are thus *not* equal to one another; their inequality corresponds to
the unequal labors that produced them. At the same time,
however, a commodity is also an object of exchange, or an
exchange-value: it exists and is valued not only, and not
immediately, because it is used but also and rather because it can
be exchanged for another commodity. The existence of exchange-
value, or what Marx simply calls value, thus presupposes that
qualitatively distinct and otherwise incommensurable commodites
enter into a formal relationship of equivalence with one another,
i.e., that qualitatively different objects become what they are not:
equal. This relationship of equivalence, in turn, is facilitated by
the existence of a particular commodity, money, which with the
development of capitalism becomes the *universal economic
equivalent* by means of which the value of every other commodity
can be expressed. Money, in other words, permits all products to
assume a formal identity so that they can become, in Marx's
suggestive phrase, "citizens of that world [of commodities]" (1967:
63), that is, they can all stand for or be *represented* by each other.
The fully developed commodity form, or the money form, thus
entails a common *form* which is an abstraction from, and masking
of, the qualitatively different *contents* of the objects and the

concrete human needs to which they correspond: "The memory of use-value, as distinct from exchange-value, has become entirely extinguished in this incarnation of pure exchange-value" (Marx, 1973:239-40).

This abstraction from, and masking of, the content or quality of the object is only made possible by a prior abstraction from, and masking of, the concrete labor that produced it. The common form that is exchange-value can only exist as the expression of the one form that is common to all the qualitatively different labors that bring objects into existence, i.e., of labor-power understood as an abstract, undifferentiated expenditure of energy over a given period of time, or what Marx calls abstract labor. Thus, in order for commodities to become equal to one another, i.e., in order for exchange-value to exist, concrete, qualitatively different labors must become what they are not: equal. The result is that the "memory" of concrete labor is "extinguished" along with that of use-value.

The logic of the commodity form is thus that of a double movement from the concrete to the abstract, a double abstraction of form from content, a twofold transmutation of quality into quantity. The transformation of commodities from unequal to equal objects parallels, and is made possible by, a transformation of the labor which produces them from unequal to equal. In order for commodities to be what they are, both the unequal objects and the unequal labor which has produced them must become what they are not, i.e., equal. Thus the commodity form has its origin in concrete human needs and creative labor, but it "possesses the peculiar capacity of concealing its own essence from the human beings who live with it and by it" (Lefebvre, 1969:47), i.e., by virtue of the double mystification inherent in the commodity form, human beings necessarily "forget" that commodities owe their existence to human needs and to the activity in which people have engaged both to produce and fulfill these needs. The commodity form, in other words, is an economic form that necessarily functions independently of, or autonomously from, the will of the subjects who set it in motion. Thus the fetishism of commodities: the masking of the link between commodities and their human origin gives rise to the appearance, the ideological inversion, that commodities have living, human powers. Products appear to take on a life of their own, dominating the very human subjects who in fact bring them into existence but who no longer "know" this. Commodity fetishism thus entails a profound reversal of the real causal relationship between humans and their products: humans, the subjects who create or cause the objects, become the object, i.e., are "caused" by the very objects which they have created and to which they now attribute subjectivity or causal power. Human life under a capitalist mode of production becomes dominated by the passion to possess the commodity's living power, especially the power of that one commodity, money, that makes possible the

possession and accumulation of all other commodities. Thus
money is transformed from a means of exchange into the very end
or goal of human life itself.

III. The Logic of the Legal Form

Although Marx never developed a full-fledged theory of the
legal form, it is nevertheless possible to reconstruct from his early
writings on law and the state in *The Critique of Hegel's
Philosophy of the State* and the essay *On the Jewish Question*, as
well as from his later, more fragmentary treatment of the same
subject in *Capital, The Grundrisse*, and the *Critique of the Gotha
Program*, an analysis of the logic of the legal form which, in its
essentials, completely parallels his more systematic, fully
developed analysis of the commodity form.[3] Thus, with the aid of
these writings, I shall argue that the logic of the legal form and
the logic of the commodity form are one and the same.

If, in a capitalist mode of production, products take on the
form of individual *commodities*, people take on the form of
individual *citizens;* the exchange of commodities is paralleled by
the exchange of citizens. A citizen, in turn, is every bit as "mysterious," twofold, and in fact contradictory a reality as a commodity.
An individual citizen, to begin with, is a qualitatively distinct,
concrete subject with qualitatively distinct human needs or
interests. In this aspect of their existence, then, individual citizens
are manifestly *not* equal to one another, an inequality which
corresponds to the uniqueness of the human activities and the
networks of social relationships from which their needs or
interests derive. At the same time, however, individual citizens
are not only, and not immediately, subjects with needs but also
and rather objects of exchange who exist in order to represent,
and be represented by, other individual citizens. The existence of
political exchange or representation thus requires that qualitatively distinct individuals with otherwise incommensurable
interests enter into a formal relationship of equivalence with one
another, *i.e.,* that the qualitatively different subjects become what
they are not: *equal.* This relationship of equivalence, in turn, is
made possible by the law which, with the development of
capitalism, becomes the *universal political equivalent* by means of
which each individual is rendered equal to every other individual,
so that any one individual can represent any other. The fully
developed legal form thus entails a common *form* which is an
abstraction from, and masking of, the qualitatively different
contents of the needs of subjects as well as the qualitatively
different activities and structures of social relationships in which
they participate. Thus the legal form, in Marx's words, "makes an
abstraction of real men"[4] which is perfectly homologous to the

abstraction that the commodity form makes of "real products." Let us look more closely at the legal form in order to clarify the way in which it is able to perform this abstraction, as well as the consequences of this operation.

A. The Law as Universal Political Equivalent

The formality, generality, and "autonomy" of the law— captured in Weber's concept of "formal legal rationality" and summarized by Professor Trubek in this issue and elsewhere (1972)—preclude the qualitatively different interests and social origins of individuals from entering into the calculus of political exchange, just as the formality, generality, and "autonomy" of money preclude the qualitatively different use-values of commodities, and the unique labor that produces them, from being recognized in the calculus of economic exchange. The "blindness" of the legal form to substantive human interests and characteristics thus parallels the blindness of the commodity form to use-value concrete labor, and if the commodity-form functions to "extinguish" the "memory" of use-value and concrete labor, so too the legal form functions to extinguish the memory of different interests and social origins. As Marx puts it:

> The [legal] state abolishes, after its fashion, the distinctions established by birth, social rank, education, occupation, when it decrees that birth, social rank, education, occupation are non-political distinctions; when it proclaims, without regard to these distinctions that every member is an *equal* partner in popular sovereignty. [1972a:31]

The legal form thus defines distinctions of interest and origin *out of political existence*, just as the commodity form defines distinctions of use and labor out of economic existence. And, just as the commodity form "replaces" use-value and concrete labor with the abstractions of exchange-value and undifferentiated labor-power, the legal form "replaces" the multiplicity of concrete needs and interests with the abstractions of *"will"* and *"rights,"* and the socially differentiated individual with the abstraction of the *juridical subject* or the legal person. Pashukanis was perhaps the first Marxist after Marx to specify what might be called the common *mode of substitution* underlying both the commodity form and the legal form:

> In the same way that the natural multiformity of the useful attributes of a product is in commodities merely a simple wrapper of the value, while the concrete species of human labor are dissolved in abstract labor as the creator of value—so the concrete multiplicity of the relationships of a man to a thing comes out as the abstract will of the owner, while all the specific peculiarities distinguishing one representative of the species *homo sapiens* from another are dissolved in the abstraction of man in general as a juridic subject. [1951:163][5]

The subject of "equal rights" substitutes for the concrete subject of needs, and the abstract legal person substitutes for the real, flesh-and-blood, socially differentiated individual. Thus we are in the presence of the same double movement from the concrete to the abstract, the same twofold abstraction of form from content, that characterizes the commodity form.

B. Equality, Individuality, and Community

The "equality" established and protected by the legal form is thus purely formal insofar as it is established in and through an abstraction from the real social inequalities of capitalist, class society, which nevertheless continue to exist, of course, even if denied "political" recognition. Thus "the political suppression of private property not only does not abolish private property, [but] actually presupposes its existence" (Marx, 1972a:31). The formality of legal equality, however, does not prevent it from having substantive consequences which are anything but equal and are in fact repressive. On the one hand, the systematic application of an equal scale to systemically unequal individuals necessarily tends to reinforce systemic inequalities; this, of course, was the force of Anatole France's famous, ironic praise of "the majestic equality of the French law, which forbids both rich and poor from sleeping under the bridges of the Seine." Thus Marx argues that the right of "equality" guaranteed by the legal form is "a right of inequality, in its content, like every other right" (1968:324.) On the other hand, and probably even more importantly, legal equality functions to mask and occlude class differences and social inequalities, contributing to a "declassification" of politics which militates against the formation of the class consciousness necessary to the creation of a substantively more equal society. Thus the "political suppression of private property" —legal equality—makes it that much harder to eliminate private property and its attendant class inequalities, since it works to prevent "property" and "class" from entering into the universe of political discourse.

Similarly, the "individuality" established and protected by the legal form is illusory insofar as it is established in and through an abstraction from the concrete, social bases of individuality and is thus a "pure, blank individuality" (Marx, 1843:481) bereft of any qualitative determinations and differences. Just as the commodity form divorces the concrete use-value existence of the commodity from its formal existence as exchange-value, recognizing only the latter as constitutive of the "individuality" of the commodity, so the legal form splits off the concrete social existence of the individual from his or her existence as a formal object of political exchange and recognizes only the latter as definitive of his or her individuality. And a form that defines individuals as individuals only insofar as they are severed from the social ties and activities that constitute the real ground of their individuality necessarily fails to contribute to the recognition of genuine individuality.

The only form of individuality common to all members of a capitalist society, moreover, is the individualism and egotism of commodity exchangers, which is in fact the real (and thus "false") content of the formal individuality produced and guaranteed by the legal form. The indifference to qualitatively different needs "announced" in and through the abstractions of "will" and "rights" parallels, and is made possible through, a system of commodity exchange whose individual agents are necessarily indifferent to reach other's reciprocal needs and are rather obliged to treat each other as a mere means to their own purely "private" ends (1973: 242, 245). The juridical person, in other words, is merely the political persona of the individual whose social existence is instrumental, self-interested, and alienated; the individual, in short, who fails to act as a *social* individual aware of the inseparable relationship between his or her development and the development of every other individual.

> Political emancipation is the reduction of man, on the one side, to the egoistic member of civil society, to the egoistic, independent individual, on the other side to the citizen, to the moral person. [1972a:44][6]

Thus the commitment of the legal form to individuality is ultimately illusory, because the individuality it recognizes and presupposes is in fact an alienated form of individuality— individualism. The commitment becomes doubly illusory, moreover, once we recognize the contributions of the legal form to the persistence of the very capitalist mode of production which makes genuine individuality impossible.

Much the same can be said about the kind of "community" produced by the legal form. Insofar as the legal order establishes its universality, and its citizens define their communality, through an abstraction from the real social differences and interests that separate the members of capitalist society and set them against one another, Marx argues that it entails an "illusory community" (1972b:159) which "satisfies the whole of man in an imaginary manner" (1969:127).

> In the [legal] state . . . the individual . . . is the imaginary member of an imaginary sovereignty; he is robbed of his real individual life and filled with an unreal universality. [1972a:32]
> In order to be a real citizen and have political significance and efficacity, he must leave his social reality, abstract himself from it and return from its whole organization into his individuality, for the only existence that he finds for his citizenship is his pure, blank individuality. [1843:494]

The community of citizens is thus purely formal, i.e., bereft of real content, because the real content of life in capitalist society is overwhelmingly particularistic, rather than universalistic, in character. As such, the community produced in and through the legal order is as "imaginary" as that produced by religion; it is a "heavenly" sphere which "soars or seems to soar above . . . the limitations of the profane world" (Lefebvre, 1969:129-30). Indeed, Marx argues that the legal form is, in essence, a *religious form:*

> Up to now, the political constitution has been the religious sphere, the religion of the people's life, the heaven of their universality in contrast to the particular mundane existence of the actuality. [1843:436]
>
> The individual leads, not only in thought, in consciousness, but in reality, a heavenly and an earthly life, a life in the political community, wherein he counts as a member of the community, and a life in civil society, where he is active as a private person, regarding other men as means, degrading himself as a means and becoming a plaything of alien powers. *The political state is related to civil society as spiritualistically as heaven is to earth.* [1972a:32, emphasis added][7]

Thus the "community" produced by the legal form is no more real than the "heaven" produced by a religious system.

Notwithstanding its purely formal, imaginary character, however, this "community" entails substantive consequences of the highest order. If citizenship is at bottom a religion, then it is an *opiate* in the twofold sense both of dulling and distorting perception of reality, and providing a substitute gratification which compensates for the misery of reality and makes it bearable. On the one hand, membership in the illusory political community blurs the perception of the real, mundane class-based and thus particularistic communities in which people live, providing the basis for appeals to an abstract "common interest" or "public interest" which militate against the recognition of class interests. On the other hand, the political community provides individuals with a compensation for the absence of communal relationships within their everyday existence in the same manner that the perfection of "heaven" compensates for, and thus allows the believer to bear, the imperfections of earthly existence. For both reasons, the "community" produced by the legal form contributes decisively to the reproduction of the very capitalist mode of production which makes genuine community impossible.

Thus the legal form both produces and reinforces illusory, rather than genuine, forms of equality, individuality, and community. At the same time, as I have suggested, these illusory forms contribute significantly to the persistence of a capitalist system which necessarily precludes the realization of genuine equality, individuality, and community. For both reasons, the legal form is a specifically "bourgeois" form; those who would simultaneously uphold this form and condemn the capitalist mode of production which "perverts" it simply fail to grasp that part they uphold is inextricably tied to the very system they condemn (Marx, 1973:245, 248-49). It follows, therefore that the legal form cannot be the basis for a fully developed, genuine socialist or communist society.

There is another way of stating the incompatibility between legalism and socialism. Legal obligations in no way transcend the *concrete particularisms* of capitalist society, but must rather be understood as *abstract universals* which owe their existence to those concrete particularisms. If a truly socialist society means anything, it means a society in which the split between the concrete particularisms of alienated self-*interest* and the abstract universalism of legal *obligation* is thoroughly transcended, such that individuals act as social individuals who are bound by neither interest nor obligation but rather by the *concrete universal* of *social need.*[8] To put it another way, the emergence of human need as the basis of social production and intercourse necessarily entails the transcendence of that form—the legal form—which, as we have seen, carries out a systematic, bloodless abstraction from human needs. Indeed, this is precisely what Marx envisions in the "higher phase of communist society . . . [in which] the narrow horizon of bourgeois *right* [is] crossed in its entirety and society inscribe[s] on its banners: From each according to his ability, to each according to his *needs*" (1968:324-25).

C. "Legitimation"

The foregoing analysis has important implications for a theory of the "legitimation" and/or "delegitimation" of the legal form, and thus of the capitalist state. Those who would argue that delegitimation can result from the failure of law to live up to its "promises" (*i.e.*, from the gap between its promises and its performance) fail to understand that the legitimation of the legal order is not primarily a function of its ability to live up to its claims or "redeem its pledges" but rather of the fact that *its claims or pledges are valued in the first place.* As long as "formality," "generality," and "equality before the law" are seen as genuine human values, even gross and systematic departures from these norms in practice will not serve to delegitimate the legal order as a whole, but will at most tend to delegitimate specific laws and specific incumbents of political office who are responsible for these laws. Consider, for example, legal practices that systematically and obviously violate the principle of "equality before the law," such as those that result in rich individuals receiving more lenient treatment than poor individuals who have been convicted of comparable crimes. Such practices may in fact delegitimate particular judges and particular court systems, but they will not delegitimate the legal order itself, insofar as the delegitimation of the former does not call into question, but rather is based on the affirmation of, a central criterion of the legal order, equal treatment irrespective of class position. In other words, those who would object to the rich individual receiving more lenient treatment than the poor, on the grounds that the law should be indifferent to the distinction between rich and poor—that rich and poor alike should receive the same penalty for the same crime—would, in that very condemnation of the judges and courts responsible for the differential treatment, be affirming the legitimacy of the legal order. Thus a "critical analysis of the relationship between claim and reality," *pace* Trubek, is *not,* in "itself a source of possible change towards a more humane society," unless and until this "critical analysis" also entails a critique of the legitimacy of the value underlying the claim itself.[9]

In other words, the objection that the rich receive more lenient treatment than the poor would only delegitimate the legal order as a whole, and thus the capitalist mode of production on which it rests and which it helps sustain, if this objection were grounded on the principle that the rich, given both their greater ability to pay the penalties resulting from conviction and also to avoid the necessity of committing crimes in the first place, should receive *more severe* penalties than the poor who have committed comparable crimes. In this case a central tenet of the legal order would be called into question and rejected—the legitimacy of the recognition of social class origins would be asserted—so that even if this order were subsequently able to make good its promise to provide equal treatment for all it would be found wanting. Delegitimation thus presupposes a fundamental break with the values and (formal) mode of rationality of the legal form itself, a break which presupposes, in turn, at least an embryonic articulation of a qualitatively different set of values and mode of rationality. An adequate theory of legitimation and/or delegitimation would therefore have to explain why the *logic* of the legal order as such, in contrast to particular laws or legal practices, is ordinarily accepted as unproblematical and is not called into question in the name of a radically different logic.

D. The Fetishism of the Law

The legal form is normally not called into question, I would argue, because the form itself ordinarily precludes the possibility of performing this critical operation. The calling into question of the legal order presupposes individuals who conceive themselves as subjects evaluating an object which they have created and over which they have control. It is just this presupposition, however, which is nullified by the perverse logic of the legal form; this form creates a fetishized relationship between individuals and the Law in which individuals attribute subjectivity to the Law and conceive themselves as its objects or creations. Under these conditions, the calling into question and subsequent delegitimation of the legal order is literally "unthinkable."

The fetishism of the Law of which I am speaking appears in many guises. The most sublime is probably the formalist theory of law itself, insofar as this theory conceptualizes the law as an "independent," "autonomous" reality to be explained according to its own "internal dynamics," i.e., conceives it as an independent subject, on whose creativity the survival of the society depends. The most ridiculous is undoubtedly the celebration of "Law Day," during which we are asked to pay homage to the God—Law. The most frequent, if it is possible to judge from the numerous discussions I have had with undergraduate students over the past decade, is the common refrain: "If we didn't have the Law everyone would kill each other." All these instances, and many others, are simply variations on the common theme of legal fetishism, in which individuals affirm that they owe their existence to the Law, rather than the reverse, inverting the real causal relationship between themselves and their product. And all these instances thus preclude the possibility of evaluating the legal form, since it is impossible to evaluate an entity which is conceived of as the independent source of one's existence and values. When Society is held to be a result of the Law, rather than the Law to be a result of one particular kind of society, then the Law by definition is unproblematical. Or, to put it another way, the answer to the legitimation question—why do citizens support the legal order?—is, above all, the fact that *the citizens of this order ordinarily do not and cannot ask this question.*

Thus under conditions of legal fetishism the legal order appears not as an object or rational choice undertaken by autonomous subjects, but rather as an autonomous subject itself, whose very existence requires that individuals "objectify" themselves before it. According to Marx, the legal State is a power

> which has won an existence independent of the individuals . . . a social power . . . [which] appears to the individuals . . . not as their own united power, but as an alien force existing outside of them, of the origin and goal of which they are ignorant, which they thus cannot control, and which on the contrary passes through a peculiar series of phases and stages independent of the will and the action of men, nay even being the prime governor of these.[10]

Here Marx is arguing that legal fetishism parallels commodity fetishism, that the legal form, like the commodity form, necessarily functions *independently* of, or *autonomously* from, the power or will of the subjects who originally set it in motion but do not know, or have forgotten, that they have done so. And, as in the case of the commodity form, the "deification" of the universal equivalent rests on the obfuscation of "origins" produced by the abstraction of the legal form. Just as the masking of the link between commodities and their human origins in use-value and concrete labor necessarily gives rise to the appearance or ideological inversion that commodities, and especially their universal equivalent, money, have living, human powers, so the abstraction from and masking of the different human needs and social origins carried out by the legal form necessarily produces the illusion that the Law—as the universal political equivalent— has a life of its own. The corollary to human relationships becoming abstract and reified (thing-like) is that things—be they material products or legal "products"—become personified, *i.e.*, take on human characteristics. Commodity fetishism and legal fetishism are thus two inseparably related aspects of an inverted, "topsy-turvy" existence under a capitalist mode of production in which *humans are first reduced to abstractions, and then dominated by their own creations.*

E.   The Semiotics of Formal Rationality

The "rationality" or logic of both the commodity form and the legal form can be grasped as a specific mode of *encoding* reality, a specific *language* for which a linguistic or semiotic analysis can therefore be developed.[11] On the most general level, the homology between legal form and commodity form can be schematically expressed in the following semiotic formula:[12]

$$\frac{\dfrac{\$}{\text{U-V, CL}}}{\text{``Commodities''}} = \frac{\dfrac{\text{Law}}{\text{Social Interests \& Origins}}}{\text{``individual citizens''}} = \frac{\dfrac{\text{Signifier}}{\text{Signified}}}{\text{Signified}}$$

In both cases, the same semiotic process is at work. A Signifier ($, the Law) is ultimately related to, and brought into existence by, a Signified (Use-Value and Concrete Labor, different social interests and origins). In both cases, however, the peculiarly abstract character of the Signifier functions to mask or obfuscate the original Signified, so that *meaning is systematically distorted and lost,* to the point where the original Signified slips from view or is barred from discourse (thus the diagonal bar above) and the Signifier appears able to call into existence an entirely new Signified ("commodities," "individual citizens"). The abstract, formal "language" of both the commodity form and the legal form is thus an *impoverished, duplicitous* language which simul- taneously prohibits qualitatively different human needs and activities from being encoded, or recognized, and appears to possess powers of "speech" completely independent of, or autono- mous from, the human beings whom it addresses.

Thus the comprehension of both the commodity form and the legal form requires an identical *decoding*. This decoding reunites the abstract and the concrete, Signifier and (original) Signified, thus overcoming the abstraction and reversing the reversal that characterize the perverse "language" of both forms. In the process meaning is restored and individuals can recapture the powers of "speech" of which they have been deprived. The "decoding" in which I have engaged, then, is no mere "academic" exercise. Insofar as the delegitimation of the legal form and the capitalist mode of production to which it is tied presupposes precisely the capacity of individuals who are dominated by this mode of production to perform such a decoding operation, my effort to develop such a decoding purports to contribute to the delegitimation of both the legal form and the capitalist mode of production, a delegitimation which is a necessary condition for the creation of a less abstract, more concrete, i.e., more human, society.

IV. Conclusion

It should now be clear why the "relative autonomy" of the law does not preclude, but rather necessarily entails, an essential identity or homology between the legal form and the commodity form. The homology between the legal form and the commodity form guarantees both that the legal form, like the commodity form, functions and develops autonomously from the preferences of social actors *and* that it does *not* function and develop autonomously from the system in which these social actors participate. Stated otherwise, the autonomy of the Law from the preferences of even the most powerful social actors (the members of the capitalist class) is not an obstacle to, but rather a prerequisite for, the capacity of the Law to contribute to the reproduction of the overall conditions that make capitalism possible, and thus its capacity to serve the interests of capital as a *class*.

The demonstration of the homologous relationship between the legal form and the commodity form which I have provided, however, is a theoretical starting point which in many ways has already been historically surpassed. The transformation from competitive, laissez-faire capitalism to monopoly, State-regulated capitalism has resulted in a partial transformation of the content of the homology between economic and political exchange. On the one hand, the growing role of the State as a "productive force" entails the increasing production of use-values—welfare, medical services, infrastructure, etc.—which do not take on the direct form of exchange-values, i.e., which are not produced as commodities. This includes the production of labor-power itself, insofar as the law of value is increasingly superceded by the political negotiation of wages as the determinant of the cost of this most central of all use-values. To this extent, it is possible to argue that the unchallenged supremacy of the commodity form is in decline, and that we are in the presence of a *certain kind* of restoration of the content and quality from which the commodity form abstracts.[13] On the other hand, the development of State-regulated, monopoly capitalism has also witnessed an erosion of the rule of Law and emergence of less formalistic, more instrumentalist and technocratic modes of social and political control; the Law as universal political equivalent gradually gives way to a series of relatively *ad hoc techniques* which, by their very nature, recognize specific interests and specific social origins.[14] For example, whereas formal rationality in the criminal justice system precludes the consideration of the individual's motive or social class position from entering into the determination of guilt and punishment, these considerations necessarily come to the forefront in technocraticrehabilitative modes of criminal justice. In short, technocratic modes of social control imply a certain reemergence of the content and quality from which the legal form abstracts, and thus parallel the restoration of content and quality entailed in the increasing political production of use-values. Thus one could argue that a homologous relationship continues to exist between the exchange of products and the exchange of human beings, but that the terms of the relationship have assumed values different from those they possessed during the period of competitive capitalism.

The demonstration of this "new" homology, however, is only a starting point. It does not and cannot tell us why the values of the two terms (economic and political) have changed, *i.e.*, why we have witnessed a still incomplete transformation from competitive capitalism-legalism to monopoly capitalism-technocracy, or what the values of the two terms of the relationship will be in the future. It does not, in other words, explain how and why human beings came to create this new homology or for that matter, how and why they came to create the earlier one I have outlined in this essay; nor does it tell us how and why they might further transform them in the course of history. Thus the demonstration of structural or synchronic homologies is not intended as a substitute for an analysis of *praxis* which would serve to reunite structure and history, synchrony and diachrony.[15] It merely suggests that such an analysis would have to proceed from the understanding that the task is to explain how one social whole with a distinctive logic originates and how it transforms itself into a different social whole with another, distinctive logic: that is, from the understanding, in Hegel's words, that "the truth is the whole."

NOTES

1.   Despite their obvious opposition, there is no *theoretical* difference between a Pluralist and an Instrumentalist-Marxist approach to law. Both bypass entirely the problem of the form or structure of the legal order in order to conceive it as a direct reflection of consciously articulated and

organized pressures. Thus the difference between them is merely empirical: Pluralists deny that there is a systematic bias to the interplay of pressures; Instrumentalist Marxists argue that this interplay is dominated by specifically capitalist interests. For a powerful critique of Legal Pluralism, see Tushnet (1977). For an influential critique of Instrumentalist Marxism, which contributed significantly to its rejection, by now almost universal, see Poulantzas (1973). The debate between Nicos Poulantzas and Ralph Miliband, which has been carried out over the past decade in the pages of *New Left Review*, is also instructive, as is the critique of Marxist Instrumentalism developed by Claus Offe (1972), as well as the analysis of David Gold, Clarence Lo, and Erik Wright (1975).

2.   Tushnet (1977) occasionally lapses into this formalist position in his otherwise excellent critique of Lawrence Friedman's Pluralist Instrumentalism.

3.   This reconstruction has profited from my encounter with the work of Lefebvre (1969), as well as that of Jean-Joseph Goux (1972). At the risk of a certain redundancy at points in this reconstruction I have deliberately employed language that is virtually identical to language in the previous section. The identity of language is designed to underscore the identity in logic between the two forms.

4.   Quoted in Lefebvre (1969: 127).

5.   Only after "working out" the homology between the commodity form and the legal form did I discover that Pashukanis had developed essentially the same analysis roughly fifty years ago! Almost all subsequent Marxist work on the law is, unfortunately, a regression from the standard established by Pasukanis's pioneering effort. The concept "mode of substitution" derives from Goux (1972).

6.   The legal state, like monotheistic religion, presupposes an individual who is incapable of acting as a social being in his or her everyday life.

> Political democracy is Christian in the sense that man . . . every man, is there considered a sovereign being, but it is uneducated unsocial man . . . man as he has been corrupted, lost to himself, alienated, subjected to the rule of inhuman conditions . . . by the whole organization of our society—in short man who is not *yet* a real species-being (1972a: 37).

7.   Thus, as Goux (1972) has noticed, Marx argues that the monotheistic religious form, as well as the legal form, is homologous with the commodity form. "Money is . . . the god among commodities" (1973: 221).

8.   For readers unfamiliar with the Hegelian terminology employed in this paragraph, I offer the following translation. In the context of our discussion, a "concrete particularism" is an internal want or desire that is, however, a-social; an "abstract universal" is a demand that is social in nature but externally imposed; and a "concrete universal" is an internal want or desire that is socially directed. Thus "social need" is a concrete universal because it creates a bond among individuals for whom sociality is an inner desire rather than either a means to a self-interested end or an obligation that limits the pursuit of self-interest.

9.   In arguing that the gap between "ideals" and performance in and of itself can be delegitimating, Trubek appears to misunderstand Habermas's

account of the possibilities of a "legitimation crisis." The latter requires "a questioning . . . of the norms that . . . underlie . . . action," and not merely a demonstration that these norms are violated in practice (1975: 69). Habermas, on the other hand, fails to develop a theory of fetishism, proposed in the following section of this essay, which would account for why this "questioning" ordinarily does not and cannot take place.

10.   *The German Ideology*, quoted in Ollman (1971: 219). Ollman's conception of the State as a "value relation" was an insightful contribution to my effort to work out the homology between legal form and commodity form.

11.   Marx himself occasionally speaks of the "language" of the commodity form, and Henri Lefebvre (1966) and Jean Baudrillard (1972) have each developed from these hints a linguistic or semiological analysis of the commodity.

12.   Readers unfamiliar with semiological terminology should note that any social practice that is sign-ificant or "meaningful" can be understood as a language whose constituent elements are *signs*. The sign, in turn, whether it be verbal, economic, legal, etc., can be understood as the association or relationship between a signifier and a signified, the former functioning to express or refer to the content of the latter.

13.   Claus Offe (1973) develops this thesis of "decommoditification." It should be emphasized however, that this "restoration of quality and content" only surfaces within a continuing framework of domination and thus in no way constitutes the emergence of socialism.

14.   This trend is by no means complete, and has from the very beginning been accompanied by the apparently contradictory extension of the legal form to a range of activities to which it did not apply in the nineteenth century; see Galanter (1976).

15.   For an analysis that makes a start in this direction by conceptualizing the state both as a form which conditions struggle *and* as an object struggle itself, see Esping-Anderson *et al.* (1976).

REFERENCES

Baudrillard, Jean, *Pour une Critique de l'Economie Politique du Signe*. Paris: Gallimard, 1972.

Esping-Anderson, Gosta, Friedland, Roger, and Wright, Erick Olin, "Modes of Class Struggle and the Capitalist State," *Kapitalistate*. 4-5 (Summer, 1976): 186.

Galanter, Marc, "Theories of Legalization and Delegalization. "Paper presented to the Annual Convention of the American Political Science Association, Chicago, Sept. 2-5, 1976.

Gold, David A., Lo, Clarence Y.H., and Wright, Erik Olin, "Recent Developments in Marxist Theories of the Capitalist State", *Monthly Review* 27(5) (Oct. 1975): 29; *Monthly Review* 27(6) (Nov. 1975): 36.

Goux, Jean-Joseph, *Freud, Marx: Economie et Symbolique*. Paris, 1972.

Habermas, Jurgen, *Legitimation Crisis*. Boston: Beacon Press, 1975.

Lefebvre, Henri, *Le Language et la Société*. Paris: Gallimard, 1966.

_____, *The Sociology of Marx*. New York, Vintage Books, 1969.

Marx, Karl, *The Critique of Hegel's Philosophy of the State*. Mega I i (1) 481, 1843.

_____, *Capital*. vol. 1, New York: International Publishers, 1967.

_____, "Critique of the Gotha Program," in *Karl Marx and Friederick Engels, Selected Works*. vol. 1, New York: New World Paperbacks, 1968.

_____, "On the Jewish Question," in Robert C. Tucker (ed.), *The Marx-Engels Reader*. New York: Norton, 1972a.

_____, "The German Ideology," in Robert C. Tucker (ed.), *The Marx-Engels Reader*. New York: Norton, 1972 b.

_____, *Grundrisse: Foundations of the Critique of Political Economy*. Martin Nicolaus (trans.), Harmondsworth, England: Penguin Books, 1973.

Offe, Claus, *Class Rule and the Political System: On the Selectiveness of Political Institutions*. Unpublished, 1972.

_____, "The Abolition of Market Control and the Problem of Legitimacy," *Kapitalistate* 1 (1973): 109; *Kapitalistate* 2 (1973): 73.

Ollman, Bertell, *Alienation: Marx's Conception of Man in Capitalist Society*. Cambridge: Cambridge University Press, 1971.

Pashukanis, E.B. "The General Theory of Law and Marxism," in Hugh W. Babb (trans. and ed.), *Soviet Legal Philosophy*. Cambridge, Mass.: Harvard University Press, 1951.

Poulantzas, Nicos, "The Problem of the Capitalist State," in Robin Blackburn (ed.), *Ideology in Social Science*. New York: Vintage Books, 1973.

Trubek, David M. "Max Weber on Law and the Rise of Capitalism" [1972] *Wisconsin Law Review* 720.

Tushnet, Mark, "Perspectives on the Development of American Law: A Critical Review of Friedman's 'History of American Law'," [1977 (1)] *Wisconsin Law Review* (forthcoming).

PART TWO

JURISPRUDENCE AND SOCIOLOGY

Legal philosophy (jurisprudence) has long been a subject of discourse among the world's great thinkers.[1] Meanings of justice, law, fairness and other ideals have been the basis for much jurisprudence. Schools of jurisprudence include natural law, formalism, cultural and historical schools, legal realism and sociological jurisprudence. Some major issues surrounding the sociological use of jurisprudence are the questions of values, morals, bias, objectivity, empiricism, and ideology in the study of law. By its very nature jurisprudence addresses such topics as morality, values, etc., through philosophical reasoning while sociology has been more empirically oriented and wary of stating value preferences and ideological bias. The following articles by Black and Nonet present two divergent assessments of the "proper" approach to the sociology of law.

Black

Black squarely confronts the issues of value bias, objectivity and advocacy in his essay concerning legal sociology. He identifies a confusion of science and policy with normative considerations subtly implicated in much legal sociology. Black contends that a purely sociological approach to law involves a scientific analysis of legal life as a system of behavior rather than as assessment of legal policy. Ultimately, the legal sociologist will be able to develop a general theory of law which would predict and explain every instance of legal behavior. Thus, legal sociology should divorce itself from value-added policy analysis.[2]

Black identifies the study of legal effectiveness as the basis for contemporary sociology of law. This involves comparing legal reality to a legal ideal, e.g., Pound's distinction between "law in action" and "law in books".[3] While such "applied" sociology of law may be helpful, when an ideal with no empirical referent is used to compare with legal reality, the investigator's personal ideals may be substituted as society's legal ideals. Therefore, social science ceases and advocacy begins. Of course the issues of values, objectivity and advocacy are relevant not only to the sociology of law, but also to the larger discipline.[4]

The author believes that sociology has become part of the larger technocratic "world view" in society, based on the assumption that all problems reduce to questions of technique. Therefore, given the many social problems identified today, the sociologist has been identified as a major consultant in finding "technocratic solutions". Thus, crime, race relations, obscenity and pornography, poverty, mass media, and immigration (among other areas of life) have been the subject of governmental commissions armed with social scientists.[5] However, Black notes that the "typical" sociologist knows little about moral or social philosophy.

According to Black, law consists of observable acts for the sociologist to empirically investigate. A sociology of law based upon positivism has certain limitations: (1) science can only know phenomena and never essences; (2) every scientific idea requires a concrete empirical referent; and (3) value judgements cannot be discovered in the empirical world and thus have no meaning in science. Therefore, science cannot evaluate the effectiveness of law because that necessitates standards of value foreign to science. In addition, Black finds disturbing the fact that evaluative studies of law are presented as "scientific" findings. Although Black acknowledges that values influence the choice of one's problem and may bias its analysis, he asserts that "the fact that scientific statements are influenced by values does not make them value statements." Value statements cannot be empirically verified while scientific statements can.

A general theory of law is needed which can be applied to all social control systems (i.e., Nazis, U.S., China) and most aspects of social life (i.e., social stratification, group size). Comparative analysis is particularly important to Black, since single society analysis may lead to ethnocentrism and time boundaries. He then discusses his own police research within the context of theoretical generalization. Black concludes that applied sociology of law will only be as good as is pure theory in legal sociology.

Nonet

In the second article, Nonet presents a compelling criticism of the position taken by Black and other adherents of the "pure" sociology perspective. He asserts that although Black's arguments are "loose, inconsistent and uninformed" they constitute an orthodoxy which prevails in the social science enterprise. This orthodoxy is characterized by a distrust of evaluative elements in social science and is underpinned by a "positivism" molded after an idealized version of the "hard" sciences.[6]

Nonet maintains that contraire to the idealized version of sociology as a pure science, the intellectual significance of sociology is based upon the meaning of social inquiry for contributions to political, economic, legal and other "normative" thought. That is, the meaning of, support for, and popularity of sociology is to be found in its addressing the human condition as it is and as it could be within the context of such ideals as justice, democracy, etc. As another sociologist has noted, sociology may be necessarily tied to a certain form of socio-political structure.[7]

Nonet presents the first two principles of the Berkeley program in legal sociology: (1) sociology of law must be jurisprudentially informed; and (2) sociology of law must have redeeming value for policy. He notes that Black's definition of the focus of legal sociology (observable dispositions) is the basis of much "debunking sociology." However, Nonet agrees with Black that debunking per se is too limited and we need to take values, rules and other normative elements more seriously, rather than dismissing them as "unscientific." This leads to the third principle: (3) the sociology of law must take legal ideas seriously. According to Nonet, Black's "pure" sociology offers two prescriptions for ignorance: (1) ignore problems, values and doctrines of jurisprudence; and (2) ignore the rules, principles, and policies that constitute law, as understood by all but the pure sociologist.

He then points out that Black's own work is based upon values and ideological preferences which are unstated, but evident. Nonet states that we are asked to "prefer the risks of error by ignorance to the risks of error from bias" by Black's insistence that bias is the arch enemy of "good science". While Nonet observes that there may be reasons for preferring ignorance to bias, it is not due to greater risks of error. He then proceeds to identify the faulty logic in Black's argument and asserts that biases—interests, sympathies, sensibilities, tastes—are essential to science and make it better. While Black distinguishes between "applied" sociology of law (good) and "evaluative" sociology of law (bad) on the basis of clarity of standards and lack of researcher bias, such distinctions are according to Nonet, nebulous and illogical.

The Berkeley programs next principle is (4) the sociology of law must integrate jurisprudential and policy analysis. Nonet suggests that Black's distinction prescribes ignorance of the purpose of the policies one evaluates, so that the "applied" sociologist of law becomes the technocrat which he admonishes. Finally, Nonet asserts that sociologists should be explicit about their own personal preferences or bias rather than "hiding" them by references to the values of others, e.g., legislature, judge.

Although "pure sociology" rests on weak intellectual grounds, Nonet observes that it might be recommended as a sound managerial practice for the social scientific establishment. However, the bureaucratic option is not open to sociologists, because the study of human affairs necessitates value analysis and support. Since jurisprudence by itself has blinders similar to those of pure sociology, Nonet advocates a jurisprudential sociology addressing the issues and one that is informed by the ideas of jurisprudence.

Conclusion

The presentation by Black and subsequent critique by Nonet does not end the issue.[8] Such issues have a history equivalent to that of science and will increasingly be debated. Such debates will not only be among social scientists, but also among physicists, chemists, biologists and other "hard" scientists involved in such areas as nuclear power, manipulation of man's environment and life processes, etc.

NOTES

1.   This initial discussion is based upon Edwin M. Schur, *Law and Society*. New York: Random House, Inc., 1968, pp. 17-67.

2.   For a more recent discussion of such distinctions see C.M. Campbell and Paul Wiles, "The Study of Law In Society in Britain," *Law and Society Review* 10 (Summer, 1976): 547-578. The authors divide the field into "sociology of law" (theoretical analysis) and "socio-legal studies" (applied).

3.   Schur, *Law and Society*. pp. 37-43.

4.   See Alvin W. Gouldner, "Anti-minotaur: The Myth of a Value-free Sociology," *Social Problems* 9 (Winter, 1962): 199-213; C. Wright Mills, *The Sociological Imagination*. London: Oxford University Press, 1959; Alvin W. Gouldner, *The Coming Crisis of Western Sociology*. New York: Basic Books, Inc., 1970; Howard S. Becker, "Whose Side Are We On?" *Social Problems* 14 (Winter, 1967): 239-247; Alvin W. Gouldner, "The Sociologist As Partisan: Sociology and the Welfare State," *The American Sociologist* 3 (May, 1968): 190-116.

Howard S. Becker and Irving Louis Horowitz "Radical Politics and Sociological Research: Observations on Methodology and Ideology," *American Journal of Sociology* 78. (July, 1972): 48-62.

5.   The technocratic mentality maintains and produces many problems. For example see John McDermott, "Technology: The Opiate of the Intellectual," *New York Review of Books* (July 31, 1969).

6.   For an excellent discussion of this issue see Gideon Sjoberg and Roger Nett, *A Methodology for Social Research*. New York: Harper and Row, 1968.

It is interesting that certain disciplines are continuously identified as the "pure" "natural," or "hard" sciences. The implication is that other sciences are somehow unnatural, impure and soft. The observations of a "hard" scientist seem appropriate here:

> Particularly I was struck by the number and extent of overt disagreements between social scientists about the nature of legitimate scientific problems and methods. Both history and acquaintance made me doubt that practitioners of the natural science possess firmer or more permanent answers to such questions than colleagues in the social sciences. (emphasis added).

Thomas S. Kuhn, *The Structure of Revolutions* (2nd ed.). Chicago: University of Chicago Press, 1970, p. vii.

7.   Thomas Ford Holt, "Who Shall Prepare Himself for Battle?" *The American Sociologist* 3 (February, 1968): 3-7.

8.   An editor's note states that Professor Black was invited to reply to Nonet's paper, but he declined and stated one could evaluate his perspective by reading his recent book *The Behavior of Law*. New York: Academic Press, 1976.

Chapter 4

The Boundaries of Legal Sociology*

Donald Black†

I

Contemporary sociology of law is characterized by a confusion
of science and policy. Its analysis proceeds in the disembodied
tongue of science, in the language of "system," "structure,"
"pattern," and "organization," or in the vocabulary of technique, of
"needs," "functions," and "viability." Rarely does the language
impart emotion, indignation, or even personal involvement on the
part of the investigator. But while legal sociology is presented in
this scientific language and scientific tone, normative considerations—the "ought" and the "just"—become subtly implicated.
     Although legal sociologists[1] typically criticize one another
according to the usual scientific standards of methodological
precision and theoretical validity, they frequently become
preoccupied with the "policy implications" of their research.

* Donald Black, "The Boundaries of Legal Sociology." Reprinted by permission of
The Yale Law Journal Company and Fred B. Rothman & Company and the author
from The Yale Law Journal, Vol. 81, pp. 1086-1100.
     This paper has benefited from the reactions of several readers: Leon Lipson,
Maureen Mileski, David Trubek, and Stanton Wheeler. In March, 1972, an early
draft occasioned an informal seminar at the Center for the Study of Law and
Society of the University of California at Berkeley. I thank the following
participants in that seminar for helping me to sharpen my ideas: David Matza,
Sheldon Messinger, Philippe Nonet, Jerome Skolnick, and Philip Selznick. Finally,
I want to express appreciation to Henry M. Fields, a law student who first
suggested that I write this paper and then went on to contribute his considerable
scholarly and editorial abilities to its preparation.
† Assistant Professor of Sociology and Lecturer in Law, Yale University.

Occasionally, in assessing one another, they shed the mantle of science and become unabashedly political. Recently, for instance, a sociologist characterized the literature of legal sociology as bourgeois, liberal, pluralist, and meliorist.[2] He went on to argue that a more radical sociology is required, one that is "more critical in its premises and farther-reaching in its proposals."[3] Whether liberal or radical, however, legal sociologists tend to share a style of discourse that deserves attention and comment.

It is my contention that a purely sociological approach to law should involve not an assessment of legal policy, but rather, a scientific analysis of legal life *as a system of behavior.* The ultimate contribution of this enterprise would be a general theory of law, a theory that would predict and explain every instance of legal behavior. While such a general theory may never be attained, efforts to achieve it should be central to the sociology of law. By contrast, the core problems of legal policymaking are problems of value. Such value considerations are as irrelevant to a sociology of law as they are to any other scientific theory of the empirical world.

Invoking the language of science and relying upon its aura of respectability, sociologists move, in a special and almost imperceptible way, beyond science and deal with questions of legal evaluation. Because they confuse scientific questions with policy questions, they severely retard the development of their field. At best, they offer an applied sociology of law—at worst, sheer ideology.

After examining the type of discourse that passes for a sociology of law and noting its apparent shortcomings, I shall discuss more directly the nature and aims of a pure sociology of law.

II

With one phrase, *legal effectiveness,* we capture the major thematic concern of contemporary sociology of law. The wide range of work that revolves around the legal-effectiveness theme displays a common strategy of problem formulation, namely a comparison of legal reality to a legal ideal of some kind. Typically a gap is shown between law-in-action and law-in-theory. Often the sociologist then goes on to suggest how the reality might be brought closer to the ideal. Law is regarded as ineffective and in need of reform owing to the disparity between the legal reality and the ideal.[4]

Legal-effectiveness studies differ from one another, however, in the kinds of legal ideals against which their findings are measured. At one extreme are "impact studies" that compare reality to legal ideals with a very plain and specific operational

meaning. Here the legal measuring rod it likely to be a statute
whose purpose is rather clearly discernible or a judicial decision
unambiguously declarative of a specific policy. The *Miranda*
decision, for example, requiring the police to apprise suspects of
their legal rights before conducting an incustody interrogation, has
a core meaning about which consensus is quite high.[5] Soon after
Miranda was handed down by the Supreme Court, research was
initiated to evaluate the degree of police compliance with the
decision.[6] When the core meaning of a decision thus is clear, this
type of research can be expected to show whether or not a
decision has, in fact, been implemented.

Sociologists, however, may launch these implementation
studies where legislation or judicial opinion is considerably more
ambiguous than in *Miranda*. In such instances, the "impact" may
be difficult to measure. What must be done, for example, to
implement *In re Gault?*[7] Though it is generally recognized that
Gault guarantees to juvenile suspects constitutional rights
previously accorded only to adults, the extent of these juvenile
rights is not at all clear.[8] Hence it becomes difficult, perhaps
impossible, to identify the degree to which *Gault* has been
implemented.[9]

Finally, the sociologist may attempt to compare legal reality to
an ideal grounded in neither statutory nor case law. Here the
investigator assesses his empirical materials against standards of
justice such as "the rule of law," "arbitrariness," "legality," or a
concept of "due process" not explicitly anchored in the due
process clause of the Constitution. Jerome Skolnick, for instance,
asserts that the police employ the informer system in narcotics
enforcement "irrespective of the constraints embodied in principles
of due process."[10] But there is no indication of where Skolnick
locates these principles. Presumably he realizes that no court in
the United States has declared the practice illegal, and there is no
reason to think such a decision is likely in the near future.[11] In
another study, Skolnick investigates plea-bargaining in the courtroom, concluding that the cooperation underlying this practice
"deviates" from some unarticulated adversarial ideal.[12] Similarly,
Leon Mayhew, in arguing that the Massachusetts Commission
Against Discrimination failed to define discrimination adequately
and thereby ignored much illegal conduct, provides neither a legal
argument nor an empirical referent for his interpretation of the
Commission's proper mission.[13] In short, then, some studies in
legal sociology seem to move beyond the law when they measure
legal reality against an ideal.

At its most useful, legal-effectiveness research may be
valuable to people in a position to reform the legal order. In this
sense it consists of studies in *applied* sociology of law. This would
appear to be particularly true of those investigations that relate
empirical findings to legal ideals which are clearly expressed in
the written law. Such research might provide legal reformers with

a kind of leverage for change, though the mere evidence of a gap between law-in-action and law-in-theory would not in itself overwhelm all resistance to change. Who can imagine a study, after all, that would not discover such a gap? Little is more predictable about the law than that these gaps exist.

However, legal-effectiveness research sometimes moves beyond applied sociology. When legal reality is compared to an ideal with no identifiable empirical referent, such as "the rule of law" or "due process," the investigator may inadvertently implant his personal ideals as the society's legal ideals. At this point social science ceases and advocacy begins. The value of legal-effectiveness research of this kind is bound to be precarious, for it involves, perhaps unwittingly, moral judgment at the very point where it promises scientific analysis.

III

As I have described it, the sociology of law significantly resembles a broader style of thought that has come to be known as *technocratic* thought,[14] or, to use an earlier term, scientism. In the technocratic world-view, every problem—factual, moral, political, or legal—reduces to a question of technique. A good technique is one that works, and what works can be learned through science. Any problem that cannot be solved in this way is no problem at all, hardly worthy of our attention. In theory, moreover, every problem can be solved if only the appropriate expertise is applied to it. Among the key words in the technocratic vocabulary are efficiency and, one I noted earlier, effectiveness. It is a style of thought in some respects akin to pragmatism, but it is a pragmatism with unstated goals, a search for the most rational way to go somewhere that is never clearly specified. Rather, we must infer what these goals are, and that is how some technocratic approaches come to be known as liberal and bourgeois, others as radical and critical. Technocrats do not make political arguments in the usual sense; they do not moralize. They simply want to get the job done.

The technocratic style dominates much discussion of social controversy at the higher reaches of American life. We are given to understand that scientific research will reveal whether marijuana should be legalized, that the Vietnam War was a miscalculation, and that economic analysis will determine the most "rational" tax program. The new nations of Africa and Asia are studied to determine what their modernization "requires." Riots, violence, and pornography give rise to government study commissions and research grants for the universities. Moral problems of every sort are translated into problems of knowledge and science, of know-how. To discuss the criminal in the moral terms of right and wrong comes to be seen as primitive and unschooled; medical terminology is introduced into the discussion of the treatment of criminal offenders. In the name of science and progress, what was once seen as evil is studied and treated, not condemned.

The logic of this technocratic mentality has helped to catapult sociology to a position of some prominence in these times of rapid social change and conflict. Sociology, it is thought, will point the way to solutions to the many problems before us. The sociologists themselves have shown little reluctance to accept this responsibility. The typical sociologist knows almost nothing about moral or social philosophy, but if public policy is no more than a matter of scientific technique, why should he? In a technocratic era, moral philosophy is an oddity in the real world of action, a quaint remnant of the nineteenth century, something for the undergraduates.

IV

Law can be seen as a thing like any other in the empirical world. It is crucial to be clear that from a sociological standpoint, law consists in observable acts, not in rules as the concept of rule or norm is employed in both the literature of jurisprudence and in every-day legal language.[15] From a sociological point of view, law is not what lawyers regard as binding or obligatory precepts, but rather, for example, the observable dispositions of judges, policemen, prosecutors, or administrative officials.[16] Law is like any other thing in the sense that it is as amenable to the scientific method as any other aspect of reality. No intellectual apparatus peculiar to the study of law is required. At the same time, a social science of law true to positivism, the conventional theory of science, cannot escape the limitations inherent in scientific thought itself.[17] Perhaps a word should be said about these limitations.

Within the tradition of positivist philosophy, three basic principles of scientific knowledge can be noted. First, science can know only phenomena and never essences.[18] The quest for the one correct concept of law or for anything else "distinctively legal" is therefore inherently unscientific.[19] The essence of law is a problem for jurisprudence, not science. Second, every scientific idea requires a concrete empirical referent of some kind.[20] A science can only order experience, and has no way of gaining access to non-empirical domains of knowledge. Accordingly, insofar as such ideals as justice, the rule of law, and due process are without a grounding in experience, they have no place in the sociology of law. Third, value judgments cannot be discovered in the empirical world and for that reason are without cognitive meaning in science.[21]

It is for this last reason that science knows nothing and can know nothing about the effectiveness of law. Science is incapable of an evaluation of the reality it confronts. To measure the effectiveness of law or of anything else for that matter, we must import standards of value that are foreign to science.[22] What is disturbing about the contemporary literature on legal effectiveness then is not that it evaluates law,[23] but rather, that its evaluations and proposals are presented as scientific findings. Far from denying this confusion, Philip Selznick[24] has gone so far in the opposite direction as to claim that "nothing we know today precludes an effort to define 'ends proper to man's nature' and to discover objective standards of moral judgment."[25]

Legal sociologists involved in the study of effectiveness have thus come to advance a conception of scientific criticism of law. This is illogical; it is a contradiction in terms.

It is apparent by now that my critique of contemporary legal sociology is premised on the notion that sociology is a scientific enterprise and, as such, can be distinguished from moral philosophy, jurisprudence, or any other normatively oriented study—in other words, that the study of fact can be distinguished from the study of value. This is not to say that I am unaware of the criticisms that have been levied against a purely value-free social science. But while accepting these criticisms, I cannot understand the conclusion that the effort to develop an objective science of man should be abandoned.

It is important to understand precisely how values become involved in social science. One widely recognized intrusion of values occurs at the first stage of scientific inquiry: the choice of the problem for study. The values of the investigator may determine, for example, whether he selects a problem with great relevance for public policy or one of wholly academic interest. This intrusion of values was long ago noted by Max Weber, perhaps the most illustrious proponent of value-free sociology. Weber contended that the role of values in the choice of a problem is unavoidable and should be faced squarely, but he insisted that the problem, once selected, could and should be pursued "non-evaluatively."[26]

But I would go further than Weber and grant that these value orientations may bias the analysis of the problem as well as its selection. Though various methodological techniques have been developed to minimize the effects of these biases, good social science still requires a disciplined disengagement on the part of the investigator—so disciplined, in fact, that it may rarely be achieved. Various arguments can be made to the effect that bias is built into social science at its very foundations. For example, the claim has been made that every social science study necessarily implicates the investigator in the perspective of an actual hierarchical position, seeing social life from either the social top or the bottom, and is therefore inherently biased.[27] For purposes of discussion I grant even this. Similarly it is arguable that all social science is, beyond science, a form of ideology, if only because it is by its nature an instance of social behavior subject to the scrutiny of the very discipline of which it is a part. Sociology, that is, can be analyzed sociologically. Sociology does not occur in a vacuum and is undoubtedly influenced by social forces. Accordingly, sociology may be viewed as ideology supporting either the defenders of the status quo or their opponents.[28]

Finally, because much social science can be interpreted in an ideological framework, its theories and findings can be used as weapons in the arena of public policymaking. The polemical impact of social science may be particularly great at this historical moment, given the enormous prestige of science in modern society. Not only do these theories and findings feed into existing policy debates, but they also can stimulate controversy and change by drawing attention to empirical situations that might otherwise be unknown or ignored by policymakers and social critics. Thus social science performs—willingly or not—an intelligence function in the political process.[29] Because of such political ramifications, the argument has been put forward that the sociologist remains responsible for the consequences of his work. Only by making an explicit moral commitment can the social scientist hope to protect himself and others from the unintended consequences of his work.[30] It is apparent that social science resonates into the realm of ideology, thereby raising serious questions about the scholar's responsibilities to his fellow man.

In several senses, then, values enter into the activity of social science. While values may play a similar role in science of all kinds, it can at least be admitted that their role is especially visible and dramatic when man is studying himself. Values may be all the more prominent in the study of man's moral life, of which legal sociology is one branch. The major arguments against the possibility of a pure science of man, in short, seem to have some merit.[31] But the crucial question is what all of this implies for the traditional distinction between fact and value. I say it implies nothing. In fact, much of the criticism of value-free sociology itself rests upon observable patterns of value impact upon social science and for that reason relies upon the fact-value distinction for its own validity.

We have seen that a social scientist may be affected by values in the choice of his problem and may be biased in his approach to it. Critics of a value-free social science assert that these psychological effects, along with the ideological character of social science when viewed as the object of analysis itself, undermine the validity of social science. But this is to confuse the origins and uses of a scientific statement with its validity.[32] *The fact that scientific statements are influenced by values does not make them value statements.* The psychological and social influence of values on scientific inquiry has no logical implications for the validity of a scientific proposition. Its validity is determined only by empirical verification. A value statement, by contrast, is not subject to such a test.[33] How, for example, is the following statement to be empirically verified: "Democratic process is an ultimate good"? The fact that we can distinguish between scientific propositions and such value statements is all we need to assert the possibility of social science. In short, values may affect social science profoundly, but that is no reason to abandon the enterprise.[34]

V

The proper concern of legal sociology should be the development of a general theory of law. A general theory involves several key elements that may not at first be obvious. To say that a theory of law is general means that it seeks to order law wherever it is found. It seeks to discover the principles and mechanisms that predict empirical patterns of law, whether these patterns occur in this day or the past, regardless of the substantive area of law involved and regardless of the society. By contrast, the contemporary study of law is ideographic, very concrete and historical. Legal scholars tend to rebel at the suggestion of a general theory of their subject matter. Nevertheless, unless we seek generality in our study of law, we abandon hope for a serious sociology of law.

If the sweep of legal sociology is to be this broad, a correspondingly broad concept of law is required. I like to define law simply as *governmental social control*.[35] This is one possibility among many consistent with a positivist strategy. It is a concept easily employed in cross-societal analysis, encompassing any act by a political body that concerns the definition of social order or its defense. At the same time it excludes such forms of social control as popular morality and bureaucratic rules in private organizations. It is more inclusive than an American lawyer might deem proper, but more selective than anthropological concepts which treat law as synonymous with normative life and dispute settlement of every description, governmental or otherwise. If we are to have a manageable subject matter, our concept must construe law as one among a larger array of social control systems. And if we are to have a strategically detached approach, our concept must be value neutral. We need a theoretical structure applicable to the law of the Nazis as well as American law, to revolutionary law and colonial law as well as the cumbersome law of traditional China. What do these systems share, and how can we explain the differences among them?

Ultimately a theory is known and judged by its statements about the world. These statements both guide and follow empirical research. They propose uniformities in the relation between one part of reality and another. Thus a general theory of law is addressed to the relation between law and other aspects of social life, including, for instance, other forms of social control, social stratification, the division of labor, social integration, group size, and the structure and substance of social networks. At the moment we have only a small inventory of theoretical statements, or propositions, of this kind. The relevant literature is sparse, and many of our leads must come from the classic works of Maine,[36] Durkheim,[37] Weber,[38] Ehrlich,[39] Pound,[40] and the like. Marx, too, should not be forgotten, though he gave law only passing attention.[41] Apart from classical sociology and comparative jurisprudence, anthropological literature, notably the work of such scholars as Malinowski,[42] Hoebel,[43] Gluckman,[44] Bohannan,[45] and Nader,[46] has contributed more than sociology to a general theory of law. Contemporary sociologists tend to limit their attention to the American legal system, and even there, disproportionate emphasis is given the criminal justice system. Rarely do they compare American law to governmental social control in other societies; yet if legal sociology is not comparative, its conclusions will inevitably be time-bound and ethnocentric.

This is not to suggest that American criminal justice is unworthy of study. But one must address problems at a higher level of generality, thereby contributing to and benefiting from scholarship in other realms of law. If we investigate the police, for example, our fundamental interest as sociologists must be in what police work can teach us about law, generically understood, and we must bring to a study of the police whatever we know about other forms of legal life. From my standpoint, in other words, the major shortcoming of most sociological literature on the police is that it concerns the police alone, instead of treating police behavior as an instance of law. Often sociologists occupy themselves with the unique world of the policeman, his attitudes, hopes and fears, his relations with his fellow officers, his social isolation in the wider community—in brief, with the "human" dimensions of police work.[47] Insofar as such studies rise above descriptive journalism or ethnography, then, they tend to focus upon the psychology of the policeman on his day-to-day round. Yet from a purely sociological point of view it is not important to know that policemen are, after all, "human" or to know how their minds work. A pure sociology of law does not study humans in the usual sense. It studies law as a system of behavior.[48] Taken in this sense, law feels nothing. It has no joy or sorrow or wonderment. Scientifically conceived as a social reality in its own right, law is no more human than a molecular structure. It has no nationality, no mind, and no ends proper to its nature.

I do not mean to criticize categorically the rather impressive body of police research that has accumulated in recent years, but only to suggest that its contribution to the sociology of law is limited. We must give up the notion that the sociology of law embraces any and all forms of empirical research relating to the legal system. A scientific discipline is defined by its theoretical mission, by what it tries to explain, not by its sources of data. Thus, research on the human body may contribute to any of a variety of disciplines—biochemistry, genetics, endocrinology, physiological psychology, or whatever. The same is true of research on law or the police. Accordingly, a study of the police contributes to legal sociology only if it provides insights into legal behavior, its empirical profile, the social conditions under which it occurs, and its social implications. I am not saying that every sociologist must be a theorist, but only that any sociologist who does research on a legal topic without knowing, roughly, its theoretical relevance does so at his peril.

Police research should tell us something about the social control function of the police: What legal matters do they handle? How do they come to deal with those matters? What are the principles according to which they process their cases? Ideally a study would also tell us how police behavior resembles other known patterns of legal behavior and how it differs. We know, for example, that the police make arrests relatively infrequently when some other form of social control is available in the situation. Thus, they rarely make an arrest when one family member criminally offends another, a situation where other means of social pressure typically are at hand, whereas the same offense committed by one stranger against another is very apt to result in arrest.[49] This pattern of legal behavior is known to have analogues in a wide variety of legal settings, in civil as well as criminal cases, in the invocation of law as well as its application, in many countries and historical periods, and even in the evolution of law itself.[50] We may state the pattern as a theoretical proposition: Law tends to become implicated in social life to the degree that other forms of social control are weak or unavailable.[51] Hence, what we discover in the behavior of policemen turns out to be simply an instance of a much more general pattern in the conditions under which the law acts upon social life. We thereby add systematically to existing knowledge of this pattern, and, what is more, we can *explain* the behavior of the police, since it can be predicted and deduced from a more general proposition about law.[52] If the likelihood of legal control is greater where other forms of social control are absent, it follows that the police are more likely to arrest a stranger who, let us say, assaults a stranger than a son who assaults his father. To be able to explain something so mundane and microscopic as behavior in a police encounter with the same proposition that we use to explain the historical emergence of law itself is exciting and encouraging. It provides a glimpse of general theory in action. This kind of theoretical structure is built up and elaborated over time through a process of give-and-take between data and tentative propositions stated at a high level of abstraction. It is the classical pattern of scientific advance, and I cannot see why the sociology of law should be any less ambitious or any less rigorous.

VI

We should be clear about the relation between sociological and legal scholarship. There is, properly speaking, no conflict of professional jurisdiction between the two. A legal problem is a problem of value and is forever beyond the reach of sociology. Jurisdictional conflict arises only when the sociologist makes policy recommendations in the name of science: In matters of legal policy, the lawyer must rely on his own wits.

But a more significant matter than jurisdictional clarity is the relation between pure and applied sociology of law. My view, hardly novel, is that the quality of applied science depends upon the quality of pure science. Just as major advances in mechanical and chemical engineering have been made possible by theoretical formulations in pure physics and chemistry, so legal engineering ultimately requires a general theory of how legal systems behave as natural phenomena. The case for a pure sociology of law does not rest solely on its social usefulness, but if utility is at issue, then in the long run the type of work I advocate is crucial. At present, applied sociology of law has little to apply. What more serious claim could be brought against it?

NOTES

1.   In what follows I shall use the term "sociologists" as a matter of convention, though I intend to refer not only to Ph.D.'s in sociology but also to lawyers and political scientists and anyone else claiming to contribute to the scientific study of law as a social phenomenon. Most of my examples, however, derive from the scholarly literature explicitly labeled "sociology of law" and authored by academic sociologists.

2.   Currie, "Book Review," The Yale Law Journal 81 (1971): 134, reviewing Law and the Behavioral Sciences. L. Friedman & S. Macaulay eds., 1969 and Society and the Legal Order, R. Schwartz & J. Skolnick eds., 1970. These two collections of the legal sociology literature not only collect representative materials but also attempt to explain the relevance of the materials, thereby providing excellent examples of the style of discourse now dominating the field.

3.   Currie, op.cit., 145. A striking feature of Currie's review is that he pays little attention to the scientific adequacy of the work he criticizes. Instead, he focuses more upon the reform implications of the existing work and condemns it on political rather than methodological or theoretical grounds. Thus, while he suggests that the work could greatly benefit from the perspectives of Marxian scholars, he fails to show that the Marxian approach to law has a superior explanatory power.

4.   Because research in legal sociology consistently shows these disparities, the field has become identified with debunkery and the unmasking of law. In legal scholarship this debunking spirit goes back to the legal realism movement which has haunted American law schools since it emerged around the turn of the century. Much legal sociology, then, is a new legal realism, appearing in the prudent garb of social science, armed with sophisticated research methods, new language, and abstract theoretical constructs.

5.   *Miranda v. Arizona*, 384 U.S. 436 (1966). Although there may be some disagreement as to the peripheral meanings of "custody" and "interrogation" (see, e.g., *Mathis v. United States*, 391 U.S. 1 (1968); *Orozco v. Texas*, 394 U.S. 324 (1969)), there is little doubt that a suspect under arrest in a police station who is probingly questioned about his involvement in a crime is both in custody and under interrogation as these concepts are used by the Court. Moreover, no question remains as to the required *content* of an apprising of rights, 384 U.S. at 478-79. Yet, there may even be disagreement as to what constitutes an "adequate" and "effective" appraising of rights. *Ibid.* at 467. Compare *United States v. Fox*, 403 F.2d 97 (2d Cir. 1968), with *State v. Renfrew*, 280 Minn. 276, 159 N.W.2d 111 (1968). For example, would a police procedure of giving the suspect a preprinted card listing his rights meet the requirement of an adequate and effective apprisal? Would that procedure meet the *Miranda* test if the suspect were illiterate?

6.   See, e.g., Project, "Interrogations in New Haven: The Impact of *Miranda*," *Yale Law Journal* 76 (1967): 1519.

7.   387 U.S. 1 (1967).

8.   See generally Foster, "Notice and Fair Procedure: Revolution or Simple Revision?" in Gault, *What Now for the Juvenile Court?* (V. Nordin ed. 1968), p.51. For examples of judical conflict in the applicability of specific rights, compare: (1) *Stanley v. Peyton*, 292 F. Supp. 213 (W.D. Va.—1968), cert. denied, 400 U.S. 828 (1970) (*dictum*) and *State v. Acuna*, 78 N.M. 119, 428 P. 2d 658 (1967), with *Steinhauer v. State*, 206 So. 2d 25 (Florida Dist. Ct. App.—1967), quashed and remanded on other grounds, 216 So. 2d 214 (1968), cert. denied, 398 U.S. 914 (1970) (Douglas J., dissenting on denial of cert.) (right to counsel at waiver of juvenile court jurisdiction hearing); (2) *In Re Fletcher*, 251 Md. 250, 248 A. 2d 364 (1968), cert denied, 396 U.S. 852 (1969), with *In Re D.*, 30 App. Div. 2d 183, 290 N.Y.S. 2d 935 (1968) (necessity of giving *Miranda* warnings to *both* juvenile and parents at pre-trial custodial interrogation); (3) *In Re Wylie*, 231 A. 2d 81 (D.C. Ct. App.—1967), with *In Re Urbasek*, 38 Ill. 2d 535, 232 N.E. 2d 716 (1967) (right to standard of proof beyond a reasonable doubt.)

9.   See, e.g., Lefstein, Stapleton & Teltebaum, "In Search of Juvenile Justice: Gault and its Implementation," *Law & Society Review* 3 (1969): 491, in which these problems of operationalization are evident.

10.   J. Skolnick, *Justice Without Trial* (1966), p. 138.

11.   Much less than viewing the use of informers as a violation of constitutional safeguards, the Supreme Court has refused even to require that an infomer's identity be revealed. Specifically, police reliance upon anonymous informants to provide the requisite information for probable cause to sustain an arrest or search warrant has been held not to violate

either the Fourth Amendment or due process clause. See *McCray v. Illinois*, 386 U.S. 300 (1967); *Draper v. United States*, 358 U.S. 307 (1959). Information supplied by an unnamed informer of apparent reliability under certain circumstances may provide sufficient cause for a search without a warrant. *Adams v. Williams*, 40 U.S.L.W. 4724 (U.S. June 12, 1972). But if the police utilize an informant as a participant in an illegal narcotics transaction, even where there is no question of entrapment the government will be required to disclose the identity of the informant at trial when such disclosure may be "relevant and helpful to the accused's defense." The failure to disclose in this context would violate due process. *Roviaro v. United States*, 353 U.S. 53 (1957).

12.   Skolnick, "Social Control in the Adversary System," *J. Conflict Resolution* 11 (1967): 52.

13.   L. Mayhew, *Law and Equal Opportunity* (1969), reviewed Black, "Book Review," *Soc. Inquiry* 40 (1970): 179. See Mayhew, "Teleology and Values in the Social System: Reply to Donald J. Black," *Soc. Inquiry* 40 (1970): 189.

14.   For a recent discussion of technocratic thought, see L. Roszak, *The Making of a Counter Culture* (1969), pp. 5-22.

15.   Hence this sociological concept of law is very different from and not logically incompatible with the legal positivism of Hans Kelsen and his "pure theory of law." See *e.g.*, H. Kelsen, *General Theory of Law and State* (1945). Similarly, to take another well-known example, a sociological approach does not conflict with the rule-oriented jurisprudence of H.L.A. Hart in *The Concept of Law* (1961).
    At the level of social life in its narrow sense, law is behavior and nothing more. If the concept of rule or norm is used in a sociological analysis, it should always refer to a behavioural pattern of some kind. See *e.g.*, E. Durkheim, "The Determination of Moral Facts," in *Sociology and Philosophy*, (D.F. Pocock trans. 1953), pp. 35-62.

16.   At a later point, I shall propose a sociological definition of law. See p. 104 *infra*.

17.   A good introduction to positivism is L. Kolakowski, *The Alienation of Reason: A History of Positivist Thought* (N. Guterman trans. 1968.).

18.   This has been called the principle of phenomenalism. See *Ibid.*, at 3-4.

19.   Philip Selznick, one of the most ambitious and influential students of legal effectiveness, considers the "cardinal weakness" of the sociological approach to law to be its "failure to offer a theory of the distinctively legal." Selznick, "The Sociology of Law," *International Encyclopedia of the Social Sciences* (D.L. Sills ed.) 9 (1968): 51.

20.   This is the principle of nominalism. See Kolakowski, *supra* note 17, at 5-7.

21.   *Ibid.*, at 7-8. Some legal sociologists are willing to tolerate an obfuscation of factual and normative discourse. Selznick, for instance, while conceding that the separation of fact and value has some merit, nevertheless suggests that this distinction is meant for "unsophisticated minds." We must, he continues, unlearn this "easy and reassuring" formula from our "intellectual youth." Selznick finds a natural-law

approach more appropriate for the mature thinker. Selznick, "Sociology and Natural Law," 6 *Natural L.F.* 86 (1961).

22.   This does not say that scientific studies of legal effectiveness are impossible. As long as a social goal is introduced into the analysis and is adequately defined for purposes of the investigation, the study of effectiveness is perfectly feasible. Such applied science can be as rigorously conducted as any other research. *Cf.* pp. 99-100 *supra.*

23.   As a rule I do not personally find the policy criticisms and proposals of legal sociologists to be particularly objectionable, the exception being those proposals that increase the power of the government to intervene in citizens' lives. Thus, for instance, I find the therapeutic approach to criminal offenders a frightening advance of an already too powerful criminal justice system. In fact, I align myself more broadly and precisely in the philosophical tradition of anarchism. For me, the validity of law is at all times contingent upon my own assessment of its moral validity, and thus I recognize no a priori legitimacy in the rule of law. For a brief introduction to this political ethic, see R. Wolff, *In Defence of Anarchism* (1970).

I would add that the students of legal effectiveness I am discussing are, politically speaking, the elite of our society, however critical of the legal process they may seem. Indeed, the government often finances their research on its own effectiveness. It is my view that the confusion of fact and value operates as a form of mystification that helps to keep the established order intact. Nevertheless, I do not wish to use my status as a scientist to promote my political philosophy. See M. Weber, *From Max Weber: Essays in Sociology* (H.H. Gerth & C.W. Mills transl. and eds. 1958), pp. 124-56.

24.   See note 19 *supra.*

25.   Selznick, *supra* note 21, at 93-94.

26.   See M. Weber, *The Methodology of the Social Sciences* (E.A. Shils & H.A. Finch, transls. 1949), pp. 21-22. For a direct attack on Weber's approach to these questions, see Gouldner, "Anti-Minotaur: The Myth of a Value-Free Sociology," *Soc. Problems* 9 (1962): 199.

27.   Becker, "Whose Side are We On?," *Soc. Problems* 14 (1967): 239.

28.   This is a major theme of a recent critique of sociological theory. See A. Gouldner, *The Coming Crisis of Western Sociology* (1970).

29.   It should be clear that the policy impact of science is never direct but is always mediated by normative analysis, whether explicit or implicit. Policy cannot be deduced from scientific propositions alone. All of this is dramatically illustrated by the relation between the Marxian theory and public policy. Surely no theory of social science has had more impact upon the world. It has been an important weapon in ideological debate, and it has alerted policymakers and the public to the situation of the working class and the role of class conflict in social change. Yet as a scientific theory the Marxian analysis of society and history has no logical implications for political action. Without passing judgment upon the exploitation and growing misery of the proletariat, one could just as well sit back passively and watch history unfold as join the revolution. Both responses are logically independent of the theory.

30.   R. Dahrendorf, "Values and Social Science: The Value Dispute in Perspective," in *Essays in the Theory of Society* (1968), p. 17.

31.   Of course in this brief discussion I cannot begin to review the sizable literature on the subject. Perhaps I should note, however, one criticism of the value-neutral strategy that bears directly on the study of law—one, moreover, that seems to me to be wholly without merit. This criticism asserts that the study of normative life, because it is normative, requires a partially normative approach on the part of the investigator if he is to comprehend its empirical character. The investigator must take the normative view of the participants if he is to understand their normative behavior. Selznick, for instance, suggests that the sociologist should make an "assessment" of the degree to which a normative system reaches an ideal "from the standpoint of the normative system being studied" though "the student of a normative system need not have any personal commitment to the desirability of that system." Selznick, supra note 21, at 88. In the study of law, therefore, it seems we must include an assessment of legal reality in terms of the ideals of the legal system we study.

In my view this argument incorrectly assumes that such normative ideals can be identified at a wholly empirical level. I do not believe, for example, that the degree of conformity of law with, let us say, a constitutional ideal, is a wholly empirical question. The nature of the ideal is itself a normative question, a question of normative interpretation. In the study of law such interpretation is the heart of legal scholarship, and from a positivist standpoint that activity is, at its core, normative rather than scientific. It advances an "ought" as the proper measure of reality, and it does not matter whether or not the interpreter himself subscribes to the "ought." It remains an unavoidably normative judgment. In effect, then, Selznick's view is that in order to understand normative life we must be normative. This view, I believe, is a non-sequitur.

32.   See Dahrendorf, supra note 30, at 9-10.

33.   Although not subject to empirical verification, a value statement may be subject to other criteria such as its logical status in relation to a more general axiological principle.

34.   My critique of contemporary legal sociology arises from a very conventional conception of scientific method, a conception associated with the broader tradition of positivist thought. I have not made and do not intend to make a philosophical defense of this tradition. I wish only to advocate a sociology of law true to basic positivist principles as they have come to be understood in the history of the philosophy of science.

35.   I mention this only as a means of delineating the subject matter of legal sociology. A definition of the subject matter is a prerequisite to any scientific inquiry. Just as a physicist must first define motion before he can describe its characteristics, a sociologist of religion, for example, must first define the pattern of social behavior that constitutes religion before he can proceed with his research. This does not mean that there is only one proper definition. Law itself has been defined non-normatively in a variety of ways. See e.g., M. Weber, The Theory of Social and Economic Organization 127 (T. Parsons ed. & transl. 1964): p. 127:

An order will be called law when conformity with it is upheld by probability that deviant action will be met by physical or psychic sanctions aimed to compel conformity or to punish disobedience, and applied by a group of men especially empowered to carry out this function.

I have chosen "governmental social control" as a definition of law for the reasons that follow in the text. I should add, however, that for me the choice of a particular sociological concept of law is not at all critical to my larger aim, since my ultimate interest goes beyond law per se to all forms of social control. For me, the study of law is preliminary and subordinate to the more general study of social control systems of all kinds. Therefore, if my concept of law is too narrow or too broad it does not matter *theoretically*, since it will in any case be relevant to a sociology of social control.

36.   See, e.g., *Ancient Law* (1861); *Village-Communites in the East and West* (1871).

37.   *The Division of Labor in Society* (G. Simpson transl. 1933); *Professional Ethics and Civil Morals* (C. Brookfield transl.1957); *Two Laws of Penal Evolution* (M. Mileski transl. 1971) (available in my files).

38.   *Max Weber on Law in Economy and Society* (M. Rheinstein ed., E.A. Shils & M. Rheinstein transl. 1954).

39.   *Fundamental Principles of the Sociology of Law* (M. Moll transl. 1936).

40.   E.g., *Social Control through Law* (1942); "The Limits of Effective Legal Action," *Int'l J. Ethics* 27 (1917): 150; "A Survey of Social Interests," *Harvard Law Review* 57 (1943): 1.

41.   Marx did, however, inspire some interesting sociological work on law. See e.g., K. Renner, *The Institutions of Private Law and Their Social Functions* (O. Kahn-Freund ed., A. Schwartzchild transl. 1949); Pashukanis, "The General Theory of Law and Marxism," in *Soviet Legal Philosophy* (H. Babb. transl. 1951), p. 111.

42.   The standard work is *Crime and Custom in Savage Society* (1926). This study is considered the first ethnography of law.

43.   *The Law of Primitive Man* (1954); K. Llewellyn & E. Hoebel, *The Cheyenne Way: Conflict and Case Law in Primitive Jurisprudence* (1941).

44.   See, e.g., *The Judical Process among the Barotse of Northern Rhodesia* (1955). Gluckman provides a useful overview of legal anthropology in *Politics, Law and Ritual in Tribal Society* (1965).

45..   *Justice and Judgment among the Tiv* (1957); "The Differing Realms of the Law," in *The Ethnography of Law* (1965), p. 33 (supplement to *Am. Anthropologist* 67 (1965): 33).

46.   E.g., "An Analysis of Zapotec Law Cases," *Ethnology* 3 (1964): 404; "Choices in Legal Procedure: Shia Moslem and Mexican Zapotec," *Am Anthropologist* 67 (1965): 394.

47.   E.g., Skolnick, supra note 10; W. Westley, *Violence and the Police: A Sociological Study of Law, Custom and Morality* (1970); Bittner, "The Police on Skid-Row: A Study of Peace-Keeping," *Am. Soc. Rev.* 32 (1967): 699; Werthman and Piliavin, "Gang Members and the Police," in *The Police: Six Sociological Essays* (D. Bordua ed. 1967), p. 56.

48.   See page ???? supra.

49.   Black, "The Social Organization of Arrest," *Stan. L. Rev.* 23 (1971): 1087, 1107.

50.   *Ibid.*, at 1107-08, nn. 30-34.

51.   *Ibid.*, at 1108.

52.   For a discussion of this type of explanation, see R. Braithwaite, *Scientific Explanation: A Study of the Function of Theory, Probability and Law in Science* (1953).

Chapter 5

For Jurisprudential Sociology*

Philippe Nonet†

Ten years ago, in the first issue of this review, Carl A.
Auerbach criticized some early statements of an emerging
"Berkeley perspective" in the sociology of law (Auerbach, 1966).[1]
Selznick, Skolnick, Carlin, and I were chided for proposing in
various terms that a central concern of the sociology of law should
be to study the social foundations of the ideal of legality (Selznick,
1961; 1968; Skolnick, 1965; Carlin and Nonet, 1968).

In part, Auerbach was troubled by the seeming lapse of logic
in an approach which appeared to claim evaluative conclusions (x
is or is not "legal") could be reached by purely factual social
scientific inquiry. Some of us at Berkeley had apparently forgotten the distinction between factual and normative statements. But
that was not the main objection. Although he faulted our logic,
Auerbach endorsed our larger program. Writing from the standpoint of the "reform-minded law professor" (1966: 104), he
expressed strong agreement with a statement by Selznick to the
effect that the objective of the sociology of law should be to
establish "principles of criticism to be applied to existing positive
law," principles based on "scientific generalizations, grounded in
warranted assertions about men, about groups, about the effects of
law itself" (Selznick, 1961; Auerbach, 1966: 93).

Auerbach's basic concern was that a focus on legality alone

* Philippe Nonet, "For Jurisprudential Sociology," Law & Society Review, Vol. 10
(1976): 525-545. Reprinted by permission of the Law and Society Association.
I am grateful to Leo Lowenthal, Philp Selznick, Pamela Utz and Paul Van Seters
for helping me improve the draft of this paper.
† Professor, University of California, Berkeley.

"would unnecessarily constrict social studies of law" (Auerbach, (1966: 91). It was premature, he feared, for sociology to impose stringent criteria of theoretical relevance, whatever these might be. A quest for orthodoxy could only narrow the scope, impoverish the sources, and reduce the promise of social inquiry. Intellectual growth required casting a wide net, setting aside issues of definition, crossing disciplinary boundaries, following multiple paths of inquiry, and (in practice, and therefore most important) facilitating an integration of legal and social research.

Ten years (and countless hours of lecturing and discussion) later, the idea that sociology might properly seek to develop a normative theory of law remains unpopular. In fact, if we are to judge from its most recent manifestos, the opposition has hardened and escalated. In two recent essays (Black, 1972a; 1972b), Donald Black, who describes himself as "an uncompromising adherent of the positivist approach" (1972a: 709), reaffirms the doctrine that "value judgements cannot be discovered in the empirical world" (1972b: 1092). Hence, he argues, "value considerations are as irrelevant to a sociology of law as they are to any other scientific theory" (1972b: 1087), and "the quest for the . . . 'distinctively legal' is . . . inherently unscientific" (1972b: 1092). Black's point is not just to remind us of a problem of logic, or to warn us against a possible source of bias. Nor is it to urge a larger vision of the task of social science in the study of law. On the contrary, it is to define *limits* within which social inquiry must be confined, or lose its "purity."

According to Black, "a purely sociological approach to law should involve not an assessment of legal policy, but rather, a scientific analysis of legal life as a system of behavior" (1972b: 1087). When "sociologists move . . . beyond science and deal with questions of legal evaluation" (1972b: 1087), they "severely retard the development of their field. At best they offer an applied sociology of law—at worst, sheer ideology" (1972b: 1087). If research "relate[s] empirical findings to legal ideas which are clearly expressed in the written law" (1972b: 1089), then it constitutes applied sociology. But "when legal reality is compared to an ideal with no identifiable empirical referent, such as 'the rule of law' or 'due process,' the investigator may inadvertently implant his personal ideals as the society's legal ideals. At this point social science ceases and advocacy begins" (1972b: 1090). The investigator "leaves sociology and enters jurisprudence" (1972a: 712), which is inevitably "saturated with ideology and evaluation and interest" (1972a: 712).

At one point, Black concedes that "applied" sociology of law may be valuable to people interested in law reform (1972b: 1089). But eventually the concession is retracted, on the theory that "the quality of applied science depends upon the quality of pure science . . . At present, applied sociology of law has little to apply. What more serious claim could be brought against it?" (1972b: 1100).

Hence, the sociologist should return to his basic mission—the formulation of a "general theory of law," i.e., a theory that "seeks to discover the principles and mechanisms that predict empirical patterns of law, whether these patterns occur in this day or the past, regardless of the substantive area of law involved and regardless of the society" (1972b: 1096).

It would be uncharitable to assess these ideas as a philosophical point of view. Although Black says he reasons from "basic positivist principles" (1972b: 1096 n.34) (which he regards as the unqualified orthodoxy of contemporary philosophy of science), his statements are less than a model of philosophical lucidity. They are loose, inconsistent, and uninformed by any criticism of the doctrine they purport to articulate. Unfortunately, it does not follow that the views Black advocates need not be taken seriously. They are widely shared. They express a mentality, and outline a program, which may shape future work in the sociology of law. It is necessary, and fair, that we ask what they promise. The answer, I believe, is intellectual sterility.

To say that the mentality of "pure sociology" is widely shared is not to claim that most, or even many, social scientists would subscribe precisely to the way Black formulates its tenets. In fact, I should expect most would prefer a more cautious and qualified version; few have Black's taste for dogmatic integrity. Nevertheless, Black articulates a prevailing orthodoxy of the social scientific enterprise, and it is to his credit that he does so without waffling. Only Glendon Schubert comes anywhere close to him in that respect (Schubert, 1975: 1-56 passim, and especially at 15). The core of that orthodoxy is a deep distrust towards evaluative elements in social scientific discourse, especially when evaluation is compounded with ambiguity (another mortal sin). This distrust is most clearly apparent in the canons that govern ritual social science writings, such as grant proposals for "basic" research, articles for professional journals, or the inevitable, methodological comments by which social scientists preface their own thoughts, and criticize their colleagues. Perhaps many social scientists, like Black, think these canons (for "general theory," "clearly defined" concepts, "objectively identifiable behavioral referents," etc. . . .; against "normative" judgments, "biased and ethnocentric" concepts, "vague terms that require subjective or impressionistic judgments," etc. . . .) follow from logical positivism. More aptly, they are the result of a feverish rush to mold social knowledge after a grossly idealized model of the "hard" sciences. Unfortunately, the rush has meant only that a few selected, and highly formal, ends of science—the quest for objectivity, the clarification of ideas—have, by edict, been transformed into prerequisites of research. The outcome is a set of rules that proscribe work on the more obscure, elusive, and problematic aspects of human experience, and confine social science to (dis)confirming the obvious or the trivial.

As Black observes, "pure sociology" is deeply alien to the perspectives that have governed the growth of sociology. Even today, although the vast majority of social scientists sing and dance in ritual reaffirmation of its canons, in fact they all cheat constantly in their actual work. There, the focus (explicit or implicit) is on the clarification of values, the assessment of institutions, the evaluation of policy, the conditions that frustrate or facilitate aspirations. In that respect, the sociology of law does not differ from other fields in the discipline, e.g. stratification (read: distributive justice), or socialization (read: moral development). Obviously, sociology bears birthmarks of its origins in the normative study of politics, law, economics, culture. Furthermore, like it or not the intellectual significance of sociological ideas remains largely derivative. In the absence of any autonomous (and persuasive) body of sociological theory, the conclusions of social inquiry continue to gain meaning and resonance primarily from what they contribute to political, legal, economic, and other branches of "normative" thought,—in other words, to our understanding of the conditions and costs of the pursuit of various human aspirations, such as democracy, fairness, efficiency, intimacy.

Judging from past experience, that situation is not likely to change. If we were to teach only "pure sociology," we would have to graduate illiterates; and research so limited would only add to an already over-great indulgence in intellectual onanism. Having law, politics, economics to think about, we manage to retain some facts, some history, and some ideas to teach, thus saving our students from radical ignorance. Furthermore, law, politics, economics are not just subjects of theory; they are also key contexts of action within which social experience accumulates. That is of course why they have been and remain foci for thought. In these contexts, experience organizes around the needs, interests, purposes, aspirations, that are the stuff of human life. And the lessons drawn from that experience naturally take the form of statements about the "adequacy, " "effectiveness," "achievements," "limitations," "growth," "decline," of various social arrangements. Why this "normative" manner of speaking should, in the eyes of some of our contemporaries, render these statements unworthy of scientific inquiry, is one of the more obscure mysteries of modern thought.

Given its past accomplishments, "pure sociology" would seem a high-risk and very speculative intellectual investment. We should of course tolerate, and even encourage, the few who may try it. But it does not follow we should allow it to become a program for the rest of us. On the contrary, experience recommends what has been a cardinal tenet of the "Berkeley program" in legal sociology: just as other branches of sociology need to be informed by the normative thought on which they comment, *so sociology of law must be jurisprudentially informed* (Principle I).

Even if a "pure sociology of law were to develop, we should still want to invest most of our resources in more tangibly fruitful ventures. The reason for that is the relatively low yield of purely theoretical work of any kind, in all sociology and all philosophy, in jurisprudence as well as in sociology of law. Hence another tenet of the Berkeley program (also, regrettably, the least observed): *sociology of law must have redeeming value for policy.* Never let any project stand on its theoretical merits alone (Principle II).

Prescribed Ignorance

Black does not deny the factual foundation of these principles. He deplores it, and urges instead that sociology sever its continuity with normative philosophy, and with its own history. Unfortunately, such a rupture entails serious and tangible intellectual costs, against which the speculative future of "pure" sociology cannot weigh heavily. The main cost is, of course, a severely impoverished education. In the event the point is not as obvious as I think it is, I shall let Black himself illustrate it. Our critic would have the sociology of law cut itself loose from its jurisprudential past. Thus he finds it regrettable that "normative" legal sociology "has become identified with debunkery and the unmasking of law." This orientation, he argues, "goes back to the legal realism movement . . . . Much legal sociology, then, is a new legal realism, appearing in the prudent garb of social science" (1972b: 1087 n.4). A "pure" sociology of law would liberate itself from this unfortunate history. In this purified approach, we are told, law is seen

> as a thing like any other in the empirical world. It is crucial to be clear that from a sociological standpoint, law consists in observable acts, not in rules as the concept of rule is employed in both the literature of jurisprudence and in everyday legal language. From a sociological point of view, *law is not what lawyers regard as binding or obligatory precepts, but rather, for example, the observable dispositions of judges, policemen, prosecutors, or administrative officials* (1972b: 1091. Italics mine).

Now it should be apparent that this allegedly "sociological" approach to law has its own jurisprudential pedigree: it was last, and most forcefully, advocated by some legal realists.[2] It should also be clear that familiarity with its jurisprudential history would help inform the sociologists of the powerful objections to which this approach is vulnerable. Specifically, a jurisprudentially informed social scientist would be more likely to understand, along with H.L.A. Hart, that the sentence quoted above in italics is internally contradictory (in that the office of judge, policeman, etc. . . . . is constituted by, and hence, cannot even be identified without reference to, rules), and seriously misleading as a guide for an empirical account of legal phenomena (in that it disregards the element of authority in legal phenomena) (Hart, 1961: especially 79-88; 132-144). Hence, he could hardly agree with Black's statement that the "sociological approach" so defined "does not conflict with the rule-oriented jurisprudence of H.L.A. Hart" (Black, 1972b: 1091 n.15). Finally, he would be able to appreciate that, however "scientifically" inadequate, a focus on "the observable dispositions" of officials makes special sense if one's purpose is to expose the discrepancy between what officials do and what they ought to do. It presumes that very "debunking spirit" from which Black wants to rescue legal sociology.

If one agrees with Black (as I do) that debunking is too limited, too unpromising, and too easy a goal for sociological inquiry, perhaps the alternative is not to dismiss or ignore the role of values, rules, and other normative elements in legal phenomena, but rather to take them more seriously. This is part of the program H.L.A. Hart proposed for jurisprudence. It is also what Selznick proposed for legal sociology when, for similar reasons but in different words, he argued against the anti-formalist (read: rule-skeptical) mood that had pervaded the field and its immediate parents, i.e. legal realism and sociological jurisprudence (Selznick, 1968). Although Auerbach criticized a statement drawn from that argument (Auerbach, 1966: 92), it is not clear he understood, or even read,[3] the argument as a whole. But judging from what he advocates elsewhere in the paper, I cannot imagine that Auerbach could have disagreed with the main thrust of Selznick's essay, and with another basic tenet of the Berkeley program, which is: *the sociology of law must take legal ideas seriously.* (Principle III. Corollary: sociologists who want to study law should become legally literate.) Perhaps a difference between Auerbach and Selznick was that the former had greater confidence in the promise of legal realism, and the good sense of social science, than the latter could muster. In fact, legal realism was fraught with ambiguity in its posture towards legal ideas. On the one hand, it hoped to make legal thought more purposive, more policy-oriented, more aware of consequences, and hence, more informed by the problems of law in action. On the other hand, its impatience towards legal formalism suggested a more radical critique of the inherent impotence of any legal thought. It was inevitable that such a perspective appeal to social scientists bent on demystification. Besides, it is all too comforting for the student of sociology to think he can study "pure" legal "behavior" (without bothering to learn about the complicated and obscure arguments that occupy lawyers), and still hope to capture all that "really" matters about the legal order.

It would be perverse, though not unthinkable, to interpret Selznick's argument as urging, like Black, that sociology reject its jurisprudential heritage. The remedy to a simplistic reading of legal realism is not less but more study of jurisprudence. As Black demonstrates, a little bit of philosophy is inevitable, and inevitably vulnerable to serious blunders. It is obscure by what reasoning one might move from the premise that moral judgments are not amenable to scientific testing, to the conclusion that such judgments (i.e., the fact that some people under some conditions express some moral preferences) cannot be objects of scientific inquiry. But Black seems to think that his commitment to positivism requires him to rule normative statements out of factual existence: in his view, rules and other materials "lawyers regard as binding or obligatory precepts" (Black, 1972b: 1091)[4] are not facts the sociology of law can study. By now, it should be clear that Black's program for a "pure" sociology of law offers not just one, but two prescriptions for ignorance. Sociology should (1) ignore the problems, values, and doctrines of jurisprudence; (2) ignore the rules, principles, and policies that constitute law, as understood by all but the pure sociologists.

Even the best intentioned and the strongest willed would find such vows of ignorance impossible to honor without breach. Black himself violates his religion in the very sermon he preaches. Thus he proposes that a definition of law as "governmental social control" (1972b: 1096) would satisfy the requirements of pure sociology. He finds that definition simple, as well as "consistent with a positivist strategy" (1972b: 1096). For example, it is obvious to Black that such a definition excludes from law "such forms of social control as . . . bureaucratic rules in private organizations" (1972b: 1096). Thus, it turns out, (a) rules are a "form of social control," and fall within the ambit of legal sociology if they are governmental; (b) the identification of the legal requires distinguishing between the "public" and the "private" sphere, a problem that has haunted jurisprudence and political theory, and which is the central preoccupation of the book Black rules out of sociology as an argument in jurisprudence (1972a).

Shortly thereafter, Black offers a "theoretical proposition" which, he thinks, exemplifies the kind of idea that pure sociology should aim to develop and test: "Law tends to become implicated in social life to the degree that other forms of social control are weak or unavailable" (1972b: 1099). It should be obvious that the conclusion that some form of social control is " weak or unavailable" presupposes the identification of some standard of need, or adequacy, or (might I venture) effectiveness, by which the control mechanism can be assessed. Thus, although pure sociology is barred from studying "legal effectiveness" (1972b: 1087) (because that involves unscientific evaluation), it appears it may, indeed must, evaluate the adequacy of non-legal forms of control. It is to Black's credit that his common sense is not always blinded by his positivist faith. One can hardly imagine a sensible study of social control that would not ask in one way or another:

control to what end? by what means? with what results? at what cost? and other such evaluative questions. Black avoids the words, but does the job.

From this "theoretical proposition," Black argues, more specific generalizations can be "predicted and deduced" (1972b: 1099). He offers an example from a study he did of the conditions under which police resort to arrest: "The greater the relational distance between a complainant and a suspect, the greater the likelihood of arrest" (1971: 1107). Black explains that the police (i.e. law, governmental social control) will likely refrain from arresting a son who (allegedly) assaulted his father, because the family (i.e. another "means of social pressure") can probably handle "the situation;" by contrast, if one (e.g. a stranger) assaults a more distantly related other (e.g. another stranger), the probability of arrest is higher. This highly schematic story summarizes a complicated cost-benefit analysis of alternative means of control. It is unclear whether that analysis is made only by the police (whose conduct Black is just describing), or also by Black (who might then be arguing that the police's cost-benefit analysis usually comes to the same conclusion as his own). But whoever does the analysis, it involves assessing a problematic situation (a family quarrel) in which (a) several ends must be taken into account (punishing the offender? restraining the participants to prevent further offenses? upholding parental authority? facilitating a reconciliation? reducing risks and costs for law enforcement?), and (b) alternative policies (to arrest or not to arrest?) must be evaluated in the light of these normative criteria. This evaluation may be more or less routinized, more or less sensitive, more or less prompt, more or less accurate; and we may want to assess the conditions under which the quality of the policeman's analysis varies. We would then be evaluating the evaluation. Furthermore, the practical conclusions one might draw from the evaluation would depend in part upon how the many relevent ends would be ordered in a priority ranking. Thus a legal order that gave high priority to upholding the authority of the criminal law, allowed police considerable resources, and had little regard for the family as an institution, would give its policemen decision criteria quite different from the criteria that would prevail if the family were highly valued, the criminal law were held in contempt, and the police were kept stingily understaffed.

Thus understood, Black's story makes new sense. Clearly, it no longer supports his "theoretical proposition," that is, the "purely sociological" "prediction" that police will "behave" (after having done all the thinking Black would like to ignore) in accordance with the stated pattern. The proposition is far too general, and has to be restated to incorporate the major conditions under which the predicted pattern can plausibly be expected. Note that at least some of these conditions would refer, implicitly or explicitly, to values, principles, and policies of the legal order, e.g., to how the legal order ranks the various ends its police must consider in deciding whether or not to arrest. Now it becomes apparent that Black's "theoretical proposition" is in fact the poorly disguised statement of a *principle of economy or restraint* by which some governments (or some officials of some governments, including the police Black studied) are sometimes guided.[5] The "prediction" is a norm which directs government officials to save their resources for situations in which no other agency can take responsibility. The norm may itself reflect considerations of economy (avoid wasting scarce resources), or a more affirmative principle of deference to "private" institutions, or a general preference for minimal government. One must then wonder whether Black's enthusiasm for his "theoretical proposition" (he finds it "exciting and encouraging") (1972b: 1100) might not be a manifestation of his ideological preference for "the philosophical tradition of anarchism" (1972b: 1092 n.23). For elsewhere in the paper he confesses that he finds "particularly objectionable" the policy proposals of legal sociologists that "increase the power of the government to intervene in citizens' lives" (1972b: 1092 n.23).

Bias and Ideology

I could not resist making this last point, not because I find it important, but because to *Black* the ultimate sin of evaluative sociology is that the investigator is given opportunities, perhaps encouraged, to "inadvertently implant his personal ideals" (1972b: 1090) and drift from science to ideology. The arch-enemy of "good science" is bias. That is why "good social science . . . requires a disciplined disengagement on the part of the investigator—so disciplined, in fact, that it may rarely be achieved" (1972b: 1093). Perhaps this principle of disengagement is the reason why Black urges upon us his program of willful ignorance. Of course, ignorance and impoverished education create their own risks of scientific error. In effect, we are asked to *prefer the risks of error by ignorance to the risks of error from bias.*

There may be reasons for preferring ignorance to bias (assuming the choice must be made), but they cannot be that the risks of error from bias are greater than the risks of error from ignorance. It does not matter much that the cause of Black's errors in arguing for his pure proposition might be his preference for anarchism. His argument is flawed not because of his perferences, but because of its faulty logic. With good reasoning, his preference for anarchism might have helped him produce a rigorous, insightful, and altogether compelling argument, say, to demonstrate that some legal policy will encourage intrusive government surveillance. As Black himself points out, we should not "confuse the origins and uses of a scientific statement with its validity"

(1972b: 1095). In other words, from the standpoint of "scientific validity," a bias is bad when it causes a flawed argument; it is not bad *per se*. It is somewhat suprising then to find Black complaining that Selznick approves the growth of "due process" standards in private employment, at the same time as he gives evidence of the pattern and of the conditions that sustain it (Selznick, 1969). One can of course, be persuaded by Selznick's evidence and reasoning (which Black does not criticize), and yet deplore the pattern on the (perhaps) equally true ground that "legalism" is now "creeping" into yet another sphere of social life (Black, 1972a: 714). (Hence, perhaps Black's disagreement is only with Selznick's values, not with his argument. But that is far from clear, because Black wrongly infers that the work reflects a "liberal jurisprudence," which "interprets the law in the interest of labor" and encourages "an ever greater involvement of the state and law in the private affairs of the citizenry" (Black, 1972a: 713-714). In fact, the argument points to the emergence of principles of industrial *self*-government, fashioned through collective bargaining and largely without the state, hence capable of taking account of the purposes and needs of management as well as labor. Any reasonably articulate socialist would protest such a thesis as anti-labor, anti-government, and perhaps smacking of a proto-fascist corporatism. Would Black have agreed with Selznick had he understood what the argument "advocates?")

More important for the scientific enterprise is the fact that "biases"—interests, sympathies, sensibilities, tastes,—generate the energy that makes us think; on that ground, the more (the greater the number of) biases we have, the better science is served. The growth of knowlege may not be as well served when inquiry is more (more intensely) biased, that is, when it is blind to all values except for the one with which it is especially concerned. This single-minded regard for one end at the expense of all others is what we have in mind when we criticize ideology. Even then, the "scientific validity" of the conclusions of ideologically inspired inquiry may be unimpeachable; our objections to these conclusions is not that they are false (in which case we would not have to criticize them for being ideological) but that they are partial. They ignore problems and considerations that might influence our judgment in a direction contrary to that which is advocated. Thus although Black might be factually correct in criticizing a policy that fosters intrusive surveillance, he would be ideological if he ignored that the same policy might help government design more just and more efficient social programs. Compared to bias, ignorance is far more damaging to the scientific enterprise. It diminishes the resources we have to analyze complex ideas, to make distinctions, to uncover hidden assumptions, briefly to correct faults in one's own as well as others' thinking. Furthermore, it reduces the chances that one will have many rather than few biases, and therefore none too strongly held, as each necessarily conflicts with some other. To prefer ignorance is to choose ideology as well as incompetence.

On close scrutiny, it turns out that ideology (in the sense just discussed) does not trouble Black too much. To assess police conduct *only* from the standpoint of its compliance with *Miranda* is to assume an ideological posture. But Black uses a study of this kind as an example of "applied" sociology (Black, 1972b: 1988), which he regards as scientifically legitimate. Two features seem to distinguish "applied" sociology from what Black regards as illegitimate evaluative sociology. First, the standard of evaluation has "a very plain and specific operational meaning" (1972b: 1088). To the extent criteria of evaluation are complex and obscure, the assessment loses its scientific integrity. Second, the standard is drawn from a source other than the researcher's own preferences (although it may be congruent with them). Thus, if the standard is "a statute whose purpose is rather clearly discernible or a judicial decision unambiguously declarative of a specific policy" (1972b: 1088), the research is "applied" science. It should be obvious that these two criteria are likely to conflict with one another. A standard of evaluation borrowed from *one* statute or decision may be clear; but the relevant law is likely to comprise many statutes and decisions, and hence to be confused and ambiguous. To select one of these many criteria is to assume a partial and partisan standpoint. Similarly, one can have a "plain and specific operational" standard of judgment only if one agrees to defend a highly partisan viewpoint. The more complex, multiple, and hence obscure, are one's evaluation criteria, the wider the array of interests and values (other than one's own or any party's) they are likely to take into account.

Because Black's two ways of distinguishing applied from illegitimate evaluative sociology conflict with one another, I shall consider each separately. Let us begin with "clarity."

According to Black, clarity of meaning is what distinguishes narrow, specific policies (the kind of standards by which "applied" sociology evaluates legal behavior) from larger, more general ends (such as due-process, the Rule of Law, and other such standards which are the concern of jurisprudence, moral, and political philosophy, and by which illegitimate evaluative sociology assesses legal "reality"). To draw the line on that ground is to reduce scientific inquiry to the role of a bureaucratic investigation of compliance. As defined, "applied" legal sociology is perhaps less difficult than jurisprudential sociology. It is certainly not more scientific; on the contrary, it retreats from a major scientific responsibility of policy research, that is, the clarification of purpose. Whatever meaning a specific policy may have, it owes that meaning to some larger purpose(s) or interests(s) it helps achieve in a particular context. Therefore, to evaluate the implementation of a policy is inevitably to further determine (clarify) what the pursuit of some larger ends requires (means) in the context under study. Research can, of course, determine whether the racial composition of classrooms meets the quantitative guidelines established by court decrees in school integration cases. But all judicial, bureaucratic, and "affirmative action" authorities to the contrary notwithstanding, that information alone would be meaningless, as full compliance with the guidelines is as compatible with increased racial conflict and poorer education, as it is with exactly opposite achievements. Good policy research would require that compliance with the guidelines be assessed in light of the ends of education and racial justice. This kind of assessment is precisely what we wish bureaucracies did more often, when we criticize them for transforming means (rules and routines of all kinds) into ends. Thus clarity, or rather the progressive clarification of values, is a *purpose, not a condition,* of policy research, as it is of jurisprudence and jurisprudential sociology. For this reason, a fourth tenet (Principle IV) of the Berkeley program is: *The sociology of law must integrate jurisprudential and policy analysis.*

Black's distinction between applied and jurisprudential sociology rejects that principle and amounts to yet another prescription for ignorance: it directs the sociologist to ignore the purpose of the policies he evaluates. Such a directive would sterilize policy-research. If the distinction also suggests that the purposes and logic of jurisprudential inquiry differ fundamentally from those of policy research, then it is doubly sterilizing. Jurisprudence lives and grows from what it learns from policy. For policy is the realm of action where abstract ideals are tested, redefined, and elaborated. Only by examining that experience can jurisprudence remain factually informed, and hope to clarify the dilemmas of moral and political choice.

Moral dilemmas, not moral causes, are the stuff of jurisprudence, as well as of moral and political theory. With this observation, let us turn to Black's second criterion for distinguishing philosophers from applied sociologists. The former, he thinks, *advocate* their "personal" preferences, whereas the latter *evaluate* in the light of standards set by others. The equation of normative thought and social advocacy is painfully naive. If philosophical education makes any difference in this respect, it is (I should think) to diminish the fervor with which any view can be espoused, and to encourage skepticism and cautious evaluation. Anyhow, as we saw earlier, Black agrees that the quality of an argument is logically independent from the preferences of its author. But perhaps Black's objections to jurisprudential sociology are not that it advocates, but that it bases advocacy or evaluation upon the *personal* preferences of the analyst, rather than preferences imposed by some other source. Why the source of the standard should matter, if the intrusion of evaluation into the argument does not necessarily corrupt its logic, is the next obscurity we must consider.

Authority and value

Obscure at it is, that question points to a central element in the creed of "pure sociology." Believers in that faith claim that science should not be used to give authority to values.

Clearly Black is not arguing that the "scientific validity" of evaluative research depends upon the source of the standard invoked. An "applied sociologist" might well personally believe in the policy by which he assesses legal behavior without thereby jeopardizing the legitimacy of his analysis. Conversely, an American jurisprudential sociologist who personally values and studies fidelity to "due process of law" is not exculpated by the fact that the Constitution of the United States gives authority to that standard.

What really matters to Black is that the applied sociologist usually makes *explicit* the authority for the standard he studies, whereas the jurisprudential sociologist is less apt to do so. Failing to disclose the source of one's standard makes one vulnerable to the charge of failing to separate clearly the normative from the factual elements in one's analysis, thus possibly misleading one's readers to believe that some normative statements are scientifically demonstrated truths. "What is disturbing about the contemporary literature on legal effectiveness then is not that it evaluates, but rather, that its evaluations and proposals are presented as scientific findings" (Black, 1972b: 1092-1093).[6] To disown evaluative statements by indicating their authors are a legislature, or a judge, or for that matter anyone but a scientist, is a convenient way to avoid that risk.

There are good reasons why social scientists do not always clearly disclose the authority for their normative statements. For example, the sources may be too many, too diffuse, or simply too obvious. Consider the following statement, which is paraphrased from another obscure text of Black: "Democracy perpetuates inequality" (Black, 1973: 149).[7] However one might read it, this is a statement about values, and a good example of the kind of vague proposition with which normative political sociology begins to think. It says that two values, democracy and equality, conflict with one another, so that, to the extent we pursue the one, we should be prepared to accept some loss of the other. Quite properly, Black cites no authority for either of these values. Hence, Black's rule is not that the scientist should disown his normative statements by citing authority for them; it must be rather, that he should disown them, period. He could do so, for example, by prefacing his statements on democracy with such disclaimers as "in the hours when my mind is not governed by the canons of science, I, along with many of you, believe in democracy, but now that I must think rigorously . . ."; or "I don't believe in democracy, but because some of you do, I think that, as a scientist, I should

tell you . . ."; or "I am quite ambivalent about democracy, because
as a scientist I have found . . . ." Perhaps simply saying that
"democracy perpetuates inequality" is sufficient indication of
reservations, doubt, disbelief, or ambivalence. Any of the above
ways of disowning normative statements would satisfy the all too
well known rule that, when social scientists deal with a problem
of value, they should be explicit about their own "personal"
preference, or "bias." That rule, in turn, is just another way to
satisfy the principle that scholars should not mislead their
audiences about the scholarly merits of what they say or write qua
scholars. With that principle, no one can reasonably disagree, even
though reasonable men may differ about what specific conclusions
they should draw from it. (The conclusions will vary in part with
the assumptions one makes about one's audience's vulnerability to
being misled. To establish an absolute requirement that normative
statements be explicitly disowned is to assume all audiences suffer
from excessive naiveté or debilitating deference to professorial
authority.)

By now we should understand that this principle ("don't
mislead") is not what Black has in mind, for it cannot distinguish
him from those he criticizes, nor pure from jurisprudential
sociology. In fact, a rigorous application of the disowning rules
Black proposes would result in systematic violations of his major
taboo, i.e., that the social scientist shall not make "policy
recommendations in the name of science" (Black, 1972b: 1100), or
"use [his] status as a scientist to promote [a] political philosophy"
(1972b: 1092 n.23). The disclaimers discussed above, including the
citing of authority, may indeed be understood as formulas by
which scientists, using proper understatement, dissociate
themselves from the irrationality with which legislatures, judges,
and other people (including at times themselves) often make moral
and political decisions. Thus understood, and slightly more
pointed, the disclaimers read: "As a scientist I must say there is no
justification for what the legislature (the court) decided;" or "no
reasonable man can want democracy and equality to the same
extent at the same time;" or "it is foolish to want to have one's
cake (modern industrial organization; democracy) and eat it too
(have no standards of due process; have no further obstacles to
equality)." Implicitly or explicitly, correctly or incorrectly, such
statements criticize moral preferences on the ground that relevant
factual problems or factual knowledge have been overlooked. They
must assume that moral judgements can be better informed of the
conditions under which, or means by which, values can be
pursued, as well as of the costs attached to the realization of
values. And they suggest that a more informed moral judgment is
also likely to be better, because it is more likely to reach its
purpose and to avoid unnecessary costs.

To Black, the suggestion that science can assess, and
knowledge can improve, the quality of moral judgments, is

anathema. Thus he sees no justification for the view that law can benefit from "an accurate sociological analysis" (1972a: 713) of the world it governs. It is not clear why he objects to this view. Sometimes, it would seem, his quarrel is only with theses that by any reasonable judgment *overstate* what knowledge can do for moral choice. For example, he disagrees with "technocratic thought" (1972b: 1090) according to which "moral problems of *every sort* are translated into problems of knowledge and science, of know how" (1972b: 1090-1091. Italics mine.). But jurisprudential sociology is not committed to such overreaching. Sometimes, Black argues on moral or political grounds. If his anarchism entails a distaste for all kinds of authority, one can understand that he would object to the authority science is allegedly accorded, and to the alleged fact that "students of legal effectiveness . . . are . . . the élite of our society" (Black, 1972b: 1092 n.23). But then one wonders why he should agree that moral philosophy has any competence, and legitimate authority, in the assessment of moral issues (Black, 1972b: 1092). If Black accepts that value statements be criticized on the basis of their "logical status in relation to a more general axiological principle" (Black, 1972b: 1095 n.33), how can he object to criticism based upon the presence or absence of an empirically verified causal relation between (a) behavior that accords with a given value statement and (b) a class of outcomes defined by "general axiological principles?" Both kinds of criticism are based on the authority of reason. It is hard to see why it might be proper to reduce incoherence, but improper to reduce ignorance in moral discourse.

But most of the time, Black is not arguing that scientifically legitimate uses of science be restricted for moral reasons. Rather he is proposing that some uses of scientific inquiry, which might conceivably increase the quality of moral and political choice, be proscribed to preserve the "purity" of science. If there is any argument for the view that science should not be used to give or deny authority to values, it cannot be that the proposition follows any requirement of logic. Although Black does not offer it, there is an argument, and it is quite empirical. When scientific inquiry touches highly controversial and divisive moral issues, it creates a risk that the integrity and the authority of science as an institution will be threatened and undermined. Scientific debates may become politicized, the fervor of faith may displace dispassionate inquiry, and even the factual assertions of "scientists" may lose credibility. Undeniably, this risk exists, especially in the social sciences. The first citation in Black's manifesto is to a piece (Currie, 1971) that illustrates what one may fear when scientists "shed the mantle of science and become unabashedly political" (Black, 1972b: 1086 nn.2 and 3). The risk is avoided, or at least reduced, if the scientific establishment commits itself to a principle of prudence: "Stay away from hot issues; leave politics to the politicians, morals to the moralists, law to the lawyers." Translated for publication in textbooks on the ethics and methods of science, this counsel becomes the dogma of the separation of fact and value. The principle has considerable precedent in institutional experience. It is the foundation of bureaucracy: there, the separation of administration and policy protects the autonomy and integrity of bureaucratic expertise. In effect, "pure sociology" is an extension of bureaucratic principle to the management of the social scientific establishment.

Hence, although "pure sociology" rests on rather weak intellectual foundations, one might nevertheless recommend it as a sound managerial practice. Perhaps one would do so, for the long term welfare of the scientific enterprise, if (a) the risks its principles help reduce were of such magnitude as to outweigh (b) the intellectual losses its rules of ignorance would inflict upon science and culture. It would be far more difficult to opt for "pure sociology" if the calculation of costs and benefits had to consider (c) the social harms that would follow this intellectual impoverishment. What if morals and politics, condemned by science to ignorance, lost their capacity to recognize harms?

For Jurisprudential Sociology

Fortunately or unfortunately, the bureaucratic option is not truly open to the social sciences. There is no way to study human affairs and not to make statements about issues that matter deeply for the satisfaction of needs, the furthering of interests, the achievement of purposes, the fulfillment of aspirations, the development of capacities, in short, about values. The pure sociologist may try to remove all normative words from his language. But all he can do is to ban the words whose moral connotations he sees (fears? dislikes?), or define the connotations out of existence. Obviously he cannot help using the words whose normative meanings escape his attention. The effect is a social scientific Newspeak, which prohibits access to a vast and precious stock of cognitive resources. For the connotations that surround words such as law, government, control, democracy, equality, arrest, police, family, are the inchoate knowledge with which we think about the denoted phenomena. In attempting to rule normative meanings out of existence, "pure sociology" either deprives itself and its readers of that knowledge ("system of social stratification" is far purer than "inequality"), or requires denying the existence of that knowledge even as we use the words that evoke it (for either a word has been purified by definition, or the writer has overlooked the need for purification thus leaving the job to the reader). How else could we make sense of the following text: "By legal intelligence I mean the knowledge that a legal system has about law violations in its jurisdiction. . . . From a

sociological standpoint, however, there is no 'proper' or even
'effective' system of legal intelligence. . . . [Let us therefore
examine the limits of legal intelligence.] Any legal system relying
upon the active participation of ordinary citizens must absorb
whatever naiveté and ignorance is found among the citizenry"
(Black: 1973, 130-132). Either the language is English, and the
reasoning incoherent, or the logic is proper, but we are forbidden
to think of "intelligence," "naiveté," "ignorance," and "limits" as
aspects of the quality and effectiveness of knowledge. Pure
sociology cannot mean what it says.

Unfortunately, jurisprudence is no alternative to "pure"
sociology. To prefer it would only be to choose another set of
blinders. In fact, jurisprudence and pure sociology are deeply
involved with one another: there is no better match for a sociology
that denies the normative aspects of legal phenomena, than a legal
philosophy blind to factual issues in the analysis of normative
ideas. To Black, jurisprudence is as "logically" incapable of failing
for lack of knowledge, as sociology is of failing for philosophical
naiveté. What can disturb such a solid and comfortable relation of
mutually respectful ignorance?

Perhaps sociology can do so, if it returns to its historic
intellectual task: that is, to enlarge the intellectual horizons of
legal, political, economic, and other modes of normative thought;
to broaden the concerns of these disciplines beyond the limits of
their *specialized* institutional domains; to blur, not to draw,
"boundaries," as between fact and value, law and politics,
economy and society, policy and administration; to help all kinds
of social thought recognize the relevence of facts, problems,
interests, and values, of which they would not otherwise take
account. Philosophy shared that intellectual responsibility until
positivism sterilized it. Must sociology go through the same crisis?
And if it must, where will that responsibility be assumed?

We need a jurisprudential sociology, a social science of law
that speaks to the problems, and is informed by the ideas, of
jurisprudence. Such a sociology recognizes the continuities of
analytical, descriptive and evaluative theory. Analytical issues—
e.g., the role of coercion in law; the relation of law to the state; the
interplay of law and politics; the distinction between law and
morality; the place of rules, principles, purpose, and knowledge in
legal judgment; the tension between procedural and substantive
justice;—are taken as pointing to variable aspects of legal
phenomena. The extent to which the law is coercive, vulnerable to
politics, purposive, or open to social knowledge, is subject to
variations that require empirical inquiry. At the same time, those
jurisprudential-sociological variables condition the ends law can
pursue, and the resources it can muster to serve those ends. To
study such questions as: the kinds of sanctions and remedies that
are available to legal institutions; the principles and structures of
authority that characterize various legal processes; the way law

receives and interprets political and moral values; the administrative resources legal agencies can deploy; the authority of purpose in legal reasoning;—is also to assess the competences and limitations of different kinds of legal orders or legal institutions. Whatever knowledge is gained about these problems should contribute to formulating principles of institutional design, and guides for the diagnosis of institutional troubles.

There is nothing arcane or novel about jurisprudential sociology. In fact, as I pointed out at the beginning of my argument, and as a glance at the index of this Review would confirm, most socio-legal studies are informed by concerns for legal values or legal policy—normative concerns whose rational pursuit would require close observance of the principles of jurisprudential sociology. If the social study of law had remained free to be true to its purposes, and to be responsive to the requirements of its research tasks, all its practitioners would hold the truth of those principles to be self-evident. Unfortunately, since the ascent of bureaucratic orthodoxy in the social sciences, confessing that truth, and resisting the ritual, pseudo-scientific rigors of "pure sociology," exposes one to excommunication, to being expelled out of "the boundaries of legal sociology." The practice of jurisprudential sociology is alive; it has only been driven under ground.

NOTES

1.   The phrase "Berkeley perspective" or "Berkeley program" is mine. It is not meant to suggest all my colleagues at Berkeley agree with the propositions I have gathered under that convenient label. Such a consensus is too improbable at such a place.

2.   The realists were fascinated by Holmes: "The prophecies of what the courts will do in fact, and nothing more pretentious, are what I mean by the law." (Oliver Wendell Holmes, 1897; 460-461).

3.   He refers to it only as quoted in Skolnick (1965).

4.   See, however, Black, 1972a: 712, where he concedes that "science may tell us what others define as just or good," thus contradicting himself once more.

5.   Other examples of the normative propositions of "pure" sociology are discussed later pp. 127, 128, and 131.

6.   See also Black, 1972a: 714, where he criticizes Selnick for not being "explicit about his legal philosophy."

7.   "The more democratic a legal system, the more the citizenry perpetuates the existing system of social stratification" (Black, 1973: 149). This is how one writes when one attempts to "purify" his statements of their normative connotations.

[Editor's Note: Professor Black was invited to reply to Professor Nonet's paper, but he declined on the ground that readers may judge the scientific value of his approach by his recently completed book, The Behavior of Law (New York: Academic Press, 1976).]

REFERENCES

Auerbach, Carl A., "Legal Tasks for the Sociologist," *Law & Society Review* 1 (1966): 91.

Black, Donald J., "The Social Organization of Arrest," *Standford Law Review* 23 (1971): 1087.

—————— , "Book Review" (reviewing P. Selznick, (1969)), *American Journal of Sociology* 78 (1972a): 709.

—————— , "The Boundaries of Legal Sociology," *Yale Law Journal* 81 (1972b): 1086.

—————— , "The Mobilization of Law," *Journal of Legal Studies* 2 (1973): 125.

Carlin, Jerome and Nonet, Philippe, "The Legal Profession," *International Encyclopedia of the Social Sciences* 9 (1968): 66. New York: Macmillan.

Currie, Elliot, "Sociology of Law: The Unasked Questions," (Book Review), *Yale Law Journal* 81 (1971): 134 (reviewing L. Friedman and S. Macaulay (eds.), *Law and the Behavioral Sciences* (1970) and R. Schwartz and J. Skolnick (eds.), *Society and the Legal Order* (1970)).

Hart, H.L.A., *The Concept of Law.* Oxford: Clarendon Press, 1961.

Holmes, Oliver Wendell, "The Path of the Law," *Harvard Law Review* 10 (1897): 457.

Schubert, Glendon, *Human Jurisprudence: Public Law as Political Science.* Honolulu: University Press of Hawaii, 1975.

Selznick, Philip, "Sociology and Natural Law" *Natural Law Forum* 6 (1961): 84.

—————— , "The Sociology of Law," *International Encyclopedia of the Social Sciences* 9 (1968): 50, New York: Macmillan.

—————— , with the collaboration of Nonet, Philippe and Vollmer, Howard M., *Law, Society and Industrial Justice.* New York: Russell Sage Foundation, 1969.

Skolnick, Jerome H., "The Sociology of Law in America: Overview and Trends," *Social Problems* 12 (1965): 4 (Supplement on "Law and Society").

PART THREE

COMPETING PARADIGMS

Paradigm Definitions

A paradigm is defined as a collection of the major assumptions, concepts, and propositions in a substantive area. Paradigms serve to orient theorizing in an intellectual discipline and resemble models. A conceptual model is a picture of social reality. It is a set of assumptions that are accepted as true and that influence one's perception of the working of society. A model only reflects limited aspects of the totality of social reality and is thus biased. A model is not a theory since it is more general. Thus, models cannot be proved wrong but consist of generally more than one related theory of specific phenomena that can be tested in reality.[1]

Thomas Kuhn's research on paradigms in the early 1960's was modified in the early 1970's to apply to the field of sociology. The initial application of this approach to sociology was made by Friedrich followed by further analyses by Lakatos and Musgrave, Lodahl and Gordon, Phillips, Effrat, and Ritzer. It was not until 1973 that the paradigmatic approach was applied to the field of criminology by Chambliss followed by Reasons. Finally, it was not until 1976 that this perspective was applied to the sociology of law division of criminology by Rich.[2]

Rich

In his two recent books, The Sociology of Law: An Introduction to its Theorists and Theories and Theory and Practice of Criminal Justice, Rich examines sociological paradigms as they apply to the evolution of the sociology of law field.[3] A summary of this research is presented in the first article. An attempt has been made to examine the major theorists representative of the several subdivisions of sociology of law (i.e., sociology of civil law, sociology of criminal law, and sociological jurisprudence) for several reasons. First, to perceive the theoretical starting point and evolution of the field as a whole; second, to examine the theoretical convergence and divergence of each subdivision within the field as a whole and its specific subdivisions.

Two paradigmatic perspectives were considered with which to analyze the forty-seven theorists selected for analysis. There are three paradigms proposed by Ritzer: the social facts paradigm composed of structural-functional and conflict theories; the social definition paradigm composed of action theory, symbolic interactionism, and phenomenology; and the social behavior paradigm. The latter paradigm does not appear to be suitable for the analysis of sociology of law.

A detailed analysis of each theorist's statements about, and definitions of, law present a consistent image of the sociology of law field. Most theorists have been or are adherents to structural-functional theory of the social facts paradigm. In particular there is a consistent orientation toward functional theory among sociological jurisprudents and anthropologists of law. Only a few civil law theorists have been oriented toward either action theory or phenomenology of the social definition paradigm. Even fewer theorists have a conflict orientation and these are from the classical period of sociology of civil law theory development. Thus, most sociologists of civil law are structural-functionalists. The sociology of criminal law subdivision is the only area of legal sociology that shows a change in theoretical direction from classical to contemporary theory. Classical theorists were either social interactionists (the social definition paradigm) or structural-functionalists, while contemporary theorists tend to be moving toward the conflict perspective.

Why is the sociology of criminal law virtually the only area of legal sociology where one is currently preoccupied with conflict theory? This is probably due to the fact that criminology has taken a radical or critical turn in theory building since the 1960's. As Taylor *et al.*, states, criminology must concern itself with the abolition of inequalities of wealth and power, particularly inequalities in property and life-chances.[4] It must deal with people's relationship to structures of power, domination, and authority and the ability of individuals to confront these structures in acts of crime, deviance, and dissent. One must create a society in which human diversity (*i.e.*, personal or social) is not subject to the power to criminalize.

Conflict theory studies of sociology of criminal law are characterized by a

> conception of the complex interaction between developments in institutional and social structures and the consciousness of people living within such structures, not by a static conception of pathological and/or anomic individuals colliding with a simple and taken-for-granted set of institutional orders.

Conflict oriented sociologists of criminal law have largely failed to address the more general propositions of conflict sociologists such as Dahrendorf because the requisite links between the more general and the more specific concepts and propositions have not been made (*i.e.*, theorists have failed to establish precise links between criminological propositions and the more general sociological concepts they generally reflect).

Sociology of criminal law theorists who are conflict oriented are basically adherents to the social facts paradigm, according to Rich. This is basically due to their interest in the development of grand, abstract theory and their concern with social institutions, structures, and processes. These theorists are preoccupied with debunking myths about society and trying to change what they regard as harmful social structures and processes that exist in today's post-industrial social order.

Chambliss

Chambliss has identified two dominant paradigms within the field of criminology: functional and conflict.[5] Ritzer and Rich both feel that the structural-functional and conflict approaches to sociology are theoretical not paradigmatic. Although there may be initial disagreement as to the definition of paradigm, there is no disagreement with Chambliss as to the importance of both the functional and conflict theories in the field of criminology.[6] It is the contention of both Ritzer and Rich that both functional and conflict theory are a part of the "social facts" paradigm. Both theories tend to be holistic (i.e., look at society as composed on interrelated parts with an interest in the interrelationship between the parts). Both theories ignore each other (i.e., one emphasizes societal conflict). Both share an evolutionary view of social class and both are basically equilibrium theories.[7]

The functional "paradigm" underscores the importance of socialization into criminality, of ascribed status characteristics, and societal reaction to the causation of criminal behavior with Durkheim as exemplar while the conflict "paradigm" stresses interest group competition as the main source of societal conflict, utilizes the concept of social power, and is oriented toward the methodology of dialectic materialism with Marx as exemplar.[8] Further functionalism assumes value-consensus as the starting point for comprehension of criminality while the conflict view begins with the Marxian orientation toward historical materialism.

Durkheim states that crime is behavior which occurs when an institution or structure of society does not properly socialize its members with the customs of the culture. The criminal law is a reflection of societal value-attitudes. Criminality and criminal law have their basis in the culture of society. Durkheim felt that only an act punishable by law is a crime. The act must be offensive and opposed by the total community, and the act must be clearly understood by all. Thus, crime serves as an establisher and preserver of community value-attitudes.

Marx states that customs are only a reflection of the status of the economic institution of society. Criminality and criminal law are products of a particular type of society in a particular social order (i.e., capitalist society where there are owners of property and those who work for these owners). The criminal law evolves as a result of the struggle between the class that rules and the class that is ruled. The state serves the interests of the rulers and creates laws that preserve the status quo (i.e., prevent those who are ruled from overthrowing those who rule). Thus, criminality and the criminal law are the result of the socio-economic order of capitalist society (i.e., the rulers exploit the labor of the ruled for their self-betterment). Therefore, as capitalism evolves more and more frequent conflict will occur between the ruling class and the exploited class which will result in more behavior of the latter group being defined as criminal.

Functional theory is ahistorical, that is, it perceives society as a reality which is unconnected with a particular social order with its peculiar social needs and problems. On the other hand, conflict theory states that society is connected with a particular social order (i.e., reflection of the needs, characteristics, and problems at a particular point time in that society's history). Structural-functional theory accepts the social order as given while conflict theory stresses the need to change societal institutions. With respect to criminality, functional theory states that criminal behavior can be comprehended by asking why some individuals adopt value-attitude systems (i.e., norms) conducive to criminal behavior while most people accept the value-attitude systems of the culture of society. Secondly, the criminal law is commonly accepted as a body of rules which reflect social consensus. Conflict theorists do not accept value consensus as the dominating factor in theory building and see it as a reflection of elitist control of both the economic and educational institutions (i.e., value-attitudes) of society. Finally, the elites create a myth about the value-attitude system of society which allows oppression of the masses so that they will more easily serve the elites.

Chambliss has clearly demonstrated that there are differences between the two perspectives. Functional theory perceives the criminal law as representing societal value-attitudes that are fundamental to social order (i.e., a standard reflecting societal social consensus); the law as upholding the normative system which protects the public interest; the legal system as value-free; the law as representing the neutral state which through the law mediates disputes between competing interest groups; criminal behavior as a violation of key community customs; criminal behavior as reinforcing the sacred nature of community standards.

Conflict theory sees the criminal law as a set of rules created by the state in the interest of the elite, not as a reflection of community normative systems. The criminal law is the result of either alienation from the myths put forth by the establishment or from competition for control of societal institutions with the elite. Criminal behavior is the end product of the capitalist economic and political systems.

The functionalist premise that criminal law is a body of rules reflective of societal morality (i.e., normative systems) is false since the elite of society are truly the major power in the creation of criminal laws (i.e., those who own or control societal resources or occupy authority positions in political bureaucracies). Furthermore, societal class structure conflicts are an important force in legal change (i.e., struggles of idealists and moralists, riots, rebellions, and revolutions all force new criminal law enactments).

Both functional and conflict theories suggest different

expectations for the sociology of criminal law according to Chambliss. Functional theory states that responses to deviance move toward reliance on restitution rather than repression as society evolves from a gemeinschaft to gesellschaft social order. Conflict theory suggests the opposite (i.e., gesellschaft societies will use the criminal law increasingly as a means to keep the lower classes in their place as technology changes society). Chambliss feels that the criminal law in capitalist societies has shown no trend toward dependence on restitutive law rather than repressive law as Durkheim predicted. In fact there appears to be a greater use of the criminal law to resolve disputes involving areas of morality (i.e., crimes without victims). Furthermore, traditional societies show a reliance on restitutive rather than repressive law as Durkheim hypothesized. Thus, functionalist theory apparently does not stand the test of empirical analysis according to Chambliss.

The statement that criminal acts are more often committed by the lower classes is rejected by Chambliss who feels that criminal acts (i.e., acts which violate the criminal law) are widely distributed throughout the stratification structure of capitalist societies. What apparent class differences which exist are really differences in type of criminal act, not in the prevalence of criminality. The comparison of crime and criminal law in Nigeria and the United States provides support for the Marxist conflict perspective.

It can be concluded that Chambliss is clearly an adherent to the conflict perspective. He feels that criminality that serves the interests of the elite will be sanctioned while acts that do not coincide with elitist interests will be punished. Further, criminal activity in capitalist society is a reflection of one's position in the class structure.

One would have to concur with Chambliss that conflict theory is the emerging perspective in the analysis of sociology of criminal law. It is true that several contemporary theorists have shifted their attention from the deviant person to the social structures and institutions which "create" such deviance. However, Marxian conflict theory is not adhered to by most theorists since the majority of those oriented toward the conflict perspective are non-Marxian in their analyses.

Turk

Turk attacks what he calls the "moral functionalist" (i.e., structural-functionalist) conception of law. This concept is defined as essentially a means for settling or precluding disputes by articulating the requirements of an idea of justice and retaining those whose actions are incompatable with such requirements. A

major weakness of the functional conception of law is its
intellectual bias toward defining away the conflictual aspects of
law. Thus, the legal means of conflict management are peaceful
and an assumption is made that consensual, non-coercive methods
are the only effective means of conflict prevention or control. A
second weakness of the functional approach is its tendency to
equate legal with consensual means of conflict resolution which is
assumed to be more effective than coercive means. Law can be
perceived here as an ideological tool to be utilized in the
maintenance of social order by providing a constant means for
channeling and limiting conflicts. Law is thus viewed as a
normative system which is a weak and inconsistent conflict
resolver. Finally, the functional view assumes that theory should
be based on the concept of natural law. Therefore, the theory of
justice proposed by functionalism is based on faith, not upon
empirical inquiry.

A more value-neutral and empirical conception of law is
offered by Turk based on the conception of law as a form of social
power. Central to Turk's definition of law as the process of
formally articulated normative expectations is the concept of
conflict. The law appears to be a set of resources about which
individuals contend, and with which they are able to put forth
their ideas and interests against others in order to work out and
resolve conflictual situations (i.e., people use law as an instrument
of power).

Power is defined by Turk as the control of resources in an
attempt to maximize the chance of acceptable solution of potential
or actual conflict. Law can thus be considered as a form of power
or resource control. There are several kinds of power contained in
the legal concept: (1) police power (i.e., state sanctioned control of
coercion)—police power means having the law on your side in
conflictual situations with the implied use of coercion against
one's adversaries if there is refusal to conform to legal agreement
or a court order; (2) economic power (i.e., control of production,
allocation, and use of resources)—economic power can enhance or
erode an individual's life chances and economic changes can be
facilitated by law but the law has difficulty in causing radical
economic changes; (3) political power (i.e., control decision-making
processes)—the law provides the format for articulating,
interpreting, and implementing organizational norms and
decisions, contributes to private as well as public order, and is
the record of events and arbiter of rightness; (4) ideological power
(i.e., control of knowledge and value-attitudes)—the law has
authoritative force upon people's intellectual frames of reference
and the concept of legality promotes adherence to the political
order and gives prestige and approval to traditional conceptual
frameworks while denying legitimacy to other conceptions through
legal rejection or refusal of legal recognition; and (5) diversionary
power (i.e., control of mass media and leisure)—pre-occupation
with the law as human interest or information diverts attention

from potentially dangerous problems. This aspect of the law also reinforces the feeling that the law is all powerful, part of everyday life, and thus a constituent of social reality.

Turk states that the conception of law as power is a more useful concept than law as conflict arbitor since the former concept utilizes conflict theory and is empirical while the latter concept is more deductive in nature and based on normative assumptions. A structural-functional orientation to sociology of law creates ideological limitations since it does not question the motives of those who control and use legal power. The power orientation questions those who wield legal power and thus assumes that the law and the legal institution are not value-neutral but oriented to special interests. A particular advantage of the power approach to law is that it shows how laws become formally binding upon members of society who have neither created these laws nor been socialized into the acceptance of such laws (i.e., the power conception is more concerned with analysis of social processes rather than with social structures). Further, the power approach to law is concerned with the human actions creating the legal/non-legal distinction. Finally, this conceptual approach of the law is concerned with the concept of social order, conflict and change. Law is a source and means of conflict according to Turk. He states twelve propositions indicating the major ways that law promotes or facilitates conflict.

The use of the power conception of law as an empirical tool for the study of sociology of law is the basic contribution made by Turk. He correctly perceives the need for further historical and anthropological studies in an attempt to determine the origins and evolution of law in traditional and industrial societies. Also, he feels that there is a need to have an objective conception of law which is not structural-functionalist oriented. What is not wanted is the reifying of the legal/non-legal distinction as is made by most functionalists. He therefore proposes that the main research concern should be development of a useful comprehension of the control and mobilization of legal resources. Finally, Turk perceives law as something other than an essence, property, or function to be found in cultural and social institutions, structures, and processes but an "empirically specifiable set of objects of specific attention". Turk is essentially examining both the concept of social norm as applied to the legal institution of society and the norm of reciprocity as applied to interpersonal and larger group relationships.[9]

Conclusion

The theoretical viewpoints presented by Chambliss and Turk show a gradual drift toward the Marxian position. This drift in ideological position is even more evident from the most recent work of Quinney.[10] It is apparent from Rich's analysis that conflict theorists have turned to such theorists as Dahrendorf and Taylor et. al., rather than to Renner in order to rediscover the conflict and Marxian perspectives. Unfortunately, Renner's sociology of law has been overlooked by most contemporary theorists who have either gone back to Marx or accepted Dahrendorf's views. Renner's analysis of law and society would afford a more comprehensive view of Marxian theory than any other classical theorist.[11]

Turk and Renner are basically conflict theory oriented while Quinney and Chambliss typify what is considered by some as critical theory oriented. Conflict theory and its sociology of criminal law applications can best be explained by reference to Dahrendorf.[12] Critical theory is Marxist in orientation and consists of several basic principles. It perceives man as both active and historically limited; is concerned with political authority and the exploitation, alienation, and repression of powerless members of society; and wants to create a society which is crime free.[13] Analysis of the political economy of crime provides a basis for critical theory informed by Marxist principles.

NOTES

1.   Encyclopedia of Sociology. Guilford, Connecticut: The Dushkin Publishing Group, 1974, pp. 203 and 189.

2.   Thomas Kuhn, The Structure of Social Revolutions. Chicago: University of Chicago Press, 1962; Robert Friedrich, A Sociology of Sociology. New York: Free Press, 1970; Lakatos and Musgrave, Criticism and the Growth of Knowledge. Cambridge: Cambridge University Press, 1970; Lodahl and Gordon, "The Structure of Scientific Fields and the Functioning of University Graduate Departments", American Sociological Review 37 (1972): 57-72; Derek Phillips, "Paradigms, Falsifications and Sociology", Acta Sociologica 15 (1973): 13-31; Andrew Effrat, "Power to the Paradigms: An Editorial Introduction", Sociological Inquiry, 42 (1972): 3-33; George Ritzer, Sociology: A Multiple Paradigm Science. Boston: Allyn and Bacon, 1975; Charles E. Reasons, "Social Thought and Social Structure: Competing Paradigms in Criminology", Criminology 13 (November, 1975): 336-349; Robert Rich, "The Sociology of Law: Toward a Paradigmatic Perspective", paper presented to the American Sociological Association, August, 1976; Rich, "The Sociology of Criminal Law: Toward a Paradigmatic Perspective", paper presented to the American Society of Criminology, November, 1976; Rich, "Toward a Sociology of Law Paradigm", in Rich, Essays on the Theory and Practice of Criminal Justice. Washington, D.C.: University Press of America, 1977, pp. 1-40; Rich, The Sociology of Law: An Introduction to its Theorists and Theories. Washington, D.C.: University Press of America, 1977.

3.   Robert Rich, The Sociology of Law: An Introduction to its Theorists and Theories. Washington, D.C.: University Press of America, 1977; Theory and Practice of Criminal Justice. Washington, D.C.: University Press of America, 1977.

4.   Taylor, Walton, and Young, *The New Criminology: For a Social Theory of Deviance*. London: Routledge and Kegan Paul, 1973, p. 28.

5.   William J. Chambliss, "Functional and Conflict Theories of Crime", *Module 17*, New York: MSS Modular Publications, 1973.

6.   George Ritzer, *Sociology: A Multiple Paradigm Science*. Boston: Allyn and Bacon, 1975, pp. 86-87; Ritzer, "Sociology: A Multiple Pagadigm Science", *The American Sociologist* 10 (August, 1975): 162; Rich, *The Sociology of Law: An Introduction to its Theorists and Theories*. Washington, D.C.: University Press of America, 1971.

7.   For a recent empirical assessment of the influence of functional and conflict perspectives upon post World War II criminological writing see Diana Bloom and Charles E. Reasons, "Ideology and Crime: A Study in the Sociology of Knowledge", *International Journal of Criminology and Penology*, Forthcoming, 1978.

8.   For other discussions of the methodological differences between functional and conflict theories see T. Lehmann and T.R. Young, "From Conflict Theory to Conflict Methodology: An Emerging Paradigm for Sociology", *Sociological Inquiry* 44: 15-28. T.R. Young, "Some Theoretical Foundations for Conflict Methodology" *Sociological Inquiry* 46 (1975): 23-29. For an attempt to test conflict propositions with a functional methodology see T.G. Chiricos and G.P. Waldo, "Socioeconomic Status and Criminal Sentencing: An Emprical Assessment of a Conflict Proposition", *American Sociological Review* 40 (1975): 752-72. Possible shortcomings of this approach are noted by Charles E. Reasons, "On Methodology, Theory and Ideology", *American Sociological Review* 42 (1977): 177-181; David F. Greenberg, "Socioeconomic Status and Criminal Sentences: Is there an Association?" *American Sociological Review* 42 (1977): 174-175; Andrew Hopkins, "Is There A Class Bias In Criminal Sentencing?" *American Sociological Review* 42 (1977): 176-177. For a recent review of functional and conflict theories see Lynn McDonald, *The Sociology of Law and Order*. Montreal: Book Center, Inc., 1976. Also see Richard J. Lundman and Paul T. McFarlane, "Conflict Methodology: An Introduction and Preliminary Assessment", *The Sociological Quarterly* 17 (Autumn, 1976): 503-512; Robert M. Christie, "Comment on Conflict Methodology: A Protagonist Position" *The Sociological Quarterly* 17 (Autumn, 1976): 513-519.

9.   For another formulation of an empirically based conflict criminology see Austin Turk, "Law, Conflict and Order: From Theorizing Toward Theories", *The Canadian Review of Sociology and Anthropology* (August, 1976): 282-294.

10.   Richard Quinney, *Class, State and Crime: On the Theory and Practice of Criminal Justice*. New York: David McKay Company, 1977.

11.   Karl Renner, *The Institutions of Private Law*. London: Routledge and Kegan Paul, 1949.

12.   Ralf Dahrendorf, *Class and Class Conflict in Industrial Society*. Standford, California: Stanford University Press, 1959.

13.   Trent Schroyer, "Toward a Critical Theory for Advanced Industrial Society", in Peter Drietzel (ed.), *Recent Sociology*. New York: Macmillan, 1970.

Chapter 6

Sociological Paradigms and the
Sociology of Law:
An Overview*

Robert M. Rich

Introduction

The author has subjected the writings of selected major theorists in the sociology of law field to analysis utilizing the paradigmatic perspective proposed by Ritzer. The theorists selected for analysis were chosen as those most clearly presenting original thoughts on the topic rather than those theorists whose main purpose was criticism of a particular theorist or rehashing what had previously been stated by others in the field.

Model Building

In 1975 a theorist published his thoughts on what sociological models of society existed based on his interpretation of the writings of Thomas Kuhn.[1] George Ritzer in his book *Sociology: A Multiple Paradigm Science* attempted to bring order to a subject that has been noted for its multiplicity of theories.

---

* This is a revised version of "The Sociology of Law: Toward a Paradigmatic Perspective," paper presented to the American Sociological Association Annual Meetings, August, 1976, New York.

The Paradigms of Ritzer

According to Ritzer, there are currently only three basic paradigms in sociology. These are the social facts paradigm, social definition paradigm, and social behavior paradigm.[2] A paradigm is defined as

a fundamental image of the subject matter within a science. It serves to define what should be studied, what questions should be asked, and what rules should be followed in interpreting the answers obtained. The paradigm is the broadest unit of consensus within a science and serves to differentiate one scientific community or sub-community from another. It subsumes, defines, and interrelates the exemplars, theories, and methods/tools that exist within it.[3]

Criminolgy and its subdivision, sociology of law should fit into one or more of these paradigms. We will begin the analysis of Ritzer's work by first defining the various applicable paradigms and describing their theories.

Social Facts Paradigm

The social facts paradigm is composed of two theories, structural-functionalism and conflict theory. Structural-functionalists feel that structures and institutions can contribute to the maintenance of other social facts and can also have negative consequences for them (i.e., utilize the concepts of function and dysfunction). Followers of this theory justify the status quo and tend to have a conservative societal orientation (i.e., emphasize order in society and de-emphasize conflict and change).[4] In particular structural-functionalists are oriented toward the analysis of social structures and institutions. Concern is with relationships between structures, between institutions, and between structures and institutions. The individual is largely controlled by social facts that are external and coercive. Functionalists view society as static or in a state of moving equilibrium. They strongly emphasize the fact that society is orderly; that every societal element contributes to stability; and that society is kept together informally by norms, values, and common morality.[5]

Conflict theory for the most part is simply a series of positions directy antithetical to structural-functionalist ideas according to Ritzer. Thus, conflict theorists are oriented toward the study of social structures and institutions like functionalists but perceive society as based on conflict and consensus emphasizing the role of power in maintaining societal order.[6] In particular, conflict theorists see every structure and institution of society subject to change, conflict ridden, and riddled by dissension. Whatever order there is in society stems from the coercion of the powerless by those in authority. Differential authority is an attribute of various societal positions. Authority does not reside in individuals but in these positions. Thus the individual is concerned with societal positions and the differential distribution of power among these positions. Hence the structural origins of conflicts must be sought in the arrangement of social roles endowed with expectations of domination or subjection (i.e., authority implies both superordination and subordination). Finally, the identification of various authority roles within society is the primary focus of conflict theorists.[7]

Social Definition Paradigm

The social definition paradigm is composed of three theories— action, symbolic interactionism, and phenomenology. Action theorists (ala Weber) view the individual as possessing a dynamic, creative, voluntaristic mind. They see Weber's verstehen concept as a method for gathering data on social institutions and social structures, not as a method for understanding the mental process. The action theorist attempts to put himself in the place of the actor, not in order to comprehend the person but to understand the cultural and societal milieu in which the actor exists.[8] Social action theorists examine the problem solving process through the minds of the actor under study. They examine the actor's means to ends whether both are valued in the same manner or differently utilizing the verstehen concept (i.e., empathy and reliving the experiences of the actor). The feelings, emotions, and habits of the actor are sometimes receptive to analysis using this concept (i.e., interpretive understanding).[9]

Symbolic interactionism theory deals with covert aspects of behavior. Theorists view behavior as a process of interpretation inserted between the environmental stimulus and response of the actor. Social facts are not viewed as things controlling or coercing the individual but only as the framework within which symbolic interaction takes place. Individuals fit their actions to those of others through a process of interpretation. Through this process actors form groups, the action of the group serving as the action of all actors within it. The world of the actor is found in the process of interpretation or orientation of himself vis-a-vis the group. The mind is a process in which the individual interacts with himself and others through symbol utilization.[10]

Phenomenological theory is more philosophical than sociological. These theorists state that man constitutes and reconstitutes what is real (i.e., objective social reality is not independent of the individual). Thus to define a situation as real makes it real. Phenominologists try to comprehend the meaning that the actor's behavior has for him by both studying the process through which social facts are created by the actor rather than the social facts themselves and by examining the ongoing process of reality construction in society as social facts do not possess an objective existence. By uncovering the processes through which social order emerges from the negotiative behaviors of everyday life, phenomenologists hope to learn how people engage in the process of creating the social facts that are coercive on them. Order and meaning cannot have an objective existence since people impose order and meaning on themselves through manipulation and molding of norms. Reality is what one makes of it. Thus order and social reality have a tenuous existence according to this theory.[11]

Social Behavior Paradigm

Sociology of criminal law theorists tend not to be oriented toward the social behavior paradigm by definition if one goes according to Sutherland. He states that this division of criminology "is an attempt at systematic analysis of the conditions under which criminal law develop."[12] The crime causation and crime control divisions of criminology appear to be primarily concerned with the social behaviorist paradigm as they tend to be individual oriented. On the other hand, sociology of criminal law is theoretically both group and individual-group oriented since it deals with people on the basis of laws and legal institutions, not on the basis of individual behavior patterns. Thus sociology of criminal law theorists would tend to either fit into the social facts or social definition paradigms. Therefore we will not deal with the theories of the social behavior paradigm in this paper (see Ritzer, *Sociology: A Multiple Paradigm Science*, Allyn & Bacon, 1975).

Sociology of Law Theorists

The field of sociology of law has been divided into the three generally recognized divisions: (1) sociology of civil law, (2) sociology of criminal law, and (3) sociological jurisprudence.

The following theorists from each division have been selected for analysis: (1) civil law—Ehrlich, Weber, Marx, Engels, Renner, Timasheff, Gurvitch, Davis, Parsons, Aubert, Selznick, Sawer, Skolnick, Schur, Akers, Black, and Nonet; (2) criminal law— Beccaria, Bentham, Tarde, Durkheim, Hall, Allen, Jeffery, Turk, Hills, Chambliss, Quinney, Reasons, Akers, Schur, and Gibbs; (3) jurisprudence—Pound, Cardozo, Llewellyn, Stone, Hart, and Fuller.

The substantive ideas of each theorist are presented by

sociology of law division in chronological order within each division in the following sections of this paper and subsequently placed into appropriate paradigms.

Sociology of Civil Law

Ehrlich

Law is defined by Ehrlich as the rules, etc. which actually order or regulate a society, in particular the roles which constitute the inner ordering of associations (i.e., corporations, churches, family, etc.) that regulate society.[13] Thus the legal order of associations constitutes the basis and original form of law in society.[14] Ehrlich relates law in the sense of the body of norms that constitute the inner order of the groups, associations, and relations that compose society. His idea of the inner order of associations represents true law (i.e., "living law") as opposed to lawyer's law.[15] Ehrlich does not convey the meaning that the inner social order of all groups and institutions in society constitute the legal order but his definition of law does not provide a precise distinction between those associations that do and those that do not. This would give the appearance that any social control of a group, association, or institution constitutes law.[16]

Ehrlich states that law is not synonymous with commands of a sovereign or a state, not with the rules known to judges, not with those rules introduced by legislators, and not with legal propositions (i.e., the precise, universally binding formulation of the legal precept).[17] He shows that law when enacted is usually for the purpose of ordering activities, protecting and delimiting interests, and resolving conflicts which have already established themselves within the everyday functioning of associations and organizations.[18]

The task of sociology of law is to identify the main types of law that exist within society; show how the different levels of law are connected with each other; and show how each law level intereacts with the system of activity of relations that composes the social system.[19] The most important function of sociology of law is the separation of those portions of the law that regulate, order, and determine society from the norms for decision (i.e., those rules and criteria which are employed by courts in adjudicating legal conflicts). Norms of decision control judicial behavior, not the normal behavior of societal members. Normal behavior is controlled by the living law (i.e., the rules, norms, or codes which develop by practice or usage within the many associations to one another).[20]

Weber

An order shall be called law when it is guaranteed by the
likelihood that (physical or psychological) coercion aiming at
bringing about conduct in conformity with the order, or at
avenging its violations, will be exercised by a staff of people
especially holding themselves ready for this purpose.[21] This is
Weber's classic definition of law which is quite comprehensive and
covers such phenomena as ecclesiastical, family, corporate,
international, and primitive law.[22] Use is made of the concept of
coercion by Weber which is an essential element in any definition
of law.[23]

Weber's definition of law recognizes that the political state in
society has a monopoly on the right to apply force to secure
conformity to societal norms. He also recognizes the existence of
extra-legal state law (i.e., law exists other than where legal
coercion is guaranteed by political authority). Thus, Weber's
definition does not rely upon the existence of a political state,
retains coercion as an essential aspect, and allows for distinction
between convention (i.e., a form of custom which is externally
validated by others responding to deviation from it by approval)
and law.[24] Law is also seen as an order system by Weber (i.e., a set
or normative or ought ideas held in the minds of members of a
community or its subdivisions). He is concerned with the basic
constituents of social order (i.e., normative order) such as social
conduct.[25]

The focal point of Weber's sociology of law is his concern for
the general process of legal thought, rather than with the special
phenomena of judicial thought.[26] He analyzes in detail the fields of
substantive law. In particular Weber deals with public and private
law; right-granting law and regulations; government and
administration; criminal law and private law; tort and crime;
concept of imperium; limitation of power and separation of power;
and substantive law and procedure.[27]

A scheme of ideal type categories is formulated by Weber
which allows one to understand the variety of kinds of legal
thought as found in the world's legal systems.[28] Weber perceives
the relation of the legal and the authoritative in his analysis of the
concept of domination (i.e., the probability that certain commands
will be obeyed by a definable group of people).[29] He distinguishes
three ideal types of legitimate domination based on the degree of
rationality of legal thought which are: (1) charismatic (i.e., the
heroic or extraordinary force in an individual which attracts and
holds obedience on the part of others); (2) traditional (i.e.,
acceptance of authority due to old custom or a social tradition);
and (3) rational (i.e., a conscious, rational system which bestows
legality upon the commands of certain people provided that both

the commands and commanders comply with the conditions designated by the system).[30]

Marx and Engels

According to Lloyd, Marx defines law as a coercive system devised to maintain the privileges of the propertied class. Law arises from the economy and is an institutionalized ideology which allows the elite to control the masses.[31] Cain states that Marx and Engels do not define law. They assume that law is commonly understood by all dealing with the concept. Further mention of the concept is made in connection with legislation formation and law enforcement.[32] In order to understand the legal concept, one must examine the bases of power in society, the societal social stratification structure, and examine the structure of the state.[33]

Cain perceives Marxian sociology of law as consisting of three major themes: (1) law ideology, (2) law as social function, and (3) law as an instrument of social change.

Legal ideology influences behavior which otherwise would have been directly determined by the economy of the society. The law can set the rules on which struggles must be fought and influence the outcome of such struggle. Legal institutions in the control of the economically powerful facilitate and expedite real economic change.[34] Engels states that the particular legal form within which and in terms of which conceptual development takes place is irrelevant. State, public, and private law are determined by economic relations. It does not matter whether these relations are founded on Roman, feudal, or bourgeois base.[35]

The second theme in their sociology of law is three functions of law: (1) mystifying function (i.e., the state develops to quell class antagonisms and is seemingly autonomous thus obscuring the real power relationships within society); (2) legitimating function (i.e., real power is legitimated by stating that legal forms of power are available to all but in reality belong to only a few). Both Marx and Engels are aware that by emphasizing the autonomy of the state and law, it was possible to create the mythology of a total society in whose interests these institutions operated, coupled with the belief that the state and law by reason of their apparent autonomy are value neutral; (3) law represents the average interests of the ruling class—the interests of the class as a whole rather than of particular individuals or groups (i.e., law irons out conflicts in the best interest of all and maintains the unity and integrity of the class).[36]

The third theme sees law as an instrument of social change. Thus, Marx and Engels analyze the development of private property, the relationship between social and legal change, the usefulness of law in the class struggle, and law as a means of social reform.[37]

Renner

Law is defined as a series of imperatives (i.e., commands addressed by one individual to another) according to Renner. He feels that law can never fully control social organization or groups although it may enhance their efficiency.[38] The social function of law is to keep society organized. Thus law consists of the basic circumstances of life. Law helps keep society functioning by aiding in the establishment of a hierarchy of authority and power and helping distribute goods among members of society.[39]

Renner is not really concerned with the concept of law in general but with societal legal institutions. He defines a legal institution as a governing legal relationship regulating a basic circumstance of life (i.e., marriage, family, property, heirship, insolvency, contract, tenancy, hiring and wage relationship, corporate structure, etc.).[40] It can be seen that Renner deals with the impact of economic forces and social changes upon the functioning of legal institutions from a Marxian perspective.[41] The social function of law in capitalist society is its use as a tool in the maintenance of the socioeconmic processes of production and reproduction of societal institutions according to Renner. Further the economic function of law is subservience to the economic processes. Thus the law is only concerned when an individual withholds possession or disturbs the owner's enjoyment of his property. The law is also concerned with the acquisition and loss of ownership rights.[42]

The sociology of law of Renner does not explore the social forces which bring about the creation and alteration of legal norms and institutions. Renner does not investigate the problem of legal principle origins since he presupposes the stability and relative immutability of legal institutions (i.e., property, contract, and succession).[43] His sociology of law also states that legal institutions may thoroughly change their social function as a consequence of a transformation in their environment.[44] Thus Renner demonstrates that adaptability is inherent in certain kinds of legal rules that regulate social institutions within society (i.e., the agricultural paternalism of Medieval England that became the wage slavery of Industrial England). This study of the relation between legal rule and social institution illustrates the tendency of society to associate a particular set of legal norms with a particular social institution, even though the legal norms are formally stated in a manner which does not make this connection explicit (i.e., use of "legal fiction" concept).[45]

The adaptability of legal rules and institutions has been

emphasized by Renner. Thus particular laws, legal concepts, and techniques have a quality of being adaptable to changing social purposes in society. Renner deals in particular with the larger social transitions from the last stages of feudalism to the early stages of modern capitalism in western society.[46] He illustrates the way the "property norm" was adapted to serve the complex purposes of European capitalist society in the eighteenth and nineteenth centuries. Renner's concern with the property norm was adapted from the Marxian view of legal and economic histories of the evolution of capitalism.[47]

Timasheff

Timasheff defines law as a specific social force or of socially imposed rules acting on human behavior (i.e., law as a form of social coordination).[48] He considers law as existing in any societal group or association which has a body of norms backed by the authority of the group or association.[49] Law helps maintain societal social equilibrium (i.e., criminal law inhibits the urge to cause dysequilibrium; civil law secures and restores social equilibrium; and constitutional law maintains the balance of power between haves and have-nots).[50] Timasheff advocates a structural-functional analysis of the legal system.[51]

The object of sociology of law is the determination and coordination of societal behavior patterns by legal norms (i.e., imposing norms of conduct or patterns of social behavior on the individual will). The sociology of law, according to Timasheff, should study the system of social actions and reactions composing "social coordination", the differences between legal and non-legal power as well as conditions establishing and destroying legal power, and the relation of law to other societal institutions and social processes.[52]

Gurvitch

Law is a relationship between claims and duties made to correspond with each other by a social guarantee of normative facts according to Gurvitch.[53] Timasheff states that Gurvitch defines law as an attempt to realize in a given social environment the idea of justice through multilateral attributive-imperative regulation deriving its validity from normative facts that give it social guaranty and may (but not must) be conductive to precise and external constraint.[54] Pound feels that Gurvitch defines law as general social control (i.e., the inner order of groups and associations).[55]

Gurvitch feels that every societal group or organization possesses a particular form of law which is controlled or rests upon a greater law found within society.[56] This view of law is akin to that of Ehrlich. Law unfolds itself through a series of graduated levels of social reality. Gurvitch states that law can be placed in two vertical classification systems which are mutually exclusive. There is organized and unorganized law in one scheme and fixed, flexible, and intuitive law in the other scheme.[57] Every type of law consists of six levels (i.e., fixed organized, flexible organized, organized intuitive, fixed spontaneous, flexible spontaneous, and intuitive spontaneous).[58]

Sociology of law thus analyzes the full social reality of all levels of society according to Gurvitch. The field is divided into three parts: (1) the systematic sociology of law (i.e., law as a function of the form of sociality and of levels of social reality); (2) the differential sociology of law (i.e., law as a function of real collective units such as groups and institutions); and (3) genetic sociology of law (i.e., law as a change agent in society).[59] Finally Gurvitch sees law as corresponding to types of groups (i.e., union, state, and canon law) which correspond to systems of law which in turn correspond to types of inclusive societies (i.e., feudal law, primitive law, Western law, etc.). Thus sociology of law is a study of the multiplicity of groups composing society.[60]

Davis

Davis defines law as the formal means of social control that involves the use of rules that are interpreted and are enforceable by the courts of a political community.[61] Davis' definition of law was influenced by legalism and its emphasis on abstract rules according to Pospisil.[62] Davis states that his legal definition is similar to those of MacIver and Pound.[63] He restricts his definition of law to the political community. Davis' definition is neither intended to support the idea that the expressed will of the state is absolutely sovereign nor is it intended to preclude systems of social control that do not have courts or other requisites of law.[64]

Law should be viewed ideally as a type of formal social control according to Davis since it is characterized by explicit rules of conduct, planned use of sanctions to support the rules, and designated officials to interpret, enforce, and make the rules.[65] Davis perceives law as a set of social institutions, as an index of values, and as an index of social solidarity. As an institutional part of culture, law is interrelated with other societal institutions. Law cannot exist independently of other societal institutions since all legal acts concern and are instrumental in making choices and in organizing value systems of the family, economy, military, school, and mass media. Political as well as voluntary associations place pressures upon the legal institution.[66]

Parsons

Parsons defines law as a set of rules backed by certain types of sanctions, legitimized in certain ways and applied in certain ways.[67] Law should be treated as a generalized mechanism of social control that operates diffusely in all sectors of society. Law is also partly a function of societal social equilibrium since acute societal value conflict or serious enforcement problems cause law to be ineffectual.[68]

Law concerns patterns, norms, and rules that are applied to the acts and to the roles of people and to the collectivities of which they are members.[69] In particular law is an instrumental aspect of the social structure; deals with normative patterns to which various kinds of sanctions are applied; is non-specific with respect to functional content; and regulates social relationships.[70]

The primary function of a legal system is integrative as it serves to mitigate potential elements of conflict and maintains social intercourse.[71] A second function of law is legitimation (i.e., enactment of statutes by duly authorized bodies using proper procedures). A third function of law is interpretation. The interpretative function has two aspects: rule-focused (i.e., integrity of the rule system) and client-focused (i.e., relation of rules to individuals, groups, and collectivities upon whom they impinge).[72]

Aubert

Law is defined as a regularity of behavior, primarily an invariant in judicial decision-making.[73] Law functions to create conformity with norms and to settle disputes among societal members according to Aubert. He states that a sociological analysis of law cannot be clearly separated from logical or philosophical analysis of law (i.e., from jurisprudence).[74]

Aubert appears to hold views similar to those of the Upsala school of sociology of law as he deals with law as normative interpretation of reality, legal rules as ideas of conduct, especially respect and obligation.[75] The primary task of sociology of law is relating the structure of legal thinking to the recurrent types of social interactions on which it is brought to bear. Aubert declares that a sociological analysis of law cannot be clearly separated from jurisprudence.[76]

Skolnick

Skolnick utilizes Selznick's views on the sociology of law to a considerable extent. Thus he would accept Selznick's definition as basically his own (i.e., law as a general element in the structure of many different groups and associations in society as well as the political structure of the state).[77] Skolnick utilizes Selznick's view that legality is a normative system found in all groups and associations within society.

The most general contribution that sociology of law can make to social theory is comprehension of the relationship between law and societal social organization.[78] Skolnick is a social factist who is attempting to make the transition from structural-functional theory to conflict theory. This is demonstrated by his concern for societal structural and institutional inconsistencies (i.e., myths of equalitarianism, Gemeinschaft-like relations myth, and power myth). However, Skolnick approaches these legal myths from a functional-dysfunctional perspective rather than conflict perspective.

Sawer

Sawer does not directly define law but comes closest to a definition by following the definition proposed by Pound[79] (i.e., the systematic and orderly application of force by the appointment of agents of politically organized society).[80]

The content of a legal system reflects the needs or demands of society according to Sawer.[81] The relation between law and society has been shown by the interests approach (i.e., Kohler's theory of jural postulates, Ihering's theory of social interests, and Pound's use of both theories in his interests theory).[82] Sawer feels that the interests approach is the clearest way of stating the relationship between the law and other societal institutions. An interest is defined as a claim advanced by certain individuals, groups, or collectivities and considered and dealt with by defined legislative bodies and courts.[83]

Law is conceived as a method of giving effect to interests according to Sawer.[84] The task of the law is to classify interests on the basis of the societal value system in order to determine which interests are to be given effect and which are to be rejected. Sociology of law to Sawer is an analysis of societal institutions and structures utilizing a theory of interests. He utilizes the concepts of norm and value; implies that there exists in society a social balance between competing interests; and implies that the legal institution maintains the balance between all interests.

Selznick

Law is defined by Selznick as a general element in the structure of many different groups and associations in society, not limited to the political structure of the state.[85] The law is an important agency of social control but is oriented more toward the persuasive than toward the coercive end of the social control continuum. Thus law can be seen as the normative system of societal groups, associations, and institutions.[86] In other words law can be viewed as the purposive enterprise of subjecting individual conduct to the governance of rules (i.e., corporate, church, fraternal, collegial).[87]

Authority, consensus, and rationality are important elements in the definition of law according to Selznick. Law attempts to maintain societal stability by preventing and reducing conflict through the rule of law (i.e., legality).[88] Law identifies claims and obligations that merit official recognition or enforcement. Thus the law acts as an authority apparatus whose purpose is norm enforcement.[89] The legal institution functions as the determiner of the rights and duties of all members of society. It also is affected by the social conditions surrounding it (i.e., other societal institutional pressures). There is an implicit recognition that law operates on several levels, not all law being of uniform quality (i.e., judge-made and legislative law).[90]

Selznick states that the main task of sociology of law is the study of legality. Legality is based on a combination of sovereign will and objective reason (i.e., an authoritative ideal).[91] Authoritative decision-making and rule finding is the chief element in law, whether the authority resides in the political state or in the normative structures of formal organizations such as university, church, military, and commercial-industrial bureaucracies.[92]

Schur

Schur thinks it would be a mistake to single out any one definition of law and label it "the definition,"[93] although he points out that most theorists have formulated or accepted a particular definition of law or legal.[94]

The legal institution of society consists of formal mechanisms of social control which compliment the informal control mechanisms of other societal institutions. The formal control mechanisms of the legal institution come into play when the informal control mechanisms prove inadequate.[95] Law to Schur is predominantly an outcome of societal social processes but not totally shaped by the environmental context in which it occurs.[96] Law constitutes both an important means of fostering individual freedoms, insuring human rights, and furthering broad social goals of equity and general well being as well as a powerful tool for the control of the individual (i.e., a means by which some segments of a society can maintain social and economic superiority over others). Thus one finds that both the freedom-enhancing and freedom-reducing aspects of the law are constantly combining in society to maintain a balance between the rights and restrictions of various societal groups over time.[97]

Akers

Akers defines law as social control exercised by the political community and ultimately backed by coercive sanctions.[98] He reviews some of the major formulations of law (i.e., as social control through legitimized coercion; as a system of rules made and enforced by the sovereign political community; as the assumed basis for or predictions of authoritative decisions; and as authoritative decision and procedure).[99]

All definitions of law agree that law is a form of social control; that laws are social norms; and that a system of norms enacted and enforced by the coercive power of the modern political state is law according to Akers.[100] There is some disagreement among theorists about how law differs in societies with developed political institutions with specialized law-making and law-enforcing agencies from societies that are stateless and with generalized or no clear law-making and law-enforcing agencies. All theorists agree that the key elements in law are identified as the use or threat of coercion in a regularized way by authorized persons, whether or not these are agents of the state.[101]

Those theorists who reject coercion as a criterion of law place emphasis on authoritative decisions between primary and secondary norms according to Akers, who defines norms as legitimized rules or principles of conduct which guide people's behavior and for which there is a possibility that sanctions will be applied for compliance or noncompliance.[102] Primary norms prescribe how people should or should not behave while secondary norms specify the way persons, who are authorized to react to instances of violation or conformity to primary norms, should behave.

Black

Black defines law simply as governmental social control although he recognizes several non-normative definitions of the concept. He states his definition is easily employed in cross-cultural analysis, encompassing any act by political bodies that concerns the definition of social order or its defense. At the same time it excludes such forms of social control as popular morality and bureaucratic rules in private organizations.[103]

From a sociological viewpoint, law consists in observable acts, not in rules as the concept of rule or norm is employed in both the literature of jurisprudence and in everyday legal language. Further, law is not what lawyers regard as binding or obligatory precepts but rather the observable dispositions of judges, policemen, prosecutors, or administrative officials.[104]

The quest for one correct concept of law is unscientific. Non-empirical concepts such as justice, rule of law, and due process have no place in the sociology of law but are appropriate to sociological jurisprudence. Value judgments that are made in the name of sociology of law, say in the area of legal effectiveness, are unscientific.[105]

The proper concern of legal sociology should be the development of a general theory of law. To say that a theory of law is general means that it seeks to order law wherever it is found. It seeks to discover the principles and mechanisms that predict empirical patterns of law, whether these patterns occur yesterday or today, regardless of the substantive area of law involved and regardless of the society.[106]

A purely sociological approach to law should involve not an assessment of legal policy but a scientific analysis of legal life as a system of behavior. The ultimate contribution of this enterprise would be a general theory of law, a theory that would predict and explain every instance of legal behavior.[107]

A general theory of law is addressed to the relation between law and other aspects of social life, including other forms of social control, social stratification, the division of labor, and social integration, group size, and the structure of social networks.[108]

Nonet

Sociology should develop a normative theory of law according to Nonet. Sociology of law must be jurisprudentially informed. Further, sociology of law must have redeeming value. Thus, the field cannot cut itself off from its jurisprudential past.[109] Sociology of law evolved from the branch of sociological jurisprudence known as legal realism. Thus, familiarity with sociological jurisprudence would be a valuable asset to the sociologist of law.[110]

One must take seriously the role of values, rules, and other normative elements in legal phenomena.[111] The sociology of law must take legal ideas seriously. The sociologist of law cannot study "pure" legal "behavior" without learning about the complicated and obscure arguments that occupy lawyers.[112] Black's program for a "pure" sociology of law offers two prescriptions for intellectual ignorance according to Nonet. It should ignore the problems, values, and doctrines of jurisprudence and ignore the rules, principles, policies that constitute law.[113]

The sociology of law must integrate jurisprudential and policy analysis research according to Nonet. Black's distinction between applied and jurisprudential sociology rejects this tenet and as such directs the sociologist to ignore the purpose of the policies he evaluates.[114] Jurisprudence is based on and thrives on what it learns from policy for the latter is the realm of action where abstract ideals are tested, redefined, and elaborated. Jurisprudence can remain informed only by examining that experience. Moral dilemmas are the stuff of jurisprudence.[115]

In attempting to rule *normative meanings* out of existence, Black's "pure" sociology of law either deprives itself of that knowledge or requires denying the existence of that knowledge even as we use the words that evoke it.[116] Jurisprudence is no alternative to "pure" sociology of law. In fact jurisprudence and "pure" sociology of law are interdependent. There is no better match for a sociology that denies the normative aspects of legal phenomena than a legal philosophy blind to factual issues in the analysis of normative ideas.[117]

Nonet states there is a need for a jurisprudential sociology, a social science of law that speaks to the problems and is informed by the ideas of jurisprudence. Such a sociology recognizes the continuities of analytical, descriptive, and evaluative theory.[118]

Sociology of Criminal Law

Beccaria

Cesare Beccaria indirectly defines criminal law through his reliance on the social contract theory of Rousseau which was partially an expansion of the writing of Hobbes and Locke. According to this theory, laws result from the combination of men who agree for mutual protection to surrender individual freedom of action. Thus, the government must rest on the consent of the governed.[119] Therefore legislative law is more important than judge-made law since only those creating statutes can alter them since the legislative body represents the will of the governed.[120]

The essence of social contract to Beccaria is that it is constituted by the meeting of persons who relate to each other in value-attitudes, life-styles, and behavior patterns. Societal laws apply to everyone on an equal basis since all accept the social contrast doctrine.[121]

Bentham

The co-founder of the sociology of criminal law with Beccaria does not directly define law. The criminal law is a method of making the interests of the individual coincide with those of the community. Thus it is to the community's interest that one abstain from theft, but only to one's interest where there is an effective criminal law.[122] Bentham would probably concur with the statement that behavior is not criminal unless it is prohibited by the criminal law which in turn is considered as a body of specific rules regarding human conduct made known by the government on behalf of the community.[123]

Bentham deals with the concept of social control and feels that only explicit social controls keep the average person from becoming a criminal. He states that individuals are to be punished by the criminal law in order to maintain order and prevent feuding. But punishment should be certain to be effective.[124]

Tarde

Tarde does not directly define criminal law but sees crime as related to value-attitudes of one's reference group (i.e., crime results from the influences of one's social environment). One's orientation to the criminal law is dependent upon the influence of primary and secondary group standards upon the individual.[125] Crime is explained as a socially acquired conduct (i.e., learned through imitation or the product of the socialization process).[126]

Crime to Tarde is a social-psychological product and represents the relation of the criminal's social self to his cultural and subcultural environments (i.e., concept of moral responsibility). Tarde noted the causal relationship between the individual and his degrees of freedom in a given environment.[127] His laws of imitation constitute his basic theory (i.e., behavior patterns or laws of fashion, custom, and substitution). As Schafer states Tarde never clearly explains why the first offender committed his crime which sets the imitative patterns in operation or why only a small percentage of the general population imitate criminal types.[128]

Durkheim

Durkheim explains law as the expression of a basic social fact. He makes a distinction between repressive law (criminal law) (i.e., those law that repress anti-social conduct) and restitutive law (civil law) (i.e., laws that prescribe remedies for wrongs).[129] Durkheim states that law is a measure of the type of solidarity or unity in a society (i.e., homogeneous society = mechanical solidarity = repressive law; heterogeneous society = organic solidarity = restitutive law).[130] Thus, he reaches the conclusion that crime is a necessary component of society, and its presence allows the criminal law to evolve.[131]

According to Durkheim, in a homogeneous undifferentiated society, punishment is meant to protect and preserve social solidarity. Punishment is a mechanical reaction to preserve solidarity and there is no thought of correction of the offender. The wrongdoer is punished as an example to the community.[132] In an advanced and differentiated urban society, punishment is centered upon the individual and deals with restitution and reparations. Crimes are thought of as acts which offend others and not the total community. Punishment is evaluated in terms of what is good for the individual and is applied to the offender in order to reform him.[133]

The concept of anomie is utilized by Durkheim to explain crime in gesellschaft type societies. Heterogeneity and increased division of labor weaken traditional societal norms and the resultant social changes loosen traditional social controls upon people, ultimately creating an environment producing crime and deviant behavior on a large scale.[134]

Hall

Hall has attempted to determine the relationship between legal changes and value changes in society through an analysis of the law of theft. He expresses four theories concerning sociology of criminal law. First, the functioning of courts is related to accompanying cultural needs. This applies to both procedural and substantive law. Second, legal change follows a definite order. First a lag occurs between the substantive law and the social needs of society followed by an attempt by judges, officials, and the laymen to make adaptations (i.e., use of legal fictions). The last step in legal change is the enactment of new legislation to eliminate the lag. Third, technicality and legal fiction function both to link the old law to the new and as indexes to solutions of societal legal problems between social orders. Fourth, sociology of criminal law is represented by the "law process" of the norm-oriented and directed conduct of large sectors of a societal population.[135]

Allen

Allen feels that the concentration of interests on the nature and needs of the criminal law has resulted in an absence of concern in the nature of crime. The behavioral scientist has all but forgotten how to deal with the types of behavior that should be declared criminal.[136] Allen states there has been a systematic lack of attention to the substantive criminal law which is due to the positivist bias against authoritative rules in any form and even challenges the reality of such rules. Instead of considering the law as a set of rules or authoritative norms, positivists have considered the law as a process according to Allen.[137] Interest has shifted from dealing with substantive law problems and definition of crime to dealing with procedural law and enforcement problems. Thus the systematic disconcern in the law of crimes has not stopped the enthusiastic enactment of penal laws which has created the problem of over-criminalization in our society. Allen refers to both offenses that affect or are believed to affect the security of the state as well as those crimes created by legislatures in large numbers to effect certain objectives of economic regulation or public welfare (i.e., regulatory offenses).[138]

Jeffery

The law is a measure of social rather than individual responsibility and assumes that individuals are responsible for their actions. The law is utilized to evaluate behavior and establish norms of conduct. The offender is one who has been judged by the social group to have violated the code of conduct and is punished accordingly.[139] Jeffery rejects the argument that criminology be independent of the criminal law. He has resurrected the views of the classical school that the sociology of criminal law should be an essential and necessary part of criminology.[140]

There is a basic dilemma between the classical (i.e., legal reform) and positive (i.e., scientific criminal study) schools of criminology. The classical school defines crime in legal terms and examines it as a legal entity while the positive school examines crime as a psychological entity. What Jeffery is alluding to is that most positivistic theorists are adherents of the social behavior paradigm while most classical theorists are social factists. The classical school defines crime within the strict limits of criminal law while the positive school attached the legal definition of crime and replaces it with sociological definitions of crime.[141]

The rejection of the legal definition of crime has left many theorists with no agreement as to the definition of crime. The positivists confuse crime and criminal behavior since they reject the legal definition of crime and try to explain criminal behavior without explaining what is crime. It is Jeffery's contention that positivists are not interested in the sociology of criminal law since they are crime control oriented and concerned with social problems solution.[142]

The positivists believe that crime should be defined as anti-social behavior. In particular they have substituted scientific categories of behavior for legal categories (i.e., accept deviant behavior as criminal, not one who violates a criminal statute).[143] Positivistic theorists seek a universal category of behavior that can be explained in terms of behavioral theory, not in terms of legal definitions of crime.[144]

The positivistic position consists of several basic postulates. It rejects the legal concept of crime; rejects criminal law study; rejects the concept of punishment.[145] Positivists by ignoring the criminal law have abandoned the traditional legal safeguards of society (i.e., law protects society against the individual and the latter against arbitrary state actions). Thus legal process by which crimes are created is ignored by positivistic theorists. Finally positivism's entry into criminal law has created an untenable position wherein the legal rights of juveniles, alcoholics, addicts, and the mentally ill have been ignored in the name of treatment.[146]

Turk

Turk accepts the conflict perspective of the law as the most relevant for sociology of criminal law. He perceives legality as an attribute of whatever words or deeds are defined as legal by those able to use to their advantage the machinery for making and enforcing rules. Political power then determines legality.[147] Law is directly related to social conflict in society according to Turk. A law is a set of words about behavior, either describing what people actually do or specifying what they ought to do.[148] Legality depends upon the ability of some social groupings jointly to seize upon the mechanisms for creating, maintaining, changing, and destroying laws. For those powerful enough to have some impact on the legal process, law will be viewed as compromise. For those who have no power in the struggle to control legal mechanisms, law will assume the form of edicts.[149]

The focus in sociology of criminal law should be upon patterns of conflict (i.e., overt and covert). This focus is between different kinds of social groups who manifest different value-attitude systems. Society is composed of authorities (i.e., those holding dominant, decision-making positions) and subjects (i.e., those holding subordinate positions). Legal norms vary in regard to the proportion of a population affected according to Turk. Thus subjects can be distinguished from authorities by their inability to influence the processes of norm creation or enforcement.[150]

There is an attempt by Turk to construct a theory about authority-subject conflict over legal norms and about the conditions under which subjects are likely to be criminalized in the course of conflict. He states that the study of criminality is the analysis of relations between the statuses and roles of legal authorities (i.e., creators interpreters, and enforcers of right-wrong standards of society) and those of subjects (i.e., acceptors or resisters but not makers of such standards).[151]

The legality of norms according to Turk depends upon how they are defined by authorities. A norm is a law if the authorities say that it is (i.e., they are prepared to use force to make people comply). The ultimate legal norm is the rule that the final decision of the authorities is binding. If the expectations of the authorities regarding their legal treatment of subjects is unclear, there is room for normative conflict to arise.[152]

In an authority relationship the control ordering of the parties should be clear as both authorities and subjects should continue to perform their roles in a way that the relationship does not become either too coercive or too consensual. Obvious and repeated failure by the authorities to sanction violators of any legal norms constitutes inadequate role performance and contributes to weakening the authority structure over time.[153] The increasing estrangement of authorities and subjects can be reversed only if the authorities exercise restraint in dealing with the norm-violators. The law is an instrument of order no matter how receptive the authorities are to making legal changes. Should the authorities fail to achieve conditioning of norm-violators, there will be an eventual dissolution of the social order, a period of explicit power struggles, and establishment of a new social structure in which new groupings have emerged and take their places in the new power struggle.[154]

Hills

Law is not defined by Hills who accepts the conclusions of interest-group theorists that criminal laws change as the interest-power structure of society changes. Thus, criminal law definitions change and adapt themselves to the changes in the societal social order.[155]

Hills states there are two competing major theoretical perspectives to the sociology of criminal law: the value-consensus and interest-group theories. The value-consensus position states that criminal laws reflect those societal values which transcend the immediate, narrow interests of various individuals and groups, expressing the social consciousness of the whole society. The legal process thus regulates, harmonizes, and reconciles all conflicting claims to enhance the welfare of the social order.[156]

The interest-group position states that criminal laws will change with modification in the interest-power structure of society. As societal social conditions change, the criminal law will adapt to these changes in the distribution of power of various interest groups. Interest-group theorists emphasize the ability of particular groups to shape the societal legal system to serve their needs and safeguard their interests.[157]

Akers

The central theoretical issue in the study of law and society is the nature of interrelationships between law and other institutions and normative systems in society.[158] In examining law in the political state, Akers reviews what he calls the two major models or theoretical approaches to understanding modern politically organized society (i.e., consensus or conflict). The first of these theories states that the law evolves from normative consensus in society and serves the broad interests and functions of society as a whole. The second theory views law as formed out of the conflict of values and actions of various groups in society and reflects the narrow interests of societal groups which wield economic, social, and political power.[159]

After a review of the literature that includes the writings of several theorists, Akers states that most evidence is in support of the conflict model. He notes that the law supports the norms of groups who have been politically successful in society. Accepted as fact is that the law is most often the outcome of group conflict. More important to Akers is whether the nature of group conflict can best be described as due to either the power elite or pluralistic concepts.[160]

Akers states that neither pluralistic nor power elite concepts deny the importance of power, domination, and conflict in society. He also feels that either model (i.e., pluralistic or power elite) more closely fits reality than a consensus model. But admitting the primary importance of power and conflict should not deny a place for the consensus model of law in society. Akers states there can be little doubt that the core of the criminal law is designed to protect the life and property of everyone although differentially enforced against the less powerful in society. He concludes that powerful groups in society make the law reflect their interests to a great extent but the law also reflects the views of all of society at any given time.[161]

Chambliss

Law defined by Chambliss and Seidman as not merely a body of rules but as a dynamic process involving every aspect of state action, for this action involves either creation of a norm, adjudication about its content, adjudication that has been violated, or a sanctioning process. This set of processes comprises the law.[162]

In his writings, Chambliss refers to the consensus model or theoretical approach to law and society as the value-expression hypothesis and to the conflict model as the interest-group hypothesis.[163] In 1971, he renamed the two models of law and society value-consensus and value-antagonism.[164] In 1973 Chambliss referred to the models as positivist (i.e., functionalist) and conflict.[165] In 1975 he updated his 1969 theoretical viewpoint and re-utilizes the terms consensus and conflict models in reference to the legal system of society.[166] Here Chambliss refers specifically to both structural-functional and conflict perspectives.[167]

Sociology of criminal law is presently dipolar in theoretical orientation according to Chambliss. The functionalist view states that acts are defined as criminal because they offend the moral beliefs of society. Those who violate the criminal law are punished according to prevailing mores of society. Individuals are labeled criminal because their behavior exceeds tolerance limits set by the community. The lower classes are more likely to be arrested because they commit more crimes. Criminal law becomes more restitutive rather than repressive (i.e., penal) as society becomes gesellschaft. The conflict view states that acts are defined as criminal because it is to the interest of the ruling class. Ruling class members are able to violate the laws while members of the subject classes will be punished. Individuals are labeled criminal because it is in the interest of the ruling class, regardless of community tolerance. The lower classes are labeled criminal more often because the bourgeoisie's control of the state protects them from stigmatization. As capitalist society becomes more gesellschaft and the gap between the bourgeoisie and proletariat widens, penal law will expand in an effort to coerce the proletariat into submission.[168]

With respect to the sociology of criminal law, the consensus and conflict models of society present quite different fundamental assumptions according to Chambliss. The consensus model emphasizes the shared interests of everyone in society and the consensus over fundamental values which this shared interest creates. The conflict model emphasizes the role of conflicts between social classes and interest groups as the moving force behind the creation and implementation of criminal laws.[169]

Chambliss lists the theories derived from the consensus perspective. There are theories that see the law as a reflection of "perceived social needs" which all reasonable men agree must be met if society is to continue; theories that see the criminal law as an expression of what is in the "public interest"; theories that perceive the law as a reflection of the "moral indignation" of a particularly influential segment of society; and theories that see the law as an expression of the most fundamental values that are inherent in society.[170] Chambliss also lists the theories derived from the conflict perspective. There are theories that emphasize the role of "moral entrepreneurs" (i.e., groups that organize to achieve legal changes which they think are essential for societal well-being); theories that emphasize the importance of bureaucratic interests in the rationalization of problems that are inherent in society; theories that emphasize the conflicts that inhere between interest groups competing for the favors of state power; and theories that emphasize the inherent conflicts between those who rule and those who are ruled and who perceive the criminal law as incorporating rules for enforcing the interests and ideologies of the ruling classes.[171]

The structural-functional perspective has dominated sociology of criminal law for many years according to Chambliss. The basic assumption of this perspective is that the criminal law is a set of rules stipulated by legislatures and courts which reflect societal beliefs. This perspective also sees the criminal law as fulfilling certain basic societal needs. The problem with this perspective is its failure to specify whose interests, views, and needs are being satisfied by the societal legal system. The emergent perspective in sociology of criminal law is the one emphasizing social conflict as the moving force behind the criminal law in action. The social relations which are part of the class, labor, and productive systems of capitalist societies are viewed as more important in determining the content and functioning of the criminal law process than are societal values, norms, and beliefs.[172]

Quinney

The most significant developments in criminology today are awareness of the criminal law and inquiries into its formulation, enforcement, and administration. Criminal law is established to govern the lives and affairs of members of politically organized society. Behind all law formulation are special interests groups. The criminal laws are formulated to promote the interests of certain societal groups. Thus, the criminal justice system caters to special interests and is influenced by socio-economic considerations.[173] Quinney believes that law is both a social product (i.e., developing its own internal logic and preceeding along its own lines) and a social force (i.e., operating simultaneously as a reflection of society and an influence on society).[174]

Quinney's sociological theory of interests provides a theoretical perspective for comprehending the sociology of criminal law. The theory of interests postulates that law is created by interests; assumes a conflict-power model of society; and proposes a conceptual scheme for analyzing the law-interests relationship. Quinney's conceptual scheme consists of several propositions. The law consists of specialized rules that are created and interpreted in politically organized society. Such a society is based on an interests structure. This structure is characterized by unequal distribution of power and by conflict. The law is formulated and administered within the interest structure of society.[175]

Sociology of criminal law accepts and supports the legal order as it exists and studies the legal system in terms of the existing social order. Thus there is no critique of the capitalist legal order in the sociology of criminal law. The source of crime is not located in the person who violates the law but in the authority structure that defines behavior as criminal. The state is not the ultimate crime control agency of society but a source of crime according to Quinney.[176]

A critical theory of criminal law based on a Marxist understanding of and orientation toward the legal order is presented by Quinney. Law in capitalist society gives political recognition to powerful social and economic interests. The legal system provides the mechanism for the forceful and violent control of the majority in society as the state reflects and serves the needs of the ruling class.[177]

Sociology of criminal law theorists neglect the state as a focal point of inquiry, thus ignoring the fact that the civil society is secured politically by the state which serves an economic elite. The American state is based on an advanced capitalist economy which is organized to serve ruling class interests. Thus the criminal law is an instrument of the ruling class used to maintain and perpetuate the existing socio-economic order. Crime control is accomplished by a government elite in order to establish domestic order for the ruling class, thus keeping the subordinate classes oppressed through utilization of coercion and violence supplied by the criminal justice system. Only the replacement of capitalist society with socialist society can resolve the crime problem according to Quinney.[178]

Reasons

It is important to analyze the criminal law as there is a definite need for data dealing with the emergence of criminal statutes within a socio-historical context.[179] Theorists have not been concerned with laws but with crime control. There is nothing inherent in criminal behavior since criminality is a status conferred upon specific behavior by the state's political apparatus.[180] Crime may be viewed as phenomena created by individuals in concert who wish their definitions of rightness to triumph and become the laws of society according to Reasons.[181]

Reasons creates what he calls three major paradigms for the field of criminology. The kinds of people paradigm asserts that the causes of criminality are in the characteristics of the criminal (i.e., positivistic view).[182] The kinds of environments paradigm asserts that crime is a product of the social system (i.e., social deterministic view).[183] Both these paradigms accept a legalistic definition of crime (i.e., behavior violating criminal laws) according to Reasons.[184] The third paradigm, power/conflict, recognizes the importance of power, politics, and people in creating, sustaining, and shaping conditions conductive to criminality.[185]

Schur

Schur thinks it would be a mistake to single out any one definition of law and label it "the definition." The closest he comes to a definition is his statement that the criminal law consists of the rules established by the legislatures and courts, and backed up by sanctions imposed by the courts.[186]

Criminal law theorists have noted that those criminal laws that do not have the support of the dominant social norms of society have limited effectiveness. Attempts to utilize the criminal law in order to regulate private morality causes problems for both the legal system and other societal institutions. Theorists should concern themselves with what the criminal law should be and place the burden of justifying applications of the law on those who seek to impose their conception of the criminal law on the behavior of all societal members.[187]

For example, there is a growing recognition among theorists that the criminal law is the inappropriate means to use in dealing with deviance and that social, medical, and psychological services are more appropriate means.[188] Schur states that some criminal laws are so ineffective and unenforceable that they are of criminological significance because of conflict of interest and value inconsistencies. These unenforceable laws (i.e., crimes without victims) attempt to legally proscribe the willing exchange of socially disapproved but demanded goods or services (i.e., homosexuality, drug addiction, prostitution, gambling, etc.). These types of crimes involve a consensual transaction or exchange and no direct and clear harm is inflicted by one person against another so no legal complaint is made by either party.[189] Further our reliance upon a criminal law solution to most social problems leads to overcriminalization of situations that really do not concern the criminal justice system. Thus there has been overcriminalization in the area of deviance (i.e., sexual behavior, vice, drugs, and political activity) in our society that leads to a doubting of the effectiveness of our legislative process and criminal justice system.[190]

Gibbs

Theorists tend to employ a statutory criterion of criminality which Gibbs criticizes (i.e., the idea that crime is an act so designated by a statute). But as inadequate as the statutory conception of crime appears to be, alternative conceptions have not been easily formulated largely because many of the attributes commonly ascribed to criminality are of doubtful nature.[191]

Some of the alternatives to the statutory conception of crime are examined by Gibbs. Sellin's proposal that criminology abandon the concept of criminal law and study norms of conduct is rejected by Gibbs. The social evaluation of crime (i.e., reaction to behavior that is publicly considered criminal) proposal is also rejected by Gibbs.[192] Using Sutherland's definition of crime as any conduct which is contrary to the criminal law, one can formulate an analytical definition of the criminal law. Thus the criminal law can be defined from politicality, penal sanction, specificity and uniformity (i.e., the criminal law's four characteristics). Gibbs accepts this definition as applied to modern industrial society.[193]

Gibbs states that any definition of criminal law should recognize that crimes are acts contrary to criminal law and not laws in general.[194] A law then is an evaluation of conduct held by at least one person in a social unit. Further there is a high probability that one or more people in a special status on their own initiative or at the request of others will attempt by non-coercive or coercive means to prevent, rectify, or revenge behavior that is contrary to the evaluation with a low probability of retaliation by individuals other than those at whom the reaction is directed.[195]

Sociological Jurisprudence

Pound

Pound discusses several areas in which the concept of law has been defined by jurisprudents before defining the concept himself.[196] Law is defined by Pound as a system of authoritative materials for grounding or guiding judicial and administrative action recognized or established in a politically organized society.[197] Thus law means social control through the systematic application of force of the politically organized society.[198]

Law is categorized into three social processes by Pound. These are (1) the legal order (i.e., regime of adjusting relations and ordering of conduct by the systematic application of force of politically organized society); (2) the authoritative grounds of or guides to determination of disputes in society (i.e., body of authoritative precepts, developed and applied by an authoritative technique in the light of, or on the basis of, authoritative traditional ideals); and (3) the judicial and administrative processes.[199]

The eight jural postulates of Pound, based on the writings of

Kohler reflect right and justice which civilization presupposes. The first five postulates have been derived as generalizations from legal evolution and the last three are the expectations of the community concerning the law's societal purpose.[200] The postulates have been summarized by Sawer as (1) security of the person from intentional aggression; (2) security of possession and property in the things discovered and appropriated, created by one's own labor, or acquired under the existing socio-economic order; (3) assumption of good faith in the making of representations and promises; and (4) assumption that things inherently dangerous unless controlled by society will be kept under control.[201]

Pound's theory of interests perceives a multiplicity of human claims or demands in society. The task of law is recognizing and securing certain of these interests (i.e., interests are claims, wants, or demands of a person to have something or to do something) within the limits imposed by effective legal action and the law itself.[202] Pound classifies interests as individual, social, and public (i.e., those involved in the individual, social, and public life and asserted in title of that life respectively).[203]

The goal of law is to satisfy the maximum of human claims, wants, and desires with the minimum of friction and waste. In order to achieve these claims, wants, and interests, they must be categorized (individual or social) and then competing interests weighed so that justice will be served.[204]

Cardozo

Law is defined by Cardozo as a principle or rule of conduct so established as to justify a prediction with reasonable certainty that it will be enforced by the courts if its authority is challenged.[205] Law is thought of as a system of fluid reality subject to the process of growth and change since legal rules and precepts are essentially relative in nature according to Cardozo.[206] He feels that the law follows a body of general rules which cannot be altered by judge or legislative body. Thus Cardozo's conception of law follows the theoretical position that denies value-choice by lawmakers and is naturalistic.[207] The law is a body of relatively stable rules and standards having prior existence to court decisions through pursuit of the concept of *stare decisis*.[208]

The law is not reducible to socially sanctioned custom of any kind since law can be differentiated from other social concepts. There is a continuous lag between law and culture. The law must allow "extra-legal" standards from societal mores to intrude upon the legal system if one wants to avoid legal subjectivism.[209] The mores from differing communities within society are the source and criterion of legal hypotheses. Thus, law like other values will have to be interpreted in terms of its place in the cultural context.[210]

Llewellyn

Law is a direct product of society and can be defined as that which officials do about disputes.[211] According to Llewellyn, the legal is the patterned normative regularity in the law-ways and the law-stuff (i.e., the legal consists of a projection and idealization of right patterns of different degrees in precision and generality from any group).[212] Akers feels the defining characteristic of law to Llewellyn is not just force, but force applied in a regular way and authorized within a social order or political state.[213]

The legal institution deals with law and order as well as law and government. There is a basic interaction of men acting under and within rules, and under and within a tradition both of goodwill and of know-how each of which is part of what we know under law.[214] There are also lesser legal-governmental institutions (i.e., regulatory law) and buttressing institutions which are only partly legal-governmental (i.e., family and economic law).[215] The legal institution also organizes and directs through effective leadership and administration what Llewellyn calls the law-team. Lastly it develops, maintains, and betters craft know-how among the law specialists (i.e., legislator, lawyer, trial judge, and appellate judge).[216]

Llewellyn deals with a number of concepts: law-jobs, law-crafts, law-ways, and law-stuff. Law-jobs (a juridical technique) consists of the disposition of trouble cases, in preventive channeling, in the allocation of authority and arrangement of procedures, and in the organization of the group, institution, or society.[217] A law-craft is a recognizable line of work practiced by recognizable craftsmen. Most lawyers practice more than one law-craft (i.e., advocate, counsellor, and legislator, for example).[218] Law-ways is any legal behavior or practice.[219] Law-stuff is any cultural phenomena which relate to the legal. This includes rules of law, legal institutions of any kind, lawyers, law-libraries, courts, habits of obedience, and anything else cultural whose reference is legal.[220]

Stone

Stone accepts Pound's definition of law as social control through the systematic application of force of the politically organized society. As a disciple of Pound, Stone's sociological jurisprudence is a study of the relationship of the legal order with the wider societal social order. The legal institution is influenced both positively and negatively by other societal institutions, especially the economic and political institutions. On the other

hand, the legal institution is also influential in the functioning
of other societal insitutions.[221]

Sociological jurisprudence is concerned with the effects of
theories of justice upon the legal order in practice. But the study of
theories of justice is concerned with such questions as whether
ideals are valid or invalid, demonstrable or undemonstrable, useful
or useless, and what ought to be or ought not to be.[222] Sociological
jurisprudence deals with the influences of social, economic,
psychological, and other non-legal factors on the process of change
in the content of the substantive law as well as the effect of non-
legal factors on both the legal profession and its traditions.[223]

Hart

Law is conceived by Hart as having a certain quality not
because it fits some abstract standard relating to the values which
it expresses but because of its formal utterance by a body of a
a certain sort (i.e., an organ of the state).[224] Hart states law
consists of particular kinds of rules. The essence of a legal system
lies in the union of primary and secondary rules. Primary rules are
informal rules of obligation through which the basic conditions of
social existence are satisfied while secondary rules are formal and
clarify, authorize, and empower.[225]

Secondary rules consist of rules of recognition which clarify
what the authoritative primary rules are and order them in
a hierarchy of importance. They are also considered as rules of
change which authorize the introduction of new primary rules.
Lastly, secondary rules are adjudicators which empower indivi-
uals to make authoritative determinations as to whether a primary
rule has been broken on a particular occasion.[226]

Fuller

Law is viewed as the purposive enterprise of subjecting
human conduct to the governance of rules by Fuller.[227] He insists
that the internal morality of law is neutral toward its substantive
aims although denying that it is possible to conceive of a system
of law at once faithful to the imperatives of legality and
indifferent to justice and human welfare.[228]

Fuller's eight criteria of legality presupposes that the central
concern of the law ought to be its predictability. To assume that
the primary value to be realized by law is predictability of the
action of state organs is to assume a common set of values for
all.[229] He points out the ways in which it is possible to fail in the
creation and maintenance of law.[230] A system that does fail in

meeting these criteria is considered law.[231] The criteria are (1) having no rules at all so that only *ad hoc* decisions reign; (2) making rules unknown or unavailable to those who are expected to obey them; (3) creating retroactive rules; (4) failing to have rules which can be understood; (5) having contradictory rules; (6) having rules which the affected individuals are incapable of following; (7) making such frequent changes in the rules that the persons subject to them cannot properly orient their conduct with regard to them; and (8) lacking congruence between the rules as announced and the same rules as they are administered or enforced.

Conclusion

Paradigms Applied to the Sociology of Law

The results of this research reveal some interesting findings. The major finding is that most theorists have been and continue to be adherents of structural-functional theory (*i.e.*, consensus theory).

In the area of sociology of civil law, most classical (Ehrlich, Weber, Timasheff, and Gurvitch) and contemporary theorists (Davis, Parsons, Aubert, Selznick, Skolnick, Sawer, Schur, Akers, and Nonet) are basically structural-functionalists. I say basically since there is some problem of fit utilizing the Ritzer typology where Ehrlich, Weber, Timasheff, and Gurvitch are concerned. First of all Weber is the type theorist for the social definition paradigm in general and action theory in particular. But his sociology of law is a model example of structural-functional theory. Thus there is a problem of classification as to where Weber should be placed ideologically. Ritzer notes that his paradigms are not exact and there is room for adjustments in a field such as sociology. Therefore, Weberian theory may be social definitionist in general but his sociology of law tends to be social factist in particular.

On the other hand, Ehrlich, Timasheff, and Gurvitch tend toward phenomenological theory of the social definition paradigm. This is more true of Timasheff and Gurvitch than Ehrlich. But the key statements made by all three theorists strongly are more structural-functionalist than phenomenological. Therefore, as in the case of Weber, some theorists cannot be totally classified as an adherent to one theory in particular or another.

This brings us to the case of Marx, Engels, and Renner. On the basis of the statements made by all three theorists they could be classified as conflict theorists. This would clearly place them as adherents of the social facts paradigm. This is not at odds with

Ritzer as he states that Marx, like Weber, is a paradigm bridger (i.e., some ideas can be classed as social factist and others as social definitionist).

Black is the only theorist that can be placed clearly in the social definition paradigm. He appears to be strongly advocating use of action theory (ala Weber) as the tool to best study the sociology of civil law. Black has been strongly criticized by Nonet for his intellectual views. The latter is clearly a structural-functionalist, an intellectual view that is not really at odds with action theory since both theories do stress observation of social facts.

Turning now to sociological jurisprudence one finds that all are clearly structural-functionalists. Within this division of sociology of law, Pound and Cardozo of the classical period and Llewellyn, Stone, Hall, Allen, Fuller, and Hart of the contemporary period are all adherents to the social facts paradigm.

When dealing with sociology of criminal law theorists, one finds a mix of theoretical positions. Beccaria, Bentham, and Tarde are social interactionists while Durkheim is a structural-functionalist. The contemporary theorists are either struc-tural-functionalists or conflict theorists. Jeffery, Schur, Gibbs, and Akers are adherents to the consensus view while Turk, Hills, Chambliss, Quinney, and Reasons are adherents to the conflict view. It is of interest to note the evolution of intellectual thought in this division of sociology of law from a predominantly social definitionist perspective to social factist. Within the latter paradigm, emphasis has evolved from a structural-functional to a conflict theory perspective since the late 1960's. This is due in part to the influence of radical ideologies introduced by European theorists and the growing recognition that traditional consensus criminal law theory has increasingly failed to provide answers to problems within our criminal justice system.

It can be concluded that most sociology of law theorists are adherents to structural-functional theory. Some adhere to conflict theory, and a few identify with either action theory or symbolic interactionist theory. Thus, according to the Ritzer paradigmatic scheme, most theorists would fall within the social facts paradigm. The majority of sociology of law theorists analyzed in this paper would probably concur that law is a social norm and a form of social control. Thus, all theorists probably view man as manipulated by normative systems (i.e., value-attitudes) and social control agencies. Finally the source of control over the individual would be for the most part societal social structures and institutions that would be coercive in nature.

NOTES

1.   Thomas Kuhn, The Structure of Scientific Revolutions (2nd ed.). Chicago: University of Chicago Press, 1970.

2.   George Ritzer, *Sociology: A Multiple Paradigm Science*. Boston: Allyn and Bacon, 1975, p. 24.

3.   *Ibid.*, 189.

4.   *Ibid.*, 48-57.

5.   George Ritzer, "Sociology: A Multiple Paradigm Science," *The American Sociologist*, 10 (August, 1975): 159-160.

6.   George Ritzer, *Sociology: A Multiple Paradigm Science*. Boston: Allyn and Bacon, 1975, pp. 57-67.

7.   George Ritzer, "Sociology: A Multiple Paradigm Science," *The American Sociologist*, 10 (August, 1975): 160.

8.   George Ritzer, "Sociology: A Multiple Paradigm Science," *The American Sociologist*, 10 (August, 1975): 161-162.

9.   George Ritzer, *Sociology: A Multiple Paradigm Science*. Boston: Allyn and Bacon, 1975, pp. 86-87; George Ritzer, "Sociology: A Multiple Paradigm Science", *The American Sociologist*, 10 (August, 1975): 162.

10.   George Ritzer, *Sociology: A Multiple Paradigm Science*. Boston: Allyn and Bacon, 1975, pp. 96-115; George Ritzer, "Sociology: A Multiple Paradigm Science," *The American Sociologist*, 10 (August, 1975): 162.

11.   George Ritzer, *Sociology: A Multiple Paradigm Science*. Boston: Allyn and Bacon, 1975, pp. 96-115; George Ritzer, "Sociology: A Multiple Paradigm Science," *The American Sociologist*, 10 (August, 1975): 162.

12.   E.H. Sutherland and D.R. Cressey, *Criminology*. Philadelphia: J.B. Lippincott Company, 1970, p. 3.

13.   P.H. Partridge, "Ehrlich's Sociology of Law," in *Studies in the Sociology of Law*. Geoffrey Sawer (ed.), Canberra: Australian National University, 1961, pp. 5-7.

14.   Ronald Akers and Richard Hawkins (eds.), *Law and Control in Society*. Englewood Cliffs, New Jersey: Prentice-Hall, 1975, p. 7.

15.   Roscoe Pound, "Sociology of Law," in *Twentieth Century Sociology*. Georges Gurvitch and Wilbert Moore (eds.), New York: The Philosophical Society, 1945, pp. 299-300.

16.   Ronald Akers and Richard Hawkins (eds.), *Law and Control in Society*. Englewood Cliffs, New Jersey: Prentice-Hall, 1975, p. 8.

17.   P.H. Partridge, "Ehrlich's Sociology of Law," in *Studies in the Sociology of Law*. Geoffrey Sawer (ed.), Canberra: The Australian National University, 1961, pp. 9-12.

18.   *Ibid.*, 14-15.

19.   *Ibid.*, 16-19.

20.   *Ibid.*, 22-26.

21.   Max Weber, *Law in Economy and Society*, Cambridge, Massachusetts: Harvard University Press, 1954, pp. xiii-xix.

22.   *Ibid.*, Julien Freund, *The Sociology of Max Weber*, New York: Random House, 1968, pp. 245-249; Philip Selznick, "The Sociology of

Law," International Encyclopedia of the Social Sciences, New York: Free Press, 1968, pp. 73-74.

23.   Jerome Skolnick, "The Sociology of Law in America: Overview and Trends," Social Problems, 13(1) (Summer, 1965): 8-11; Julien Freund, The Sociology of Max Weber, New York: Random House, 1968, pp. 245-251.

24.   Ronald L. Akers and Richard Hawkins (eds.), Law and Control in Society. Englewood Cliffs, New Jersey: Prentice-Hall, 1975, pp. 8-9; Philip Selznick, International Encyclopedia of the Social Sciences. New York: Free Press, 1968, p. 54; Edwin Schur, Law and Society: A Sociological View. New York: Random House, 1968, pp. 10-15; S.J. Stoljar, "Weber's Sociology of Law", in Studies in the Sociology of Law, Geoffrey Sawer (ed.), Canberra: The Australian National University, 1961, pp. 37-39.

25.   Max Weber, Law in Economy and Society. Cambridge, Massachusetts: Harvard University Press, 1954, pp. lxii-lxv; S.J. Stoljar, Weber's Sociology of Law," in Studies in the Sociology of Law, Geoffrey Sawer (ed.), Canberra: The Australian National University, 1961, pp. 41-44.

26.   Max Weber, Law in Economy and Society. Cambridge, Massachusetts: Harvard University Press, 1954, pp. 11-15.

27.   Ibid., 41-45; Julien Freund, The Sociology of Max Weber. New York: Random House, 1968, pp. 251-253.

28.   Max Weber, Law in Economy and Society. Cambridge, Massachusetts: Harvard University Press, 1954, pp. 56-59.

29.   Philip Selznick, "The Sociology of Law," International Encyclopedia of the Social Sciences. New York: Free Press, 1968, p. 56; S.J. Stoljar, "Weber's Sociology of Law," in Studies in the Sociology of Law, Geoffrey Sawer (ed.), Canberra: The Australian National University, 1961, pp. 47-50.

30.   Jerome Skolnick, "The Sociology of Law in America: Overview and Trends," Social Problems, 13(1) (Summer, 1965): 37-39; F. James Davis, "Law As A Type of Social Control," in Society and the Law, F. James Davis et al., New York: Free Press, 1962, pp. 41-44; Julien Freund, The Sociology of Max Weber. New York: Random House, 1968, pp. 263-265; S.J. Stoljar, "Weber's Sociology of Law," in Studies in the Sociology of Law, Geoffrey Sawer (ed.), Canberra: The Australian National University, 1961, pp. 51-52.

31.   Maureen Cain, "The Main Themes of Marx and Engels' Sociology of Law," British Journal of Law and Society (Winter, 1974): 136.

32.   Ibid., 138.

33.   Ibid., 139.

34.   Ibid., 141, 145.

35.   Ibid., 142.

36.   Ibid., 137, 142-143.

37.   Ibid., 144.

38.   Karl Renner, The Institutions of Private Law. London: Routledge and Kegan Paul, 1949, pp. 3-6.

39.   Ibid., 9-11.

40.   Geoffrey Sawer, "Law as Socially Neutral: Karl Renner," in Studies in the Sociology of Law, Geoffrey Sawer (ed.), Canberra: The Australian National University, 1961, pp. 137-142; Geoffrey Sawer, Law in Society. London: Oxford University Press, 1965, pp. 12-16.

41.   Karl Renner, The Institutions of Private Law. London: Routledge and Kegan Paul, 1949, pp. 8-11.

42..   Ibid., 15-17.

43.   Ibid., 25-27.

44.   Ibid., 31-34.

45.   Geoffrey Sawer, "Law as Socially Neutral: Karl Renner," in Studies in the Sociology of Law, Geoffrey Sawer (ed.) Canberra: The Australian National University, 1961, pp. 147-150.

46.   Ibid., 151.

47.   Ibid., 155-157.

48.   Nicholus S. Timasheff, An Introduction to the Sociology of Law. Cambridge, Massachusetts: 1939, pp. 19-21.

49.   Ronald Akers and Richard Hawkins (eds.), Law and Control in Society. Englewood Cliffs, New Jersey: Prentice-Hall, 1975, pp. 9-10; Roscoe Pound, "Sociology of Law", in Twentieth Century Sociology, Georges Gurvitch and Wilbert Moore (eds.), New York: The Philosophical Society, 1945, pp. 334-335.

50.   Nicholus S. Timasheff, An Introduction to the Sociology of Law. Cambridge, Massachusetts: Harvard University Press, 1939, pp. 26-30.

51.   Ibid., 34-37.

52.   Ibid., 39-40.

53.   Georges Gurvitch, "Major Problems of the Sociology of Law," Journal of Social Philosophy, 6(3) (April, 1941): 198-200.

54.   Nicholus S. Timasheff, "Growth and Scope of Sociology of Law," in Modern Sociological Theory in Continuity and Change, Howard Becker and Alvin Boskoff (eds.), New York: The Dryden Press, 1957, pp. 432-435.

55.   Roscoe Pound, "Sociology of Law", in Twentieth Century Sociology, Georges Gurvitch and Wilbert Moore (eds.), New York: The Philosophical Society, 1945, pp. 338-341.

56.   Georges Gurvitch, "Major Problems of the Sociology of Law," Journal of Social Philosophy, 6(3) (April, 1941): 199-200.

57.   Ibid., 202-203.

58.   Ibid., 204-206.

59.   Ibid., 208-211.

60.   Ibid., 213-215.

61.   F. James Davis, "Law as a Type of Social Control", in Society and the Law, F. James Davis et al., New York: Free Press, 1962, pp. 39-41.

62.   Leopold Posposil, "Law and Order," in *Introduction to Cultural Anthropology*, James Clifton (ed.), Boston: Houghton Mifflin Company, 1968, pp. 212-213.

63.   F. James Davis, "Law as a Type of Social Control, in *Society and the Law*, F. James Davis *et al.*, New York: Free Press, 1962, pp. 342-343.

64.   *Ibid.*, 44-46.

65.   *Ibid.*, 47-48.

66.   *Ibid.*, 50-53.

67.   Talcott Parsons, "The Law and Social Control", in *Law and Society*, William E. Evan (eds.), New York: Free Press, 1962, pp.56-59.

68.   *Ibid.*, 60-61.

69.   *Ibid.*, 62-63.

70.   *Ibid.*, 64-65.

71.   *Ibid.*, 66-67; Edwin M. Schur, *Law and Society: A Sociological View*. New York: Random House, 1968, pp. 72-75.

72.   Talcott Parsons, "The Law and Social Control", in *Law and Society*, William E. Evan (ed.), New York: Free Press, 1962, pp. 69-71.

73.   Vilhelm Aubert, "Researches in the Sociology of Law," *The American Behavioral Scientist*, 7(4) (1963): 16.

74.   *Ibid.*, 17.

75.   Nicholus S. Timasheff, "Growth and Scope of Sociology of Law", in *Modern Sociological Theory in Continuity and Change*, Howard Becker and Alvin Boskoff (eds.), New York: The Dryden Press, 1957, pp. 432-435.

76.   Vilhelm Aubert, "Researches in the Sociology of Law", *The American Behavioral Scientist*, 7(4) (1963): 17.

77.   Jerome Skolnick, "The Sociology of Law In America: Overview and Trends", *Social Problems*, 13(1) (1965): 7-10; Ronald Akers and Richard Hawkins (eds.), *Law and Control in Society*, Englewood Cliffs, New Jersey: Prentice-Hall, 1975, p. 10.

78.   Jerome Skolnick, "The Sociology of Law In America: Overview and Trends," *Social Problems*, 13(1) (1965): 27-30.

79.   Geoffrey Sawer, *Law in Society*. London: Oxford University Press, 1965, pp. 23-26.

80.   F. James Davis, "Law as a Type of Social Control," in *Society and the Law*, F. James Davis *et al.*, New York: Free Press, 1962, pp. 51-53.

81.   Geoffrey Sawer, *Law in Society*. London: Oxford University Press, 1965, pp. 12-16.

82.   *Ibid.*, 30-31.

83.   *Ibid.*, 46-47.

84.   *Ibid.*, 147-150.

85.   Ronald Akers and Richard Hawkins (eds.), *Law and Control in Society*. Englewood Cliffs, New Jersey: Prentice-Hall, 1975, p. 12.

86.   *Ibid.,* 13.

87.   Philip Selznick, "The Sociology of Law", in *The Sociology of Law,* Rita J. Simon (ed.), Scranton, Penn.: Chandler Pub. Co. 1968, pp. 190-191.

88.   Philip Selznick, "The Sociology of Law", *International Encyclopedia of the Social Sciences.* New York: Free Press, 1968, pp. 50-51.

89.   Jerome Skolnick, "The Sociology of Law in America: Overview and Trends", *Social Problems,* 13 (1) (1965): 37-39; Philip Selznick, "The Sociology of Law", *International Encyclopedia of the Social Sciences.* New York: Free Press, 1968, pp. 52-53.

90.   Philip Selznick, "The Sociology of Law", in *The Sociology of Law,* Rita J. Simon (ed.), Scranton, Pennsylvania: Chandler Publishing Company, 1968, pp. 193-194.

91.   *Ibid.,* 195-196; Philip Selznick, "The Sociology of Law", in *International Encyclopedia of the Social Sciences.* New York: Free Press, 1968, pp. 54-55.

92.   Ronald Akers and Richard Hawkins (eds.), *Law and Control in Society.* Englewood Cliffs, New Jersey: Prentice-Hall, 1975, p. 13; Philip Selznick, "The Sociology of Law."

93.   Edwin M. Schur, *Law and Society: A Sociological View.* New York: Random House, 1968, pp. 4-8.

94.   *Ibid.,* 10-13.

95.   *Ibid.,* 14-15.

96.   *Ibid.,* 68-72.

97.   *Ibid.,* 73-76.

98.   Ronald Akers and Richard Hawkins (eds.), *Law and Control in Society.* Englewood Cliffs, New Jersey: Prentice-Hall, 1975, pp. 5-6.

99.   *Ibid.,* 7-8.

100.   *Ibid.,* 9-10.

101.   *Ibid.,* 11-12.

102.   *Ibid.,* 12-13.

103.   Donald Black, "The Boundaries of Legal Sociology", *Yale Law Journal* 81 (June, 1972): 1096.

104.   *Ibid.,* 1091.

105.   *Ibid.,* 1092.

106.   *Ibid.,* 1096.

107.   *Ibid.,* 1087.

108.   *Ibid.,* 1097.

109.   Philippe Nonet, "For Jurisprudential Sociology", *Law and Society Review,* 10 (Summer, 1976): 526, 529.

110.   *Ibid.,* 530.

111.   *Ibid.,* 530.

112.   *Ibid.,* 531.

113.   *Ibid.,* 531-532.

114.   *Ibid.,* 537.

115.   *Ibid.,* 538.

116.   *Ibid.,* 542-543.

117.   *Ibid.,* 543.

118.   *Ibid.,* 543.

119.   Henry C. Black, *Black's Law Dictionary.* St. Paul, Minnesota: West Publishing Company, 1968, p. 1561; Elio Monachesi, Cesare Beccaria, in *Pioneers in Criminology,* Hermann Mannhein (ed.), Montclair, New Jersey: Patterson Smity, 1972, pp. 38-39.

120.   Elio Monachesi, Cesare Beccaria, in *Pioneers in Criminology,* Hermann Mannheim (ed.), Montclair, New Jersey: Patterson Smith, 1972, pp. 39-40.

121.   Julius Gould & William Kolb (eds.), *A Dictionary of the Social Sciences.* New York: Free Press, 1964, p. 650; Elio Monachesi, Cesare Beccaria, in *Pioneers in Criminology,* Hermann Mannheim (ed.), Montclair, New Jersey: Patterson Smith, 1972, pp. 41-44.

122.   Bertrand Russell, *A History of Western Philosophy.* New York: Simon and Schuster, 1959, p. 775.

123.   Edwin Sutherland and Donald Cressey, *Criminology.* Philadelphia: J.B. Lippincott, 1970, p. 4; Stephen Schafer, *Theories in Criminology.* New York: Random House, 1969, p. 33.

124.   Gilbert Geis, Jeremy Bentham, in *Pioneers in Criminology,* Hermann Mannheim (ed.), Montclair, New Jersey: Patterson Smith, 1972, pp. 53-66; Bertrand Russell, *A History of Western Philosophy.* New York: Simon and Schuster, 1959, p. 775.

125.   Margaret Vine, Gabriel Tarde, in *Pioneers in Criminology,* Hermann Mannheim (ed.), Montclair, New Jersey: Patterson Smith, 1972, pp. 292-295; Stephen Schafer, *Theories in Criminology.* New York: Random House, 1969, p. 238.

126.   Stephen Schafer, *Theories in Criminology.* New York: Random House, 1969, p. 238.

127.   Margaret Vine, Gabriel Tarde, in *Pioneers in Criminology,* Hermann Mannheim (ed.), Montclair, New Jersey: Patterson Smith, 1972, pp. 296-299; Stephen Schafer, *Theories in Criminology.* New York: Random House, p. 239.

128.   Stephen Schafer, *Theories in Criminology.* New York: Random House, 1969, p. 239.

129.   Roscoe Pound, Sociology of Law, in *Twentieth Century Sociology,* Georges Gurvitch and Wilbert Moore (eds.), New York: The Philosophical Society, 1945, pp. 316-319.

130.   F. James Davis, "Law as a Type of Social Control", in *Society and the Law,* F. James Davis *et al.,* New York: Free Press, 1962, pp. 41-43;

Roscoe Pound, "Sociology of Law", in *Twentieth Century Sociology,* Georges Gurvitch and Wilbert Moore (eds.), New York: The Philosophical Society, 1945, pp. 318-319; Georges Gurvitch, Emile Durkheim, in *Sociology of Law,* London: Routledge and Kegan Paul, 1947, pp. 83-96.

131.   Walter Lunden, Emile Durkheim, in *Pioneers in Criminology,* Hermann Mannheim (ed.), Montclair, New Jersey: Patterson Smith, 1972, pp. 390-391; Stephen Schafer, *Theories in Criminology.* New York: Random House, 1969, p. 243.

132.   Walter Lunden, Emile Durkheim, in *Pioneers in Criminology,* Hermann Mannheim (ed.), Montclair, New Jersey: Patterson Smith, 1972, pp. 392-393.

133.   *Ibid.,* 394-395.

134.   *Ibid.,* 396-397; Stephen Schafer, *Theories in Criminology.* New York: Random House, 1969, pp. 245-246.

135.   Jerome Hall, *Theft, Law and Society.* Indianapolis: The Bobbs-Merrill Company Inc., 1952, pp. xii-xiii.

136.   Francis Allen, *The Borderland of Criminal Justice: Essays in Law and Criminology.* Chicago: University of Chicago Press, 1964, pp. 29 and 31.

137.   *Ibid.,* 125.

138.   *Ibid.,* 126-130.

139.   C. Ray Jeffery, "Criminal Justice and Social Change", in *Society and the Law,* F. James Davis et al., New York: Free Press, 1962, pp. 264-269.

140.   *Ibid.,* 270-275.

141.   *Ibid.,* 276-281.

142.   *Ibid.,* 282-284.

143.   *Ibid.,* 285-288.

144.   *Ibid.,* 289-294.

145.   *Ibid.,* 295-301.

146.   *Ibid.,* 302-304.

147.   Austin Turk, *Criminality and Legal Order.* Chicago: Rand McNally, 1969, pp. 30-32.

148.   *Ibid.,* 36.

149.   *Ibid.,* 32.

150.   *Ibid.,* 33.

151.   *Ibid.,* 35.

152.   *Ibid.,* 37-38.

153.   *Ibid.,* 43 and 45.

154.   *Ibid.,* 46-48.

155.   Stuart Hills, *Crime, Power, and Morality: The Criminal-Law Process in the United States.* Scranton, Pennsylvania: Chandler Publishing Company, 1971, p. 5.

156.   Ibid., 3-4.

157.   Ibid., 4-5.

158.   Ronald Akers and Richard Hawkins (eds.), Law and Control in Society. Englewood Cliffs, New Jersey: Prentice-Hall, 1975, p. 41.

159.   Ibid., 43-44.

160.   Ibid., 47.

161.   Ibid., 48-49.

162.   William Chambliss and Robert Seidman, Law, Order, and Power. Reading, Massachusetts: Addison-Wesley Publishing Company, 1971, p. 9.

163.   William Chambliss (ed.), Crime and the Legal Process. New York: McGraw-Hill Book Company, 1969, pp. 8 and 10.

164.   William Chambliss and Robert Seidman, Law, Order, and Power. Reading, Massachusetts: Addison-Wesley Publishing Company, 1971, pp. 17 and 40.

165.   William Chambliss, "Functional and Conflict Theories of Crime", (New York, MSS Modular Publications) Module 17 (1973): 1-23.

166.   William Chambliss (ed.), Criminal Law in Action. Santa Barbara, California: Hamilton Publishing Company, 1975, pp. 5-6.

167.   Ibid., 476-477.

168.   William Chambliss, "Functional and Conflict Theories of Crime", (New York, MSS Modular Publications) Module 17 (1973): 1-23.

169.   William Chambliss (ed.), Criminal Law in Action. Santa Barbara, California: Hamilton Publishing Company, 1975, p. 5.

170.   Ibid., 6.

171.   Ibid., 6.

172.   Ibid., 476-477.

173.   Richard Quinney, "Toward a Sociology of Criminal Law", in Crime and Justice in Society. Boston: Little, Brown and Company, 1969, p. 1-10.

174.   Ibid., 11-20.

175.   Ibid., 21-30.

176.   Richard Quinney, "A Critical Theory of Criminal Law", in Criminal Justice in America. Boston: Little, Brown and Company, 1974, pp. 8-13.

177.   Ibid., 14-20.

178.   Ibid., 21-25.

179.   Charles Reasons, "Law and the Making of Criminals", in The Criminologist: Crime and the Criminal. Pacific Palisades, California: Goodyear Publishing Company, 1974, pp. 99-100.

180.   Ibid., 101-102.

181.   Ibid., 103-104.

182.   Charles Reasons, "Social Thought and Social Structure: Competing Paradigms in Criminology", *Criminology* 13(3) (November, 1975): 336-337.

183.   *Ibid.*, 337-339.

184.   *Ibid.*, 342.

185.   *Ibid.*, 342-343.

186.   Edwin Schur, *Law and Society: A Sociological View.* New York: Random House, 1968, pp. 4-13.

187.   Edwin Schur, "Unnecessary Crimes: The Perils of Overlegislating", in *Our Criminal Society.* Englewood Cliffs, New Jersey: Prentice-Hall, 1969, pp. 191-197.

188.   *Ibid.*, 198-201.

189.   *Ibid.*, 219-223.

190.   *Ibid.*, 224-227.

191.   Jack Gibbs, "Crime and the Sociology of Law", in *Crime, Criminology, and Contemporary Society*, Richard Knudten (ed.), Homewood, Illinois: The Dorsey Press, 1970, pp. 397-398.

192.   *Ibid.*, 399.

193.   *Ibid.*, 400-401.

194.   *Ibid.*, 402,

195.   *Ibid.*, 403-404.

196.   Roscoe Pound, "Sociology of Law", in *Twentieth Century Sociology*, Georges Gurvitch and Wilbert Moore (eds.), New York: The Philosophical Society, 1945, pp. 316-323.

197.   *Ibid.*, 325-332.

198.   *Ibid.*, 334-335.

199.   *Ibid.*, 337-340.

200.   E.K. Braybrooke, "The Sociological Jurisprudence of Roscoe Pound", in *Studies in the Sociology of Law*, Geoffrey Sawer (ed.), Canberra: The Australian National University, 1961, pp. 57-63.

201.   Geoffrey Sawer, *Law in Society.* London: Oxford University Press, 1965, pp. 147-150.

202.   E.K. Braybrooke, "The Sociological Jurisprudence of Roscoe Pound", in *Studies in the Sociology of Law*, Geoffrey Sawer (ed.), Canberra: The Australian National University, 1961, pp. 64-71.

203.   *Ibid.*, 72-80.

204.   *Ibid.*, 83-88.

205.   Benjamin Cardozo, *The Growth of the Law.* New Haven, Connecticut: Yale University Press, 1924, p. 52.

206.   Moses Aronson, "Cardozo's Doctrine of Sociological Jurisprudence", *Journal of Social Philosophy*, 4(1) (October, 1938): 5-9.

207.   *Ibid.*, 10-15; William Chambliss and Robert Seidman, *Law, Order, and Power*. Reading, Massachusetts: Addison-Wesley Publishing Company, 1971, pp. 40-41.

208.   Moses Aronson, "Cardozo's Doctrine of Sociological Jurisprudence", *Journal of Social Philosophy*, 4(1) (October, 1938): 11-15.

209.   *Ibid.*, 24-31.

210.   *Ibid.*, 34-39.

211.   Georges Gurvitch, K.N. Llewellyn, in *Sociology of Law*. London: Routledge and Kegan Paul, 1947, pp. 135-138.

212.   *Ibid.*, 138.

213.   Ronald Akers, "The Concept of Law", in *Law and Control in Society*, Ronald Akers and Richard Hawkins (eds.), Englewood Cliffs, New Jersey: Prentice-Hall, 1975, p. 11.

214.   Karl Llewellyn, "Law and the Social Sciences—Especially Sociology", in *Jurisprudence*. Chicago: University of Chicago Press, 1962, pp. 352-358.

215.   *Ibid.*, 359-363.

216.   *Ibid.*, 364-367.

217.   Georges Gurvitch, K.N. Llewellyn, in *Sociology of Law*. London: Routledge and Kegan Paul, 1947, p. 139.

218.   Karl Llewellyn, "Law and the Social Sciences—Especially Sociology," in *Jurisprudence*. Chicago: University of Chicago Press, 1962, pp. 368-371.

219.   Georges Gurvitch, K.N. Llewellyn, in *Sociology of Law*. London: Routledge and Kegan Paul, 1947, pp. 139-140.

220.   *Ibid.*, 141-144.

221.   Julius Stone, "Where Law and Social Science Stand", in *Law and the Social Sciences*. University of Minnesota Press, 1966, pp. 3-11.

222.   *Ibid.*, 12-23.

223.   *Ibid.*, 34-41.

224.   William Chambliss and Robert Seidman, *Law, Order, and Power*. Reading, Massachusetts: Addison-Wesley Publishing Company, 1971, p. 48.

225.   H.L.A. Hart, *The Concept of Law*. London: Oxford University Press, 1961, pp. 78-79.

226.   *Ibid.*, 77-96.

227.   Lon Fuller, *The Morality of Law*. New Haven, Connecticut: Yale University Press, 1964, p. 106.

228.   William Chambliss and Robert Seidman, *Law, Order, and Power*. Reading, Massachusetts: Addison-Wesley Publishing Company, 1971, p. 43.

229.   *Ibid.*, 44.

230.   Ronald Akers, "The Concept of Law", in *Law and Control in Society*, Ronald Akers and Richard Hawkins (eds.), Englewood Cliffs, New Jersey: Prentice-Hall, 1975, p. 13.

231.   Lon Fuller, *The Morality of Law*. New Haven, Connecticut: Yale University Press, 1964, p. 39.

Chapter 7

Toward a Political Economy of Crime

*William J. Chambliss**

In attempting to develop a Marxist theory of crime and
criminal law we are handicapped by the fact that Marx did not
devote himself very systematically to such a task. There are
nonetheless, several places in his analysis of capitalism where
Marx did direct his attention to criminality and law.[1] Furthermore,
the logic of the Marxian theory makes it possible to extrapolate
from the theory to an analysis of crime and criminal law in ways
that are extremely useful. Thus, in what follows I will be focusing
on the implications of the Marxist paradigm as well as relying
heavily on those Marxist writings that directly addressed these
issues.

As with the general Marxist theory, the starting point for the
understanding of society is the realization that the most fundamental feature of peoples' lives is their relationship to the mode of
production. The mode of production consists of both the means of
production (the technological processes) and the relationship of
different classes to the means of production—whether they own
them or work for those who do. Since ultimately, the only source
of an economic surplus is that amount of goods which is produced
beyond what the worker consumes, then the distinction between
those who own and those who work for others is crucial to
understanding the control of the surplus in the society.

All of this is of course elementary Marxism and was only
briefly summarized here to get us started.

We must then speak of historical periods according to the

mode of production which characterizes them. The most fundamental distinction would be between those societies where the means of production are owned privately, and societies where the means of production are not. Obviously there are many possible variations on these two ideal types: societies where the means of production are owned by the state (for example the Soviet Union) as contrasted with societies where the means of production are controlled by small groups of workers (for example Yugoslavia), or where the means of production are owned by collective units of workers, farmers, peasants and other strata (China for example). Each of these different modes of production would of course lead to quite different social relations and therefore to different forms of crime and criminal law.

Capitalist societies, where the means of production are in private hands and where there inevitably develops a division between the class that rules (the owners of the means of production) and the class that is ruled (those who work for the ruling class), creates substantial amounts of crime, often of the most violent sort, as a result of the contradictions that are inherent in the structure of social relations that emanate from the capitalist system.

The first contradiction is that the capitalist enterprise depends upon creating in the mass of the workers a desire for the consumption of products produced by the system. These products need not contribute to the well being of the people, nor do they have to represent commodities of any intrinsic value; nonetheless, for the system to expand and be viable, it is essential that the bulk of the population be oriented to consuming what is produced. However, in order to produce the commodities that are the basis for the accumulation of capital and the maintenance of the ruling class, it is also necessary to get people to work at tedious, alienating and unrewarding tasks. One way to achieve this, of course, is to make the accumulation of commodities dependent on work. Moreover, since the system depends as it does on the desire to possess and consume commodities far beyond what is necessary for survival, there must be an added incentive to perform the dull meaningless tasks that are required to keep the productive process expanding. This is accomplished by keeping a proportion of the labor force impoverished or nearly so.[2] If those who are employed become obstreperous and refuse to perform the tasks required by the productive system, then there is a reserve labor force waiting to take their job. And hanging over the heads of the workers is always the possibility of becoming impoverished should they refuse to do their job.

Thus, at the outset the structure of capitalism creates both the desire to consume and—for a large mass of people—an inability to earn the money necessary to purchase the items they have been taught to want.

A second fundamental contradiction derives from the fact that the division of a society into a ruling class that owns the means of production and a subservient class that works for wages *inevitably* leads to conflict between the two classes. As those conflicts are manifest in rebellions and riots among the proletariat, the state, acting in the interests of the owners of the means of production will pass laws designed to control, through the application of state sanctioned force, those acts of the proletariat which threaten the interests of the bourgeoisie, In this way, then, acts come to be defined as criminal.

It follows that as capitalism develops and conflicts between social classes continue or become more frequent or more violent (as a result, for example, of increasing proletarianization), more and more acts will be defined as criminal.

The criminal law is thus *not* a reflection of custom (as other theorists have argued), but is a set of rules laid down by the state in the interests of the ruling class, and resulting from the conflicts that inhere in class structured societies; criminal behavior is, then, the inevitable expression of class conflict resulting from the inherently exploitative nature of the economic relations. What makes the behavior of some criminal is the coercive power of the state to enforce the will of the ruling class; criminal behavior results from the struggle between classes whereby those who are the subservient classes individually express their alienation from established social relations. Criminal behavior is a product of the economic and political system, and in a capitalist society has as one of its principal consequences the advancement of technology, use of surplus labor and generally the maintenance of the established relationship between the social classes. Marx says, somewhat facetiously, in response to the functionalism of bourgeois sociologists:

> . . . . crime takes a part of the superfluous population off the labor market and thus reduces competition among the laborers—up to a certain point preventing wages from falling below the minimum—the struggle against crime absorbs another part of this population. Thus the criminal comes in as one of those natural "counterweights" which bring about a correct balance and open up a whole perspective of "useful" occupation . . . the criminal . . . produces the whole of the police and of criminal justice, constables, judges, hangmen, juries, etc.; and all these different lines of business, which form equally many categories of the social division of labor, develop different capacities of the human spirit, create new needs and new ways of satisfying them. Torture alone has given rise to the most ingenious mechanical inventions, and employed many honorable craftsmen in the production of its instruments.[3]

Paradigms, as we are all well aware, do much more than supply us with specific causal explanations. They provide us with a whole set of glasses through which we view the world. Most importantly, they lead us to emphasize certain features of the world and to ignore or at least de-emphasize others.

The following propositions highlight the most important implications of a Marxian paradigm of crime and criminal law.[4]

A. On the content and operation of criminal law

1. Acts are defined as criminal because it is in the interests of the ruling class to so define them.
2. Members of the ruling class will be able to violate the laws with impunity while members of the subject classes will be punished.
3. As capitalist societies industrialize and the gap between the bourgeoisie and the proletariat widens, penal law will expand in an effort to coerce the proletariat into submission.

B. On the consequences of crime for society

1. Crime reduces surplus labor by creating employment not only for the criminals but for law enforcers, locksmiths, welfare workers, professors of criminology and a horde of people who live off of the fact that crime exists.
2. Crime diverts the lower classes' attention from the exploitation they experience, and directs it toward other members of their own class rather than towards the capitalist class or the economic system.
3. Crime is a reality which exists only as it is created by those in the society whose interests are served by its presence.

C. On the etiology of criminal behavior

1. Criminal and non-criminal behavior stem from people acting rationally in ways that are compatible with their class position. Crime is a reaction to the life conditions of a person's social class.
2. Crime varies from society to society depending on the political and economic structures of society.
3. Socialist societies should have much lower rates of crime because the less intense class struggle should reduce the forces leading to the functions of crime.

The remainder of this paper will be an attempt to evaluate the degree to which the Marxian perspective on crime and criminal law is consistent with some empirical research findings.

On the Content and Operation of the Criminal Law

The conventional, non-Marxian interpretation of how criminal law comes into being sees the criminal law as a reflection of widely held beliefs which permeate all "healthy consciences" in the society. This view has been clearly articulated by Jerome Hall:

> The moral judgements represented in the criminal law can be defended on the basis of their derivation from a long historical experience, through open discussion . . . . the process of legislation, viewed broadly to include participation and discussion by the electrorate as well as that of the legislature proper, provides additional assurance that the legal valuations are soundly established . . .[5]

The Marxian Theory of Criminal Law

There is little evidence to support the view that the criminal law is a body of rules which reflect strongly held moral dictates of the society.[6] Occasionally we find a study on the creation of criminal law which traces legal innovations to the "moral indignation" of a particular social class.[7] It is significant, however, that the circumstances described are quite different from the situation where laws emerge from community consensus. Rather, the research points up the rule by a small minority who occupies a particular class position and shares a viewpoint and a set of social experiences which brings them together as an active and effective force of social change. For example, Joseph Gusfield's astute analysis of the emergence of prohibition in the United States illustrates how these laws were brought about through the political efforts of a downwardly mobile segment of America's middle class. By effort and some good luck this class was able to impose its will on the majority of the population through rather dramatic changes in the law. Suend Ranulf's more general study of *Moral Indignation and Middle Class Psychology* shows similar results, especially when it is remembered that the lower middle class, whose emergence Ranulf sees as the social force behind legal efforts to legislate morality, was a decided *minority* of the population.[8] In no reasonable way can these inquiries be taken as support for the idea that criminal laws represent *community* sentiments.

By contrast, there is considerable evidence showing the critically important role played by the interests of the ruling class as a major force in the creation of criminal laws. Jerome Hall's analysis of the emergence of the laws of theft and Chambliss' study of vagrancy laws both point up the salience of the economic interests of the ruling class as the fountainhead of legal changes.[9] A more recent analysis of the legislative process behind the creation of laws attempting to control the distribution of amphetamine drugs has also shown how the owners of the means of production (in this case, the large pharmaceutical companies) are involved in writing and lobbying for laws which affect their profits.[10]

The surface appearance of legal innovations often hides the real forces behind legislation. Gabriel Kolko's studies of the creation of laws controlling the meat packing and railroad industries in the United States have shown how the largest corporations in these industries were actively involved in a campaign for federal control of the industries, as this control would mean increased profits for the large manufacturers and industrialists.[11]

Research on criminal law legislation has also shown the substantial role played by state bureaucracies in the legislative process.[12] In some areas of criminal law it seems that the law enforcement agencies are almost solely responsible for the shape and content of the laws. As a matter of fact, drug laws are best understood as laws passed as a result of efforts of law enforcement agencies which managed to create whatever consensus there is. Other inquiries point up the role of conflicting interests between organized groups of moral entrepreneurs, bureaucrats, and businessmen.[13]

In all of these studies there is substantial support for the Marxian theory. The single most important force behind criminal law creation is doubtless the economic interest and political power of those social classes which either (1) own or control the resources of the society, or (2) occupy positions of authority in the state bureaucracies. It is also the case that conflicts generated by the class structure of a society act as an important force for legal innovation. These conflicts may manifest themselves in an incensed group of moral entrepreneurs (such as Gusfield's lower middle class, or the efforts of groups such as the ACLU, NAACP or Policemen's Benevolent Society) who manage to persuade courts or legislatures to create new laws.[14] Or the conflict may manifest itself in open riots, rebellions or revolutions which force new criminal law legislation.

There is, then, evidence that the Marxian theory with its emphasis on the role of the ruling classes in creating criminal laws and social class conflict and as the moving force behind legal changes is quite compatible with research findings on this subject.

The Consequences of Crime and Criminal Law

A. Moral Boundaries or Class Conflict?

One of the few attempts to systematically investigate the consequences that crime has for society at large is Kai Erikson's imaginative study of deviance among the Puritan settlement in New England.[15] Erikson sets out to investigate the hypothesis that

.... crime (and by extension other forms of deviation) may actually perform a needed service to society by drawing people together in a common posture of anger and indignation. The deviant individual violates rules of conduct which the rest of the community holds in high respect; and when these people come together to express their outrage over the offense and to bear witness against the offender, they develop a tighter bond of solidarity than existed earlier.[16]

Erikson's conclusion from his study of deviance among the Puritans is that several "crime waves" were in effect created by the community in order to help establish the moral boundaries of the settlement. Yet his conclusion is hardly supported by the data he presents. During the relatively short period of some sixty-odd years, this small community had three major crime waves: the Antinomian controversy of 1636, the Quaker prosecutions of the late 1650's, and the witchcraft hysteria of 1692.[17] This suggests, at the very least, that each crime wave failed as a source of community consensus and cohesion; otherwise so small a group of people would certainly not have needed so many serious crime waves in so short a period of time.

More importantly, Erikson's description of the Puritan settlement and of these three "crime waves" makes it very clear that they were not precipitated by crises of morality in the community, but by power struggles between those who ruled and those who were ruled. As Erikson points out:

> . . . . the use of the Bible as a source of law was [a problem in that] many thoughtful people in the colony soon became apprehensive because so many discretionary powers were held by the leading clique . . . - "the people" themselves (which in this instance really means the enfranchised stockholders) were anxious to obtain an official code of law; and so a constitutional battle opened which had a deep impact on the political life of the Bay. On one side stood the people, soon to be represented in the General Court by elected Deputies, who felt that the Bible would supply a clearer and safer guide to law if the elders would declare at the outset how they intended to interpret its more ambiguous passages. On the other side stood the ruling cadre of the community, the ministers and magistrates, who felt that the whole enterprise would be jeopardized if they were no longer able to interpret the World as they saw fit.[18]

Thus the lines were drawn between what Erikson calls "The Ruling Cadre" and "The People." When Anne Hutchinson, a particularly sharp-witted and articulate woman, began gathering large numbers of the people to her house where she rendered interpretations of the bible and the ruling cadre at odds with the rulers' interests, she was labelled a deviant—an "antinomian." She and her followers who "thought they were engaged in a local argument about church affairs," found themselves banished as criminals, disarmed as potential revolutionaries, or asked to recant crimes they had never known they were committing.[19]

Only twenty years later, the Quakers entered Massachusetts Bay. Once again the ruling class hegemony was threatened. By October of 1658, there were perhaps two dozen Quakers traveling around the countryside and a hundred or more local converts.

The constables and courts responded in the time-honored fashion of the law as an arm of the ruling class. Laws were passed making the preaching of Quakerism severely punishable, and constables broke up meetings.[20] Two of their members were publicly executed, and local constables conducted household raids, public floggings and confiscated property.[21]

In 1670, the ruling class was again threatened: this time by a costly war with the Indians, a power struggle between factions of the ruling class, and the English Crown's attempt to restructure or perhaps even revoke the colony's charter. In addition, there were increasing numbers of disputes between landowners.

Into this sea of conflicts threatening the ruling class, came the witchcraft mania, which was conveniently adopted and encouraged by the courts and the constables under the guidance of the "ruling cadre."

In all three instances, deviance was indeed created for the consequences it had. But it was not created by the community in order to establish "moral boundaries;" rather, it was created by the ruling class in order to protect and perpetuate its position of control.

The Etiology of Criminal Behavior

It is obviously fruitless to join the debate over whether or not contemporary theories of criminal etiology are adequate to the task. The advocates of "family background," "differential association," "cultural deprivation," "opportunity theory," and a host of other "theories" have debated the relative merits of their explanations ad infinitum (one might even say ad nauseam). I should like, however, to present a summary of data from a study of crime and criminal law which compares selected aspects of these phenomena in Nigeria and the United States. In so doing I hope to shed some light on the Marxian paradigm without pretending to resolve all the issues.

My data come from research in Seattle, Washington, and Ibadan, Nigeria. The research methods employed were mainly those of a participant observer. In Seattle the research spanned almost ten years (1962—1972), and in Ibadan the research took place during 1967—1968. In both cities the data were gathered through extensive interviewing of informants from all sides of criminal law—criminals, professional thieves, racketeers, prostitutes, government officials, police officers, businessmen and members of various social class levels in the community. Needless to say, the sampling was what sociologists have come to call (with more than a slight bit of irony) "convenience samples." Any other sampling procedure is simply impossible in the almost impenetrable world of crime and law enforcement into which we embarked.

Nigeria and America both inherited British common law at the time of their independence. Independence came somewhat later for Nigeria than for America, but the legal systems inherited are very similar. As a result, both countries share much the same foundation in status and common law principles. While differences exist, they are not, for our purposes, of great significance.

In both Nigeria and the United States, it is a crime punishable by imprisonment and fine for any public official to accept a bribe, to solicit a bribe or to give special favors to a citizen for monetary considerations. It is also against the law in both countries to run gambling establishments, to engage in or solicit for prostitutes, to sell liquor that has not been inspected and stamped by a duly appointed agency of the government, to run a taxi service without a license, etc. And, of course, both nations share the more obvious restrictions on murder, theft, robbery, rape and the standard array of criminal offenses. In both countries there is a striking similarity in the types of laws that do not and those that do get enforced.[22]

Crime and Law Enforcement in Nigeria

In both Nigeria and the United States, many laws can be, and are, systematically violated with impunity by those who control the political or economic resources of the society. Particularly relevant are those laws that restrict such things as bribery, racketeering (especially gambling), prostitution, drug distribution and selling, usury and the whole range of criminal offenses committed by businessmen in the course of their businesses (white collar crimes).

In Nigeria the acceptance of bribes by government officials is blatantly public and virtually universal. When the vice president of a large research organization that was just getting established in Nigeria visited the head of Nigerian Customs, he was told by the Customs Director that "at the outset it is important that we both understand that the customs office is corrupt from the top to the bottom." Incoming American professors were usually asked by members of the faculty at the University if they would be willing to exchange their American dollars on the black market at a better exchange rate than banks would offer. In at least one instance the Nigerian professor making this request was doing so for the military governor of the state within which the university was located. Should the incoming American fail to meet a colleague who would wish to make an illegal transfer of funds, he would in all likelihood be approached by any number of other citizens in high places. For example, the vice president of the leading bank near the university would often approach American professors and ask if they would like to exchange their money through him personally, and thereby receive a better exchange rate than was possible if they dealt directly through the bank.

At the time of my study, tithes of this sort were paid at every level. Businessmen desiring to establish businesses found their way blocked interminably by bureaucratic red tape until the proper amount of "dash" had been given to someone with the power to effect the result desired. Citizens riding buses were asked for cigarettes and small change by army soldiers who manned check points. The soldiers, in turn, had to pay a daily or weekly tithe to superior officers in order to be kept at this preferential assignment. At the border one could bring French wine, cigarettes and many other prohibited commodities into Nigeria, so long as prior arrangements had been made with the customs officers either in Lagos (the capital of the country) or at the check point itself. The prior arrangements included payment of a bribe.

As a result of bribes and payoffs, there flourished a large and highly profitable trade in a wide variety of vices. Prostitution was open and rampant in all of the large cities of Nigeria—it was especially well developed in those cities where commerce and industry brought large numbers of foreigners. Gambling establishments, located mainly in large European style hotels, and managed incidentally by Italian visitors, catered to the moneyed set with a variety of games of chance competitive with Monte Carlo or Las Vegas. There was a large illicit liquor trade (mostly a home-brewed gin-like drink), as well as a smaller but nevertheless profitable trade in drugs that received political and legal protection through payoffs to high level officials.

In at least Ibadan and Lagos, gangs of professional thieves operated with impunity. These gangs of thieves were well organized and included the use of beggars and young children as cover for theft activities. The links to the police were sufficient to guarantee that suspects would be treated leniently—usually allowed to go with no charges being brought. In one instance an entire community within the city of Ibadan was threatened by thieves with total destruction. The events leading up to this are revealing. The community, which I shall call Lando, had been victimized by a gang of thieves who broke into homes and stole valuable goods. The elders of Lando hired four men to guard the community. When thieves came one evening the hired guards caught and killed three of them. The next day the Oba of the community was called on by two men from another part of the city. These men expressed grave concern that some of their compatriots had been killed in Lando. The Oba informed them that if any other thieves came to Lando they would be dealt with similarly. The thieves' representatives advised the Oba that if such a thing happened the thieves would burn the community to the ground. When the Oba said he would call the police, it was pointed out to him that the chief of police was the brother-in-law of one of the thieves. Ultimately an agreement was reached whereby the thieves agreed to stop stealing in Lando in return for the Oba's promise that the thieves could sell their stolen property in Lando on market day.

Iban is a very cosmopolitan city which lies in the Yoruba section of western Nigeria. Although dominated by the Yoruba, there are nonetheless a large number of Hausa, Ibo and other ethnic groups in the city. The Hausa who are strongly Muslim (while the Yoruba are roughly 50% Christian) occupy a ghetto within Ibadan which is almost exclusively Hausa. Despite the fact that the Hausa are an immigrant group where one might expect the crime rate to be high, there are very few Hausa arrested for crime. (See Table 1.) This is particularly impressive since there is general belief that the Hausa are responsible for some of the more efficient and effective groups of professional thieves in the area. The explanation for this apparently lies in the fact that the Hausa have a strong leadership which intervenes with payoffs and cash to government and police officials whenever a member of their community is in any difficulty.

Table 1

Arrest Rate for 1,000 Population,
Ibadan, Nigeria 1967

Immigrant Areas	Indigenous Area	Hausa Area
1.41	.61	.54

Payment of bribes to the police is usually possible whenever an arrest is likely. An incoming American who illegally photographed an airport was allowed to go (without even destroying his film), upon payment of $15.00 to the arresting officer. Six dollars was sufficient for the wife of an American professor to avoid arrest for reckless driving. A young son of a wealthy merchant was arrested on numerous occasions for being drunk, driving without a license, stealing and getting into fights. On every occasion the police returned him to the custody of his parents without charges being filed when the father paid the arresting officer (or the policeman on the desk) thirty to forty-five dollars.

Such practices were not atypical, but were instead the usual procedure. It was said, and research bears this out, that one with money could pay to be excused from any type or amount of crime.

Who, then, did get arrested? In general, those who lacked either the money or the political influence to "fix" a criminal charge. The most common youth arrest was for "street trading"—that is selling items on the street. The second most frequent offense was "being away from home" or "sleeping out without protection." Among adults, "suspiciousness," public indecency, intoxication and having no visible means of support were the most common offenses. Although robbery, theft and burglary were common offenses (in a sample of 300 residents of Ibadan, 12.7% reported having been the victim of burglary), arrests for these offenses were much less frequent.

Anyone who has lived or traveled in foreign countries will not be suprised by these findings. What is usually not recognized, however, is that these same kinds of things characterize crime and criminal law enforcement in the United States (and possibly every other nation) as well.

Crime and Law Enforcement in Seattle

Seattle, like Ibadan, is a city of 1,000,000 people with its own police, government, and set of laws inherited from Great Britain. In Seattle, as in Ibadan, any type of vice can be found. It is only necessary to travel away from the middle and upper class suburbs that ring the city, and venture into the never-never land of skidrow derelicts, the Black ghetto or a few other pockets of rundown hotels, cafes and cabarets that are sprinkled along freeways and by the docks. Here there is prostitution, gambling, usury, drugs, pornography, bootleg liquor, bookmaking and pinball machines.

The most profitable of these are gambling and usury. Gambling ranges from bookmaking (at practically every street corner in the center of the city), to open poker games, bingo parlors, off-track betting, casinos, roulette and dice games (concentrated in a few locations and also floating out into the suburban country clubs and fraternal organizations), and innumerable two and five dollar stud-poker games scattered liberally throughout the city.

The most conspicuous card games take place from about ten in the morning (it varies slightly from one "fun house" to the next) until midnight. But there are a number of other twenty-four hour games that run constantly. In the more public games the limit ranges from one to five dollars for each bet; in the more select games that run twenty-four hours a day there is a "pot limit" or "no limit" rule. These games are reported to have betting as high as twenty and thirty thousand dollars. I have seen a bet made and called for a thousand dollars in one of these games. During this game, which was the highest stakes game I witnessed in the six years of the study, the police lieutenant in charge of the vice squad was called in to supervise the game—not, need I add, to break up the game or make any arrests, only to insure against violence.

Prostitution covers the usual range of ethnic groups, age, shape and size of female. It is also found in houses with madams as in New Orleans, on the street through pimps, or in suburban apartment buildings and hotels. Prices range from five dollars for a short time with a street walker to two hundred dollars for a night with a lady who has her own apartment (which she usually shares with her boyfriend who is discreetly gone during business operations).

High interest loans are easy to arrange through stores that advertise "your signature is worth $5,000." It is really worth considerably more; it may, in fact, be worth your life. The interest rates vary from twenty per cent for three months to as high as one hundred per cent for varying periods. Repayment is demanded not through the courts, but through the help of "The Gaspipe Gant" who call on recalcitrant debtors and use physical force to bring about payment. The "interest only" repayment is the most popular alternative practiced by borrowers, and is preferred by the loan sharks as well. The longer repayment can be prolonged, the more advantageous it is to the loan agents.

Pinball machines are readily available throughout the city, and most of them pay off in cash. The gambling, prostitution, drug distribution, pornography, and usury (high interest loans) which flourish in the lower class center of the city do so with the compliance, encouragement and cooperation of the major political and law enforcement officials in the city. There is, in fact, a symbiotic relationship between the law enforcement-political organizations of the city and a group of *local* (as distinct from national) men who control the distribution of vices.

The payoffs and briberies in Seattle are complex. The simpler and more straightforward are those made by each gambling establishment. A restaurant or cabaret with cardroom attached had to pay around $200 each month to the police and $200 to the "syndicate." In reality these were two branches of the same group of men, but the payoffs were made separately. Anyone who refused these payments was harassed by fire inspectors, health inspectors, licensing difficulties and even physical violence from enforcers who worked for the crime cabal in the city. Similarly, places with pinball machines, pornography, bookmaking or prostitution had to pay regularly to the "Bagman" who collected a fee for the police.

Payoffs to policemen were also required of two truck operators, cabaret owners and other businesses where police cooperation was necessary. Two truck drivers carried with them a matchbox with $3.00 in it and when asked for a light by the policeman who had called them to the scene of an accident, they gave him the matchbox with the $3.00 inside. Cabaret owners paid according to how large their business was. The police could extract payoffs because the laws were so worded as to make it virtually impossible to own a profitable cabaret without violating the law. For example, it was illegal to have an entertainer closer than 25 feet to the nearest customer. A cabaret, to comply with this ordinance, would have had to have a night club the size of a large ballroom, at which point the atmosphere would have been so sterile as to drive customers away, not to mention that such large spaces are exceedingly expensive in the downtown section of the city. Thus, the police could, if they chose to, close down a cabaret on a moment's notice. Payoffs were a necessary investment to assure that the police would not so choose.

The trade in licenses was notoriously corrupt. It was generally agreed by my informants that to get a tow truck license one had to pay a bribe of $10,000; a card room license was $25,000; taxi cab licenses were unavailable, as were licenses for distributing pinball machines or juke boxes. These licenses had all been issued to members of the syndicate that controlled the rackets, and no outsiders were permitted in.

There were innumerable instances of payoffs to politicians and government officials for real estate deals, businesses and stock transactions. In each case the participants were a combination of local businessmen, racketeers, local politicians and government officials.

Interestingly, there is also a minority ghetto within Seattle where one might expect to find a high crime rate. In Seattle this is the Japanese American section of the city.

It is widely believed that the Japanese-Americans have a very low propensity to crime. This is usually attributed to the family centered orientation of the Japanese-American community. There is some evidence, however, that this perspective is largely a self-fulfilling prophecy.[23] Table 2 shows a comparison between the self-reported delinquency and arrest rates of Japanese-American youth for a selected year. The data suffers, of course, from problems inherent in such comparisons, but nonetheless, the point cannot be gainsaid that the actual crime rate among Japanese-American youth is considerably higher than the conventional view would suggest.

Table 2

Comparison of Arrests (for 1963) and Self-Reported Delinquency Involvement by Radical Groups[a]

Radical Group	Per Cent Arrested	Per Cent Self-reporting High Delinquency Involvement[b]
White	11	53
Negro	36	52
Japanese	2	36

[a]Based on data from Richard H. Nagasawa, *Delinquency and Non-Delinquency. A Study of Status Problems and Perceived Opportunity,* unpublished M.A. thesis, University of Washington, 1965, p. 35.

[b]A self-reported delinquency scale was developed and the respondents were divided, so that 50 per cent of the sample was categorized as having high, and 50 per cent as having low delinquent involvement.

Thus we see that in both the Hausa area of Ibadan and the Japanese-American section of Seattle there is reason to suspect a reasonably high crime rate, but official statistics show an exceptionally low one. When discussing Hausa crime earlier, I attributed this fact to the payoffs made by Hausa leaders to the police and other government officials.

Somewhat the same sort of system prevails in Seattle as well, especially with regard to the rackets. Whereas prostitutes, pornography shops, gambling establishments, cabaret operators and tow truck operators must pay off individually to the police and the syndicate, the Japanese-American community did so *as a community*. The tithe was collected by a local businessman, and was paid to the police and the syndicate in a group sum. Individual prostitutes and vice racketeers might at times have to do special favors for a policeman or political figure, but by and large the payoffs were made collectively rather than individually.

This collective payoff was in large measure attributable to a common characteristic present in both the Hausa and the Japanese-American communities, namely, the heterogeneous social class nature of the community. Typically, wealthy or middle-class members of the lower class white slum or the Black ghetto moved out of these areas as rapidly as their income permitted. So too with Yoruba, Ibo or other ethnic groups in Ibadan. But many, though certainly not all, upper and middle-class Hausa in Ibadan, and Japanese-Americans in Seattle retained their residence in their respective communities. As a result, the enforcement of any law became more problematic for law enforcement agencies. Arrests made of any youth or adult always carried with it the possibility that the suspect would have a politically influential parent or friend. There was also the possibility that a payoff of some sort (including political patronage) would override the policeman's efforts. Since there was also the necessity to hide from the middle- and upper- class the extent to which the police closed their eyes to the rackets, it was then convenient to avoid having many police in the Hausa and Japanese-American community. The myth of these areas as "no crime" sections of the city was thus very convenient. By contrast, since only those members of the middle- and upper-class who were seeking vice would come to the skidrow area, or the Black ghetto, then the presence of the police was not problematic, and in fact helped to assure the "respectable" citizen that he could partake of his purient interests without fear of being the victim of robbery or violence.

As in Nigeria, all of this corruption, bribery and blatant violation of the law was taking place, while arrests were being made and people sent to jail or prison for other offenses. In Seattle over 70% of all arrests during the time of the study were for public drunkenness.[24] It was literally the case that the police were arresting drunks on one side of a building while on the other side a vast array of other offenses were being committed with police support and management.

What then are we to conclude from these data about the etiology of criminal behavior? For a start, the data show that

criminal behavior by *any reasonable* definition is *not* concentrated
in the lower classes. Thus, to the extent that a theory of the causes
of criminal behavior depends on the assumption that there is a
higher rate of criminality in the lower classes, to that extent, the
theory is suspect. These data on Seattle and Ibadan link members
of the ruling class, legal and political officials and racketeers in
joint ventures which involve them actively and passively in
criminal activities as part of their way of life.

This conclusion, ironically, is identical with Edwin
Sutherland's only he came to this view from his study of
corporation ("white collar") crime. However, he then went on to
propose an explanation for criminality which was essentially
socio-psychological: Sutherland asked why some *individuals*
became involved in criminal behavior while others did not. My
contention is that this question is meaningless. Everyone commits
crime. And many, many people whether they are poor, rich or
middling are involved in a way of life that is criminal; and
furthermore, no one, not even the professional thief or racketeer or
corrupt politician commits *crime all the time*. To be sure, it may be
politically useful to say that people become criminal through
association with "criminal behavior patterns," and thereby remove
the tendency to look at criminals as pathological. But such a view
has little scientific value, since it asks the wrong questions. It
asks for a psychological cause of what is by its very nature a
socio-political event. Criminality is simply *not* something that
people have or don't have; crime is not something some people do
and others don't. Crime is a matter of who can pin the label on
whom, and underlying this socio-political process is the structure
of social relations determined by the political economy. It is to
Sutherland's credit that he recognized this when, in 1924, he noted
that:

> An understanding of the nature of Criminal law is necessary in order
> to secure an understanding of the nature of crime. A complete
> explanation of the origin and enforcement of laws would be, also, an
> explanation of the violation of laws.[25]

But Sutherland failed, unfortunately, to pursue the implications of his remarks. He chose instead to confront the prevailing
functionalist perspective on crime with a less class-biased but
nonetheless inevitably psychological explanation.

The argument that criminal acts, that is, acts which are a
violation of criminal law, are more often committed by members of
the lower classes is not tenable. Criminal acts are widely
distributed throughout the social classes in capitalist societies.
The rich, the ruling, the poor, the powerless and the working
classes *all* engage in criminal activities on a regular basis. It is in
the enforcement of the law that the lower classes are subject to the
effects of ruling class domination over the legal system, and which
results in the appearance of a concentration of criminal acts among
the lower classes in the official records. In actual practice,

however, class differences in rates of criminal activity are probably negligible. What difference there is would be a difference in the type of criminal act, not in the prevalence of criminality.

The argument that the control of the state by the ruling class would lead to a lower propensity for crime among the ruling classes fails to recognize two fundamental facts. First is the fact that many acts committed by lower classes and which it is in the interests of the ruling class to control (e.g., crimes of violence, bribery of public officials, and crimes of personal choice, such as drug use, alcoholism, driving while intoxicated, homosexuality, etc.) are just as likely—or at least very likely—to be as widespread among the upper classes as the lower classes. Thus, it is crucial that the ruling class be able to control the discretion of the law enforcement agencies in ways that provide them with immunity. For example, having a legal system encumbered with procedural rules which only the wealthy can afford to implement and which, if implemented, nearly guarantees immunity from prosecution, not to mention more direct control through bribes, coercion and the use of political influence.

The Marxian paradigm must also account for the fact that the law will also reflect conflict between members of the ruling class (or between members of the ruling class and the upper class "power elites" who manage the bureaucracies). So, for example, laws restricting the formation of trusts, misrepresentation in advertising, the necessity for obtaining licenses to engage in business practices are all laws which generally serve to reduce competition among the ruling classes and to concentrate capital in a few hands. However, the laws also apply universally, and therefore apply to the ruling class as well. Thus, when they break these laws they are committing criminal acts. Again, the enforcement practices obviate the effectiveness of the laws, and guarantee that the ruling class will rarely feel the sting of the laws, but their violation remains a fact with which we must reckon.

It can also be concluded from this comparative study of Ibadan and Seattle that law enforcement systems are *not* organized to *reduce crime* or to enforce the public morality. They are organized rather to *manage* crime by cooperating with the most criminal groups and enforcing laws against those whose crimes are minimal. In this way, by cooperating with criminal groups, law enforcement essentially produces more crime than would otherwise be the case. Crime is also produced by law enforcement practices through selecting and encouraging the perpetuation of criminal careers by promising profit and security to those criminals who engage in organized criminal activities from which the political, legal and business communities profit.

Thus, the data from this study generally support the Marxian assertion that criminal acts which serve the interests of the ruling class will go unsanctioned while those that do not will be

punished. The data also support the hypothesis that criminal
activity is a direct reflection of class position. Thus, the
criminality of the lawyers, prosecuting attorneys, politicians,
judges and policemen is uniquely suited to their own class position
in the society. It grows out of the opportunities and strains that
inhere in those positions just as surely as the drinking of the
skidrow derelict, the violence of the ghetto resident, the drug use
of the middle class adolescent and the white collar crimes of
corporation executives reflect different socializing experiences.
That each type of criminality stems from social-psychological
conditioning is to say nothing unique about crime and criminality,
but only to posit what would have to be a general theory of human
psychology—something which places the task beyond the scope of
criminology and which has also been notoriously unsuccessful.

The postulates in the paradigm that deal with expected
differences between capitalist and socialist societies have not been
tested by the data presented, because our data come from two
capitalist societies. Crime statistics which might permit a
comparison are so unreliable as to be useless to the task. A
comparison between East and West Germany would be most
enlightening in this regard, as would a comparison between
Yugoslavia and Italy, Cuba and Trinidad, or China and India. I
have the impression that such a series of comparisons would
strongly support the Marxist hypothesis of crime rates being
highest in capitalist societies.

Summary and Conclusion

As Gouldner and Fredrichs have recently pointed out, social
science generally, and sociology in particular is in the throes of a
"paradigm revolution."[26] Predictably, criminology is both a
reflection of and a force behind this revolution.

The emerging paradigm in criminology is one which
emphasizes social conflict—particularly conflicts of social class
interests and values. The paradigm which is being replaced is one
where the primary emphasis was on consensus, and within which
"deviance" or "crime" was viewed as an aberration shared by some
minority. This group had failed to be properly socialized or
adequately integrated into society or, more generally, had suffered
from "social disorganization."

The shift in paradigm means more than simply a shift from
explaining the same facts with new causal models. It means that
we stretch our conceptual framework and look to different facets
of social experience. Specifically, instead of resorting inevitably to
the "normative system," to "culture" or to socio-psychological
experiences of individuals, we look instead to the social relations
created by the political and economic structure. Rather than

treating "society" as a full-blown reality (reifying it into an entity with its own life), we seek to understand the present as a reflection of the economic and political history that has created the social relations which dominate the moment we have selected to study.

The shift means that crime becomes a rational response of some social classes to the realities of their lives. The state becomes an instrument of the ruling class enforcing laws here but not there, according to the realities of political power and economic conditions.

There is much to be gained from this re-focusing of criminological and sociological inquiry. However, if the paradigmatic revolution is to be more than a mere fad, we must be able to show that the new paradigm is in fact superior to its predecessor. In this paper I have tried to develop the theoretical implications of a Marxian model of crime and criminal law, and to assess the merits of this paradigm by looking at some empirical data. The general conclusion is that the Marxian paradigm provides a long neglected but fruitful approach to the study of crime and criminal law.

NOTES

1.   In the United States the proportion of the population living in poverty is between 15 and 30% of the labor force.

2.   Primary source materials for Marx's analysis of crime and criminal law are: *Capital, v. 1,* pp. 231—298, 450—503, 556—557, 574, 674—678, 718—725, 734—741; *The Cologne Communist Trial,* London: Lawrence and Wishart; *The German Ideology (1845—6),* London: Lawrence and Wishart, 1965, pp. 342—379; *Theories of Surplus Value, v. 1,* pp. 375—376; "The State and the Law," in T. B. Bottomore and Maxmillien Rubel (eds.), *Karl Marx: Selected Writings in Sociology and Social Philosophy.* New York: McGraw-Hill, 1965, pp. 215—231.

3.   *Ibid, Theories of Surplus Value,* pp. 375—376.

4.   For an excellent statement of differences in "order and conflict" theories, see John Horton, "Order and Conflict Approaches to the Study of Social Problems," *American Journal of Sociology,* May 1966; see also Gerhard Lenski, *Power and Privilege.* New York: McGraw-Hill, 1966; William J. Chambliss, *Sociological Readings in the Conflict Perspective.* Reading, Mass.: Addison-Wesley, 1973.

5.   Jerome Hall, *General Principles of Criminal Law.* Indianapolis: Bobbs-Merrill, 1947, pp.: 356-357.

6.   For a more thorough analysis of this issue, see William J. Chambliss "The State, The Law and the Definition of Behavior as Criminal or Delinquent," in Daniel Glaser (ed.), *Handbook of Criminology.* Chicago: Rand McNally, 1974, Ch. 1, pp. 7—43.

7.   Svend Ranulf, *The Jealousy of the Gods,* Vols. 1 & 2, London: Williams and Northgate, 1932; and *Moral Indignation and Middle Class*

Psychology, Copenhagen: Levin & Monkagord, 1938; Joseph Gusfield, *Symbolic Crusade: Status Politics and the American Temperance Movement.* Urbana: University of Illinois Press, 1963.

8.   *Ibid.;* see also Andrew Sinclair, *Era of Excess: A Social History of the Prohibition Movement.* New York: Harper & Row, 1964.

9.   Jerome Hall, *Theft, Law and Society.* Indianapolis: Bobbs-Merill and Co., 1952; William J. Chambliss, "A Sociological Analysis of the Law of Vagrancy," *Social Problems.* Summer 1964, pp. 67-77.

10.   James M. Graham, "Profits at all Costs: Amphetamine Profits on Capitol Hill," *Transaction,* January 1972, pp. 14—23.

11.   Gabriel Kolko, *Railroads and Regulations.* Princeton: Princeton University Press, 1965; and *The Triumph of Conservatism,* New York: The Free Press of Glencoe, 1963.

12.   Alfred R. Lindesmith, *The Addict and the Law.* Bloomington: Indiana University Press, 1965; Edwin M. Lemert, *Social Action and Legal Change: Revolution Within the Juvenile Court.* Chicago: Aldine, 1964; Troy Duster, *The Legislation of Morality: Law, Drugs and Moral Judgement.* New York: The Free Press, 1970.

13.   Pamela A. Roby, "Politics and Criminal Law: Revision of the New York State Penal Law on Prostitution," *Social Problems,* Summer, 1969, pp. 83—109.

14.   William J. Chambliss and Robert B. Seidman, *Law, Order and Power.* Reading, Mass.: Addison-Wesley, 1971.

15.   Kai T. Erikson, *Wayward Puritans: A Study in the Sociology of Deviance.* New York: John Wiley and Co., 1966.

16.   *Ibid.* p. 4.

17.   *Ibid.* p. 67.

18.   *Ibid.* p. 59.

19.   *Ibid.* p. 71.

20.   *Ibid.* p. 118.

21.   *Ibid.* p. 121—122.

22.   Throughout the paper we rely on data from Ibadan and Seattle as a basis for discussing the patterns in both countries. This lead may disturb some, and if so, then the study may be considered as directly referring only to the two cities—with only a possible application more generally. From a variety of research studies and my own impressions, I am convinced that what is true of Ibadan and Seattle is only true of Nigeria and the United States, but whether or not this is the case should not affect the overall conclusions of this inquiry.

23.   Richard H. Nagasawa, *Delinquency and Non-Delinquency: A Study of Status Problems and Perceived Opportunity,* Unpublished M.A. thesis, Seattle: University of Washington, 1965. See also William J. Chambliss and Richard H. Nagasawa, "On the Validity of Official Statistics," *Journal of Research in Crime and Delinquency,* January, 1969, pp. 71—77.

24.   James Q. Spradley, *You Owe Yourself a Drunk.* Boston: Little Brown and Co., 1970, p. 128.

25.   Edwin H. Sutherland, *Criminology*. Philadelphia: J.P. Lippincott, 1924, p. 11.

26.   Alvin W. Gouldner, *The Coming Crisis in Western Sociology*. New York: Basic Books, 1970: Robert W. Frederichs, *A Sociology of Sociology*. New York: The Free Press, 1970. For a more personal discussion of paradigm revolution in science, see Thomas S. Kuhn, *The Structure of Scientific Revolutions* (2nd ed.). Chicago: University of Chicago Press, 1970.

Chapter 8

Law as a Weapon in Social Conflict*

Austin T. Turk†

Explicit or implicit in most research on law and society is the "moral functionalist" conception of law as essentially a means for settling or precluding disputes. The major limitations of this conception are that it (1) introduces cultural bias into research by defining away the disruptive and exploitive aspects of law, (2) tends to equate legal with consensual methods or processes of conflict management, which are presumed to be more effective than coercive ones, and (3) encourages research in which natural law and/or functional-systems assumptions are taken for granted. A superior alternative is the conception of law as power, *i.e.* a set of resources whose control and mobilization can in many ways—as indicated in a series of propositional statements—generate and exacerbate conflicts rather than resolving or softening them.

Despite persistent challenges by proponents of a wide range of alternative theoretical and ideological perspectives,[1] the most prevalent conception of law explicit or implicit in recent research

---

* Austin T. Turk, "Law as a Weapon in Social Conflict," *Social Problems* 23(3) (Feb., 1976): 276—291. Reprinted by permission of The Society for the Study of Social Problems and the author.

Substantially revised and expanded version of a working paper discussed at the annual meetings of the American Sociological Association, New York, 1973, and published in German translation by R. Hahn and W. Kaupen as "Recht als Waffe in sozialen Konflikt" in the newsletter of the section on sociology of law of the German Sociological Association (*Informationsbrief*, Nr. 3, February 1974).

For their comments and advice, seriously considered though not always followed, I am especially grateful to Ilene Bernstein, William Chambliss, Donald Cressey, Allen Grimshaw, Sheldon Stryker, and the participants in the discussion at the 1973 ASA meetings.
† Professor, University of Toronto.

213

on law and society is that articulated most notably in the works of Fuller (1964, 1971) and Selznick (1961, 1968, 1969) and prominent in such influential sourcebooks as Aubert (1969), Nader (1969), and Schwartz and Skolnick (1970). Law is characterized as essentially a means for settling or precluding disputes by (a) articulating the requirements of an idea of justice (expressed as prerequisites for sustained interaction and the viable organization of social life), and (b) restraining those whose actions are incompatible with such requirements. Accordingly, the presumptive aims of socio-legal research are to determine how legal concepts, institutions, and processes function in preventing, minimizing, or resolving conflicts; how such legal mechanisms emerge or are created; how they relate to complementary non-legal mechanisms; and how they can be made more effective.

Not to deny either that law often does contribute to conflict management or that the quest for a just and secure social order is honorable and necessary, the objectives in this paper are (1) to note certain fundamental limitations of what may be termed the moral functionalist conception of law; (2) to marshal arguments for a conception of law free of those limitations—i.e., the conception of law as a form or dimension of social power (as empirically more a partisan weapon in than a transcendent resolver of social conflicts); and (3) to formulate a set of basic empirical propositions about law and social conflict to which the power conception of law directs socio-legal research.

Law as Conflict Management

To *define* law as a means of conflict management is to leave theory and research on law and society without an analytical framework independent of particular ethical and theoretical preferences and aversions. While it may facilitate critiques of totalitarian or bureaupathic decisions and actions taken "in the name of law," such a definition appears at the same time to impede the development of an understanding of law in which evidence of its regulatory functions is integrated with evidence of its disruptive and exploitive uses and effects. Merely condemning the seamier side of law as perversions or departures from "the rule of law," and attributing them to human fallibility or wickedness, encourages neglect of the possibly systemic linkages between the "good" and "bad" features of law as it is empirically observed. Moreover, insofar as the moral functionalist conception of law has directly or by default encouraged such neglect, it has left socio-legal research vulnerable to charges of bias favoring certain culture-specific ideas and institutions, and helped to provoke the radical counter-assertion that exploitation and disruption constitute the defining reality of law while regulation is only illusion and suppression (see Lefcourt 1971; Zinn, 1971; Quinney, 1974).

A related difficulty with the moral functionalist conception of law is that *legal* means of conflict management tend to be equated with *peaceful* ones; and there is a strong inclination to assume that consensual, non-coercive methods are the only really effective ways of preventing or managing conflicts. The difficulties with such assumptions are exemplified in Barkun's (1968) volume appropriately entitled *Law Without Sanctions*. From his useful analysis of conflict management in segmentary lineage primitive societies and in international relations Barkun adduces evidence of the development of legal controls in the absence of any Weberian (or Austinian) enforcement staff. Instead of coercion, he finds the bases of legal control in these instances to be "consensus on procedures and on perceived mutual self-interest" (Barkun, 1968; 123)—a consensus produced by "the human craving for order" (160, and see 78-92) in conjunction with the human propensity to fix upon the features of initial dispute-settlements as conceptual and procedural models for handling subsequent conflicts (132).

Interaction experiences are by a process of social learning transformed into shared normative perceptual frames that constrain behavior by defining the availability and meaning of various behavioral alternatives. Rather than upon the social structuring of enforcement power, the binding impact of law is found to depend upon acceptance of the value of continued interaction and of the reality and usefulness of the normative framework, including procedural rules for determining the meaning and applicability of particular rules. Though the achievement of order by such means, as by any others, is assumed to be necessarily a matter of degree, Barkun concludes that the evidence does confirm the empirical possibility of non-coerced legal order.

Barkun is able to reach such a conclusion because he combines a severely restricted definition of coercion with a virtually unrestricted definition of law (*cf.* Pospisil, 1971: 41). Coercion is taken to mean only the most obvious exercise or threat of physical force by a central enforcement agency—thus excluding the many other direct and indirect ways social control for political purposes is effected. In contrast, apparently any behavioral or interactional pattern may be construed as a legal norm (especially where such patterns are reflected in linguistic conventions as "rules"); and any order or system of social interaction may be viewed as a legal order (especially where such an order is explicitly recognized and accepted as a constraining—though not necessarily determining— social reality). Thus, any continuing relation in the absence of a physically threatening formally instituted "umpire" becomes evidence for his thesis, as does any case in which sanctioning is accomplished by other means and agencies.

What Barkun does accomplish, admirably, is to demonstrate that law as a cultural, or ideological, structure can contribute greatly to the maintenance of social orders by providing perceptual guides for channeling and limiting disputes. He fails, however, to demonstrate that "law without sanctions" is possible except within the narrow bounds of his definitional assumptions. To the contrary, he himself observes repeatedly that such normative frameworks are very much subject to rejection and deterioration when the costs of acceptance become too high for a conflicting party. In addition, he makes it clear that such frameworks can in their creation and application be manipulated on behalf of partisan interests, noting especially manipulation by parties external to particular conflicts but interested in preserving the ordered context of the conflicts (i.e., the tribal, international, or other system). Given that social relationships are evidently quite vulnerable when sustained only by self-defined interests, and that the rules for defining and defending such interests are not immune to partisan manipulation, the more tenable conclusion to be drawn from Barkun's study is that "norms" (whether or not legal in some sense or other) are weak and unreliable conflict-regulators to the extent that they (a) rest only upon conventional understandings unsupported by any "teeth" in the event of serious misunderstanding, (b) reflect only the bargaining and maneuvering of current or potential adversaries, or (c) are not accompanied by the replacement or adequate modification of those social arrangements that generate conflicts.

At a more general theoretical level, the moral functionalist conception of law impedes efforts to approach the scientific ideal of unbiased inquiry by encouraging investigators to define their research problems in terms of theoretical models derived from "natural law" and/or "functional-systems" assumptions. First, the bias introduced by natural law philosophy, even though secularized (cf. Selznick, 1961), leaves researchers unable to deal convincingly (i.e., in strictly naturalistic and empirically demonstrable propositions) with the observation or view that any idea of justice is founded ultimately upon faith, not upon empirical criteria (Stone, 1965). Second, many crucial methodological and theoretical issues are not resolved but evaded to the extent that research begins with, instead of testing, the assumptions (a) that legal phenomena constitute a system, (b) that the system-referent is empirically obvious, or at least readily determined, and (c) that the system embodies the meritocratic or egalitarian prerequisities for social welfare. In particular, boundedness and the other assumptions of systems modeling are left unexamined, as are the conventional or traditional understandings of what are "legal things," while—despite the recognition of structured inequities in particular instances (e.g., Nonet, 1969)—there is no conceptual resolution of the issues raised by the fact that the prerequisites, however, defined, for the welfare or survival of *some* are not necessarily consistent with the prerequisites for the welfare or survival of *all*.

To summarize briefly, the major limitations of the moral functionalist conception of law for the purpose of socio-legal research are that it (1) introduces cultural bias into research by defining away the disruptive and exploitive aspects of law, (2) tends to equate legal with consensual methods or processes of conflict management, which are presumed to be more effective than coercive means, and (3) encourages research in which natural law and/or functional-systems assumptions are taken for granted. If research on law and society is to be even relatively unbiased by culturally, ethically, methodologically, and politically partisan asumptions, a more neutral and empirically-grounded conception of law is needed. The remainder of this paper is devoted to an attempt to develop such a conception.

Law as Power

It must be granted that people may use the language of norms and generally, more or less consciously, accept their constructions as binding in the absence of a centralized enforcement agency, or indeed of any reliable means of forcing conformity. However, as has already been observed, it is equally clear that they may come to believe that their interests are better served by violating the normative expectations of others. In this connection, the increasingly formal articulation of such expectations and the recognition or invention of the right to seek or attempt their enforcement (Hoebel, 1954; 28) implies the increasing inability of people to get along with one another solely on the basis of tacit or consensual understandings. Furthermore, the persistence and growth of law as a cultural (symbolic, perceptual) and social (interactional, relational) reality is at least a kind of evidence that people have not yet found that they can do without such formalization, whether by a return to primitivism or by attaining some new consensual plateau. The effort to develop an adequate conception of law must, therefore, begin by recognizing the centrality of diversity and conflict in social life wherever law— provisionally understood as the process of formally articulating normative expectations—is discernable.

Given that law is intimately linked with social diversity and conflict, the most parsimonious explanation of the linkage seems to be that people find they cannot trust strangers. As the scale and complexity of social relatedness increase, so does the diversity of human experiences. The more diverse the experiences people have had, the more diverse their perceptions and evaluations of behavioral and relational alternatives may be. The greater the diversity of perceptions and evaluations, the greater may be the variability in what is perceived as justice in the specific terms of everyday life. (The implied distinction is between "norms in action" versus whatever similarities might be found in terms either of a general belief in justice as an abstract value, or of verbal responses to hypothetical questioning regarding the substantive meanings and relative importance of various normative statements or labels.) Aware that others' ideas of justice may vary from their own, people try—in accord with their own ideas and interests as they understand them—to maintain or gain control of, or to contest or evade, the processes by which normative expectations come to be formally articulated and enforced across, rather than only within, the boundaries of culturally homogeneous groups (whether the salient boundaries be those of families, clans, tribes, nations, or other groupings).

The empirical reality of law—apparently well understood in practice if not in theory seems, then, to be that it is a set of resources for which people contend and with which they are better able to promote their own ideas and interests against others, given the necessity of working out and preserving accommodative relationships with strangers. To say that people seek to gain and use resources to secure their own ideas and interests is, of course, to say that they seek to have and exercise *power*. While the meaning of power is far from settled, a convenient starting point is to view power as the control of resources, and the exercise of power as their mobilization in an effort to increase the probability of acceptable resolutions of actual or potential conflicts.[2] Although it helps to recognize that "law is power," a more specific conceptualization of what *kinds* of resource control are possible is necessary if we are to arrive at a useful understanding of what the general proposition means. I see five kinds of resource control, all represented in the cultural and social structural reality of law. These are (1) control of the means of direct physical violence, *i.e.*, *war* or *police* power; (2) control of the production, allocation, and/or use of material resources, *i.e.*, *economic* power; (3) control of decision-making processes, *i.e.*, *political* power; (4) control of definitions of and access to knowledge, beliefs, values, *i.e.*, *ideological* power; and (5) control of human attention and living-time, *i.e.*, *diversionary* power.[3]

1. Having the law on one's side in a conflict implies that one can rightfully use or call upon others (allies, champions, or the authorities claiming jurisdiction over the area, people, or matters involved) to use violence to support one's claims against others. Modern polities are characterized by the presence and availability of control agencies specializing in the accretion, organization, and use of the means of violence, and asserting the principle that violence is—excepting more and more narrowly defined emergency situations—a resource reserved for official use only. Decisions by authorities, including decisions regarding the respective claims of disputing parties, are accompanied by the implied threat of

physical coercion should any of the affected parties refuse to act in accord with such decisions.

2. People's life chances are affected just as decisively by how much their economic power is enhanced or eroded by law. The invention and elaboration of property and tax laws, in particular, reflect and help implement decisions on (1) what kinds of activities, products, and people should be rewarded more and what kinds less, and (2) how great should be the range between maximum and minimum rewards. "Radicals" seek modifications of law so as to change the criteria for reward, and very often also to reduce the range of rewards; "liberals" seek modifications so as to insure at least a "decent" minimum in the range of rewards, and may accept—if they do not seek—some reduction in the range; "conservatives" resist modification, but may accept some "decent minimum." Though orderly (usually meaning limited and gradual) economic changes can be facilitated by law, economic decisions once articulated in and supported by law become postulates which further elaborations and even modifications of the law must satisfy. Radical economic changes, therefore, become increasingly difficult to effect by legal means because they require not legal reasoning to satisfy the postulates of a body of law, but rather a new set of postulates and thus a new body of law.

3. The formulae and procedures of legal decision-making are integral to the workings of politically organized societies. Organizational decisions are in significant ways influenced by and expressed through legal decisions. Most important, the law as culture and as social structure provides the rubric for articulating, interpreting, and implementing organizational norms and decisions. As a substantive and procedural model and as an ultimate support for institutional normative structures, the law contributes—as Selznick (1969) and many others have demon-strated—to private as well as public social ordering, and provides some of the weightiest criteria for assessing proposed changes and resolving internal as well as inter-organizational conflicts. While non-legal factors clearly affect political struggle in general and organizational decision-making in particular, the law—as the most authoritative record of events and as the definitive model, criterion, and arbiter of rightness—is itself a political resource of major importance.

4. Legal concepts and thought-ways develop in the course of pragmatic efforts by men to comprehend problems of social interaction so as to manage them—including the problematics of dominating the lives of other people. Though not in this regard different from other products of such efforts, law as culture has an especially strong impact upon the frames of reference people use to give meaning to their situations. Those definitions of the real, the true, and the worthy given legal expression or approval are thereby given the support of what is not only one of the most prestigious of cultural structures, but also that structure most

directly supported by the apparatus of political control. The reality or value of alternative conceptions can be denied either by simply denying recognition in law, or else more forcefully by explicitly rejecting them in ways ranging from the most extreme forms of suppression to the most subtle forms of rejection in practice conjoined with verbal acceptance or toleration. Censorship by omission or commission is nonetheless censorship. Yet, the greatest importance of law as an ideological resource probably lies not in the facts of deliberate or inadvertent intervention on behalf of some perceptual alternatives versus others, but in the fact that legalism is the cultural bedrock of political order. The very concept of legality is designed to promote adherence to the ground rules of conventional politics (Turk, 1972: 15-16)—which amount to agreement among contending parties on the supreme value of their common memership in a polity which must be preserved.

5. Human attention and living-time are finite resources—a trite but profoundly consequential observation. Insofar as the rhetoric and the real workings of law occupy men's attention and time to the exclusion of other phenomena—perhaps of greater import for the probability and quality of life—the law exerts diversionary power. As entrepreneurs of the news, publishing, advertising, and entertainment industries have long known, at least the more reassuring, titillating, or lurid aspects of law can in the name of "human interest" and "information" be presented to capture and hold the public's attention. Nor have the obviously close links between diversionary and ideological power been neglected. Preoccupation with the law, especially in its more attractive and innocuous aspects, not only diverts attention from potentially more dangerous concerns (from the perspective of authorities, de facto including loyal oppositions) but also reinforces the sense of law as an overwhelming, scarcely challengeable reality and criterion of reality.

The conception of law as a set of resources, as power, is methodologically superior to the conception of law as conflict regulator in that the relationship between law and conflict is not assumed, but left open for investigation, and the distinction between legal and non-legal phenomena is grounded in empirical observations rather than normative assumptions. Instead of asking *how* law regulates conflict, the investigator is encouraged to ask *whether* law regulates or generates conflict, or in what ways and in what degree the use of legal power does both. Instead of assuming that legal and non-legal actions and relations are somehow differentiated by criteria of moral legitimacy or functional necessity, the investigator asks whether and how the invocation of such criteria and the introduction of the distinction itself exemplify the control and mobilization of ideological and diversionary resources. Freed from arbitrary ideological and theoretical constraints, the investigator directly confronts the empirical realities that legal power can be used in ways inconsistent as well as consistent with normative criteria of legality, that the empirical relevance of such criteria is decided by the actions rather than the claims of those who wield legal power, and that the law—since it is necessarily promulgated, interpreted, implemented, or enforced by people with specific social and cultural involvements—can never really be neutral vis-a-vis social conflicts.

A particular advantage of the power conception of law is that it facilitates analysis of the *processes* (as distinct from particular structures) by which normative expectations are given "cross-group" as well as "intra-group" significance—i.e., how they become formally binding upon people who themselves have neither generated such norms nor been socialized as children to accept them. At the most general analytical level, the processes are those—stigmatization and other forms of manipulation—any group uses to achieve some behavioral and relational coherence despite the varying idiosyncracies of its members. Nonetheless, as one's attention shifts from the most ephemeral and least differentiated forms of group life to more durable and complex social entities, the processes come more sharply into focus as the distinction between legal and nonlegal emerges and acquires increasing social and cultural reality. The power conception of law suggests analysis of these processes in the specific empirical terms of how people actually deal with one another, regardless of any conventional understandings or rationales about the existence and significance of particular legal phenomena. Thus, socio-legal research is cast not in terms of the assumed concreteness or meaningfulness of the legal-nonlegal distinction, but in terms of the human actions creating the distinction, giving it empirical substance, and altering or erasing it.

Finally, the power conception of law gives socio-legal research a distinctive focus, related to but not confused with the general concerns of the social sciences with social order, conflict, and change. Instead of losing the legal-nonlegal distinction in the quest for knowledge useful in conflict management (as in Barkun's case), the distinction itself becomes in two ways the basis for defining research problems. First, the problematic status of the distinction implies the need for historical and anthropological studies to determine the specific conditions where it is introduced (and perhaps to suggest the conditions where it may be transcended) in social life.[4] Second, as the core task of socio-legal research is taken to be that of developing a predictively useful understanding of the control and mobilization of legal resources, the availability of such resources is necessarily presupposed. That is, scientifically meaningful research questions about law and society become possible only when the concept of law is empirically grounded by the differentiation of legal from other cultural and social phenomena in one or more of the following ways: (1) verbal articulation of a set, in some degree a sytem, of explicit norms; (2)

establishment of procedures for making, interpreting, implementing, and changing normative decisions; (3) occupational
specialization in knowing the substantive law and in using the
established procedures; (4) institution of explicit provisions for the
enforcement of substantive and procedural norms, by actual or
threatened deprivations; and (5) associated with any or all of the
other ways, the display of symbolic trappings designed to
emphasize the reality, rightness, and might of law.[5] Rather than
some kind of essence, property, or function to be sought in an
apparently unlimited variety of cultural and social configuration,
"law" thus becomes an empirically specifiable set of objects of
scientific attention.

In sum, in the power conception of law students of law and
society are offered a methodologically tenable definition of the
scope of their inquiry that includes it within the social scientific
enterprise without reifying, mystifying, or obscuring the legal-
nonlegal distinction. Given then the availability and amorality of
legal power, the formulation and testing of propositions about the
exercise of such power become central concerns for the scientific
study of law as it is, as distinquished from doctrinal or applied
research on behalf of law as someone believes it should or must
be.[6] Because of the availability of so much work on law as a
regulator and the relative paucity of work on law as a source and
means of conflict, there is a particular need for propositions about
ways in which law may generate or sharpen social conflicts.
Accordingly, an effort has been made to develop several
propositions indicating what seem to be the major ways law
promotes or facilitates conflict. To the extent that these and
related propositions are sustained and elaborated with greater
precision in further research, they are expected to constitute the
basis for a theory of law able to explain the conditions when and
how conflict management may be accomplished by the control and
mobilization of legal resources—i.e., a theory able to deal with
conflict management as a problematic outcome instead of a defining characteristic of law as a social and cultural phenomenon.

Propositions: Law and Social Conflict

1. The availability of legal resources is in itself an impetus to
social conflict, because conflicting or potentially conflicting parties
cannot risk the possible costs of not having the law—or at least
some law—on their side. When legal resources are not available or
are negligible, parties are forced or able to rely upon nonlegal
power to deal with the problematics of social interaction; law is
irrelevant except perhaps in the loose sense of a generally
recognized right of self-help for aggrieved parties able to assert it
(cf. Hoebel, 1954: 25-28). As law becomes available, it becomes

relevant as a contingency which must be met. It then becomes necessary to act so as to gain or increase control of legal resources, if only to neutralize them as weaponry an opponent might employ. The point is illustrated in the long effort by American southern whites to use the "white primary" and other ostensibly legal devices (Wirt, 1970: 56-71), supplemented by extralegal and illegal ones, to prevent blacks from using resources formally granted them by emancipation and subsequent legal enactments and decisions.

2. Given pressure to contend for control of legal resources, differential nonlegal power can be expected to result at least initially in corresponding differences in legal power. The party with greater legal as well as non-legal power may then be able to increase its edge over weaker parties, even to the extreme of excluding the weaker altogether from access to the legal arena, cutting him off from even the opportunity to advance his claims and defend his interests "legally." For instance, since the formation of the inegalitarian South African nation in 1910, the weaker nonwhites have had their legal position steadily eroded, losing between 1936 and 1955 even voting rights guaranteed by the "entrenched clauses" of the South Africa Act (May, 1955: 47-78; see also Sachs, 1973: 143-145 and passim)—South Africa's constitution until it was superseded by the Republic of South Africa Consititution Act, 1961.

3. Legal power provides both the opportunity and the means to accomplish the effective denial of the reality of conflicts by making it impossible or inordinately difficult for them to be articulated and managed—as amply demonstated in the long and stubborn effort to deny legal recognition and support for the effective unionization of agricultural laborers (McWilliams, 1942; Tangri, 1967; Galarza, 1970).

However, the persistent recurrence of struggles against economic, racial, and other forms of domination and exploitation make it clear that issues which cannot be couched in the language of law, or will not be accepted as actionable or justiciable, eventually have to be fought out in non-legal arena—where resolutions may be achieved, but often at greater cost and with less durability. It is, of course, true that the lack of appropriate legal mechanisms for managing some issues may result from unintended as well as intended actions. Nonetheless, even though the denial of access to law may be explicable in objective terms, "objective" denial appears to be just as real in its consequences as "subjective."

4. Where power differences are rather less extreme, the availability of legal resources may encourage litigiousness—a word indicative of the fact that the presence of law encourages its use by parties hoping to improve their positions by methods relatively less dangerous or costly than non-legal power struggles, especially with formidable opponents. Parties confronting more

powerful opponents may be encouraged to hope that by threatened or actual recourse to law they will be able to reduce, eliminate, or reverse initial power differences, or merely to extract some concession. For example, Nonet (1969: 81-83, 133-137) concluded that the New Deal turned law into an ally rather than an enemy of American trade unionism, so that the unions were encouraged to pursue a policy of self-help through legal advocacy instead of relying upon administrative procedures for handling workmen's compensation claims. On the other hand, stronger parties moving against weaker ones may find it advantageous to cloak their moves with legitimacy, especially to minimize the chance of third-party intervention on behalf of the underdog—as in the use of antitrust, conspiracy, right-to-work, and other laws to impede the development of effective labor unions (Blumrosen, 1962; Nonet, 1969: 81-83).

5. Apart from encouraging litigiousness, the availability of legal facilities decreases the pressure upon conflicting parties to resolve disputes in terms of the non-legal resources they can mobilize. Informal and private settlements, or at least accommodations to non-legal power differences (e.g., race relations "etiquette") seems less likely where the parties have the option or hope of legal recourse. Similarly, where an older legal system is giving way to a newer one, as in the Northern Rhodesian (Zambian) copperbelt, parties without recourse in the older system (e.g., young men protesting against the power of their wife's kin to intervene in marital and familial affairs) may be encouraged to appeal "to norms irreconcilably opposed to those of the traditional tribal system" (Epstein, 1958: 222).

6. Articulation in law of social categories, boundaries, and roles—with their associated rights and obligations—can sharpen old conflicts and produce new ones. Heightened awareness of the problematics of social interaction and relatedness can decrease the chances of resolving or avoiding conflicts, because "bringing things out into the open" frequently hardens existing boundaries, cleavages, and inequities (whether objectively or perceptually "real") by making it less easy to ignore, tacitly live with, or quietly and informally erase or change them. Rather than a transformation of conflict into a form more amenable to a reasonable resolution, legalization of a conflict can amount to an escalation that makes genuine settlement more difficult. Recognition of such possibilities has often been used for resisting the use of law as an instrument of social change—e.g., the views of some southern moderates, as well as conservatives, in the 1950's regarding the probable impact of the U.S. Supreme Court's desegregation decisions (Tumin and Rotberg, 1957).

7. Legal procedural norms are often used to exclude or distort information essential to an adequate comprehension of empirical problems, and thus can impede or prevent conflict resolution. In particular, legal distinctions between admissible and inadmissible

evidence tend to work against consideration of perceptual, or subjective factors—those perhaps not objectively important or recognizable by legal criteria but extremely important in terms of what is significant to some or all of the involved parties. European, especially Anglo-American, legal systems have frequently been critically contrasted with non-European systems (e.g., Epstein, 1958, 198-223; Gibbs, 1963; several of the selections in Nader, 1969) in which there are few if any restrictions upon what may be considered in determining the contextual significance of facts. These non-European systems emphasize the qualitative more than the formal aspects of what is seen as a continuing rather than an episodic relationship between the disputing parties. Similarly, though in a different vein, "bourgeois legalism" has been rejected by Marxists in favor of "socialist legality," where the emphasis is asserted to be (and in non-political cases normally is) upon the education of disputants and offenders to social awareness and responsibility (Berman, 1966: 277-384).

8. Legal formulae and processes tend to emphasize the limitation and cessation of overt conflict behavior, discouraging not only all-out battles of principle but even the recognition that at least some social conflicts are zero-sum, not variable-sum (e.g. czars vs. communists: white racists vs. black revolutionaries).[7] To a considerable extent, law is oriented to regulating the *symptoms* of conflict without getting at the more intractible problems of removing the *sources* of conflict. However tactical concern with symptoms may sometimes be dictated by a strategic concern to minimize political or other costs of dealing with those sources. Consider the frequently noted judicial preferences, supported by and expressed in such operating principles as *stare decisis* and *certiorari*, for carefully delimited case-specific issues rather than open confrontations over the political and economic premises of "the given order." Nonetheless, insofar as the legalization of conflicts does no more than limit the means of conflict and/or obfuscate the real issues, as in zero-sum struggles, some or all of the conflicting parties may come to view legalization as simply another device for out-positioning an opponent or for gaining time to mobilize or regroup one's non-legal forces—an attitude characteristic of both revolutionaries and counter-revolutionary police agents.

9. The tactics required to accomplish a legal settlement can conflict with those required to accomplish a genuine settlement. Where communication between disputants may be essential for them to become aware of common interests with priority over those at issue, communication may be precluded by the risk of disclosing injurious facts, violating rules against collusion, or otherwise weakening or contaminating the case at hand. The terminology and style of public legal conflict—as in verbal exchanges in legislative and judicial proceedings—may emphasize instead of correcting the affective and cognitive biases associated

with conflict. Obtaining formal, open concessions from opponents in the course of legal struggle can make it more difficult for them to back down or accept defeat, and can reduce the chances of building a fund of mutual trust with them as a way of making further conflicts more amenable to resolution. Such considerations appear to explain the reluctance of businessmen to conduct their transactions in strictly legalistic terms (Macaulay, 1963), as well as the opposition of many academics to the more explicit legalization of faculty-student relationships.

10. Legal decisions may prematurely signal the end of conflicts without actually resolving them. The processes of legal hearing, trial, and appeal often amount to rituals of dispute-settlement resulting in only illusory resolutions of conflicts, i.e., formal decisions that seem to settle disputes but do not do so on terms acceptable or even tolerable to the losers (and sometimes also the winners). Not only may dissatisfied parties be forced to seek redress by non-legal means in such present conflicts but the pretense of conflict resolution which they have experienced as the reality of law in action may make them far less willing to enter the legal arena in future conflicts. To the extent that law produces illusory instead of real conflict resolutions, it not only aggravates existing conflicts but also makes future conflicts more likely, and likely to be worse. Racial conflicts, for instance, have clearly not been resolved in South Africa by the legalization of a policy of racial separation—to be gradually accomplished during a "transitional" period of *dejure* white domination (Sachs, 1973), or in North America by the legalization of a policy of racial integration—to be gradually accomplished during a "transitional" period of overcoming *de facto* white domination "with all deliberate speed" (compare Blaustein and Ferguson, 1962, with Swett, 1969, Moore, 1971 and Balbus, 1973).

11. Insofar as legal culture is incongruent with the social-behavioral realities of legal power as exercised by authorities, the law itself promotes cynicism, evasion, and defiance with respect to normative expectations and decisions—even among its represen-tatives and practitioners (on lawyers, see Blumberg, 1967; on police, see Galliher, 1971). The law provides authorities with the cloak of claimed impartiality, a difficult claim impossible to live up to always and entirely. Apart from predispositions arising from their social origins, legal officials develop at least a partiality on behalf of their own organizational and career interests (Aubert, 1963) and routines for categorizing and handling cases with as little effort and risk as possible (Cicourel, 1968: 170-242).

Moreover, whether or not authorities try to be unbiased, the intent of the law can never be identical with the effect of the law as experienced. Even the most "understandable" differences between interpretation and interpretation, interpretation and action, or action and action, may not be "understandable" to affected parties who believe themselves—probably correctly—to be disadvantaged by the outcome. Credit, tenancy, welfare, and other laws affecting economic opportunities, privileges, and liabilities have often been shown to work systematically against the poor (Caplovitz, 1963; Carlin, Howard, and Messinger, 1966; tenBroek, 1966).

The crucial point is that bias is not just a matter of intention or even objective behavior, much less a matter only of due process under formal rules. Bias is also—and for the tasks of conflict regulation most important—a matter of perception and inference. Law *believed* to be biased may be just as ineffective, or worse, as law that *is* biased.

12. Legal changes that precipitate or facilitate non-legal social and cultural changes inevitably—barring the improbable case of unanimity on the meaning and desirability of the changes— sharpen and produce conflicts. As new law supersedes old, older ideas and interests may be shunted aside or demoted to lower priority ratings—as will be those people whose identifications and commitments are defined in terms of those ideas and interests. Nowhere is the fact of law as a party with its own interests to safeguard and enhance, potentially in conflict with others, more inescapable to people than when legal power serves to override, subvert, or simply reject their values and ways. Regardless of the possible long-run impact of legally promoted changes, the short-run impact will certainly be some contribution to increasing and exacerbating conflicts—most especially conflicts between legal authorities and at least some of those over whom authority is claimed. The degree of conflict resulting from legal changes will, of course, vary with the type of innovation, the social characteristics of those affected, and other factors (Zimring and Hawkins, 1971), from the relatively mild conflicts of conventional politics to the extreme conflicts resulting from legal intrusions into matters of sacred belief and practice—as in the Bolshevik attempt of the 1920's to impose sexual equality upon the largely Moslem peoples of Soviet Central Asia (Massell, 1968).

Conclusion

As many others have said in various ways, those engaged in socio-legal research must constantly question the assumptions so easily received from jurisprudence if the social science of law is to be more than a servant of established power, albeit a servant with critical intelligence. Socio-legal inquiry that assumes the goodness or badness of any set of cultural and social phenomena cannot be expected to produce valid and reliable knowledge of the full range of problematic relationships within that set and between that set and others.[8] It had been argued in this paper that the most prevalent conception of law orienting contemporary socio-legal research—the "moral fuctionalist" conception of law as in essence a means of conflict regulation—is in this and other respects demonstrably inadequate for the purposes of scientific research, however useful it may be for other purposes. A far more adequate alternative, it has been further argued, is the power conception of law, which recognizes in law a set of resources whose control and mobilization can in many ways—as indicated in a series of propositional statements—lead toward instead of away from conflicts. While the specifics undoubtedly need extension, elaboration, and qualification, the formulation offered here will have served its purpose if it stimulates socio-legal theorists and researchers to be more alert to the often subtle realities of power and conflict. In any case, there should be no quarrel over the fact that law may indeed contribute to conflict management—not least by its role in creating, sustaining, denying, and changing the perceptions and understandings by which people live.

NOTES

1.   Some recent formulations of historically familiar positions may be found in Black 1972, 1973; Chambliss and Seidman, 1971; Diamond, 1971; Gibbs, 1968; Pospisil, 1971; Quinney, 1974; Turk, 1969, 1972; and Wolff, 1971.

2.   "Control" means the availability or accessibility of resources, varying from the extremely limited access of the helpless, through the shared access of competitors or allies, to the exclusive access of the almighty. "Resource" means anything of biological or cultural significance for human welfare. The distinction here between controlling and mobilizing resources is analogous to that which Etzioni (1968: 314-317) makes between "assets" and "power." However, his concept of "power" is much more restricted, or truncated, in that it refers only to mobilization against resistance and excludes much of what is involved in the control and mobilization of symbolic resources. With rather unnecessary inconsistency, he defines "persuasive power" as "exercised through the manipulation of symbols" (358) after suggesting that "the assets from which power is generated are much more scarce than the symbols which are the main base of communication" (335) and arguing that "communication" can be substituted for "power" (336).

3.   My conscious indebtedness for terms and ideas used in this effort to sort out the forms and dimensions of power is mainly to Russell (1938), Schermerhorn (1961), and Gamson (1968).

4.   This formulation is intended to emphasize that the legal-nonlegal distinction is a problematic human invention rather than an inevitable product of some supra-human evolutionary process. Against any emergentist conception of "legal evolution" as an unavoidable and/or irreversible linear progression, the differentiation of legal from nonlegal phenomena is simply recognized as an historically specific accomplishment that has occurred, may occur, and may continue.

5.   The extent to which sequential or functional relationships may be found among these indicants of the five kinds or dimensions of legal power is an empirical question. Though not directly pertinent, the

mediation-courts-punishment-police-counsel cumulative scale order that seems to be emerging from the work of Schwartz and others (Schwartz and Miller, 1964; Wimberley, 1973; Baxi, 1974; Schwartz, 1974) suggests that some such relationships may well exist.

6.   While the distinction is essentially that proposed by Jerome Hall (1963: 42) between "normative" or "humanistic legal sociology" (which he approves) and "scientific legal sociology" or "legal science" (which he disapproves), there is no compelling reason to oppose these two kinds of inquiry to each other. The point is merely that for those whose primary aim is to develop scientific knowledge of law as a social and cultural phenomenon an appropriately objective conception of law is essential. For those with other primary objectives, the moral functionalist or some other "committed" conception may well be more useful.

7.   Whether or not all human conflicts are in principle transformable into variable-sum terms, and therefore resolvable by consensual means, it appears that in empirical, historically specific, rather than philosophical terms there are limits to the ability and willingness of people collectively to accomplish such transformations.

8.   In this connection, the social science of law can benefit from the history of criminology, blindered and retarded by just such assumptions. Only as criminological research has become informed by larger and more neutral perspectives on social organization and human behavior has it been able to move toward becoming even a useful servant.

REFERENCES

Aubert, Vilhelm, "Competition and Dissensus: Two Types of Conflict Resolution," *Journal of Conflict Resolution* 7 (1963): 26-42.

_____, (ed.), *Sociology of Law*. Baltimore: Penquin Books, 1969.

Balbus, Isaac D., *The Dialectics of Legal Repression: Black Rebels before the American Criminal Courts*. New York: Russell Sage Foundation, 1973.

Barkun, Michael, *Law Without Sanctions*. New Haven: Yale University Press, 1968.

Baxi, Upendra, "Comment-Durkheim and Legal Evolution: Some Problems of Disproof," *Law & Society Review* 8 (Summer, 1974): 645-651.

Berman, Harold J., *Justice in the U.S.S.R.: An Interpretation of Soviet Law*. Cambridge: Harvard University Press, 1966.

Black, Donald J., "The Boundaries of Legal Sociology," *Yale Law Journal* 81 (May, 1972): 1086-1100.

_____, "The Mobilization of Law," *Journal of Legal Studies* 2 (Jan. 1973): 125-149.

Blaustein, Albert P. and Ferguson, Clarence C., Jr., *Desegregation and the Law: The Meaning and Effect of the School Segregation Cases*. New York: Vintage Books, 1962.

Blumberg, Abraham S. "The Practice of Law as a Confidence Game: Organizational Cooptation of a Profession." *Law & Society Review* 1 (June, 1967): 15-39.

Blumrosen, Alfred W., "Legal Process and Labor Law: Some Observations on the Relation between Law and Sociology," in William M. Evan (ed.), *Law and Sociology*. New York: Free Press of Glencoe, 1962, pp. 185-225.

Caplovitz, David, *The Poor Pay More*. New York: The Free Press, 1963.

Carlin, Jerome E., Howard, Jan, and Messinger, Sheldon L., "Civil Justice and the Poor: Issues for Sociological Research," *Law & Society Review* 1 (Nov. 1966): 9-89.

Chambliss, William J. and Seidman, Robert B., *Law, Order and Power*. Reading, Mass.: Addison-Wesley, 1971.

Cicourel, Aaron V., *The Social Organization of Juvenile Justice*. New York: Wiley, 1968.

Diamond, Stanley, "The Rule of Law Versus the Order of Custom," in Robert P. Wolff (ed.), *The Rule of Law*. New York: Simon and Schuster, 1971, pp. 115-144.

Epstein, A.L., *Politics in an Urban African Community*. Manchester: Manchester University Press, 1958.

Etzioni, Amitai, *The Active Society*. New York: Free Press, 1968.

Fuller, Lon. L., *The Morality of Law*. New Haven: Yale University Press, 1964.

_____, "Human Interaction and the Law," in Robert P. Wolff (ed.), *The Rule of Law*. New York: Simon and Schuster, 1971, pp. 171-217.

Galarza, Ernesto, *Spiders in the House and Workers in the Field*. South Bend: University of Notre Dame Press, 1970.

Galliher, John F., "Explanations of Police Behavior: A Critical Review and Analysis," *Sociological Quarterly* 12 (Summer, 1971): 308-318.

Gamson, William A., *Power and Discontent*. Homewood, Ill.: Dorsey, 1968.

Gibbs, James L., Jr., "The Kpelle Moot: A Therapeutic Model for the Informal Settlement of Disputes," *Africa* 33 (1963): 1-11.

Hall, Jerome, *Comparative Law and Social Theory*. Baton Rogue: Louisiana State University Press, 1963.

Hoebel, E.A., *The Law of Primitive Man*. Cambridge: Harvard University Press, 1954.

Lefcourt, Robert (ed.), *Law Against the People*. New York: Vintage Books, 1971.

Macaulay, Stewart, "Non-contractual Relations in Business: A Preliminary Study." *American Sociological Review* 28 (Feb. 1963): 55-67.

Massell, Gregory J. "Law as an Instrument of Revolutionary Change in a Traditional Milieu: The Case of Soviet Central Asia," *Law & Society Review* 28 (Feb. 1963): 55-67.

May, Henry J., *The South African Constitution* (3rd ed.). Cape Town: Juta, 1955.

McWilliams, Carey. *Ill Fares the Land: Migrants and Migratory Labor in the United States*. Boston: Little, Brown, 1942.

Moore, Howard, Jr., "*Brown v. Board of Education:* The Court's Relationship to Black Liberation," in Robert Lefcourt (ed.), *Law Against the People.* New York: Vintage Books, 1971, pp. 55-64.

Nader, Laura (ed.), *Law in Culture and Society.* Chicago: Aldine, 1969.

Nonet, Philippe, *Administrative Justice: Advocacy and Change in a Government Agency.* New York: Russell Sage Foundation, 1969.

Pospisil, Leopold, *Anthropology of Law: A Comparative Theory.* New York: Harper and Row, 1971.

Quinney, Richard. *Critique of Legal Order.* Boston: Little, Brown, 1974.

Russell, Bertrand, *Power: A New Social Analysis.* London: Allen and Unwin, 1938.

Sachs, Albie, *Justice in South Africa.* Berkeley: University of California Press, 1973.

Schermerhorn, Richard A., *Society and Power.* New York: Random House, 1961.

Schwartz, Richard D., "Legal Evolution and the Durkheim Hypothesis: A Reply to Professor Baxi," *Law & Society Review* 8 (Summer, 1974): 653-668.

Schwartz, Richard D. and Miller, James C., "Legal Evolution and Societal Complexity," *American Journal of Sociology* 70 (Sept. 1964): 159-169.

Schwartz, Richard D. and Skolnick, Jerome H. (eds.), *Society and the Legal Order.* New York: Basic Books, 1970.

Selznick, Philip, "Sociology and Natural Law," *Natural Law Forum* 6 (1961): 84-108.

_____, "The Sociology of Law" in David L. Sills (ed.), *International Encyclopedia of the Social Sciences,* vol. 9. New York: Macmillan and The Free Press, 1968, pp. 50-59.

_____, *Law, Society, and Industrial Justice.* New York: Russell Sage Foundation, 1969.

Stone, Julius, *Human Law and Human Justice.* Stanford: Stanford University Press, 1965.

Swett, Daniel H., "Cultural Bias in the American Legal System," *Law & Society Review* 4 (Aug. 1969): 79-110.

Tangri, Beverly S., *Federal Legislation as an Expression of United States Public Policy Toward Agricultural Labor, 1914-1954.* Berkely: University of California, unpublished Ph. D. dissertation, 1967.

tenBroek, Jacobus (ed.), *The Law of the Poor.* San Francisco: Chandler, 1966.

Tumin, Melvin M. and Rotberg, Robert, "Leaders, the Led, and the Law: A Case Study in Social Change." *Public Opinion Quarterly* 21 (Fall, 1957): 355-370.

Turk, Austin, T., *Criminality and Legal Order.* Chicago: Rand McNally, 1969.

————, *Legal Sanctioning and Social Control.* Washington, D.C.: Supt. of Docs., U.S. Government Printing Office, DHEW Pub. No. (HSM) 72-9130, 1972.

Wimberley, Howard, "Legal Evolution: One Further Step." *American Journal of Sociology* 79 (July, 1973): 78-83.

Wirt, Frederick M., *Politics of Southern Equality: Law and Social Change in a Mississippi County.* Chicago: Aldine, 1970.

Wolff, Robert P. (ed.), *The Rule of Law.* New York: Simon and Schuster, 1971.

Zimring, Franklin, and Hawkins, Gordon, "The Legal Threat as an Instrument of Social Change," *Journal of Social Issues* 27 (2) (1971): 33-48.

Zinn, Howard, "The Conspiracy of Law," in Robert P. Wolff (ed.), *The Rule of Law.* New York: Simon and Schuster, 1971, pp. 15-36.

PART FOUR

LAW AND SOCIO-POLITICAL STRUCTURE

The fact that law as we know it is basically a political phenomenon is often lost in a dominant ideology which emphasizes its apolitical nature. The trite observation that "law is the formal cause of crime" suggests that we need to analyze the emergence of law in order to understand its contemporary ramifications. Contrary to the popular ideology, law is a relatively recent phenomenon in man's history, with other means of dispute resolution evident throughout history.[1] The emergence of the nation-state and subsequent ideological variations (e.g., capitalism, socialism, communism) provide dramatic examples of the relationship between legal form and content and socio-political structure. The following articles present both historical and contemporary examples of this relationship.

Diamond

In the first article, Diamond illustrates through historical analysis that the relation between custom and law is basically one of contradiction, not continuity.

As Chambliss noted in the previous section, the functionalist approach views the cause of law as the codification of custom. However, it appears this may be quite the opposite since custom is spontaneous and automatic and law is the product of organized force. Law is the basis of the politically organized state while custom is the modality of primitive society.[2]

Through a number of historical examples, Diamond shows how political society creates the disaffiliated and alienated person. In intermediate societies he finds the beginning of civil law based upon the interrelated census-tax-conscription system. Thus, law arose in support of bureaucracy and the sovereign.

Laws against suicide epitomize the alienation of man since he is the property of the state and has no right to take his life. Thus, the state is evidence of the divisiveness and conflict in society and law is the antonym and not the synonym of order. Diamond believes our last line of defense against the totalitarianism of the state is procedure e.g., due process.

Tiruchelvam

In "The Ideology of Popular Justice", Tiruchelvam discusses the deprofessionalization of the administration of justice in certain socialist societies in an attempt to find the causes of such change.[3] He divides the countries into three categories (1) Soviet Union, Poland, Cuba, and Chile; (2) Tanzania, India and Burma; and (3) People's Republic of China. After noting limitations in his analysis, he proceeds to discuss each group of countries.[4]

A number of factors emerged which seem to account for the emergence of popular tribunals. In all of the societies an alien or domestic regime was replaced through revolution or reform. Also, most of these societies are committed to a social and economic program radically different from the previous regimes. Therefore, popular justice is an extension of the new ideology to the judicial sphere and, thus, a rejection of the inherited legal system.

While there were variations in the degree of repudiation of previous governments and their legal systems, they all tend to approach the nature of law, organization of legal institutions, the role of law professionals, and the nature of legal thought in a fundamentally different way. Therefore, as Diamond notes in the previous article, the state largely determines the legal system, not the legal system the state. The relationship between socio-political structure and the law is most dramatically evident in the above cases.

Pepinsky

A specific comparison of the legal and socio-political systems of the People's Republic of China and the United States is provided in the next article. The contrasts between these two nation states are striking.[5] While in the United States (as in most other Western capitalist nations), the use of formal written law and attorneys abounds, the People's Republic of China has practically no reliance on formal written law or attorneys. Pepinsky suggests that the degree of reliance on formal written law is related to the freedom of citizen's actions and ultimately to the socio-political nature of society.

He notes that individual freedom of social mobility (geographic, occupational, marital) is much greater in the United States, while in the People' Republic stability (geographically, occupationally and maritally) is emphasized. For example, divorce is relatively easily obtained in the United States while in the People's Republic reconciliation and persuasion are emphasized in attempts to avoid dissolution. Resolution of conflicts is much more of a responsibility to the Chinese citizen. Thus, one knows one's neighbours and neighborhoods and intervenes to resolve conflicts rather than calling upon an agent of the state e.g., policeman, school official, etc.

The freedoms more typical for the Chinese are collective (thus individual) improvements in their life situation. The five guarantees of enough food, clothes, fuel, an honourable funeral and education are provided. Furthermore, freedoms offered by a social system geared to collective accomplishment rather than individual social mobility are evident in less reliance on (thus control of) state agents.

Pepinsky notes that official pronouncements in the People's Republic of China prescribe how individual conduct is to be decided upon within community groups, not what each individual's conduct shall be. The written law of the United States prescribes what conduct is required by individuals. Thus, in the United States decisions about individual behavior are taken out of the hands of individuals, while in the People's Republic individuals are given the responsibility to make such decisions.

He concludes that use of formal written law preserves a certain type of social order, and plays a role in establishing or maintaining one form of individual freedom at the expense or enjoyment of another form.

Christie

The increased reliance on formal written law and legal professionals has taken conflict away from the participants. In our urbanized, industrialized, professionalized society, conflicts are too few for the citizen, according to Christie. He uses an example from Tanzania to point out how conflict is dealt with in an informal, personal way with the disputants the major participants. Professionals, particularly lawyers, have "stolen" conflicts from the participants and established them as their property.

Conflicts are also stolen due to the basic social structural arrangements of society. Segmentation in terms of space (e.g., mobility) and castebase (e.g., sex, age, colour) leads to a de-personalization of social life, premature destruction of conflicts, and a masking of conflicts.

Christie proposes a model of neighborhood courts which are victim-oriented and lay-oriented. Thus, de-professionalization is a basic requisite for his model. However, as he notes, professionalism and professionalization is increasing. More importantly, the basic nature of our socio-political life (as noted by Pepinsky) suggest such modifications will be difficult without more substantial social change.

Pepinsky

While somewhat similar to Christie's attempt to wed traditional Anglo-Saxon procedure with a more "populist" style of justice, Pepinsky does this with reference to bureaucracies. After describing two models of social control—due process and anarchist-communist—he discusses their respective contributions to new types of social control strategies in the American context. These, according to the author, show promise of facilitating reason and understanding as the basis of social control.

Conclusion

All the authors in this section have identified important issues in the study of law and society. Diamond critically assessed the assumption that law is merely the codification of custom while Tiruchelvam describes the emergence of "popular justice" in several nations and explains its origins. An excellent comparison law in the People's Republic and the United States is provided by Pepinsky. Christie's notion of conflict as property addresses the significant issue of professionalization, while his proposed changes suggest an alternative approach to conflict resolution. In the last article, Pepinsky attempts to combine the best features of two different models of social control. The efforts by the above writers are provocative and hopefully will stimulate further critical thought and action.

NOTES

1.   For extended discussions of "primitive" methods of dispute resolution see Laura Nader (ed.) *Law in Culture and Society*. Chicago: Aldine Publishing Company, 1969; William J. Chambliss and Robert B. Seidman, *Law, Order, and Power*. Reading, Massachusetts: Addison-Wesley Publishing Company, 1977, pp. 1-74; Jan N. Sutherland and Michael S. Werthman (eds.), *Comparative Concepts of Law and Order*. Glenview: Scott, Foresman and Company, 1971.

2.   For an excellent discussion of the emergence of the nation-state and notions of law, crime and punishment, see Mark C. Kennedy, "Beyond Incrimination" *Catalyst* 6 (Summer, 1970): 1-37.

3.   For a more general discussion of socialist law see Rene David and John E.C. Brierley, *Major Legal Systems in the World Today*. New York: Stevens and Sons, 1968.

4.   It should be noted that his discussion of Chile is based upon materials written during the early stages of Allende's government and, thus, prior to his assassination.

5.   For other discussions of Chinese law see Derk Boodle, "Age, Youth, and Infirmity in the Law of Ching China", *University of Pennsylvania Law Review* 121 (1973): 437-470; William C. Jones, "A Possible Model for the Criminal Trial in the People's Republic of China", *The American Journal of Comparative Law* 24 (1973): 229-245; Alice Erch-Soon Tay, "Law in Communist China, Part I and II," *The Sydney Law Review* 6 (1969): 153-172, 335-370; and the journal *Chinese Law and Government*.

Chapter 9

The Rule of Law Versus the
Order of Custom*

Stanley Diamond

Creon: Knowest thou the edict has forbidden this?
Antigone: I knew it well. Why not? It was proclaimed.
Creon: But thou didst dare to violate the law?
Antigone: It was not God above who framed that law,
            Nor justice, whispering from the underworld,
            Nor deemed I thy decrees were of such force
            As to o'er ride the sanctities of heaven;
            Which are not of today or yesterday.
            From whom—whence they first issued, no one knows.
            I was not like to scant their holy rites
            And brave the even justice of the gods
            For fear of someone's edict.
                                            (Sophocles, *Antigone*)

The lowest police employee of the civilized state has more "authority" than all
the organs of gentilism combined. But the mightiest prince and the greatest
statesman or general of civilization may look with envy on the spontaneous
and undisputed esteem that was the privilege of the least gentile sachem. The
one stands in the middle of society, the other is forced to assume a position
outside and above it.
                                    (Friedrich Engels, *Origin of the
                                    Family, Private Property and the State*)

There's too much due process of law. The electric chair is a cheap crime
deterrent to show these criminal elements that law and order is going to
triumph.
                                    (Detective Sergeant John Heffernan,
                                    current vice-president of the
                                    International Conference of Police
                                    Associations and head of the
                                    New Jersey State Police Benevolent
                                    Association)

---

* Stanley Diamond, "The Rule of Law Versus the Order of Custom," *Social
Research* 38 (Spring, 1971): 42-72. Reprinted by permission of *Social Research*.
This article, in slightly different form, appears in *The Rule of Law*, Robert Paul
Wolff, ed., New York: Simon & Schuster.

I

We must distinguish the rule of law from the authority of custom. In a recent effort to do so (which I shall critically examine because it is so typical), Paul Bohannan, under the *imprimatur* of the *International Encyclopedia of the Social Sciences*,[1] contends that laws result from "double" institutionalization. He means by this no more than the lending of a specific force, a cutting edge, to the functioning of "customary" institutions: marriage, the family, religion. But, he tells us, the laws so emerging assume a character and dynamic of their own. They form a structured, legal dimension of society; they do not merely reflect, but interact with given institutions. Therefore, Bohannan is led to maintain that laws are typically out of phase with society and it is this process which is both a symptom and cause of social change. The laws of marriage, to illustrate Bohannan's argument with the sort of concrete example his definition lacks, are not synonymous with the institution of marriage. They reinforce certain rights and obligations while neglecting others. Moreover, they subject partners defined as truant to intervention by an external, impersonal agency whose decisions are sanctioned by the power of the police.

Bohannan's sociological construction does have the virtue of denying the primacy of the legal order, and of implying that law is generic to unstable (or progressive) societies, but it is more or less typical of abstract efforts to define the eternal essence of the law and it begs the significant questions. Law has no such essence but a definable historical nature.

Thus if we inquire into the structure of the contemporary institutions which, according to Bohannan, stand in a primary relation to the law, we find that their customary content has drastically diminished. Paul Radin made the point as follows:

> A custom is, in no sense, a part of our properly functioning culture. It belongs definitely to the past. At best, it is moribund. But customs are an integral part of the life of primitive peoples. There is no compulsive submission to them. They are not followed because the weight of tradition overwhelms a man . . . a custom is obeyed there because it is intimately intertwined with a vast living network of interrelations, arranged in a meticulous and ordered manner.[2]

And, "What is significant in this connection," as J.G. Peristiany indicates, "is not that common values should exist, but that they should be expressed although no common political organization corresponds to them."[3]

No contemporary institution functions with the kind of autonomy that permits us to postulate a significant dialectic between law and custom. We live in a law-ridden society; law has cannibalized the institutions which it presumably reinforces or with which it interacts.

Accordingly, morality continues to be reduced to or confused with legality. In civil society we are encouraged to assume that legal behavior is the measure of moral behavior, and it is a matter of some interest that a former Chief Justice of the Supreme Court proposed, with the best of intentions, that a federal agency be established in order to advise government employees and those doing business with the government concerning the legal propriety of their behavior. Any conflict of interest not legally enjoined would thus tend to become socially or morally acceptable; morality becomes a technical question. Efforts to legislate conscience by an external political power are the antithesis of custom: customary behavior comprises precisely those aspects of social behavior which are traditional, moral, and religious, which are, in short, conventional and non-legal. Put another way, custom *is* social morality.[4] The relation between custom and law is, basically, one of contradiction not continuity.

The customary and the legal orders are historically, not logically related. They touch coincidentally; one does not imply the other. Custom, as most anthropologists agree, is characteristic of primitive society, and laws of civilization. Robert Redfield's dichotomy between the primitive "moral" order and the civilized "legal" or "technical" order remains a classic statement of the case.

William Seagle writes,

> The dispute, whether primitive societies have law or custom, is not merely a dispute over words. Only confusion can result from treating them as interchangeable phenomena. If custom is spontaneous and automatic, law is the product of organized force. Reciprocity is in force in civilized communities too but at least nobody confuses social with formal legal relationships.[5]

Parenthetically, one should note that students of primitive society who use the term "customary law" blur the issue semantically, but nonetheless recognize the distinction.

It is this overall legalization of behavior in modern society which Bohannan fails to interpret. In fascist Germany, for example, laws flourished as never before. By 1941, more edicts had been proclaimed than in all the years of the Republic and the Third Reich [sic]. At the same time, ignorance of the law inevitably increased. In a sense, the very force of the law depends upon ignorance of its specifications, which is hardly recognized as a mitigating circumstance. As Seagle states, law is not definite and certain while custom is vague and uncertain. Rather, the converse holds. Customary rules must be clearly known; they are not sanctioned by organized political force, hence serious disputes about the nature of custom would destroy the integrity of society. But laws may always be invented, and stand a good chance of being enforced: "Thus, the sanction is far more important than the rule in the legal system . . . but the tendency is to minimize the sanction and to admire the rule."[6]

In fascist Germany, customs did not become laws through a

process of "double institutionalization." Rather, repressive laws, conjured up in the interests of the Nazi Party and its supporters, cannibalized the institutions of German society. Even the residual customary authority of the family was assaulted: children were encouraged to become police informers, upholding the laws against their kin. "The absolute reign of law has often been synonymous with the absolute reign of lawlessness."[7]

Certainly, Germany under Hitler was a changing society, if hardly a progressive one, but it was a special case of the general process in civilization through which the organs of the state have become increasingly irresistible. It will be recalled that Bohannan takes the domination of law over custom to be symptomatic of changing societies. But the historical inadequacy of his argument lies exactly here: he does not intimate the overall direction of that change and therefore fails to clarify the actual relation between custom and law. Accordingly, the notion that social change is a function of the law, and vice versa, implies a dialectic that is out of phase with historical reality.

Plato, it deserves note, understood this well enough when he conceived the problem of civilization as primarily one of injustice, which he did not scamp by legalistic definition. His remedy was the thorough restructuring of society. Whether we admire his utopia or not, *The Republic* testifies to Plato's recognition that laws follow social change and reflect prevailing social relationship, but are the cause of neither. Curiously, this view of the relationship between law and society accords with the Marxist perspective on the history of culture. Customary societies are said to precede legal societies, an idea which, semantics aside, most students of historical jurisprudence would accept. But Marxists envision the future as being without laws as we know them, as involving a return to custom, so to speak, on a higher level, since the repressive, punitive and profiteering functions of law will become superfluous. Conflicts of economic and political interest will be resolved through the equitable reordering of institutions. Law, for the Marxists and most classical students of historical jurisprudence, is the cutting edge of the state—but the former, insisting on both a historical and normative view of man, define the state as the instrument of the ruling class, anticipating its dissolution with the abolition of classes and the common ownership of the basic means of production. Whatever our view of the ultimate Marxist dynamic, law is clearly inseparable from the state. Sir Henry Maine equates the history of individual property with that of civilization:

> Nobody is at liberty to attack several property and to say at the same time he values civilization. The history of the two cannot be disentangled. Civilization is nothing more than the name for the . . . order . . . dissolved but perpetually re-constituting itself under a vast variety of solvent influences, of which infinitely the most powerful have been those which have, slowly, and in some parts of the world

much less perfectly than others, substituted several property for collective ownership.[8]

In the words of Jeremy Bentham, "Property and law are born together and die together."

Law, thus, is symptomatic of the emergence of the state; the legal sanction is not simply the cutting edge of institutions at all times and in all places. The "double institutionalization" to which Bohannan refers needs redefinition. Where it does occur, it is an historical process of unusual complexity and cannot be defined as the simple passage of custom into law. It occurs, as we shall see, in several modes. Custom—spontaneous, traditional, personal, commonly known, corporate, relatively unchanging—is the modality of primitive society; law is the instrument of civilization, of politcal society sanctioned by organized force, presumably above society at large, and buttressing a new set of social interests. Law and custom both involve the regulation of behavior but their characters are entirely distinct; no evolutionary balance has been struck between developing law and custom, whether traditional or emergent.

II

The simple dichotomy between society and civilization does not illustrate the passage from the customary to the legal order. The most critical and revealing period in the evolution of law is that of *archaic societies*, the local segments of which are the cultures most often studied by anthropologists. More precisely, the earlier phases of these societies, which I call proto-states, represent a transition from the primitive kinship-based communities to the class-structured polity. In such polities, law and custom exist side by side; this gives us the opportunity to examine their connections, distinctions, and differential relationship to the society at large. The customary behavior typical of the local groups—joint families, clans, villages—maintains most of its force; the Vietnamese, for example, still say: "The customs of the village are stronger than the law of the emperor." Simultaneously, the civil power, comprising bureaucracy and sovereign, the dominant emerging class, issues a series of edicts that have the double purpose of confiscating "surplus" goods and labor for the support of those not directly engaged in production while attempting to deflect the loyalties of the local groups to the center.

These archaic societies are the great historical watershed; it is here that Sir Henry Maine and Paul Vinogradoff located the passage from status to contract, from the kinship to the territorial principle, from extended familial controls to public law. One need not be concerned with the important distinctions among archaic societies, or with the precise language or emphases of those

scholars who have recognized their centrality for our understanding of the law. The significant point is that they are
transitional. Particularly in their early phase they are the agencies
that transmute customary forms of order into legal sanction. Here
we find a form of "double institutionalization" functioning
explicitly; we can witness, so to speak, what appears to be the
emergence of a custom, in defense of the kinship principle against
the assault of the state, and the subsequent shift of the customary
function into its own opposite as a legal function. The following
example from the archaic proto-state of Dahomey, prior to the
French conquest in 1892, will make this process clear.

   Traditionally, in Dahomey each person was said to have three
"best" friends, in descending order of intimacy and importance.
This transitional institution, a transfiguration of kin connections,
of the same species as blood brotherhood, reinforced the extended
family structure, which continued to exist in the early state, but
was being thrown into question as a result of the political and
economic demands made by the emerging civil power. So, for
example, the best friend of a joint-family patriarch would serve as
his testator, and, upon the latter's decease, name his successor to
the assembled family. It seems that the ordinary convention of
succession no longer sufficed to secure the family's integrity, since
the central authority was mustering family heads as indirect
rulers. In this instance, the institution of friendship was
assimilated to the form and purpose of customary behavior. On the
other hand, the best friend of a man charged with a civil "crime"
could be seized by the king's police in his stead. However, these
traditional friendships were so socially critical, so deeply held that
the person charged, whether or not he had actually committed a
civil breach, would typically turn himself in rather than implicate
a friend in his punishment. The custom of friendship was thus
given a legal edge and converted by the civil power into a means
of enforcing its will. This example of "double institutionalization"
has the virtue of explicitly revealing the contradiction between
law and custom; but there are others in which law appears as a
reinforcement of customary procedure.

   In eleventh century Russia, for instance, Article 1 of the
codified law states,

> If a man kills a man . . . the brother is to avenge his brother; the son,
> his father; or the father, his son; and the son of the brother (of the
> murdered man) or the son of his sister, their respective uncle. If there
> is no avenger (the murderer) pays 40 grivna wergeld . . .[9]

Similarly, circa A.D. 700, the law of the Visigoths states,

> Whoever shall have killed a man, whether he committed a homicide
> intending to or not intending to (volens aut nolens) . . . let him be
> handed over into the potestas of the parents or next of kin of the
> deceased . . . .[10]

In these instances, a custom has been codified by an external agency, thus assuming legal force with *its punitive character sharpened.* Such confirmation is both the *intimation* of legal control and the antecedent of institutional change beyond the wish or conception of the family. "Whatever princes do, they seem to command," or, as Sir Henry Maine put it, "What the sovereign permits, he commands."[11] Maine had specifically in mind,

> . . . the Sikh despot who permitted heads of households and village elders to prescribe rules, therefore these rules became his command and true laws, which are the solvent of local and domestic usage.

Simpson and Stone explain this apparent reinforcement of custom by the civil power as follows:

> Turning then to the role of law in the emergent political society . . . it is true that political institutions, independent of the kin and the supernatural, had risen to power; yet these institutions were young, weak and untried. Their encroachment on the old allegiance was perforce wary and hesitating. Social cohesion still seemed based on nonpolitical elements, and these elements were therefore protected. It is this society which Pound has perceived and expressed when he says that the end of law envisaged in his period of strict law, is the maintenance of the social *status quo.* In modern terminology this means the primacy of the interest in the maintenance of antecedent social institutions. (italics added)[12]

This sort of confirmation, which betrays the structural opportunism of the early civil power, inheres in the limitations of sovereignty, and is further apparent in the sovereign's relation to the communally held clan or joint-family land. In Dahomey, for example, where the king was said to "own" all property, including land, it is plain that such ownership was a legal fiction and had the effect of validating the pre-existent joint-family tradition. That is, the king "permitted" the joint families, by virtue of his fictional ownership, to expand into new lands and continue transmitting their property intact, generation after generation. The civil power could not rent, alienate or sell joint-family property, nor could any member of a joint family do so.[13] This is borne out by A.I. Richards, who informs us that

> in Northern Rhodesia (Zambia) the statement that 'all the land is mine' does not mean that the ruler has the right to take any piece of land he chooses for his own use . . . I have never heard of a case where a chief took land that had already been occupied by a commoner.[14]

The same point is made by Rattray on the Ashanti[15] and Mair on the Baganda,[16] among others. Civil validation, then, expresses the intention but not yet the reality of state control. We might more realistically formulate Maine's epigram as: What he cannot command, the sovereign permits.

Ultimately, local groups have maintained their autonomy when their traditional economies were indispensable to the functioning of the entire society. They could be hedged around by restrictions, harassed by law, or, as we have seen, they could be "legally" confirmed in their customary usage; but, so long as the central power depended on them for support, in the absence of any alternative mode or source of production, their integrity could be substantially preserved. This certainly seems the case during the early phases of state organization in the classic nuclear areas (e.g., Egypt, Babylonia, Northern India) before the introduction of large-scale irrigation and analogous public works, and it was true of precolonial Africa. But in all archaic societies, whether incipient, as in sub-Saharan Africa, florescent, as in the ancient peasant societies of the Middle East or China, or in cognate contemporary societies which probably still embrace most of the world's population, the extensive kin unit was more functional, in spite of varying degrees of autonomy, than the family in commercial and industrial civilization.

As the state develops, according to Maine, "the individual is steadily substituted for the family as the unit of which civil laws take account."[17] And in Jhering's words, "The progress of law consists in the destruction of every natural tie, in a continued process of separation and isolation."[18] That is to say, the family increasingly becomes a reflex of society at large. Hence, one might add, the legal stipulation that spouses may not testify against each other appears as one of the last formal acknowledgements of familial integrity, and the exception that proves the historical case. Clearly, the nuclear family in contemporary urban civilization, although bound by legal obligations, has minimal autonomy; obviously, the means of education, subsistence and self-defense are outside the family's competence. It is in this sense that, given the absence of mediating institutions having a clearly defined independent authority, the historical tendency of all state structures vis-à-vis the individual may be designated as totalitarian. Indeed, the state creates the disaffiliated individual whose bearings thus become bureaucratic or collective; the juridical "person," who may even be a corporation doing business, is merely the legal reflection of a social process. If "totalization" is the state process, totalitarianism cannot be confined to a particular political ideology but is, so to speak, the ideology, explicit or not, of political society.

This étatist tendency has its origins in archaic society; we can observe it with unusual clarity in the proto-states of sub-Saharan Africa. In East Africa, pastoralists, competing for land, and in West Africa, militaristic clans, catalyzed by the Arab, and, later, the European trade, notably in slaves, conquered horticulturalists, thereby providing the major occasions for the growth of civil power. Since the basic means of exploiting the environment in these polities remained substantially unchanged, and, to some extent, survived under colonialism, we can reconstruct through chronicles extending back for centuries and by means of contemporary field work, the structure of early state controls, which evolved in the absence of writing and the systematic codification of law. The absence of writing *should* relieve the scholar from that dependence on official records that has so thoroughly shaped our sense of European history; unfortunately, rubbing shoulders with the upper class in a non-literate state creates equivalent distortions.

In such societies, Rattray tells us, referring to Ashanti,

> . . . the small state was ever confronted with the kindred organization which was always insidiously undermining its authority by placing certain persons outside its jurisdiction. It could only hold its own, therefore, by throwing out an ever-widening circle to embrace those loyalties which were lost to it owing to the workings of the old tribal organization which has survived everywhere.[19]

Further,

> the old family, clan and tribal organization survived in the new regime which was ever striving to make territorial considerations, and not the incidence of kinship, the basis of state control.

Rattray concludes that,

> . . . corporate responsibility for every act was an established principle which survived even the advent of a powerful central public authority as the administration of public justice.[20]

Nadel asserts, concerning the Islamized Nupe of the Nigerian Middle Belt, that what emerged from his analysis was,

> . . . a much more subtle development and a deeper kind of antagonism (than interstate warfare), namely, the almost eternal antagonism of developed State versus that raw material of the Community which, always and everwhere, must form the nourishing soil from which alone the state can grow.[21]

And Engels refers to the "irreconcilable opposition of gentile society to the state."[22]

I have documented this conflict in detail in a study of the Dahomean proto-state. There, as elsewhere, it is apparent that the contradictory transition from customs to specified law, "double institutionalization," if you will, *is by no means the major source of law*. Whether the law arises latently in "confirmation" of previous usage, or through the transformation of some aspect of custom, which the law itself may have, in the first instance, provoked, as in the example of the "best friend," neither circumstance brings us to the heart of the matter. For we learn by studying intermediate societies that the laws so typical of them are *unprecedented*; they do not emerge through a process of "double institutionalization," however defined. They arise in opposition to the customary order of the antecedent kin or kin-equivalent groups; they represent a new set of social goals pursued by a new and unanticipated power in society. These goals can be reduced to a single complex imperative: the imposition of the inter-related census-tax-conscription system. The territorial thrust of the early state, along with its vertical social entrenchment, demanded conscription of labor, the mustering of an army, the levying of taxes and tribute, the maintenance of a bureaucracy, and the assessment of the extent, location, and numbers of the population being subjected. *These were the major direct or indirect occasions for the development of civil law.*

The primary purpose of a census is indicative. Census figures (in non-literate societies, pebbles, for example, would be used as counters) provided the basis on which taxes were apportioned among the conquered districts and tribute in labor exacted from the constituent kin units. The census was also essential for conscripting men into the army. This information was considered so important in Dahomey that each new king, upon his enstoolment, was escorted by his two leading ministers to a special hut in the royal compound and there admonished as he knelt: "Young man, all your life you have heard Dahomey, Dahomey, but you have never until today seen the true Dahomey, for Dahomey is its people and here they are."[23]

With this declaration, the two elders pointed to sacks of pebbles, each pebble representing a person, each sack representing a sex or age group. The young king was then told that he must never allow the contents of the sacks to diminish and that every year the pebbles would be counted to see whether their number had increased or declined. He was then given an old gun (in earlier times a hoe handle) and advised, "Fight with this. But take care that you are not vanquished."[24]

The census figures represented the potential power of the state and were carefully guarded; perhaps they were the first state secret. The act and intent of the census turned persons into ciphers, abstractions in civil perspective; people did all they could to avoid being counted. Suspicion persists; even in the United States the authorities during the period of census taking find it necessary to assert that census information will not be used to tax or otherwise penalize the individual, and, in fact, to do so is said to be against the law.

The double meanings of certain critical terms in common English use—"custom," "duty," and "court," reveal this conflict between local usage and the census-tax-conscription system of the early state. We have been speaking of custom as traditional or conventional non-legal behavior, but custom also refers to a tax routinely payable to the state for the transportation of goods across territorial borders. All such taxes are clearly defined legal impositions, frequently honored in the breach, and they do not have the traditional command of custom. In Dahomey, the "Grand Customs" held at the unveiling of a new king, presumably in honor of his ancestors, were the occasion for the payment of taxes, the large-scale sentencing and sacrifice of criminals, and the prosecution of other state business. Camus has Caligula describe such an event in a passage that could have been extrapolated from a Dahomean chronicle:

It's only the Treasury that counts. And living is the opposite of loving
. . . and I invite you to the most gorgeous of shows, a sight for gods to
gloat on, a whole world called to judgment. But for that I must have a
crowd—spectators, victims, criminals, hundreds and thousands of
them. Let the accused come forward. I want my criminals, and they
are all criminals. Bring in the condemned men. I must have my public.
Judges, witnesses, accused—all sentenced to death without a hearing.
Yes, Ceasonia, I'll show them something they've never seen before, the
one free man in the Roman Empire.[25]

Along with the annual "customs," the "Grand Customs" paralleled
the form of local ceremonies, but the substance had entirely
changed. Fiscal or legal coercion, political imposition were not the
purpose of these ancestral ceremonies which ritually re-enacted
reciprocal bonds. The "customs" of the sovereign were laws, the
ceremonies of the kin groups were customs.

Similarly, the term "duty" implies a moral obligation on the
one hand and a tax on the other. Naturally, we assume that it is
the duty of citizens to pay taxes: the paradox inherent in the term
becomes more obvious, as one might imagine, as we examine
archaic civilizations.

The term "court" is analogously ambivalent. On the one hand,
it refers to the residence or entourage of the sovereign; on the
other, to a place where civil justice is dispensed, but at their root
the functions fuse. The prototypical juridical institution was, in
fact, the court of the sovereign where legislation was instituted,
for which no precedent or formal analogue existed on the local
level. Peristiany, speaking of the Kipsigis, sharpens the latter
point:

> One of the most significant differences between the . . . council of
> elders and a European judicature is to be found in the relation
> between officer and office. The Council elders do not hold their office
> from a higher authority. They are not appointed . . . [26]

As Seagle, among others, indicates, the court is the first, most
important, and perhaps the last legal artifact. In Montaigne's
words, "France takes as its rule the rule of the court."[27] Put
another way, the court is a specialized legal structure and it
embraces all those particular and determinate legal bodies which
are peculiar to civilization.

Clearly, the function of the court was not primarily the
establishment of order. In primitive societies, as in the traditional
sectors of proto-states, there already existed built-in mechanisms
for the resolution of conflict. Generally speaking, as Max
Gluckman, among others, has shown, in such societies conflicts
generated by the ordinary functioning of social institutions were
resolved as part of the customary ritual cycle integral to the
institutions themselves.

With regard to more specific breaches, we recall Rattray's
observation on the Ashanti: "Corporate responsibility for every act
was an established principle which survived even the advent of

. . . the administration of public justice." That is to say the kin
unit was the juridical unit, just as it was the economic and social
unit. Furthermore,

> Causes which give rise to the greater part of present 'civil' actions
> were practically nonexistent. Inheritance, ownership of moveable and
> non-moveable property, status of individuals, rules of behavior and
> morality were matters inevitably settled by the customary law, with
> which everyone was familiar from childhood, and litigation regarding
> such matters was . . . almost inconceivable. Individual contract,
> moreover, from the very nature of the community with which we are
> concerned, was also unknown, thus removing another possible,
> fruitful source of litigation.[28]

The primary purpose of the historically emerging court, the
sovereign's entourage and habitation, was to govern. The
distinguished British jurist Sir John Salmond has observed, "Law
is secondary and unessential. . . . The administration of justice is
perfectly possible without law at all."[29] And Sir William Markby
writes, "Tribunals can act entirely without law."[30] The perhaps
unintended point here is that justice, commonly defined, is neither
deducible from the law, nor was the legislation of the court a
measure of justice, but of the political thrust of the early state, and
that flowed from the implementation of the census-tax-
conscription system.

In the census-tax-conscription system, every conceivable
occasion was utilized for the creation of law in support of
bureaucracy and sovereign. We observe no abstract principle, no
impartial justice, no *precedent*, only the spontaneous opportunism
of a new class designing the edifice of its power. It should be re-
emphasized, however, that in certain instances formal analogues
for civil imposition existed on the local level, but no formal or
functional precedents. Civil taxation, for example, can be
rationalized in the context of reciprocal gift-giving in the localities,
but the latter was not confirmed by law, or specifically used by
the sovereign; similarly, corvée labor is a political analogue of
local cooperative work groups. But such evolutionary, and
dialectical, relationships are most important for their distinctions.

Stubbs writes about the Norman kings that "it was mainly for
the sake of the profits that early justice was administered at all."[31]
Burton relates that at Whydah, in native Dahomey, in the event of
a financial dispute the Yevogan, the leading bureaucrat in the
district, sat in judgment. For his services, he appropriated half
the merchandise involved, in the name of the king, and another
quarter for various lesser officials. The remainder presumably
went to the winning contestant in the judicial duel.[32] Among the
Ashanti, the central authority relied on the proceeds of litigation
as a fruitful means for replenishing a depleted treasury. Litigation,
Rattray notes, came actually to be encouraged.[33]

Tolls were an important source of revenue. In Ashanti, the
king had all the roads guarded; all traders were detained until

inquiries were made about them, whereupon they were allowed to pass on payment of gold dust.[34] W. Bosman writes that in early eighteenth century Whydah, the king's revenue,

> . . . in proportion to his country is very large, of which I believe, he hath above one thousand collectors who dispose themselves throughout the whole land in all market roads and passages, in order to gather the king's toll which amounts to an incredible sum, for there is nothing so mean sold in the whole kingdom that the king hath no toll for it. . . .[35]

The punishment for the theft of property designated as the king's was summary execution by "kangaroo courts" organized on the spot by the king's agents.[36] This is echoed in the code of Hammurabi: "if a man steals the property of a god (temple) or a palace, that man shall be put to death; and he who receives from his hands the stolen (property) shall also be put to death."[37] Where the king's property was concerned, no judicial duel was possible. In these instances, which could be endlessly multiplied, we witness the extension of the king's peace, the primary form of the civil "order," actually the invention and application of sumptuary law through the subsidiary peaces of highway and market. In Maitland's words, "the king has a peace that devours all others." If in these proto-states, the sovereign power is not yet fully effective, it nonetheless strives to that monopoly of force which characterizes the mature state.

The purpose and abundance of laws inevitably provoked breaches. The civil authority, in fact, continually probed for breaches and frequently manufactured them. In Dahomey, for example, a certain category of the king's women were distributed to the local villages and those men who made the mistake of having intercourse with them were accused of rape, for which the punishment, following a summary trial, was conscription into the army.[38] Thus, rape was invented as a *civil* crime. If rape had, in fact, occurred in the traditional joint-family villages—and such an occurrence would have been rare, as indicated by the necessity of civil definition—the wrong could have been dealt with by composition (the ritualized giving of goods to the injured party), ritual purification, ridicule, and, perhaps, for repeated transgressions, banishment; the customary machinery would have gone into effect automatically, probably on the initiative of the family of the aggressor. Such instances as this only sharpen the point that in early states crimes seem to have been invented to suit the laws; the latent purpose of the law was punishment in the service and profit of the state, not prevention or the protection of persons, not the *healing* of the breach. As Seagle indicates, "The criminal law springs into life in every great period of class conflict," and this is most obviously the case during the initial phases of state formation.

In its civil origins, then, a correlation existed between law and crime which partook of entrapment. One may even state that the substantial rationale for law developed *after* the fact of its emergence. For example, civil protection of the market place or highway was certainly not necessary to the degree implied in the archaic edicts at the time they were issued. Joint-family markets and village trails were not ordinarily dangerous places if we are to believe the reports of the earliest chroniclers, as well as those of more contemporary observers. Moreover, if trouble had developed, the family, clan or village was capable of dealing with it. But, in an evolving conquest state, the presence of the king's men would itself be a primary cause of disruption Indeed, as M. Quénum, a descendant of Dahomean commoners, informs us in a remarkable work, the soldiers were referred to as bandits and predators who victimized many people. Sometimes their forays were confined to a single compound, where someone, whether man, woman or child, resided who had spoken badly of the sovereign or whom the king suspected.[39] In common parlance, the very names of the elite army units became insults; one meant "nasty person," another "arrogant person," and one would say of a tragic event that it was worthy of yet another military cadre. It is, therefore, understandable that the peace of the highway became an issue.[40]

As the integrity of the local groups declined, a process which, in the autochthonous state, must have taken generations or even centuries, conditions doubtless developed which served as an *ex post facto* rationalization for edicts already in effect. In this sense, laws became self-fulfilling prophecies. Crime and the laws which served it were, then, co-variants of the evolving state.

Just as entrapment was characteristic of early civil law, the idea of protection, in the sense of a protection racket, also inheres in its origins. In Dahomey, we are told by Norris and others, prostitution was encouraged by the civil power and prostitutes were distributed through the villages, the price of their favors being set by civil decree. They were obliged to offer themselves to any man who could pay the moderate fee and once a year were convened at the "annual customs" where they were heavily taxed.[41] Skertchly notes that the prostitutes were licensed by the king and placed in the charge of the Mew, the second leading bureaucrat, who was entrusted with the task of "keeping up the supply."[42] Bosman observes at Whydah that "for every affair that can be thought of, the king hath appointed a captain overseer."[43] *What the king permits, he commands; what he "protects," he taxes.*

The intention of the civil power is epitomized in the sanctions against homicide and suicide, typical of early polities; indeed they were among the very first civil laws. Just as the sovereign is said to own the land, intimating the mature right of eminent domain, so the individual is ultimately conceived as the chattel of the state. In Dahomey, persons were conceived as *les choses du monarque.* Eminent domain in persons and property, even where projected as a fiction, is, of course, the cardinal prerequisite of the census-tax-conscription system. We recall that Maine designated the individual the unit of which the civil law steadily takes account. Seagle stated the matter as follows: "By undermining the kinship bond, they (the early civil authorities) made it easier to deal with individuals, and the isolation of the individual is a basic precondition for the growth of law."[44]

Homicide, then, was regarded as an offense against the state. In Rattray's words, "The blow which struck down the dead man would thus appear to have been regarded as aimed also at the . . . central authority."[45] In Ashanti homicide was punishable by death in its most horrible form; in Dahomey, by death or conscription into the army. There is a nuance here which should not be overlooked. By making homicide, along with the theft of the king's property, a capital offence, the sovereign power discouraged violent opposition to the imposition of the civil order.

Traditionally, murder in a joint-family village was a tort—a private, remediable wrong—which could stimulate a blood feud, not to be confused with the lex talionis, until redress, which did not imply equivalent injury, was achieved. But a breach was most often settled by composition. As Paul Radin put it: "The theory of an eye for an eye . . . never really held for primitive people . . . rather it was replacement for loss with damages."[46] And this is echoed by Peristiany: ". . . they claim restitution or private damages and not social retribution."[47] In any case, the family was fully involved. "The family was a corporation," said Rattray, "it is not easy to grasp what must have been the effect . . . of untold generations of thinking and acting . . . in relation to one's group. The Ashanti's idea of what we term moral responsibility for his actions must surely have been more developed than in peoples where individualism is the order of the day."[48] This more or less typical anthropological observation makes it clear that the law against homicide was not a "progressive" step, as if some abstract right were involved which the state, coming of age, finally understands and seeks to establish. "Anti-social conduct (is) exceptional in small kinship groups," writes Margery Perham of the Ibo.[49] Crimes of violence were rare, Richard Burton reported of Dahomey, and "murder virtually unknown."[50] Of course, as with other crimes defined by civil law, they may have increased as the social autonomy, economic communalism, and reciprocity of the kin units weakened. But this is much less important than Dalzel's observation that in Dahomey "many creatures have been put to death . . . without having committed any crime at all,"[51] thus exemplifying the power of the sovereign literally to command the lives of his citizens. The threat and example of summary execution, especially but by no means exclusively evident at the mortuary celebrations of "Grand Customs" on the enstooling of a king, encouraged obedience to civil injunctions.

The law against suicide, a capital offense, was the apotheosis of political absurdity. The individual, it was assumed, had no right to take his own life; that was the sole prerogative, presumably, of the state, whose property he was conceived to be.

The fanatical nature of the civil legislature in claiming sole prerogative to the lives of its subjects is conclusively revealed among the Ashanti, where, if the suicide was a murderer,

> . . . the central authority refused to be cheated thus and the long arm of the law followed the suicide to the grave from which, if his kinsmen should have dared to bury him, he was dragged to stand trial.[52] (One recalls Antigone's defiance.)

This contrasts remarkably, if logically, with the behavior of the more primitively structured Ibo, as reported by Victor Uchendu, an anthropologist who is himself an Ibo:

> Homicide is an offense against ala—the earth deity. If a villager is involved, the murderer is expected to hang himself, after which . . . daughters of the village perform the rite of . . . sweeping away the ashes of murder. If the murderer has fled, his extended family must also flee, and the property of all is subject to raids. When the murderer is eventually caught, he is required to hang himself to enable the daughters of the village to perform their rites. It is important to realize that the village has no power to impose capital punishment. In fact, no social group or institution has this power. Everything affecting the life of the villager is regulated by custom. The life of the individual is highly respected; it is protected by the earth-goddess. The villagers can bring social pressure, but the murderer must hang himself.[53]

It can hardly be argued that the purpose of the civil sanction against suicide was a diminish its incidence or to propagate a superior moral consciousness. Dare we say, as with other crimes, that attempts at suicide increased as society became more thoroughly politicized? The law against suicide reveals, in the extreme, the whole meaning and intent of civil law at its origins. In the proto-state, the quintessential struggle was over the lives and labor of the people, who, still moving in a joint family context, were nonetheless conceived to be *les choses du monarque.*

III

If revolutions are the acute, episodic signs of civilizational discontent, the rule of law, in seven millennia of political society, from Sumer or Akkad to New York or Moscow, has been the chronic symptom of the disorder of institutions. E.B. Tylor stated, "A constitutional government, whether called republic or kingdom, is an arrangement by which the nation governs itself by means of the machinery of a military despotism."[54]

The generalization lacks nuance but we can accept it if we bear in mind Tylor's point of reference: "Among the lessons to be learnt from the life of rude tribes is how society can go on without the policeman to keep order."[55] When he alludes to constitutional government, Tylor was not distinguishing its ultimate sanction from that of any other form of the state: all political society is based on repressive organized force. In this he was accurate. For pharaohs and presidents alike have always made a public claim to represent the common interest, indeed to incarnate the common good. Only a Plato or a Machiavelli in search of political harmony, or a Marx in search of political truth, has been able to penetrate this myth of the identity between ruler and ruled, of equality under law. The tradition of Plato and Machiavelli commends the use of the "royal" or "noble lie," while that of Marx exposes and rejects the power structure (ultimately the state) that propagates so false a political consciousness. On this issue, I follow Marx.

Tylor distinguishes the civilized from the primitive order. Such a distinction has been made at every moment of crisis in the West but nowhere so pertinently as in Montaigne's contrast of a primitive society with Plato's ideally civilized republic:

> This is a nation, I should say to Plato, in which there is no sort of traffic, no knowledge of letters, no science of numbers, no name for a magistrate or for political superiority, no custom of servitude, no riches or poverty, no contracts, no successions, no partitions . . . no care for any but common kinship. How far from this perfection would he find the Republic he imagines![56]

The issue of law and order implicit in Montaigne's contrast between primitive and civilized societies has been a persistent underlying theme for the most reflective and acute minds of the West. The inquiry into the nature of politics probably demarcates most accurately the boundaries of our intellectual landscape. The evolution of the state toward what Max Weber called maximally politicized society, the unprecedented concentration of bureaucratic and technological power, which economically and culturally dominates the rest of the world, creates a climate in which all problems cast a political shadow. We may flee from the political dimension of our experience or we may embrace it in order to do away with it, but we are obsessed by politics. It was perhaps Plato's primary virtue that, at the very origin of the Western intellectual tradition, he understood that, in civilization, all significant human problems have a political aspect and he insisted upon the solution of the latter as a coefficient of the creative resolution of the former. The Republic is the first civilizational utopia, and it maintains its force both as a model of inquiry and as antithesis to all projections of the nature of primitive society. Any contrary view of the possibilities of human association must take The Republic into account.

The legal order, which Plato idealized, is as Tylor maintained and Marx understood, synonymous with the power of the state. Paul Vinogradoff writes,

> The state has assumed the monopoly of political co-ordination. It is the state which rules, makes laws and eventually enforces them by coercion. Such a state did not exist in ancient times. The common-

wealth was not centered in one sovereign body towering immeasurably above single individuals and meting out to everyone his portion of right.[57]

And Engels, reflecting on the origins of the state, asserts:

The right of the state to existence was founded on the preservation of order in the interior and the protection against the barbarians outside, but this order was worse than the most disgusting disorder, and the barbarians against whom the state pretended to protect its citizens were hailed by them as saviors.[58]

Moreover,

The state created a public power of coercion that did no longer coincide with the old self-organized and (self) armed population.[59]

Finally, in a passage that epitomizes the West's awareness of itself, Engels writes:

The state, then, is by no means a power forced on society at a certain stage of evolution. It is the confession that this society has become hopelessly divided against itself, has estranged itself in irreconcilable contradictions which it is powerless to banish. In order that these contradictions, these classes with conflicting economic interests may not annihilate themselves and society in a useless struggle, a power becomes necessary that stands apparently above society and has the function of keeping down the conflicts and maintaining 'order.' And this power, the outgrowth of society, but assuming supremacy over it and becoming more and more divorced from it, is the state. . . .[60]

In a word, the state is the alienated form of society: and it is this process which has fascinated the Western intellect and which may, in fact, have led to the peculiar intensity of the reflective, analytic, and introspective consciousness in the West, to our search for origins and our inexhaustible concern with secular history. A knowledge of one's present, as Montaigne maintained, implies not only a knowledge of one's past but of one's future.

However we project, imagine, or reconstruct the past, we recognize the division, the objective correlate of the division within ourselves, between primitive and civilized society, between moral and civil order, between custom and law. Interpretation of the nature of the primitive and the civilized has, of course, not been uniform. Hobbes versus Rousseau is paradigmatic. But most theorists tend to see civilization as a kind of fall from a "natural," or at least more natural, to a legal or more repressive order. No matter how the virtues of civilization are weighed, the price exacted is inevitably noted. This is as true of Plato as of Freud or Engels. Plato, for example, notes, however inadequately, a condition of existence prior to the city-state, a type of rusticity which he views nostalgically and whose destruction he maintains was socioeconomically determined. I suspect that even the great majority of anthropologists, despite professional illusions of dissociated objectivity, sense that primitive societies are somehow closer than civilized societies to the realization of "natural" law and "natural" right. I believe this emphasis in the Western tradition to be the sounder, and it serves as the basis of my own thinking. There is, as Montaigne noted, an "amazing distance" between the primitive character and our own. In the contrast between these two sides of our historical nature, which we existentially re-enact, we come to understand law as the antonym and not the synonym of order.

IV

I agree with Nadel that in the transition from primitive to political society the means of control and integration employed were, in a wider sense, "all . . . deliberately conceived and (executed): they are agencies of an assimilation conscious of itself and of the message which it carries."[61] Finally, we are led to ask, as did Nadel about the Nupe:

> What did the tax-paying law-abiding citizen receive in return for allegiance to king and nobility? Was extortion, bribery, brutal force, the only aspect under which the state revealed itself to the populace? The people were to receive, theoretically, on the whole, one thing: security—protection against external and internal enemies, and general security for carrying out the daily work, holding markets, using the roads. We have seen what protection and security meant in reality. At their best, they represented something very unequal and very unstable. This situation must have led to much tension and change within the system and to frequent attempts to procure better safeguards for civil rights.[62]

The struggle for civil rights, then, is a response to the imposition of civil law. With the destruction of the primitive base of society, civil rights have been defined and redefined as a reaction to drastic changes in the socioeconomic structure, the rise of caste and class systems, imperialism, modern war, technology as a means of social exploitation, maldistribution and misuse of resources, racial hatred. The right to socially and economically fruitful work, for example, which did not come into question in a primitive society or in a traditional sector of an early state (and therefore was not conceived to be a stipulated right) becomes an issue under capitalism. The demand implies a need for profoundly changing the system and indicates that our sense of the appropriately human has very ancient roots indeed. However, we are reminded by the struggle for civil rights, that legislation alone has no force beyond the potential of the social system that generates it. From the study of proto-states we also learn that the citizen must be constantly alert to laws which seek to curb his rights in the name of protection or security. Restriction legislation is almost always a signal of repressive institutional change, but is, of course, not the cause of it.

The major focus of the defense of the citizen as a person can only be on procedure or, as we call it in our own society, due process. Quénum reports, of the early state of Dahomey, "There was no penal code promulgated . . . punishment had no fixity . . . the Miegan (leading bureaucrat, chief judge, and executioner) would become restive if capital punishment would be too long in coming."[63] In the words of Dalzel, "There was a vast disproportion between crimes and punishments."[64] And in early states, most if not all civil breaches were what we would define as crimes, just as in primitive societies "civil crimes" were considered, where they were not unprecedented, torts or private remediable wrongs. As every intelligent lawyer knows, the substance of the law can hardly be assimilated to morality. It is clear, therefore, why Jhering insisted that "Form is the sworn enemy of unlimited discretion (of the sovereign power) and the twin sister of freedom."[65] The degrees of theft or homicide, the question of double jeopardy, habeas corpus, the right to counsel, the question of legitimate witness, trial by jury and the selection of jurors, protection against summary search and seizure, the very division between civil and criminal law—these intricacies of procedure are the primary, but far from absolute, assurance of whatever justice can be obtained under the rule of law.

For example, the only way dissidents in Russia can defend themselves against summary punishment and make their cases universally understandable is by calling attention to abuses of procedure. The spirit of the laws, mummified in the excellent constitution of 1936, is irrelevant, abstract. The tribunal that discharges the intentions of the state can discard, suspend, reinterpret, and invent laws at will. The court, not the constitution, is the primary legal reality. And the politically inspired charge of insanity, which can remove dissidents from the body politic altogether, is the ultimate étatistic definition of the person—a non-being incapable of autonomy. And that, I should note, is fore-shadowed in the consummate anti-Socratic Platonism of the Laws, the heavenly city brought to earth, wherein the ordinary citizen is "to become, by long habit, utterly incapable of doing anything at all independently."

Procedure is the individual's last line of defense in contemporary civilization, wherein all other associations to which he may belong have become subordinate to the state. The elaboration of procedure then, is a unique, if fragile, feature of more fully evolved states, in compensation, so to speak, for the radical isolation of the individual. In the proto-states, the harshness of rudimentary procedure was countered by the role of the kinship units which, as we recall, retained a significant measure of functional socioeconomic autonomy and, therefore, of local political cohesion.

But "law has its origin in the pathology of social relations and functions only when there are frequent disturbances of the social equilibrium."[66] Law arises in the breach of a prior customary order and increases in force with the conflicts that divide political societies internally and among themselves. Law *and* order is the historical illusion; law versus order is the historical reality.

In the tradition of Rousseau, Lévi-Strauss, in a moment of candor, declares,

> We must go beyond the evidence of the injustices and abuses to which the social order gives rise, and discover the unshakable basis of human society . . . Anthropology shows that base cannot be found in our own civilization, ours is indeed perhaps the one furthest from it.[67]

The progressive reduction of society to a series of technical and legal signals, the consequent diminution of culture, *i.e.*, of reciprocal, symbolic meanings, are perhaps the primary reasons why our civilization is the one least likely to serve as a guide to "the unshakable basis of human society."

NOTES

1.   Paul Bohannan, "Law," *International Encyclopedia of the Social Sciences* (New York, 1968), pp. 73-78.

2.   Paul Radin, *The World of Primitive Man*, New York, 1953, p. 223.

3.   J. C. Peristiany, *The Institutions of Primitive Society*, Glencoe, Illinois, 1956.
    In the words of V.C. Uchendu, writing about the Ibo:

> . . . the use of force is minimal or absent; . . . there are leaders rather than rulers, and . . . cohesion is achieved by rules rather than by laws and by consensus rather than by dictation. In general, the Igbo have not achieved any political structure which can be called a federation, a confederacy, or a state.

V.C. Uchendu, *The Igbo of Southeast Nigeria*, N.Y., 1965, p. 46.

4.   Sydney P. Simpson and Julius Stone, *Law and Society in Evolution*, Book I, Saint Paul, 1942, p. 2.

5.   William Seagle, *The History of Law*, Tudor, 1946, p. 35.

6.   *Ibid.*, pp. 19-20.

7.   *Ibid.*

8.   Henry Maine, *Village Communities and Miscellanies*, New York, 1889, p. 230.

9.   George Vernadsky, *Medieval Russian Laws*. 1917, pp. 26-27.

10.   Quoted by Simpson and Stone, *op. cit.*, p. 78.

11.   Henry Maine, *Early History of Institutions*, 1897, p. 383.

12.   Simpson and Stone, *op. cit.*, p. 177.

13.   Stanley Diamond, *Dahomey, a Proto-state in West Africa*, Ann Arbor, Microfilm, 1951, p. 109.

14.   Quoted by Max Gluckman, "Studies in African Land Tenure," *African Studies*, vol. III. 1944, pp. 14-21.

15.   R.S. Rattray, *Ashanti, Law and Constitution*, London, 1929.

16.   L.P. Mair, "Baganda Land Tenure," *Africa*, vol. VI, 1933.

17.   Henry Maine, *Ancient Law*, p. 140.

18.   R. von Jhering, *Geist des Romishchen Recht*, 1866, vol. II, p. 31.

19.   Rattray, *op. cit.*, p. 80.

20.   *Ibid.*, p. 286.

21.   S.F. Nadel, "Nupe State and Community," *Africa*, vol. VIII, p. 303.

22.   Engels, p. 133 (see N. 58).

23.   M.J. Herskowitz, *Dahomey, an Ancient West African Kingdom*, New York, 1938, p. 73.

24.   *Ibid.*

25.   Albert Camus, *Caligula and Three Other Plays*, Stuart Gilbert (trans.), New York, 1958, p. 17.

26.   Peristiany, *op. cit.*, p. 42.
The contrast is well remarked by V.C. Uchendu:

Under a constitution like that of the Igbo, which does not provide for a specialized court, judicial matters are ad hoc affairs. The injured party takes the initiative. He may appeal to the head of the compound of the offender or to a body of arbitrators . . . Since the arbitrators have no means of enforcing their decision, for it to be respected it must be acceptable to both parties.
Uchendu, *op cit.*, p. 43.

27.   Montaigne, (see N. 56 for full citation) p. 197.

28.   Rattray, *op. cit.*, p. 286.

29.   Sir John Salmond, *Jurisprudence*, 1920, p. 13.

30.   Sir William Markby, *Elements of Law*, 1905, p. 21.

31.   William Stubbs, *The Constitutional History of England*, London, 1890, vol. I, p. 48.

32.   Burton, Richard F., *A Mission to Gelele, a King of Dahomey*, London, 1864, vol. II, p. 211.

33.   Rattray, *op. cit.*, p. 292.

34.   Rattray, *op. cit.*, p. 111.

35.   W. Bosman, *A New and Accurate Description of the Coast of Guinea*, London, 1705, p. 362.

36.   R. Norris, *Reise nach Abomey, der Hofstadt des Konigs von Dahomey an von Guinea im Jahr 1772*, Leipzig, 1790, p. 221. et seq.

37.   *Code of Hammurabi*, Harper translation, 1904, paragraph 6, p. 13.

38.   A. Le Herisse, *L'Ancien Royaume du Dahomey*, Paris, 1911, p. 72.

39.   M. Quénum, *Au Pays des Fons*, Paris, 1938, p. 7.

40.   Quénum, pp. 21-22.

41.   Norris, *op. cit.*, p. 257.

42.   Skertchly, *Dahomey As It Is*, London, 1874, p. 283.

43.   Bosman, *op. cit.*, p. 361.

44.   Seagle, *op. cit.*, p. 64. Quénum had a poor opinion of the ethnographers who claimed to understand and interpret his country. They failed, he believed, because of inadequate sources of information, and (or) ignorance of social customs. "Most of our ethnographers," he wrote, "have had as collaborators princes and ex-ministers of state and have believed their tales." He adds that ignorance of the native language and deficient sympathy compounded the problem. The point to note here is that Quénum is objecting to the view from the top which is a critical issue in the writing of all political history.

45.   Rattray, *op. cit.*, p. 295.

46.   Radin, *op. cit.*, p. 252.

47.   Peristiany, *op. cit.*, p. 43.

48.   Radin, *op. cit.*, p. 62.

49.   Margery Perham, *Native Administration in Nigeria*, London, 1962, pp. 229. *et seq.*

50.   Burton, *op. cit.*, p. 56.
       Acts of violence must be distinguished from *crimes* of violence. The incidence, occasions for, and character of violence in primitive, as opposed to civilized societies, is a subject of the utmost importance, which I have discussed elsewhere (see footnote 52). But the question here has to do with crimes in which violence is used as a means for, e.g., the theft of property. In contemporary societies unpremeditated acts of personal violence which have no ulterior motive, so-called crimes of passion, may not be penalized or carry minor degrees of guilt, that is, their status as legally defined crimes is ambiguous. This would certainly seem to reflect a historically profound distinction between crime and certain types of violence. In primitive societies violence tends to be personally structured, nondissociative, and, thereby, self-limiting.

51.   A. Dalzel, *The History of Dahomey, An Inland Kingdom of Africa,* etc., London, 1793, p. 212.

52.   Rattray, *op. cit.*, p. 299.

53.   Uchendu, *op. cit.*, pp. 42-43.

54.   E.B. Tylor, *Anthropology*, vol. II, London, 1946, p. 156.

55.   *Ibid.*, p. 134.

56.   Michel de Montaigne, *The Complete Essays*, trans. Donald Frame, Stanford, 1965. In ignorance of Montaigne's contrast between primitive society and Plato's ideal republic, I published an article, "Plato and the Definition of the Primitive," *Culture in History*, New York, 1960, which explicates some of the points briefly noted above. For a more comprehensive model of primitive society see my "The Search for the Primitive" in *Man's Image in Medicine and Anthropology*, New York, 1963, edited by I. Galdston, pp. 62-115. In order to understand the functioning of custom in primitive society fully, one should have such a model in mind. Unfortunately, in this article I can only suggest its outlines.

57.   Paul Vinogradoff, *Outlines of Historical Jurisprudence*, vol. I, London, 1920. p. 93.

58.   Friedrich Engels, *Origin of the Family, Private Property and the State*, Chicago, 1902, p. 179.

59.   *Ibid.*, p. 207.

60.   *Ibid.*, p. 206.

61.   S.F. Nadel, *A Black Byzantium*, London, New York, Toronto, 1942, p. 144.

62.   Nadel, "Nupe State and Community," *Africa*, vol. VIII, p. 287.

63.   Quénum, *op. cit.*, p. 22.

64.   Dalzel, *op. cit.*, p. 212.

65.   Jhering, *op. cit.*, vol. II, p. 471.

66.   Seagle, *op. cit.*, p. 36.

67.   Claude Lévi-Strauss, *A World on the Wane*, New York, 1961, p. 390.

Chapter 10

The Ideology of Popular Justice

Neelan Tiruchelvam

The de-professionalization of the administration of the justice
in the historical or planned development of a number of socialist
societies is one of the more intriguing phenomena in comtemporary
legal history. It is reflected in the emergence of diverse institutional forms for facilitating popular participation in
conflict-management and law enforcement, distinctively labelled
in each society and generally referred to as "popular tribunals".
While each of these institutions reflects in varying degrees the
state's committment to the ideal of participation by non-law-
professionals in legal administration; a cursory survey of the
organic law relating to these institutions reveals that the rubric,
"popular tribunals" often conceals fundamental differences in
form, organization, recruitment patterns, jurisdiction, degree and
nature of procedural regulation, sanctioning power and types of
supervisory control. The different configuration of structural and
functional features represented by each of these institutions points
to differences in the legal ideology of each of these societies; which
are in turn related to and shaped by their traditional and
contemporary authority structures, legal and social organizations.

In this paper we shall analyze the goals of popular justice
with a view to isolating some of the forces which may account for
the emergence of these institutions in different countries. In doing
so we shall group the countries which have adopted some form of
popular tribunal into three categories. In the first category we

---

* Neelon Tiruchelvam, "The Ideology of Popular Justice", lecture given at the
  University of Windsor, Oct. 1973. Reprinted by permission of the author. This is
  the unrevised edition of the lecture.

shall place the Soviet Union, and other countries which seem to
have been stimulated by the Soviet experience to initiate similar
institutional innovations such as Poland and Cuba. We shall also
place in this category and briefly discuss for their academic
significance the abortive proposals to institute neighborhood
tribunals in Chile. In the second category we shall place Tanzania,
India and Burma. The popular tribunals in these countries appear
to be of indigenous inspiration and represent post colonial
reactions to an imposed British court structure. Popular justice in
China appears to be of a different order and will be dealt
separately in the third category. While many scholars see the
origins of the general emphasis on people's mediation as a
technique for coping with conflict and anti-social conduct in the
Traditional Confucian preference for conciliation, Chinese
ideologists, on the other hand, rationalize it as a distinctive
Maoist contribution to Marxist-Leninist thought. The general
discussion of popular justice in these three categories would
provide a backdrop for a more detailed examination of the
significance of popular tribunals in the socialist development of
Sri Lanka.

Before we begin such an analysis we should be sensitive to
some of the difficulties inherent in such an approach. Firstly, the
goals of popular justice in design may be quite distinct from what
they are in operation. State rhetoric may assert the principal
objective of popular justice as the encouragment of local jural
autonomy, but in operation these institutions may be used to
facilitate the penetration of the national legal order. Conversely,
tribunals designed to facilitate the implementation of national
policies may in actual fact articulate local values and interests and
cushion the impact of these policies. Secondly, there tends to be an
ambiguity or lack of unanimity amongst a nation's ideologists as
to the goals of popular justice. Policy makers may oscillate
between the 'policy implementation' and 'self-management'
conceptions of local tribunals. Thirdly, the legal ideology of a
society may be subject to shifts, and correspondingly popular
courts acquire a new significance at different periods of time.
State propagandists may at an early phase of the establishment of
popular tribunals emphasize its conflict management function, but
as the regime becomes more radicalized, place greater emphasis
on its pedagogic functions. Fourthly, different popular tribunals
may occupy contradictory positions in the legal ideological
landscape. One popular tribunal by being empowered to dispose of
minor crimes and anti-social conduct by the application of
informal social pressure may represent the withdrawal of the
central legal order, while another tribunal by being vested with
coercive sanctioning power over a wide range of social behavior
not previously subject to state regulation may represent a
contradictory trend.

The re-emergence of popular tribunals in the Soviet Union

followed the repudiation by the Twenty-First and Twenty-Second Party Conferences of the public order concepts of the Stalinist era. Khrushchev in his address to the latter Conference, underscored the importance of popular participation in the maintenance of public order and the effectiveness of informal social pressure in the anticipation and deterence of anti-social conduct. Lipson emphasizing the lack of "full-time paid professional staff, formal procedural rules and bureaucratic traditions" described the institutions which emerged to give expression to this policy as "the non-courts (in the first place the comrades courts and the anti-parasite tribunals) and the im-police (the D.N.D. or the volunteer people's guard)". The most important of these, the comrades courts, were re-constituted in 1961. The organic law relating to comrades courts provides that the more important objectives of this court would include "the prevention of violations of law and misconduct that cause harm to society, the education of people through persuasion and social pressure, and the creation of conditions of intolerance towards any anti-social conduct". A more detailed analysis of four goals emphasized by Soviet commentators as being served by comrades courts would contribute towards a more general understanding of the significance of popular justice in Soviet society.

The first is the ideal of popular participation in the operation of the legal system, which must be seen in the broader context of the political role assigned to the "people" by the Soviet ideology. A problem central to Marxist-Leninist thought is the proper balance between centralized direction and localized popular control in the organization and management of a socialist society. Lenin after a review of the history of the trade union movement concluded that the working class could not be relied on to spontaneously evolve a revolutionary socialist consciousness consistent with the objective conditions of its class, and that it required an elite party to direct the process of socialist transformation. Lenin, therefore, assigned to the revolutionary party, by reason of its organization superiority and the discipline and ideological unanimity of its cadres, an active interventionist role in the period of transition to communism. The people, however, were not to be totally excluded from this process, and were allocated the role of participation in the administration of state functions. Lenin urged that the "whole of the population" be educated in the art of administration. "Our aim" he said, "is to draw the whole of the poor in the practical work of administration . . . to ensure that every toiler after having finished his eight hours' lesson in productive labor, shall perform state duties gratis". Popular participation was to extend to the administration of legal institutions and the enforcement of laws. Lenin pointed out "every citizen must be placed in conditions which would enable him to participate in the discussion of state laws, in the election of his representatives and in putting the state laws into practice". In the Soviet Union the Communist Party is therefore recognized as "the highest form of socio-political organization, the guiding and directive force of Soviet society. Leninist conceptions of popular participation, although discarded during the Stalinist era, have been reaffirmed by Stalin's heirs in 1957. Accordingly, popular tribunals are rationalized as implementing a broad program for the transfer of state functions from governmental organs to "social" agencies.

This is clearly seen in the 1961 statute on comrades courts. The statute gives strong expression to the concept of local control by providing that "comrades courts shall be invested with the trust of the collective, shall express its will and shall be responsible to it." Accordingly the local Soviet work and residential units were vested with the power to constitute, elect members, review sanctions and exercise overall supervision over comrades courts. These provisions contrast sharply with earlier legislation entrusting central state agencies with supervisory control over comrades courts.

Lipson is, however, less convinced than Soviet commentators that the comrades courts, the toiler's collective under the anti-parasite laws (1957-65), lay prosecutors and defenders, and the voluntary peoples militia represent a shift towards participatory institutions in the legal sphere. By drawing attention to the centrality of party control in the operation of these institutions, he alleges that these tribunals are only "nominally" popular courts. He further adds that the withdrawal of toiler's collectives from the investigation of violations of the parasite laws is indicative of the containment of even the "apparent" movement towards participatory legal organs.

Secondly, with regard to the ideal of legal nihilism, Soviet jurists have often viewed law as a coercive instrument of the dominant social class. The classical Marxist vision is that, in the final stage of the classless communist society, both the state and law as a coercive instrument of the state would disappear. The emphasis on non-coercive social pressures in the design of comrades courts, therefore, led some Soviet commentators to regard the establishment of comrades courts as signalling early stages in the gradual withering away of law.

Other commentators, however, draw attention to the fact that the anti-parasite laws, by expanding the use of coercive sanctions over a wide range of social behavior and attitudes not previously subject to state regulation, reflect a trend in the opposite direction. It has also been emphasized that the coercive powers vested in the comrade courts were enhanced in 1965 by increasing the maximum fine they may impose for theft within their jurisdictions.

Thirdly, both in Krushchev's speech to the Twenty-First Party Congress and the organic law relating to comrades courts, there is strong emphasis on their educational role. Berman regards the pedagogic function as central to Soviet law and legal institutions, and often determinative of the procedure, style and outcome of judicial proceedings. Soviet jurists have remarked that the most "important task of the courts is the fundamental remaking of the conscience of the people". The courts are accordingly enjoined to explore the causes that underline crime and anti-social conduct and take steps to eliminate them. The establishment of comrades courts and other popular legal organs reinforces the "paternalistic" elements in the legal system. The relative absence of status differentiation between tribunal and disputants, the informality and the flexibility of their procedures, the social and physical proximity of the proceedings to the location of the dispute or the violation, enhance the effectiveness of the popular courts in reshaping the attitudes and behavioral patterns of workers and residents. With respect to the comrades courts, the 1961 statute explicated the values which the courts should instill in the parties and others present in the court to include "the communist attitude towards labor and socialist property and the rules of socialist community life, . . . a sense of collectivism and comradely mutual assistance and respect for the dignity and honor of citizens".

Fourthly, Soviet ideologists and jurists have strongly emphasized the role of participatory institutions in the protection of the public order through the identification of potenial law-breakers and the deterence of anti-social conduct by the application of social pressure. To enable these institutions to expose and correct criminal conduct at its earliest stage they are empowered to overview "not only questions of behavior on the job, but also questions of everyday behavior and morality." Some commentators believe that these institutions may provide an ingenious solution to the problems of delinquency in post-industrialized societies caused by the breakdown of primary group loyalties and the disruption of old patterns of recreation, and the resulting anomie and depression. Others regard the popular courts as part of the elaborate Soviet machinery for political control. The latter commentators concede that the Soviet regime has become less repressive, but they draw attention to the wide range of conduct subject to the institutional supervision of popular legal organs in urging that the regime has become more comprehensive.

At this point we may also briefly note that Eastern European commentaries on popular courts also highlight the value of the popular tribunals in the protection of the public order. Podgorcki points out that the constitution of workers' courts in Poland was inspired by the belief that "old means of mass repression are becoming obsolete and are no longer sufficient to prevent certain forms of socially harmful behavior; and that in such the pressure of opinion of the occupational groups is more effective than legal sanctions."

We may now turn to the Cuban popular tribunals, which were organized on an experimental basis in the rural areas in 1964, and were subsequently extended through out the country. It has been recently estimated that there are about 5,000 popular tribunals in operation. In the absence of an organic law regulating the constitution of these tribunals, we must turn to a Judges' manual issued by a panel of lawyers, for a statement of the goals of Cuban popular justice. The preamble to the manual contains a coherent statement of the ideological basis of popular tribunals. It equates the establishment of popular tribunals with fundamental changes in the economic sphere such as the transfer of the ownership of basic means of production from private to public sectors. It then reiterates the familiar critique of law in capitalist society as an instrument of oppression servicing the interests of the dominant social class. By way of contrast the popular tribunals are thought to complete on the one hand and reiterate on the other a new conception of popular socialist legality. In contrasting "bourgeois" legality with the new legality, attention is drawn to the fact that the former is "something official, something alien to the people, that comes down from above." Popular tribunals symbolize on the other hand that socialist legality is something "that arises from the people", in that the tribunals are organized and managed by the people. The close involvement of the tribunal in the life of the neighborhood is also emphasized. Its personnel is drawn from the local community. It is located within and otherwise intimately linked with the neighborhood. The justice it administers is therefore the "expression of the power of the working people in the socialist state".

Besides giving expression to this vaguely defined new legality, the tribunal also was to educate the masses and protect the public order. They would not only be instruments of coercion but also apply non-coercive sanctions such as a public admonition to rehabilitate offenders. It also served important pedagogic functions in extolling the values of the new socialist man and of explaining the norms of the revolutionary regime, and thereby consolidating the socialist social order.

Other commentators, however, perceive the significance of popular tribunals differently. They point out that these tribunals merely created a parallel legal order, which worked in disharmony with and had little impact on the pre-liberation legal order. The regular courts of law continued to operate with almost the same personnel and with little difference in procedure, style or in the codes of law they administered. This evaluation seems, however, to be over-stated. Even though the same court structure has been retained, the fundamental changes in outlook, role conception and function of the Cuban law professional must clearly inform the working of the official legal organs. More recently, however, an attempt is being made to unify the dual court structures and extend the concept of popular participation to all levels of the integrated judicial organization, and thereby "synthesize the contradictions inherent in the legal system."

We may by way of contrast briefly refer to the abortive

proposal to institute neighborhood tribunals in Chile. Chilean ideologists have been repeatedly critical of the failure of the central legal order to reach important sectors of Chilean society represented by slum dwellers and workers and they have attributed this lack of penetration to the contradictions between the legal system and the "social and cultural reality" which these sectors represented. The popular tribunals therefore presented an alternative legal framework for these alienated social groups to organize their daily lives in a "more humane and dignified way". The tribunals would be managed by the working classes and deal with problems "which have little significance for the social groups of higher income but have a crucial importance for the working class". The procedure would be public, oral and informal and the sanctions directed towards correction and re-education. The norms would be simplified to exclude the need for law professionals, and the technique of norm application would be changed. The tribunal would be required to be less conscious of the rule itself and be more attentive to "the social and human reality to which the rules are to be applied." Accordingly, in the evaluation of evidence the tribunal was required to take into account 'the degree of culture of the parties and the moral values relevant to the social group' in which it functioned. The expectation was that the values of these social groups would be drawn into this process by the adoption of a new technique of norm application. The attempt here then was not to absorb the working classes and the slum dwellers into the existing legal framework, but to create a structure outside of this framework which would be informed by and be responsive to the needs and aspirations of these groups.

The next category of societies consists of Tanzania, India and Burma. We shall first deal with the new mechanisms in Tanzania for facilitating popular involvements in legal administration, namely the Primary Courts, the arbitration councils and the TANU cell-leaders. The Primary Courts, established in 1964, are composed of one professional magistrate and two lay assessors. They replace the Local Courts which were created during the colonial period to apply customary norms and follow indigenous procedures in dealing with the controversies and the crimes of the African population. The Africans however developed a deep distrust of the Local Courts and made little use of it. Three factors seem to have contributed towards this situation; a) resentment over the discriminatory colonial court structure which excluded Africans from all but the lower courts, b) the negative image of the courts as one of the instruments through which the colonial power exercised its domination and c) the availability of adequate processes within the community to deal with these problems. Since independence, several basic changes were instituted, including the integration of the dual court structure and the separation of the exercise of judicial functions from that of the administration. The establishment of Primary Courts also appears to give expression to a more general desire to provide persons in rural Tanzania expeditious and more easily accessible judicial institutions. Unlike its precursors, the Primary Courts were also required to be subject to the Penal Code and the Criminal Procedure Code, thereby reinforcing the determination of the architects of the Primary Courts to bring them within the fold of the central legal order.

Judicial administrators in recent years have also focused attention on the arbitration of disputes by local elders pointing out that while these elders helped ease the overcrowding of court dockets, in many instances they abused their powers and disregarded basic standards of even-handedness. Accordingly, they moved "to formalize and institutionalize" the resolution of disputes by such elders through the creation of arbitration councils. Here again an attempt is made to extend the control of the central legal order over local remedy agents, by determining which elders are competent to resolve disputes, by strictly defining their jurisdiction and powers, by subjecting them to an appellate process, and by requiring them to adhere to certain basic procedural standards.

Another popular institution which we should note is the TANU cell-leader, the lowest unit of the Tanzanian mass party organization. The cell-leaders were created in the expectation that they would primarily devote themselves to transmitting and explaining party policies and mobilizing popular support towards these policies; they were, on the other hand, found to devote most of their efforts towards the settlement of inter-personal disputes. Very few TANU cell-leaders also seized upon the conflict-solving situation as an opportunity to articulate party policies, and some commentators urge that there is an incompatibility between the reconciler role which they perceive creates a need to draw on traditional values, and the mobilizational role and the resultant attempt to instill new values. Since the TANU cell-leaders are not often drawn from the traditional leadership of the clan, their role as para legal agents has also been interpreted as an encroachment by the party into the conflict management functions of traditional elders. The cell-leaders have also found to be involved in policing duties and in the execution of court-decrees, and thereby relieving state agencies of some of the reponsibilities of law enforcement.

The Indian counterparts of popular judicial institutions are the statutory nyaya panchayats, the judicial limbs of the village level panchayat which in turn is a component of a three tiered elective participatory structure of local self government. [The two others are the block level panchayat samati and the zillad panshad (the district panchayat)]. The panchayat raj concept derives its more immediate rationale and inspiration from the interrelated but relatively unsystematically developed body of social ideas which we shall herein refer to as "Gandhian collectivism". Gandhi, like his counterparts in western social thought, the anarchists and utopian socialists, believed in the benign goodness of human nature and attributed the debasement of individual man to the evils of industrialization, the oppression of hierarchical political structure and the artificial wants created by a capitalistic economic order. He believed that individual needs and aspirations find their highest level of material and spiritual fulfilment and expression in the solidarity of small groups and communites. Gandhi described this social order as follows:

> In this structure composed of innumerable villages there will be ever-widening, never ascending circles. Life would not be a pyramid with the apex sustained by the bottom. But it will be an oceanic circle where center will be the individual always ready to perish for the circle of villages, till at last the whole becomes one life composed of individuals, never aggressive in their arrogance but ever humble, sharing the majesty of the oceanic circle of which they are integral units. Therefore the outermost circumference will not wield power to crush the inner circle but will give strength to all within and derive its own strength from it.

This non-acquisitive equalitarian social order was to be accomplished not by class antagonism but by moral suasion, by which the propertied classes would be urged to forgo their social and economic priviliges and hold property (in exess of their basic needs) in trust for the welfare of the group. In the ideal Gandhian collective there would be no groups or individuals competing for power or wealth and therefore one assumes that there would be little need for an autonomous legal order to reconcile their claims. The cohesiveness of the group is conserved by the internalization of collective standards and values and by the resolution of disputes and differences by compromise and conciliation.

At a programmatic level, despite the abortive efforts of some Gandhians at the Constituent Assembly to establish an Indian polity composed of a federation of village governments, Gandhi himself was enough of a realist to recognize the inevitability of the modern state. He did, however, feel that the autonomous and self-contained village could serve as a buffer between the individual and the state, by containing the penetration of the central bureaucratic apparatus, and by cushioning the impact of the forces of industrialization released by it. As a concession to the Gandhian collectivists, the Constitution contains a provision favouring the establishment of village *panchayats* as units of local self government. The state's committment to the *panchayat* movement took more concrete shape with the recommendations of a Planning Ministry study team, headed by a Gandhian, Balwantry Mehta. The Mehta team proposed a scheme which served as a model to subsequent state *panchayat* legislation.

Alternative explanations have also been suggested to account for the statutory *panchayats*. Some, while conceding the establishment of statutory *panchayats* to the Gandhian collectivist movement, perceive the latter as essentially a revivalist program based upon a romanticized image of traditional organizational forms. But such an explanation tends to overlook the antitraditional elements in Gandhian social thought. Gandhi denied the immutability of what many believed to be religiously sanctioned hierarchical social arrangements, and believed that the social order is susceptable to change through collective effort. Further, the social organization and the distribution of authority and economic power in the equalitarian Gandhian collective was envisioned to be radically different from that in the traditional village model.

At the other extreme there are others who view the statutory *panchayats* as instruments of modernization, representing the expansion and not the containment of the modern state and the central legal order. They argue that the Indian elites regarded statutory *panchayats* as successors to the ineffective base level organizations in the community development program, a centrally planned and directed effort to integrate the rural into the national polity. The expectation was that an elective *panchayat* would be more successful than its bureaucratically conceived precursors in generating local enthusiasm and support for the program of rural development. Traditional symbolism and the emphasis on traditional values merely served the function of providing legitimacy to the new institutional forms. These considerations compelled one commentator to conclude, "the movement to *panchayats* then is . . . not an abandonment of the modern legal system but its extension in the guise of tradition."

There is a third group which regards judicial *panchayats* as no more than an imaginative judicial reform providing a creative fusion of modern and traditional elements. This group, therefore, perceives a continuity between the efforts of sensitive British administrators, such as Munro and Elphinstone, to devise judicial reforms which capture the features of indigenous procedures, and the post-independent judicial *panchayats*. Both reforms are directed towards minimizing some of the negative consequences of the British court system, arising from its lack of congruence with traditional jural postulates and resulting in frivolous and vexations suits, the use of falsified documents and the prevalence of perjured testimony, which in turn add to the expense and duration of litigation. The traditional elements in the judicial *panchayats*, the simplicity of the procedure, the absence of law professionals, the emphasis on compromise and the physical and the social proximity to the disputants, on the one hand, facilitate the cheap, informal and expeditious disposition of disputes. On the other hand, the precise delineation by statutes of the jurisdiction and powers of these tribunals, and their integration into the national court system, ensure the adherence to some of the basic procedural safeguards of the new legal order and impose consistency and uniformity in the disposition of like disputes. From this perspective, the statutory *panchayats* tend to mediate between the modern and traditional components of the dual legal order.

The establishment of popular courts in Burma has been described as a "judicial revolution" which clearly goes beyond the reforms in Tanzania and India. It envisages the replacement of the court structure with a "people's judicial system" consisting of tribunals staffed by popular judges working in rotation and a law professional serving as its secretary. The popular judges do not merely participate in the proceedings but exercise control, as the ultimate power of disposition rests with them. The participation of the law professional on the other hand is strictly limited to that of an advisor. Local control in the recruitment of the popular judges is ensured by delegating this function to a three member judicial committee composed of the local representatives of the party, worker and peasant organizations. The Popular Courts are accessible and informal, their "language is simple, and proceedings now better understood, are speedier."

The significance of the newly instituted popular judicial system can only be understood in the context of Burma's legal history. The traditional Burmese system of justice has been represented as the archtype of the informal conciliatory model of dispute resolution. The headman and other village elders mediated family problems and disputes between villagers with the aim of maintaining the peace and harmony of the family and the village. Early British adminstrators contained for some time efforts to superimpose English laws and judicial forms on Burmese society. They desired, on the one hand, to retain the expeditiousness and informality of the Burmese system and were determined, on the other, to render it more impartial, and, as a result, applied Burmese customary norms and devised an adjudicatory system which combined "British and Burmese notions of justice". The pressure for more basic changes, however, came from those who regarded the Burmese customary laws appropriate to an "isolated agricultural people" but no longer adequate to sustain the expanded commerce and economic life of an industrializing society. By the turn of the nineteenth century, customary norms were almost entirely replaced by the Anglo-Indian codes and the British common law. The relatively informal and hybrid adjudicatory system was systematically replaced by a hierarchical court organization. This process by which a formal-rational legal system and certain basic postulates such as formal equality and procedural regularity which underline it, were transposed into Burma has been described as the introduction of the "rule of law." Perspectives on the rule of law and its impact have, however, varied amongst the Burmese elite. On the one hand, several prominent leaders read "rule of law" to mean the exercise of authority in accordance with the law and the related principle of equality before the law, and regard it as one of the most valuable legacies of British rule. Others, associate the concept with the sanctity of formal rules and procedural technicalities and believe that it leads to the isolation and alienation of the courts from the social life it is expected to regulate. Those of the latter persuasion

see the undermining of the authority of the village headmen and
the destruction of the traditional social order as one of the more
pernicious effects of the introduction of the rule of law. Furniwall
seems to echo the concern of some of these persons when he notes
that "the substitution of the rule of law for custom encouraged
wasteful litigation, favoured private interests, defeated social
justice, sapped the foundations of communal life, and resulted in
general impoverishment."

The more recent socialist indictments of the judicial system
tend, however, to be more intense and assume a more consciously
ideological quality. One commentator summarizing these criticisms
notes,

> (the judicial) system has been accused of being a creation of the
> ruling elite designed to preserve its supremacy and impose its will on
> the ruled; of giving too much power to individual judges and
> magistrates; of excluding the people from the work of administering
> justice; of being beneficial only to the rich, the crafty and the
> influential, of fostering 'legal sophistry'. Above all it has been
> condemned as a powerful and exclusive bureaucracy of bourgeoisie
> days, totally out of place in a socialist democracy.

These perspectives seem to have shaped the hostility of the
present military dominated socialist regime to the existing judicial
institutions. One of the first steps taken by General Ne Win when
he assumed power a decade ago was to terminate the Supreme and
the High Courts. This policy of hostility towards the judicial
organization is further reflected in the recent efforts to establish
an alternative adjudicatory framework.

Besides being a repudiation of an alien structure, the
establishment of popular courts is also consistent with the
regime's overall ideological position on the role of the people in the
organization and management of Burmese society. From this point
of view it is closely related to the decentralization of the political
organization through the creation of base-level security and
administrative committees throughout the country, and the
debureaucratization of the administrative apparatus by the
abolition of the Secretariat and the district unit of administration.
Another related development has been the efforts of the regime "to
base its organization primarily on the strength of peasants and
other working masses" through the creation of peasants councils
and workers councils.

Another factor which seems to have influenced these
developments is the view shared by Burma's ruling elite that most
law related roles do not require legal expertise. Some commentators perceive in this a continuity between the traditional and
contemporary approaches to conflict and its management.
Proponents of the popular institutions have also drawn attention
to the persistent involvement of family elders and parents in the
hearing and disposition of domestic disputes. "To decide which
side is wrong, and which is right", the Burmese Justice Minister

adds "is a life-long work of everyone . . . [and] administering justice means doing just that." On the other hand one clearly detects important differences in recruitment, jurisdiction and powers between the traditional and contemporary models. While the evidence is unclear, it is also probably that the regime may require the popular courts, like other base-level organizations to play a mobilizational role. Different role conceptions may correspondingly give rise to important differences in function. We may, therefore, tentatively conclude that while the traditional judicial experiences may have influenced the government's decision to institute popular courts, in other respects the continuities between the traditional and the contemporary systems may be more apparent than real.

In the third category we have contemporary China, in which mass involvement in the administration of justice is one of the most distinct features of its legal system. It is realized through diverse institutional innovations such as popular assessors who participate in the limited adjudicatory work of official legal organs; mediation committees and base level mass organizations which deal with an overwhelming majority of disputes and anti-social conduct in urban and rural China; and the peoples militia, the street committee, the residents committee and the "commune" which are parts of the complex public security and law enforcement apparatus.

The emphasis on people's mediation as a principal instrument of legal policy had induced some scholars to search for continuities between the traditional and contemporary attitudes towards conflict and its resolution. Confucian thought which dominated traditional Chinese political and social life viewed disputation as disruptive of the state of natural harmony which "linked the individual, the group, society and the entire universe". Accordingly it was virtuous to "yield to another's claim and thereby restore the harmony which had been disturbed by the state of conflict." The Confucian tenets of "yielding", compromise, and non-litigiousness combined with the state's institutional structure and the traditional social order (family, clan, village, guild) to produce a preference for mediation as a technique of social control. While at a superficial level both Traditional and Contemporary China seem to share a preference for dispute resolution through mediation, a closer comparison reveals important differences in the identity, style and role of mediators and more significantly in the functions of mediation. These dissimilarities in turn point to different ideological approaches to conflict and its resolution in Confucian and Maoist thought. More significant continuities may, however, be detected between the legal experience in the Yenan province and other areas "liberated" by the Communists before 1949, and contemporary people's mediation.

The objectives of people's mediation may be understood through an analysis of the People's Mediation Committees, which by themselves or fused with other base level legal organs such as the security defense committees dispose of most of the interpersonal conflict. Both the Provisional Rules for the Organization of Mediation Committees and the authoritative party statement on these Committees place special emphasis on two specific goals. Firstly, it is stated that one of the principal objectives of Mediation Committees is to promote the internal unity of the people. The argument runs that conflict and dissension weaken the collectivist spirit and the sense of unity of the masses which are deemed necessary to propel economic production and to realize social reconstruction. The base level courts and cadres are, however, overburdened with these disputes, which interfere with other "productive" work by these agencies and weaken their capacity to expeditiously and correctly deal with the problems of the people. The Mediation Committee is therefore presented as an "effective organizational form and work method" for the prompt resolution of disputes. Secondly, the mediation committees are also regarded as "mass organizations for the people's self-education." The Rules accordingly instructed the Committee to conduct through mediation "propaganda education" concerning policies, laws and decrees. To retain this pedagogic element, mediation must be "principled" in that it should be in conformity with the central program of the state. To ensure "principled" mediation, mediators are required to be in constant touch with party cadres and base level courts and to frequently consult them and obtain their advice. Mediators are also warned against the application of coercive sanctions to compel parties into accepting or implementing an agreement. They are instead required to encourage the parties to resolve their differences through the application of "criticism and self-criticism".

On a more general ideological level, people's mediation is rationalized as one aspect of the extension of the mass-line to legal work. Such a rationale underscores the need to see popular mediation in the context of the evolution of the legal system as a whole, and more specifically those changes wrought in the legal system as a result of the extension of the "mass-line" doctrine. To do so we shall now summarize the mass-line concept and evaluate its extension into legal work through a brief review of Chinese legal developments.

The "mass-line" concept is the Maoist answer to a problem which we referred to earlier as one central to Marxist-Leninist thought, namely the proper allocation of power and initiative between the "party" and the "people" in the program of socialist transformation. There are two elements to this concept. The first underscores a deep reverence "for the political and inspirational powers of the masses," and therefore asserts the general need for constant intimate contact between the "party" and the "people." The second sets out a technique for co-ordinating the efforts of the party and the "masses" in the formulation and execution of policy.

This technique requires party cadres to study and synthesize the unsystematic views of the masses on questions of policy, to turn them into policy statements and to exhort the masses through discussion and persuasion to translate them into action. This prolonged process of dialogue has been referred to as "from the masses to the masses". While this procedure, on the one hand, enables the party to make out that all policies originate from the masses, on the other hand, the party has also asserted its ultimate authority to control policy. Where therefore, by reason of "low level of consciousness" some of the masses resist the implementation of policy, the mass-line would require the cadres to raise through non-coercive techniques, such as persuasion, criticism and thought reforms, their level of consciousness.

The mass-line concept thus subsumes Maoist ideas on mobilization", "popular participation", "re-education", and "thought reform".

As we turn to the Chinese legal system, we note that one of the first steps the Communists took after Liberation was to decree the abolition of "all laws, decrees and judicial systems of the Kuomingtang reactionary government which oppress the people". The immediate practical impact of this provision was, however, less dramatic. Several judicial and law enforcement organs were retained with often no more than a change of name. Many pre-liberation judicial and police personnel continued to work until they were removed during the anti-rightest campaigns in the early fifties. From 1950-57, coinciding with the Soviet-style economic reconstruction, we witness the Chinese legal system evolving along different lines. Concerted efforts were made to structure judicial institutions, establish a procuracy, draft codes and other legislation, and to reorganize legal education and the profession on Soviet lines. There was even a brief period of experimentation with Comrades Courts. However, since 1957, the identification of the existing legal organs with "feudalism, capitalism and Soviet revisionism" accelerated the de-professionalization of the legal system during the anti-rightest movement and more recently during the cultural revolution. Under the further influence of Maoist ideology and more specifically the tenets of the mass-line concept, the legal system assumed the following characteristics which are now regarded as distinctive of the Chinese legal model.

Firstly, efforts to rationalize and systematize centralized normative directives through the enactment of codes and statutes was suspended, on the ground that such legislation would be both premature in a society in a state of revolutionary flux and a constraint on a radical program of change. This was a hardening of an earlier approach, where there was some recognition of the importance of codes of law but as evolution of a new legislative process. This process required the party to issue preliminary drafts embodying the people's experience and their view on specific problems; to select and evaluate the responses of the

masses and other local state organs and social organizations to
these drafts; to put the amended draft into effect on an experimental basis; and finally to issue a law after scrutiny and approval
by the legislative organs.

With the decline in legislative activity the program of the
party has taken the place of what we may regard as "law". The
articulation of the central party policy often in abstract and
flexible terms has also facilitated the diffusion of norm making
authority to base level units of government and party cadres
through techniques as diverse as newspaper editorials, pamphlets,
radio broadcasts and public meetings.

Secondly, there were important changes in the relative
importance of formal legal organs, law professionals and the
informal political-legal apparatus. The role of law professionals
was gradually eliminated, and in judicial work they were replaced
by party cadres recruited more for their ideological correctness,
than their legal expertise. The judicial cadres informalized the
procedures and transformed the work style of legal institutions to
render them more accessible to the masses. On the one hand they
"penetrated the masses" by investigating complaints at the scene
of the dispute, and on the other hand "received the masses" in
person to advise them on the resolution of their problems. Since
the cultural revolution, however, the formal legal organs were
limited to the review of the more serious criminal offenses. Almost
total reliance is therefore placed on a network of base level
participatory organs, which are often active in other spheres of
political life, to manage conflict and protect the public order.

Thirdly, with the fusion of the mobilizational and conflict
management elements in judicial and mediational activity, legal
thought and the techniques of norm application became
transformed. With the emphasis on "criticism", "re-education", and
"thought reform" the vocabulary, style and technique of norm
aplication was less distinct from that of political discourse and
administrative policy implementation.

To conclude this survey we may briefly summarize some of
the factors which seem to account for the emergence of popular
tribunals in the countries we have referred to above. All of these
societies have recently replaced an alien or domestic regime either
through a violent social upheaval or through a more orderly
process of succession. In addition, many of them are also
committed to a program of social and economic change radically
different from that of the prior regime. Where the substantive ends
are broadly similar there is a committment to a radically different
strategy for realizing these ends. Popular justice in these
situations represents the extension of the new "ideology" to the
legal and specially the judicial sphere. As a result many of the
efforts to establish popular tribunals are often preceded or
accompanied by an indictment of the inherited legal system. This
takes the form of either a critique of the legal system for having

served the social or political group represented by the dethroned regime as an "instrument of oppression", or for reflecting conceptions of the law and certain assumptions about the social and economic organization of society which are repudiated by the new regime. The theoretical foundation upon which the rejection of the inherited legal system is based in turn conditions the rationalization of the new participatory institutions. Popular tribunals are therefore rationalized as responding to the needs and aspirations of emergent social groups and of reflecting in varying degrees an approach to the nature of law, the organization of legal institutions, the role of law professionals, and of the nature of legal thought fundamentally different from that represented by the inherited legal system. This pattern is repeated in each of the three categories of societies.

The revival of comrades courts (and the emergence of other forms of popular participation in the legal sphere) in the Soviet Union was preceded by a denunciation by the Twenty-First and Twenty-Second Party Congress of the Stalinist conceptions of the state and the approach to law as a coercive instrument to secure popular compliance to state policies and to protect the public order. This critique revived the vision of the withering away of the state and the disappearance of law as a coercive instrument in the ultimate stage of communism, and provided a doctrinal base for the rationalization of popular tribunals. Correspondingly, the Soviet explanation is that these tribunals illustrate the transfer of state functions to social agencies and emphasize the efficacy of non-coercive techniques for the protection of the public order and for the mobilization and education of the masses. Similarly in Cuba (and perhaps in Chile) the perception of the inherited laws and institutions as being informed by the values and class interests of the dethroned social groups, led to the expectation that the popular legal institutions in the sectors in which they were established would express the values and interests of the working classes. They would, therefore, reflect a new popular legality and propagate the norms and values of the new social order.

When we turn to the next category of countries which inherited a British court structure we perceive a difference in the post-colonial approach to the alien institutions in Tanzania on the one hand and in India and Burma on the other. In Tanzania the complaint has been that the British established a discriminatory court structure which barred Africans from the superior courts and thereby denied them many of the benefits of the western adjudicatory process. In India and in Burma (until recently) the complaint has been an opposite one. It is charged that the policy of Anglicization was pursued with such vigour that the British courts often undermined and eroded the traditional mechanisms for dispute resolution. In the latter case, it it further alleged that the clash of values underlying the indigenous and imposed legal orders contributed towards litigiousness and the further disruption

of the traditional social order. As a result in Tanzania the
establishment of popular courts represents the containment of
conflict-managing role of traditional elders and the expansion of
the inherited western legal order. The Indian *panchayats* present a
more confused picture. While some perceive the *panchayats* as
reviving traditional forms of social and legal organization, the
better view would be that they express a creative systhesis of
elements of the inherited and traditional systems. There is an
additional element in the Burmese situation. More recently the
indictments of the inherited judicial system besides being infused
with nationalistic sentiments assume a more consciously
socialistic dimension. Accordingly, the establishment of popular
tribunals is presented as part of a broader program of debureaucratization and the decentralization of the political
structures. While the Tanzanians and Indian institutions are
viewed as merely instituting "reforms" in the judicial system, the
popular courts in Burma are regarded as establishing a "judicial
revolution".

In China, we find the most extreme expression of the
repudiation of the laws and legal institutions inherited from the
Kuomingtand Government. The abolition of the inherited legal
institutions precipitated the need to formulate a state policy
towards the management of conflict and the protection of the
public order. The concept of mass-line crystalized out of the
mobilizational efforts in the provinces liberated before 1949, and
reflecting the Maoist reaction to the bureaucratization and the
consolidation and abuse of power by Traditional and Kuomingtan
governments, helped shape the state policy towards people's
mediation. This doctrine which extols the value of, and provides
a technique for, extensive mass participation in the discharge of
state functions transformed the law making process, the work
style and techniques of norm application of mediation committees
and of the entire public security apparatus. At later periods
the reaction against soviet-style legal reforms and the "struggle"
by party cadres against legal specialists for the latter's adherence
to the procedures, forms and even values of the "bourgeois legal
systems" further accelerated the pace of de-professionalization.
The mass-line concept also provides the link between people's
mediation and the legal experience in Yenan and other areas
"liberated" before 1949.

Chapter 11

Reliance on Formal Written Law, and Freedom and Social Control in the United States and the People's Republic of China*

Harold E. Pepinsky†

Introduction

The use of formal written law is highly developed in the United States (U.S.). Agents of the state publish innumerable substantive rules as to how people shall and shall not act, and procedural rules as to how agents of the state shall react to transgressions of the substantive rules. This rule-making, and the tradition that the rules generally can be expected to be followed both by citizens and by agents of the state, form the basis of an American strategy of social control.

In the People's Republic of China (P.R.C.), agents of the state have promulgated few substantive rules, and it has been established that agents of the state are not found to follow the relatively few written rules as to how they are to respond to citizens' acts.[1] In the latter society today, it is rare to find someone 'punished according to law'. In the U.S., such punishment is frequently declared to have been given. Four hundred thousand Americans have been specially trained (as attorneys) to apply the

* Harold E. Pepinsky, "Reliance on Formal Written Law, and Freedom and Social Control in the United States and The People's Republic of China," *The British Journal of Sociology* 26 (Sept., 1975): 330-342. Reprinted by permission of Routledge & Kegan Paul Ltd. and the author.
† Harold E. Pepinsky B.A. J.D. PH.D. Forensic Studies, Indiana University.

written law to particular cases, while today in the P.R.C. there are no lawyers to speak of.

In the U.S., the practical absence of utilized formal written law is generally seen as a fearsome prospect.[2] On the one hand, the prospect is that of a breakdown of social order, of rampant social conflict, of anarchy. On the other hand, the prospect is that of totalitarian state restriction of citizens' actions, of unfettered social control. Obviously, the prospect is paradoxical. Conversely, reliance on a formal written law is seen to restrict both each citizen's freedom to act uncontrolled by the demands of others and others' freedom to control each citizen's freedom of action. This view is also paradoxical. Each notion implies that citizens' freedom from control by agents of the state co-varies directly with state agents' control of citizens' freedom of action. The paradoxes are eliminated only by making logically tenable the possibility of a simultaneous increase and decrease in citizens' freedom from control by state agents, accompanied by a simultaneous decrease and increase in state agents' control of citizens' freedom of action.

It is therefore possible that Americans' typical visions of the consequences of lesser reliance on formal written law might be qualifiedly valid. In one sense, freedom of citizens' actions from control by state agents might be increased, while in another sense it would be decreased. The way in which citizens' freedom would be increased and that in which it would be restricted remain to be predicted.

The P.R.C. is the only large, complex social system in which there is practically no reliance on formal written law. That society thus presents the only comparative empirical base from which to draw an inference as to which social changes might be expected to accompany a decreased reliance on formal written law in the U.S. The next section will isolate the differences between the U.S. and the P.R.C. in two respects. In one respect, it will isolate an area of citizens' action in the U.S. that is relatively *less* restricted by agents of the state than is the case in the P.R.C. In another respect, it will isolate an area of citizens' action in the U.S. that is relatively *more* restricted by agents of the state than is the case in the P.R.C.

The comparison is not in itself adequate evidence that a decreased reliance on formal written law can be expected generally to be related to particular changes in citizens' freedom of action. However, as the succeeding section of the paper will show, there is a logical basis for inferring a general relationship. By way of preliminary hypothesis, a prediction can plausibly be made of the effect of reduced use of formal written law on freedom of citizens' action from control by state agents.

The Freedom of Social Mobility vs. that of
Collective Accomplishment

Indications are that commitment of Americans to maintaining particular relationships is lower in the United States (U.S.) than it is of Chinese in the People's Republic of China (P.R.C.). Commitment as used here is the probability that social relationships with the same persons will be maintained over time.

Social statistics are easier to obtain in the U.S. than in the P.R.C., though ordinal comparisons between the two polities remain possible. To begin with, geographical mobility is higher in the U.S. than in the P.R.C. One-fifth of all Americans move from one residence to another each year.[3] In China, one lives where assigned. Unauthorized and authorized movement from countryside to cities are both apparently held low in a predominantly rural country. Apparently, most of those who are sent to the countryside are sent only temporarily to learn the meaning of working with the masses, though some stay in the countryside for long periods of time. Community members sent to cities are generally sent temporarily for education and training to use back at home. To be sure, a number of Chinese are permanently assigned to work far away from their homes. However, the rate of geographical mobility, especially from one neighbourhood to the next in the same metropolitan area, appears to be far higher in the U.S. than in the P.R.C.

Occupational mobility is rather high in the U.S. if one includes horizontal mobility as well as the less frequent vertical mobility. The latest data on frequency of job change are unfortunately a bit old (from 1949), but there is no reason to believe that frequency of job changes has decreased since that time. The findings, by Lipset and Bendix[4] in Oakland, showed unskilled workers having held an average of more than ten jobs. Business managers and executives, at the other extreme, had averaged over three jobs apiece. The overall average number of jobs held by all those sampled was 6.3.

The rate of change of occupation would have to be lower than the rate of change of jobs, but even in this category only 29.3 per cent of American males between the ages of 25 an 64 were found not to have changed occupations as of 1962.[5]

Apparently, in the P.R.C. occupational mobility is minimal. Once trained, urban workers are reported to change jobs either only as a job is eliminated in favour of another or temporarily from managerial status to work among the masses. Rural workers may perform different jobs as local needs change, such as from cultivating to harvesting of crops or to construction of irrigation facilities. Very much like the small American farmer the rural Chinese is apt to be more a generalist than a specialist. However, the work setting is not apt to change for the rural resident.

Hence, at home and at work, Chinese tend to stay with the

same people far longer than their American counterparts.

While divorce is rather commonplace and ever easier to obtain in the U.S., divorce is seemingly rather difficult to obtain in the P.R.C. since the Cultural Revolution. Lubman[6] describes a divorce trial he attended in Peking. The district judge went to the tractor factory where the estranged husband and wife worked. He 'had already interviewed husband and wife singly and together as well as their neighbours, fellow workers and supervisors. All past attempts to keep them together had failed, however, and the wife had persisted in her demand for a divorce.'

The judge interviewed the couple singly and together once again. With him were a group of the couples' neighbours and fellow workers or 'masses' representatives'. Duties under two of the few laws in the P.R.C., the Constitution of 1954 and the Marriage Law of 1950, were vaguely described—to 'mutually love and respect each other' and to participate in Socialist construction'. The husband had admitted adultery and had struck his wife in a quarrel, but these were considered past problems to be overcome in a reconciliation, not grounds for a separation. Following the counsel of the 'masses' representatives', the judge ordered the husband to sign a 'statement of guarantee' that he would not again strike his wife. Failure to keep the guarantee would ostensibly be grounds for a divorce and injury to the wife would result in 'punishment according to law' (threatening, but remote). The representatives would continue to 're-educate' the husband and 'assist' in the reconciliation process. Continues Lubman, 'The trial expressed the ideal of Chinese justice—to avoid formal adjudication of disputes between citizens and to strengthen the social solidarity of the working class.'

Professor Victor Li of Stanford University Law School had a similar reconciliation attempt described to him during a visit to the P.R.C. This author's reconstruction of that description is that a husband had constantly been late to work and was making mistakes on the job. His work group had asked him for an explanation. He replied that he and his wife were fighting because they saw so little of each other so that he was losing sleep and could not focus on his work. The wife worked another shift at the same plant. The group sent the husband's supervisor to the wife's supervisor to arrange for the husband and wife to work on the same shift. The husband was exhorted to study his mistakes and improve his work.

Two contrasts in domestic relations with the U.S. are noteworthy. First, much greater emphasis in the P.R.C. than in the U.S. (with parades of faceless people moving through routine and often uncontested divorce hearings) is put on keeping spouses together in the same relationship. For a spouse simply to abandon a family would be inconceivable in the P.R.C. Second, one's co-workers and supervisors get much more thoroughly involved in the intimate details of a person's home life than would characteristically be the case in the U.S.

As Cohen[7] describes, groups and mediation mechanisms exist for residents of urban areas similar to those for workers. 'Mediation' is something of a misnomer, for it is practically unheard of for disputants not to defer to the counsel of their 'mediators', though the process lacks the formal written guarantees of authority of what we know as arbitration. The point is that reconciliation and persuasion will be tried repeatedly and with involvement of many familiar faces at work and in the neighbourhood before the disputants may be released from the burden of trying to resolve their differences within ongoing relationships.

Extended observations of the police, corroborated by police officers from various parts of the country, have suggested that the situation in U.S. urban neighbourhoods is different.[8] A large portion of citizen complaints to patrolmen call for the patrolmen to act as the citizens' agents in resolving petty problems with relatives and neighbours. One common complaint, especially in apartment buildings, is that neighbours are playing music too loudly. Usually in these cases, the complainant has not approached his neighbour directly and stays away while the police convey his demand. The complainant is apt not even to know the neighbour. Other common complaints would be of neighbours parking in front of the complainant's home, of neighbours' children or pets causing minor damage or simply a disturbance on the complainant's property, of landlords locking tenants out of apartments or rooms, of alcoholic or infirm elderly neighbours of family members needing removal (somewhat like garbage) or of petty but voluble family arguments. The police may not enjoy being called upon to handle such problems, but in practice generally concur in the wisdom of their separating the disputants. The police also generally consider it good practice to end their own involvement as rapidly as possible, figuring the most they can do is to cool down the conflict of the moment.

This is a second type of mobility far more commonly found in the U.S. than in the P.R.C. Not only are American citizens more apt to move from one place of residence or work to the next and to do so at will, but Americans in a number of cases use third persons to take care of (removing, if necessary) people with whom the Americans get into conflict in residence situations. According to Rothman,[9] both forms of mobility became salient simultaneously in the Jacksonian era in the U.S. The American does not rely solely on removing himself from others; he can have the others removed or restrained while he remains aloof from them, and, literally, relatively unmoved himself. Characteristically, a Chinese would not be permitted to absolve himself of responsibility for carrying on relationships with family and neighbours throughout periods of conflict and need. He can remove himself or others from troublesome situations only rarely, and then in the guise and with the consensus of his fellows that in the overall task of socialist construction he is more valuable elsewhere.

Commonly, juveniles who are institutionalized in the U.S. are so treated because they have caused trouble in school. [10] Cicourel and Kitsuse[11] have described the process by which troublemakers in American schools get picked out and isolated from their peers. Contrast this to the report that in the P.R.C. 'a MS (middle school) class receives the grade of its poorest achiever'.[12] Frank criticism of others and of oneself, as a prelude to reintegration of a 'deviant' back into a group, and continuing to help someone who is not making his fair contribution to do so, are acceptable ways of handling social conflict and disruption, but in school and elesewhere isolation of a person would seldom be considered a viable solution to any problem. If anything, the opposite tends to be the case, for a person causing trouble is considered to require more rather than less intensive interaction with and attention from his peers. In general, while stress is conventionally associated with mobility in the U.S.,[13] stress is conventionally associated with 'criticism' and 'struggle' in the P.R.C.

This set of examples indicates consistently a greater tendency in the U.S. for citizens to move among relationships than is the case in the P.R.C. Presumably, too, there is more occasion for citizens to express themselves in private, as by painting, alone, than would be the case in the P.R.C., where all action is to be public. The right to privacy has in fact been held to be implicit in law as law is known in the U.S.[14] On the other hand, P.R.C. citizens seem more consistently to stay involved in ongoing relationships through problem situations than do their U.S. counterparts. As a result, the scope of the relationships in the P.R.C. appears characteristically to extend beyond that of corresponding relationships in the U.S.

Hence, the state which restricts less—and even encourages— social mobility is also the one that relies more heavily on formal written law.

The freedom more typical for Chinese than for Americans is difficult to describe. It is a kind of freedom with which Americans are largely unfamiliar. For Americans this freedom has a subtlety corresponding to its salience for the Chinese. The freedom is that of developing access to new economic and social resources within the context of existing relationships.

The improvement in the economic lot of the average Chinese over the last twenty-five years is dramatic and well known. Where famines periodically took millions of lives, all people have enough to eat. All in the cities have shelter, where many once had only the streets on which to live. Middle school education has become universal where illiteracy was the norm. Myrdal and Kessle[15] found that through collective effort the 'five guarantees' of enough food, enough clothes, enough fuel, an honourable funeral and education for the children had become a reality for everyone even in a relatively poor village in Yenan in 1969. Myrdal and Kessle provide perhaps the most detailed, vivid and credible description of the form of the collective effort in the P.R.C.

However, for those accustomed to relative affluence in the U.S., any description of collective accomplishment in the P.R.C. is apt to seem trivial. The general strength of interpersonal competition has become an American assumption. The following scenario has been developed to translate the recent Chinese experience into an American context.

The President has just made a nationwide television address telling Americans of a fuel crisis and asking them to curtail automobile gasoline consumption as much as possible. No formal action is contemplated; full faith is being placed in the voluntary co-operation of the citizenry, in accord with the political ideology that has become nationally dominant in the past several years.

Outside the city of Gotham, at the 2100 block of Rich Street in the suburb of Pleasantview, darkness has fallen. It is 8 p.m.—time for the nightly block meeting. Jack and Doris Stormann generally host the meeting in their spacious home. Tonight is no exception.

Almost everyone has arrived. The children are being watched tonight by Dan and Barbara Spinoza, who are taking their turn in the babysitting rotation. In the living-room, about thirty people are sitting in a circle—each already engaged with his neighbours in discussions of the President's speech. Conversation among them is relaxed for most of them have known each other, in and out of these meetings, for years. Then block chairman Mary Geller, bearing in mind that her responsibility is to elicit a co-operative response to the fuel crisis, calls the meeting to order.

'Obviously, the President's speech is on all our minds,' she begins. 'Anyone who wants to comment on it may speak.'

'Apparently, the fuel crisis is real. We simply have to use our cars a lot less than we've been doing.' Heads nod in agreement. Bill Samuch has verbalized a preliminary consensus of the meeting.

Discussion moves quickly to how members of the group can help one another to meet the-agreed-upon objective. Use of the bus service is suggested, but a number of disparaging remarks about the service lead to abandonment of this idea.

Then a member of the group raises the notion of a car pool. A car pool is acceptable to everyone but George Jones, who likes to be alone on the way to work. 'How can you be so selfish in a matter of such importance?' he is asked. George argues awhile for his conception of his rights, but eventually his resistance gives way to assent. Even if he had left the meeting to escape the group pressure, he soon would have been visited by a delegation seeking to 'help' him with 'his problem'. It has come to be taken for granted by all participants that no one can expect to get away with pursuit of private interests in matters of public concern.

And so it is agreed that eight car pools will be established to take the neighbours to and from places of work in various areas of the community. The membership of each pool is established, and each pool is asked to work out its own schedule, rotation of driving and plan of sharing expenses.

Then it is noted that a substantial number of housewives in the neighbourhood have shopping to do and other errands to run. With little deliberation, the notion of car pools is extended to meet these needs. On a rotating schedule, individual housewives accept the responsibility for taking calls from those who plan to go out during the day. The first to call who has use of a car and who cannot make use of transportation in a car already scheduled to go on a trip is to be a driver, and the co-ordinator of the day refers subsequent callers to her as passengers. Also on a rotating basis, two housewives a day are enlisted for child care while both parents are away. Thus, mothers and fathers are freed from having to take small children with them on their various trips. Such a child-care programme has already been tried and proved for evening babysitting. Children have learned to look forward to staying as long as overnight with neighbours as a kind of adventure. From prior experience, any inequities in allocation of responsibilities versus utilization of services are left to be adjusted as they arise in future meetings.

The meeting has been going on for nearly an hour. By convention, it is about time to adjourn. Alice Ladinsky mentions that she and her husband have been having marital difficulties, and asks leave to discuss them in the next meeting. Her husband, Mack, concurs. Without objection, the chairwoman approves the request. The meeting is over.

Over the years, the need for social services in the block has declined markedly. The police have not been called for the past two years. A few would-be burglars have been scared off by watchful neighbours. Loans have been arranged by the group for families in a financial crisis. Members of the group have effectively acted as informal therapists for one another. The rate of movement in and out of the neighbourhood has declined to insignificance, for the social support provided there has proved generally more valuable to the residents than occupational mobility.

The scenario is designed to highlight the kind of freedom offered by a social system geared to collective accomplishment rather than to social mobility. The co-operative effort of a stable group (or groups) provides opportunities and services closely tuned to the needs of the members. Each member has a freedom to choose among services that would otherwise be unavailable or not so well suited to his or her requirements. In the process of restricting social mobility by organizing people into groups and, initially at least, trying to enforce members' participation in them, the role of the state in providing rules and institutions especially for conflict resolution and provision of services tends to become superfluous. The kind of individual freedom from control by state agents changes as one moves from a social system relying heavily on formal written law to one resisting such reliance. However, the overall quantum of freedom cannot be shown to differ between the two systems. How the use of formal written law tends to imply the freedom of social mobility rather than that of collective accomplishment remains to be explained.

The Impact of Societal Reliance on Formal Written Law

Weber has translated the meaning of law, including its formal written form, into functional terms:

> An order will be called *law* if it is externally guaranteed by the probability that coercion (physical or psychological), to bring about conformity or average violation, will be applied by a *staff* of people holding themselves specially ready for that purpose.[16]

When a law is formal and written, the law carries the additional promise that the order of coercion is knowable in advance and that the probability of coercion is tied to the knowable order. Commitment to formal written law by members of society seems logically to imply that 'a general function of law in any society is that of enabling members of the society to calculate the consequences of their conduct, thereby securing and facilitating voluntary transactions and arrangements.[17]

As the system of formal written law serves this function of creating security, it engenders a dependence by the society's members and thereby restricts their freedom of action. As long ago as 1840, Tocqueville found a role for formal written law in a kind of despotism which he foresaw coming to the U.S. He wrote:

> [Despotism] covers the surface of society with a *network of small, complicated rules, minute and uniform*, through which the most original minds and the most energetic characters cannot penetrate, to rise above the crowd. The will of man is not shattered, but softened, bent, and guided; men are seldom forced by it to act, but they are constantly restrained from acting: such a power does not destroy, but it prevents existence; it does not tyrannize, but it compresses, enervates, and stupifies a people, till each nation is reduced to nothing better than a pack of animals, of which the government is the shepherd.[18] [Emphasis added.]

There has been a tendency to analogize exhortations in newspapers, on radio and in Party directives in the P.R.C. to the formal written law in the U.S. There is a significant difference between the published exhortations in the P.R.C. and the terms of the law in the U.S. however. The exhortations in the P.R.C. contain three elements: (a) statements of what social products are needed from collective actions (e.g., the level of industrial output must be increased), (b) descriptions of tools that can be used by groups to shape social action to obtain the products (e.g., criticism and persuasion) and (c) specification of attitudes or general approaches to action which are obstacles to production (e.g., bureaucratism). Attempts at formal statements of what particular products of action are required from *individuals* have been practically abandoned since the disaster of 'The Great Leap Forward' programme in the latter part of the 1950's, when it proved ineffective, for instance, to set quotas on production of pig iron by individuals in backyard furnaces. Official pronouncements in the P.R.C. prescribe *how* individual conduct is to be decided upon within community groups. Official pronouncements do not designate *what* each individual's conduct shall be.

The formal written law of the U.S., on the other hand predominantly prescribes *what* conduct is required by individuals. Indeed, the U.S. Supreme Court has held that the criminal law, as law is traditionally conceived, can only address concrete acts by people.[19] The 'rules' to which Tocqueville refers are those which prescribe specific acts that an individual must or must not carry out. Rules of substantive conduct take decisions as to courses of action towards particular others out of the hands of individuals, while directives as to how and why decisions must be made place responsibility for these decisions squarely in the hands of the citizen, while tending to take away responsibility for when and where the decisions are made.

Experience in the U.S. and the P.R.C. suggest two modifications of the role of rules—including those in formal written law. First, people are not restrained by use of the rules from moving among relationships with others; they are encouraged to do so. Second, the restraint takes the form of providing a structural substitute for reliance on others for co-operation.

Reliance on formal written law reinforces a distrust of interpersonal support from particular others. The structure provided by rules indicates that the state through its agents will take care of the arrangements of interpersonal relations where these relations are necessary. People are seen as trouble; the only thing they characteristically can and will provide not supplied by the legal order is capricious, unpredictable obstinacy and resistance to the furthering of one's personal interests. Associations with others tend to become those of momentary convenience. When another stands in one's way, it is best to move along.

By its explicit emphasis on the ordering of acts rather than the ordering of status, formal written law replaces the attempted definition of where one is with that of what one does. Consistently, our formal written law even stresses a freedom of movement for its citizens. So long as the citizens do as the law commands, they are free to do it wherever they please. With its invitation to citizens to enjoy one kind of freedom, formal written law helps discourage them from attempting to enjoy another.

The promulgation of formal written law dampens efforts to collective accomplishment in other ways, too. Such promulgation helps establish the conventional wisdom that the substance of appropriate and inappropriate action tends to be immutable and unvaried from one relationship and situation to the next. The idea that one can customarily create a novel form of action to meet the demands of a particular situation, changing the form in the next situation merely by the exercise of personal judgment, tends to be met with considerable scepticism.

By contrast, the system in which use of formal written law is eschewed essentially requires just one rule. The citizen shall stay with the group or groups in which he is placed by agents of the state. To some extent agents of the state may also be relied on for information as to what social needs and problems are, and for feedback as to whether the needs are being met and the problems resolved. However, agents of the state tend to refrain from promulgating rules as to what each citizen is to do to work to meet even those needs and resolve the problems the agents attempt to define. The individual is restricted from moving among relationships, and forced to rely for survival on the relationship he or she is given. Survival seemingly requires that the individual be resourceful, adaptable and innovative in choosing a form of action to meet the demands of the moment. Such an environment is apparently conducive to experiencing and learning the potential of collective accomplishment.

The apparent relationship between the use of law and the form of individual freedom from control by state agents is symbiotic, rather than recursively causal. That is, the predominant form of the use of law and the predominant form of freedom can be expected to change together rather than a change in one being logically prior to a change in the other. Thus, as social support grows for reinforcing opportunities for collective accomplishment, use of formal written law can be expected to become an undesirably restrictive anachronism, while as use of formal written law declines, individual reliance on collective accomplishment can be expected to tend to displace reliance on social mobility.

Conclusion

It is beyond the scope of this article to predict what change, if any, is to be anticipated in the reliance on use of formal written law in the U.S. As the article is composed there is, to say the least, scant indication that such reliance is on the wane. There are currently as many law students in U.S. schools as there are attorneys in the country. Now legislation is frequently and conventionally seen as the major tool needed to respond to domestic crises such as that known under the rubric of 'Watergate' and the energy crisis.

The argument here is that *if* attenuation of reliance on formal written law should occur in this or another society, the change will not occur in isolation. The hypothesis advanced here is that any such attenuation will be accompanied by a change in the form of individual freedom from control by state agents that predominates in the society. Thus, by the terms of the hypothesis, use of formal written law does not preserve *social order;* it plays an important role in preserving *a* social order. It does not preserve or establish *individual freedom* from social control by state agents; it plays an important role in establishing or maintaining one *form* of individual freedom at the expense of enjoyment of another form. The hypothesis implies that it is overly simplistic to associate a reluctance to use formal written law with 'dictatorship' (as does Nagel)[20] or to call a failure to adhere to the terms of formal written law 'undemocratic' (as does Evan).[21] There is more than one way in which citizens can rule themselves without state interference, and in the process of availing themselves of one kind of self-rule the citizens must give up another. No method suggests itself for weighing the quality of one form of individual freedom from control by state agents against that of its antithetical form. For the time being, perhaps it is sufficient that we understand the possible trade-off in freedom we make by a transition from reliance on formal written law to reliance on its non-use order that our choice of whether to use formal written law may be better informed.

NOTES

1.   See Jerome A. Cohen, *The Criminal Process in the People's Republic of China: 1949-1963.* Cambridge, Mass.: Harvard University Press, 1968; Stanley Lubman, "Form and Function in the Chinese Criminal Process", *Columbia Law Review* (April, 1969): 535-75; Victor H. Li, "The Role of Law in Communist China," *China Quarterly* 44 (Oct.-Dec., 1970): 66-111; Victor H. Li, "Law and Penology: Systems of Reform and Correction" in Michel Oksenberg (ed.), *China's Developmental Experience.* New York: Praeger Publishers, 1973; Harold E. Pepinsky, "The People v. the Principle of Legality in the People's Republic of China," *J. Crim. Justice* I (March, 1973): 51-60.

2.   Richard Quinney, "The Ideology of Law: Notes for a Radical Alternative by Legal Oppression", *Issues in Criminology* 7 (Winter, 1972): 1-35.

3.   See James W. Simmons, "A Review of Interurban Mobility", *Geogr. Rev.* 58 (Oct., 1968): 622-57, at 622.

4.   Seymour M. Lipset and Reinhard Bendix, *Social Mobility in the United States,* Berkeley: University of California Press, 1959.

5.   United States Bureau of the Census, "Lifetime Occupational Mobility of Adult Males, March 1962", *Current Population Reports,* series P-23, no. II (May 1964).

6.   Stanley Lubman, "A Divorce Trial—Peking Style", *Wall St. J.* (5.6.73).

7.   Cohen, *op. cit.*

8.   Harold E. Pepinsky, "Police Decisions to Report Offences", Philadelphia: University of Pennsylvania dissertation, 1972, pp. 72-8.

9.   David J. Rothman, The Discovery of the Asylum: Social Order and Disorder in the New Republic. Boston: Little, Brown & Co., 1971, pp. 57-9.

10.   See Graeme R. Newman, "Deviance and Removal", Philadelphia: University of Pennsylvania dissertation, 1972.

11.   Aaron B. Cicourel and John I. Kitsuse, "The Social Organization of the High School and Deviant Adolescent Careers", in Earl Rubington and Martin S. Wemberg, Deviance: The Interactionist Perspective. New York: Macmillan, 1968, pp. 124-35.

12.   Albert H. Yee, "School and Progress in the People's Republic of China", Educational Researcher 2 (July, 1973): 5-15.

13.   See W. A. V. Clark and Martin Cadwallader, "Locational Stress and Residential Mobility", Environment and Behaviour 5 (March, 1973): 29-41.

14.   United States Supreme Court, Griswold v. Connecticut (1965), 381 U.S. 479.

15.   Jan Myrdal and Gun Kessle (Paul B. Austin (trans.)), China: The Revolution Continued. New York: Pantheon Books, 1970, pp. 52-5.

16.   Max Weber (Max Rheinstein (ed.), and Edward Shils and Max Rheinstein, trans.), Max Weber on Law in Economy and Society. New York, Simon & Schuster, 1967, p. 5.

17.   Harold D. Berman and William R. Greiner, The Nature and Function of Law (2nd ed.), Brooklyn: The Foundation Press, 1966, p. 31.

18.   Alexis de Tocqueville in Richard D. Heffner (ed.), Democracy in America. New York: The New American Library 1956, pp. 303-4.

19.   United States Supreme Court, Robinson v. California, (1962), 370 U.S. 660.

20.   Stuart S. Nagel, "Culture Pattern and Judicial Systems", Vanderbilt Law Rev. 16 (Dec., 1962): 1-157.

21.   William M. Evan, "Public and Private Legal Systems" in William M. Evan (ed.), Law and Sociology: Exploratory Essays. New York: The Free Press, 1962.

Chapter 12

Conflicts as Property*

Nils Christie†

Abstract

Conflicts are seen as important elements in society. Highly
industrialised societies do not have too much internal conflict,
they have too little. We have to organise social systems so that
conflicts are both nurtured and made visible and also see to it that
professionals do not monopolise the handling of them. Victims of
crime have in particular lost their rights to participate. A court
procedure that restores the participants' rights to their own
conflicts is outlined.

Introduction

Maybe we should not have any criminology. Maybe we should
rather abolish institutes, not open them. Maybe the social
consequences of criminology are more dubious than we like to
think.

* Nils Christie, "Conflicts as Property", Brit. J. Crimin. 17
(Jan. 1977): 1-15. Reprinted by permission of the British Journal of Criminology
(The Institute for the Study and Treatment of Delinquency).
† Foundation Lecture of the Centre for Criminological Studies. University of
Sheffield, delivered March 31, 1976. Valuable comments on preliminary drafts of
the manuscript were received from Vigdis Christie, Tove Stang Dahl and Annika
Snare. Professor of Criminology. University of Oslo.

I think they are. And I think this relates to my topic—conflicts as property. My suspicion is that criminology to some extent has amplified a process where conflicts have been taken away from the parties directly involved and thereby have either disappeared or become other people's property. In both cases a deplorable outcome. Conflicts ought to be used, not only left in erosion. And they ought to be used, and become useful, for those originally involved in the conflict. Conflicts *might* hurt individuals as well as social systems. That is what we learn in school. That is why we have officials. Without them, private vengeance and vendettas will blossom. We have learned this so solidly that we have lost track of the other side of the coin: our industrialised large-scale society is not one with too many internal conflicts. It is one with too little. Conflicts might kill, but too little of them might paralyse. I will use this occasion to give a sketch of this situation. It cannot be more than a sketch. This paper represents the beginning of the development of some ideas, not the polished end-product.

On Happenings and Non-Happenings

Let us take our point of departure far away. Let us move to Tanzania. Let us approach our problem from the sunny hillside of the Arusha province. Here, inside a relatively large house in a very small village, a sort of happening took place. The house was overcrowded. Most grown-ups from the village and several from adjoining ones were there. It was a happy happening, fast talking, jokes, smiles, eager attention, not a sentence was to be lost. It was circus, it was drama. It was a court case.

The conflict this time was between a man and a woman. They had been engaged. He had invested a lot in the relationship through a long period, until she broke it off. Now he wanted it back. Gold and silver and money were easily decided on, but what about utilities already worn, and what about general expenses?

The outcome is of no interest in our context. But the framework for conflict solution is. Five elements ought to be particularly mentioned:

1. The parties, the former lovers, were in *the centre* of the room and in the centre of everyone's attention. They talked often and were eagerly listened to.

2. Close to them were relatives and friends who also took part. But they did not *take over*.

3. There was also participation from the general audience with short questions, information, or jokes.

4. The judges, three local party secretaries, were extremely inactive. They were obviously ignorant with regard to village matters. All the other people in the room were experts. They were experts on norms as well as actions. And they crystallised norms

and clarified what had happened through participation in the procedure.

5. No reporters attended. They were all there.

My personal knowledge when it comes to British courts is limited indeed. I have some vague memories of juvenile courts where I counted some 15 or 20 persons present, mostly social workers using the room for preparatory work or small conferences. A child or a young person must have attended, but except for the judge, or maybe it was the clerk, nobody seemed to pay any particular attention. The child or young person was most probably utterly confused as to who was who and for what, a fact confirmed in a small study by Peter Scott (1959). In the United States of America, Martha Baum (1968) has made similar observations. Recently, Bottoms and McClean (1976) have added another important observation: "There is one truth which is seldom revealed in the literature of the law or in studies of the administration of criminal justice. It is a truth which was made evident to all those involved in this research project as they sat through the cases which made up our sample. The truth is that, for the most part, the business of the criminal courts is dull, commonplace, ordinary and after a while downright tedious".

But let me keep quiet about your system, and instead concentrate on my own. And let me assure you; what goes on is no happening. It is all a negation of the Tanzanian case. What is striking in nearly all the Scandinavian cases is the greyness, the dullness, and the lack of any important audience. Courts are not central elements in the daily life of our citizens, but peripheral in four major ways:—

1. They are situated in the administrative centres of the towns, outside the territories of ordinary people.

2. Within these centres they are often centralised within one or two large buildings of considerable complexity. Lawyers often complain that they need months to find their way within these buildings. It does not demand much fantasy to imagine the situation of parties or public when they are trapped within these structures. A comparative study of court architecture might become equally relevant for the sociology of law as Oscar Newman's (1972) study of defensible space is for criminology. But even without any study, I feel it safe to say that both physical situation and architectural design are strong indicators that courts in Scandinavia belong to the administrators of law.

3. This impression is strengthened when you enter the courtroom itself—if you are lucky enough to find your way to it. Here again, the periphery of the parties is the striking observation. The parties are represented, and it is these representatives and the judge or judges who express the little activity that is activated within these rooms. Honoré Daumier's famous drawings from the courts are as representative for Scandinavia as they are for France. There are variations. In the small cities, or in the

countryside, the courts are more easily reached than in the larger towns. And at the very lowest end of the court system—the so-called arbitration boards—the parties are sometimes less heavily represented through experts in law. But the symbol of the whole system is the Supreme Court where the directly involved parties do not even attend their own court cases.

4. I have not yet made any distinction between civil and criminal conflicts. But it was not by chance that the Tanzania case was a civil one. Full participation in your own conflict presupposes elements of civil law. The key element in a criminal proceeding is that the proceeding is converted from something between the concrete parties into a conflict between one of the parties and the state. So, in a modern criminal trial, two important things have happened. First, the parties are being *represented*. Secondly, the one party that is represented by the state, namely the victim, is so thoroughly represented that she or he for most of the proceedings is pushed completely out of the arena, reduced to the triggerer-off of the whole thing. She or he is a sort of double loser; first, vis-à-vis the offender, but secondly and often in a more crippling manner by being denied rights to full participation in what might have been one of the more important ritual encounters in life. The victim has lost the case to the state.

Professional Thieves

As we all know, there are many honourable as well as dishonourable reasons behind this development. The honourable ones have to do with the state's need for conflict reduction and certainly also its wishes for the protection of the victim. It is rather obvious. So is also the less honourable temptation for the state, or Emperor, or whoever is in power, to use the criminal case for personal gain. Offenders might pay for their sins. Authorities have in time past shown considerable willingness, in representing the victim, to act as receivers of the money or other property from the offender. Those days are gone; the crime control system is not run for profit. And yet they are not gone. There are, in all banality, many interests at stake here, most of them related to professionalisation.

Lawyers are particularly good at stealing conflicts. They are trained for it. They are trained to prevent and solve conflicts. They are socialised into a sub-culture with a surprisingly high agreement concerning interpretation of norms, and regarding what sort of information can be accepted as relevant in each case. Many among us have, as laymen, experienced the sad moments of truth when our lawyers tell us that our best arguments in our fight against our neighbour are without any legal relevance whatsoever and that we for God's sake ought to keep quiet about them in court. Instead they pick out arguments we might find irrelevant or even wrong to use. My favourite example took place just after the war. One of my country's absolutely top defenders told with pride how he had just rescued a poor client. The client had collaborated with the Germans. The prosecutor claimed that the client had been one of the key people in the organisation of the Nazi movement. He had been one of the master-minds behind it all. The defender, however, saved his client. He saved him by pointing out to the jury how weak, how lacking in ability, how obviously deficient his client was, socially as well as organisationally. His client could simply not have been one of the organisers among the collaborators; he was without talents. And he won the case. His client got a very minor sentence as a very minor figure. The defender ended his story by telling me—with some indignation—that neither the accused, nor his wife, had ever thanked him, they had not even talked to him afterwards.

Conflicts become the property of lawyers. But lawyers don't hide that it is conflicts they handle. And the organisational framework of the courts underlines this point. The opposing parties, the judge, the ban against privileged communication within the court system, the lack of encouragement for specialisation—specialists cannot be internally controlled—it all underlines that this is an organisation for the handling of conflicts. *Treatment personnel* are in another position. They are more interested in *converting the image of the case from one of conflict into one of non-conflict.* The basic model of healers is not one of opposing parties, but one where one party has to be helped in the direction of one generally accepted goal—the preservation or restoration of health. They are not trained into a system where it is important that parties can control each other. There is, in the ideal case, nothing to control, because there is only one goal. Specialisation is encouraged. It increases the amount of available knowledge, and the loss of internal control is of no relevance. A conflict perspective creates unpleasant doubts with regard to the healer's suitability for the job. A non-conflict perspective is a precondition for defining crime as a legitimate target for treatment.

One way of reducing attention to the conflict is reduced attention given to the victim. Another is concentrated attention given to those attributes in the criminal's background which the healer is particularly trained to handle. Biological defects are perfect. So also are personality defects when they are established far back in time—far away from the recent conflict. And so are also the whole row of explanatory variables that criminology might offer. We have, in criminology, to a large extent functioned as an auxiliary science for the professionals within the crime control system. We have focused on the offender, made her or him into an object for study, manipulation and control. We have added to all those forces that have reduced the victim to a nonentity and the offender to a thing. And this critique is perhaps not only relevant for the old criminology, but also for the new criminology. While the old one explained crime from personal defects or social handicaps, the new criminology explains crime as the result of broad economic conflicts. The old criminology loses the conflicts, the new one converts them from interpersonal conflicts to class conflicts. And they are. They are class conflicts also. But, by stressing this, the conflicts are again taken away from the directly involved parties. So, as a preliminary statement: Criminal conflicts have either become *other people's property*—primarily the property of lawyers—or it has been in other people's interests to *define conflicts away.*

Structural Thieves

But there is more to it than professional manipulation of conflicts. Changes in the basic social structure have worked in the same way.

What I particularly have in mind are *two types of segmentation* easily observed in highly industrialised societies. First, there is the question of segmentation *in space.* We function each day, as migrants moving between sets of people which do not need to have any link—except through the mover. Often, therefore, we know our work-mates only as work-mates, neighbours only as neighbours, fellow cross-country skiers only as fellow cross-country skiers. We get to know them as *roles,* not as total persons. This situation is accentuated by the extreme degree of division of labour we accept to live with. Only experts can evaluate each other according to individual—personal—competence. Outside the speciality we have to fall back on a general evaluation of the supposed importance of the work. Except between specialists we cannot evaluate how good anybody is in his work, only how good, in the sense of important, the role is. Through all this, we get limited possibilities for understanding other people's behaviour. Their behaviour will also get limited relevance for us. Role-players are more easily exchanged than persons.

The second type of segmentation has to do with what I would like to call our re-establishment of caste-society. I am not saying class-society, even though there are obvious tendencies also in that direction. In my framework, however, I find the elements of caste even more important. What I have in mind is the segregation based on biological attributes such as sex, colour, physical handicaps or the number of winters that have passed since birth. Age is particularly important. It is an attribute nearly perfectly synchronised to a modern complex industrialised society. It is a continuous variable where we can introduce as many intervals as we might need. We can split the population in two: children and adults. But we also can split it in ten: babies, pre-school children, school children, teenagers, older youth, adults, pre-pensioned, pensioned, old people, the senile. And most important: the cutting points can be moved up and down according to social needs. The concept "teenager" was particularly suitable 10 years ago. It would not have caught on if social realities had not been in accordance with the word. Today the concept is not often used in my country. The condition of youth is not over at 19. Young people have to wait even longer before they are allowed to enter the work force. The caste of those outside the work force has been extended far into the twenties. At the same time departure from the work force—if you ever were admitted, if you were not kept completely out because of race or sex-attributes—is brought forward into the early sixties in a person's life. In my tiny country of four million inhabitants, we have 800,000 persons segregated within the educational system. Increased scarcity of work has immediately led authorities to increase the capacity of educational incarceration. Another 600,000 are pensioners.

Segmentation according to space and according to caste attributes has several consequences. First and foremost it leads into a *depersonalisation* of social life. Individuals are to a smaller extent linked to each other in close social networks where they are confronted with *all* the significant roles of the significant others. This creates a situation with limited amounts of information with regard to each other. We do know less about other people, and get limited possibilities both for understanding and for prediction of their behaviour. If a conflict is created, we are less able to cope with this situation. Not only are professionals there, able and willing to take the conflict away, but we are also more willing to give it away.

Secondly, segmentation leads to destruction of certain conflicts even before they get going. The depersonalisation and mobility within industrial society melt away some essential conditions for living conflicts; those between parties that mean a lot to each other. What I have particularly in mind is crime against other people's honour, libel or defamation of character. All the Scandinavian countries have had a dramatic decrease in this form of crime. In my interpretation, this is not because honour has become more respected but because there is less honour to respect. The various forms of segmentation mean that human beings are inter-related in ways where they simply mean less to each other. When they are hurt, they are only hurt partially. And if they are troubled, they can easily move away. And after all, who cares? Nobody knows me. In my evaluation, the decrease in the crimes of infamy and libel is one of the most interesting and sad symptoms of dangerous developments within modern industrialised societies. The decrease here is clearly related to social conditions that lead to increase in other forms of crime brought to the attention of the authorities. It is an important goal for crime prevention to re-create social conditions which lead to an increase in the number of crimes against other people's honour.

A third consequence of segmentation according to space and

age is that certain conflicts are made completely invisible, and thereby don't get any decent solution whatsoever. I have here in mind conflicts at the two extremes of a continuum. On the one extreme we have the over-privatised ones, those taking place against individuals captured within one of the segments. Wife beating or child battering represent examples. The more isolated a segment is, the more the weakest among parties is alone, open for abuse. Inghe and Riemer (1913) made the classical study many years ago of a related phenomenon in their book on incest. Their major point was that the social isolation of certain categories of proletarised Swedish farm-workers was the necessary condition for this type of crime. Poverty meant that the parties within the nuclear family became completely dependent on each other. Isolation meant that the weakest parties within the family had no external network where they could appeal for help. The physical strength of the husband got an undue importance. At the other extreme we have crimes done by large economic organisations against individuals too weak and ignorant to be able even to realise they have been victimised. In both cases the goal for crime prevention might be to re-create social conditions which make the conflicts visible and thereafter manageable.

Conflicts as Property

Conflicts are taken away, given away, melt away, or are made invisible. Does it matter, does it really matter?

Most of us would probably agree that we ought to protect the invisible victims just mentioned. Many would also nod approvingly to ideas saying that states, or Governments, or other authorities ought to stop stealing fines and instead let the poor victim receive this money. I at least would approve such an arrangement. But I will not go into that problem area here and now. Material compensation is not what I have in mind with the formulation "conflicts as property". It is the conflict itself that represents the most interesting property taken away, not the goods originally taken away from the victim, or given back to him. In our types of society, conflicts are more scarce than property. And they are immensely more valuable.

They are valuable in several ways. Let me start at the societal level, since here I have already presented the necessary fragments of analysis that might allow us to see what the problem is. Highly industrialised societies face major problems in organising their members in ways such that a decent quota take part in any activity at all. Segmentation according to age and sex can be seen as shrewd methods for segregation. Participation is such a scarcity that insiders create monopolies against outsiders, particularly with regard to work. In this perspective, it will easily be seen that

conflicts represent *a potential for activity, for participation.*
Modern criminal control systems represent one of the many cases
of lost opportunities for involving citizens in tasks that are of
immediate importance to them. Ours is a society of task-
monopolists.

The victim is a particularly heavy loser in this situation. Not
only has he suffered, lost materially or become hurt, physically or
otherwise. And not only does the state take the compensation. But
above all he has lost participation in his own case. It is the Crown
that comes into the spotlight, not the victim. It is the Crown that
describes the losses, not the victim. It is the Crown that appears
in the newspaper, very seldom the victim. It is the Crown that gets
a chance to talk to the offender, and neither the Crown nor the
offender are particularly interested in carrying on that conversation. The prosecutor is fed-up long since. The victim would not
have been. He might have been scared to death, panic-stricken, or
furious. But he would not have been uninvolved. It would have
been one of the important days in his life. Something that belonged
to him has been taken away from that victim.[1]

But the big loser is us—to the extent that society is us. This
loss is first and foremost a loss in *opportunities for norm-
clarification.* It is a loss of pedagogical possibilities. It is a loss of
opportunities for a continuous discussion of what represents the
law of the land. How wrong was the thief, how right was the
victim? Lawyers are, as we saw, trained into agreement on what is
relevant in a case. But that means a trained incapacity in letting
the parties decide what *they* think is relevant. It means that it is
difficult to stage what we might call a political debate in the court.
When the victim is small and the offender big—in size or power—
how blameworthy then is the crime? And what about the opposite
case, the small thief and the big house-owner? If the offender is
well educated, ought he then to suffer more or maybe less, for his
sins? Or if he is black, or if he is young, or if the other party is an
insurance company, or if his wife has just left him, or if his
factory will break down if he has to go to jail, or if his daughter
will lose her fiancé, or if he was drunk, or if he was sad, or if he
was mad? There is no end to it. And maybe there ought to be none.
Maybe Barotse law as described by Max Gluckman (1967) is a
better instrument for norm-clarification, allowing the conflicting
parties to bring in the whole chain of old complaints and
arguments each time. Maybe decisions on relevance and on the
weight of what is found relevant ought to be taken away from
legal scholars, the chief ideologists of crime control systems, and
brought back for free decisions in the court-rooms.

A further general loss—both for the victim and for society in
general has to do with anxiety-level and misconceptions. It is
again the possibilities for personalised encounters I have in mind.
The victim is so totally out of the case that he has no chance, ever,
to come to know the offender. We leave him outside, angry, maybe

humiliated through a cross-examination in court, without any
human contact with the offender. He has no alternative. He will
need all the classical stereotypes around "the criminal" to get a
grasp on the whole thing. He has a need for understanding, but is
instead a non-person in a Kafka play. Of course, he will go away
more frightened than ever, more in need than ever of an
explanation of criminals as non-human.

The offender represents a more complicated case. Not much
introspection is needed to see that direct victim-participation
might be experienced as painful indeed. Most of us would shy
away from a confrontation of this character. That is the first
reaction. But the second one is slightly more positive. Human
beings have reasons for their actions. If the situation is staged so
that reasons can be given (reasons as the parties see them, not
only the selection lawyers have decided to classify as relevant), in
such a case maybe the situation would not be all that humiliating.
And, particularly, if the situation was staged in such a manner
that the central question was not meting out guilt, but a thorough
discussion of what could be done to undo the deed, then the
situation might change. And this is exactly what ought to happen
when the victim is re-introduced in the case. Serious attention will
centre on the victim's losses. That leads to a natural attention as
to how they can be softened. It leads into a discussion of
restitution. The offender gets a possibility to change his position
from being a listener to a discussion—often a highly unintelligible
one—of how much pain he ought to receive, into a participant in a
discussion of how he could make it good again. The offender has
lost the opportunity to explain himself to a person whose
evaluation of him might have mattered. He has thereby also lost
one of the most important possibilities for being forgiven.
Compared to the humiliations in an ordinary court—vividly
described by Pat Carlen (1976) in a recent issue of the *British
Journal of Criminology*—this is not obviously any bad deal for the
criminal.

But let me add that I think we should do it quite
independently of his wishes. It is not health-control we are
discussing. It is crime control. If criminals are shocked by the
initial thought of close confrontation with the victim, preferably a
confrontation in the very local neighbourhood of one of the parties,
what then? I know from recent conversations on these matters that
most people sentenced are shocked. After all, they prefer distance
from the victim, from neighbours, from listener, and maybe also
from their own court case through the vocabulary and the
behavioural science experts who might happen to be present. They
are perfectly willing to give away their property right to the
conflict. So the question is more: are *we* willing to let them give it
away? Are we willing to give them this easy way out?[2]

Let me be quite explicit on one point: I am not suggesting
these ideas out of any particular interest in the treatment or

improvement of criminals. I am not basing my reasoning on a belief that a more personalised meeting between offender and victim would lead to reduced recidivism. Maybe it would. I think it would. As it is now, the offender has lost the opportunity for participation in a personal confrontation of a very serious nature. He has lost the opportunity to receive a type of blame that it would be very difficult to neutralise. However, I would have suggested these arrangements even if I was absolutely certain they had no effects on recidivsm, maybe even if they had a negative effect. I would have done that because of the other, more general gains. And let me also add—it is not much to lose. As we all know today, at least nearly all, we have not been able to invent any cure for crime. Except for execution, castration or incarceration for life, no measure has proven minimum of efficiency compared to any other measure. We might as well react to crime according to what closely involved parties find is just and in accordance with general values in society.

With this last statement, as with most of the others I have made, I raise many more problems than I answer. Statements on criminal politics, particularly from those with the burden of responsibility, are usually filled with answers. It is questions we need. The gravity of our topic makes us much too pedantic and thereby useless as paradigm-changers.

A Victim-Oriented Court

There is clearly a model of neighbourhood courts behind my reasoning. But it is one with some peculiar features, and it is only these I will discuss in what follows.

First and foremost; it is a *victim-oriented* organisation. Not in its initial stage, though. The first stage will be a traditional one where it is established whether it is true that the law has been broken, and whether it was this particular person who broke it.

Then comes the second stage, which in these courts would be of the utmost importance. That would be the stage where the victim's situation was considered, where every detail regarding what had happened—legally relevant or not—was brought to the court's attention. Particularly important here would be detailed consideration regarding what could be done for him, first and foremost by the offender, secondly by the local neighbourhood, thirdly by the state. Could the harm be compensated, the window repaired, the lock replaced, the wall painted, the loss of time because the car was stolen given back through garden work or washing of the car ten Sundays in a row? Or maybe, when this discussion started, the damage was not so important as it looked in documents written to impress insurance companies? Could physical suffering become slightly less painful by any action from

the offender, during days, months or years? But, in addition, had
the community exhausted all resources that might have offered
help? Was it absolutely certain that the local hospital could not do
anything? What about a helping hand from the janitor twice a day
if the offender took over the cleaning of the basement every
Saturday? None of these ideas is unknown or untried, particularly
not in England. But we need an organisation for the systematic
application of them.

Only after this stage was passed, and it ought to take hours,
maybe days, to pass it, only then would come the time for an
eventual decision on punishment. Punishment, then, becomes that
suffering which the judge found necessary to apply *in addition to*
those unintended constructive sufferings the offender would go
through in his restitutive actions *vis-à-vis* the victim. Maybe
nothing could be done or nothing would be done. But neighbourhoods might find it intolerable that nothing happened. Local courts
out of tune with local values are not local courts. That is just the
trouble with them, seen from the liberal reformer's point of view.

A fourth stage has to be added. That is the stage for service
to the offender. His general social and personal situation is by now
well-known to the court. The discussion of his possibilities for
restoring the victim's situation cannot be carried out without at
the same time giving information about the offender's situation.
This might have exposed needs for social, educational, medical or
religious action—not to prevent further crime, but because needs
ought to be met. Courts are public arenas, needs are made visible.
But it is important that this stage comes *after* sentencing.
Otherwise we get a re-emergence of the whole array of so-called
"special measures"—compulsory treatments—very often only
euphemisms for indeterminate imprisonment.

Through these four stages, these courts would represent a
blend of elements from civil and criminal courts, but with a strong
emphasis on the civil side.

A Lay-Oriented Court.

The second major peculiarity with the court model I have in
mind is that it will be one with an extreme degree of lay-
orientation. This is essential when conflicts are seen as property
that ought to be shared. It is with conflicts as with so many
good things: they are in no unlimited supply. Conflicts can be
cared for, protected, nurtured. But there are limits. If some are
given more access in the disposal of conflicts, others are getting
less. It is as simple as that.

Specialisation in conflict solution is the major enemy;
specialisation that in due—or undue—time leads to professionalisation. That is when the specialists get sufficient power to

claim that they have acquired special gifts, mostly through education, gifts so powerful that it is obvious that they can only be handled by the certified craftsman.

With a clarification of the enemy, we are also able to specify the goal; let us reduce specialisation and particularly our dependence on the professionals within the crime control system to the utmost.

The ideal is clear; it ought to be a court of equals representing themselves. When they are able to find a solution between themselves, no judges are needed. When they are not, the judges ought also to be their equals.

Maybe the judge would be the easiest to replace, if we made serious attempt to bring our present courts nearer to this model of lay orientation. We have lay judges already, in principle. But that is a far cry from realities. What we have, both in England and in my own country, is a sort of specialised non-specialist. First, they are used *again and again*. Secondly, some are even *trained*, given special courses or sent on excursions to foreign countries to learn about how to behave as a lay judge. Thirdly, most of them do also represent an extremely *biased sample* of the population with regard to sex, age, education, income, class[3] and personal experience.

Should lawyers be admitted to court? We had an old law in Norway that forbids them to enter the rural districts. Maybe they shoud be admitted in stage one where it is decided if the man is guilty, I am not sure. Experts are as cancer to any lay body. It is exactly as Ivan Illich describes for the educational system in general. Each time you increase the length of compulsory education in a society, each time you also decrease the same population's trust in what they have learned and understood quite by themselves.

Behaviour experts represent the same dilemma. Is there a place for them in this model? Ought there to be any place? In stage 1, decisions on facts, certainly not. In stage 3, decisions on eventual punishment, certainly not. It is too obvious to waste words on. We have the painful row of mistakes from Lombroso, through the movement for social defence and up to recent attempts to dispose of supposedly dangerous people through predictions of who they are and when they are not dangerous any more. Let these ideas die, without further comments.

The real problem has to do with the service function of behaviour experts. Social scientists can be perceived as functional answers to a segmented society. Most of us have lost the physical possibility to experience the totality, both on the social system level and on the personality level. Psychologists can be seen as historians for the individual; sociologists have much of the same function for the social system. Social workers are oil in the machinery, a sort of security counsel. Can we function without them, would the victim and the offender be worse off?

Maybe. But it would be immensely difficult to get such a court to function if they were all there. Our theme is social conflict. Who is not at least made slightly uneasy in the handling of her or his own social conflicts if we get to know that there is an expert on this very matter at the same table? I have no clear answer, only strong feelings behind a vague conclusion: let us have as few behaviour experts as we dare to. And if we have any, let us for God's sake not have any that specialise in crime and conflict resolution. Let us have generalised experts with a solid base outside the crime control system. And a last point with relevance for both behaviour experts and lawyers: if we find them unavoidable in certain cases or at certain stages, let us try to get across to them the problems they create for broad social participation. Let us try to get them to perceive themselves as resource-persons, answering when asked, but not domineering, not in the centre. They might help to stage conflicts, not take them over.

Rolling Stones

There are hundreds of blocks against getting such a system to operate within our western culture. Let me only mention three major ones. They are:
1. There is a lack of neighbourhoods.
2. There are too few victims.
3. There are too many professionals around.

With lack of neighbourhoods I have in mind the very same phenomenon I described as a consequence of industrialised living; segmentation according to space and age. Much of our trouble stems from killed neighbourhoods or killed local communities. How can we then thrust towards neighbourhoods a task that presupposes they are highly alive? I have no really good arguments, only two weak ones. First, it is not quite that bad. The death is not complete. Secondly, one of the major ideas behind the formulation "Conflicts as Property" is that it is neighbourhood-property. It is not private. It belongs to the system. It is intended as a vitaliser for neighbourhoods. The more fainting the neighbourhood is, the more we need neighbourhood courts as one of the many functions any social system needs for not dying through lack of challenge.

Equally bad is the lack of victims. Here I have particularly in mind the lack of personal victims. The problem behind this is again the large units in industrialised society. Woolworth or British Rail are not good victims. But again I will say: there is not a complete lack of personal victims, and their needs ought to get priority. But we should not forget the large organisations. They, or their boards, would certainly prefer not to have to appear as victims in 5000 neighbourhood courts all over the country. But maybe they ought to be compelled to appear. If the complaint is serious enough to bring the offender into the ranks of the criminal, then the victim ought to appear. A related problem has to do with insurance companies—the industrialised alternative to friendship or kinship. Again we have a case where the crutches deteriorate the condition. Insurance takes the consequences of crime away. We will therefore take insurance away. Or rather: we will have to keep the possibilities for compensation through the insurance companies back until, in the procedure I have described, it has been proved beyond all possible doubt that there are not other alternatives left—particularly that the offender has no possibilities whatsoever. Such a solution will create more paper-work, less predictability, more aggression from customers. And the solution will not necessarily be seen as good from the perspective of the policy-holder. But it will help to protect conflicts as social fuel.

None of these troubles can, however, compete with the third and last I will comment on: the abundance of professionals. We know it all from our own personal biographies or personal observations. And in addition we get it confirmed from all sorts of social science research: the educational system of any society is not necessarily synchronised with any needs for the product of this system. Once upon a time we thought there was a direct causal relation from the number of highly educated persons in a country to the Gross National Product. Today we suspect the relationship to go the other way, if we are at all willing to use GNP as a meaningful indicator. We also know that most educational systems are extremely class-biased. We know that most academic people have had profitable investments in our education, that we fight for the same for our children, and that we also often have vested interests in making our part of the educational system even bigger. More schools for more lawyers, social workers, sociologists, criminologists. While I am *talking* deprofessionalisation, we are increasing the capacity to be able to fill up the whole world with them.

There is no solid base for optimism. On the other hand, insights about the situation, and goal formulation, is a pre-condition for action. Of course, the crime control system is not the domineering one in our type of society. But it has some importance. And occurrences here are unusually well suited as pedagogical illustrations of general trends in society. There is also some room for manoeuvre. And when we hit the limits, or are hit by them, this collision represents in itself a renewed argument for more broadly conceived changes.

Another source for hope: ideas formulated here are not quite so isolated or in dissonance with the mainstream of thinking when we leave our crime control area and enter other institutions. I have already mentioned Ivan Illich with his attempts to get learning away from the teachers and back to active human beings.

Compulsory learning, compulsory medication and compulsory consummation of conflicts solutions have interesting similarities. When Ivan Illich and Paulo Freire are listened to, and my impression is that they increasingly are, the crime control system will also become more easily influenced.

Another, but related, major shift in paradigm is about to happen within the whole field of technology. Partly, it is the lessons from the third world that now are more easily seen, partly it is the experience from the ecology debate. The globe is obviously suffering from what we, through our technique, are doing to her. Social systems in the third world are equally obviously suffering. So the suspicion starts. Maybe the first world can't take all this technology either. Maybe some of the old social thinkers were not so dumb after all. Maybe social systems can be perceived as biological ones. And maybe there are certain types of large-scale technology that kill social systems, as they kill globes. Schumacher (1973) with his book *Small is Beautiful* and the related Institute for Intermediate Technology come in here. So do also the numerous attempts, particularly by several outstanding Institutes for Peace Research, to show the dangers in the concept of Gross National Product, and replace it with indicators that take care of dignity, equity and justice. The perspective developed in Johan Galtung's research group on World Indicators might prove extremely useful also within our own field of crime control.

There is also a political phenomenon opening vistas. At least in Scandinavia social democrats and related groupings have considerable power, but are without an explicated ideology regarding the goals for a reconstructed society. This vacuum is being felt by many, and creates a willingness to accept and even expect considerable institutional experimentation.

Then to my very last point: what about the universities in this picture? What about the new Centre in Sheffield? The answer has probably to be the old one: universities have to re-emphasise the old tasks of understanding and of criticising. But the task of training professionals ought to be looked into with renewed scepticism. Let us re-establish the credibility of encounters between critical human beings: low-paid, highly regarded, but with no extra power—outside the weight of their good ideas. That is as it ought to be.

NOTES

1.   For a preliminary report on victim dissatifaction, see Vennard (1976).

2.   I tend to take the same position with regard to a criminal's property right to his own conflict as John Locke on property rights to one's own life—one has no right to give it away. (*cf* C.B. MacPherson (1962)).

3.   For the most recent documentation, see Baldwin (1976).

REFERENCES

Baldwin, J., "The Social Composition of the Magistracy," *Brit. J. Criminol.* 16 (1976): 171-174.

Balm, M. and Wheeler, S., "Becoming an Inmate," in Wheeler, S. (ed.), *Controlling Delinquents.* New York: Wiley, 1968, ch. 7, pp. 158-157.

Bottoms, A.E. and McClean, J.D. *Defendants in the Criminal Process.* London: Routledge and Kegan Paul, 1976.

Carlen, P., "The Staging of Magistrates' Justice," *Brit. J. Criminol.* 16 (1976): 48-55.

Gluckman, M., *The Judicial Process Among the Bartose of Northern Rhodesia.* Manchester University Press, 1967.

Kinberg, O., Inghe, G., and Riemer, S., *Incest-Problemeti Sverige. Sth.*

MacPherson, G.B., *The Political Theory of Possessive Individualism: Hobbes to Locke.* London: Oxford University Press, 1962.

Newman, O., *Defensible Space: People and Design in the Violent City.* London: Architectural Press, 1972.

Schumaker, E.F., *Small is Beautiful: A Study of Economics as if People Mattered.* London: Blond and Briggs, 1973.

Scott, P.D., "Juvenile Courts: The Juvenile's Point of View," *Brit. J. Delinq.* 9 (1959): 200-210.

Vennard, J., "Justice and Recompense for Victims of Crime," *New Society* 36 (1976): 378-380.

Chapter 13

Communist Anarchism as an Alternative to the Rule of Criminal Law*

Harold E. Pepinsky†

The logic of the rule of criminal law is so straightforward. It seems that it ought to work. Never mind the extended, recent arguments of American theorists like Van den Haag[1] and Wilson[2]. Beccaria's[3] short book, first published in 1764, makes the case neatly and compellingly. Make criminal law penalties just severe enough, and apply them swiftly and surely, and practically everyone should be deterred from committing any crime at all. If Americans in particular are inflicted with the disease of rising crime rates, and if there is no indication that imprisonment acts as a cure[4], the fault lies not with the theory of law-imposed deterrence, but with a flawed application of the theory. Americans are simply not devoting sufficient resources to making imposition of the sanctions swift and sure.

Some argue that Beccarian logic itself is flawed, in that crime is really caused by class oppression, of which the rule of law is but an instrument[5]. If law can be seen as a cause at all, law causes, not prevents, crime, by defending the injustice of private ownership. Those holding this position do so as fallaciously as would the proponent of the view that blood pressure cannot be controlled by bio-feedback because blood pressure is in reality controlled by the autonomic nervous system. Even if class oppression is granted to be a cause of crime, and if one grants the

* Reprinted by permission of Elsevier Scientific Publishing Company, publishers of *Contemporary Crises*, and the author.
† Forensic Studies, Indiana University.

moral argument that the real harm is done by the oppressors rather than by those treated as criminals, there is still no reason to question the logic that the all-powerful oppressors can keep the oppressed people from violating the terms of the law by applying the law swiftly, surely and severely enough. One can posit that the spirit of oppressed people is indomitable, but the proponents of Beccarian logic need only respond that this remains to be seen, just as it remains to be seen whether class oppression can be transcended.

On the other hand, Beccaria's logic is no refutation of the neat compelling logic—pre-eminently of Berkman[6]—that to eliminate government and its laws, and to permit people to partake of goods and services regardless of what they do in return, would also largely eliminate the injuries people do to one another—currently known as crimes. Communist anarchism is, even in theory, no easier to perfect than the rule of law, but the logic of communist anarchism has no more been impeached by proponents of the rule of law than have proponents of communist anarchism impeached the logic of the rule of law. And yet, in part no doubt because the two strategies are diametrically opposed means to the end (among others) of preventing crime, proponents of each side are viscerally opposed to one another.

Their opposition to one another is ill-considered. Progress toward the rule of criminal law and progress toward communist anarchism are symbiotic. One will not happen without the other. The failure of each set of proponents to support the success of its counterpart strategy of crime control is an impediment to its own success. The partisans of the rule of criminal law and of communist anarchism are locked in a mixed-sum not a zero-sum game. Analyzing the issue in the American context, this essay is directed to showing that it behooves legalists and communist anarchists to co-operate with one another to achieve progress in crime control.

More Means Less: The Paradox of Perfecting the Rule of Criminal Law

Throughout the United States, as this essay is written, Americans are caught up in the latest flood of attempts to perfect the rule of criminal law. The watershed from which these attempts flow is a decade old: the report of the President's Commission on Law Enforcement and Criminal Justice[7], a grand attempt—as an element of building the Great Society—to set the agenda for American crime control. Since then, scholars and researchers have set about helping localities, states and the federal government make application of the law swift, sure and severe enough to deter crime. Criminal and juvenile codes have been revised in many states. Not to be out-done, the federal government first enacted the Omnibus (imagine!) Crime Control and Safe Streets Act in 1968, and now appears to be on the verge of enacting a comprehensive re-codification of federal criminal law. Educational and training standards for all manner of criminal justice functionaries have been increased. New programs have proliferated to fill gaps in the old. Personnel and hardware (and now even software!) have been added to make application of the law swifter and surer. Systems analysts and social science evaluators have been employed to rationalize criminal justice operations. The federal government, especially through the agency of the Law Enforcement Assistance Administration, has lavished funds on finding and attempting to solve problems of perfecting the rule of criminal law. State and regional planning agencies have been established to apply these funds. Together with their federal counterparts, the state and regional planning agencies have in most cases made religious use of the scriptures from the latest Presidential commission: the National Advisory Commission on Criminal Justice Standards and Goals[8]. Recent scholarly re-inventions of Beccarian logic have gained tremendous popularity.

For all this effort, crime rates have in general continued to increase, if anything faster than ever. So glaring has the failure been to make application of American criminal law swift, sure and severe enough to deter crime, that (again as this essay is written) even the Law Enforcement Assistance Administration is rumored to be on the brink of an ignominious demise. All this occurs just as victim data are becoming regularly available, which show the amount of crime in need of criminal justice management to be as much as ten times as great as had been revealed in police data.

The faster Americans go in trying to perfect the rule of criminal law, the more behind they get.

Why?

The rule of criminal law will fail for want of any of its three elements: swiftness, sureness and severity. Imagine each of these elements to be the south pole of a magnet, and imagine further the problem of perfecting the rule of criminal law to be like the problem of drawing these poles of all three magnets together, and you have a fair approximation of the paradox of the rule of criminal law. Strengthen the field of any of the magnets, and it will repel the others further than ever. Make criminal justice functionaries apply the law more swiftly, and the capacity to apply the law surely (without error) to every crime will grow more remote. The more severe the sanction to be imposed, the greater the complexity of review of that imposition—the American extremes being the summary imposition of traffic fines and the elaborate trial and appellate procedures for review in capital cases. The more complex the review of the imposition of a sanc-tion, the longer the delay in imposing the sanction. It has repeatedly been found that raising sanctions lowers the propensity of officials to arrest and prosecute (as happened following enactment of the "Rockefeller drug law" mandating life sentences for drug sale in New York State[9]), while lowering the severity of penalties makes arrest and prosecution surer (as happened following the reduction of statutory penalties for marihuana possession in Nebraska[10]). Ross[11] and Wilson[12], too, find an inverse relation between sureness and severity. Swiftness, sureness and severity are mutually exclusive.

If the magnets are to rest closer to each other, their fields must be weakened. Similarly, if the rule of criminal law is to be approached, the force with which swiftness, sureness and severity of imposition of criminal sanctions is pursued must be reduced. This is reflected in experimental and quasi-experimental findings on deterrence. It is where the severity of sanctions is lowest, in traffic law, that sporadic campaigns of swift, sure enforcement have been found to have temporary deterrent effects on parking and moving violations. The campaigns are bound to be sporadic, and the effects only temporary, because swift and sure enforcement cannot be routinely sustained. The magnet analog: weaken the field on one of the magnets to a bare minimum, suddenly push the magnets together, and you will succeed in bringing them close, but you will have trouble holding them long without somehow losing your grip.

(As it happens, it has been found in research on learning that the magnitude of a reinforcer has much less to do with the rate of response than do the swiftness and sureness of reinforcement[13]. Beccaria himself emphasized the waste of making penalties more severe than minimally necessary, which in part contributed to his argument against capital punishment. Americans would do well to note that Scandinavian countries and the Netherlands appear to be doing relatively well at crime control with, by American standards, remarkably low-level sanctions.)

To sustain an approximation of the rule of criminal law, to sustain deterrence of crime, as in bringing the magnets closer by weakening their fields, the force with which law is applied must be reduced. In theory, in any community, the fewer the resources invested in applying the law to any form of behavior, the more effectively the rule of criminal law will operate to deter that behavior from occurring. Practically speaking, this means that the lower the rate—by population of the community—at which criminal justice agencies take jurisdiction over a kind of crime, the less likely it will be that that kind of crime will occur.

Note that this relationship is the same that would be predicted, but interpreted differently, by proponents of communist anarchism. As Berkman puts it,

> The truth is that what is called 'law and order' is really the worst disorder, as we have seen in previous chapters. What little order and peace we do have is due to the good common sense of the joint efforts of the people, mostly in spite of the government . . . . the interference of any government or authority can only hinder their efforts.[14]

Is the bottle half empty or half full? Whether one concludes that the most effective deterrent is the one that needs invoking least, or that if people get along it is because they are left alone, the result is the same. In either case, the criminal justice system works best where it works least.

This is consistent with the findings of a number of recent studies, notably those conducted by American economists, interpreted to indicate that more severe and more sure criminal sanctions deter crime more[15]. Literally, the findings are that the more rarely the criminal justice system takes jurisdiction over an offence (i.e., the more rarely an offence appears in police offence reports or in arrest figures), the more likely and more severe the sanctions imposed for that offence will be. This is interpreted to indicate that sure, severe sanctions reduce the likelihood of crime. Now it also happens generally that the more rarely officials report an offence, the more serious the offence is in the eyes of the community. At extremes, disorderly conduct is commonly reported and regarded as a trivial offence, while assassinations of popular political figures and multiple murders are rarely reported and are (perhaps, in part, therefore) regarded as especially heinous. Restated, the findings of the so-called deterrence studies are intuitively obvious: community sentiment will most probably support successful prosecution of crimes and imposition of heavy sanctions in the relatively rare instances in which the criminal justice system is mobilized to respond to what, in that community, will be regarded as especially heinous crimes. That is, the criminal justice system responds most surely and severely to those forms of behavior that—for whatever reason—seldom occur and receive the weight of official attention. The government best deters those acts which people are least likely to commit in the first place. Or, the more rarely the law is applied to a form of behavior, the better it deters.

Thus, the findings of deterrence studies are consistent with the logic of the magnet analog to deterrence, which supports the communist anarchist premise that the less the government reacts to people's behavior, the better people behave. If perfection of the rule of criminal law is to be pursued with apparent success, it will only be as communities manage their affairs with less resort to criminal justice intervention. Those who would arrange for the law to be a stronger deterrent to crime had best help develop community mechanisms which disengage the communities from utilization of criminal justice services, lest the burden of crime control impede the swift, sure, severe application of the law.

I will return to a sketch of some ways in which a communist anarchist program for strengthening the rule of criminal law might be implemented. Meanwhile, let us consider the corollary argument that progress toward communist anarchism requires that criminal justice workers be made more free to perform their functions as they see fit.

The Ambiguous Status of the Communist Anarchist's Criminal Justice Worker

American governments employ a large and rapidly growing number of criminal justice workers. In 1971, the criminal justice labor force[16] grew to more than one percent of the total American labor force, including nearly three million armed forces personnel[17]. The number of criminal justice workers passed the million mark in 1973[18]. The total American labor force grew just over eight percent from 1970 to 1974[19], while the criminal justice labor force grew more than twenty-eight percent.[20] As of October 1975[21], there were reported to be 1,128,569 criminal justice employees in the country, of which 97,623 worked for the federal government, 274,319 worked for state governments, and 756,627 (half a million of them in law enforcement) for local governments[22].

Criminal justice workers are becoming unionized and occasionally even striking for better pay and job conditions. Even grassroots criminal justice workers can wield considerable political power. About five years ago, a reformist commissioner of corrections was appointed, with strong words of gubernatorial endorsement, in the politically liberal State of Minnesota. The commissioner announced his intention to close down the reformatory in the town of St. Cloud. The community rose in anger; the community kept its reformatory and its members their jobs, while the commissioner resigned his. Criminal justice workers are a large, rapidly growing political force with which to be reckoned in planning crime control strategy.

Workers are the hero(in)es in the communist anarchist scenario. At the heart of the communist anarchist revolution is the workers' expropriation of the industries in which they work. "In expropriating, . . . you *stay* on the job and you put the boss out. He may remain only on equal terms with the rest: a worker among workers."[23] Berkman emphasizes the "constructive" nature of this aspect of the revolutionary process. Presumably, the workers continue producing, having now become their own bosses.

What if the product of the workers happens to be arrests, prosecutions, confining inmates or the like? Literally, as Berkman puts it, ". . . anarchism means doing away with the state or government altogether."[24] The enigmatic position of government workers whose product is force or violence had presented itself by the time Berkman wrote (most of all in the case of professional soldiers in standing armies), but Berkman and (as far as I can see) every other communist anarchist writer has overlooked the problem. The writer who has come closest to addressing the matter is Godwin, first published in 1793:

> If juries might at length cease to decide, and be contented to invite, if force might gradually be withdrawn, and reason trusted alone, shall we not one day find, that juries themselves, and every other species of

public institution, may be laid aside as unnecessary? Will not the
reasonings of one wise man, be as effectual as those of twelve? Will
not the competence of one individual to instruct his neighbours, be a
matter of sufficient notoriety, without the formality of an election?[25]

"At length," perhaps. For the time being, it would be pretty
difficult to get criminal justice workers out of the habit of giving
orders, or to get citizens to interpret official invitations as devoid
of coercion. There is no particular indication that the mass of
criminal justice workers would readily be accepted as sages in
their communities. Until communism were sufficiently perfected
that former criminal justice workers could maintain decent
standards of living without earning their pay, criminal justice
officials who gave up coercion would be hard pressed to make
their livelihood.

Suppose the problem were resolved in favour of trying to
dispense with criminal justice workers. To get to know criminal
justice workers—especially those in lower status occupations (e.g.,
police officers and prison guards rather than judges and
prosecutors)—is to find the view prevailing among them that a
major effort is required to defend against this very treatment.
Many criminal justice workers see themselves as engaged in a
struggle against much of the citizenry for their professional
survival. The defense is quite reasonable and fairly straightforward: organize, make oneself more desperately needed, and
proliferate. Parkinson's Law aside[26], defense against attacks on
their social standing encourages criminal justice workers to help
swell their own ranks into a larger fighting force.

The most potent political weapon criminal justice workers
have is the authority they are given to define the size of the crime
problem they are called upon to manage. As long ago as 1858, the
police in New York City discovered that if they made more arrests,
they could show thereby that they had a bigger problem to manage
and hence required an enlarged budget[27]. A little more than a
century later, the same police force revised its offence reporting
practices and arranged for the overall offence rate to increase 72%
between 1965 and 1966[28]. In the courts, case backlogs can be
extended to support the call for increased resources. In prisons,
complaints by inmates can serve as a basis for lobbying to enlarge
facilities and staffs. Probation and parole revocation proceedings
can be used as evidence that more personnel are needed to give
greater attention to clients. Just as the species, like the rabbit, that
are most heavily preyed upon breed the fastest, and as the human
beings that are most destitute tend to reproduce at the highest
rates in order to survive, so the species of worker—in criminal
justice—that is especially heavily criticized proliferates in order
to survive. Communist anarchists and others who seek to defeat
the criminal justice system by attacking it defeat their own
purposes instead, for the criminal justice bureaucracy expands in
response.

The phenomenon is familiar. Bomb the British in London or the Vietnamese in Hanoi, and you have more British and more Vietnamese fighting for their cause with greater determination than ever. Try to take heroin away from those who depend on it, and the supply and demand for heroin is apt to increase. Communist anarchists in general and Berkman in particular are especially sensitive to the self-defeating character of complusion. The fundamental principle of communist anarchism—that people who themselves are liberated from force and compulsion will be least likely to use force and complusion against others—suggests that criminal justice workers will most readily give up their use of force when, instead of being attacked and threatened with loss of livelihood and community respect, they are entrusted with the management of their own pursuits and given respect and dignity.

There is some indication that the granting of respect can be effective in diverting criminal justice workers from acts of compulsion. It is a common feature of American traffic enforce-ment that a show of respect to a police officer is the best way for the motorist to avoid a traffic citation[29]. Criminal justice workers can—and do—rationalize that the respect they want for their own sakes is the best indicator they can get that persons whom they meet in the course of their work are inclined to respect and follow the law itself. From the vantage point of the criminal justice worker, the better she/he is treated, and the less conflicts she/he encounters, the less serious "the crime problem" appears.

Part of the insecurity that criminal justice workers suffer is the threat of job curtailment or of salary increases insufficient to maintain current standards of living for him/ herself or—more especially in many cases—for his/her dependents. If all criminal justice workers were given life tenure—in the manner of federal judges—and guaranteed that their incomes would minimally keep pace with the cost of living, they would not have reason to go to the trouble of drumming up more business and creating a pretext for public support. There would be greater reluctance to authorize new positions in the criminal justice system if each involved a lifetime commitment to keep someone's standard of living safe against inflation, and so the growth of the criminal justice labor force would be further retarded. Life tenure with high enough pay increments would also serve to delay retirement of criminal justice workers. Younger police officers I rode with used to tell me what a problem it was that veteran officers stopped enforcing the law with vigor and enthusiasm. There is probably a general tendency for criminal justice workers, with age and experience, to become more jaded about their capacity to reform others. From the point of view of relieving the citizenry from compulsion and interven-tion, it would be so much the better if the criminal justice system grew to be composed mainly of easygoing service veterans. Such a work force would be especially amenable to helping turn its business back over to communities for their self-management.

With the threat of doing themselves out of jobs absent, the workers would respond to any extra pay incentive to reduce their caseloads, although this incentive would have to be kept low enough so that the capacity of private persons to manage their own affairs could keep pace with reduction in the force of crime control. Otherwise, the panic people suffered at being suddenly denied the criminal justice protection they had thought they had had would set a self-fulfilling prophecy in motion. Fear of vulnerability to violence would promote exaggerated, violent acts of self-defense, against which people would have to defend themselves more forcefully than they had previously needed to do, and so on until—like Germans forty years ago—Americans panicked by the threat of social chaos would welcome a political order that promised control through terror if necessary.

Berkman recognizes the importance of the thrust of a communist anarchist social revolution's being "not destruction but construction."[30] He argues that extensive preparation, particularly of workers learning to practice communist anarchist principles among themselves, is a necessary pre-condition of the social revolution he seeks[31]. In these days in the United States in which corporate ownership of the means of production of goods and services has so far replaced private ownership and in which the middle class is so preponderant—now that the distinction between workers and owners has gotten so blurred—one wonders how preparation for the sudden, dramatic social revolution could proceed far enough for the revolution to succeed unless success had already been achieved by the preparation itself. For the time being, at least, the insecurity of people inside and outside the criminal justice system needs to be recognized and attended to. The increased security that leads criminal justice workers to give up their use of force must lead them to do so gradually, or the insecurity of the citizenry will produce a backlash that will eventually make government more tyranical than ever. In the interest of progress toward communist anarchism, respect must be afforded the security and protection symbolized by criminal justice workers.

"Let's be Realistic," or "Optimization in Defense of Idealsim is No Vice"

It is a tribute to the abiding optimism of Americans that so many of them can respond to their mounting crime problem with such naive romanticism. Were Berkman alive today, he might well be encouraged by the failure of Americans to be discouraged into nihilism by the growing levels of violence and predation they suffer at one another's hands. Instead, many Americans confidently proclaim that an ideal that has never come close to being achieved in practice—deterrence of crime by perfection of the rule of law—can indeed be attained.

Communist anarchists are themselves often accused of naive romanticism for believing that what has at most been achieved for short periods in small communities could be achieved enduringly in large societies. They, too, should be commended for their enduring optimism.

But to be practical, proponents of the rule of law and of communist anarchism should recognize that as purists—rejecting one another's positions out of hand—they only make their own ideals more elusive than ever. If the rule of law is ever to move from fantasy into practice, people must learn to get along without government. If communist anarchism is ever to move from fantasy into practice, people must give dignity and respect to those who work to serve them in their government. Rule-of-law and communist-anarchist proponents make porgress together or not at all. Although on their face the establishment of the rule of criminal law and the abolition of government protection of rights (basically of property holdings and entitlements) are antithetical, the strategy that optimizes progress toward both objectives also maximizes progress toward each.

The basic principle upon which the mutual progress toward the rule of law and communist anarchism rests is simple. Regardless of whether people in society happen to work in government, if they have the courage to trust, respect and dignify one another for their ability to get along together fairly, the prophecy will tend to fulfill itself, while if people act out of fear and distrust for one another, their fears will be realized instead. At the societal level, as manifested in the growth of crime, and at the individual level, as manifested in what Lemert describes as "paranoia and the dynamics of exclusion," [32] the course of distrust and fear is all too familiar to Americans. Given Americans' history, interpersonal fear and distrust are—"empirically" and "objectively"—established for them, regardless of ideological persuasion. Practically all Americans share the view that progress requires that some personal enemy be destroyed. Whether their particular enemy happens to be anarchists, capitalists, communists, conservatives, criminals, Jews, liberals, hippies, Indians, mafiosi, men, niggers, Nixon, owners, politicians, rednecks, rulers, or others, Americans are remarkably united in the wisdom—yea, even the necessity—of pursuing a self-defeating strategy to achieve social harmony. "They" must be subjugated by whatever weapons (the grander the better) "we" can develop.

If Americans are to make progress toward crime control, they must learn to subjugate their own distrust—not other people—and empower those they now fear to act fearlessly. This is no more or less practicable than is progress either toward the rule of law or toward communist anarchism.[33] If American criminal justice workers, whose job currently is to distrust the citizenry, cannot afford to trust and empower them instead, and if the citizenry cannot afford to trust and empower their criminal justice workers, then they deceive themselves by believing that either the rule of law or communist anarchism is approachable.

Except for tenure and guaranteed pay increments for criminal justice workers, a set of concrete proposals for optimizing deterrence and anarchism appears elsewhere. Besides tenure with assured cost-of-living pay increases, it is proposed that criminal justice workers be given bonuses for filing official reports of any kind (not just selected reports as was done with police in Orange, California[34]). To encourage private settlement of disputes without resort to official arbitration, it is proposed that state mediation services be established, which would be forbidden (a) to set conditions on initiation or termination of client contact, (b) to keep files of otherwise unavailable information, (c) to act as legal representatives for clients, or (d) to take any action on clients' behalf outside of their physical presence, lest the mediation turn into another form of arbitration. I would add that mediation workers could be given pay bonuses for declines in arrest rates (which would signify reduced entry of cases into the criminal justice process).

To encourage the private sector of the community to stabilize its relations, thereby having less occasion to resort to government intervention in people's affairs, it is proposed that a tax/subsidy mechanism be established to encourage employers to profit most by decreasing class disparities in their society. Employers would qualify for the subsidy by *simultaneously* (a) employing more full-time workers and (b) raising the income of their lowest paid full-time workers faster than the rate of inflation. Otherwise, they would be taxed. This would reward and dignify employers for making progress toward communism, while increasing the respect, dignity and material welfare of workers. The challenge of optimizing progress toward the rule of law and communist anarchism is to empower and dignify all citizens equally, whether they work in or out of government, and whether or not they manage production. In place of the impotence Americans now feel that tends to make everyone believe that the solution of social problems must be someone else's responsibility, everyone must be made freer to take her/his social position and survival for granted as she/he helps and allows others to pursue their own interests more freely.

Whether, as proponents of the rule of law, they look to written standards of fair exchange for their salvation, or as proponents of communist anarchism, they look instead to the obsolescence of standards of exchange, Americans are misled by assuming a dualism between what Kalven and Zeisel[35] refer to as a government of law and a government of men. The two are symbiotic. Law rules more the less it is imposed, and law is imposed less the more its agents are respected. Were the rule of law to become absolute, people would have ceased reckoning the equation of value given and value received among themselves, as deterrence perfected made referral to formal standards of exchange obsolete.

Proponents of the rule of law and of communist anarchism are equally correct in their diagnosis: the growth of crime reflects both a failure of deterrence and a failure to leave people free to tend their own affairs. On the other hand, the treatment prescribed by both sides is equally wrong, for increasing the force of criminal justice and generating resistance to criminal justice workers both promote crime. Americans would do well to accept the twin diagnosis and have confidence in the promise underlying two romantic and as yet remote visions of how to control crime. If Americans have enough faith in deterrence to help people to act without government intervention, and enough faith in freedom from government compulsion to give dignity to government workers, crime will become less of a problem for them.

NOTES

This was to be a revision of a paper, Anarchist-Communism as an alternative to due process, delivered at the Society for the Study of Social Problems Meeting, New York, 1976. As it turns out, the spirit is the same but the content is entirely different. Special thanks for criticism through versions of both papers go to Jill Bystydzienski, Drew Humphries, John Laub, Barton Parks, Harold E. Pepinsky, Pauline Pepinsky, Vic Streib, an anonymous anarchist in New York City, and from Contemporary Crises, Bill Chambliss and anonymous reviewers. Special thanks for typing this and the remainder of the pile I have recently laid on, go to Martha Geter and Donna Littrell.

1.   Van den Haag, E., Punishing Criminals: Concerning a Very Old and Painful Question. New York: Basic Books, 1975.

2.   Wilson, J.Q., Thinking About Crime. New York: Basic Books, 1975.

3.   Beccaria, C., (H. Paolucci, trans.), On Crimes and Punishments. Indianapolis: Bobbs-Merrill, 1968.

4.   Von Hirsch, A., Doing Justice: The Choice of Punishment. New York: Hill and Wang, 1976.

5.   As, for instance, has R. Quinney, Critique of Legal Order: Crime Control in Capitalist Society. Boston: Little, Brown, 1974.

6.   Berkman, A., ABC of Anarchism. London: Freedom Press, 1971 [1929].

7.   President's Commission on Law Enforcement and Administration of Justice, The Challenge of Crime in a Free Society. Washington, D.C.: United States Government Printing Office, 1967.

8.   National Advisory Commission on Criminal Justice Standards and Goals, Courts, Corrections. Police. (3 reports) Washington, D.C.: United States Government Printing Office, 1973.

9.   New York Times (September 5, 1976), "Study Backs Critics of New York Drug Law," pp. 1, 40.

10.   Galliher, J.F., McCartney, J.L. and B. Baum, "Nebraska's Marihuana Law: A Case of Unexpected Legislative Innovation," *Law and Society Review* 8 (Spring, 1974): 441-455.

11.   Ross, H.L., "The Neutralization of Severe Penalties: Some Traffic Law Studies," *Law and Society Review* 10 (Spring, 1976): 403-413.

12.   Wilson, J.Q. (1975), *Op. cit.*

13.   Rachlin, H., *Introduction to Modern Behaviorism*. San Francisco: W.H. Freeman, 1970.

14.   Berkman, A. (1971), *Op cit.*

15.   See Palmer, J, "Economic Analyses of the Deterrent Effect of Punishment," *Journal of Research in Crime and Delinquency* 14 (Jan., 1977): 4-21.

16.   National Criminal Justice Information and Statistics Service, *Trends in Expenditure and Employment Data for the Criminal Justice System: 1971-1974*. Washington, D.C.: United States Government Printing Office, 1976, p. 18.

17.   United States Bureau of the Census, *Statistical Abstract of the United States: 1974*. Washington, D.C.: United States Government Printing Office, 1974, p. 336.

18.   National Criminal Justice Information and Statistics Service (1976), *Op. cit.*

19.   United States Bureau of the Census (1974), *Op cit.*

20.   *Ibid.*, p. 156.

21.   National Criminal Justice Information and Statistics Service (1976), *Op. cit.*

22.   National Criminal Justice Information and Statistics Service, *Expenditure and Employment Data for the Criminal Justice System: 1975*. Washington, D.C.: United States Government Printing Office, 1977.

23.   Berkman, A. (1971), *Op. cit.*, p. 60.

24.   *Ibid.*, p. 11.

25.   Godwin, W., "Enquiry Concerning Political Justice," in S. Schatz (ed.), *The Essential Works of Anarchism*. New York: Bantam Books, 1971, pp. 3-41.

26.   Costello, A.E. (1885). *Our Police Protectors: History of the New York Police from the Earliest Period to the Present Time*. New York: author's edition, as reported in J.A. Inciardi, "Criminal Statistics and Victim Survey Research for Effective Law Enforcement Planning," pp. 177-189, in E. Viano (ed.), *Victims and Society*. Washington, D.C.: Visage Press, 1976, at pp. 179-180.

27.   Villaume, A.C. (1977), "Parkinson's Law and the United States Bureau of Prisons," *Contemporary Crises* (in press), makes a persuasive case that Parkinson's Law operates in the federal corrections bureaucracy, as it probably operates elsewhere.

28.   Weinraub, B., "Crime Reports Up 72% Here in 1966: Actual Rise is 6.5%," *New York Times* (February 21, 1967).

29.   Pepinsky, H.E., *Crime and Conflict: A Study of Law and Society*. London: Martin Robertson. New York: Academic Press, 1976, pp. 64-65.

30.   Berkman, A. (1971), *Op cit.*, p. 41.

31.   *Ibid.*, pp. 50-62.

32.   Lemert, E.M., "Paranoia and the Dynamics of Exclusion," *Sociometry* 25 (March, 1962): 2-25.

33.   Pepinsky, H.E. (1976), *Op. cit.*, pp. 119-132.

34.   Greiner, J.M., *Tying City Pay to Performance: Early Reports on Orange, California, and Flint, Michigan.* Washington D.C.: Labor-Management Relations Service of the National League of Cities, National Association of Counties, United States Conference of Mayors, 1974.

35.   Kalven, H., Jr., and Zeisel, H., *The American Jury.* Boston: Little, Brown, 1966, p. 8.

PART FIVE

LAW, ORDER AND SOCIAL CHANGE

The relationship between the law and social change has been the object of much speculation and research.[1] The previous section described how law and order are related to the socio-political structure of a society and when that socio-political order changes dramatically e.g., China, Cuba, the legal system may also be changed. However, the law may also be used as a mechanism for social change, in combination with other efforts. The nature of this dual relationship between the legal order, social order and social change is best investigated historically and cross-nationally in order to understand which way the relationship is working. The following articles provide such analysis and understanding.

McConnell

The political nature of justice is often most evident when threats to the status-quo are addressed.[2] McConnell reviews five books which deal with political trials in the United States, Hungary and the Soviet Union.[3] All of these political criminals were protesting governmental policies and practices and/or were believed to be engaged in activity threatening the very viability of the state. They were political activists who thought "dangerous thoughts" and were a menace to the ideological and political hegemony of the state. Although the cases cover both totalitarian and democratic regimes, they all provide examples of the fact that all states have limits on the extent to which their citizens are allowed to protest government.

Burns

McConnell noted that the quality of a political culture may be determined by the toleration of dissent, and thus, democratic societies are relatively better off. However, as he points out, the right to dissent may not obtain for some in even democratic societies. Burns provides an historical and contemporary analysis of the manner in which the legal system has oppressed black Americans and subsequently repressed attempts at social change.[4] Notwithstanding certain legal gains in the civil rights movement, black people are still largely oppressed in day to day administration of the law. Increased police surveillance, judicial harassment and the warehousing of an increasing number of blacks in jails gives evidence to the way in which the legal system thwarts social change. Finally, he addresses the racism in the legal professions and suggests that blacks must develop their own legal perspective and priorities. This will better contribute to needed social change through maximization of control over those decisions affecting the black community.

Reasons

One perspective which has increasingly been applied to the situation of black, brown and red people in North America is the colonial approach. Reasons compares the traditional order/assimilationist model of race and ethnic relations with the more recent conflict/pluralist model (which incorporates the colonial approach). He then notes how the order/assimilationist model has been the dominant approach toward native people by both governments of the United States and Canada. The colonial approach provides the best explanation of both the historical and contemporary situations of native people in the United States and Canada. While the traditional order/assimilationist model has been evident in corrections, it has largely failed to habilitate native and non-native offenders. Given the facts of the movement for native cultural revitalization, emergence of red power and the beginning of the establishment of minimum civil and human rights for prisoners, the conflict/pluralist model should be the basis of white/native relationships both inside and outside prison.

Goode

Law has been both an obstacle and promoter of social change. Goode critically assesses the underlying ideology of the Law Reform Commission of Canada. Such commissions have increasingly been used in more recent years to address major socio-political issues.[5] Using selected quotations, Goode describes the political ideology of the commissions reports to be a "liberal-positivist ideology." (Similar to the functionalist/perspective approach discussed in section 3 of this book). While ideology is a basis for the emergence and operation of law, he criticizes the commission for not recognizing and acknowledging that they are taking only one of several possible ideological positions.[6] The other model which the commission fails to address is the "value antagonism" (conflict in section 3 of this book) model. This model provides a quite different analysis of the law and subsequently the types of social change needed. Nonetheless, the commission has failed to address this model and, in fact, clearly provides an ideal system based upon the liberal-positivist model. Goode provides three examples of the moral ideology surrounding the commission's approach and concludes that debate and discussion of alternative models should be pursued.

Petras

A specific example of lawlessness in Latin America is provided by Petras' study of Chile.[7] While economic crimes by the corporate elite have periodically been investigated,[8] little attention has been given to systematic criminality of the bourgeoisie in attempts to destroy a political regime and/or undermine an emerging order. Petras illustrates how the bourgeoisie violated the law systematically when their socio-economic interests were threatened by the new Allende government. Thus, while expousing law and order when the law operates in their interests, they became a major lawless force within Chilean society. The crimes of the bourgeoisie included political assassinations and physical assaults, formation of illegal para-military organizations, lockouts, speculation and black market transactions, sabotage of production, riots and mob rule, and receipt of illegal support from the United States for various criminal activities. He points out that Allende's committment to democratic ideals and the "fiction" that the legal system is non-political, contributed to his downfall. In the transition from capitalism to socialism bourgeois political crime becomes extensive and violent. In the case of Chile, such criminal activity resulted in the destruction of a democratically elected government and the establishment of a totalitarian regime. The function of law in social change is thus very dependent upon the power relationships within a society and how they are used to flaunt or support the legal system.

Conclusion

All of the articles in this section have explored an aspect of the place of law in relationship to social change. The use and abuse of the law to stifle dissent (McConnell), oppress minorities (Burns and Reasons), influence broader social policy (Goode), and subvert needed social change (Petras) suggests the varied ways in which the law reflects and effects the economic and socio-political arrangements in various societies. Ultimately, law and legal institutions and their use and abuse reflect both the historical and contemporary political (in the broad meaning of the word) relationships evident in a society. Power is at the base of such relationships and consequently of any subsequent change.

NOTES

1.   See Harvey U. Ball, et al., "Law and Social Change: Summer Reconsidered" American Journal of Sociology 67 (March, 1962): 532-40; Donald J. Black, "The Mobilization of Law", The Journal of Legal Studies 2 (1973): 125-49; Lawrence M. Friedman, "Legal Rules and the Process of Social Change", Standford Law Review 19 (April, 1967): 786-840; Adam Podgarecki, "Law and Social Engineering", Human Organization 21 (Fall, 1962): 177-181; Arnold Rose, "Law and the Causes of Social Problems", Social Problems 16 (Summer, 1968): 33-43; Richard D. Schwartz and

James C. Miller, "Legal Evolution and Society Complexity", *American Journal of Sociology* 70 (September, 1964): 159-169; Upendra Boxie, "Durkheim and Legal Evolution: Some Problems of Disproof", *Law and Society Review* 8 (Summer, 1974): 645-668; Lawrence M. Tiedman, "Legal Culture and Social Development", *Law and Society Review* 4 (August, 1969): 30-44; Robert M. Unger, *Law in Modern Society*. New York: The Free Press, 1976.

2.   For further discussion of such issues see Otto Kirchheimer, *Political Justice: The Use of the Legal Procedure for Political Ends*. Princeton: Princeton University Press, 1961; Charles E. Reasons, "The Politicizing of Crime, the Criminologist and the Criminal", *Journal of Criminal Law and Criminology* (December, 1973): 471-477; S. Schafer, *The Political Criminal: The Problem of Morality and Crime*. New York: Free Press, 1974; J.M. Clements, "Repression: Beyond the Rhetoric", *Issues in Criminology* 6 (Winter, 1971): 1-31.

3.   For an analysis of the nature of "radical" political trials in the United States see David Steinberg, "The New Radical-Criminal Trials: A Step Toward a Cross-for-Itself in the American Proletariat?" *Science and Society* (Fall, 1972): 274-301.

4.   For other discussions of racism in the law see George W. Crockett, Jr., "Racism in the Law", *Science and Society* (Spring, 1969): 223-30; Jack Greenber, *Race Relations and American Law*. New York: Columbia University Press, 1959; Lewis L. Knowles and Kenneth Prewitt, *Institutional Racism in America*. Englewood Cliffs: Prentice-Hall, 1969; Loren Miller, *The Petitioners: The Story of the Supreme Court of the United States and the Negro*. Cleveland: World Publishing, 1966; Kenneth M. Stampp, *The Civil Rights Record: Black Americans and the Law, 1849-1970*. New York: Thomas Y. Cromwell, 1970.

5.   For a discussion of such commissions see Ray C. Rist, "Polity, Politics, and Social Research: A Study in the Relationship of Federal Commissions and Social Science", *Social Problems* 21 (Summer, 1973): 113-128; W. Lehman, "Crime, the Public and the Crime Commission; A Critical Review of the Challenge of Crime in a Free Society", *Michigan Law Review* 66 (May, 1968): 1487-1540; Gary Hogarth, "The Law Reform Commission as a Powerful Agent of Change: Fact or Fantasy?", *Crime and/et Justice* 4 (May, 1976): 24-31.

6.   For varying ideological positions on crime see Walter B. Miller, "Ideology and Criminal Justice Policy: Some Current Issues", *The Journal of Criminal Law and Criminology* 64 (June, 1973): 141-162; J. Griffiths, "Ideology in Criminal Procedure or a Third Model of the Criminal Process", *Yale Law Journal* 79 (January, 1970): 359.

7.   For an excellent discussion of such "colonial criminology" see G.H. Boeringer, "Imperialism, Development and the Under-Development of Criminology" *Mclanesian Law Journal* (1976).

8.   For an overview of such offenses see Richard Quinney, *Criminology*. Boston: Little, Brown and Company, 1975, Chapter 8: "Crimes of Business in the American Economy," pp. 131-145; Colin Goff and Charles E. Reasons, *Corporate Crime in Canada: A Critical Analyses of Anti-Combines Legislation*. Scarborough, Ontario: Prentice-Hall of Canada, 1978.

Chapter 14

Political Trials East and West*

W.H. McConnell†

Louis Nizer, *The Implosion Conspiracy*, (Doubleday, New York, 1973), $10.00.
Cardinal Mindszenty, *Memoirs*, (Macmillan, New York, 1974), $10.00
William Van Etten Casey, S.J., ed., *The Berrigans*, (Avon Books, New York, 1971), $1.25.
Angela Davis, *An Autobiography*, (Random House, New York, 1974), $8.95.
Alexander Solzhenitsyn, *The Gulag Archipelago, 1918-1956*, (Harper & Row, New York, 1973). $12.95.

Socrates, Charles I and Patty Hearst, despite their widely varied times, circumstances and beliefs, shared the common characteristic that at a certain time in their lives they were placed on trial because of behaviour found reprehensible by the political elite of their day, for activities thought highly prejudicial to the welfare of the state, and tried in legal proceedings from which a large political element and an inflamed public opinion could not be severed. And they were tried, moreover, by bodies seeking to foster official values or notions of public policy which the victims repudiated. One of the great perennial problems of legal and political theory is to devise adequate safeguards to protect dissenting minorities from insensitive majority rule. The Founding Fathers of the American Republic considered that an entrenched

---

* W.H. McConnell, "Political Trials East and West," *Saskatchewan Law Review* (1974): 131-146. Reprinted by permission of the *Saskatchewan Law Review*.
* Ph. D. (Toronto), LL.M. (Sask.), Professor of Law, College of Law, University of Saskatchewan.

Bill of Rights was the answer, but widely divergent judicial interpretations (e.g., the heretical assertion by Black and Douglas that First Amendment freedoms are "absolute" and should prevail whenever they come into conflict with lesser rights) and uneven implementation have cast some doubt on the efficacy of such a resource. Dicey felt that a vigilant, independent judiciary and the subjection of all to the common law would protect the individual, but even in his own day his analysis of the judicial process was anachronistic.

Five books are discussed below dealing with the plights of individuals in the United States, Hungary and the Soviet Union, who were placed on trial for thoughts and acts deemed unworthy by the official majority, or the ruling faction, in the countries concerned, and the various processes were carried on in a general climate which was distinctly hostile to the accused. There are certain similarities and dissimilarities between the cases which will be examined briefly in conclusion.

The Rosenbergs:

In *The Implosion Conspiracy*, New York Attorney Louis Nizer tells the story of Julius and Ethel Rosenberg who were sentenced to death in the electric chair by Judge Irving R. Kaufman on April 5, 1951, for transmitting vital information on the atomic bomb to the Soviet Union during the war years of 1944 and 1945. Nizer played no direct part in the espionage case, but his law firm, Phillips, Nizer, Benjamin & Krim, has represented many Hollywood personalities, as well as the Paramount and Rank studios, and he was once asked by Otto Preminger to write a motion picture script on the spy case, a task which he declined. His interest in the case, however, has resulted in a book which is, in turn, both sympathetic and critical, relating the warm love story of the principals right up to their execution in Sing Sing on June 20, 1953, but concluding that there was sufficient evidence for the jury to convict the couple, without himself unequivocally affirming his own conclusion as to their guilt. Despite his reluctance in this respect, one gets a strong impression that Nizer believes the pair to be guilty as charged.

Nizer has deep respect for the father and son team of Alexander and Emanuel Bloch who defended the Rosenbergs. He relates how counsel, beset by difficulties on all sides, attempted to refute with little success the testimony of David Greenglass, Ethel's 29-year old brother, who allegedly was recruited in the spy plot by the couple but agreed, despite the closest blood ties, to testify against them. Greenglass got off with a fifteen-year sentence. It was Greenglass, an ex-Army technical Sergeant who sketched and described at Los Alamos, New Mexico, the atomic bomb triggering mechanism, comprising a high explosive lens, a detonator and a tube which "imploded" ('implosion', from which the book's title is taken, refers to the terrific inward confluence of waves resulting in a concentration of energy and of an atomic blast). When examined by prosecuting attorney Irving H. Saypol, Professor Walter S. Koski of the physical chemistry department at John Hopkins said that Greenglass's sketch accurately depicted the experiments carried on at Los Alamos in 1945 by Oppenheimer, Fermi, Fuchs and others, that to the best of his knowledge no other nation at that time had been conducting similar experiments, and that information on the experiments continued to be classified up to the time of the 1951 trial. In due course, Nizer relates, espionage courier Harry Gold went to Los Alamos and produced the jagged edge of a half-Jello-O box front to the Greenglasses for identification; when it matched their half he was given the sketch and returned East where the classified information was transmitted via the Rosenbergs to the Soviets.

Despite the fact that nobody had ever been executed for a similar crime in peacetime, the jury which found the Rosenbergs guilty of conspiracy to commit wartime espionage made no recommendation for mercy and Judge Kaufman showed none. In the context of the Korean War and the anti-Communist hysteria ignited by Senator Joseph R. McCarthy the widespread public sentiment against the Rosenbergs is understandable, but it detracted from the intellectual climate and political conditions which were essential for a fair trial. In sentencing the pair to death, Judge Kaufman, who at just over forty was the youngest judge on the federal bench, described the defendant's crime as "worse than murder." He added that the very fact that the Soviets possessed the secret and the sense of security it (the A-Bomb) brought would have influenced them in inciting their North Korean allies to commence the Korean War in which so many Americans had died.[1]

After the sentence, defence counsel Emanuel Bloch said on behalf of his clients: "I repeat that these defendants assert their innocence and will continue to assert it as long as they breathe. They believe that they are victims of political hysteria, and that their sentence was based upon extraneous political considerations having no legitimate or legal connection with the crime charged against them."

After being removed to temporary detention cells in the United States Courthouse, Mrs. Rosenberg, a former music student, sang the aria "One Fine Day" from Puccini's Madame Butterfly, as well as "Good Night Irene", while Julius sang "The Battle Hymn of the Republic." During the more than two years that were to elapse before their execution, as the appellate process was wearily grinding on, defence counsel Emanuel Bloch bestowed countless kindnesses on 4-year-old Robert and 8-year-old Michael Rosenberg, the children of the couple who were innocent victims of the tragedy.[2]

In a dramatic last-minute development two lawyers not previously connected with the case, Fyke Farmer of Nashville, Tennessee, and Daniel G. Marshall of Los Angeles persuaded Justice William O. Douglas to grant a stay of execution to the Rosenbergs on the basis that the General Espionage Act of 1917 under which the pair had been sentenced was superceded by the 1946 Atomic Energy Act which provided that the death sentence might be imposed only on recommendation of the jury. There was, of course, no such recommendation in the Rosenberg case.

After an emotional hearing, six justices vacated the stay with Justices Black and Douglas dissenting and Justice Frankfurter announcing neither a concurrence nor a dissent. The latter contended that the points raised by the "interloping" counsel were "complicated and novel" and demanded more lengthy study than the six-judge majority was apparently willing to allow. The majority held that each statute was independent of the other, having its own distinct rationale and field of operation, and that the later statute neither expressly nor by implication repealed the earlier one. The defendants, moreover, had commenced their crime on June 6, 1944, substantially before the 1946 Act was passed, and the Government could appropriately invoke the earlier law.

It remained only for President Eisenhower to reject Mrs. Rosenberg's second eloquent appeal for executive clemency (e.g., . . . I ask this man, himself no stranger to the humanities, what man there is that history has acclaimed great, whose greatness has not been measured in terms of his goodness?") In rejecting their plea the President said: "I can only say that by immeasurably increasing the chances of atomic war, the Rosenbergs may have condemned to death tens of millions of innocent people all over the world. The execution of two human beings is a grave matter. But even graver is the thought of the millions of dead whose deaths may be directly attributable to what these spies have done."[3] One might ask Eisenhower whether, granted his premises, the cases of Ethel and Julius should not have been distinguished. Julius was seen by the prosecution as the main actor of the two,[4] and Ethel was only the ninth woman executed in New York, all the others having been convicted of murder.

An international cause celebre, the plight of the Rosenbergs inspired mass demonstrations throughout the U.S. and in London, Paris, Rome, Toronto, and many other cities throughout the world. The couple were widely seen as victims of political hysteria betrayed by the self-serving evidence of unprincipled government informers who had much to gain through their conviction. The case even now raises nagging doubts about the fairness of the trial, and the detachment of the court. As Nizer relates, most of the individuals playing a major role in the trial were Jewish, and there was discernible in much of the American Jewish community a strong sentiment that the Rosenbergs had reflected adversely on their patriotism and loyalty. The Jews were not alone in extolling loyalty in the fifties, of course, but in the anti-Communist spirit of the times it could be a most serious matter which could prejudice the accused.

Nizer has written a fast-paced and very humanly interesting book. In some places, as in his detailed recounting of the execution in Chapter 52, he verges, however, on morbidity. The book is perhaps of greater interest to the general reader than to the practising or academic lawyer, but it does vividly recapture the frenetic atmosphere of the early fifties in the United States. With such an extensive cast of characters and such a convoluted series of events, however, the lack of an index is absolutely inexcusable.

Cardinal Mindszenty:

In his *Memoirs* published in 1974 shortly before his death, Cardinal Mindszenty, Archbishop of Esztergom, (the archbishopric was established in 1001 with the present nineteenth century Cathedral being modelled after St. Peter's) and primate of Hungary, narrates his life of constant trial and torment instigated by both the political left and right. In striving to uphold the ancient prerogatives and moral authority of the Church in the face of implacable foes, the besieged Cardinal showed a steel will that eventually brought him into conflict with his own Church. A proud and stubborn man, he would not compromise with what he conceived to be moral evil.

His first arrest, on February 9, 1919, was by the socialist Karolyi government which he had opposed in the preceding elections as a spokesman for the Christian Party. Brought to the county courthouse, he was confronted by a Lutheran pastor who enquired what his offence had been. "That is exactly what I would like to know," retorted Mindszenty. Rearrested on March 20 when the Communist ruler Bela Kun seized power, he was locked in a cell formerly used for prostitutes. With the cellar of the Parliament buildings in Budapest used as an execution ground, the prisoners constantly expected to be put before the firing squad, but the Hungarian dictatorship of the proleteriat in this case was brief and the prisoners were finally released. Kun's nationalization of banks, large businesses and estates and all private property above a stipulated minimum consolidated opposition to his regime and he was finally defeated and forced to flee by a Rumanian Army of intervention.[5] His eventual fate is uncertain, but he is believed to have returned to the U.S.S.R. and been a victim of the Stalinist purges in 1939.

One obvious criticism of the Cardinal's autobiography is that his obsession with the wickedness of Communism causes him to devote more than three hundred pages of a book of 341 pages to his relations with the Communist regime. Of his life before the age

of fifty-three we are told very little. For him, of course, the
dreadful significance of what the Stalinist regime was accomplish-
ing in Hungary was critically important, but we are deprived
through his microscopic concentration on this later period with
what would have been a most fascinating glimpse of Hungary
between the wars, and the historical context which caused land
reform and nationalization to loom as such important issues after
1945. A description of his ecclesiastical duties and his views on
theology, philosophy, and the mission of the Church would also
have added great interest to the narrative.

Cardinal Mindszenty's second arrest occurred late in 1944
when, as Bishop of Veszprem, he forbade a priest in his diocese
from conducting a service for the Arrow Cross (the Hungarian
version of the Nazis) to celebrate the "successful liberation" of
Veszprem from the Jews, who had been rounded up and sent to
concentration camps. The complications following from this
incident brought him into confrontation with the authorities. On
this occasion the local prosecutor, who was a believer in "legal
process" refused to draw up an indictment, but the Cardinal
remained in jail until April, 1945, when in the confusion attending
the Red Army's advance into Eastern Europe he managed to get on
a cattle car at Sopron and escape.

Appointed primate of Hungary in 1945, and raised to the
cardinalate in 1946, he was thrust into a position where
confrontation again was inevitable and not being a particularly
diplomatic man by nature, he incurred the wrath of the government by his stern opposition to many of its initiatives. In
particular, he mentions a new law permitting divorce on the
ground of "mere separation"; the official denigration of Saint
Stephen, a towering figure in Hungarian history who was the
country's first King (1001-1038) and the "Apostle of Hungary"; the
assault on the Catholic School system according to which teachers
were to make Marxism, instead of "outmoded Christian Theology"
the basis of their work, and the conversion of Catholic youth
hostels into Marxist youth organizations. His attitude at this time
is shown by his reply to a message of congratulations sent by the
provisional government when he was named primate: "Many
Thanks for the Warm Congratulations. The Highest Constitutional
Authority of the country stands ready to serve his native land."
There would appear to be something splendidly mediaeval in the
Cardinal's conception of the fusion in the primatial office of both
ecclesiastical and civil authority; sadly, as the sequel shows, his
conception of the organic law of Hungary was not shared by
others.

On December 26, the Cardinal was arrested and charged with
treason and currency manipulations. Whatever plausibility the
charge of treason possessed stemmed from his supposed desire to
re-establish the thousand-year-old Hungarian monarchy, an
institution of a mixed religious and political character originating

with the now much maligned St. Stephen. The Communists
charged that after his attendance at the Marian Congress in
Ottawa in 1947, the Cardinal had met with Otto von Habsburg, the
pretender to the Hungarian throne, and drawn up a list of
potential cabinet ministers for a restored monarchist government.
The count on currency manipulation was predicated on the fact
that the Cardinal had accepted donations from foreign benefactors,
such as a $30,000 check from New York's Cardinal Spellman,
which he had refrained from converting into Hungarian currency,
as required by law, at the official exchange rate. In reply to the
charge of treason, the Cardinal admitted meeting von Habsburg in
Chicago for a half-hour audience, but emphatically denied any
aspiration to overthrow the government. He had beseeched the
noblemen to help him obtain and transfer charitable gifts from
America, and he denied drawing up a list of members for a rival
regime. In reply to the charge of currency manipulation, he
conceded that he possessed foreign currency as charged, but
contended it was necessary to have such currency to buy food for
the destitute in the inflation years of 1945-46. The official
exchange rate, he added, meant that the government would skim
off a profit of from 70-75 percent on alms from abroad which
"would scarcely have been moral." He added that none of the
purchases authorized by him had been for his own benefit, but
that the monies had been used exclusively to carry on the work of
the Church.

Cardinal Mindszenty recounts in great detail the dehumanizing
process, "the shattering of personality" which preceded his formal
show trial. He was endlessly interrogated at all hours of the day
and night, dressed in clown's garb, beaten with a rubber
truncheon, and "ate almost nothing because of the fear that mind
impairing drugs would be smuggled into the food." He would be
stripped naked and asked who his collaborators were and who
helped him formulate his political programme. Finally, when his
physical stamina was gone and his once formidable intellectual
abilities were severely strained, he "confessed" his guilt, and his
state-appointed defence counsel, in an incredible summation,
conceded virtually all points in the indictment and recommended a
sentence of life imprisonment rather than the death penalty. The
Cardinal, however, had taken the precaution to disavow
beforehand any "confession" he might make under duress during
the trial, and after his vitality revived he continued steadfastly to
maintain his innocence. It was believed widely at the time that his
confession was induced by drugs.

Cardinal Mindszenty relates the travail of his subsequent
imprisonment with moderation, praising his occasional good
treatment and condemning brutality where it existed. He relates
hearing about the proclamation by Pius XII of the dogma of Mary's
bodily ascension into Heaven, and the canonization of Pius X,
while he was in prison. He acknowledges his gratitude to Pius XII

who never divested him of the primacy, despite his conviction, and expresses his vexation against a growing number of Hungarian "peace priests" who supported the Communist regime.

In conclusion, he narrates the story of the brief-lived Hungarian uprising of 1956 during which Premier Imre Nagy proclaimed the country's "perpetual neutrality" on the model of Switzerland, and promised free elections and an early end to one-party rule. The Cardinal's entry into the capital in triumph was followed shortly by the arrival of Soviet tanks after which he was forced into exile for some fifteen years in the American Embassy in Budapest. In September, 1971, implored for purposes of detente by Pope Paul VI and President Nixon, the Cardinal finally agreed to leave Budapest for the Pazmaneum Seminary in Vienna, which was to be his permanent residence thereafter. Cardinal Mindszenty's unhappy disagreement with the Vatican after his departure from Hungary is well known. He contends that there was an understanding that he would remain Primate, but nevertheless the Vatican released a communique indicating that the Cardinal had voluntarily retired; to the Vatican's embarrassment, he denied such an assertion, stating blandly in a release of his own dated February 6, 1974, "Cardinal Mindszenty has not abdicated his office as archbishop nor his dignity as primate of Hungary. The decision was taken by the Holy See alone." Soon after he died.

The Berrigans:

It was said of the martyred Thomas à Becket by one of his contemporaries, as it might be said of the Berrigans, *zelo justitiae fervidus, utrum autem plene secundum scientiam novit Deus:* "burning with zeal for justice, but whether altogether according to wisdom God knows." Few would now doubt that their moral indictment of the Vietnam adventure was richly deserved, although some might question the appropriateness of the means the Berrigans used to protest it and their eventual flight from the F.B.I. to avoid imprisonment. One of the best witnesses against iniquity, after all, results from publicized imprisonment for ideas.

Daniel Berrigan, a Jesuit whose sensitive poetry has won national awards, was sent to the federal prison in Danbury, Connecticut with his brother Philip, a Josephite priest, for napalming draft files on May 17, 1968, on the second floor of the Knights of Columbus Hall at Catonsville, Maryland. They realized at the time that sooner or later they would go to prison for their protest. In defence of their stand they invoked natural law premises.[6] The War in Vietnam was both immoral and illegal. It was horrible beyond belief. Countless examples of brutality and of failure to discriminate between civilian and military targets, as required by international law, could be invoked to show this. Such a venture violated "the universal conscience of mankind," and laws invoked to justify it were not "true laws." The War was illegal because it contravened both the U.N. Charter and the U.S. Constitution. Taking a natural law or "higher law" approach, the War was an "unjust war"[7] fought with almost any means by a bullying superpower not in self defence but for overriding political purposes involving the drawing of an imaginary perimeter between the Communist and non-Communist worlds. In the context of 1968 this type of thinking was already obsolete for it was based on a concept of monolithic world Communist Empire that was negated by the existence of a dissident Peking, a disenchanted Yugoslavia and restive satellites throughout Eastern Europe, as Russian tanks rumbling through the streets of Prague would soon reaffirm.

In burning the draft records in Catonsville, Maryland, the Berrigans were avowing that certain types of property had no "right" to exist. The U.S. government was using these files to help prosecute an iniquitous, brutalizing and immoral war, involving the wholesale killing of innocent civilians, and property used to promote such a purpose should simply be destroyed. It had no right to exist. Only the moral insensitivity of a Washington bureaucracy which had suppressed all qualms of conscience could think otherwise. There would be here a natural law analogy to a borrower who was asked to return a knife or gun which he knew the owner meant to use for murder; in such a case the owner had no present "right" to the return of his property.

The Berrigans argued, moreover, that they had resorted to all other means to register their disapproval of the war and the destruction of the draft files was a last resort. Philip Berrigan had engaged in a prayer vigil outside the homes of the Joint Chiefs of Staff at Fort Myers, Virginia, and of Secretary McNamara in Washington; he had interviewed senators and spoke at numberless public meetings; he had poured blood on draft files in the United States Custom House in Baltimore. Daniel had been co-chairman of "Clergy and Laymen Concerned About Vietnam" and was jailed in the aftermath of a mass demonstration at the Pentagon; he too had been one of the most probing, articulate and uncompromising opponents of the War at public meetings throughout the country. Their action at Catonsville reflected their sense of futility and desperation.

The Court, however, took no cognizance of the "higher law" to which the Berrigans were appealing. The right of draft records to exist depended not on natural law premises but on the *lex scripta* enacted by Congress. In charging the jury Judge Roszel Thomsen stated flatly: "The law does not recognize political, religious, moral convictions, or some higher law, as justification for the commission of a crime, no matter how good the motive may be." The Berrigans were convicted, and a subsequent Gallup Poll disclosed that 82 percent of Americans disapproved of their destruction of draft records as a form of protest. The Berrigans, however, became a symbol for a growing number of people who felt a revulsion for the Vietnam War and it is clear from post-Watergate disclosures that an important calculation influencing President Nixon and Secretary Kissinger in their determination to scale down U.S. participation and end the War was their appreciation that much of the country's youth were totally disenchanted and would not support seemingly purposeless hostilities indefinitely. The simple question of "Why we were in Vietnam?" had no meaningful answer.

Despite the conflagration at Catonsville, the aim of the Berrigans was one of moral, nonviolent protest. In an interesting essay in the book reviewed "Dan Berrigan: Fugitive From Justice," Paul Cowan attempts to delineate the moral and religious wellsprings of his action:

> "I turn my back on Cardinal Cooke's visits to the troops, but I stay with the life and death of Jesus."
> Then he began to talk about Jesus's belief in nonviolence—and, I think, about the hope that undergirds his own act.
> "Jesus decided in his own life that it was more important to undergo violence than to inflict it. He wasn't just offering that as one man's opinion. The Sermon on the Mount was a blueprint. It helps show how to look for the points of resistance that have to do with vindicating the dignity of man."[8]

One of the few authentic prophets and revolutionaries of our time, Dan Berrigan's prophecy is of a world in which compassion and kindness will be more widespread for the revolution he speaks of is of the heart rather than the sword.

Angela Davis:

In this *Autobiography,* the Marxist intellectual, Angela Davis, tells the story of her life through her trial in 1972 in which she was charged with Ruchell Magee on three counts of murder, kidnapping and conspiracy for allegedly smuggling guns into a Marin County California courthouse as a result of which, on August 7, 1970, two San Quentin inmates, a young black revolutionary and a Superior Court judge who was being abducted were killed in a crossfire. Sought for her alleged complicity in the Marin County shoot-out, she became a fugitive eluding the pursuing F.B.I. until apprehended in a Howard Johnson motel in New York City on October 13, 1970. Professor Davis was indicted for the above-mentioned crimes by a Marin County Grand Jury approximately one month later.

In the absence of significant concrete evidence, Assistant Attorney General Albert W. Harris, Jr., argued that the former

U.C.L.A. philosophy instructor and pupil of Herbert Marcuse had been induced to bring the murder weapons to the Marin County courthouse not out of political idealism but through sexual passion for the now dead Soledad Brother George Jackson, an associate of the men arraigned there. Acting as her own Attorney, she denied the allegation:

> Now he will have you believe that I am a person who would commit the crimes of murder, kidnapping and conspiracy, having been motivated by pure passion. He would have you believe that lurking behind my external appearance are sinister and selfish emotions and passions which, in his words, know no bounds.
> Members of the jury, this is utterly fantastic. It is utterly absurd. Yet it is understandable that Mr. Harris would like to take advantage of the fact that I am a woman, for in this society women are supposed to act only in accordance with the dictates of their emotions and passions. I might say that this is clearly a symptom of the male chauvinism which prevails in our society.[9]

Her defence was not to deny the existence of the facts on which any of the counts in the indictment were based, but to steadfastly maintain that she was completely innocent of any of the crimes mentioned. She and the attorneys associated with her proved to be more than a match for the prosecution, remaining the epitome of calmness, coolness and dignity throughout the trial, which ended in her acquittal and a victory party where "our joy knew no bounds and our celebration no restraints."

The fact that the last few pages only of the book deal with the actual trial may reflect the author's firm belief that there were no grounds on which she could reasonably have been indicted: " . . . I didn't have a fair trial . . . the only fair trial would have been no trial at all."

The earlier, and by far the larger, portion of the book deals with the author's early life in her native city of Birmingham, Alabama, her studies at Brandeis University in Waltham, Massachusetts, in Paris and in Frankfurt, Germany, and later her studies under Herbert Marcuse and her philosophy teaching at U.C.L.A. until she was forced to retire by the California Board of Regents when it became known that she was an avowed Communist. The latter incident precipitated a zealous but unsuccessful endeavour by civil libertarians to keep her on the academic staff in spite of her political views and activities.

Angela Davis was born in Birmingham in 1944. Her mother and father were both teachers. While her mother has continued to teach, her father has now opened a service station, and her brother Ben is well known for his defensive playing for the Cleveland Browns of the NFL. Growing up in Alabama in the fifties, she became thoroughly familiar with the activities of the Ku Klux Klan and similar groups, and the bias of the local police against "black agitators." She attended Elizabeth Irwin High School in New York City on a scholarship after which she went to Brandeis to study French literature, and became a member of the Brandeis chapter of Phi Beta Kappa. She became one of the favorite students of neo-Marxist philosopher Herbert Marcuse at Brandeis, switching from French literature to political philosophy and going, on his recommendation, to the Institute for Social Research at the University of Frankfurt where Marcuse had formerly taught along with Max Horkheimer, Theordor Adorno, Erich Fromm and others. On her return, she went with Marcuse to the University of California at San Diego where she completed her master's degree in philosophy in one year, together with all the classes required for her doctorate. It was arranged that Marcuse would be her thesis supervisor. She soon became a regular visitor to the Black Panthers in Los Angeles and a member of the Che-Lumumba all-black collective arm of the Communist Party. Her troubles, leading to her dismissal from her academic post, then began with the State House in Sacramento and the Board of Regents. In June, 1970, the regents refused to reappoint her as an acting assistant professor of philosophy because of public speeches which were "so extreme, so antithetical to the protection of academic freedom and so obviously deliberately false in several respects as to be inconsistent with qualifications for appointment to the faculty of the University of California." An investigating committee, however, comprised of Richard Brandt of the University of Michigan and law professor Hans Linde of the University of Oregon, after interviewing Governor Reagan, Lieutenant Governor Max Rafferty, the Board of Regents, Angela, and various members of the U.C.L.A. faculty concluded that while her language was "strong", her outside activities appeared in no way to interfere with her performance in the classroom, and recommended her re-hiring. These latest events happened in mid-1970 just before the Marin County incidents leading to Professor Davis's indictment. At that time, as mentioned above, she became a fugitive, and was eventually apprehended, tried and acquitted.

The *Autobiography* is the work of an extraordinarily brilliant and sensitive mind, acutely aware of the many injustices and contradictions in American society and earnestly seeking a remedy. One can only hope that she will find it. The absence of an index, however, is a great inconvenience to the reader.

Alexander Solzhenitsyn:

Possibly the most famous Russian writer next to Tolstoy living in this century, in the *Gulag Archipelago* Nobel laureate Alexander Solzhenitsyn has written his personal indictment of the Soviet prison system. Much like Cardinal Mindszenty in his total rejection of Communism, Solzhenitsyn's Christian mysticism and yearning for a Russian return to what the Soviets regard as decadent bourgeois values give a highly personal flavour to what he has to tell us. Conformity to the norms of dialectical materialism for him is equivalent to spiritual stultification. The very assumptions underlying the Soviet system are a monstrous perversion of the truth, a truth which is objective, eternal and knowable. Events have shown that the Soviet version of Communism which was once welcomed with eagerness by progressive minded people throughout the globe as a long awaited harbinger of social reform, has instead brought with it a repressive police apparatus, harsh penalties for speaking or writing anything not approved by the state, and generally one of the most highly centralized and tyrannical governmental bureaucracies existing anywhere.

The plight of the non-conforming intellectual in the Soviet Union emerges on every page of the book in which Solzhenitsyn describes in great detail his own and others' experiences.

Born at Kislovodsk on December 11, 1918, Solzhenitsyn early acquired an inclination to write. He was raised by his mother, a shorthand-typist, since his soldier father had died on the German front six months before his birth. Meeting with small success in finding publishers for his youthful writings, Solzhenitsyn turned momentarily to the study of physics and mathematics at Rostov University, graduating from the University in 1941 just before the German invasion of Russia. Because of his mathematical training he was sent to artillery school and served at the front as an artillery officer without a break from November, 1942, to February, 1945, when he was arrested because of certain disrespectful remarks on Stalin which the censors found in a letter he wrote to a school friend:

> Mine was, probably, the easiest imaginable kind of arrest. It did not tear me from the embrace of kith and kin, nor wrench me from a cherished home life. One pallid European February it took me from our narrow salient on the Baltic Sea, where, depending on one's point of view, either we had surrounded the Germans or they had surrounded us, and it deprived me only of my familiar artillery battery and the scenes of the last three months of the war.
>
> The brigade commander called me to his headquarters and asked me for my pistol: I turned it over without suspecting any evil intent, when suddenly, from a tense, immobile suite of staff officers in the corner, two counterintelligence officers stepped forward hurriedly, crossed the room in a few quick bounds, their forehands grabbed simultaneously at the star on my cap, my shoulder boards, my officer's belt, my map case, and they shouted theatrically:
> "You are under arrest!"
> Burning and prickling from head to toe, all I could exclaim was: "Me? What for?"[10]

There followed the gruelling interrogations characteristic of the system with repeated attempts to get Solzhenitsyn to disclose those of his acquaintances who might also be "enemies of the State." Sentenced *in absentia* to eight years in a detention camp under the notorious section 58 of the Criminal Code (in a division of the Code dealing with "organized gangsterism" and "crimes against the state") Solzhenitsyn spent the years from 1945 to 1953 in detention, being exiled for life at the end of this period to Southern Kazakhstan. His first published book *One Day in the Life of Ivan Denisovich* describes his experiences in the latter area. Among his tribulations at this time was a severe case of cancer from which he almost died, but from which he recovered finally in 1954 in a clinic at Tashkent. His personal experiences were again used as the basis for his novel *The Cancer Ward*.

According to the journal *Sovetskaya Rossiya*, (28 November, 1962) he was finally rehabilitated in 1957 when the authorities retroactively determined that he had committed no offence. His highly individualistic spirit and his absolute refusal to compromise his artistic integrity by conforming to the literary norms of the Writers' Union or the political norms of the Communist Party brought him, however, repeatedly into collision with the Soviet authorities. Subjected to harrassment of a continuous and petty character, he confined himself to his Moscow house where he wrote, on the basis of the actual experiences relayed to him by many victims, the present work. When a woman possessing a manuscript copy of the work was forced to yield it up to the authorities, she committed suicide and Solzhenitsyn prepared for what he anticipated could have been his death. Instead, early in 1974, in the interest of detente and to the massive relief alike of Nixon and Brezhnev he was forced into exile in Western Europe. Since then he has been a homeless wanderer seeking a refuge in Switzerland, France, South America, or perhaps even Canada, and a highly vocal critic of the Soviet regime. One wonders whether he would have preferred the traditional exile to Siberia to that outside of the country which he both bitterly criticizes and passionately loves.

While the *Gulag* remains a terrible condemnation of the Soviet prison system, it might have been a better book had Solzhenitsyn eliminated some of the repetition (he is obviously trying to make a cumulative case by piling incident on incident but after a time it becomes numbing), and had he not sought so fervently to draw unfavourable comparisons between the Soviet and the preceding Czarist penal systems. While there is little doubt that in magnitude and terror the excesses of the Soviets surpass those of their predecessors, a candid admission that the Czar's system was also very cruel would have served Solzhenitsyn better. The plight of Czarist political prisoners in the late nineteenth century is described as follows in the 1911 edition of the Encyclopedia Britannica: "Wholesale arrests were made by the police, and many of the accused were imprisoned or exiled to distant provinces, some by the regular tribunals, and others by so called "administrative procedure" without a formal trial. The activity of the police and the sufferings of the victims naturally produced intense excitement and bitterness . . ."[11]

Incidental flaws notwithstanding, however, Sozhenitsyn has performed a great service by permanently recording the savage treatment of dissenters by a regime dedicated, paradoxically, to the betterment of the human condition.

Conclusion:

In all of the above cases, the accused were seen by the prosecution as engaging in activities constituting a direct threat to important public interests. The Rosenbergs were accused of transmitting the most closely guarded American secret weapon of the twentieth century to Soviet agents; Cardinal Mindszenty's significance was symbolic as well as real, he was summoning the hallowed moral authority of his country's thousand-year-old Church for a final battle against the atheistic regime in Budapest, and unless he was stopped there was a real danger of political disintegration, as events in 1956 demonstrated; the Berrigans likewise were appealing to a higher law against an immoral war, they were appealing to the conscience of the nation to defy interests to which the Pentagon and the State Department attached the highest priority; Angela Davis and Alexander Solzhenitsyn in their different ways were both challenging the fundamental assumptions of a political society, Angela seeing in a Commmunist ideology purged of some of its crasser elements by Marcuse's neo-Marxism an antidote to racism and poverty, while Alexander looked back nostalgically to a mystical Christian liberal nationalism.

Although in the case of the Berrigans and Solzhenitsyn the pretexts for their arrests were relatively insignificant, all of the above persons were political activists thinking "dangerous thoughts" and capable of greatly expanding their influence and posing, to a considerable extent, a menace to the ideological and political integrity of the state. While it is true that a larger range of viewpoints is tolerated in the pluralistic liberal-democratic West than in the Soviet Union, the Berrigans assertion that property used to prosecute an immoral war had no right to exist, and Angela Davis's and the Rosenberg's espousal of Communist principles placed them in the margins of society, beyond the limits of dissent officially tolerated. It can be, indeed, a terrible thing to enter the courtroom confronted not only by all the panoply of State power, but by an enraged public opinion from which there can be no secure refuge. A problem of great difficulty in such a case is simply to empanel a reasonably unbiased jury, or to obtain a judge who will try to offset and discount any bias he might feel against the accused.

It may be that where significant cleavages of opinion do exist the jury system could serve as a check on an overzealous prosecutor or a biased judge. It is noteworthy that in Bentham's England juries in the early nineteenth century refused to convict accused of relatively minor offences, carrying a capital penalty, often in direct contravention of the evidence.[12] So might the Berrigans have been acquitted. The acquittal of Angela Davis suggests that in appropriate circumstances this will be done. In the Soviet Union or Hungary with their inquisitorial processes the result is usually, however, predetermined, and Solzhenitsyn's case, where he was given an eight year "administrative" sentence without even formally appearing in court, reveals the grave inadequacies of Stalinist justice.

One may wonder, finally, if the quality of a political culture may not be measured by its toleration of dissent. To many marxist and neo-Marxists "social solidarity" is of more importance, and pluralism is decadent liberal mythology. Perhaps, in a spirit of wonder and dread, we can only await the higher synthesis of freedom and authority at some future date in a Hegelian Heaven.

NOTES

1.   The strong political biases of Judge Kaufman are revealed in the following words pronounced while sentencing the Rosenbergs:

> They [the Rosenbergs] made a choice of devoting themselves to the Russian ideology of denial of God . . . and aggression against free men everywhere . . . . I believe your [the Rosenbergs'] conduct . . . . has already caused the Communist agression in Korea with the resultant casualties exceeding 50,000, and who knows but that millions more of innocent people may pay the price of your treason? Indeed by your betrayal you undoubtedly have altered the course of history to the disadvantage of your country . . . I . . . assume that the basic Marxist goal of world revolution and the destruction of capitalism was well known to the defendants . . . . I must pass such sentence upon the principles in this diabolical conspiracy to destroy a Godfearing nation which will demonstrate with finality that this nation's security will remain inviolate (quoted in Eric Bentley, *Thirty Years of Treason*. New York: 1971. p. 939).

Judge Kaufman's role in the case has dogged him throughout his entire subsequent judicial career. See the *New York Times*, Sunday, June 8, 1975, VI. 36, on a threatened student disruption of his visit to Pomona College in California arising out of the cause celebre over which he presided twenty-four years ago.

2.   The Rosenberg brothers, who now use the surname "Meeropol" of the family who adopted them, contend that their parents were completely innocent and find Nizer's book a tendentious travesty of the truth as they see it. In June, 1975, they obtained the right to examine portions of F.B.I. files used by the U.S. Government in the prosecution of their parents. Attorney-General Edward H. Levi overruled both the F.B.I. and the U.S. Attorney in New York to make more extensive portions of the files available. The F.B.I. still strongly opposes the use of information that might give away its informants or its methods of operation, even after

many years. See the New York Times, Friday, July 11, 1975, 8. Apparently concerned about the inadequacy of the material released to them by the Government, the Rosenbergs decided on July 14 to file suit against the U.S. Government in the U.S. District Court under the new Freedom of Information Act to secure the release of all the files in their parents' case. Their suit was inspired in part by the revelation that the U.S. Attorney in New Mexico had destroyed records on Greenglass who, of course, was a key witness against their parents. See the New York Times, Tuesday, July 15, 1975, 12.

3.   In his book on the Eisenhower administration Eisenhower and the American Crusades. New York: 1972, Herbert S. Parmet mentions the global movement to save the Rosenbergs and certain undisclosed evidence (the nature of which is not specified) which was not used at the trial but which "corroborated" the pair's guilt to the satisfaction of the Eisenhower cabinet (see p. 259):

> . . . . Efforts to spare the lives of the young parents were made by a group of one hundred Protestant clergymen, by Cardinal Feltin and three French bishops, by forty-one members of the British Parliament and by French President Vincent Auriol. In London, the American embassy was surrounded by protestors. Many thousands paraded around the White House. Finally, on the nineteenth of June, the Supreme Court set aside a stay of execution that had been granted by Mr. Justice William O. Douglas and thereby upheld the validity of the death sentence under the Espionage Act of 1917. During the thirty-six years of the First World War-inspired law, it had brought no capital punishment.
>
> The Rosenbergs then awaited the President's action on the clemency appeal. At that morning's cabinet meeting, Attorney General Brownell reviewed the case and said that the government had information corroborating their guilt which could not have been used in the trial. Robert Donovan reported that the President declared that any intervention by him could be justified only, in Donovan's words, "where statecraft dictated in the interests of American public opinion or of the reputation of the United States Government in the eyes of the world.

4.   See, however, Judge Kaufman's remarks at p.356 of Nizer's book that Ethel" . . . was a full-fledged partner in the crime."

5.   On Kun see Oszkar Jaszi, Revolution and Counter-Revolution in Hungary. New York: 1924.

6.   The Berrigans were not the only clergymen to invoke natural law to justify civil disobedience. The black Nobel Peace Prize laureate Dr. Martin Luther King whose assassination in Memphis in April, 1968, set off a nation-wide rampage of looting, arson and criminal activity (including 711 fires in Washington alone), appealed to a higher law when imprisoned for defying segregationist ordinances in the South. After receiving his doctorate at Harvard in 1955, Dr. King became minister of a Baptist church in Montgomery, Alabama, and led the fight in 1955-56 against the segregated bus lines in that city. An almost insignificant incident had inspired the bus boycott in that case. Forty-two year old Rosa Parks had refused, on December 1, 1955, to move to the rear of the bus when ordered by a bus driver so that a white man could have her seat. The black community became enraged when she was subsequently fined ten dollars for violating a local law and since the 25,000 black residents of

Montgomery accounted for 75 per cent of the bus company's local patronage their boycott was able to exert tremendous financial pressure on the local transit service. Dr. King gained a major victory and national prestige when approximately one year later, on December 21, 1956, the city instituted a desegrated bus service.

His *Letter from Birmingham City Jail* enunciated the natural law principles underlying passive resistance to unjust laws:

> . . . . One may well ask, "How can you advocate breaking some laws and obeying others?" The answer is found in the fact that there are two types of law: There are *just* and there are *unjust* laws. I would agree with Saint Augustine that "An unjust law is no law at all."
>
> Now what is the difference between the two? How does one determine when a law is just or unjust? A just law is a man-made code that squares with the moral law or the law of God. An unjust law is a law that is out of harmony with the moral law. To put it in the terms of Saint Thomas Aquinas, an unjust law is a human law that is not rooted in eternal and natural law. Any law that uplifts human personality is just. Any law that degrades human personality is unjust. All segregation statutes are unjust because segregation distorts the soul and damages the personality (see Edward Kent, ed., *Revolution and the Rule of Law*. Englewood Cliffs, N.J.: 1971, 17).

7.   The Doctrine of the "just war" has a very long pedigree in Christian theology, one of its principal proponents being the seventeenth century Spanish Jesuit Suarez, but it can be traced back at least as far as the fifth century to Augustine:

> As far back as the early fifth century St. Augustine laid the foundations of the doctrine of a just war. Succeeding theologians and canonists sought to define it more exactly and apply it to the circumstances of their time. In the thirteenth century the greatest of the theologians, St. Thomas Aquinas, gave more logical form to the doctrine; and there was little to add to his analysis when, three hundred years later, Victoria and the Spanish theologians sought to interpret it in terms of the problems of the newly discovered Western Hemisphere. War, said St. Augustine, was permissible to the Christian when resorted to in a just cause, in defence of the state against external enemies and in punishment of wrongdoing. Moreover, war must be declared by the competent authority; and when so declared the responsibility for the justice of the war rested with the ruler, not with the individual soldier; soldiers were in such cases not murderers but ministers of the law. St. Thomas, elaborating on these principles, pointed out that wars must not only be waged in a just cause but the intention of the ruler must be a right intention. Even if the other conditions of a just war were present, it would not do for the ruler to wage war from wrong motives (Charles G. Fenwick, *International Law* (4th ed.). New York: 1965, 57).

8.   190.

9.   Angela Davis, *op. cit.*, 363.

10.   Alexander Solzhenitsyn, *op.cit.*, 18.

11.   *Encyclopedia Britannica*, 11th ed., article "Russia", vol. 23, p. 905.

12.   Cf.

The haphazard list of two hundred crimes punishable by death had not even consistent severity to recommend it. It was death to steal from a boat on a navigable river, but not on a canal. To cut down trees in a garden was a capital offence, and also to slit a person's nose; but not so the most aggravated murderous assault which the victim managed to survive with nose intact. The unjust laws often resulted in a leniency as injurious to justice as the severity that had been decreed. Juries were unwilling to convict and witnesses to give evidence, in cases of theft that were capitally punishable. The burglar on his part was strongly tempted to escape the rope by murdering the householder who had witnessed his robbery. The chance of escaping capture for want of an efficient police, and in case of capture the uncertainty of what would happen in court, made a life of crime an agreeably exciting gamble. (G.M. Trevelyan, *British History in the Nineteenth Century and After: 1782-1919.* Pelican, Harmondsworth: 1965, 46-47.)

Chapter 15

Black People and the Tyranny of American Law*

Haywood Burns

Abstract:

The American legal system has not managed to escape the
racism that permeates American life. Both historically and
contemporaneously, the law has been the vehicle by which the
generalized racism in the society has been made particular and
converted in policies and standards of social control. Notwithstanding many countervailing experiences, many black Americans
see their dominant experience with the law as that of the law's
victim. Present efforts at using the law as an instrument of social
change in order to relieve this victimization are encumbered by a
lack of black direction of and control over the resources, policy,
and personnel ostensibly organized to combat racism. The tyranny
of a racist legal structure and the powerlessness of blacks in the
face of white hegemony over most of the major legal institutions—
public and private—which have been established to attempt to
eradicate white racism, must both be answered by the reassertion
by the black bar and black community of their interests in shaping
the decisions which so profoundly affect their lives. If leadership
of this character articulates black priorities from the perspective
of the community centrally affected, then all willing elements of
the society can contribute usefully to the attainment of the goals of
freedom with dignity for all.

* Haywood Burns, "Black People and the Tyranny of American Law", *The Annals*
407 (May, 1973): 156-166. Reprinted by permission of the American Academy of
Political and Social Science and the author.

In classical theories of democracy, the laws are supposed to reflect "the will of the people"—or at least of the majority. From the point of view of black people in this country, American law has been all too successful in this regard; for, in a country permeated by white racism,[1] the legal system has been and continues to be racist in character. More than a century ago, in analyzing democracy in America, Alexis de Tocqueville warned of the "tyranny of the majority," pointing out that in the absence of safeguards for the protection of minority rights, American democracy becomes just another form of tyranny.[2] Tocqueville might have gone further and pointed out that in a majority racist society what obtains these circumstances is a racist tyranny over the racial minority. For American blacks, too often the safeguards either do not exist, or are not applied. Too often blacks have known the law only as a sword, and not as a shield.

There have, of course, been myraid countervailing experiences with the law, where it has been used as an instrument of constructive social change to the benefit of blacks—more so in the most recent past than throughout our history.[3] However, the dominant experience has been one in which the law acted as the vehicle by which the generalized racism in the society was made particular and converted into standards and policies of subjugation and social control. Most white Americans tend to view the historic role of the law in this country as that of a tool for the expansion of liberty, and they are largely correct as to themselves—especially if they are not poor (which most are not). However, etched deep in the collective consciousness of American blacks is the role that the law has played in their oppression. It is a present perception which comports with both the historical and contemporary reality.

The Past

Slavery

The institution of American chattel slavery is unique in the experience of human kind—unique in its brutality, unique in its drive to degrade and depersonalize those persons enslaved.[4] The American slave system relied heavily upon the American legal system for the creation and the perpetuation of the institution of American chattel slavery. This is not to say that the law itself was responsible for bringing slavery into existence. It was, to a large extent, recognizing as de jure a de facto situation that had been developing for some time. What is true, though, is that the law played a critical role in the institutionalization of American slavery, defining, sanctioning, and ossifying it, and protecting its presence upon the American landscape for centuries.

It is not often recalled that in the early seventeenth century, during the days of the first settlements in this country, there was at first no clearly defined status of "slave." White Europeans and black Africans existed side by side in various stages of unfreedom. Some form of bondage was a very common experience, and there was considerable confusion over and imprecision about the use of the term "slave." It certainly was not synonymous and interchangeable with the word "Negro"—as it later grew to be. Black persons sometimes served a term of years and were then to be released from service and even in some instances to own or hold other blacks in servitude.[5]

Increasingly, however, throughout the seventeenth century the situations of the blacks in bondage and the whites in bondage diverged: the plight of the white steadily improved and that of the black became more debased. It was the law that was responsible for the crucial developments in this whole process, which by century's end had defined the perimeters of a slave system and had permanently locked the black, by reason of his blackness, on the inside. This was accomplished by white men who, sitting in Colonial legislatures, passed laws making bondage for *blacks* (1) a lifetime condition and (2) a hereditary condition.[6] Thus the law not only fastened onto the captive African for all of his days, but it marked as well the unborn, condemning not an individual or a generation, but an entire people to the night of slavery.

Nation-building

With a revolution for liberty and the birth of a new nation, the so-called founding fathers were presented with a prime opportunity to resolve in favor of freedom the contradictions of a nation which was established in the interest of liberty, yet everywhere kept men and women enslaved. After much debate, the opportunity was missed. Slavery was to be a part of the new America. Apparently, even the more progressive of the founding fathers, those with scruples against slavery, were unprepared to tamper with so much private property and unable to accept fully the notion of blacks being their equals.[7] Blacks were, at this point in time—as they would be many times thereafter—the victims of an American pragmatism that bartered and compromised their lives away in a process from which they had been totally excluded—sacrificed to the exigencies of certain white imperatives. Black school children of today must still look at the Constitution of 1789 and see enshrined in our fundamental law, the guaranteed continuation of the slave trade,[8] the required return of fugitive slaves,[9] and the counting of enslaved, disfranchised blacks as three-fifths persons for purposes of political representation.[10]

Pre-Civil War

It was the law, through the slave codes of the eighteenth and nineteenth centuries, which governed in oppressive detail the lives of millions of black slaves. The slave codes, by their terms, denied a legal personality to blacks, barring them from bringing law suits or testifying against a white person. Through elaborate statutory schemes, the slave codes regulated the movement of blacks, denied any family relationship, and applied criminal sanctions according to a different and harsher standard than applied to whites.[11] The law confirmed and guaranteed the debased situation of the slave, and the entire legal apparatus was ultimately reinforced by the Taney dictum, in the *Dred Scott* case, that the Negro "had no rights which the white man was bound to respect."[12]

Neither was the oppressive role of the law in this period entirely a regional phenomenon. North of the Mason-Dixon line it was the law which relegated so-called free blacks to an inferior status, barring blacks from certain types of employment, banning them from within the borders of certain territories, requiring segregated schools, and withholding from blacks the franchise.[13]

Post-Civil War

A northern victory in the Civil War and the passage of the Thirteenth, Fourteenth, and Fifteenth Amendments were not sufficient to arrest this process completely; for immediately after the Civil War whites turned to the law once again hoping to duplicate in so far as was possible, the vertical white-black relationship that existed prior to emancipation. The wholesale passage of black codes was designed to keep blacks: close to the land, away from certain types of occupations, away from white women, and subservient.[14] In fact, without an identifying date, it is often difficult to tell a post-Civil War black code from a pre-Civil War slave code.

After Reconstruction the law was once again a major white weapon for wrenching rights from the hands of blacks, destroying the many black gains that had been made during that period. It was the law which launched the strange career of Jim Crow, codifying the customs and usages of segregation and giving them universal application in the southern states.[15] It was the law— aided by the extra-legal, though community sanctioned, force of lynch law—which disfranchised hundreds of thousands of blacks in the late nineteenth and early twentieth century, stripping from black people the hard won black political power. The grandfather clause, the literacy test, and the poll tax were all legal devices designed to block black people from the polls. It was in this period, as well, that an increasingly conservative Supreme Court cut back on the breadth of the Civil War Amendments, giving them an increasingly narrow intepretation to the detriment of black people, a trend that finally culminated in acceptance as the law of the land of the *Plessy* v. *Ferguson* "separate, but equal" pronouncement.[16] The citadel of legally established and sanctioned apartheid remained largely inviolate throughout most of the twentieth century, until the major legal assaults of the U.S. Supreme Court decision in *Brown* v. *Board of Education*[17] in 1954 and the Civil Rights Act of 1957[18]—the first federal civil rights legislation in the country since Congress had passed the Civil Rights Act of 1875.[19]

The Present

The numerous successful legal attacks upon segregation have not solved the problem of racism and the law for black people today. Racism is still part and parcel of the daily reality of the functioning of the justice system. Black lawyers, plaintiffs, defendants, and witnesses are still subjected to the overtly racist attitudes, actions, and comments of an overwhelmingly white justice system. Black people are likewise affronted by a legal system that so often works against them and too seldom works for them, when they have been victimized and the state should be under an obligation to prosecute the white perpetrators of the wrong.

At one point in our history the law reserved exclusively for white men the right to sit on juries.[20] Though jury statutes no longer state this exclusion, blacks are still systematically excluded from juries through unfair procedures for compiling prospective jury rolls and through racial use of the peremptory challenge by the prosecutor. As a result, legions of black men and women are continually having their liberty and property taken away and their lives put in jeopardy by juries from which their peers have been systematically excluded.[21]

In the nineteenth century there were legal provisions that prevented blacks from bringing law suits against whites, or from testifying when white interests were involved. Though this situation no longer legally obtains, it is the common experience of black litigants that judges and juries are often likely to outweigh the testimony of several black witnesses with the testimony of one white one; that in a personal injury case the leg or arm of a white litigant is valued more highly than that of a black one.[22]

In the past, in some statutes different penalties were set out for whites and blacks for the same offense. Though this is no longer the case, sentencing patterns, when taken as a whole, often reveal a significant disparity between sentences meted out to blacks and whites for the same offense.[23] One of the most egregious areas in this regard is in death sentences, in particular, death sentences for interracial sex crimes. Sexual mutilation was at one time the statutory penalty reserved almost exclusively for blacks and Indians for interracial sex crimes.[24] In modern times it seems to have been the death penalty. Since the 1930s, 455 persons have been executed for rape in this country. Four hundred five of these persons have been black.[25] In other areas of law related to sentencing, where great amounts of discretion are involved—such as commutation of sentences—overall patterns of disparity of treatment can also be discerned.[26]

Quite apart from any direct or explicit considerations, the law, by reason of its structure—its procedural rules and substantive doctrines—operates to the disadvantage of the poor and minority person. This structural inequality brings about a type of institutional subordination[27] based on class and caste—class, because so much of this institutional unfairness is related to the amount of money a person has; caste, because such a vastly disproportionate number of the poor in this country are also members of the nation's racial minorities.

A prime example can be seen in the operation of the money bail system, which jails one group of citizens for weeks, months, and sometimes years before trial, while another group goes free. Both are equally presumed innocent; money is the only discriminating factor. As a result, the country's jails are packed to overflowing with the nation's poor—with red, brown, black, and yellow men and women showing up in greatly disproportionate numbers.[28]

These problems of institutional subordination along racial lines due to the law's structural inequality are not, however, limited to matters of criminal justice. There is structural inequality in the owner-biased landlord-tenant law[29] and creditor bias in the commercial law.[30] In adminstrative law as measured by the standard due process required, there is often less respect and protection for the matters of concern to poor and minority citizens than that accorded major commercial and propertied interests.[31] Further, in the previous century black people were barred from certain states and territories by law. Today, large-acre zoning laws effectively put certain geographical areas off-limits to blacks.[32] In addition, the law continues to be used as a tool for depriving black people of effective political participation through the exercise of the franchise, for example, where "at-large" systems of voting can be used to assure that a black minority will never be in a position in the particular locale in question to elect a political representative of its own choosing.[33]

Political repression

Black people are, as well, increasingly victimized by the growing political uses of the law against the unpopular and the politically controversial, as the law is used for a tool of political repression in the service of racism, and in opposition to the legitimate aspirations of the black community for change. Political uses of the law certainly are not directed exclusively at black community activists, but since members of the black community make up such a large part of the cutting edge of the movement for social change in this country, the black community takes a large part of the brunt of the abuses of state power. Contemporary concern in the black community focuses upon the passage of new legislation that can be used as an instrument of repression; for example, prevention detention, "no-knock," and "stop and frisk" legislation, while not racially directed in its terms, is seen to pose a decided threat to the freedom of blacks. The Interstate Riot Act, or so-called Rap Brown Act,[34] which, in effect, makes certain thoughts criminal if one happens to be thinking them while crossing a state line, is a ready weapon to attack politically active black spokesmen. Legislation that limits grand jury immunity and, in effect, compels grand jury testimony upon pain of imprisonment, flies in the face of traditional notions concerning the privilege against self-incrimination.[35] It is part of a much larger phenomenon which supports governmental use of the grand jury process to suppress and inhibit political activism—a phenomenon of special moment to the black community at a time when it is attempting to coalesce and organize its efforts to secure change.

The fact that the U.S. Supreme Court apparently looks with favor upon such practices,[36] coupled with what is perceived as a more generalized trend in Supreme Court decisions toward the erosion of fundamental rights, is another source of distress for black people.

Wholly apart from statutes or appellate decisions, it is the day-to-day administration of the law—particularly, the criminal justice system—which shapes the attitudes of black people about the law. There is concern about the street-level abuse—verbal, psychological, and physical—attendant upon the enforcement of the law in black communities. The para-military aspect of law enforcement has taken on an even more decided emphasis in recent times with police resorting to some of the latest technological advances in equipment and weaponry, greatly aided by grants under the federal Law Enforcement Assistance Administration to patrol and control black communities. The harshness of the developments are exacerbated by the rampant police corruption and the selective enforcement of the law witnessed by minority persons in their communities.[37]

Of late, the violence of officialdom has gone beyond unprovoked police attacks upon the headquarters and offices of political activists or upon the persons of political activists as they come to court, to the murders at Kent State, Jackson State, South Carolina State (Orangeburg), Southern University, Attica, Chicago (Fred Hampton and Mark Clark), and elsewhere.

Police practices in dealing with black political spokesmen give black people further cause for pause and further support the view that the law continues to be an instrument of racism and repression where they are concerned. There is the questionable manner in which informants are being employed. All too often they are either unsound individuals, or persons with serious charges or possible long sentencing facing them, who are told to produce evidence under circumstances that invite entrapment. There is, as well, the use of the *agent provocateur*, the person who infiltrates political groups and instigates activity that may subject the members and leadership of the group to arrest and imprisonment. This unsavory police practice has been used against black political activists to the overall detriment of the image of the police and the law in the mind of much of black America.[38]

These practices must be seen against a backdrop of increased police surveillance of private citizens in many sectors of life—but especially political activity. The amassing of dossiers and keeping of data banks on persons quite unrelated to criminal activity has served both to anger and to chill those who seek to exercise First Amendment rights.

Electronic surveillance or "bugging," to the level of wholesale invasions of privacy and encroachments upon fundamental rights, is a source of deep concern for a people who for centuries had their lives constantly monitored and governed in minutest detail. In recent years the federal government had even gone so far as to maintain that it could conduct electronic surveillance in certain kinds of cases involving domestic security without first having to obtain judicial approval. The U.S. Supreme Court, however, was unanimous in its view that the government had no authority to contravene our fundamental liberties.[39]

Fear of the law as an instrument of repression on the part of a racial group that has experienced the law in this role is enhanced when the government blithely ignores constitutional safeguards to accomplish what it may view as a superior political purpose. The mass arrest of hundreds of persons during the Washington, D.C., May Day activity without any semblance of "probable cause" raised just such a specter.

The money bail system is inequitable in its normal operation, making pretrial liberty depend on the size of a person's wallet. The inequity of the system is compounded in political cases, however, by the extremes to which the state goes in demanding exorbitant amounts of money as a condition of pretrial release. Often these amounts seem to bear no relationship to the likelihood of appearance at trial, but are, in fact, a species of political ransom.

The frequent charge of conspiracy in cases involving political activists is viewed as another example of political use of the law. Conspiracy has long been a charge to which the state would resort in attacking the controversial and/or politically disfavored defendant. The rules of evidence become much more elastic under such a charge, and no substantive crime need be proven. The amorphous nature of the law of conspiracy makes it a useful prosecutorial device. Angela Davis, Bobby Seale, Erika Huggins, the Panther Twenty-one, the Chicago Seven, the Harrisburg Eight: all were faced with conspiracy charges—though none was convicted.

A further difficulty with the law that faces blacks in modern times is the harassment of those who would plead their cause. Increasingly, lawyers—black and white—who have taken on the defense of black activists have themselves become the subject of official sanctions—facing contempt, bar discipline, or even criminal charges. This has happened to the degree that part of the struggle of black people with American law today is to protect their protectors.

The inequities and failings of the legal system, as far as black people are concerned, are capped by the barbarity and racism of a punishment system that is itself a crime. The warehousing of human beings that goes on in our nation's prisons is a well-documented national disgrace, which, once again, falls with disproportionate severity upon minority group prisoners— especially those who would organize in an effort to change their lot and end the crime of punishment.[40]

Thus, from the sidewalk to the big house, the ugly specter of legal racism still stalks today's American black man and woman.

Structure of the Profession

The law's racism—past and present—has been a substantial obstacle to black advance in this country. Despite this fact, the legal system still carries with it the possibilities of positive change in the direction of remedying many of the deprivations black people face in America. Offensive civil actions, criminal defense of activists working for change, and the test case all have their merit. As long as the law is regarded as only a component in a much larger change process, and not a panacea, it is evident that it is much too valuable a tool for black people to abandon at this point in time—if ever.

What is ironic, but perhaps not surprising, is that not only are black people afflicted by the legacy of a legal structure permeated with racism, but much of the structure of the institutional apparatuses that have grown up to attack this racism operates in ways inimical to black interests. At one point in time, black people played a major role in shaping and carrying out the legal strategies addressed to the problems of their own liberation. Under the guidance and direction of such legal giants as Charles Houston, William Hastie, Thurgood Marshall, James Nabrit, Jr., and others, and with the intellectual support of the Howard Law School, great civil rights advances through law were plotted and carried out.[41]

However, the situation of black leadership in the legal arena in the definition and solution of the major problems of black society in white America no longer obtains.

Of course, racism is a problem that affects all who live in America—black or white. All have a stake in its eradication—including those of its beneficiaries who would hate to see it go. However, to say that all are victimized by racism is not to say that all are victimized by it equally or in the same way. Blacks, as the chief direct victims, should have a critical say in the way in which their victimizers and victimization are to be addressed. In the presence of the villainous white racism, fair-minded persons should respect black people sufficiently to permit them to define their problems and lead in shaping the solutions. This is a crucial aspect of black's empowerment, self-determination, and decolonization. It is, as well, rightfully a part of white people's liberation—liberation from paternalism, from patronizing, from dictating to blacks what black problems are and how they are to be solved. It is not an excuse for white abdication of responsibility or inaction in these areas. In the past, great contributions by lawyers of all races have been made to the legal struggle against racism. History has seen to it that there are very few black lawyers at the bar.[42] A major portion of the legal assault upon racism has been and will continue to be carried on by white attorneys—which is entirely appropriate, since white racism is all our problem. Close cooperation and close working relationships between the white and black bar in these areas certainly are indicated. However, representatives of the white bar need to relinquish their hold on the claim to control and direct black people's destinies, and be prepared to accept black leadership on matters of social policy where black people are primarily affected.

Today, most of the major decisions concerning legal strategies designed to address the issues having widest impact upon black America are made in institutions—private and public—that are not under black direction or control and which lack sufficient black input from either the black bar or the black community. The major financing of legal efforts on issues of critical importance to the black community goes to these institutions, for, despite the burgeoning efforts of black people at organization and self-help and the ever increasing number of well-credentialed blacks interested in applying legal skills in the service of their communities, foundations and other philanthropic sources continue to fund in their own image. The result of this set of circumstances is that choices are made of the greatest moment to the black community—concerning what issues are important, what is their priority, what political activists are worthy of defense, what political activists are not, where will the millions of dollars of private and public funds be allocated, and so forth—without the assistance of the legally trained persons from the community most affected, or without the ability of members of those communities to exercise much control over these decisions which so deeply affect their lives.

One of the most serious, if not the ultimate, of indignities is the tyranny of those who control the gathering and dissemination of the written and spoken word concerning the black situation. Even there the majority group would have black people submit themselves to the will and the power of those non-blacks who control. For example, not only are black people disadvantaged by a white racist legal structure and hindered in their efforts to correct this situation by a white-dominated civil rights legal establishment, but the interpretation of their situation is given over to persons from outside the group centrally involved. They cannot tell their own story without having it screened through white interpreters. This is not to negate the right of white writers and editors to write and prepare publications on blacks; nor is it to disparage personally the white individuals, often persons of great ability, who follow this course. It is only to say that in the 1970's, in the presence of so many fine, trained, and talented black legal personages equipped by training and sensitivity to address and interpret the black situation, it is a great affront to the black bar and the black community, and the product of the grossest racial myopia, when those responsible for generating major commentaries on black people and their legal situation ignore and pass over all black scholars, writers, and practitioners in the decision of who will structure, guide, and control the content and nature of that publication. The audacity involved is overwhelming.

The lesson from the exercise of so much white power—in the legal system and in the legal profession—is that black people, the black bar, and the black law schools must reassert their right of leadership and their right to maximize control over the decisions affecting the lives of the black community. They must fashion an independent thrust based on a black perspective and on black priorities. All who wish to join in and contribute to the effort should be welcomed, for it is only in the pooling of all available resources that any real hope of eradicating racism lies. This can be the first step in the forging of a new majority, which will avoid the pitfalls of operating in a manner that perpetuates the very evils sought for elimination.

Sic semper tyrannis.

NOTES

1.   See *Report of the National Advisory Commission on Civil Disorders.* New York: Bantam, 1968, p. 10.

2.   Alexis de Tocqueville, *Democracy in America.* (1841; reprint ed.), New York: Vintage, 1945, p. 269.

3.   See William H. Hastie, "Toward an Equalitarian Legal Order: 1930-1950," *The Annals* (May, 1973): 18-31.

4.   See Kenneth M. Stampp, *The Peculiar Institution: Slavery in the Ante-Bellum South*. New York: Random House, 1956.

5.   See Winthrop D. Jordan, *White over Black*. Chapel Hill: University of North Carolina Press, 1968, p. 74; Paul C. Pahner, "Servant into Slave: The Evolution of the Legal Status of the Negro Laborer in Colonial Virginia," *South Atlantic Quarterly* 65 (1966): 355-70.

6.   See Jordan, *White over Black*, pp. 44-98; Assembly Proceedings, September 1664, Liber WH 8J., 28-29, Maryland Archives, I, 533-34, as quoted in *Civil Rights and the American Negro*, Albert P. Blaustein and Robert L. Zangrando (eds.), New York: Trident, 1968, p. 9.

7.   See Staughton Lynd, "Slavery and the Founding Fathers," in *Black History*, Melvin Drimmer (ed.), Garden City, N.Y.: Doubleday, 1968, pp. 115-31.

8.   U.S. Constitution, article I, s. 9.

9.   U.S. Constitution, article IV, s. 2.

10.   U.S. Constitution, article I, s. 2.

11.   For cases and statutes in this area see William Goodell, *The American Slave Code*. (1853; reprint ed.), New York: New American Library, 1969; George M. Stroud, *A Sketch of the Laws Relating to Slavery in the several states of the United States of America* (2nd ed.). Philadelphia: Henry Longstreth, 1856; Helen Catterall, *Judicial Cases Concerning American Slavery and the Negro*. Washington, D.C.: Carnegie Institution of Washington, 1926-37. See also Pauli Murray, "Roots of the Radical Crisis: Prologue to Policy" (J.S.D. thesis, Yale University, 1965).

12.   *Scott v. Sanford*, 60 U.S. (19 How.) 393 (1857).

13.   See Leon Litwack, *North of Slavery*. Chicago: University of Chicago Press, 1961; *Roberts v. City of Boston*. 59 Mass. (Cush.) 198 (1849).

14.   See, for example, an act to establish and regulate the domestic relations of persons of color, and to amend the law in relation to paupers and vagrancy, Acts of General Assembly of the State of South Carolina, 1864-1865, pp. 291-304, quoted in Blaustein and Zangrando, *Civil Rights*, pp. 218-25; see also W. E. B. Dubois, *Black Reconstruction in America*. London: Cass and Co., 1964, pp. 196-97, 331, 351; John Hope Franklin, *From Slavery to Freedom, A History of Negro Americans* (3rd ed.), New York: Random House, 1969, pp. 187-90, 303, 327.

15.   See Blaustein and Zangrando, *Civil Rights*, pp. 283-88, 294-321; C. Vann Woodward, *The Strange Career of Jim Crow* (2nd rev. ed.). New York: Oxford University Press, 1966, pp. 67-109.

16.   163 U.S. 537 (1896).

17.   347 U.S. 483 (1954).

18.   71 Stat. 634 (1957).

19.   18 Stat. 335 (1875).

20.   See *Strauder v. West Virginia*, 100 U.S. 303 (1880).

21.   See *Swain v. Alabama*, 380 U.S. 202 (1965); Charles Morgan, "Segregated Justice," in *Southern Justice*, Leon Freidman (ed.), New York: Pantheon, 1965; note, "Fair Jury Selection Procedures," *Yale Law Journal* 75 (1965): 322.

22.   See Morgan, note 21 above, p. 157.

23.   Marvin Wolfgang and Bernard Cohen, *Crime and Race: Conceptions and Misconceptions.* New York: Institute of Human Relations Press, 1970, p. 81.

24.   Jordan, *White over Black*, p. 155.

25.   U.S. Department of Justice, National Prisoner Statistics: Capital Punishment, 1930-1968 (1969), p. 10.

26.   Wolfgang and Cohen, *Crime and Race*, p. 85.

27.   Institutional subordination is the placing or keeping of persons in a position or status of inferiority by means of attitudes, actions, or institutional structures which do not use color itself as the subordinating mechanism, but instead use other mechanisms indirectly related to color. This definition is derived from the U.S. Commissions on Civil Rights study, "Racism in America and How to Combat It" (1970), p. 6.

28.   See National Conference on Bail and Criminal Justice, "Bail in the United States" (1964); Caleb Foote, "The Coming Constitutional Crisis in Bail," *University of Pennsylvania Law Review* 113 (1965): 959.

29.   See Emily Goodman, *The Tenant Survival Book.* Indianapolis: Bobbs-Merrill, 1972; *Project on Social Welfare Law, Housing for the Poor, Rights and Remedies.* New York: New York University School of Law, 1967.

30.   See *The Law and the Low Income Consumer*, Carol Hecht Katz (ed.), New York: New York University School of Law, 1968.

31.   See Charles Reich, "The New Property," *Yale Law Journal* 73 (1964): 733.

32.   See John D. Johnston, Jr., "Land Use Control," *Annual Survey of American Law* 49 (1970).

33.   See, for example, *Chavis v. Whitcomb*, 305 F. Supp. 1364 (S.D. Ind. 1969); *Petersburg v. U.S.*, — U.S. — (March 5, 1973).

34.   18 U.S.C. 2101, 2102.

35.   18 U.S.C. 6002-6003.

36.   See *Kastigar v. U.S.*, 406 U.S. 441 (1972).

37.   See Paul Chevigny, *Police Power.* New York: Pantheon, 1969; Commission to Investigate Allegations of Police Corruption and the City's Anti-Corruption Procedures, *Commission Report 1972* (New York City's Knapp Commission).

38.   See Paul Chevigny, *Cops and Rebels.* New York: Pantheon, 1972.

39.   *U.S. v. U.S. Dist. Court for the Eastern District of Michigan*, 407 U.S. 297 (1972).

40.   See Karl Menninger, *The Crime of Punishment.* New York: Viking, 1968; *Black Law Journal* 1 (2) (Summer, 1971).

41.   See Robert L. Carter, "The Black Lawyer," *Humanist* (September-October, 1969): 12, 13.

42.   Though black people make up well over 11 percent of the overall population, there are only about 3,845 black lawyers in the country comprising about 1½ percent of the bar. See Christine and Leroy Clark, "The Black Lawyer," *Black Enterprise* (February, 1973): 15.

Chapter 16

Two Models of Race
Relations and Prison Racism:
A Cross Cultural Analysis

Charles E. Reasons*

Two Models for the Study of Race and Ethnic Relations

The dominant approach among students of race and ethnic relations in North America has been the order/assimilationist perspective.[1] Emphasis is placed upon analysis of individual prejudice and discrimination within a context of changing both those specific individuals who evidence such attitudes and behaviour and helping racial/ethnic group members to adjust to dominant group standards.[2] From the order approach, problems of racial and ethnic relations are largely a product of members of subordinate racial and ethnic groups who need to become adapted to the dominant group culture.

While attention is given to problems of the few dominant group members who are prejudiced and discriminate, most effort is directed toward the analysis of racial and ethnic group members and their problems. For example, white-native relations are viewed as the "Indian problem" from this perspective, with specific attention given to the characteristics of natives, interpreted as evidence of their lack of adequate socialization and assimilation, anomy, etc.

+ The author would like to give his special thanks to Ms. Elsie Wingeno, research
 assistant, for her excellent help in gathering the relevant materials and to the
 Native Brotherhood of Drumheller Penitentiary. Paper presented to "The State of
 the Prison" Conference, University of Kent, Canterbury, June 1977.

Therefore, from an order perspective existing values and policies of dominant institutions are viewed as healthy and good and problems of racial and ethnic groups are due largely to subordinate racial and ethnic groups' failure in adjustment. Assimilation, or the shedding of unique cultural traits and identity, and adoption of those of the dominant group is felt to be the primary way to bring about a stable and healthy society. The order/assimilationist perspective minimizes the significance of power and coercion in everyday life between subordinate and superordinate groups, emphasizing the social psychology of individual and group adaptation to dominant group values and practices. Society is viewed as made up of competing individuals who carry out their competition within the context of neutral social institutions.Thus, everyone is equal and has equal opportunity. The significance of competing groups and classes, as far as one's social, political and economic opportunities are concerned, is largely neglected.

While the above noted order/assimilationist model has been the dominant perspective of students of race and ethnic relations in North America, it has come under increasing attack in more recent years. More specifically, it has been assailed as lacking in cross-cultural comparative analysis; having largely a short sighted policy emphasis rather than theoretical integration with the rest of sociology; having a liberal bias emphasizing the basic goodness of society and its institutions; defining race and ethnic problems as those of integration and assimilation into the mainstream of a consensus-based society (Van den Berghe, 1967). For example, Myrdal's (1944) analysis of black-white relations in the United States viewed the problem as a moral dilemma in the hearts and minds of men rather than a complex dynamic of group conflict resulting from the differential distribution of power, wealth, prestige and other social rewards.

> The problem with sociological thought has been defined in the narrow sense of providing adequate, if not equal, opportunity for members of minority groups to ascent as individuals into the mainstream culture (Metzger, 1971: 627).

Due to the above mentioned limitations, another approach has emerged largely within the last few decades to challenge the order/assimilationist view. The conflict/pluralist approach to race and ethnic relations views society as a contested struggle between groups with opposed aims and perspectives. Differentials between race and ethnic groups in economic, political and social power are emphasized as significant for analysis. Conflict is viewed as an essential facet of societies and the unit for analysis is largely that of race and ethnic groups and social class, with emphasis upon collective situations and definitions.

Pluralism is viewed as a viable alternative to assimilation which considers the point of view of race and ethnic minority group members. Pluralism as used in the following discussion is given a "cultural" meaning emphasizing differences in language, religion, kinship forms, nationality, tribal affiliation, and/or, other traditional values and norms distinguishing an ethnic group from the dominant group and the ethnic minority group's desire to preserve their own way of life even though it differs from the dominant group (Schermerhorn, 1970).

The conflict/pluralist approach emphasizes the significance of the historical analysis of racial and ethnic conflict and the subsequent pluralism which emerged. Colonial societies are the classical form of plural societies. After reviewing ethnic relations throughout the world in terms of recurrent intergroup processes, Schermerhorn noted (1970: 156) that:

> First and foremost it appears that the great bulk of ethnic group formations attain subordinate or minority status as the result of coercive subjugation by dominant groups . . . evidence shows conclusively that the overriding relationship has been one of force and compulsion. Two implications follow from this conclusion: (1) studies of ethnic relations based chiefly on data from voluntary migrations cannot serve as the model or foundation for ethnic relations as a whole; (2) some form of power or conflict theory has first claim to relevance in approaching ethnic relations historically.

Therefore, power, conflict and coercion are viewed as important factors in analyzing the dynamics of race and ethnic relations and the emergence and development of pluralism. Within the context of the conflict/pluralist approach, the "Indian problem" of the order/assimilationist perspective becomes a "white problem." Ameliorative action is one of lessening the extent of dominant group social control and exploitation. Collective efforts at fostering and controlling one's group and individual fate are pursued through the various forms of pluarlism previously mentioned. The negative aspects of colonial pluralism are to be replaced by the positive aspects of racial and ethnic group liberation and self-control. This approach emphasizes the aims and aspirations of subordinate groups and the need for large scale structural change.

The significance of socio-historical analysis becomes very important in understanding the contemporary dynamics of race and ethnic relations. This is particulary the case when one is discussing racial minorities in North America. A race is a human group that defines itself and/or is defined by other groups as different from other groups by virtue of innate and immutable physical characteristics which are believed intrinsically related to moral, intellectual, and other non-physical attributes or abilities (Van de Burghe, 1967: 9). While the existence of races is arguable on the basis of phenotypical and genotypical traits (Comas, 1961; Lieberman, 1968), sociologically the use has and continues to have a great deal of influence upon man's relationships (Gossett, 1963).

The significance of distinguishing between racial and ethnic groups is that while one might change his language, religion, values, etc., it is near impossible to change one's colour.

Proponents of the order/assimilationist approach have been particularly negligent in combining analysis of ethnic group assimilation and acknowledgement of the social meaning and significance of the colour line. The assumption that racial minority group members will assimilate like ethnic immigrants has been a major assumption underlying North American race and ethnic relations theory.

The Colonial Model and Government Policies

In recent years there have been a number of students of race and ethnic relations who have criticized the myopia of such a a belief. The history and contemporary situation of blacks, chicanos and native people in North America[3] may be viewed more appropriately from a colonial perspective (Blauner, 1972; Moore, 1970; Hagen, 1962; Frideres, 1974). Regarding native people in Canada, for example, Frideres has carefully documented how the colonial model is the most appropriate one for the analysis of native-white relationships. More specifically, Frideres (1974: 157-90) views colonization as a process consisting of seven parts: (1) forced entry—conquering of native people; (2) destruction of native institutions, e.g., political, legal, economic, kinship; (3) external political control through the IAB; (4) native economic dependence upon the colonizer; (5) social services provided native people are of a low standard, e.g., differentials between native and white health statistics; (6) racism through the belief in the genetic superiority of one group (white) and inferiority of another group (natives); and (7) a colour line which establishes and institutionalizes symbols allowing groups to be quickly and easily identified, i.e., skin pigmentation and body structure.

All of the above facets of the colonization complex are largely applicable historically and contemporarily to white-native (superordinate-subordinate) relationships in Canada and the U.S. The reserves and native "ghettos" in urban areas are the contemporary colonies which exemplify this legacy. In order to assess the worth of contemporary white majority policies toward the native minority, it is necessary to recognize the significance of the colonization process as evidenced in governmental policies.

Simpson and Yinger (1972: 16-24) have identified six types of majority policies toward minorities: (1) assimilation (forced or permitted); (2) pluralism; (3) population transfer (peaceful or forced migration); (4) legal protection of minorities; (5) continued subjugation; and (6) extermination.

All of these policies have been applied in varying degrees and at different times to native people in North America. The colonization of native people provided a forced type of pluralism with subsequent forced population transfer to reserves, and special legislation and treaties to respect certain rights. These policies have largely maintained continued subjugation of the native population on reserves which are politically, legally, and economically controlled by the colonizer. Extermination was a particularly prevalent policy in the United States where two-thirds of the native population was decimated in westward expansion. For example, one of the first debates in the Colorado legislature was over a measure to offer bounties for the destruction of Indians and skunks (Reasons and Kuykendall, 1972). The matter of dealing with native people has, in many respects, been quite similar in Canada and the United States (Mickenberg, 1971). A cornerstone of the policy of both countries has been assimilation, i.e., the "native problem" would be solved by making them like whites (Smith, 1975; Cohen and Mause, 1968).

White Man's Policy and the Red Man's Response

The assimilationist approach is exemplified in the Canadian federal government's White Paper on Indian Affairs presented in 1969 (Department, 1969; Frideres, 1974).[4] One of the basic contentions was that for the Canadian Indian to become integrated into the mainstream of Canadian society their separate legal status must be eliminated. Therefore, everyone was to be treated as equal with the elimination of the Indians' special legal status. Unfortunately, such a policy ignores that the declaration of equality and the substantive achievement of equality are often two quite distinct matters. By declaring equality one does not wipe out the effects of nearly 400 years of subjugation. Of course, if such a policy of equal treatment had in fact been in effect historically, there would be no need for subsequent distinctions. The liberal ideal of equality for all must be squared with the reality of a history of inequality. One of the unintended consequences of such liberal theorizing is that natives are bound to fail, given their greatly disadvantaged position in competitive Canadian society. Such an approach almost ensures continued deprivation, subjugation and suffering among native peoples. This could be construed as a form of cultural genocide.[5]

The response of most native people to termination was to reject it as largely cultural genocide, the general argument being that natives must be allowed to remain as distinct ethnic groups and to control their own affairs. While many specific alternative recommendations have been presented by natives, the thrust is based upon a pluralist policy, respecting the economic, political and social control of native institutions and policy by natives. Unlike the colonial pluralism that was imposed upon natives and subsequent assimilationist policies, this type of pluralism would be based upon native control of native people.

The official response of native organizations and leaders to the termination policy reflected the increasing assertion of rights by natives in both Canada and the United States. The attempts to gain an increasing degree of autonomy and self-control among native people followed in the wake of other Movements to democratize North American institutions in the 1960's by the relatively powerless, e.g., welfare rights movement, black power movement, anti-war movement, student rights movement, French Canadian liberation movement, among others (Dolbeare and Dolbeare, 1973; Marchak, 1975).

Increasingly native spokesmen have challenged the ability and legitimacy of whites to run their affairs. Deloria's *Custer Died for Your Sins: An Indian Manifesto* (1969) and Cardinal's *The Unjust Society: The Tragedy of Canada's Indians* (1969) both eloquently present the case of the native people in the U.S. and Canada. Furthermore, periodical literature directed to a native readership and written largely by natives has come into prominance in recent years (Price, 1972). Much of this literature protests current governmental policy and practices and suggests alternatives. Through such media, native people are increasingly presenting an alternative view of native-white relations, e.g., a native perspective. The definition of the problem is not an "Indian problem" but a "white problem".

Events at Wounded Knee, Alcatraz, Kenora, Akwesasne, Parliament Hill, among others, have given notice to North American white society that natives will no longer passively accept their fate. One author believes that the native protest movement in Canada will become stronger than that in the United States due to their proportion of the Canadian population (2.5% versus .4% in the U.S.); the greater cultural contrast in Canada because Canadian natives are more traditional and; the fact that Canadian natives have a stronger potential political base on reserves since 70% of enrolled natives live on reserves (only 30% in U.S.).

The continuation of great disparities between natives and whites in employment, income, housing, health standards, education and other indices of well-being portends further conflict in the future. (Hawthorn, 1966 and 1967; Frideres, 1974; Elliot, 1971; Bahr, Chadwick and Day, 1972; Abler, Sanders, and Weaver, 1974; la Graze, Kruszewski, Arcintega, 1973; Hughes and Kallen, 1974). A major area of conflict between natives and whites both historically and contemporarily has been the law.

Natives and the Criminal Law

Native people are more disproportionately involved with the criminal law in North America than any other racial or ethnic minority (Canadian Corrections Association, 1967; Bienvenue and Latif, 1974; Hagen, 1974; Schmeiser, 1974; Reasons and

Kuykendall, 1972; Forsland and Meyers, 1974). From arrest to incarceration native people are very much overrepresented in official statistics on crime.[6] While there is an increasingly large volume of literature concerning minorities and the police, (Bayley and Mendelsohn, 1969; Kuykendall, 1970; Rafky, 1973, 1975; Spitzer, 1976) administration of justice to minorities, (Wolfgang and Cohen, 1970; Reasons and Kuykendall, 1972; U.S. Commission on Civil Rights, 1970; Reid, Sr., 1972; Swett, 1969; Blacks and the Law, 1973; Thornberry, 1973; Wynn and Hartnagel, 1975; Kelly, 1975; Hall and Simkus, 1975) and minorities in corrections, (Reasons, 1974a; Dandurand, 1974; Badcock, 1976) relatively little attention has been given specifically to native people and the law.

Increasing national efforts to address the issue of natives and the law will undoubtedly arise in part as a response to the growing conflict between natives and whites. This will likely be more evident in Canada than in the U.S. where blacks and chicanos are the largest racial minorities.[7] Such conflict has emerged in recent years due to the various minority liberation movements in North America. With the emergence of these social movements there has arisen an alternative view of crime and criminality. The traditional (order) and emerging (conflict) perspectives may be briefly outlined in table form.

Table I.

Order and Conflict Theories of Crimes*

	Criminal Law		Criminal Behavior	
	Cause	Consequence	Cause	Consequence
Conflict Paradigm	Ruling class interests	Provide state coercive force to repress the class struggle and to legitimize the use of this force	Class divisions which lends to class struggle	Crime serves the interests of the ruling class by reducing strains inherent in the capitalist mode of production
Order Paradigm	Customary beliefs that are codified in state law	To establish procedures for controlling those who do not comply with customs	Inadequate socialization	To establish the moral boundaries of the community

* Adapted from William J. Chambliss, Functional and Conflict Theories of Crime (New York: MSS Modular Publications, Inc.) 1974.

From the order perspective criminal behaviour is largely due to inadequate socialization including various deficiencies of native people regarding education, training and subsequent employability, among others. Thus the focus is upon the personal characteristics of native people and their causal significance. The laws reflect the customs of all peoples (natives and white) according to the order approach and are necessary for controlling deviants. From a conflict perspective emphasis is placed upon group (class) position and the laws are viewed as representing superordinate class (white) interests and repressive of subordinate class (natives) interests. Such class divisions are reflected in the higher involvement in crime by native people which lessens the potential collective power and energies of native people.

While the above positions are an ideal-type representation of polar opposites which magnify differences, they nonetheless provide examples of the varying interpretations of crime from the order and conflict perspectives. As Horton (1966) noted, these perspectives are largely socially situated vocabularies. That is, those who are in positions of power and influence (for our analysis whites) will tend to view crime from the order perspective, while those in positions of relative powerlessness and subordination (natives) will tend to be more conflict oriented in their interpretations.

A dramatic example of the two perspectives is to be found in prisoner riots in recent years. As Pallas and Barber (1972) note, prison riots and prisoner protest have greatly changed in the last few decades. From the demands of the 1950's for better food, more recreational time, more treatment staff, better health standards, increased visiting hours, among others, has emerged demands for amnesty, unions, negotiating rights with authorities, a part in the decision-making process, and other more political demands. What has happened in the last few decades?

> The politicization of prisoners can only be understood within the context of the attempts at democratization of major social institutions. For example, universities, which have been traditionally characterized as apolitical, became the brunt of a rapid politicizing and conflict during the 1960's. The Civil Rights Movement, anti-war movement, poor people's movement, welfare rights movement, among others, challenged the legitimacy of power distribution in our society. The law and legal institutions increasingly came under fire as they were exposed as being highly political. Youth, nonwhites, the poor and other previously powerless groups were increasingly politically sensitized and since they are the prime 'recruits' for correctional insitutions, this undoubtedly has had many ramifications for the prisons. (Reasons, 1973)

While prisons have been largely out of sight and out of mind in North America, the riots in the 1960's and 1970's have brought increasing attention to the area of corrections. More significantly, increased attention has been given to the significance of race in prison conflict. In one of the worst prison riots in North American history, Attica, institutionalized racism was found to be a major factor.

> The relationship was probably inevitable when predominately poor, urban, black, and Spanish-speaking inmates were placed under the supervision of white officers from rural areas equipped with only three weeks of training. Most whites in society have not met blacks on equal social terms and except for their service in the military, many Attica officers were exposed to blacks only after they were convicted animals. They began with little or nothing in common, and Attica was not a catalyst which made people want to learn about each other (Attica, 1972).

Therefore, increasing attention has been given to the fact that racial and ethnic minorities are disproportionately evident in correctional institutions in North America. In the United States one author notes:

> Nationally, 58% of the inmates in federal and state correctional institutions were white in 1970, compared to 41% black and 1% Native American. If one considers people of Spanish origin as an ethnic/racial goup (which we do), then only 51% of the incarcerated population is white, with 7% being of Spanish origin (Mexican, Puerto Rican, Cuban, others). For these racial/ethnic groups the ratio of their representation in prisons compared to their representation in the U.S. population is White, .6; Blacks, 3.7; Indian, 3.4; Spanish origin, 1.8. The disproportionate incarceration rates of non-whites is greatest in state institutions and the least in federal. The above ratios remain essentially the same for local jails and workhouses in 1970 (Reasons, 1974a: 5).

Thus, native people have an incarceration rate nearly four times their proportion of the population.

In Canada, native people are greatly over-represented in corrections, generally three to four times their proportion in provincial and federal institutions (Schmeiser, 1974). While such data is subject to enumeration errors, nonetheless, it dramatically outlines the differential representation of native people in correctional institutions.

The following analysis is a critical assessment of pertinent literature regarding the application of the previously discussed models of race and ethnic relations to correctional institutions and habilitation.[8]

Order/Assimilationist Approach to Corrections

The order/assimilationist approach to corrections assumes that current institutional policies and practices are correct and attention is placed upon changing members of the racial/ethnic minority to fit into the institutional structures. Of course the emphasis upon changing the inmate so that he will blend in with the "law abiding" general population has been a long standing goal of prisons. Thus, in one sense, the order/assimilationist model has been the approach toward that minority group labelled prisoners.[9] Therefore, this approach is applicable to all inmates.

The goal of rehabilitation has been to strip the convict of his previous identity and help produce a new person who would make it in society. Rehabilitation is to "restore a dependent, defective, or criminal to a state of physical, mental, and moral health through treatment and training (Webster's, 1964: 1225). Early proponents of the penitentiary saw it as "a grand theatre, for the trials of all new plans in hygiene and education, in physical and moral reform" (Rothman, 1971: 84). Rothman described the birth of the penitentiary in the mid-nineteenth century, an era of profound pessimism about the multitude of temptations ever present in society and incredible optimism about the potential of the penitentiary as a change agent:

> The prison would train the most notable victims of social disorder to discipline, teaching them to resist corruptions. And success in this particular task would inspire a general reformation of manners and habits. The institution would become a laboratory for social improvement. By demonstrating how regularity and discipline transformed the most corrupt persons, it would reawaken the public to these virtues. The penitentiary would promote a new respect for order and authority (Rothman, 1971: 107).

While the optimism evident in this quote is hardly found today, treatment and rehabilitation are still major acknowledged functions of prisons (Reasons and Kaplan, 1975). A cornerstone of treatment and rehabilitation efforts is the medical model of deviance.

Traditional correctional policies and practices have been based upon the medical model of deviance which draws an erroneous analogy to the physician's practice. Thus, like a disease, an individual is to be diagnosed, prognosed, prescribed, treated and cured of his "illness", i.e., criminality. While the medical model has produced many labels, e.g., psychopathis, dangerous offenders, asocial, little evidence of the effectiveness of this labeling has emerged.

A recent review of this model concludes:

> In spite of its popularity in scientific and correctional circles, the medical model of delinquency is open to question on theoretical, practical, and ethical grounds. The medical perspective obscures the nature of delinquency by neglecting the critical role social audiences play in defining behavior as delinquent or non-delinquent. It has also hampered preventive and correctional efforts because of the undue emphasis given to the problems of individual delinquents rather than the institutional framework within which delinquency occurs. Finally, the medical model of delinquency raises serious ethical questions about the treatment of pre-delinquent children, the indeterminate sentence, and the individualization of correctional programs—all of which have traditionally been justified by the medical analogy (Balch, 1975: 116).

The above is equally applicable to criminality and criminals
(Thomas, 1973; Johnson, 1971; Irwin, 1970; American Friends
Service, 1971).

Contemporary criminological thought is based upon a largely
different conception of causality. While an individual is legally
culpable for certain actions, it is acknowledged that many societal
factors, e.g., economic, family, peer group, infinge upon and affect
everyone's behaviour, including those who commit criminal acts
and are officially labelled criminal. The circle of causality and
thus treatment has broadened from the individual to the family,
peer group and community, with community-based corrections
currently emerging as the "new" penology. Thus, this "kind of
environment" model has become the dominant model in criminology and is increasingly making inroads into the prison, which has
been a stronghold of the "Medical Model" (Reasons, 1975).
Therefore, the "Medical Model" underlying the order/
assimilationist approach to inmates is found to be lacking in light
of criminological data.

The native offender bears the double burden of two minority
identities—native and criminal. Therefore, such an approach as
applied to natives must attempt to eliminate the racial/ethnic
minority status of natives as through correctional policies which
ostensibly provide equal treatment of all inmates irregardless of
their racial/ethnic status. Since correctional institutions and their
rules and policies are determined by the dominant group members
(whites), based upon their culture, it is inherently discriminatory.
The equal application and enforcement of policies and rules based
upon one culture upon members of other cultures represents a
classic example of culture conflict and cultural oppression.

The appearance of equality masks the oppression of cultural
annihilation and worsening conditions. Within this context, the
concept of institutionalized racism is increasingly being used.
Institutional racism has two general meanings: (1) the institutional
extention of individual racist beliefs, such as de jure segregation
or (2) the by-product of certain institutional practices which
operate to restrict on a racial basis the choices, rights, mobility,
and access of groups or individuals, such as meritocratic
standards (Willhelm, 1969). As one student of race relations
states:

> Institutional racism can be defined as those established laws,
> customs, and practices which systematically reflect and produce
> racial inequities in American society. If racist consequences accrue to
> institutional laws, customs, or practices, the institution is racist,
> whether or not the individuals maintaining those practices have
> racist intentions . . . Institutional racism can be either overt or covert
> (corresponding to de jure and de facto respectively) and either
> intentional or unintentional (Jones, 1972: 35).

The major form of institutionalized racism today is covert and
unintentional through equal treatment and meritocratic standards.

For example, using the meritocratic standard of a high school diploma as necessary for employment, one systematically eliminates a disproportionate number of native applicants, due to group differences in formal educational attainment (which is itself a matter of differential opportunities). Such rules may exist regardless of the job relatedness of the requirement. Therefore, by using such dominant group standards and ignoring alternative relevant factors, e.g., work in native community, speaking native language, being native, etc., few natives are hired.

In the correctional setting, for example, the lack of recognition of cultural differences in the inmate population and the failure to address these differences in the inmate population through the recruitment of minority group members is a form of institutionalized racism. Whether the lack of natives on the industrial and vocational training staff or other habilitative staffs is the result of individual racist policies or institutionalized meritocratic standards the result is the same, i.e., no natives on the staff. The form of advertising (white newspapers), nature of the questions on the application form, the nature of checking of background character, the personal interview, are a few possible items which contribute to the complexion of the staff. Specifically, if prior arrest is a criterion for elimination, it will obviously weigh more heavily on natives due to their disproportionate official involvement with the law. While the invoking of such standards may be applied equally to individual cases, it has the cumulative effect of largely excluding whole categories of people such as native people.

The order/assimilationist approach to corrections has a long history of application. However, with the more recent attacks upon the assumptions of this approach and its apparent inability to reform, plus the ermergence of a prisoner rights movement, such an approach is no longer assured. While the elimination of any or all human rights would probably be accepted if corrections actually corrected through such a model, the failure of corrections *and* the lack of minimum standards of civil and human rights are untenable (Tittle, 1974; Spence Jr., 1972; Price, 1974; Kaiser, 1971; Jackson, 1974). The prisoner rights movement must be understood within the context of the politics of protest.

> One way to understand the development of political protest in prisons is to view protest activity as a political resource that is used by disadvantaged groups to gain political power and influence when more traditional sorts of political activity are unavailable or unsuccessful (Atkins and Glick, 1972: 3).

If the order/assimilationist model is invalid for the general prison population, it is most certainly inapplicable to native inmates. This is particularly true with regard to the emergence of a movement among native people for self-determination, cultural revitalization and enhancement of positive self-identity. The recognition of cultural needs of native inmates will increasingly be called for as the native movement on the outside spreads to the inside. As one penologist has noted:

> The same civil rights issues, religious issues, and other social issues appear in prison as appear in the city. The prison reflects the society it serves . . . the same problems that have occurred in prison have occurred outside, the difference being that the prison is a closely confined and generally deprived environment. The result is that small things seem to be more important in prison than outside (Fox, 1974: 389).

Conflict/Pluralist Approach to Corrections

Much of the impetus for the expansion of civil and human rights to previously powerless people, including prisoners, has come from their own efforts. While the extension of such rights to inmates is met with substantial negative reaction from both public officials and segments of the general public, bringing the rule of law to corrections has increased in recent years. As one authority noted (Price, 1974), this expansion of rights has been due largely to increased recognition of the siginificance of low-visibility administrative decisions for inmates and the potential positive habilitative effects of such practices. The latter point is particulary important.

If an individual is to develop the capacity to make personal rational decisions on the outside, then the inmate should have some degree of influence over decisions affecting his life space within the institution. In order to develop responsibility one must be given responsibility. There is data to suggest the positive benefits of allowing inmates to engage in meaningful participation in institutional decision making (Zald, 1962; President's Commission, 1967; National Advisory Commission, 1973; Murton, 1976).

Both the President's Commission on Law Enforcement and Administration of Justice and the National Commission on Criminal Justice Standards and Goals in the United States have emphasized the need for inmates being involved in decision-making to combat feelings of alienation based on powerlessness. Furthermore, prison rights groups are emerging inside and outside.[10] In Canada there are signs of increased recognition of inmate rights. Some institutions are forming inmate governments and a relatively new publication by inmates and ex-inmates of federal penitentiaries—*Transition*—is advocating more changes of this nature. Further recognition of inmate rights was evidenced by the appointment by the Solicitor General on June 1, 1973 of a Correctional Investigator for all Federal penitentiaries.

As noted above, increasingly attention is being given to the establishment and maintenance of basic civil human rights for all inmates, including racial/ethnic minority group members.

The question posed by ethnic group members in the correctional system can be viewed as basically one of human rights. One
means of alleviating such problems is through administrative
solutions.

> The solutions which immediately come to everybody's mind usually
> are those pertaining to the improvement of our already existing
> institutionalized means of intervention or treatment: let us bring in
> some volunteers who speak the same language, and share the same
> culture and values as our 'problem-clients'; let us hire more staff
> from these groups; let us create special institutions and service for
> these minority groups, etc. (Dandurand, 1974: 36).

As Dandurand further notes, there is the need for minority
group members to have the free choice of assimilation of pluralism
without the current social costs involved. More specifically,
certain rights are particularly pertinent to ethnic members
including the right to be treated, the right to differential treatment
due to cultural differences, and the right to be different.

The right to be different is particularly important for racial/
ethnic minority group members. The fact that native people are
disproportionately subject to laws dealing with alcohol, hunting
and fishing suggests these "crimes" might better be handled in a
different context.

> The Canadian Bill of Rights refers to 'the right of the individual to
> equality before the law and the protection of the law', but equal
> application of laws can accentuate injustices when applied to persons
> who are unequal in condition and opportunity. In such instances, law
> can become the oppressor rather than the protector, and government
> action becomes unbearably bureaucratic (Schmeiser, 1968: 1).

Therefore, if laws which were made by whites on the basis of
their cultural standards are applied to natives with contrasting
and/or conflicting standards, the "equal application" of such laws
is manifestly oppressive.

Recognition of the significance of cultural differences within
corrections is evident in the increasing efforts to hire minority
group members in corrections. For example, in the United States
during the last few years there have been a number of minority
group members hired in corrections. Such efforts appear in three
different forms: (1) rhetoric; (2) judicial decisions and; (3)
administrative regulations (Skoler and Lowenstein, 1974). The
rhetoric to hire more minority group members comes from such
notable sources as the American Bar Association Commission in
Correctional Facilities and Services, American Correctional
Association, U.S. Attorney General, National Advisory
Commission on Criminal Justice Standards and Goals, among
others. They have noted the need for more blacks, chicanos and
native Americans in correctional service. Legally, certain criteria
which disproportionately screen out minority group members
while being unrelated to job performance include arrest and
conviction records, garnishment of wages, credit references,

parentage of illegitimate children, and minimum education requirements. Finally, administrative guidelines are mainly those of federal correctional funding agencies concerning affirmative action hiring. Little data exists testing the effectiveness of this approach. One black correctional authority completely changed the "complexion" of his staff to approximate the "complexion" of the inmates as means of creating a more humane and just atmosphere (Moore, 1971).

In Canada, increasing recognition of the need for native personnel in corrections is being given. A recent report on parole recommendations includes employing more native workers in all phases of the correctional process; parole authorities contracting with native service groups or agencies for supervision and related correctional work; a study being undertaken regarding the desirability and feasibility of establishing community correctional centres staffed mainly with natives and primarily for native offenders and; the establishment of Regional Divisions of the parole authority with native representation in appropriate regions (Report, 1974). The Federal-Provincial Ministerial Conference on Native Peoples and the Criminal Justice System also emphasized the need for more involvement of native people in corrections. Such recommendations are official recognition of the importance of cultural differences within corrections and the need for special remedies. However, if such recommendations are to go beyond the level of rhetoric, criteria for such positions should be critically assessed for possible cultural bias which would systematically eliminate most potential native applicants, *i.e.*, institutionalized racism.

The conflict/pluralist perspective emphasizes group self-determination and the fostering of cultural revitalization and positive self-concept. The significance of fostering positive group and subsequently self-identity must be understood within the context of the negative self-concept fostered by the larger society on native people (Bowker, 1972; Houts and Bahr, 1972; Hellon, 1969; Grindstaff, Galloway and Nixon, 1973). A principle means of creating such condition within the correctional setting has been formation of ethnic socio-political self-help groups. The potential value of such organizations has often been of less interest to correctional administrators than their potential for violence. However, in a recent discussion of ethnic socio-political self-help groups, a high level correctional administrator suggests they may in fact avert violence (Burdman, 1974).

The fostering of racial/ethnic socio/political groups rejects the medical treatment model since members of such groups generally define themselves as victims and society as in need of treatment. Such a change in causality necessitates a change in treatment staff function. Rather than attempting to treat the inmate for his "illness", attention should be given to his developing abilities and acquiring the skills to bring about needed social change.

Specific policies might include specialized native programs; official recognition of native organizations; more native personnel and pre-service and in-service training for non-native staff; native inmate involvement in program planning and implementation; programs for special native needs, e.g., life skills, communication, and trades directly related to lifestyle after release; ready access to community groups and information being available to native inmates upon admission regarding self-help groups; administrative encouragement of inmate newsletters for the outside; natives being informed of their basic rights upon admission; female offenders being permittted to remain in their home province; and halfway homes being staffed with natives (National Conference, 1975).

The last recommendation concerns community-based corrections. Community-based corrections has been heralded as the "new penology" that will help bring an end to the crime problem. The *ad populum* appeals of habilitation and economic savings through the increase of such programs as work-training release, temporary absences, probation subsidy, and community-based facilities have brought about much activity and hope among those concerned with corrections. As noted earlier, The Canadian Corrections Association report *Indians and the Law* emphasized reducing the use of jail sentences for Indian offenses dealing with liquor while using more probation and treatment. Both the Canadian Corrections Association and the more recent Law Reform Report on *Natives and the Law* point out the ineffective and costly nature of incarcerating native people for repeated lesser offenses.

Concerning community-based facilities the National Conference on Native Peoples and the Criminal Justice System recommends the establishment of halfway homes and community-based residential centres for parole and temporary absences, as an alternative to incarceration, which are managed and staffed by native people. While little valid empirical evidence is present clearly showing the positive effects of such centres, they are likely more humane than the large human warehouses, known as prisons.

> The long history of prison reform is over. On the whole the prisons have played out their allocated role. They cannot be reformed and must be gradually torn down. But let us give up the comforting myth that remaining facilities (and they will be prisons) can be changed into hospitals. Prisons will be small and humane; anything less is treason to the human spirit (Martinson, 1972: 23).

Summary and Conclusion

The order/assimilationist approach has historically been the dominant model for the analysis of race relations in North America. This approach is particularly apparent in government policy regarding native people. Within corrections this approach is evident since the emergence of prisons and has been the model for rehabilitating criminals.

In more recent years the order/assimilationist model and subsequent policy has been under increasing attack throughout society. This approach has been assailed within corrections as generally invalid for the entire inmate population and particularly inappropriate for native offenders.

While egalitarian principles are often used to preclude different treatment for native offenders, cultural differences necessitate different habilitative programs and services for native offenders in order to provide equal opportunities. Therefore, the rules and regulations regarding probation, parole and correctional institutions must be analyzed for possible institutionalized racism. Within the context of the larger society, the order/assimilationist model is increasingly becoming inappropriate. Given the facts of the movement for native cultural revitalization, emergence of red power and the beginning of the establishment of minimum civil and human rights for prisoners, a conflict/pluralist model is providing a viable alternative to the order/assimilationist approach. The implications of maintaining order/assimilationist policies for native inmates within the context of events external to corrections are increased tension and conflict and contained failure in attempts at habilitation.

The conflict/pluralist approach has arisen largley because of the apparent failure of the order/assimilationist approach and the collective action of native people. Some policy implications of the conflict/pluralist approach for corrections include a critical evaluation of rules and regulations for cultural bias; establishing separate habilitation programs for natives and therefore reconsidering egalitarian principles in light of cultural differences and the imposition of white standards; fostering staff support for recognition of cultural differences and their significance for habilitation through the principles of contingency management; critically analyzing criteria for employment in view of the need for culturally sensitive employees.

Ultimately the issues of racism in prisons will only be resolved with its resolution on the outside.

> The elimination of racial/ethnic oppression in prison and the establishment of basic civil and human rights for prisoners will only come about with the increasing elimination of racial/ethnic oppression in the larger society and the establishment of a more humane and just society (Reasons, 1974a: 13).

NOTES

1.   For a discussion of this general orientation see Horton, 1966.

2.   A good example of a text taking this approach is Simpson and Yinger, 1972.

3.   North America will be used to refer to Canada and the U.S.

4.   For U.S. policy see Brophey and Aberle, 1966 and Cohen and Mause, 1968.

5.   For a discussion about the negative consequences of "equal" treatment see Willhelm, 1969.

6.   It must be recognized of course that official statistics are subject to numerous limitations. See Nettler, 1974 and Silverman and Teevan, Jr., 1975.

7.   For example the following major Federal Reports and Conferences have been held in Canada while no comparable attention has been given natives and the law in the United States. (National Conference, 1975; Federal-Provincial, 1975; Schmeiser, 1974; Canadian Corrections Association, 1967).

8.   See Reasons, 1974b: 357-65.

9.   For a discussion of prisoners as a minority group see Winslow, 1972, Chapter 8, "The Convicted Minority," pp. 275-342.

10.   See any issue of the San Francisco based *The Outlaw: Journal of the Prisoners Union* for information on such efforts.

REFERENCES

Abler, Thomas A., Sanders, Douglas E., and Weaver, Sally M., *A Canadian Indian Bibliography, 1960-1970*. Toronto: University of Toronto Press, 1974.

Atkins, Burton M. and Glick, Henry R., *Prisons, Protest, and Politics*. Englewood Cliffs: Prentice-Hall, 1972.

Attica: The Official Report of the New York State Special Commission on Attica. New York: Bantam Books, 1972.

Bahr, Howard M., Chadwick, Bruce A., and Day, Robert C., *Native Americans Today: Sociological Perspectives*. New York: Harper & Row, 1972.

Balch, Robert W., "The Medical Model of Delinquency - Theoretical, Practical, and Ethical Implications", *Crime and Delinquency* 21 (April, 1975).

Bayley, David H. and Mendelsohn, Harold, *Minorities and the Police: Confrontation in America*. New York: The Free Press, 1969.

Bienvenue, Rita M. and Latif, A.H. "Arrests, Dispositions and Recidivism: A Comparison of Indians and Whites," *Canadian Journal of Criminology and Corrections* 16 (April, 1974): 105-16.

Blauner, Robert, *Racial Oppression in America*. New York: Harper and Row, 1972.

"Blacks And The Law", Special Issue of the *Annals of the American Academy of Political and Social Science* (May, 1973).

Bowker, Lee H., "Red and Black in Contemporary American History Texts: A Content Analysis", in Howard M. Bahr, Bruce A.

Chadwick, Robert C. Day, Native Americans Today: Sociological Perspectives. New York: Harper & Row, 1972, pp. 101-9.

Brophey, William A. and Aberle, Shopie D., The Indian: American's Unfinished Business. Norman: University of Oklahoma Press, 1966.

Burdman, Milton, "Ethnic Self-Help Groups in Prison and on Parole," Crime and Delinquency 20 (April, 1974): 107-18.

Canadian Corrections Association, Indians and the Law. Ottawa: Queen's Printers, 1967.

Cardinal, Harold, The Unjust Society: The Tragedy of Canada's Indians. Edmonton: Hurtig Publishing Co. 1969.

Chambliss, William J. (ed.), Sociological Readings in the Conflict Perspective. Reading, Massachusetts: Addison-Wesley Publishing Company, 1973.

Cohen, Warren H. and Mause, Phillip I., "The Indian: The Forgotten American", Harvard Law Review 81 (June, 1968): 1818-58.

Comas, Juan, "Scientific Racism Again?", Current Anthropology 2 (Oct., 1961): 303-40.

Dandurand, Yvon, "Ethnic Group Members and the Correctional System: A Question of Human Rights", Canadian Journal of Criminology and Corrections 16 (Jan., 1974): 35-52.

Deloria, Vine, Jr., Custer Died For Your Sins: An Indian Manifesto. New York: Macmillan, 1969.

Department of Indian Affairs and Northern Development, Statement of the Government of Canada on Indian Policy (The White Paper). Ottawa: Queen's Printer, 1969.

Dolbeare, Kenneth A. and Dolbeare, Patricia, American Ideologies: The Competing Political Beliefs of the 1970's. Chicago: Markham Publishing Company, 1973.

Elliott, Jean Leonard, Native Peoples. Scarborough: Prentice-Hall of Canada Ltd, 1971.

Federal-Provinical Ministerial Conference on Native Peoples and the Criminal Justice System: Verbatim Report, February 5, 1975, Document No. NCJ-80. Ottawa: Canadian Intergovernmental Conference Secretariat, 1975.

Forsland, Morris A. and Meyers, Ralph E., "Delinquency Among Wind River Indian Reservation Youth", Criminology: An Inter-disciplinary Journal 12 (May, 1974): 97-106.

Fox, Vernon, "Prisons: Reform or Rebellion?", in The Criminologist: Crime and the Criminal, Charles E. Reasons (ed.). Pacific Palisades: Goodyear Publishing Company, 1974, pp. 388-403.

Frideres, James S., Canada's Indians: Contemporary Conflict. Scarborough: Prentice-Hall of Canada Ltd, 1974.

Gossett, Thomas, Race: The History of An Idea. Dallas: Southern Methodist University Press, 1963.

Grindstaff, Carl F., Galloway, Wilda, and Nixon, Joanne, "Racial and

Cultural Identification Among Canadian Indian Children". *Phylon* 34 (1973): 368-377.

Hagen, Everett E., "Colonialism: The Case of the Sioux", in *On the Theory of Social Change*. Homewood, Illinois: The Dorsey Press, 1962, pp. 471-502.

Hagen, John, "Criminal Justice and Native People: A Study of Incarceration in a Canadian Province", *The Canadian Review of Sociology and Anthropology* (a special publication on the occasion of the VII World Congress of Sociology) (Summer, 1974): 220-236.

Hall, Edwin L. and Simkus, Albert A., "Inequality in the Types of Sentences Received by Native Americans and Whites". *Criminology* 13 (Aug., 1975): 199-222.

Hawthorn, H.B., *A Survey of the Contemporary Indians of Canada*. 2 volumes. Ottawa: Information Canada, 1966 and 1967.

Hellon, C.P., "Legal and Psychiatric Implications of Erosion of Canadian Aboriginal Culture", *University of Toronto Law Journal* 19 (1969): 76-79.

Horton, John, "Order and Conflict Theories of Social Problems as Competing Ideologies", *American Journal of Sociology* 71 (May, 1966): 701-13.

Houts, Kathleen C. and Bahr, Rosemary S., "Stereotyping of Indian and Blacks in Magazine Cartoons", in Bahr, Chadwick, Day, *Native American Today*, 1972, pp. 110-114.

Hughes, David R. and Kallen, Evelyn, *The Anatomy of Racism: Canadian Dimensions*. Montreal: Harvest House Ltd, 1974.

Irwin, John, *The Felon*. Englewood Cliffs: Prentice-Hall Inc., 1970.

Jackson, Michael, "Justice Behind the Walls - A Study of the Disciplinary Process in a Canadian Penitentiary", *Osgoode Hall Law Journal* 12 (May, 1974): 1-103.

Johnson, Elmer H., "A Basic Error: Dealing with Inmates as Though They Were Abnormal", *Federal Probation* 35 (March, 1971): 39-44.

Jones, James M., *Prejudice and Racism*. Reading, Mass.: Addison & Wesley Publishing Company, 1972.

Kaiser, Gordon E., "The Inmate as Citizen: Imprisonment and the Loss of Civil Rights in Canada", *Queen's Law Journal* 2 (1971): 208-277.

Kelly, Henry E., "A Comparison of Defense Strategy and Race as Influences in Differential Sentencing", *Criminology* 14 (Aug., 1976): 241-9.

Kuykendall, Jack, L., "Police and Minority Groups: Toward a Theory of Negative Contacts", *Police* 15 (Sept.-Oct., 1970): 47-56.

La Graza, Randolph Oide, Kruszewski, Z. Anthony, and Arcintega, Tomés A., *Chicanos and Native Americans*. Englewood Cliffs: Prentice-Hall Inc., 1973.

Lieberman, Leonard, "The Debate Over Race: A Study in the Sociology of Knowledge", *Phylon* 29 (Summer, 1968): 127-41.

Martinson, Robert, "Planning for Public Safety", *New Republic* (April, 1972): p. 23.

Metzger, Paul, "American Sociology and Black Assimilation: Conflicting Perspectives", American Journal of Sociology 76 (Jan., 1971): 627-47.

Mickenberg, Neil H., "Aboriginal Rights in Canada and the United States", Osgoode Hall Law Journal (1971): 119-55.

Moore, Joan, "Colonialism: The Case of Mexican Americans", Social Problems 17 (Spring, 1970): 463-72.

Moore, Winston E., "My Cure for Prison Riots: End Prison Racism!", Ebony 27 (Dec., 1971): 86.

Myrdal, Gunnar, An American Dilemma. New York: Harper & Row, 1944.

National Advisory Commission on Criminal Justice Standards and Goals Corrections. Washington, D.C.: U.S. Government Printing Office, 1973.

National Conference on Native Peoples and the Criminal Justice System: Verbatim Report. February 3-4, 1975, Document No. NCJ-48. Ottawa: Canadian Intergovernmental Conference Secretariat, 1975.

Nettler, Gwynn, Explaining Crime. New York: McGraw-Hill Book Company, 1974.

Pallas, John and Barber, Bob, "From Riot to Revolution", Issues in Criminology 7 (Fall, 1972): 1-19.

President's Commission on Law Enforcement and Administration, Task Force Report: Corrections. Washington, D.C.: U.S. Government Printing Office, 1967.

Price, John A., "U.S. and Canadian Indian Periodicals", Canadian Reivew of Sociology and Anthropology 9 (May, 1972): 150-62.

Price, Ronald R., "Bringing the Rule of Law to Corrections", Canadian Journal of Criminology and Corrections 16 (July, 1974): 209-55.

Rafky, David J., "Police Race Attitudes and Labelling", Journal of Police Science and Administration 1 (July, 1973): 65-86.

_____, "Racial Discrimination in Urban Police Departments", Crime and Delinquency 21 (July, 1975): 233-42.

Reasons, Charles E, "Crime and the Native American", in Charles E. Reasons and Jack L. Kuykendall, Race, Crime and Justice. Pacific Palisades: Goodyear Publishing Company, 1972, pp. 79-95.

_____, "The Politicizing of Crime, The Criminal and the Criminologist", The Journal of Criminal Law and Criminology 64 (Dec., 1973): 471-77.

_____, "Racism, Prisons and Prisoners Rights", Issues in Criminology 9 (Fall, 1974a): 3-20.

_____, "Correcting Corrections", in Charles E. Reasons (ed.) The Criminologist: Crime and the Criminal. Pacific Palisades: Goodyear Publishing Company, 1974b, pp. 357-365.

_____, "Social Structure and Social Thought: Competing Paradigms in Criminology", Criminology 13 (Nov., 1975): 332-65.

_____, and Kaplan, Russell L., "Tear Down The Walls? Some Functions of Prisons", Crime and Delinquency (Oct., 1975): 360-72.

_____, and Kuykendall, Jack L. (eds.), *Race, Crime and Justice.* Pacific Palisades, California: Goodyear Publishing Company, 1972.

Report of the Standing Senate Committee on Legal and Constitutional Affairs Parole in Canada. Ottawa: Information Canada, 1974.

Rothman, David J., *The Discovery of the Asylum.* Boston: Little, Brown, 1971.

Schermerhorn, R.A., *Comparative Ethnic Relations: A Framework for Theory and Research.* New York: Random House, 1970.

Schmeiser, Douglas A., "Indians, Eskimos and the Law", *Musk-Ox* 3 (1968): 1.

_____, *The Native Offender and the Law.* Ottawa: Information, Canada, 1974.

Silverman, Robert A. and Teevan, James J., Jr. (eds.), *Crime in Canadian Society.* Toronto: Butterworth and Co. Ltd, 1975.

Simpson, George Eaton and Yinger, J. Milton, *Racial and Cultural Minorities: An Analysis of Prejudice and Discrimination.* 4th Edition. New York: Harper & Row, 1972.

Skoler, Donnill L. and Lowenstein, Ralph, "Minorities in Corrections: Nondiscrimination, Equal Opportunity, and Legal Issues", *Crime and Delinquency* 20 (Oct., 1974): 339-46.

Smith, Derek G. (ed.), *Canadian Indians and the Law: Selected Documents, 1663-1972.* Toronto: McClelland and Stewart Limited, 1975.

Spence, Roy G. Jr., "Conditioning and Other Technologies Used to 'Treat?' 'Rehabilitate?' 'Demolish?' Prisoners and Mental Patients". *Southern California Law Review* (Spring, 1972): 616-81.

Spitzer, Steven, "Conflict and Consensus in the Law Enforcement Process: Urban Minorities and the Police", *Criminology* 14 (Aug., 1976): 189-212.

Swett, Daniel, "Cultural Bias in The American Legal System", *Law and Society Review* 5 (Aug., 1969): 79-110.

Thomas, Charles W., "The Correctional Institution as an Enemy of Corrections", *Federal Probation* 37 (March, 1973): 8-13.

Thornberry, Terrence P., "Race, Socioeconomic Status and Sentencing in the Juvenile System", *Journal of Criminal Law and Criminology* 64 (March, 1973): 90-98.

Tittle, Charles R., "Prisons and Rehabilitation: The Inevitability of Disfavor", *Social Problems* 21 (Summer, 1974): 385-95.

United States Commission on Civil Rights, *Mexican Americans and the Administration of Justice in the Southwest.* Washington, D.C.: U.S. Government Printing Office, 1970.

Van den Berghe, Pierre L., "Dialetic and Functionalism: Toward a Theoretical Synthesis", *American Sociological Review* 28 (Oct., 1963): 695-705.

_____, *Race and Racism: A Comparative Perspective.* New York: John Wiley & Sons, Inc., 1967.

Webster's New World Dictionary of the American Language. Cleveland: The World Publishing Company, 1964.

Willhelm, Sidney M., "Black Man, Red Man and White America: The Constitutional Approach to Genocide". *Catalyst* (Spring, 1969): 1-62.

Winslow, Robert W. (ed.), *The Emergence of Deviant Minorities: Social Problems and Social Change.* San Roman, Cal.: Consensus Publishers, Inc., 1972.

Wolfgang, Marvin E. and Cohen, Bernard, *Crime and Race: Conceptions and Misconceptions.* New York: Institute of Human Relations Press, 1970.

Wynn, Derek and Hartnagel, Timothy F., "Race and Plea Negotiation: An Analysis of Some Canadian Data", *The Canadian Journal of Sociology* 1 (Summer, 1975): 147-55.

Zald, Mayer N., "Organizational Control Structure in Five Correctional Institutions", *American Journal of Sociology* 68 (Nov., 1962): 335-45.

Chapter 17

Law Reform Commission of Canada—Political Ideology of Criminal Process Reform.*

M.R. Goode†

The approach of the Law Reform Commission of Canada when dealing with matters which may be conveniently subsumed under the general rubric of "the criminal process", has been avowedly philosophical,[1] and it is within the context of the philosophy revealed by the Commission's working papers on the criminal process that any debate must take over the preferable approach to the task of criminal process reform in Canada. This comment has two, rather limited, purposes. The first is to reveal the political ideology which is common to the Commission's published views upon the problem of social deviance and the appropriate reaction to it in a modern, democratic, capitalist society. The second is to examine that ideology in the context of current political-criminological debate which has begun to forcefully question many of the basic assumptions of traditional criminology.

In keeping with the approach of the Commission itself, it is not intended here to survey comprehensively the totality of the Commission's papers,[2] nor to discuss in full legal detail the specific recommendations that the Commission has not infrequently made. Rather, it is intended to identify a common ideological basis revealed by these working papers and in so doing, to open for further debate the real philosophical questions

---

* M.R. Goode, "Law Reform Commission of Canada—Political Ideology of Criminal Process Reform," *The Canadian Bar Review* (Sept., 1976): 653-674. Reprinted by permission of *The Canadian Bar Review* and the author.
† Faculty of Law, University of Adelaide, Adelaide, Australia.

at issue with which reform of the criminal process must be concerned and which the Commission has signally failed to consider. The criminal law has long been a matter for politically expedient decisions, principally by lawyers, and, as the Commission itself has pithily commented:[3] ". . . law is ultimately a branch of politics. . . ."

An Ideology Revealed: Selected Quotations from the Working Papers

The working papers published by the Commission abound in statements which, although undeniably vague, reveal to the researcher a common ideological thread. For example, the Commission states with respect to proposals to compensate certain victims of certain crimes:[4]

> . . . the Commission is of the view that one of the purposes of the criminal law is to protect core values. At the basis of any society is a shared trust, an implicit understanding that certain values will be respected.

In the conclusion to that paper:[5]

> . . . [this paper] recognizes the contribution the criminal law can make through sentencing and dispositions to preserving that mutuality or shared trust that is the basis of much of civilized society.

The working paper on obscenity and the limits of the criminal law concerned a similar philosophy:

> But what is society, if not a cooperative venture? As such it can't succeed unless its members are committed to doing what will make it succeed and to avoid what will make it fail. They have to be committed to certain values.[6]
> Certain values are essential to any society. Without them no society could survive.[7]
> And there are others which, though not essential to any society, are necessary for our society—they help to make it the sort of society it is. So when such values are contravened and threatened we call into play the use of the criminal law.
> When values are threatened, the criminal law serves various purposes: it provides a response, articulates the values threatened, helps to inculcate those values, and provides the rest of us with re-assurance.[8]

Finally, from the working paper on the principles of sentencing and dispositions:[9]

> . . . it is suggested that society's interest in having certain values upheld and protected can often be met by giving primary attention to the injured victim. . . .

Behind this collection of vague and superficially innocent statements lies a wealth of undisclosed and undiscussed

assumptions about the nature of Canadian society, and democratic
society in general, as it is and as it should be; about the nature of
crime and the criminal, about the internal validity of politically
constituted, economically determined legal authority, and about
the nature of social and legal authority itself. These, and other
examples which will follow,[10] point consistently to what may be
loosely called a liberal-positivist ideology,[11] which fails to question
the most fundamental bases of the criminal process in a
democratic capitalist society and the faiths which underlie them.[12]
This failure to question, combined with the failure to give written
consideration to present debate on these topics, has led to the
bankruptcy of the Commission's philosophical approach to
criminal process reform. This is explicit in the working paper
titled "discovery", in which it is said:[13]

> ... to assert that "justice and liberty depend not so much on the
> definition of crime as on the nature of the process ... designed to
> bring the alleged offender to justice" *necessarily assumes that society
> is justified in repressing certain acts* by the use of the criminal
> process. ... What is the aim and purpose of criminal law? Is its
> purpose to protect society, or to reduce crime, or to rehabilitate
> offenders? Or is its purpose a combination of all three of these,
> together with a recognition of society's right, indeed duty, to take note
> of an offence, to not allow it to go unchecked, and in this way to
> affirm, clarify, and support basic values? ... *However, it is
> unnecessary, perhaps even unwise, to go beyond the mere statement
> of these basic questions.*

Quite apart from the naive political equation of "society" and
"state", and quite apart from the failure of the author to perceive
that the discussion of these fundamental questions inevitably
determines the nature and scope of the criminal process and its
reform,[14] the failure to question must result in severe doubt being
cast upon the worth of the philosophical approach embraced by
the Commission, and the recommendations which flow from that
approach. Indeed, failure to question and failure to recognize the
true basis of current political-criminological debate, and the
consequent adoption of the existing social environment as a whole,
results in the Commission accepting the status quo in substance of
the social order and all that it implies.[15]

Assumptions Concerning the Nature of Social Authority: "Core Values" and the Universality of Moral Consensus

> ... the questions of how authorities become authorities, *and the ways
> in which they translate legitimacy into legality is central: for unless
> these questions are understood, we are certainly left ... with an
> inevitabilist [sic] view of bourgeois society.*[16]

The essential starting point for the indentification of the
political ideology (defined as a political philosophy as to the ideal

nature of society) underlying the published views of the Commission is to be found in the way in which the Commission regards society and social authority in the ideal state with which the Commission is philosophically concerned. It is submitted that the Commission has adopted the so-called value-consensus model of society which is characterized by the possession of two major premises: that there exists in society a fundamental agreement as to the values which the society wishes to, in some way, uphold: and that that consensus is reflected in the law making, law applying and law interpreting practices of political authority.[17] This is evident when the Commission speaks, as it is wont to do, of "certain values",[18] "core values",[19] "society's interest",[20] "shared trust"[21] and "implicit understanding".[22]

The identification of the model carries with it the indentification of other characteristics of the model, and hence a more complete picture of the political philosophy common to all the Commission papers here under consideration. For example, the value-consensus model carries with it the belief that political social authority, and hence norm creative: deviance creative and deviance controlling authority is derived from continuing consensus among the members of society about the most desirable aspects of that society.[23] The "social contract" which emerges as a result of the consensus takes the form of an initially limited surrender of personal liberty and freedom to the State in exchange for various forms of security provided by the controlled use of authoritative force.[24] This view of the basis of society leads naturally to egalitarianism,[25] for all sign equally and all equally agree to surrender liberty. It leads also to the view that society has the right, and duty, acting through the government of the day, to solve what are perceived to be current social problems by direct legislative and executive action. This is characterized in modern political terminology as a fundamentally liberal view of the basis of modern democratic capitalist society.[26]

The ideology involved, once discovered, may be variously labelled, and for introductory purposes has already been titled "liberal-positivist". Similar philosophies, or groups of philosophies, have been called "utilitarian",[27] "Fabian",[28] or even "conservative",[29] but no two labels are mutually exclusive, commonly accepted, or free from emotional taint. It would be an error to attempt to classify the descriptive characteristics of the political world-view, described above, except on an *a priori* basis. The shorthand "liberal-positivist" has been adopted here to emphasize the relationship between a political view of the basis and nature of society and a discipline of criminology based upon that view and in which "liberal" politicians and political thinkers have placed a great deal of faith.[30]

The Commission's ideology of social consensus bears a number of the characteristics of classical Liberalism. Ricci in his work on community power and democratic theory, has pointed out that philosophically, classical Liberalism and its derivatives evolved as a contradictory force to a conservative political philosophy, explanatory and protective of the old ideas and practices of feudal monarchy.[31]

> ... in general, Liberal tenets were inversely related to those of the political culture Liberals sought to replace. . . . One must seek the logic of Liberalism in Conservation, in the ideas and practices of the old aristocratic society that Liberalism opposed.[32]

The persuasive value of this theory is enhanced by the Commission's working paper on the concept of restitution, to which concept the Commission has given its wholehearted support.[33] Having pointed out that the concept of restitution as a major and widely-used "sentence" was basic to the primitive equivalents of a criminal process, the working paper then explains that the practice fell into disfavour and largely disappeared, partially because of the creation of the crime of compounding a felony.[34] Compounding an offence is still a crime in Canada, and its gist is to criminalize conduct leading to the concealment of a crime by satisfaction obtained through private settlements.[35]

The modern tendency is to rationalize the compounding offence by stating that its (laudable) purpose is to prevent a criminal from being sheltered from the public (deterrent) light and public sanction through the (consensus) legal system.[36] The original bases for the enactment of the crime were more likely to have been the following. First, the feudal monarchs of England wanted to replace the old, local, restitution based criminal process of Anglo Saxon and early Norman England, increasingly being taken over by local barons, with a centralized, unified, royal justice system. In gaining a centralized monopoly on public justice, the King could gain control of the central mechanism with which to enforce his political will, and at the same time, deprive the barons of a weapon which could be used against him.[37] As such, enactment of a whole range of offences, such as barratry, compounding, and conspiracy, was designed to serve the interests of the King in his political war with local barons. Second, a notion of public wrong implied not only public control of the territory in which the wrong occurred, but also implied a notion of recompense to the public purse. The public fine as a source of revenue and profit for the State (King) may also have led the law maker (King) to prevent diversion of cases into the competing non-revenue system.[38]

The vesting of a centralized monopoly of public justice in the State was grounded in conservative political philosophy upon the needs of social authority in conservative society. Like other adherents of classical Liberalism, the Commission has denied the policies inherent in the needs of conservative social authority,[39] but does not recommend in this paper the abolition of the crime of compounding which enforces those needs. One may presume that is because the Commission has adopted the modern rationalization of the crime described above. The presumption is strengthened by the fact that it is consistent with the value-consensus model to argue that vindication of public consensual moral standards requires a crime to be aired in the public *fora* and the criminal sanctioned publicly for public purposes.[40] Hence the Commission is prepared to recommend considerable widening in the use of restitution as a primary basis for sentencing, but only *institutionally* under the watch of the State.[41] It is evident that the Commission's view is *formed* in contradiction to conservative policy, in classical Liberal fashion: by adaptation of conservative policy to meet new social ends which are in contradiction to conservative political philosophy.

Ricci goes on to point out that the values of classical Liberalism, and, it is submitted, the values to which the Commission frequently refers, are to be found in the middle class— in the bourgeoisie:

> In the larger historical context the term "Liberal" is best reserved for the great political ideas and policies formulated by the middle class of the Western world since about 1650. . . .[42]
> The Liberal tenets marked a middle class resolve to question the legitimacy of a society controlled by hereditary aristocracy. . . .[43]

This point has not gone unremarked by other commentators. Taylor, Walton and Young comment:

> Social contract theory can be seen historically as an ideological framework for the protection of the rising bourgeoisie. . . .[44]

The consensus aspect of the philosophy of the Commission, also a major premise of classical Liberalism,[45] was and is used to provide a political and ideological basis for concepts of due process and fundamental fairness in the criminal process. The United States, a society founded upon a constitution limiting social authority on a fundamentally liberal basis,[46] has a criminal process in which due process and procedural fairness play a dominant role. Social contract theory there not only involved a citizen's duty to the State, but also the State's duty to the citizen. Hence, there was implied the notion of a citizen's correlative *rights* as a basis for protection against the excesses of a state owned by a neofeudal elite exercising political power by means of inherited wealth and, on occasion, religious *fiat*.[47] It is ironic that a concept developed to protect a citizen against State interference with *procedural* due process should now be used to defend State interference in society on a *substantive* level. But, logically, an ideology committed to the procedural protection of the rising, propertied middle class should also have substantive implications for the protection of bourgeois values: for example, the protection of newly-acquired property rights, and the philosophy of utilitariansim.[48]

The Commission may now be seen to have adopted a political-social philosophy to the approach of criminal process reform which involves major assumptions about the nature and basis of society and social authority. It is evident that the Commission has not explained, to date, why it adopts this philosophy, and its implications, nor has it considered in print the reasons for its rejection of alternative models of society, both real and ideal. Instead, the Commission has discussed, in general terms, the implications of applying the value consensus model to the Canadian criminal process. In fact, the ideology which the Commission has chosen to present has lately come under heavy and telling fire from adherents of an alternate opposing model. This contradictory model may be called the "value antagonism" model.[49]

In the fields of political philosophy and criminology, the value consensus model has been attacked as representing a false social consciousness because of the model's failure to account for present social reality.[50] In both disciplines, the debate has focused upon the influence which groups or factions[51] have upon the political norm creative and norm controlling attitudes of the State, and the fundamental values which liberal ideology attributed to an individualized social consensus. Thus, as a political scientist, Ricci comments in detailing Marxist theory:[52]

> In the capitalist social system, Marxists argued, the bourgeois middle-class own . . . the means of industrial production, and members of the working class have no choice but to labor for minimal wages. The result of Liberal freedom, then, is not a society in which groups count for little, but rather a society in which certain groups . . . are penultimately important.

Richard Quinney has made a similar point in discussing the interest analysis of law propounded by Roscoe Pound. Quinney comments:[53]

> First . . . Society is characterized by diversity conflict, coercion and change, rather than by consensus and stability. Second, law is a *result* of the operations of interests, rather than an instrument that functions outside of particular interests. Though law may control interests, it is in the first place *created* by interests. Third, law incorporates the interests of specific persons and groups; it is seldom the product of the whole society . . . .

He then goes on to identify the particular interest groups whose success or failure results in the formulation of public policy. Hence:[54]

> . . . public policy itself is a manifestation of an interest structure in politically organized society.

The influence of groups and powerful interests upon the State focused the criticism of the value consensus model of society which involved both major assumptions of that model, and in so doing, shaped the theoretical structure of opposing theory and its formulation.[55] The adherents of the value antagonism model, not all of whom are Marxists,[56] formulate their theory in logical contradiction to the essential tenets of liberalism and positivism, and hence a view of society and social authority emerges which has direct, and difficult, implications for reform of the criminal process. The "radical" criminologist, so-called because not all applications of the value antagonism model are Marxist, denies that there is fundamental social agreement as to the values of society, but rather that society is characterized by diversity and conflict on a large scale, and that social authority is wielded by and for an economic meritocracy which controls the means of production in the society.[57] Moreover, the radical criminologist would deny that law primarily reflects the will of the mass of society—rather it is a means used to protect and perpetuate the interests of the dominant groups which control social authority.[58] Hence, politically organized society is characterized by conflict and is ruled by alliances between economically determined power groupings. This view of social authority has obviously significant implications for reform of the Canadian criminal process, even if it is only partially valid.

Taylor, Walton and Young describe the implications from a Marxist point of view.[59]

> A full-blown Marxist theory of deviance . . . would be concerned to develop explanations of the ways in which particular historical periods, . . . give rise to attempts by the economically and politically powerful to order society in particular ways.

Sykes, in describing his perceptions of the foundations of radical criminology, has detailed a philosophy which is highly persuasive, but in direct opposition to the Commission's view:

> According to emerging "critical criminology" the criminal law should not be viewed as the collective moral judgments of society promulgated by a government that was defined as legitimate by almost all people. Instead, our society was best seen as a . . . territorial group living under a regime imposed by a ruling few in the manner of a conquered province. The argument was not that murder, rape and robbery had suddenly become respectable but that popular attitudes toward the sanctity of property, the sanctity of the physical person, and the rather puritanical morality embedded in the law were far less uniform than American criminology had been willing to admit.[60]

As Ricci has pointed out, the value antagonism model is determined in structure and content by that philosophy which it was created to oppose.[61] That philosophy was liberalism, its criminological arm positivism, and its perspective on society and social authority, the value-consensus model. The attack on positivist criminology, described in detail by Taylor, Walton and Young,[62] appears to have begun in the form of debate concerning the objectivity of social science and, in particular, the objectivity of criminology and criminologists.[63] The questioning of criminological and social science research on the basis of ideological bias had severe implications for the validity of legislation and criminal process reform based upon that research. In particular, if scientific objectivity was a myth, it could be argued that the primary influence, indeed the major influence, upon the criminal process, has been political expediency.[64]

The value antagonism model, while highly persuasive, has not been accepted without criticism. It has been widely argued, for example, that the value consensus model of society, as a purportedly *universal* model of society, no longer has descriptive or validating function, but that it still may serve to explain and justify part of the criminal process structure.[65] A different criticism has focused upon the assertion that the law as an agency of social control, is dominated by the ruling economic class. Denisoff and McQuarie, in criticizing Quinney, state:[66]

> In correctly denying the *absolute* autonomy of the capitalist state [*qua* "the capitalist ruling class"] Quinney fails to deal with the essential issue of the state's *relative* autonomy under certain specific conditions.

Denisoff and McQuarie go on to point out that the state bureaucracy will, for example, pursue the interests of its own class and not those of the ruling class within certain unspecified limits.[67] Thus, although they accept the value antagonism model, it is with the reservation that it, too, is an inadequate explanation of the totality of both the social functioning and political determination of the criminal process. However, that does *not* imply an even partial acceptance of the consenus model.

Akers and Hawkins, however, while conceding that the value antagonism model is the most persuasive *single* explanation of the criminal process,[68] state:[69]

> . . . a comprehensive explanation of the law must partake of both the consensus and conflict models. The politically powerful subunits of society at any given time can see to it that the law enhances their interests to a greater extent, but the law also reflects the past, current and changing functions and values of the whole society.

It is not intended here to do more than outline the bare framework of the debate that is still continuing.[70] However, the result of the debate has been a widely held political and criminological philosophy with direct relevance to generic reform of the criminal process: a theory which is highly critical of and contradictory to the political philsophy espoused by the Law Reform Commission. In a truly fundamental discussion of reform of the criminal process in Canada, which process is central to the operation of social authority,[71] both views should be canvassed before one is adopted.

Conclusion

It has been the thesis of the discussion above that the work of the Law Reform Commission of Canada has been, to date, profoundly unsatisfactory. The approach taken by the Commission to reform of the criminal process in Canada has been presented as a philosophical enquiry into the kind of criminal process which can best serve Canadian society as it presently exists: in itself a value-laden acceptance of much of the substantial status quo.[72] In actual performance, the working papers of the Commission represent the application of a particular ideology—liberal positivism—to the present framework of the criminal process. Thus Grygier has commented:[73]

> Unfortunately, the Law Reform Commission's Working Paper represents, in my view, not reform but return, or at best a stream-lining process of the old classical theory of justice, which sounds medieval to any modern criminologist.

There has been no real philosophical enquiry, no reasoned discussion of the continuing dialectic of criminal process models which keeps the area in a constant "state of crisis",[74] but rather the a priori adoption of a particular ideology of criminal process reform. In particular, the failure of the Commission to perceive that there can be no consensus as to the "core values" of a given society, except perhaps in terms of vast generalization, has led also to its failure to perceive that there can be no consensus as to the need for, or existence of, that consensus.

Three brief examples should serve to illustrate the difficulties in which the Commission has found itself as a consequence of its failure either to explain the reality of the present criminal process or the basis in detail of its ideal criminal process. All three examples focus upon the generalized and mythical "minimal consensus"[75] upon which the Commission's liberal-positivist ideology rests and in particular the morality or core values which are the subject of that consensus.

Example 1: "We-Us: They-Them"

> The ideology of most criminologists can be understood in terms of their class, sexual and racial sameness. It is likewise clear that this sameness distorts studies of the criminal and gives life to the stero-type of the criminal as being clearly inferior from the social pathologist.[76]

It is unfortunate, but revealing, that the Commission constantly speaks in the first person plural, designating a "we" and an "us". From context, it is often clear that the "we" refers to the Commission as opposed to anyone else, but sometimes the "we" is a more general reference to "we" as representing society and law-abiding citizens as opposed to "them": the criminals. Consider the following extracts from Commission papers:

> Crime uncoped with is unjust: to the victim, to potential victims and to all of us.[77]
> How people behave is *our* business if *their* behaviour causes us harm.[78] In short *we* have to make it *our* criminal law. Then, and only then, may *we* really learn to cope with crime.[79]

Sadly, there are echoes here of the old Lombrosian attitude that the criminal can be distinguished from the rest of society by factors, usually, but not always, biological, beyond the fact that the deviant has been found to have broken the law. Fox has noted in his discussion of the XYY syndrome:

> . . . it provides a convenient moral advantage for both the community at large and those responsible personally for the offenders' welfare, for all are relieved from blame for the behavioural consequences of what is a purely biological accident.[80]

The point is, of course, that there is no "us" and "them", and that the criminal law should not belong to "us".

Example 2: The Enforcement of Morality

In its report titled, significantly, *Our Criminal Law*,[81] the Law Reform Commission has shown considerable confusion on the question whether the criminal law is in the business of enforcing morality or not. Consider the following statements taken from that report:

> Crimes are not just forbidden, they are also wrong.[82]
> In truth, the criminal law is fundamentally a *moral* system. . . basically it is a sytem of applied morality and justice.[83]
> Nor is the business of the criminal law the enforcement of morality. Though wrong behaviour is the target, its wrongfulness or immorality is only a necessary condition, not a sufficient one.[84]
> . . . criminal law simply underlines our general notions of right and wrong.[85]

It is very difficult to conclude whether or not the Commission is of the opinion that criminal law is in the business of enforcing a moral system. Clearly, the Commission is of the opinion that criminal law should enforce some morality, but not all morality, but the central and unanswered question is whether or not *a* primary function of criminal law is to preserve and enforce a selected morality or whether that function is merely attendant upon any legislation of a criminal or quasi criminal nature. The vague Commission double-talk outlined above proceeds from a fundamental weakness in the ideology the Commission has chosen to adopt. But what morality? Whose morality? Who, *really* are "we"? What, *really*, is the content of "our" consensual morality?

Who decides?[86] If there is no minimal social consensus, if there is no reflection of any *possible* common morality in social legal institutional decision making, then enforcement of morality can easily become a facade for the imposition of the will of one social group upon another.

Example 3: The Delineation of Morality

If the basis of the Canadian criminal process is to be a "minimal consensus about how disputes and conflicts will be resolved in society" and that consensus is to be one shared by (a majority of?) the citizens of the society in which it shall operate, then it follows logically that it will not be necessary to detail with precision the exact parameters of the criminal law, for most or all members of society will know, *ex hypothesi*, what conduct is wrong and what conduct is not. Consistently with its reasoning, the Law Reform Commission has stated:[87]

> The individual has a right to know clearly what is forbidden. The administrator has a right to know clearly when he can legally intervene. This, it is argued, justifies spelling the details out in black and white. The argument is not totally convincing. In particular it is not convincing as regards "real" crimes. These are acts generally recognized as seriously and obviously wrong. So general is this recognition and so obvious is their wrongfulness that ignorance of the law is not allowed as a defence. Whether or not the accused is familiar with the actual language of the Criminal Code sections on homicide is quite irrelevant on a charge of murder—he knows that it is wrong to kill. . . . This being so, we contend that there is no need for detailed definitions.

This conclusion is logically consistent with the ideology of the Commission and quite as erroneous as that philosophy. The need for certainty and clarity in the criminal law could be, and should be, discussed at length, but such discussion is not within the scope of this brief comment. Nevertheless, the errors of the Commission's conclusion may be easily shown.

It is simply not true in Canadian society and Canadian criminal law to state that it is wrong to kill. On some occasions it is wrong, on some occasions it is not. Indeed, the Criminal Code is full of provisions excusing, under specified conditions, the killing of one human being by another.[88] Moreover, considerable doubt may exist as to whether the accused has "killed" and whether the accused has killed "a human being". The abortion debate is an obvious example of the latter problem, and *R. v. Blaue*[89] provides a convenient example of the former. Blaue stabbed a young woman with a knife, which penetrated her lung. The victim was taken to hospital where she was told that surgery and blood transfusion were necessary to save her life. She refused transfusion because it was contrary to her religious beliefs as a Jehovah's Witness and died the following day. Medical evidence indicated that the wound would have not been fatal had the victim accepted medical treatment. The question is, of course, whether Blaue is guilty of murder. Moreover, in the absence of legal definition of "kill", is the result obvious? It is true that the accused committed a "wrong act", and that the accused's state of knowledge as to the law was quite irrelevant to the decision. Nevertheless, do "we" say that Blaue is guilty of murder? Or is he guilty of something else? In the absence of definition, how can "we" tell?

One more example should reinforce the need for definition. In *R. v. Paquette*[90] the accused was the driver of the car used by two other persons to commit a robbery. During the course of the robbery, a person was killed. Paquette remained in the car outside the shop throughout and took no other part in the robbery or murder committed by his co-accused. By combination of s. 21 (2) and s. 213 of the Criminal Code,[91] Paquette could be found guilty of murder, despite the fact that he killed no one and did not know that anyone was to be killed, if the Crown could prove the elements of s. 21 (2). Paquette's defence was that he was compelled to drive the car at gunpoint. Assuming for the purposes of the case that Paquette's story was true, is he guilty of murder? Is he guilty of anything? Is it obvious?

The discussion in this comment has moved from general criticism of the approach of the Law Reform Commission to specific criticism of some of its proposals. Little further discussion is necessary or advisable, nor is it possible to look comprehensively at all of the work and accomplishments of the Commission. It is to be hoped that some of the issues raised herein will spark further public and academic debate concerning that matter which touches all citizens most closely: the criminal process which should be in place in Canada.

NOTES

1.   See, for example, Barnes, "The Law Reform Commission of Canada," *Dal. L. J.* 2 (1975): 62 at 72-73, in which the philosophical orientation of the Commission is discussed.

2.   The working papers from which material was drawn for this comment were: Law Reform Commission of Canada, Working Paper 2, *The Meaning of Guilt (Criminal Law: Strict Liability)*, February 1974; Law Reform Commission of Canada, Working Paper 3, *The Principles of Sentencing and Dispositions*, March 1974; Law Reform Commission of Canada, Working Paper 4, *Discovery (Criminal Procedure)*, June 1974; Law Reform Commission of Canada, Working Paper 5 + 6, *Restitution and Compensation, Fines*, October 1974; Law Reform Commission of Canada, Working Paper 10, *Limits of Criminal Law (Obscenity: A Test Case)*, 1975; Law Reform Commission of Canada, Working Paper 16, *Criminal Responsibility for Group Action*, 1976.

3.   Working Paper 10, ibid., p. 41. See also, Quinney, "The Social Reality of Crime: A Sociology of Criminal Law," in Akers and Hawkins, *Law and Control in Society*. (1975), p. 76 ". . . law in operation is an aspect of politics . . . ."

4.   Working Paper 5, *op. cit.*, footnote 2, p. 17.

5.   Working paper 5, *ibid.*, p. 25.

6.   Working Paper 10, *ibid.*, p. 21.

7.   Working Paper 10, *ibid.*, p. 21

8.   Working Paper 10, *ibid.*, p. 36.

9.   Working Paper 3, *ibid.*, p. 2.

10.   *Infra*, footnotes 77-79, 82-85, 87.

11.   See *infra*, footnotes 24-26.

12.   See Taylor, Walton and Young, "Critical Criminology in Britain: Review and Prospects", in Taylor, Walton and Young, (eds.), *Critical Criminology*. (1975), pp. 14 and 56: "The project, then, must be to build a materialist criminology which flows out of a materialist analysis of law in propertied, capitalist societies." See also *infra*. footnote 15.

13.   Working Paper 4, *op. cit.*, footnote 2, pp. 1-2. Emphasis added.

14.   See, for example, the implications for criminal procedure reform which conflicting models of society and social authority produce in Rapoport, "Theories of Conflict Resolution and the Law", in Friedland (ed.), *Courts and Trials: A Multidisciplinary Approach*. (1975), pp. 23-39, in which the adversary process of justice is examined.

15.   Acceptance of the status quo is a recurrent criticism of the liberal-positivist ideology. See, for example, Taylor, Walton and Young, *The New Criminology* (3rd ed.). (1975), p. 5: ". . . social contract theorists left the moral and rational supremacy of the bourgeoisie unquestioned."; Quinney, *Critique of Legal Order*. (1974), p. 3: "The political failure of positivist thought, as related to its intellectual failure, is its acceptance of the status quo."; Krisberg, *Crime and Privilege: Toward a New Criminology*. (1975), p. 18: "The standards of practicality are always taken from those who rule and who wish to preserve their status quo."; Taylor, Walton and Young, *op. cit.*, footnote 12, pp. 10, 22; Unger, *Law in Modern Society: Toward a Criticism of Social Theory*. (1976), p. 33: "Moreover, by suggesting that the evaluation of conduct does and must ultimately rest on consensus, it appears to sanctify whatever standards happen to prevail in a given collectivity."

16.   Taylor, Walton and Young, *op. cit.*, footnote 12, p. 46.

17.   The model is traceable to Beccaria, *Essays on Crimes and Punishments*. (1804), pp. 5-6. See also Ross, *Social Control*, (1901), pp. 56-75, 106-125; Sumner, *Folkways: A Study of the Sociological Importance of Usuages, Manners, Customs, Mores and Morals*. (1906); Durkeim, *The Division of Labour and Society*. (1964); Durkeim, *Suicide. A Study in Sociology*. (1967); all of whom arguably adopt a consensus model. For critical accounts of the consensus model, see Quinney (ed.), *Crime and Justice in Society*. (1969), pp. 20-25; Quinney, *op. cit.*, footnote 3, pp. 8-13; Ricci, *Community Power and Democratic Theory: The Logic of Political Analysis*. (1971), esp. at pp. 10-13; Hills, *Crime, Power and Morality: The*

Criminal Law Process in the United States. (1971), pp. 3-4; Chambliss and Seidman, *Law, Order, and Power.* (1971), pp. 17, 40-52; Young, "Working-class Criminology," in Taylor, Walton and Young (eds), *op. cit.,* footnote 12, p. 64; Taylor, Walton and Young, *op. cit.,* p. 10; Krisberg, *op. cit.,* footnote 15, pp. 68-70; Taylor, Walton and Younge, *op. cit.,* footnote 15, pp. 1-3, 14, 31-32; Unger, *op. cit.,* footnote 15, pp. 30-31. Taylor, Walton and Young, *op, cit.,* footnote 15, at p. 14, note 15, comment:

> The attempts by the liberal positivists, therefore, to arrive at a moral yardstick on which to build a positive science ultimately concerned with the diminution of unwanted behaviour, rests on assumptions that there is a more or less prevalent consensus on the nature of morality: that this morality can be described . . . and that the law in some way can be reformed . . . to ensure that it represents the morality . . . described.

18.   *Op. cit.,* footnotes 4, 6, 7, 9.

19.   *Op. cit.,* footnote 4.

20.   *Op. cit.,* footnote 9.

21.   *Op. cit.,* footnotes 4, 5.

22.   *Op. cit.,* footnote 4.

23.   See the material cited *supra,* footnote 17.

24.   See Beccaria, *op. cit.,* footnote 17, p. 5: "The sum of all these portions of liberty of each individual constituted the sovereignty of a nation; and was deposited in the hands of the sovereign. . . ."
See also Akers and Hawkins, *op. cit.,* footnote 3, pp. 7, 44-49. As to the central importance of the devolution of force to social authority, see *infra.*

25.   See, for example, Lenski, *Power and Privilege.* (1966), p. 11, in which the author notes the emphasis on legal equality in classical liberalism and the emphasis on natural equality in Marxism and radical political theory; Krisberg, *op. cit.,* footnote 15 p. 48, quoting Balbus, *The Dialectics of Legal Repression.* (1973), p. 4: ". . . the crucial significance of equality before the law as a legitimating principle of the liberal state."
See also Taylor, Walton and Young, *op. cit.,* footnote 15, pp. 3-4; Taylor, Walton and Young, *op. cit.,* footnote 12, p. 10: "The Fabian project can indeed be seen as the creation of such equal opportunity . . . in order that a genuinely utilitarian society, based on a universally-appropriate social contract, could be created."

26.   See, for example, Ricci, *op. cit.,* footnote 17, p. 8.

27.   By Taylor, Walton and Young, *op. cit.,* footnote 12, pp. 9, 15; Taylor, Walton and Young, *op. cit.,* footnote 15, p. 3.

28.   See, for example, *supra,* footnote 25.

29.   By Unger, *op. cit.,* footnote 15.

30.   This relationship has not been developed in the text as it must be regarded as fairly well established. See, for example, Quinney, *op. cit.,* footnote 15; Rapoport, *op. cit.,* footnote 14; Krisberg, *op. cit.,* footnote 15, pp. 15-16: "Critics of the 'Old' Criminology have commented on how that field has prostituted itself . . . fostered and disseminated the hegemonic concepts of the ruling class. . . . ", and p. 68; Taylor, Walton and Young,

op. cit., footnote 12, p. 8; Taylor, Walton and Young, *op. cit.,* footnote 15, pp. 14 and 31. Young, *op. cit.,* footnote 17, p. 71, makes a clear connection: "The positivists had declared there to be a consensus to which all normal men adhered." See also Reasons, "Paradigm Conflict in Criminology," in Riedel and Thornberry (eds.), *Crime and Delinquency: Dimensions of Deviance.* (1974), pp. 4-11, esp. note 3, p. 12; Phillipson, *Understanding Crime and Delinquency* (2nd ed.). (1974), pp. 1-21; Sykes, "The Rise of Critical Criminology," *J.C.L.C.* 65 (1974): 206; Shover, "Criminal Behaviour as Theoretical Praxis," *Issues in Criminology* 10 (1975): 95, at 96-97.

31.   Ricci, *op. cit.,* footnote 17, p. 17: "The Liberal tenets marked a middle-class resolve to question the legitimacy of a society controlled by hereditary aristocrats; the Conservative tenets reflected an aristocratic need to justify a dominant role in that society."

32.   Ricci, *op. cit.,* pp. 13-14.

33.   Working Paper 5, *op. cit.,* footnote 2.

34.   Ibid., pp. 8-9.

35.   Criminal Code, R.S.C., 1970, c. C-34, s. 129 (compounding indictable offence); s. 130 (corruptly taking reward for recovery of goods); s. 131 (advertising reward and immunity). The offences of misprison, conspiracy, compounding, barratty, champetry, and maintenance are all related. See, for example, Winfield, *The Present Law of Abuse of Legal Procedure.* (1921). See also the account given by Radzinowicz, *A History of English Criminal Law,* Vol. 2. (1956), pp. 313-318. The power of the prosecution to enter a stay of proceeding, Criminal Code, ibid., at s. 508 may be regarded as legal authority to compound an indictable offence.

36.   For example, see *R. v. Whiteford,* [1947] 1 W.W.R. 903, 4 C.R. 318, at pp. 321-322, 89 C.C.C. 74 (B.C.):

> A criminal offence is not an offence against an individual but is *an offence against society as a whole.* The King is recognized as having no partiality to any individual but as representing impartially *society as a whole.* . . . Each member of society, however, owes a duty to *society as a whole.* If he has knowledge of a crime having been committed, whether he be the particular individual against whom this particular crime be committed or not, it is his duty to inform the Crown of the commission of such crime and then it is for the Crown to take such steps or proceedings as may be considered in the best interests of *society as a whole.* (Emphasis added.)

37.   See Krisberg, *op. cit.,* footnote 15, pp. 138-139. As to the central nature of authoritative force, see *infra.* footnote 71.

38.   *Ibid.* See also the important works of Rusche and Kirchheimer. Punishment and Social Structure (1968) for very similar conclusions.

39.   At least insofar as the crime discourages what the Commission regards as proper restitution (*op. cit.,* footnote 33, p. 9). However, the paper does not identify the exact nature of the crime of compounding and appears to think that "historical developments" were "well intentioned"!

40.   Hence the Commission gives stress to the notion that public sanction provides "us" with "reassurance" (*op. cit.,* footnote 8),

"sustains public confidence" (op. cit., footnote 33. p. 19), "demonstrates a concern" (ibid.). The most obvious example of the application of the consensus view of compounding occurs (ibid., p. 15): "It is fitting that [the deviant] would be required to pay back more than he took [?? Why?]. Consequently, in many cases, a fine would be an appropriate additional sanction in recognition of the harm done to society and the costs involved in upholding values and protecting individual rights."

Compare Becearia, op. cit., footnote 17, p. 5: "He who endeavours to enrich himself with the property of another, should be deprived of part of his own."

41.   Working Paper 5, op. cit., footnote 2. Although radical community based diversion schemes may involve restitution other than through the courts, diversion is mentioned in the working paper only as an alternative to a sentence of imprisonment. Ibid., p. 15.

42.   Op. cit., footnote 17, p. 8.

43.   Ibid., p. 17.

44.   Op. cit., footnote 15, p. 3. See also Gouldner, The Coming Crisis of Western Sociology. (1971), pp. 70-71; Taylor, Walton and Young, op. cit., footnote 12, pp. 78 et seq. Krisberg. op. cit., footnote 15, pp. 48-49: "The development of a universal legal institution, under which all were equal, was a critical weapon for the rising bourgeoisie. . . ."

As to equality, see supra, footnote 25. See also Akers and Hawkins, op. cit., footnote 3, p. 45: citing further authority identifying the "values" of liberal society as being those of the middle class, and Rapoport, op. cit., footnote 14, p. 25.

45.   Ricci, op. cit., footnote 17, pp. 10-13 in particular. See also the authority cited supra, footnote 17.

46.   See, for example, Rapoport, op. cit., footnote 14, pp. 22-23, 26, and Ricci, ibid., p. 9.

47.   See, for example, Unger, op. cit., footnote 15, pp. 127 et seq., in discussing the nature of bureaucratic law, which may be characterized as law created by an instrumentalist society: "Power is justified by religion."

Until 1650 in a formal sense when power began to move from King to Parliament in England, or until 1832, in a fundamental sense when Parliament began to be representative of a wide range of voters, England was a society characterized by bureaucratic law and closely tied, in Stuart times, to religion in the "divine right of kings" and the monarch's role as head of the Church.

48.   See, for an extended analysis of the role and origin of property rights, and the rise of utilitarianism, Taylor, Walton and Young, op. cit., footnote 12, pp. 9-14, 33-44, and footnote 15, pp. 3-7. At p. 34 they state: "A society which is predicated on the unequal right to the accumulation of property gives rise to the legal and illegal desire to accumulate property as rapidly as possible."

The concept of private property is central to the Commission's "value," and in Working Paper 10, op. cit., footnote 2, pp. 21-22 it is stated:

. . . in any society there has to be some vestigial respect for property rights: whether a society holds all its property in common

or is wedded to private ownership, it couldn't make satisfactory use
of land and other items of property unless the user were to be given
some security of possession. . . . These are the basic values
necessary for society. Without them there can be no real cooperation and hence no real society.

Yet when money is involved, the principle becomes much less basic.
In Working Paper 5, *op. cit.*, footnote 2, p. 21, the Commission states with
respect to a scheme of State compensation to victims of crime:

> . . . it can be said that property loss should be covered, since such
> compensation would support core values, strengthen social bonds,
> reduce the victim's anxiety. . . . On a practical level, however, the
> cost of compensating property losses would be substantial and
> funds available for compensation are limited. . . .

49.   So called by Chambliss and Seidman, *op. cit.*, footnote 17, p. 17.
Other names are "conflict" (Quinney, *op. cit.*, footnote 17, pp. 20-25) and
"interest group" (Hills, *op. cit.*, footnote 17, p. 4).

50.   See Ricci, *op. cit.*, footnote 17, p. 20: ". . . the great flaw in our
Liberal ideology . . . has been and still is its failure to describe adequately
the political systems established or reformed in the name of Liberalism."
See also, *ibid.*, p. 23; Quinney, *op. cit.*, footnote 17; Akers and Hawkins,
op. cit., footnote 3, pp. 45, 47; Phillipson, *op. cit.*, footnote 30; Krisberg, *op.
cit.*, footnote 15, pp. 167-168; Taylor, Walton and Young, *op. cit.*, footnote
12, p. 21; Unger, *op. cit.*, footnote 15, p. 31: "The first and fundamental
drawback of the consensus doctrine is its inherent tendency to explain
both too much and too little."

51.   See generally Ricci, *op. cit.*, footnote 17, who is primarily
concerned with the sociology of group action, esp. pp. 36 *et seq.*; see, also
generally, Lenski, *op. cit.*, footnote 25. esp. ch. 2; Davis, "Law as a Type of
Social Control," in Akers and Hawkins, *op. cit.*, footnote 3, pp. 22-23;
Akers and Hawkins, *ibid.*, pp. 45, 47.

52.   *Op. cit., ibid.*, p. 24.

53.   *Op. cit.*, footnote 3, p. 75. See, to similar effect, Quinney. "Crime
Control in Capitalist Society: A Critical Philosophy of Legal Order," in
Taylor, Walton and Young, *op. cit.*, footnote 12, pp. 192-193.

54.   *Ibid.*, p. 77. See also Lenski, *op. cit.*, footnote 25, pp. 35 *et seq.*;
Herz and Hula, "Otto Kirchheimer. An Introduction to His Life and Work,"
in Burin and Shell (eds.), *Polities, Law and Social Change.* (1969), pp. xxi
et seq.; Taylor, Walton and Young, *op. cit.*, footnote 12, p. 30.

55.   Ricci *op. cit.*, footnote 17, p. 26: "In the logic of political
disputation, it was virtually predictable that Marxists, *in order to
overthrow Liberalism*, would deny the validity of Liberal tenets and
rationalize a position exactly opposite them."
Taylor, Walton and Young, *op. cit.*, footnote 12, p. 8; ". . . the
alternative positions taken appear to be little more than inversions on
orthodox perspectives. . . ."
See also p. 14; Young, *op. cit.*, footnote 17, p. 77; Unger, *op. cit.*,
footnote 15, p. 35: "The two conceptions of social order seem to be
juxtaposed in a contradictory way rather than merged. . . ."

56.   See Denisoff and McCaghy, (eds.), *Deviance, Conflict and*

Criminality. (1973). See also, for a forceful critique of Marxist
Criminology, Hirst, "Marx and Engels on Law, Crime and Morality," in
Taylor, Walton and Young, op. cit., footnote 12, p. 214.

57.   See, for example, Lenski, op. cit., footnote 25, pp. 22-23; Ricci, op.
cit., footnote 17, pp. 25-27; Quinney, op cit., footnote 15, pp. 15-16;
Reasons, op. cit., footnote 30, pp. 9-11; Johnston, "Toward a Supra-
National Criminology: The Right and Duty of Victims of National
Government to Seek Defence Through World Law," in Drapkin and Viano
(eds.), Victimology: A New Focus. (1974), p. 40; Taylor, Walton and
Young, op. cit., footnote 12, pp. 6-7, 30, 47-48; Akers and Hawkins, op.
cit., footnote 3. pp. 44-45; Sykes, op. cit., footnote 30, p. 209.

58.   Supra, footnote 51. See also Quinney, ibid.: Johnston, ibid.; Reasons
ibid.; Germann, "To All Researchers of the Criminal Justice System: A
Warning!" in Viano (ed.), Criminal Justice Research. (1975), p. 5: "The
orientation of the criminal justice system is, expectedly, overwhelmingly
conservative . . . and consequently it is not representative of the entire
community."
    See also Rapoport, op. cit., footnote 14, p. 25: ". . . the dominant class
imposes its ideology, including a value system, on the entire society."
    See also Akers and Hawkins, ibid.; Hirst, op. cit., footnote 56;
Krisberg, op. cit., footnote 15, pp. 42, 55: Unger, op. cit., footnote 15, p. 64:
"Law becomes a tool of the power interests of the groups that control the
state."

59.   Op. cit., footnote 15, p. 220. See also, for a discussion of the
implications of a Marxist view for the criminal process, Rapoport, ibid.,
p. 23.

60.   Op. cit., footnote 30, p. 209; see also Krisberg, op. cit., footnote 15,
pp. 67-71; Johnston, op. cit., footnote 57, p. 40; and see generally Viano,
op. cit., footnote 58. See also Poveda and Schaffer, "Positivism and Interactionism: Two Traditions of Research in Criminology," in Viano, ibid.,
pp. 25-29.

61.   Op. cit., footnote 17, pp. 25-27. See supra, footnote 55, for further
references.

62.   Op. cit., footnote 15.

63.   See, for example, Lenski, op. cit., footnote 25, pp. 22-23: Krisberg,
op. cit., footnote 15, pp. 2-3, 14-18, 72-73; Taylor, Walton and Young, op.
cit., footnote 12, pp. 7-8, 22-26, 41; Taylor, Walton and Youg, op. cit.,
footnote 15, pp. 3, 19-21, 281; Viano, op. cit., footnote 58, p. xiii; Tifft,
Sullivan, and Siegel, "Criminology, Science and Politics," in Viano, ibid.,
p. 10; see generally Platt, "Prospects for a Radical Criminology in the
U.S.A.," in Taylor, Walton and Young, op. cit., footnote 12, pp. 95 et seq.
For example, see Viano, ibid.:

    Criminology and criminological research are very much the
    servants, first of political values that define crime and the criminal
    as something outside society, and second, of the personal, often self-
    interested values of the criminologists who accept these political
    values and work within them.

    See also Sykes, op. cit., footnote 30, p. 206: "Sociology . . . was still
contaminated by the bias and subjectivity of particular interest groups in
society. The claim to the cool neutrality of science was a sham."

64.   See, for example, Kirchheimer, *Political Justice: The Use of Legal Procedure for Political Ends* (1961).

65.   See, for example, Taylor, Walton and Young, *op. cit.*, footnote 12, p. 6: ". . . once it is seen that an 'unjust despotism' may be hidden by the ideology of social contract utilitarianism, the classical symmetry of crime and punishment, an essential part of the theory itself, is shown to be ineffective and self-contradictory."

66.   "Crime Control in Capitalist Society: A Reply to Quinney" *Issues in Crim.* 10 (1975): 109 at 113. See also *ibid.*, at 114:

> Class factors aside, the relative autonomy of the state is, in the final analysis, a clear necessity for the state to survive and function at all. . . .the state can only function so as to organize the legionary of any ruling class *as a whole* insofar as it is relatively independent from the *immediate* control of any of the diverse factions of that class.

See, to similar *effect*, Krisberg, *op. cit.*, footnote 15, pp. 70, 74. See also Ricci, *op. cit.*, footnote 17, p. 45 where, in discussing the scholarship of Charles Merriam, it is said: "In other words, the citizenry retain some kind of ultimate reserve power which they can exercise in time of need." Again, there are implications for the relative autonomy of the State.

67.   *Ibid.*, p. 115.

68.   *Op. cit.*, footnote 3, p. 47: "All this adds up to a *preponderance of evidence* in support of the conflict model as the one which comes closer to the reality of the making and enforcing of laws in modern society."

69.   *Ibid.*, p. 49. See generally Lenski, *op. cit.*, footnote 25, who is concerned to "synthesize" the two models. At p. 33 Lenski states: "Both clearly contain an element of truth." See also Unger, *op. cit.*, footnote 15, p. 64.

70.   See, for example, Hirst, *op. cit.*, footnote 56, p. 204: "Radical deviancy theory . . . questions the value assumptions, underlying justifications of establishment interests, and the ideological stand of orthodox criminology, but it very rarely questions its own position, assumptions and interests."

71.   As to the *critical* role which the use of force through social authority is given, see Lenski, *op. cit.*, footnote 25, p. 23: Quinney, *op. cit.*, footnote 15, p. 15: "Although the legal order consists of more than criminal law, criminal law is the foundation of that order."
    See also Krisberg, *op. cit.*, footnote 15, pp. 41-42: Allen, "The Trial of Socrates: A Study in the Morality of the Criminal Process," in Friedland, *op. cit.*, footnote 14, p. 4; Akers and Hawkins, *op. cit.*, footnote 3, p. 11; Davis, *op. cit.*, footnote 51, pp. 21-23.

72.   See *supra*, footnote 15. This acceptance is explicit when the Commission speaks of the necessity for the enforcement of core-values "essential to the existence of our own particular society *as it is*". Law Reform Commission report, *Our Criminal Law*, March 1976, p. 20.

73.   "Sentencing: What For? Reflections on the Principles of Sentencing and Dispositions," *Ottawa L. Rev.* 7 (1975): 267 at 267.

74.   It is not contended here that the crisis should be resolved. See Hartt, "Some Thoughts on the Criminal Law and the Future," *Can. Bar Rev.* 51 (1973): 59 at 62.

75.   *Ibid.*, at p. 65.

76.   Krisberg, *op. cit.*, footnote 15, p. 4.

77.   *Op. cit.*, footnote 72, p. 7. See also Working Paper 2, *op. cit.*, footnote 2, p. 5: "We have, we would contend, a basic right to protect *ourselves* from harm and in particular from the harmful acts of *others.*" (Emphasis added on both quotations.)

78.   Working Paper 10, *op. cit.*, footnote 2, p. 36. (Emphasis added.)

79.   *Op. cit.*, footnote 72, p. 40 (Emphasis added.)

80.   Fox, "The XYY Offender: A Modern Myth?" *J.C.L.C. & P.S.* 62 (1971): 59 at 71-72.

81.   *Op. cit.*, footnote 72.

82.   *Ibid.*, p. 5.

83.   *Ibid.*, p. 16.

84.   *Ibid.*

85.   *Ibid.*, p. 37.

86.   See also Grygier, *op. cit.*, footnote 73, at p. 268.

87.   *Op. cit.*, footnote 72, p. 37.

88.   See, for example, Criminal Code, *supra*, footnote 35, s. 7(3) (common law defences); s. 16 (insanity); s. 25 (protection while enforcing the law); ss. 34-42 (defence of property and self-defence); and so on.

89.   [1975] 1 W.L.R. 1411, [1975] 3 All E.R. 446 (C.C.A.).

90.   (1974), 5 O.R. (2d) 1, 19 C.C.C. (2d) 154 (Ont. C.A.).

91.   See the famous case of *R. v. Trineer*, [1970] S.C.R. 638, [1970] 3 C.C.C. 289, 11 C.R.N.S. 110, 10 D.L.R. (3d) 568, 72 W.W.R. 677.

Chapter 18

Chile: Crime, Class Consciousness and the Bourgeoisie*

James F. Petras†

According to convention, the bourgeoisie is conceived of as
upholders of "law and order." Crime is associated with the lower
classes and is, according to the perspective of the observer, a
product of their deprived environment, lack of family training or
even "heredity." In most of the literature concerning "terrorism"
and political violence the actors are described as politically and
socially marginal figures, profoundly alienated from the society in
which they live. Yet in the contemporary world there are not
infrequently cases in which large numbers of prominent citizens of
the upper and middle classes engage in precisely the same kind of
terroristic, anti-social political behavior attributed to "deviants."
In the case study under consideration the major political parties
of the bourgeoisie and most of their supporters were actively
engaged in violent illegal activity directed toward destroying the
legitimately elected government. The types of violent action ranged
from political assassinations to massive boycotts—leading to a
violent seizure of power by the military, an action publicly
endorsed by all major bourgeois parties and professional
associations. The middle class' public endorsement and active

* James F. Petras, "Chile: Crime, Class Consciousness and the Bourgeoisie," *Crime
and Social Justice* 7 (Spring/Summer): 14-22. Reprinted by permission of *Crime
and Social Justice*.
Presented at the annual meeting of the Society for the Study of Social Problems,
New York City, August 1976.
† James F. Petras is Professor of Sociology at the State University of New York at
Binghamton.

support of political terror directed toward an illegitimate end is a subject which has scarcely been discussed in the social science literature since the European fascist experience of the 1930's. With the rise of right-wing terroristic bourgeois regimes throughout the South American region, it is important to rekindle that analysis.

There is substantial evidence that crime—meaning violation of existing laws—is widespread among the middle and upper classes.[1] Indeed Honoré de Balzac once noted that there was a crime behind every great fortune. The literature on the period of early industrialization in the West is replete with accounts of systematic forms of illicit behaviour. The crimes vary from bribery to the use of physical assaults—with a broad range of goals, including government concessions, bigger shares of the market, control over labor, etc. (Josephson, 1934). In the present day, accounts of "crime in the suites" overshadow reports of "crime in the streets." Public officials are bribed by multi-nationals on the five continents.[2] Business corporations overcharge government purchasing agencies. Price-fixing and scores of other clear violations of existing laws legislated by bourgeois politicians, administered by bourgeois officials and supported, at least verbally, by the capitalist class, are commonplace.[3] For some corporate executives this illegal behavior is considered necessary to keep up with the competition—it is seen as a normal part of business operations.[4] Most of the activity described is in the realm of largely economic considerations—the purpose is to secure economic favors from existing political figures. The crimes are largely economic and have the function of reinforcing the status quo. The recipients of the bribes and the donors more or less share a common outlook, at least insofar as the operation of the larger social system is concerned. The motivation of corporate executives in most cases is clearly limited to quite narrow economic considerations—increasing profits. This type of corporate criminality is not correlated with underdeveloped or developed countries, democracies or dictatorships, capitalist countries with greater or lesser degrees of social/economic inequality—but rather tends to be associated with countries which have strong social, political and economic ties with the U.S. (Badain, 1976).

In other words, this type of economic crime is part of an ongoing relationship which provides a means of reinforcing existing linkages and follows the general pattern of economic exchanges within the existing social order. The economic crimes committed by the corporate elite hence reinforce and even further the existing social and political order. These crimes are not preceded by any overt and manifest expressions of class consciousness—at the outside the only consciousness that is expressed is over the profits, sales needs or market concerns of the firm.

There is another type of bourgeois criminality, perhaps less pervasive but of greater consequences: systematic violations of the law in order to destroy a political regime, to undermine an emerging social order, to provoke chaos in the economy. The purpose of these illegal actions clearly transcend the concerns of the firm and embrace the class to which the individual corporate executive belongs. The illegal action is preceded by a series of intense political activities expressing concern with the impact of laws on the social order. In a word, the illegal action is dictated by a conception of class interest which transcends the boundaries of the legal system and which redefines the areas for political action. Insofar as the areas of social interest and political action take priority, the "law" becomes an arbitrary device subordinated to the immediate tactical and long-term strategic needs to overthrow the regime.

Bourgeois political criminality is most likely to occur in social-political contexts wherein the bourgeoisie perceives its prerogatives, power and privileges challenged by the "lower classes"—namely by labor and the peasantry. To the degree that bourgeois criminality is associated with large-scale social change, the argument that bourgeois law (and of course the political and judicial system to which it is tied) is an "autonomous" element operating independently of class interests, will have been challenged. To argue for the autonomy of law is to assume that respect for the law in the eyes of the bourgeoisie transcends their long-term, as well as immediate, interests. The assumption is that if all social strata respect the law then all can benefit from its impartial application. But if it is found that one class—in our discussion the bourgeoisie—respects the law only when it is in a position to legislate and execute the law according to its socio-economic interests and violates the law when it is not, then the other classes are not bound to obey the law except as it serves their socio-economic interests. Clearly the subordination of law to social interest, central to our discussion of bourgeois criminality, underlines the direct relevance of these issues to notions or methods of social transformation and/or restoration of the status quo. The process of change through legal measures becomes a moot question when it is clearly the case that the law is merely one more instrument in the arsenal of social conflict. Legality is in this sense an ideological weapon concealing the larger interests which inform its use. The shift from legal to illegal instrumentalities hence is explainable by the underlying social interests and the conjunctural context in which they appear.

Chile under Allende (November 1970 to September 1973) is an appropriate case for considering the politically motivated criminality of the bourgeoisie. We have chosen this period and government because it involves a sustained effort at transforming the social order within the legal framework of the Constitution. Salvador Allende was elected president and took office within the legal structures of the Constitution and followed the letter and spirit of the Constitution until he was overthrown. The socio-economic program of the Allende government included basic changes involving nationalization of foreign owned natural resources, banks and 90 monopoly firms, as well as the expropriation of large farms (Petras, 1973a; Zamonit, 1973). In each case the changes were carried out legally: the U.S. copper firms were nationalized by unanimous vote of Congress; the banks were purchased, farms expropriated and monopolies were intervened through the application of laws on the books, put there by previous regimes but never enforced. In each case, however, the segment of the bourgeoisie which was adversely affected, and their political and military cohorts, responded by taking illegal action.

I.   Types of Criminal Action, Perpetrators and its Impact

The crimes of the bourgeoisie covered a wide gamut of activity, each in turn subdivided into various types, directed at different targets, perpetrated by different segments and having varying impact on society, economy and polity.

A.   Political Assassination.[5]

There were two types of political assassination—those directed at the leaders and high officials of the government, military and left-wing parties and those directed at the rank and file members of the left parties and industrial and peasant unions. The top officials assassinated by the bourgeoisie included the commander-in-chief of the army, René Schneider, President of the Republic Salvador Allende and the naval aide of the president, Comandante Arturo Araya. The perpetrators were largely members of the upper class, funded by the upper class, and included members of the Fatherland and Liberty group, the National Party and those sectors of the armed forces allied with big business and the U.S. Central Intelligence Agency. In the cases of Schneider and Araya, the courts and police were lax in prosecuting the culprits; in the case of Allende it was the army chiefs themselves who were the assassins.

The assassination of rank and file workers was much more common, frequently involving peasants engaged in a peaceful occupation of landed property. These peasant occupations were efforts to prevent other illegal actions by landlords involved in the dismantling of landed estates (the selling off of farm machinery, slaughter of dairy cattle, etc.) prior to the legal transfer of title. These assassinations were usually carried out by groups of landlords and hired thugs, aided and abetted by the non-enforcement of the law and the tacit cooperation of courts and federal police (carabineros).

B.   Physical Assaults.[6]

This was one of the more frequent forms of terrorist activity and was directed at the person and/or property of individuals or organizations of the left. Scores of incidents involving homes, cars, businesses and government and party buildings were damaged or destroyed. Between October and November of 1972, 200 terrorist incidents were recorded—while many more probably went unrecorded. There were several aborted assaults on the President of the Republic and many more attacks on cabinet ministers, congressmen, senators and high administrative officials. Para-military groups of the right Fatherland and Liberty, Rolando Matus Commando and the shock forces of the major bourgeois parties, the National and Christian Democratic Parties were reportedly involved. In the cases of assassination and physical assaults, the purposes varied, ranging from efforts to sow disorder in order to provoke a military coup, as in the case of the assassination of the commander-in-chief, to attempts to intimidate the left and prevent it from fulfilling its mandate. It is difficult to assess the individual effects of each act—a great deal depended on when the act occurred and the circumstances surrounding it. In some cases the impact was negative in that it polarized opinion against the perpetrators, as in the case of the murder of General Schneider. At other times, when the physical terror was combined with other illegal activities, such as boycotts, lockouts and mass rioting, it probably contributed to a sense of disorder and insecurity and intimidated dissident members of the middle and upper class who might otherwise have opposed the extremism of the right-wing bourgeoisie. As in the case of assassinations, the police and the courts were very lax in their treatment of right-wing bourgeois violence; few offenders were caught, fewer were found guilty and hardly any served any time in jail.

C.   The Formation of Illegal Para-military Organizations.[7]

The widespread terror and use of force and violence was largely the product of several para-military groups whose members were well known and whose collaborators and financial supporters were found among the leaders in the National and Christian Democratic orgnizations as well as the National Agrarian Association (SNA) and the National Manufacturing Association (SOFOFA). These para-military groups provided the muscle to keep the right-wing leadership of the *gremios* (mass organizations) in control of the membership. Numerous truck owners, shop-keepers and small businessmen who refused to follow the directives of the bourgeoisie during the politically inspired lockouts had their property damaged or lost their lives. The result of the para-military activity was that the bourgeoisie had a relatively disciplined and obedient mass following among the petit bourgeoisie.

D.   Lockouts.[8]

The employer associations in industry, trucking and transport, wholesale and retail trade, finance and communications organized massive lockouts, endangering public safety, in order to overthrow the Allende government. Frequently these efforts were initiated by seizing on a local or trivial issue and through the techniques of confrontation politics, the membership was drawn into total and intransigent opposition to the government. The organizers were frequently rightist property owners, financed by the CIA and backed covertly by military chieftans and the political leaders of the Christian Democratic and National Parties. The activists of the parties were able to turn out their followers among white collar unions. Among the professional associations the same mobilization occurred, despite the danger to public health in the case of doctors, especially in the emergency wards of hospitals. The lockouts were aimed at paralyzing the economy and bringing about the resignation of the government and/or in order to provoke a military coup. The two major lockouts each cost the Chilean economy losses estimated at between 200 and 300 million dollars and seriously drained the resources of the country. The decline in production and chaos produced by the illegal and criminal action of the bourgeoisie was then cited by anti-socialist propagandists in the U.S. and Chile as evidence of the "incompetency" of the Left. The major internal political effect was to weaken the authority of the government and deprive it of resources; the loss of authority and resources then led to the alienation of the petit bourgeoisie and sections of the military. On the other side, however, the vicious right-wing physical assaults and lockouts radicalized the working class. Through numerous factory occupations, demands for arms and a hard line from the government, the working class served notice that they recognized that only the firm application of force would serve to deter bourgeois criminality.

E.   Speculation and Black Market Transactions.[9]

Practically the whole of the commercial sector, wholesale and retail, engaged in illicit commercial transactions, for both economic and political reasons. By withholding goods for sale at official prices they countermanded government policy and channeled vital food supplies from working class supporters of the regime to affluent middle and upper class opponents—and in the process enriched themselves. Practically every item from cigarettes to steaks were dealt with on the black market. Not infrequently clothing items which were produced in plentiful supply by worker run factories never found their way toward popular consumption, as retailers, wholesalers and distributors held back stocks and sold them under the counter. The breakdown of the supply networks was a prime political weapon in the efforts by the bourgeoisie to undermine middle class confidence in the government and to demoralize the regime's supporters. Efforts by the workers at barter relations or direct sales from producers to neighborhoods were attempted to circumvent bourgeois sabotage, but were not centrally planned or supported by the democratic government, which continued to coddle the opposition. The Christian Democratic and National Parties blocked all legislation which attempted to provide substantive sanctions. The courts and police followed suit. In effect, the bourgeois parties gave license to criminal commercial activity because it was directed at weakening the democratically elected government.

F.   Sabotage of Production.[10]

Illegal withdrawal of capital, remissions to foreign accounts, contraband sales of beef and cattle, illegal allocation of government credits from industrial investment to speculative and political purposes, etc., were practiced by virtually all industrialists and served to run down or destroy the productive facilities which remained in private hands. The efforts by the workers to requisition plants forced the government to intervene (with great reluctance), usually too little, too late, and not infrequently resulting in the reversion of the firm to its private owner. The employers and their associations, both in industry and agriculture, were the main perpetrators of these destructive actions informed by an "end-of-the-world" vision of "rule or ruin." The cumulative upshot was a severe decline in economic growth in the last year of the Allende government.

G.   Riots and Mob Rule.[11]

The bourgeois parties and their mass organizations frequently engaged in violent rioting, involving widespread property damage, street fighting and littering that paralyzed traffic, commerce and transport and left scores injured and maimed, sometimes on a daily basis. By openly flouting the law and commanding the

downtown sections of the capital city, the right-wing street
fighters sought to create an image of a power vacuum, inviting the
opposition civilian and/or military to seize power. The principals
involved ranged from secondary students to lumpen proletariat
and truck owner-operators.

H.   The Illegal Activity of the U.S.[12]

The U.S. played a decisive role in promoting many of the illegal
activities engaged in by the Chilean bourgeoisie. The CIA, on
orders from the White House, and representing big business,
collaborated closely in a number of areas with the parties and
organizations of the Chilean bourgeoisie, with the terrorist right
and the pro-coup military. These activities included:
1. Illegal campaign contributions and other forms of intervention
    in the political affairs of a sovereign country.
2. Attempts to bribe Congress.
3. Collaboration (including funds and guns) with terrorist groups
    which eventually assassinated the Commander-in-Chief of the
    Army.
4. Penetration and financing of a variety of political and social
    organizations which severely disrupted the normal activity of
    society.
5. Penetration and financing of the media and active collabora-
    tion with the army in actively planning and perpetrating the
    violent overthrow of the legally elected government.
6. The destruction of the existing legal and political order and
    support for an illegitimate regime.
    No doubt numerous other forms of illegal action were engaged
in, including activities promoted by the Nixon-Kissinger team in
Washington. But this inventory is sufficient to give some idea of
the scope, depth and impact of the involvement of the bourgeoisie
in criminal activity. There can be general agreement that
criminality was essential to the effort undertaken by the
bourgeoisie in overthrowing the Allende government and conversely seriously affected the capacity of the democratically
elected government to carry out its mandate. The multiple levels
of criminal action were made possible by the piecemeal type of
change. The depth of criminality, including assassinations, reflects
the profound attachment which the bourgeoisie has for its
property over and above any consideration of human and political
rights. The non-enforcement of the laws by the court officials
previously appointed by the bourgeois parties underwrote all the
violent actions. Within the "democratic consensus" Allende was
tied to the fiction of the non-political nature of the court
appointees. The same fiction affected the government's behavior
toward the police and the army. The paradox facing the

democratic-socialist government was that in complying with its part of the democratic bargain it facilitated the illegal action of its profoundly anti-democratic bourgeois opposition. The selective enforcement of the law by the bourgeois appointees in the courts illustrates the selective behavior of the bourgeoisie toward all institutions and policies.[13] First, it applies the test: does the law/appointee/agreement tie the hands of our enemies and/or does it allow us to defend or extend our property/privileges or prerogatives. Secondly, when the interests at hand coincide with democracy, the bourgeoisie proclaims the latter is a hallowed principle (and of course denounces the actions of any opponents who do not follow suit). When there is a major divergence between social interests and democracy, a higher purpose is evoked and the victims are accused of the crimes committed against them. In the case of Chile, bourgeois violence and criminality against the Left were frequently justified by falsified accounts or attributed to the Left itself.

By examining the types of bourgeois criminal action and their extent, the perpetrators and their effects, we can see that there is no single group or groups which acted to bring down the Allende government. The bourgeoisie as a whole acted on many levels to bring about the outcome. The extensive network of participants and the wide range of criminal activities had a substantive impact in overturning the government, reversing social changes and arresting the progress of the working class. In that sense, bourgeois criminality, when carried out on a societal-wide base, has great historical and sociological importance. Bourgeois illegal activity can define a new historical epoch. In the case of Chile, the reversal of the trend toward socialism through bourgeois terror has led to a quasi-totalitarian regime which rules through the permanent use of violence and the surveillance of the secret police.

II. Toward a Theory of Bourgeois Political Criminality

During the transition from capitalism to socialism, bourgeois politically motivated criminality becomes extensive and violent, involving various strata and sectors, frequently in coordinated activity. As the process of social transformation deepens, the degree of criminal violence increases, reaching proportions which paralyze the total instrumental use of law and disqualifies the bourgeoisie from judging the political lawlessness of the masses.

A government with a program proposing to realize a transition from capitalism to socialism must take account of the threats to internal safety found in the rather pervasive use of illegal actions by the bourgeois opposition. In Chile "citizen participation" was demanded and in part implemented by the workers and peasants to combat the lawlessness by the bourgeoisie (Raptis, 1975).

Workers organized networks of distribution, production and transportation. Popular tribunals were organized in certain
neighborhoods. But the absence of a popular militia and the
continuance of government support of the existing police and
military apparatus assured the bourgeoisie that they would be
protected—and this contributed to encouraging lawless behavior.

The fact that there are few studies of lawless and disorderly
behavior of the bourgeoisie is probably a function of their position
in society. As Richard Quinney (1970) noted: ". . . the most
important conceptions of crime are those held by the powerful
segments of society. Criminal definitions in their official
formulations, consequently, are the most powerful means of social
control, used to control actions which conflict with the interest of
those who create these criminal definitions."

By extending the scope of criminal definitions to include
bourgeois political action against socialist governments, and by
defining the interests of the working class cast in the form of a
government in transition to socialism, we can utilize the notion of
crime as a weapon to the advantage of those exploited sectors who
have gained control over the governmental process.

NOTES

1.   Quinney (1970: 230f.) notes, "A capitalist economy, based on
competition and free enterprise, promotes an ethic that stresses the
rightness of any activity that is pursued in the interest of one's business
or occupational activity. Consequently, otherwise "respectable" members
of society engage in activities that have been criminally defined by
various laws, but which are not considered by them or most of the public
as criminal." See also Quinney (1964) and two useful pioneering studies
by Sutherland (1949) and Clinard (1952).

2.   Cf. U.S. House of Representatives, Committee on International
Relations (1976). See also Milton Gwitzman, "Is bribery defensible?," New
York Times Magazine, October 5, 1975; Michael Jensen, "U.S. company
payoffs: way of life overseas," New York Times, May 5, 1975, New York
Times, March 2 and March 5 on Northrop and Lockheed corporate
bribery; Ann Critenden, "Closing in on corporate payoffs overseas," New
York Times, February 6, 1976; McCloy, et al. (1976).

3.   Clyde Farnsworth, "Drugs in Europe: Collision of interests—
corporate pricing abuses and payoffs reported," New York Times, March
21, 1976.

4.   The chairman of Gulf Oil explains the use of bribes in a very
matter-of-fact manner: "I just thought that the opportunity to continue a
profitable business without unwarranted and inhibiting government
influence required it." (McCloy, et al., 1976: 101, 103).

5.   Accounts of bourgeois political assassinations, usually by their
para-military organizations, can be found in Chile Hoy, probably one of
the most important independent left political literary journals in Chile
during the Allende period. It provides numerous useful accounts of

assassinations of peasants and workers, as well as the details of the
murder of Allende's aide-de-camp. On the right-wing assassination of the
Commander-in-Chief of the Army see U.S. Senate, Select Committee to
Study Govermental Operations (1975). The assassination of Allende is
reconstructed by Sandford (1975).

On peasant and worker assassinations see "Los campesinos mueren
como los pájaros," Chile Hoy 12; '2 años de la derecha: del pánico a la
prepotencia," No. 13; "San Javier donde la derecha mata con licencia," No.
17; "Cada vez más sangre entre la DC y el pueblo," No. 47. On the murder
of the naval aide see "Del hombre clave al 'comandante Sabino,'" Chile
Hoy No. 62.

In each of the major political assassinations the Christian
Democrats and the right-wing parties attempted to blame the victims for
their crimes or those committed by their collaborators.

6.   There were daily reports of physical assaults on every conceivable
aspect of society associated with the leftist government. In a survey
article, "2 años de la derecha: del pánico a la prepotencia," in addition to
the eight peasants assassinated the list of physical assaults includes
arson, destruction of public property, numerous assaults on public
officials, destruction of food supplies, etc. See Chile Hoy 13. Another
inventory of physical assaults is presented in Chile Hoy 61, "argumentos
de la derecha: 128 atentados en un mes." In this case there is the following
breakdown of the 128 violent incidents which occurred in the preceding
month (July 1, 1973 to August 6, 1973):

Target	Number of Assaults
transport, public service vehicles	34
train tracks, bridges	24
public buildings	6
highway	4
private houses	19
embassy	1
businesses	4
party offices	4
electrical power facilities	2
factories	3
TV and radio stations	5
miscellaneous	22
	123

As a result of these violent actions two persons were killed, six
were badly wounded. Of the 128 incidents, 122 remained "unsolved." For
detailed descriptions of the daily use of terror and violence by the
bourgeoisie see the following articles in Chile Hoy: "El plan Septiembre en
Octubre," No. 13; "La derecha clausura su vía pacífica," No. 41: "La
oposición está aceitando su manquinaria terrorista," No. 42; "Robo y
asesinato con 'medios electrónicos,'" No. 46; "Cada vez más sangre entre
la D.C. y el pueblo," No. 47; "Las clases: frente a frente," No. 54. All of the
violence was not committed by para-military groups but in many cases by
the military and police. For a detailed description of military terror—even
prior to the coup—against the government's supporters see Chile Hoy, "La
izquierda acosada en la marina," No. 62; "Puerta Arenas: ciudad ocupada,"
No. 62; "Torturas en la armada," No. 63; "Plan golpista en la armada," No.

63; and most of issue No. 65 devoted to the illegal seizure of town, torture of peasants and soldiers who opposed the impending coup.

7.   The formation of illegal para-military organizations and the linkage between military, para-military and bourgeoisie organizations in the preparation of violent actions is described in a number of issues of *Chile Hoy*. What was absolutely crucial for the success and continuing action of the terrorist groups was their close ties with the legal above-ground political parties and business, agricultural and professional associations. The collaboration between the two ensured the safety-in-action of the terrorists. On the linkage between the fascist terrorist group, such as Fatherland and Liberty and the industrialists' association, SOFOFA, the big landowners association, SNA, the truck owners and the Chamber of Wholesalers, see "El negocio de la sedición," *Chile Hoy* 14; "La santa alianza de fascistas de D.C. y oligarcas," No. 54. On the para-military and subversive military groups see "La derecha refuerza su comando único," No. 46; "Voz del golpe" and "La mañana del golpe" in *Chile Hoy* 56; on the Christian Democratic support for a military takeover, in addition to above, see "Otro golpe frustrado" and "Paro, golpe y gabinete: D.C. 15 días de contradicciones," *Chile Hoy* 63. For a discussion of the widespread involvement of the naval and air force officers in the key plots see "Plan golpista en la armada," *Chile Hoy* 63 and "Fuerza Aérea: el golpe está vivo," *Chile Hoy* 64. Both articles describe the conspiratorial activity and terroristic activity of the officer corp in preparing the ground for the destruction of the constitutional government in collaboration with bourgeois parties and associations. A good summary of the alliances backing two separate efforts aimed at overthrowing Allende is found in "2 vías, un solo golpe: modelo freista, model fascista," *Chile Hoy* 65.

The most revealing account of right-wing terror appears in an interview with Roberto Thieme, head of the bourgeoisie and CIA financed Fatherland and Liberty group, who took credit for 500 terrorist incidents in a 40 day period between July and August 1973 that left six persons dead. See *Chile Hoy* 63 for an analysis of Thieme's role in the terror that brought about the coup and his ties with the bourgeoisie.

8.   Lockouts, boycotts, and strikes were probably the most damaging activities engaged in by the bourgeoisie in their attack on the economy. Landowners, industrialists, wholesalers, retailers, truck owners, professionals attempted to paralyze the economy in order to discredit the government. By making it impossible to realize its program they sought to demoralize its supporters, provoke its resignation and/or provide a pretext for a military coup. In pursuit of these policies the economic measures caused hundreds of millions of dollars in losses in production, forced the standard of living of the masses downward throughout the last year of the government and successfully contributed to the coup. Many of these economic activities were financed by the CIA and received a favorable press in most of the media financially supported by the U.S.

On the closing of retail businesses see "Un duelo que terminó en asonada," *Chile Hoy* 8. A good account of the joint efforts of all sectors of the bourgeoisie to overthrow Allende is found in "El plan Septiembre en Octubre," a special issue of *Chile Hoy* 19, analyzing the October 1972 employer's lockout. On the defeat of the lockout by the organized working class see "La derrota del poder empresarial," *Chile Hoy* 21. On the role of the landowners in production boycotts see "El campo," *Chile Hoy* 21. The role of the construction contractors is discussed in "Las constructoras después del paro," *Chile Hoy* 23. One of the few trade union leaders to collaborate with the bourgeoisie in undermining the Allende government was the head of the copper workers in El Teniente (Medina), whose strike, it was later revealed (U.S. Congress, Select Intelligence Committe, 1975), was financed by the CIA. See "El teniente un conflicto deformado," *Chile Hoy* 49. On the prolonged transport lockout leading to the coup see "Transportistas: peces gordos frenan a Vilarín," *Chile Hoy* 64. The medical doctors' illegal walkout was justified by the Secretary-General of the Chilean Medical Association, Edgardo Cruz Mana, who declared "either people die or Chile dies"—six people died in the emergency ward. See "Médicos se declaran en estado de guerra," *Chile Hoy* 65. The cost of the several lockouts and illegal actions by the employers in October 1972 was estimated at 300 million dollars. See "El costo del paro,' *Chile Hoy* 21. The impact of the July-August 1973 boycott, the sabotage of a vital oleoduct which cut off the supply of petroleum, and the destruction of electrical power in 13 provinces led to " tens of million of dollars in losses," destruction of 50% of the agricultural crop, thousand of liters of milk and cut off supplies for construction and manufacturing industries. See "Paro de camioneros, zarpaza a la economía nacional." *Chile Hoy* 63.

By providing credits and financial aid to the bourgeoisie to stimulate production—as the Communist Party and other "moderates" advocated—the government was financing its own destruction. "Este gobierno ha financiado todos los paros," *Chile Hoy* 15. On U.S. financing see U.S. Congress, Select Intelligence Committee (1975).

9.   Speculation and black market transactions were probably one of the most corrosive and widespread activities and involved broad layers of the bourgeoisie and petit bourgeoisie. Bourgeois control over food processing and distribution networks provided an easy way of circumventing government controls. See "Las JAP: el poder de la canasta," *Chile Hoy* 3; "Dirinco debe apoyarse en aparatos de masas," *Chile Hoy* 12; "En busca de un dique para el mercado negro," No. 27; "Mercado negro agrícola," *Chile Hoy* 31; "Encuentro obrero-campesino: donde están nuestros productos?," *Chile Hoy* 48.

The workers' organizations and sectors of the government tried to organize alternative distributive networks to avoid the black market, with only limited success given the continuing economic influence of the bourgeoisie and the lack of punitive powers in the hands of the regime. See "La fuerza del pueblo" and Distribución en emergencia," *Chile Hoy* 20; also "Las JAP rompen el empate" and "Ahora, la batalla de la distribución," *Chile Hoy* 33. Th extent of the black market speculative activities is evident in the fact that the disposable food per inhabitant increased between 1970 and 1972 but the supply in the legal market went down precipitously. See "Un examen político," *Chile Hoy* 37.

10.   Economic sabotage of production by employers took many forms. Employers added to the production woes of the Allende government by sending capital abroad, disinvesting and dismantling installations. See for example *Chile Hoy*, "La ofensiva inversionista," No. 53. The capacity of the bourgeoisie to bleed the country of vital foreign exchange—and the capacity of the government to act—is evident in the outward flow of 40 million dollars for foreign travel in 1972, a sum which would have purchased 40 thousand tons of beef. See "Cuando escapar cuesta caro," (*Ibid.*).

11.   Riots and mob rule were features of bourgeois political opposition.

Beginning with the march of the pots in December 1971, the bourgeoisie gradually escalated its activities, combining most of its activity between riots and the above-mentioned forms of violent political action. To a large degree the street action was delegated to the women to create embarrassing incidents with public officials of the government or to secondary students and the lumpen proletariat hired to wreak havoc on recalcitrant shopkeepers not abiding with the "official" calls for a boycott. On the use of student riots to detonate broader political movements and violent action see "El facismo anticipa su invierno," Chile Hoy 47; also "Un duelo que terminó en asonada," Chile Hoy 8.

12.   On U.S. government involvement in criminal action, see U.S. Congress, Select Intelligence Committee (1975). On U.S. corporate involvement (ITT) in criminal action see Subversion in Chile: A Case Study of U.S. Corporate Intrigue in the Third World (London: Spokesman Books, 1972). For a comprehensive and detailed analysis see Petras and Morley (1973).

13.   Selective application of "justice" was evidenced in the class bias of the courts, military and police. Nothing shatters the mythology surrounding the liberal platitudes concerning the independent and professional character of the Chilean state than the behavior of government agencies during the Allende period. The capacity of the bourgeoisie and right-wing to engage in massive terror was conditioned by their control over the courts and their influence in the police and army, which allowed them to act with impunity—and to use the same courts, police and army to apply the law against the defensive responses of their class opponents, the workers and peasants. Chile Hoy reports that of 44 criminal complaints against the right, all were exonerated—including four against known terrorists from the Fatherland and Liberty organization. While right-wing terrorists were invariably freed—as was the case of a landlord who killed a peasant occupying a farm, 21 peasants engaged in peaceful protest were spending six months in jail. See Chile Hoy 13. The collusion between judges and landlords was so transparent that communist cabinet minister Orlando Millas was constrained to note that "the ruling class is not accustomed to complying with the law," see Chile Hoy 17. Other examples of judicial bias are found in Chile Hoy 33 and 35. On the selective use of repression by the military offices and police see Chile Hoy 57, 58, 60 and 61. There was substantial opposition within the ranks of the army and navy to the pro-coup orientation of the officers, but this too was stifled— ironically with the "tactical" support of Allende and the Communist Party in the name of professionalism. See "Los soldados son también explotados," Chile Hoy 58; "La izquierda acosada en la marina," Chile Hoy 62; "Persecución a los leales," Chile Hoy 65.

The legal institutions, parliament, the courts and the State Auditing Agency became staging areas for launching attacks on the government, offering legal pretexts for illegal action. See Chile Hoy 19, 21, 36 and 52. The impotence of the democratic government in dealing with lawlessness and violence was in large part a function of the legal restrictions imposed on it by legal arms of the terroristic and violent organizations. Obviously the decision of the democratic-socialist government to bind itself to that legality was its major undoing.

REFERENCES

Badain, David, "Machinery Stalled for Lack of Grease: A Study in Bribery and U.S. Corporations Abroad." Unpublished term paper, 1976.

Clinard, Marshall B., The Black Market: A Study in White Collar Crime. New York: Holt, Rinehart and Winston, 1952.

Josephson, Mathew, The Robber Barons. New York: Harcourt, Brace and Company, 1934.

McCloy, John et al., The Great Oil Spill. New York: Chelsea House Publishers, 1976.

Petras, James F., "Political and Social Change in Chile," in James F. Petras (ed.), Latin America: From Dependence to Revolution. New York: John Wiley, 1973a, pp. 9-41.

————, "Reflections on the Chilean Experience: The Petit Bourgeoisie and the Working Class," Socialist Revolution No. 17 (v. 3, no. 5), 1973b.

Petras, James and Morley, Morris, U.S. and Chile. New York: Monthly Review Press, 1973.

Quinney, Richard, "The Study of White Collar Crime: Toward a Reorientation in Theory and Research," Journal of Criminal Law, Criminology and Police Science 55 (June, 1964).

————, The Social Reality of Crime. Boston: Little, Brown and Company, 1970.

Raptis, Michael, Revolution and Counterrevolution in Chile: A Dossier on Workers' Participation in the Revolutionary Process. New York: St. Martin's Press, 1975.

Sandford, Robinson Rojas, The Murder of Allende. New York: Harper and Row, 1975.

Sutherland, Edwin H., White Collar Crime. New York: Holt, Rinehart,and Winston, 1949.

U.S. Congress, Select Intelligence Committee, Covert Action in Chile 1963-1973. Washington: U.S. Government Printing Office, 1975.

U.S. House of Representatives, Committee on International Relations, The Activities of Multinational Corporations Abroad: Hearings Before the Subcommittee on International Economic Policy. Washington: U.S. Government Printing Office, 1976.

U.S. Senate, Select Committee to Study Government Operations, Alleged Assassination Plots Involving Foreign Leaders. U.S. Government Printing Office, 1975.

Zamonit, Ann (ed.), The Chilean Road to Socialism. Austin: University of Texas Press, 1973.

PART SIX

THE SOCIOLOGY OF LAW
AND SOCIAL PRAXIS

Definition of Praxis

According to Marx, praxis refers to what people do as opposed to what people think. Praxis is a revolutionary form of social practice (i.e., it contributes to the humanization of people by transforming reality from alienation to hope for a better future). The concept is both a means of consciously shaping historical conditions and a standard for evaluating what occurs in any historical social order. Marx maintains that a dialectical relationship exists between theory and praxis.[1]

Theory offers an objective comprehension of reality, expanding on the possibilities for revolutionary praxis. Further, theory serves as a guide to praxis and is a necessary condition for the possibility of revolutionizing reality. Thus, theory is the ultimate determiner of what is true, for it falls to theory to develop an analysis of how the internal contradictions of capitalism make the transition to socialism possible. What happens in history is dependent on human behavior. However, there is no way to predict in advance when social conditions are ready for revolutionary change or the extent to which the activity of people may create a decisive difference in the outcome of conflict. Theory not only gives rise to and is tested by praxis but is also developed by praxis (i.e., theory always accompanies praxis and assesses the altering course of events adjusting itself conceptually). Therefore, Marx formulated a unity between theory and praxis pointed at both criticizing and replacing the man of thought versus the man of action dichotomy. The following articles address the issue of praxis and law.

Grace and Wilkinson

The most common problem concerning the sociology of law field is that centering around the interdisciplinary nature of the subject. Theorists have attempted to unite the disciplines of law and society to establish a new field. According to Grace and Wilkinson, a sociology cannot be defined by its ability to resolve another discipline's problems. The sociology of law can be useful in creating a common scientific language to be understood by both jurisprudents and social theorists. Also, it can show how law and sociology can accommodate each other intellectually. The key issue for the sociology of law as a field of study is the type of questions posed and their derivations from sociological methodology. Accommodation with the legal discipline does not provide a structure for the comprehension of society and the legal institution within it.

The problems which face sociology of law theorists are the

same faced in any attempt to apply sociology to any substantive area for the purpose of comprehension of social phenomena. Sociology of law theory has taken numerous forms historically according to Grace and Wilkinson. First is the work of grand theorists such as Parsons who has established an explicit theory about the social order through use of concepts, hypotheses, and explanations about the law and the legal insitution. Second is the work of theorists who view the law as either a form of social control or a form of coercion. Last are the theorists who are preoccupied and concerned with the legal institution as a source of data accumulation used for the formulation of empirical propositions.

Grace and Wilkinson are attempting to point out the direction of sociology of law theory (i.e., their examples typify the structural-functional and conflict theories). The sociology of law has failed theoretically to evolve a methodology consistent with the social nature of legal phenomena according to Grace and Wilkinson. They feel that both structural-functional and conflict theories impose a priori assumptions on the study of law and society. In particular, one should not utilize existing theory unquestioningly since practitioners apply whichever theory appears best to them. Secondly, there is the problem of perceiving any type of knowledge about the legal institution as sociological knowledge. Thirdly, there is the problem of analyzing legal sociology through the pursuit of a definition of law (i.e., finding a sociological definition of law). Finally, there is the possibility of misunderstanding the purpose of legal sociology in an attempt to achieve a totally sociological comprehension of the legal institution.

The only viable sociological orientation that can be taken in order to comprehend the sociology of law is social action (i.e., meaningful action). Thus, Grace and Wilkinson accept the action theory of Weber as the only way to analyze the legal institution of society. One must reject imposing ideas from structural-functional and conflict theories and accept the fact that law is a common part of everyday life. Therefore, we must look at legal phenomena as a part of every day life. This world of everyday life is subjective but it is also of an interpersonal nature. One must concentrate on the analysis of man as he gives meaning to what he experiences. Man can impose meaning on structures and institutions. Therefore man gives meaning to law and law exists as a phenomenon of study for sociology.

According to action theory, the major problem is approaching the law, not defining it according to a variety of characteristics which impose assumptions on it. One must approach law as an everyday phenomenon (i.e., where law categorizes experience and establishes a comprehensible structure of the social world). People act in terms of meaning and in their actions confirm the relevance of meaning structures for social life. People are not generally aware of the law in the pursuit of everyday actions.

Social action as an approach has no inherent ability to answer questions as to the nature of law or legality but concerns itself with inquiries about meaning structures (i.e., their imposition, origin, and consequences for people caught up in everyday life in the contemporary social order). Law, therefore, can be likened to a categorization of experience according to Grace and Wilkinson (i.e., the status of law in social life as an everyday occurrence). Social action is an intellectual starting point for the analysis of law in society. Law as both a type of experience and as creating structures of meaning does not imply a coercive network of experience controlling people's behavior. The categories and meaning structures established are both the result of creative social action and a beginning for creative work by other individuals. The categorization holds from within the possible origins and transformations of the conditions in terms of which social action can proceed.

Grace and Wilkinson feel that sociology of law can only be approached utilizing the theory of social action. They feel that legal propositions embody *meanings* and constitute the product of meaning-endowed social action as well as an *interpreted object* in terms of which people act. Thus, one must deal with the creation of a legal proposition, the proposition itself, and the application of the proposition at the level of meaning. One must deal with the inter-subjective aspects of social life and thus treat legal propositions as both created and creative since the inter-subjectivity of the social world is the basis of law as a rational activity.

One must analyze both the activities of those acting in terms of a proposition and the proposition itself as a meaning endowed product of creative social action. One must look at law as both a category of experience and as a sociological concept. Sociology of law theory should be consistent with the theory of social action. It should concern itself with the subjective and inter-subjective nature of the law and avoid substantive assumptions about the content of that social action (i.e., should deal with the meaning structures within a legal proposition). One must examine the behavior of people in response to a legal proposition as well as to the creation of the legal proposition itself. It is important to social action research that both aspects of the phenomenon be analyzed to determine the correct level of meaning. Thus, whatever the content of action, one must treat the persons involved in both the the creation and the application of a legal proposition in the same terms (i.e., analysis of social actors will depend on the questions revolving around their relationship in the legal proposition).

Social action as the theoretical approach to sociology of law has an inherent practical orientation to it. The theorist must be familiar with Weber's *verstehen* concept as a method for gathering data. The attempt to place oneself in the place of the individual under study is an attempt to comprehend the cultural and societal environments in which the person exists. Thus, social action examines the problem solving process through the minds of the person under study and attempts to be as value-neutral as possible with no *a priori* assumptions. One must be trained in the techniques of participant observation to be able to properly utilize action theory.

Krisberg

Krisberg feels that traditional sociological theory and methodology (*i.e.*, structural-functionalism) have little value to offer contemporary sociology of law theorists. It is felt that C. Wright Mills and his conception of the sociological imagination can provide a new perspective to sociological analysis. Krisberg utilizes five categories derived from Mills with which to define an alternative methodology for sociological research and theory development. The first category is the relating of private troubles to public issues. Thus, one wants to relate the personal problems of individuals with the societal social problems causal to individual problems. The methodology utilized by Mills was based on a study of individual value-attitudes within the sub-cultural and cultural environments. The researcher should analyze the personal interaction with social institutions. Krisberg advocates utilization of life histories, ethnographic and depth interviews, and believes that the researcher should be personally involved in the resolution of the social problem, not just aware of its existence.

The second category is the use of the perspective and substance of the "new" history. This proposition is related to Mills' emphasis upon history as a vital part of social inquiry. The theorist should approach history with skepticism and be prepared to demystify false conceptions of people, structures, processes, and institutions of society. Research should be guided by theoretical concerns, not the availability of data. Abstract empiricism should be avoided at all costs since it makes the theorist into a "toolmaker" who attempts to apply natural science methodology to social science situations which are methodologically impossible to interpret accurately and precisely.

The third category is the use of a compassionate, as opposed to an appreciative, mode in research. The sociological imagination is humanistic in orientation. The typical symbolic interaction theorist which Krisberg criticizes is able to appreciate the problems and suffering of those unfortunates observed in society but he lacks compassion. This theorist sees the world of the lower classes and can be a defender of these people but maintains his intellectual distance and retains his sense of superior status by not getting involved in "loser" causes. The sociological imagination approach demands that subject and theorist share their feelings, needs, rewards, and plans. There must be an empathetic tie and respect between researcher and subject. Thus, the theorist must select a problem for analysis not for self-gratification but for the betterment of mankind.

The fourth category is the relation of one's intellectual work to a change oriented practice and a refining of theory from the experience of that practice. The theorist must take ideological stances with respect to issues of political significance. Thus, those theorists who are to approximate the sociological imagination have a history of praxis or are engaged in change directed practice. One must have political and moral commitments and avoid what Mills calls liberal practicality (i.e., the concept of value-neutrality).

Mills was opposed to value-neutrality and advocates that one let his value-attitudes be felt but not totally destroy one's objectivity. Thus, value neutrality is an intellectual device to deny any emotional involvement on a critical social issue. Liberal practicality also tends to support authority and to serve the interests of the status quo. It serves as a source of legitimation of those in power. Liberal practicality can also be indicted for lack of interest or concern with political and economic problems of society. Any concern with the redistribution of societal resources is rejected since this would destroy the status quo and threaten the elite who control society. Also, those theorists who are adherents to liberal practicality tend to be unable to deal with political issues in proper perspective. There is no challenge of structural inequalities since this would destroy the status quo and expose the elite with all their privileges and their system of exploitation of the majority of the members of society.

Finally, the sociological imagination approach demands the careful selection of an audience with which to communicate. Thus, theorists must reach people concerned with social change. This means that one's professional standing in the academic community should be subservient to the needs of the community. Therefore, the theorist must become involved in grass roots organizations, protests, and use political pressure tactics which might place him in a delicate position regarding his academic career and standing in the intellectual community. To be adherent of the sociological imagination approach commits the theorist to social change.

The ideological position stated by Krisberg based on the writings of C. Wright Mills can only be pursued by those dedicated to the cause of eradication of social injustice who are willing to stake their personal reputation and professional careers in the cause of social change. The sociological imagination as applied to the sociology of law is generally a condemnation of structural-functionalism with its lack of comprehension of history and its myth perpetuating propensities. It is also a condemnation of Weber's action theory concept of *verstehen* with the implied notion of value neutrality. Further, it also rejects symbolic interaction theory, e.g., Goffman, since these theorists are relatively value-neutral. The sociological imagination approach is a combination of conflict theory with action theory that is value-biased. The theorist should become involved in his research in order to change societal processes, structures, and institutions. He should also destroy societal myths in order to promote social change. Thus, the sociologist of law should reform or change the legal institution wherever needed and work for the reformation of both the criminal justice system and the criminal law where needed.

Beirne

Marxist thought has been neglectful of the study of law in society according to Beirne who feels that both Marxists and analysts of Marx will not study his conception of sociology of law. Marx was only indirectly concerned with law and society which was subordinated to his analysis of the state and the class struggle concepts. He looked for basic internal contradictions in institutions analyzed. Thus, the law could be explained by reference to the contradictions of the capitalist mode of production.

Marxism stresses the need for an historically specific theory relating each aspect to the totality of a specific society and mode of production. Analysis of the state, ideology of the classes, and the inevitable class struggle precede study of the law in society. Thus, Marx's research on the law in society was secondary to and incorporated in his theory of the state in capitalist society. (i.e., his concern with law was bound up with change in the political structure of capitalist society). The main concern of Marxist theory according to Beirne is the use of empirical knowledge as a practical tool for social change. Marxist ideology aims at changing the existing social order, not the perpetuation of existing institutions, structures, and processes.

Beirne criticizes Cain's analysis of Marx as viewing law as independent of its historical and economic base. She is also criticized for leaving out of her analysis the location of revolutionary praxis and the class struggle.[2] Let us examine Cain's interpretation of Marx, among others, to see if Beirne is correct in his analysis that there can be no Marxist sociology of law.

Cain perceives Marxian legal sociology as consisting of three major themes. Legal ideology influences behavior which otherwise would have been directly determined by the economy of the society. The law can set the rules on which struggle must be fought and influence the outcome of such struggle. Legal institutions in the control of the economically powerful facilitate and expedite real economic change.

The second theme in the Marxian sociology of law is the three functions of law: (1) mystifying function (i.e., the state develops to quell class antagonisms and is seemingly autonomous, thus obscuring the real power relationships within society); (2) legitimating function (i.e., real power is legitimated by stating that legal forms of power are available to all but in reality are available to only a few). Marxists are aware that by emphasizing the autonomy of the state and law, it is possible to create the mythology of a total society in whose interests these institutions operated, coupled with the belief that the state and law by reason of their apparent autonomy are value neutral; and (3) law represents the average interests of the ruling class—the interests of the class as a whole rather than of particular individuals or groups (i.e., law irons out conflict in the best interests of all and maintains the unity and integrity of the class).

The third theme sees law as an instrument of social change. Thus, Marxists analyze the development of private property, the relationship between social and legal change, the usefulness of law in the class struggle, and law as a means of social reform. It appears that the analysis of Marx made by Cain is in general agreement with that presented by Renner, a major interpretor of the Marxian view of sociology of law.[3]

Renner states that the social function of law in capitalist society is its use as a tool in the maintenance of the socio-economic processes of production and reproduction of societal institutions. Further, the economic function of law is subservience to the economic process of society. Thus, the law is only concerned when an individual withholds possession or disturbs the owner's enjoyment of his property.

Renner's radical theory does not explore the social forces which bring about the creation and alteration of legal norms and institutions. He does not investigate the problem of legal principle origins since he supposes the stability and relative immutability of legal institutions (i.e., property, contract, and succession). Renner's theory also states that legal institutions may thoroughly change their social function as a consequence of a transformation in their environment. Thus, Renner demonstrates that adaptability is inherent in certain kinds of legal rules that regulate social institutions within society (i.e., the agricultural paternalism of Medieval England that became the wage slavery of Industrial England). This study of the relation between legal rule and social institution illustrates the tendency of society to associate a particular set of legal norms with a particular social institution, even though the legal norms are formally stated in a manner which does not make this connection explicit (i.e., use of "legal fiction" concept).[4]

The adaptability of legal rules and institutions has been emphasized by Renner. Thus particular laws, legal concepts, and techniques have a quality of being adaptable to changing social purposes in society. Renner deals in particular with the larger social transition from the last stages of feudalism to the early stages of modern capitalism in western society. He illustrates the way the "property norm" was adapted to serve the complex

purposes of European capitalist society in the eighteenth and
nineteenth centuries. Renner's concern with the property norm was
adapted from the Marxian view of legal and economic histories of
the evolution of capitalism.

Finally, there is the latest theoretical position of Quinney
which sets forth the Marxist position on crime and criminal
justice.[5] The socialist concept of the unity of theory and practice
differs from the capitalist concept of social policy or social
engineering. The latter attempts to inform the population on social
changes according to the needs of the existing society. Thus, the
professional and political elite of capitalist society control the
population by rationalizing the maintenance of the status quo. A
critical social theory attempts to inform the population as to their
status and social situation so that the masses come to the
realization that they are being oppressed by the elites of society.
Therefore, the purpose of critical social theory is not to manipulate
the population like social policy theory.

Capitalist social theory aids in the control of the working
classes in society utilizing the criminal justice system as a tool of
oppression. The research of theorists is used to manipulate and
control the majority of the polutation (i.e., working classes).
Marxist criminology is based on the concept of popular justice.
This is the attempt of people to resolve conflicts between
themselves outside of the existing criminal justice system. Thus,
in the community and its local institutions, alternatives are being
worked out to the capitalist concept of law and order. Popular
justice is a tool used in the class struggle according to Quinney.

Quinney states that a critical comprehension of criminal
justice in capitalist society is necessary if one is to make the
transition to socialist society. Theoretical analysis of the capitalist
economy in relation to its criminal justice system is a necessary
part of revolutionary praxis. The critical comprehension of
criminal justice allows theorists to make the transition from a
capitalist system that controls the working class to a socialist
system that provides people with an understanding of both their
alienation and legal status in society. Critical social theory allows
one not only to begin the socialist revolution in capitalist society
but to embark on ideological, educational, and applied social
change in society. Therefore, social theory should serve the masses
of society in their struggle for creation of a socialist society. In
this struggle social theory will have to be constantly revised and
practice altered to achieve a better type of socialism. Finally, a
thorough comprehension of capitalist criminal justice allows one to
reject the capitalist social order and accept a socialist social order.

It can be seen from the statements of Renner, Cain, and
Quinney that Beirne is wrong in thinking that there can be no
Marxist analysis of law and society. Quinney most forcefully
argues for a Marxist sociology of law. He notes that

the rule of theory in practical action will not vanish under socialism.

It will be more important than under capitalism in that social theory will become a part of the everyday life for the masses of people.

Conclusion

It can be seen that Grace and Wilkinson present a case for the analysis of the legal institution in society utilizing action theory while Krisberg argues for the utilization of both conflict and action theories in the comprehension of law in society. Beirne presents a thesis that Marxian theory cannot be utilized to analyze the legal institution in capitalist society. All three theoretical positions have a common theme—opposition to traditional structural-functional analysis of society. Thus, all are opposed to traditional sociological analysis of capitalist society, and all are searching for a theoretical orientation that is humanistic and leads one from theory to practice utilizing other than traditional research methodologies. Even though these theorists do not actively call for a socialist theory (i.e., critical or Marxist) as does Quinney, they are probably opposed to the pessimistic conclusion concerning a Marxist sociology of law as presented by Beirne.

NOTES

1.   Encylopedia of Sociology, Guilford, Connecticut: The Dushkin Publishing Group Inc., 1974, 200-221.

2.   Maureen Cain, "The Main Themes of Marx' and Engels' Sociology of Law," British Journal of Law and Society 1 (Winter, 1974); 136-148.

3.   Karl Renner, The Institutions of Private Law. London: Routledge and Kegan Paul, 1949.

4.   Geoffrey Sawer, "Law as Socially Neutral: Karl Renner," in Studies in the Sociology of Law, Sawer (ed.), Canberra: The Australian National University, 1961, 147-150.

5.   Richard Quinney, Class, State, and Crime: on the Theory and Practice of Criminal Justice. New York: David McKay Company, 1977.

Chapter 19

Social Action and a Methodology for the Sociology of Law*

Clive Grace†
Philip Wilkinson†

Recently several authors have emphasized the need to
establish a new sub-area of sociology by developing a body of
writing which would constitute a sociology of law.[1] This call
arises in the light of the present dissatisfactions with the
literature, and carries with it the implication that at present no
such sub-discipline has developed. Yet we do have sub-disciplines
of education, family, organizations, deviance. Without assuming
that these sub-disciplines exist as unproblematic, unquestioned
and unquestionable bodies of knowledge, we can usefully review
the rationale for the present call for a sociology of law, and the
relationship of this call to the existing literature.

We may assume that the recognition of a lacuna in academic
sociology has developed along with an awareness, not only of the
importance of law in social life, but also of law as a social
phenomenon, itself a valid object of study. Yet this is hardly a
revelation. The founding fathers of sociology, in their understanding of the primary characteristics of modern society, wrote
extensively about the law. Modern grand theorists have similarly
accorded law an important place in their schemes. If it is not a
lack of attention, then there must be some other reason for the

* Clive Grace and Philip Wilkinson, "Social Action and A Methodology for the
  Sociology of Law" British Journal of Law and Society 1 (Winter, 1974): 185-194.
  Reprinted by permission of the British Journal of Law and Society (University
  College Cardiff Press).
† Centre for Socio-Legal Studies, Wolfson College, Oxford.

present call for a sociology of law. Whilst no spurious uniformity
need be portrayed in the writings being discussed, they do appear
to stand on a common ground, that of "relevance". The sociology
of law being called for is seen to have the potential of being
relevant. We should know how the courts operate, in order to
reform, criticize or lubricate the mechanisms. We ought to know
the effects of laws in order to advise the law-makers and we ought
to study the operations of the law so that we can articulate
demands for higher levels of law. Of course, sociologies developed
from such disparate relevances will generate sociologies of law
which will be quite dissimilar. Some would fall into a sociology of
administration. Others would be more concerned to characterize
the law (a mixture of right reason and sovereign will) or to test
hypotheses, possibly utlilizing social surveys to locate opinions
about the law and the impact of legislation.

One might be forgiven for imagining that a call for a sociology
of law on these grounds has been somewhat overtaken by events,
for although law has been somewhat ignored as a topic of
investigation for several decades since the founding fathers broke
the ground, recently we have seen the emergence of a growing
body of empirical research which might claim to be part
of a sociology of law. Part of this research has constituted
sociological studies containing a legal element rather than the
addressing of law as a phenomenon as such.[2] Any contribution
made by these studies to a sociology of law has therefore been
fortuitous. Undertaken from another perspective and in different
terms, these studies were not intended to produce and could not
produce such a discipline. A great deal more of this recent work,
however, has claimed that particular status and potential, holding
itself ready to receive the kudos granted to empirical research
taking the first tentative steps into largely uncharted territory.[3]
It is difficult to know whether these latter studies are accepted by
the proponents of the sociology of law as such, and whether they
are calling for systematic and concentrated work of this kind. The
proponents do not state their position clearly in respect of this
body of work but it is possible to assess their stance by examining
the sorts of problems they consider need to be overcome for the
sociology of law to develop to maturity.

Just as the proponents hold similar ground in respect of
"relevance", they also share similar views on the problems to be
overcome. Those most frequently stated in the literature revolve
around the problems of inter-disciplinary study and the absence of
any one sociology to be meted out to the sub-disciplines. It can be
seen that the second "problem" cannot be a problem in respect of
the under-development of the sociology of law, for if it were, we
would also be faced with under-developed sociologies of education,
organizations, family and so on. It might indeed be the case that
these sub-disciplines are under-developed, but in that case the
"problem" ceases to distinguish and will not assist in explanations
of why a sociology of law in particular should lack maturity.

The first problem appears more substantial, while at the same time illustrating that those who call for a sociology of law do accept much of the ongoing research as valid, albeit hesitant, steps in the right direction. This research does attempt to unite the two disciplines of law and sociology and establish a union of legal and sociological science. It is our contention, however, that inter-disciplinary problems are not central, and that the misconception that they are continues to stultify development. We will argue that sociology must take its relevance structures from sociology, its touchstone must be its own endeavour and not that of another discipline or problem hierarchy. A sociology cannot be defined by its relevance for someone else's problems.

Coming to terms with legal science is seen as taking several forms, be it clarifying the language utilized by sociologists and lawyers, examining the benefits that each discipline will bring to the union or, in general terms, how best accommodation can take place. This is the crucial distinction drawn between the sociology of law and other sub-disciplines, the idea that a sociology of law somehow faces peculiar problems in this respect. On reflection, however, it becomes apparent that other provinces of sociology have had to face up to the problem of accommodation to competing disciplines. The sociology of the family has accommodated to the psychology of small groups, the sociology of crime has accommodated to the psychology of criminal motivation, and political sociology, after a particularly protracted and bitter debate, has accommodated to political theory. These sociologies have been able to develop autonomously, in opposition to competing theories, without taking their relevance structures from, or being co-opted by, established sets of explanations within their chosen domain of study. The sociology of law can do likewise when it is appreciated that such an enterprise requires neither a union of sociologists and lawyers nor a commitment to intellectual imperialism. This is no guarantee that the sociology of law will develop in any less problematic fashion than, say, the sociology of organizations. In the latter field several writers would regard the most basic questions as satisfactorily answered, while others would say that the sociological questions have yet to be asked.[4] The crucial issue in the development of a sub-discipline will be the types of questions asked and their derivations from a sociological rather then from any other perspective. Merely to accommodate or come to terms with a competing discipline is to provide the conditions for co-existence, not a framework for understanding the social world and the place of legal phenomena within it.

Clearly then we are arguing that development of the sociology of law revolves around questions as to the nature of the sociological enterprise rather than questions about how, as practising sociologists in an academic setting, we can best compete in the academic market place.

The problems which do beset the sociology of law are the same problems faced in any attempt to apply sociology to a particular substantive province for the purposes of generating an understanding of social phenomena. Conventional sociology utilizes "theory" as a means of explaining the phenomenon under study. But within sociology, generally, and sociology of law, in particular, theorizing has taken a number of forms. The first is that exemplified by the work of the grand theorists such as Marx or Parsons. Having established an explicit theory about the social world, statements, hypotheses and explanations about law and legal phenomena are deduced. Bredemeier's consideration of law as an integrative mechanism, deducing the functions of law from the Parsonian schema, is an obvious example.[5] A second, and similar, type of theorizing is employed by those authors whose view of law is embodied in axioms of the form "law as social control" or "law as coercive" though in this case the source of the characterizations is frequently obscure. The theory generating that depiction of law is unclear and unexamined, or, in cases such as Chambliss' work,[6] bears little relation to the theory supposed to have generated the depiction. The third manner of theorizing is that epitomized by the phrase "letting the data speak for itself", and constitutes merely the accumulation of empirical propositions. Ziesel and Kalven, for instance, consider that establishing five categories of reasons why judge and jury disagreed in a series of cases was to state a theory—whatever the status of these categories it is clearly not that of a theory.[7]

In achieving generalizations through theorizing in one of the ways outlined above, sociology has forgotten to address itself to a question prior to the issue of what particular theory or method of theorizing one should employ. That question concerns the development of a methodology consistent with the nature of the social world. The creation of theory is to be seen as a methodological problem. Similarly, the developing sociology of law has failed to address itself to the problem of achieving a methodology consistent with the social nature of legal phenomena. Developing a sociology of law depends on creating that methodology which would enable us to approach law as social phenomenon without imposing a priori assumptions upon it.

We turn shortly to discuss the form that one possible methodology might take, but first it is necessary to point to four temptations encountered in applying sociology to legal phenomena. These temptations must be avoided if a viable methodology is to be established.

The first temptation is to utilize existing sociological theory unquestioningly. It is impossible to imagine that issues in sociological theory can be safely left to "theorists", whilst practitioners in sub-disciplines apply whichever theory appears best developed at the time. Such a crude division of labour misconstrues the criteria on which our generalizations will stand as valid or invalid. The existence of competing theories necessitates that the adoption of any particular theory involves the exercise of choice. The assumptions which base this choice have to be open to scrutiny. The acceptance of theory can only be an imposition of assumptions, and if these assumptions should be of the nature of substantive propositions concerning the social world, then they cannot be allowed any place *a priori* within sociology. Such propositions imply that the analysis has already been undertaken and can only exist within sociology as conclusions. Accepted *a priori* they are not only illegitimate, but invite the selective collation of data for analysis.

The second temptation is to view any type of knowledge about a phenomenon as sociological knowledge. Sociology is a developing discipline which addresses itself to and speaks about the social world. If other forms of knowledge can exhaust a topic of investigation—for instance, if behaviour were determined in the strong sense—then this is not sociology, but a case where sociology has nothing to say. It is a denial of the possibility of doing sociology. Similarly, we must not presume that sociology can necessarily provide a satisfactory account of phenomena for the purposes of endeavours other than that one peculiar to sociology. Even if a sociological account can be generated, it is not so generated for the purposes of those who view the phenomenon from a problem or another orientation.

The third temptation is to see the purpose of a sociology of law as being the academic pursuit of a definition of law. Not only must we be aware of establishing the characteristics of law in terms of theory and imposing them on our subject matter, but we must also be aware of attempting to define our subject matter by our theory. Theorizing about a phenomenon necessitates that the phenomenon can be identified independently of the theory. If a sociological definition of law is impossible, we may attempt to define law "for the purposes of study". But if we do this, attention must be paid to the manner in which that definition is generated. To be consistent with the enterprise of sociology that definition can only arise in terms of the accounts given of empirical actuality. We are not allowed to accept a substantive definition *a priori* and expect to be able to utilize such a definition to understand empirical data.

Finally, we must avoid the temptation of allowing immediate purposes to blur the central attempt to achieve a sociological understanding of social phenomena. We have already mentioned the manner in which sociologists' purposes as members of a discipline competing with legal science generated problems flowing from the academic market place rather than from the sociological enterprise. Our purposes as men-in-society can be just as persuasive, if not more so. The question is not whether these purposes are correct, in some sense, but whether they are allowed to mediate between our subject matter and our endeavour to understand.

The consequences of succumbing to any of these temptations is to distort both the subject of study and the status of that study. What we take as relevant for any given study must be drawn from an understanding of the sociological enterprise. Problems, methods and explanations all derive from the sociological purpose, not our purposes as men-in-society; they are sociological problems, not problems of men-as-sociologists.

The sociological enterprise which constitutes our touchstone is one that is centrally concerned with action at the level of meaning.[8] Social action is meaningful action. The problem of sociology is clear, and is one of generating a methodology which enables us to make contact with this subject matter. It is necessary to find a way of talking about and studying phenomena in the social world, keeping us firmly within an understanding of the social world as interpretive. The essence of the solution depends on a rejection of imposing ideas from theory and a recognition that law is a common sense notion of our everyday world and is therefore open to sociological analysis. We have to make contact with the subject matter in a manner that does not rectify this sociological starting point, and we can begin this project by firmly grounding legal phenomena in the world of everyday life. The world of everyday life is a subjective world, but it is also an inter-subjective world. If it were not so, then the operation of a legal sytem could not be a rational activity. It is only man that can give meaning to the world he experiences, but men can also make classifications. He can impose meaning structures on events through the law. This is necessitated by saying that law exists as a phenomenon of study for sociology. Nothing more flows from this existence without moving to the level of assumption. The major problem is approaching the subject matter, not defining it according to a variety of characteristics which impose assumptions on the subject to be examined. We therefore approach law as an everyday phenomenon, one that in its existence categorizes experience and establishes a meaning structure on the social world. This meaning structure is not necessarily empirically prior to the actions and events in the social world, but is analytically prior and for the purposes of analysis must be treated as such. Men act in terms of meaning and in their action affirm and reaffirm the relevance of meaning structures for social life. They may only be recognized by their immanence in social action. This approach does not assume that men are cognizant of the propositions of law in constructing their actions. That this is or is not a feature of empirical actuality is the province of investigation not assumption. Indeed, the law itself is illuminating in that ignorance of the law is no defence. Action undertaken in the context of a universe of meanings unrelated to any legal propositions does not offer immunity to the specified consequences of that action. But for our purposes "ignorance of the law is no defence" is to be treated as one of those propositions of an existent legal system that in its analytic status exists as a categorization of experience. Although an actor may not be cognizant, the proposition exists as a categorization of experience in the sense that it constitutes a peculiar construction of the relationship between knowledge of the law and immunity from it.

The validity of this approach depends upon its capacity to generate a methodology sensitive to problems of meaning in social action. By "methodology" we refer to the whole issue of the sorts of questions we ask of any phenomenon and the explanations we construct. The potential for sociology is at issue, not the potential for generating arguments for reform or for any other relevances. The approach does not claim an ability to answer questions as to the nature of law or legality, but remains wedded to the subject matter in a sociological fashion, asking questions about the imposition of meaning structures, how these arise and their consequences for men living within the social world in which they have existence. The approach is utilized to allow a level of conceptualization allowing for the development of a sociological method that is both legitimate and capable of surviving the exigencies of the research situations. In saying that law is a categorization of experience, we are saying that law constitutes propositions embodying language. The law imposes meaning structures in the same way in which any sentence or proposition containing language is itself an abstraction of certain features of the phenomenon to which it refers. The abstraction of these features of the phenomenon and its embodiment in language constitutes a way of looking at that phenomenon.

We take an example from child care legislation. In looking at this example we will discuss the manner in which legislation has traditionally been studied, in terms of the types of questions asked and the level of explanation offered. Generally, traditional sociology has addressed itself to a very rich and diverse set of questions with regard to legislation, but these questions have a particular relationship to the subject matter under study. They have not been orientated to the nature of social action, but, rather, have elected to deal with issues such as the impact of legislation or the relation between "legislative intent" and the ensuing distortion of that intent. With child care legislation, impact studies would be concerned with the consequences of the legislation for a range of areas of social life. Questions might be addressed to the number of children taken into care, the impact on the family structure and the organizations delegated to apply the legislation. In the case of child care legislation these organizations are those included in social services and questions could be addressed concerning the effects of the legislation on social worker training, the increased resources required or conflicts generated between social work and other agencies.

"Intent—distortion" studies in one sense look quite different. Such studies tend not to take legislation for granted but address themselves first to legislative intent and secondly to the intent given to the legislation by agents. These studies do not view the process of rule use as a social activity, the object of the studies being to reveal the correspondence or discontinuity between intended and actual interpretation. These studies either fail to address or completely misconstrue the relationship between legislation and social action, in terms of the manner in which law is made available for social action through the routine natural activities of actors in an organizational setting. In the impact studies, mediation of legislation through social action for social action is ignored altogether as a topic for investigation. In the "intent-distortions" studies, interpretation of legislation is seen not in terms of a social activity as such but in terms of whether an interpretation is right or wrong, the validity of the assessment presumably relying on some notion of observer-competence. Some of the more sophisticated practitioners have raised this issue. They have recognized that law is made available but never address themselves to *how* law is made available and the importance of this for an understanding of the social nature of legal phenomena.

The failure to address the issue adequately flows directly from two primary characteristics of this whole *genre* of study, the nature of explanation given of legal phenomena and the particular relevance structures adopted. These explanations, offered in terms of cause or functions, divorce legal phenomena from social activity. If sociology addresses social activity it cannot offer explanations in terms of semi-automatic biologically related notions which bear no relationship to that activity. Similarly, if social action is to do with meaning it is not clear to the authors how such a subject matter can be explained in terms of casual relationships.

By the acceptance of a relevance orientation, questions concerning social actions central to sociology are similarly closed off. A relevance orientation assumes a problem to be addressed, be that problem defined by the particular sociologist, to the community at large, or the legislation in question. With this stance, each social actor's relationship to the legislation is not seen in terms of the problem faced by the actor in the construction of his activity. Such an analysis could never answer questions about social action because social action is never treated as a topic in its own right.

We have shown how certain ways of studying legislation close off sociological questions and do violence to the sociological subject matter. We suggest that the methodology we propose has more potential for a sociology of legal phenomena.

Our inquiry begins with an examination of the constitutive features of the legislation itself, an inquiry which seeks to investigate the manner in which such elements enter into the construction of social activity. An initial inquiry into Section 2 of the Children Act 1948 reveals a number of constituent elements as outlined below. Under this section a local authority may assume parental rights in respect of a child in its care if it appears

(a) that his parents are dead and that he has no guardian; or

(b) that a parent or guardian of his has abandoned him or suffers from some permanent disability rendering the said person incapable of caring for the child; or (z) is of such habits or mode of life as to be unfit to have the care of the child.

We recognize that these propositions were not created in a vacuum but were generated with reference to particular social settings. We also accept that the legislation is not immediately available for use in those settings. The propositions, therefore, constitute a part of the constructed activity of actors situated differentially in time and place. Each social actor can be treated in his own right, his action being seen not in terms of someone else's problem but in terms of his own relationship to the setting. This approach is made possible by our understanding of the nature of law. Although we begin with the constituent parts of a piece of legislation we treat them not as bounded categories but, in looking at the manner in which they enter into the constructions of activity, as social phenomena. Each of these propositions is an abstraction of certain features of the parent-child relationship and is an invitation to view the relationship in that way for the purposes of applying a certain proposition. It is not a question of whether these propositions are correct propositions for particular situations; it is merely that they constitute a taxonomy of possible experiences of a parent-child relationship. Where these propositions enter the symbolic universe of a social actor, to be taken account of in undertaking action, they constitute sets of experiences which he can endow with meaning and act accordingly. The meanings any actor can attribute to a proposition are limited in part by the proposition, in that, for instance, an actor could hardly construe "dead" in proposition (a) to mean that the parents led a fairly quiet existence. Other propositions, for instance (z) appear to offer a much wider range of interpretations. We are not, however, attempting to assess the "right" interpretation, but to understand legal propositions in terms which enable us to retain a conception of social action as meaningful and as an interpretive activity.

Whether social action is constructed in terms of categories established by law is an empirical question. That law is a categorization of experience is a statement concerning the status of law in social life as an everyday phenomenon. It constitutes a sociological starting point for the study of law in social life. It must be stressed that to talk of law as a categorization of experience and as establishing structures of meaning does not imply a fixing of experience dominating men's actions. The categories and meaning structures established are both the result of creative social action and a starting point for creative social work by other actors. The categorization holds within it the possibility for originating and transforming the conditions in terms of which social action takes place.

The validity of the approach ultimately rests on its potential for generating and handling questions of sociological importance. We use another example to demonstrate the manner in which the approach sensitizes study to sociological questions closed off by conventional treatments of topics in the sociology of law. Suppose we are looking at the role of a lawyer or legal adviser in the context of representation before tribunals.[9] The utility of representation is an important question given a particular set of relevances, and views inevitably vary on this question. But handling representation in terms of its utility closes off certain questions which have much to say about law as a social phenomenon. For example, security of tenure may be denied a claimant on the grounds that the flat is furnished. His legal needs in the tribunal situation, and subsequent eviction proceedings, can be debated, but what must be recognized is that his needs only exist on the basis of the classification of certain types of dwellings into furnished and unfurnished. If no prior division existed, then the tenant of furnished premises would have no special or peculiar legal needs. His inability to obtain security of tenure and subsequent eviction would not be an issue. It cannot be an issue separate from the propositions of law. This particular situation is, of course, well recognized and we use it merely as an example, to highlight the level of analysis to which a sociology of law must aspire in order to handle the law as a sociological topic.[10] Viewing the furnished-unfurnished dichotomy in terms of a categorization of experience opens up question as to why the categorization takes a particular form, rather than any other form, which structures of meaning are discarded, avoided or ignored, in the development of legal propositions. Viewing law in this fashion necessitates that we concern ourselves with the development of particular structures of meaning and the relation of relevant social actors to them.

So far we have not made a case for a particular methodology to be utilized in studying the law in a sociological fashion. Beyond establishing a way of viewing law consistent with the nature of the social world, we are open to develop methodologies which, developed in terms of the approach, are geared to the particularistics of the research being undertaken. The approach, as a method of conceptualization, ensures that particular methodologies do not contain assumptions of substance about what goes on in the social world under investigation. We wish to suggest one viable methodology for examining legal phenomena when they exist as propositions in case law or legislation. The discussion will refer to legislation, but applies equally to case law.

Engaging in a sociology of law requires that our commitment flows from the nature of social action.[11] What is at issue is an explanation of meaningful social action in respect of a legal phenomenon. Since legal propositions embody meanings and constitute the product of meaning endowed social action, as well as an interpreted object in terms of which men act, we must treat both the creation of a legal proposition, the proposition itself and the application of that proposition, at the level of meaning. The social world as we have said, is inter-subjective, and this inter-subjectivity is the basis of law as a rational activity. In the study of law we must have regard to the inter-subjective aspects of social life and treat legal propositions as both created and creative. One does not accept the propositions as a given objective. Whilst it may have a concrete existence as marks on a piece of paper independent of the meanings men attach to it and act in terms of, for the purposes of analysis that form of existence is not important. The marks on the paper can only become a factor in an intentional act when endowed with meaning. If our interest lies in, for instance, social workers' action in relation to propositions in child care legislation, then a full sociological analysis will require that we do not establish arbitrary cut-off points and ignore the created and creative character of the propositions themselves. These propositions constitute the sets of meanings which are the references of that social action.

This twin methodology of analysing both the activities of those acting in terms of a proposition and the proposition itself as a meaning endowed product of creative social action does not follow as of right from conceptualizing law as a categorization of experience. The method flows from the same sociological frame of reference that gave rise to the conceptualization. In examining any particular proposition a sociological account requires such a twin methodology and a view of the creation of the proposition as a social accomplishment. The methodology is for a sociology of law consistent with the nature of social action, its subjective and inter-subjective character, and allows the avoidance of substantive assumptions about the content of that social action. Whether or not a legal proposition is taken account of in social action, the manner of its relevance for that action, and the particular meaning structures embodied in it, are empirical questions to which the methodology is addressed. The methodology in no way suggests the answers *a priori*.

In approaching a legal proposition utilizing this "twin" methodology, both the activities of actors behaving in terms of the proposition and the creation of the proposition itself are signified by meaningful social action. Therefore, both aspects of the phenomenon must be analysed by a method that can reach the level of meaning. The nature of the social world encompasses all social actors. Whether a social actor is President or peasant, the *nature* of his social action is fundamentally the same, although the although the *content* varies enormously. "Content" involves both the actual activities and meanings in terms of which such activity is constructed, and also the form of that activity, for instance, the range of alternative meanings available to that actor. The implication is that, whatever the content of action, we must treat the social actors involved in both the creation and the application of a proposition, in the same terms. This does not mean that our analysis of the relevant social actors will take the same form, but that such analyses will be consistent with the nature of social activity. Analysis of particular sets of social actors will depend on the questions revolving around their relationship to the legal proposition. For instance, an analysis of the activities of social workers in relation to child care legislation outlined above, will require an analysis of the interpretive social action of the social workers in respect of these propositions, the interpretive procedures to be illuminated by a study of routine activities and accounting practices. The analysis of the propositions themselves at the level of meaning would not of necessity require a full analysis of the interpretive procedures of law makers, but would require both analysing the proposition as the product of creative social action, and a consideration of the meaning structure with which the proposition is endowed.

The conduct of inquiry utilizing the proposed twin methodology, allows analysis to be directed by questions flowing from the sociological frame of reference, consistent with the nature of social action and social actors. The method of approach is based firmly in the world of everyday life, avoids ordering assumptions, and, in being capable of surviving the exigencies of particular research settings, is open to use by working sociologists.

NOTES

1. See for instance, V. Aubert (ed.), *Sociology of Law.* Harmondsworth: Penquin, 1969; W. Evan (ed.), *Law and Sociology.* Beverly Hills: Free Press of Glencoe, 1962; J. Skolnick and R. Schwartz (eds.), *Society and the Legal Order.* New York: Basic Books, 1970; P. Morris, P. Lewis and R. White, *Social Needs and Legal Action.* London: Martin Robertson, 1973.

2. P. Rock, *Making People Pay.* London: Routledge and Kegan Paul, 1972.

3. V. Aubert, P. Morris *et al., op. cit.*

4. For instance E. Bittner in R. Turner (ed.), *Ethnomethodology.* Harmondsworth: Penquin Education, 1973.

5. H. Bredemeier, "Law as an Integrative Mechanism," in V. Aubert (ed.), *op. cit.*, pp. 52-67.

6. W. Chambliss and R. Seidman, *Law, Order and Power.* Reading, Mass.: Addison-Wesley, 1971.

7. H. Kalven and H. Zeisel, "Disagreement between Jury and Judge," in V. Aubert (ed.), *op. cit.*, pp. 237-255.

8. Most authors accept Weber's treatment of the sociological subject-matter as meaningful behaviour, though they differ in their under-standings of the methodological imperatives which thereby follow. The Weberian position can be found in M. Weber, *Economy and Society.* G. Roth and G. Wittich eds., New York: Bedminster, 1968.

9.   See for instance, P. Morris *et al., op. cit.*; and K. Bell "Advise, Assistance and Representation before Tribunals" (paper presented at a Conference at the Institute of Judicial Administration, Birmingham, 20 April 1974).

10.   This comment was written prior to the publication of the Rent Act 1974. Although it is thought that the Act affects the current application of this example it remains a valid historical illustration.

11.   Purists may object to the phrase "meaningful social action" since in Weber, social action itself includes the notion of meaning through the equation, social action=meaningful (social) behaviour. But for an audience which may not be versed in these distinctions, we choose to emphasize the meaningful nature of social action.

Chapter 20

The Sociological Imagination Revisited*

Barry Krisberg†

An important development in modern social science is the increase in researchers who find little or no value in the theory and methodology which they have inherited from their elders and teachers. Although their doubts may frustrate and confuse more seasoned practitioners of social research, this open questioning of the domain assumptions or metatheories which have dominated liberal social science promises to expose hidden bias, to make implicit bias more explicit and perhaps result in a science of human affairs which is both moral and intellectually honest.

The search for a "new" perspective has not proved entirely successful. One obvious reason for this lack of progress is the virtual stranglehold which the guardians of the heritage have over funding sources and publication. In spite of sparse professional resources, some social scientists have performed the extremely necessary task of uncovering and exposing much of the racist, ideological and oppressive work in the disciplines of anthropology (Harris, 1968), economics (Gordon, 1971), sociology (Schwendingers, 1973 and Gouldner, 1970), history (Zinn, 1970) and criminology (Snodgrass, 1972). In so doing they have cleared the path to what C. Wright Mills called "The Sociological Imagination"; these scholars have looked carefully and proclaimed loudly that "The Emporer Has No Clothes".

This critical exegesis must continue but we must build upon

* Barry Krisberg, "The Sociological Imagination Revisited," The
Canadian Journal of Criminology and Corrections 16 (April, 1974): 146-161.
Reprinted by permission of The Canadian Journal of Criminology and Corrections.
† School of Criminology, University of California, Berkeley, California.

its interpretations by doing and not merely talking about the hard work of empirical research and theory building. New paradigms need to be closely scrutinized and subjected to the test of praxis-informed empirical investigation. However, getting down to work is not so simple for those who have learned to be skeptical of the "tools" of their craft. If there is to be a new methodology where or who will provide its starting point? It is our contention that we need to look at some current practitioners of the sociological imagination and we need to read closely the works of C. Wright Mills who clearly practiced and described the components of moral and potentially liberating social science.

The Legacy of C. Wright Mills

The words "hero", "courage" and "magic" abound in the several attempts to capture and express the humanistic meaning of C. Wright Mills.[1]

Often the eulogizers make reference to the large physical stature of the man in hopes of reconstituting his largeness as an intellectual force in modern social science. Certainly scholars of the new left owe much of the spirit and direction of their work to Mills, and although they have found it a painful truth, younger scholars have learned to disagree with their radical father.

Perhaps not surprisingly, Mills has been embraced by many who continue to represent the mundane and destructive trends which Mills brilliantly unmasked and dissected in The Sociological Imagination. At the same time, he has been canonized and shelved. Professional societies use his name to glorify their latest consensus upon scholarship (Krisberg, 1972). In the face of this "liberal plot" to tolerate Mills, there is a real danger that he will be lost. To avoid this, we must first of all read Mills; this is a delightful task because he is eminently readable and we need not depend upon "official translations". Our second task is to confront Mills, challenge him, argue with him and bring to this critical dialogue the force of historical events which occurred after his untimely death in 1962. Finally, we need to analyze the method inherent in his schoolarly production. We need to discover the analytic strategies and research techniques which Mills employed in his perceptive studies of many aspects of "Power, Politics, and People" (Horowitz, 1970).

Part of that rich legacy left to us by C. Wright Mills is a straightforward and penetrating analysis of the new methodology. In the Sociological Imagination, Mills understands and critiques the limits of the "secular" social science of his time but he also offers us several important clues to the sources of a more "sacred" social inquiry. For Mills the more "sacred" social inquiry meant the joining of the moral, and political and the intellectual aspects

of all persons. The scientist should focus his work on those powerful forces which contribute to the massive suffering and
uneasiness of his fellow mortals. The foremost objective of the
sociological imagination was to help "ordinary" men and women
develop

> a quality of mind that will help them use information and develop
> reason in order to achieve lucid summations of what is going on in the
> world and of what may be happening within themselves. (Mills,
> 1959:5).

The scholar should assist others and not make monopolistic
claims upon the "gift" of interpretation. The scientific task is one
of clarification not mystification, relevance not neutrality and
theoretically informed action rather than pure reflection.

It was the fate of C. Wright Mills to die prematurely in April
1962 and thus to miss (or be spared) one of the most tumultuous
decades in world history. Speculations can run unbounded as to
the impact which world events might have had upon the
perspectives and theories of the great radical sociologist. The
agony of the Viet Nam War, which energized much of the attack
upon the complacent liberal academy, certainly would have
touched his life. The murders of the Kennedy's, Martin Luther
King and Malcolm X might have prompted changes in the intensity
of his vision. The race riots of the 1960s would have caused Mills
to study the issue of racism. One wonders about the Mills who
might have emerged as students were beaten by police on the
Columbia University campus. Some might cynically respond that
our "hero" might have disappointed us. This is possible but there
is no evidence of lack of courage in Mills' life. It is interesting to
speculate if the Third World Movement both abroad and domestic
would have affected Mills' work. Unfortunately, he shared the
problems of several of his contemporaries and virtually ignored
the subject of race. An engagement between Malcolm X and Mills,
Fanon and Mills, George Jackson and Mills—these intellectual
unifications might have produced exciting results. Ironically, it is
Third World writers who have consistently employed the
sociological imagination in the last decade. Why this is so is not
the compelling question; more important is the ongoing quest for
the spirit of the sociological imagination. Let us explore that spirit
and make some practical suggestions about how to achieve its
promise in one's own work.

Some Notes on a New Methodology

In our own reading of Mills we have identified five major
dimensions of the sociological imagination. Nothing magical
adheres to the number five or our selection. We invite our readers
to extract from Mills' work their own interpretations of the

sociological imagination. Perhaps we may create an interchange which will improve the methodology of critical research. In a sense we are engaged in the difficult process of creating our own philosophy of science. The development of a proper perspective is a prelude to any discussions of technologies or specifics of research. Once we establish the boundaries of the new meta-theories we may begin to develop the paradigms and research designs which fit the new orientation. The task is not simple.

History and Biography

The first component of the sociological imagination must be the relationship between biography and history which Mills postulated as the moral task of the social sciences.

> Know that many personal troubles cannot be solved merely as troubles, but must be understood in terms of public issues and in terms of the problems of history making. Know that the human meaning of public issues must be revealed by relating them to personal troubles and to the problems of individual life (Mills, 1959: 226).

This central element of the sociological imagination was the explicit attempt to connect "Personal problems of milieu and public issues of social structure". The task of the social sciences was to clarify the link between men suffering and the larger historical forces which created their "personal troubles". Mills argued that social inquiries must ultimately address the *intersections of biography and history* within a given society. The social analyst must work to make his audience "aware of the idea of social structure" (Mills, 1959: 5).

Mills conceived of "troubles" as threats to values cherished by individuals. These occur within the "character of the individual and within the range of his immediate relations with others" (Mills, 1959: 8). The study of personal troubles requires that we employ the method of biography in attempting to describe and understand the impact of these troubles upon humans. Issues involve some values which are cherished by publics and these overlap individual milieu. The study of issues requires investigation of how personal networks fit into the institutions of a society. History is meant to express the idea of change in such organizations or institutions, or, more simply, social structures. Mills gave the example of unemployment. If in a city of 100,000, only one man is unemployed, Mills would refer to this as a personal trouble. To find the solution to this trouble is to search the biographic features of the man. However, the case of 15 million unemployed in a nation of 50 million employees is an issue, and "we may not hope to find its solution within the range of opportunities open to any one individual" (Mills, 1959: 9). Mills would direct his study to the collapse of the very structure of opportunities and this would require a consideration of the economic and political institutions of the society.

One could explore issues of war, marriage, and urban problems among others but release of the sociological imagination depended upon the constant analytic interplay of history and biography. Consider Mills' description of the proper study of war:

> The personal problem of war, when it occurs, may be how to survive it or how to die in it with honor; how to make money out of it; how to climb into the higher safety of the military apparatus; or how to contribute to the war's termination. In short, according to one's values, to find a set of milieu and within it survive the war or make one's death in it meaningful. But the structural issues of war have to do with its causes; with the types of men it throws up into command; with its effects upon economic, political, family and religious institutions, with the unorganized irresponsibility of a world of nation-states. (Mills, 1959: 9)

It is wishful thinking to argue, as some old guardians may do, that Mills is simply talking about what most social scientists practice when they use "rates" of events and perform statistical analysis. A new group of social scientists is tired of hearing ideology such as Durkheim's study of suicide, passed off as great social science. The classic liberal social thinkers of the late 19th century whom Nisbet calls carriers of the *sociological tradition* offer us the illusion of history and biography without the change oriented perspective which Mills embodied. Mills reminds us that issues are, in fact, often crises in institutional arrangements; these are what Marxists refer to as internal contradictions or antagonisms. Perhaps Mills may be faulted in not drawing more clearly the distinction between what he meant by the sociological imagination and the traditional social science of the late 19th century. It appears that after he wrote the *Sociological Imagination* Mills moved closer to this rejection.[2]

Successful examples of the interest of biography and history can be seen in Fanon's work on "Mental Disorders of Colonial Wars" (Fanon, 1968), Mills' *White Collar* (1956) and Ben Tong's recent work on the historical psychology of Asian Americans (Tong, 1971). In each case the author begins with a set of human troubles and expands the scope of the analysis to the realm of public issues. Moreover, historical forces such as racism, imperialism, or exploitation are grounded in the daily problems confronting real human beings. There is no easy answer to the question of how one goes about ensuring the unity of trouble and issue in one's work. A place to start is to consciously employ more human sorts of data in one's studies. We need to consider the scientific value of the life history, the ethnography, and the depth interview approaches, not as they are being practiced but as they should be. A second critical point is to be aware of the pressing social issues, not only in terms of cognitive awareness but also in terms of the way in which those most intimately involved experience such historical movements. The social analyst must experience his data, not simply collect it. To be immersed in the world of human encounters is a partial fulfillment of a method which Mills proposed.

The Sociological Imagination and The New History

Mills' emphasis upon *history as a vital part of social inquiry* should be continued. We should certainly avoid the ahistorical ideology of the corporate liberals. But we do not believe that Mills would make us only historians, for surely historians have perpetuated racist and hegemonic mythologies. Zinn argues that the concern for history must be tied to a commitment to change in the present. Without the critical thrust and the constant interplay with the present, we fear that some radical scholars will conceive that the ultimate revolutionary act will take place in a university library, probably somewhere deep in the stacks. The new history implies that the researcher comes to his data with preconceived questions which will be of significance in on-going struggles. The new history doubts the findings of the establishment historians and is especially alert to "rediscover" the contributions to world history of people of colour, of women, of anyone, bar none.

The study of history to effect change in the present means avoiding the danger of what Mills referred to as abstracted empiricism. Abstracted empiricism represents the "distortion" of the sociological imagination, which transforms an interest in the study of contemporary social problems to the fetish of a precise methodology. Mills describes the model of this type of research as follows:

> In practice the new school usually takes as the basic source of its "data" the more or less set interview with a series of individuals selected by a sampling procedure. Their answers are classified, and, for convenience, punched on Hollerith cards which are then used to make statistical runs by means of which relations are sought. Undoubtedly this fact, and the consequent ease with which the procedure is learned by any fairly intelligent person, accounts for much of its appeal. The results are normally put in the form of statistical assertions; . . . There are several complicated ways of manipulating such data, but these need not concern us here, for regardless of the degree of complication, they are still manipulations of the sort of material indicated. (Mills, 1959: 50-51)

What is wrong with this mode of research, according to Mills, is that work is guided by the availability of data rather than by theoretical concerns. Abstracted empiricists transform concepts into whatever indicators they have at their disposal. Thus, the study of public opinion becomes the study of responses to polls or surveys. Mills dislikes the ahistorical character of this brand of research. He strongly objects to the tendency of the abstracted empiricist to reduce social realities to psychological variables; these researchers make extensive use of notions like "attitude", "personality", "motivation", or "psychological conflict". Mills most strongly objects to the conception, promoted by the abstracted empiricists, of the sociologist as toolmaker. The core of the problem, according to Mills, is the pretension of natural science methods which 1) does not correctly apply this philosophy of the natural sciences and 2) in fact, substitutes the questionable pursuit of the perfect method for the important goal of interpreting social life. Mills cites George Lundberg, Samuel Stouffer, Stuart Dodd and Paul Lazerfeld as the theoreticians of this ethic of scientism.

Mills does not provide us with a satisfying understanding of the emergence of abstracted empiricism. This is partially excusable because a critical history of the rise of quantitative social research has not been written. If such a history were available we might be able to provide a more compelling explanation for the emergence of this "methodological inhibition". For example we would probably learn that the abstracted empiricists were the very opposite of abstract. It can be shown that the development of most research tools is linked to direct service to business and political elites. Consider the first psychological "experiments" conducted by Wundt (1886) which sought to determine if men worked more productively in group settings. Many of the earliest works in social psychology had direct industrial uses and this tradition has remained strong throughout the history of that discipline. The famous applied statistician Karl Pearson (developed the Pearsonian "r" or correlation coefficient) employed mathematical arguments to defend the use of child labour in English factories. The development of measures of intelligence was directly related to efforts to preserve race and class distinctions and privileges. Similarly, the survey or poll has its origins in the oldest of human history as an instrument by which sovereigns could assess and control their domains.

Current critics of American social science have commented upon the prostitution of social science to the service of military, political and economic elites. Whereas the grand theorists such as Parsons have fostered and disseminated the hegemonic concepts of the ruling class, the empiricists have supplied the technology of social control which has been employed in both domestic and foreign spheres.[3] Perhaps the most dangerous aspect of work of some influential social scientists is their efforts to export American ideas on social problems to nations of the Third World. Under the guise of the prestige of American science, the executives of the social science centers justify and extend policies and programs which have failed at home to countries which can ill afford the American solutions to the problems of disorder. Such international training efforts need to be investigated and challenged by scholars who reject the imperialist thrust of these "scientific" efforts. Mills of the 1970s would have used the term "technocrat" to describe the abstracted empiricists and he probably would have taken their potential danger more seriously. Mills did understand a fundamental fact about the "political economy" of research:

> One thing, moreover, is surely clear: because of the expensiveness of the method, its practitioners have more often become involved in the commercial and bureaucratic uses of their work and this often has affected their style (Mills, 1959: 65).[4]

The "trivial" nature of some of the research serves as a cover for the more directly oppressive work and allows social scientists a way of avoiding moral issues. Zinn writes

> Most knowledge is not directly bought, however, it can also serve the purpose of social stability in another way—by being squandered on trivia (Zinn, 1970: 7).

Recently a prominent criminologist received a grant to evaluate his discipline. This, on the surface, sounds like an exciting opportunity to explore the reasons for the failure of this particular discipline to provide coherent answers to a social problem of considerable public interest. Moreover, the charges of racism and counterinsurgency bias in this area of research could be examined and clarified during this massive research venture. Instead, and typically, the project aims more precisely and trivially at affixing a number to every article or book written on the subject matter since 1945; the significance of the number will presumably have something to do with the methodological value or worth of the work. "We are interested in how well we know things, not what we know," asserted the head of the research team. The triumph of method over substance has clear political and moral meaning in this case and in countless other examples of contemporary social science.

Research oriented toward change and rooted in history can avoid a concentration on trivia as well as a technocratic perspective. Younger scholars need not become historians so much as they should be aware of the method and substance of the new history. For instance, Third World people have had to rescue their own history from the oppressive ignorance of white scholars and thus have a more intuitive sense of the struggle value of history. Marvin Harris' *Rise of Anthropological Theory* and Thomas Gossett's *Race: The History of an Idea in America* are both good examples of the application of perspective of the new history.

Compassion, Commitment and Imagination

The sociological imagination *thrives because of its humanistic impulses.* Mills meant his work to serve humans and to alleviate part of their malaise. His was the sociology of compassion not the

more vulgar form of hip sociology which presently dominates the
study of social problems in America. The hip sociologist is usually
appreciative of the "deviance" which he studies, but rarely does he
reach the level of compassion, which means, literally, co-suffering.
Under the guise of the language of the theatre, the hipsters such as
Erving Goffman, Howard Becker, Bennett Berger and others tell us
that life is less real than a set of appearances. In the world of
appearances all is leveled including the hierarchy of values which
is, after all, what motivates political struggle. The sociologist who
can see through the world of everyday life can triumph as the
cynical, liberal (very liberal) defender of the underdog; at the same
time he can preserve his sensibilities and his firm academic
position. To be compassionate is to break with the colonialist
mode of research—the superior-subordinate relationship of the
researcher and his subject. Perhaps we need to think about social
research which rewards the studied at least as much as those who
do the investigation. The research process needs to be democra-
tized. *Subject and researcher need to share feelings, needs,
rewards and plans.* A direct movement towards these principles
could be accomplished if the researcher and his subject attempt to
share the social meanings of diverse racial, sexual, class and
personal histories. Identification and communication might flow
more naturally between those who exchange elements of their
distinctiveness and accord mutual respect to one another.

   To be compassionate is to recognize that the essential fate of
men is tragic, that suffering is enormous but that the human spirit
is strong and vibrant. Thus, the compassionate scholar studies not
for himself entirely, but for others. His work does deal with life
and death issues and cannot be taken lightly. The other side of
this point is that the researcher should not see himself as the sole
spokesman for those who never had a chance to select him.
Academic humility is surely a component of the compassionate
mode.

   Another dimension of the sociological imagination is the
crucial interrelation between one's active life and one's
intellectual life. Our interpretation of Mills suggests that the
release of the sociological imagination demands that the social
analyst take positions with respect to issues of political
significance. To have bias is to be possessed of a commitment, but
from where does this commitment flow except from the individual's participation in some form of action? Mao has described
this process as follows:

> The discovery of truths through practice; and through practice the
> verification and development of them; the active development of
> perceptual knowledge into rational knowledge, and by means of
> rationale knowledge, the active direction of revolutionary practice and
> the reconstruction of the subjective and external world; practice,
> knowledge, more practice, more knowledge, the repetition ad infini-
> tum of this cyclic pattern and with each cycle, the elevation of the
> content of practice and knowledge to a higher level: such is the whole

> epistemology of dialectical materialism, such is its theory of the unity
> of knowledge and action. (Mao, 1967)

This statement on the philosophy of revolutionary science may
help us explain why the most significant insights into our society
have come from Malcolm X, Eldrige Cleaver, George Jackson and
others immersed in practice. Those social scientists who have most
closely approximated the sociological imagination have a history
of praxis (e.g., Robert Blauner or Howard Zinn), or are currently
engaged in change directed practice (e.g., Ben Tong, Paul Sweezy,
or Paul Takagi).

To take this stance is to reject what Mills refers to as "liberal
practicality". "The confusion in the social sciences is moral as well
as 'scientific', political as well as intellectual" writes Mills (1959:
76). In the section on types of practicality, Mills points to the
moral dilemmas which he sees in liberal social science. Practicality
always means some avoidance of the *political and moral
commitments* which are important to the sociological imagination.
As in the case of other issues, Mills conceived of the problem as a
distortion of an older and presumably more desirable sociological
tradition.[5]

We need to look closely at the elements of liberal practicality
to help define an alternate posture. The first issue that Mills
discusses is the claim of certain social scientists to value
neutrality. While Mills agrees that we ought to strive to use
conceptions which are not value-heavy, he places emphasis upon
making bias more explicit; this is in contrast to the fashionable
stance of denying its existence. Mills cannot accept the role of
"cheerful idiot" that would be placed upon the social researchers
by some of the "value-neutral" groups. He reminds us that Max
Weber's edict about neutrality concerns the uses of the lecture
podium and not the absence of passion in scholarship. Mills raises
the serious question as to whether the flight from stating values
reveals a deeper fear of any passionate commitment among social
scientists.

> As we all know, . . . much of the jargon of the social science, and
> especially of sociology, results from the curious passion for the
> mannerism of the uncommitted (Mills, 1959: 79).

The neutral conception of social science resonates with the second
aspect of liberal practicality, namely the tendency to support
authority and to serve bureaucratic interests.

The claim of neutrality becomes important to the degree that
social science is a source of legitimation of those in power. In
order for science to serve those who rule it must approximate the
objectivity or unbiased character of other systems of legitimation
such as religion, tradition or charisma. Mills acknowledges that
there has been a tremendous growth in new institutions and,
therefore, a resultant need for additional ideological support. The
state has become an ever more important part of the professional
life of the social scientist. Mills noted,

CHAPTER 20: THE SOCIOLOGICAL IMAGINATION REVISITED   465

> Nowadays social research if often in direct service to army generals
> and social workers, corporation managers and prison wardens (Mills,
> 1959: 80).

Every society, as Mills points out, holds views of itself, images of
its own nature. Control of these master images and slogans has
been increasingly important to the modern State (Miliband, 1969).
    The word hegemony is an important concept among left
scholars. It means that one class or ruling elite controls the
mechanisms which affect popular conceptions of common values
and norms, and thus the dominated partially believe the legitimacy
of their subordinate status. If we accept the idea that social
science holds enormous potential power in terms of the process of
legitimation, then three types of responses can be expected in the
works of social researchers. First there will be those who justify
the arrangement of power, using images and ideas to transform
power into authority. Second, there will be those who through
claims of moral neutrality or some other devices will distract
attention away from issues of power and authority. In so doing
they lead us away from "the structural realties of society itself"
(Mills, 1959: 80). The third alternative is to adopt a critical and
debunking stance relative to prevailing arrangements of power and
those who rule. Mills' work most closely fits this last posture, but
sadly the bulk of social science production is similar to Houghton's
description of U.S. research on international relations: " . . . little
more than footnoted rationalizations and huckstering of these
policies" (Mills, 1959: 84). We are reminded that social science is
"inevitably relevant to bureaucratic routines and ideological
issues" (Mills, 1959: 84), and that political meanings are best
exposed rather than allowed to remain hidden.
    The last two forms of practicality which Mills dissects are
very much related. These are the "pluralistic" or scatter approach
to causality and the concept of personal adjustment. Mills indicts
social science for its fear of discovering one or two major causal
elements, particularly if these include political and economic
dimensions. Instead we are treated to a buffet table of causes
described as "multiple factor approaches." In many social problem
areas it is not uncommon to hear scientists plead for an end to the
search for causes.
    The notion of a municipality of causes, each of equal
significance and none of primary importance, has fitted well with
liberal approaches to piecemeal social reform. Multi-causality is a
powerful justification for an endless string of demonstration
projects to be "carefully evaluated". Such approaches to social
issues like crime, racism, poverty, or war provide us with the
myth that progress and improvement can occur without major
restructuring of the social order. An explanation which poses
issues of self-determination or redistribution of societal resources
is not permissable by liberal standards and is often rejected as
impractical. Note that the standards of practicality are always

taken from those who rule and wish to preserve their status quo.

The lack of political education among social scientists, or perhaps their inability to see an issue of political import unless pounded over the head, is consistent with the concept of adjustment which completes the types of liberal practicality. The concept of adjustment may take on either a personal or group meaning but in either case the problem is always located in milieu. Various studies conclude that the solution for the deviant or criminal, the impoverished or mentally ill is their successful reintegration into the mainstream of their society. For racial and ethnic groups the white solution is assimilation and integration (Takagi, 1973). There is no room in the concept of adjustment for challenging the pathology of the mainstream. Liberal scholars may cynically admit that there are structural inequities (although such admissions are sufficiently rare as to become collector's items) but their paternalistic advice offered to the poor, the people of colour, women, and the young is to adjust, play within the system and hope for the best. Their message is practical in terms of the interests of those who gather privileges from the exploitation of others. Fortunately many of those who are oppressed are formulating new conceptions of *practical social changes that link individual success to the fate of the group.* In the interim apologists for the state will issue their justifications for "benign neglect" of our most burning social issues.[6]

By now it should be obvious that we feel that the older heritage of theory and research must be rejected. Clearly we do not wish to abandon all of the classic social thinkers. The sociological imagination, as we envision it, will draw heavily upon the words of important but often neglected authors such as W. E. B. DuBois, Charles Beard and Emma Goldman. Moreover, we do not argue for sociological or "liberal illiteracy". Quite the opposite, Mills tells us to read the works of our antagonists, so that we may understand their metatheories and avoid some historical errors in our research. In the process of the intellectual part of the struggle, it will be of strategic value to know the core of the sociological tradition in greater detail than the current keepers of the castle. The debunking of the old masters must continue and we suspect that the scholarship of reinterpretation, (often referred to as the new history, the new economics, the new philosophy, etc.) will remain the sustaining element of critical social science for some time to come.

To join the unhooked generation is to cast off the educational indoctrination which has been our experience in programs of professional training. When one realizes that the material which he or she learned in order to pass exams, get good grades or to butter powerful professors is of little or no value in attacking problems of real human concern, then the first steps toward the integration of one's political, moral and intellectual life can be successfully accomplished. Although many have made the rejection without having to confront the "literature", the completion of the break with the white liberal tradition is somewhat more satisfying.

To position oneself in the world of political issues and to apply this experience of practice to social inquiry is a demanding requirement of the sociological imagination. For some, especially those scholars from oppressed groups, there is little choice in the matter; their fate is related to the fate of their fellows by history and the current structure of domination. This category, like it or not, most probably applies to all of us and we need not look too far into other people's troubles, to locate a meaningful point of action in our own lives.

The stating of bias becomes not a chore but an integral part of the work of the active social analyst. Mills proclaimed

> My biases are, of course, no more or less biased than those I am going to examine. Let those who do not care for mine use their rejections to make their own as explicit and as acknowledged as I am going to make mine! Then the moral problem of social study—the problem of social science as a public issue will be recognized and discussion will become possible (Mills, 1959: 21).

Communicating the Sociological Imagination

One might take the importance of stating one's bias one step further; that is, by clarifying the audience which the researcher would like to reach by his writing (or teaching). Mills often abandoned the "scholarly" journals even though he did not have the tremendous variety of publication media available to the current left scholar.[7] Scientists who today practice the sociological imagination are, or should be, communicating their ideas to the community of people engaged in social change. This implies that disciplinary jargon should be eliminated and that we should pay more attention to clarity of expression, but beyond writing more clearly, we should learn to write to sympathetic audiences. We need to listen to the criticisms of our work from the liberal audience but this sensitivity should help us improve our ideas, not inhibit the production of new ideas. Radical ideas will be attacked by liberal scholars according to their own conceptual and method-ological standards. These hostile inhibitions can be partially ignored so long as the social scientist is constantly engaged in the process of self and comrade criticism.

We do not advocate a heroic "write for the people" approach. Few of us are so gifted and besides we each have special consti-tuencies which command our strongest dictated commitment. The choice of the format or the expression of our ideas ought to be dictated by the relationship of those ideas to practice. Certainly the written word, let alone scholarly journals, does not exhaust the possible mode of effective communication.

468 PART SIX: SOCIAL PRAXIS

A related matter is the very decision to communicate through some formal medium such as writing. The sociological imagination leaves no room for publications meant solely to advance one's career, in liberal academia. Marlene Dixon suggests that

> Publication occurs when errors need to be corrected, when a fuller education of participants becomes mandatory, when changes are demanded in strategy and tactics, or when theoretical and practical debates within social movements are the most urgent and immediate struggle (Dixon, 1972: 14).

Such an approach to academic production runs counter to the "publish or perish" ethos of the liberal university but for those who take up the tradition of Mills the reality may be more like "publish *and* perish." An implicit assumption in this discussion of the selection of the audience is that the social scientist is capable of resisting the temptation to impress his liberal peers.

Summary

In this paper we have argued for a rediscovery of C. Wright Mills and his conception of the sociological imagination. In its essence the sociological imagination consists of images of social science as a potentially liberating force in world history. A crucial issue remains as to how liberating insights can be translated into meaningful action.

In reviewing Mills' critique of the major tendencies of social science, we noted that Mills gives us useful categories with which we may define an alternative methodology for research and theory development. Moreover Mills provides us with practical suggestions which will allow us to work towards the promise of social science as he envisioned it. These include:

1) The relating of private troubles to public issues.
2) The use of the perspective and substance of the new history.
3) The use of a compassionate as opposed to an appreciative mode in research.
4) Relating one's intellectual work to a change oriented practice and refining one's theories from the experience of that practice.
5) The careful selection of an audience to whom one wishes to communicate the results of social research and presumably a focus to the choice of the medium of expression.

Adopting the five suggestions above does not guarantee the release of the sociological imagination, but authors who do exhibit the Millsian perpsective such as Ben Tong, Franz Fanon, Ralph Miliband, Robert Blauner and C. Wright Mills himself, incorporate most of these elements in their work. The sociological imagination may yet become the dominant cultural dynamic, as Mills hoped it would, but the success of the sociological imagination is intimately wrapped up in the struggles of oppressed people for equality, self-determination and social justice because it is these groups which are actively seeking liberation intellectually and politically. To stand for the sociological imagination is not a fashion or aesthetic choice, but ultimately it commits one to social change.

NOTES

1.   See attempts by Horowitz (1967), Gerth (1962), Domhoff (1968).

2.   See Listen Yankee (1960) and The Marxist (1962).

3.   See Janowitz (1968) or Schwitzgebel (1971).

4.   If we apply the sociological imagination to the ideology of abstracted empiricism, then we might be led to consider the relationship of social science and social service technology to the development of capitalist economies. The emergence of imperialism and the welfare state required the development of socio-political as well as military forms of domination. Influentials in such societies reward the tool-makers and in turn the tool-makers make prestige claims and mask their ideology under the pretense of the natural science method. Although this argument needs further research support, it seems a fruitful line of inquiry into the emergence of the abstracted empiricism trend in social science at the close of the 19th century.

5.   We would argue that the forms of practicality are not distortions and that they are certainly not accidental departures from the right path.

6.   There is an important reason for the absence of passion from social science and this is the process of academic repression. It is the case that the liberal shield of academic freedom has not always been applied to Third World and radical scholars. In fact, we have been treated to the rather absurd logic that the free expression of critical ideas is itself a threat to academic freedom. Critical scholars do get fired but less dramatically they are not hired, or promoted, or given salary increases so as to punish them for their deviant ideas and actions. The Academy is structured as Veblin and others have argued to ensure compliance with the existing ideology, and in this epoch it is the ideology of state domination.

7.   Works by Mills which were pitched to a mass audience such as Listen Yankee and The Causes of W.W. III, have been dismissed by liberal scholars as "polemics".

REFERENCES

Dixon, Marlene, "Academic Roles and Functions," The Insurgent Sociologist (1972): 8.

Domhoff, William, C. Wright Mills and the Power Elite. Boston: Beacon Press, 1968.

Fanon, Frantz, The Wretched of the Earth. New York: Grove Press, 1968.

Gerth, Hans, Eulogy for Charles Wright Mills. Columbia University, 1962.

Gordon, David M, "Class and the Economics of Crime", in *Union of Radical Political Economists* 3 (1971): 51.

Gossett, Thomas, *Race: The History of an Idea in America*. New York: Schocken, 1965.

Gouldner, Alvin, *The Coming Crisis in Western Sociology*. New York: Basic Books, 1970.

Harris, Marvin, *The Rise of Anthropological Theory*. New York: Thomas C. Crowell Books, 1968.

Horowitz, Irving Louis, *Power, Politics and People: The Collected Essays of C. Wright Mills*. New York: Oxford University Press, 1967.

Janowitz, Morris, *The Social Control of Escalated Riots*. Chicago: University of Chicago, 1968.

Krisberg, Barry, "Review of Tearoom Trade", in *Issues in Criminology* 7 (1972): 126.

Tse-tung, Mao, "On the Relation between Knowledge and Practice, between Knowing and Having", *Selected Works of Mao Tse-Tung,* 1, Peking: Foreign Language Press, 1967.

Miliband, Ralph, *The State in Capitalist Society*. New York: Basic Books, 1969.

Mills, C. Wright, *White Collar*. New York: Oxford University Press, 1956.

————, *The Sociological Imagination*. New York: Oxford University Press, 1959.

————, *Listen Yankee: The Revolution in Cuba*. New York: Ballantine, 1960.

————, *The Marxists*. New York: Oxford University Press, 1962.

Schwendinger, Herman and Julia, *Sociologists of the Chair*. New York: Basic Books, 1973.

Schwitzgebel, Ralph, "Development and Legal Regulation of Coercive Behavior Modification Techniques with Offenders". Washington, D.C.: National Institute of Mental Health Service Publication No. 2067, 1971.

Snodgrass, Jon, *The Ideology of American Criminology*. Philadelphia: University of Pennsylvania (Ph.D. dissertation), 1972.

Takagi, Paul, "The Concept of Assimilation", in *Amerasia Journal* forthcoming, 1973.

Tong, Ben, "The Ghetto of the Mind", in *Amerasia Journal* 1 (1971): 1.

Zinn, Howard, *The Politics of History*. Boston: Beacon Press, 1970.

Chapter 21

Marxism and The Sociology of Law:
Theory or Practice?*

Piers Beirne

Maureen Cain's recent guide to the main themes of Marx' and Engels' sociology of law is welcome as it attempted to provide a basic and possibly alternative standpoint from which to view law and legal systems in capitalist societies.[1] Her article explicitly emphasised two yawning chasms in contemporary inquiry: the divide between the juristic and Marxist perspectives on law, and that between the developed Marxist approach on the one hand and the relative dearth of Marxist studies of law on the other. I say "developed" because Marxism is a living body of thought and subsequent additions have been made to it, in this area notably by Stuchka, Lenin, Renner and Gramsci. The first distinction is of course both inevitable and irreconcilable but the second is not accidental. With the current exception of debate on the formation of the State under the capitalist mode of production, Marxist thought has in fact been singularly neglectful of law. But both to wonder at this coyness and also to recommend the "intellectual delights" of Marxism is to misportray the theoretical basis and revolutionary content of the Marxian dialectic. Cain presents Marxism as a mere heuristic device for the intellectually-complete legal scholar. Put simply, Marxist sociologists of law and Marxist studies of "intentionality and unintended consequence" are (hopefully) unlikely to be forthcoming.

* Piers Beirne, "Marxism and the Sociology of Law: Theory or Practice?", *British Journal of Law and Society* 2 (Summer, 1975): 78-81. Reprinted by permission of the *British Journal of Law and Society* (University College Cardiff Press).

Contrary to some interpretations, and Nicos Poulantzas in particular,[2] theoretical problems of the bourgeois State (armies, prisons, law, lawyers, and so on) were only central to Marx at the beginning of his intellectual life. These problems were mainly expounded in his *Critique of Hegel's Philosophy of Right* (1843),[3] *On the Jewish Question* (1844),[4] *The Economic and Philosophic Manuscripts* (1844),[5] and *The Eighteenth Brumaire of Louis Bonaparte* (1852).[6] But Marx' analysis of law was always secondary to that of the State and the class struggle, and the scattered nature of his references to law testifies to this—factory legislation and the control of wages by law,[7] the law of contract (usually veiled in a discussion of wages and prices), the law of property, the criminal position of the lumpenproletariat,[8] and the social formation.[9] A useful distinction may be drawn between Marx' analyses of the pre-and post-revolutionary State: the former were conducted on the whole early on in his life and mainly at a theoretical level, whilst the latter were part of his pragmatic correspondence against certain revisionist elements at the time of the Paris Commune.[10] The distinction itself has implications for the concept of revolutionary praxis.

In the analysis of any phenomenon Marx always looked for the basic internal contradiction which determined the movement of the whole: ideological forms such as State, law, religion, and so on are explained by reference to the contradictions of the capitalist mode of production. Karl Renner once said ". . . in a state of rest legal and economic institutions, though not identical, are but two aspects of the same thing, inextricably interwoven."[11] Renner's dualism here is misleading, but by ignoring the crucial referent of the mode of production Cain in effect advocates a Marxist methodology for "fruitful areas of research" which views law independently of its historical and economic base. Classical sociology in the form of Weber and Durkheim has succeeded in doing just this. As an aside, Cain feels Marx and Engels influenced the work of Durkheim, Weber and even phenomenology, but it is difficult to see the connections, intellectual or historical. Marx was a revolutionary wedded to scientific socialism, yet Weber's methodology was grounded in conservative political theory. Weber's *Protestant Ethic* was a polemic consciously written against the materialist conception of history, and his concept of *verstehen* is responsible for the confusion which is ethnomethodology and phenomenology.[12] The result is that the study of law has become compartmentalised, as too has political economy. And yet this is the very process which Marx derided in his critique of Hegel. That we have a "sociology of law", a separate journal (and inter-disciplinary basis if editorial comments in the first issue are to be believed)[13] and conference attests to this. As Martin Shaw says: "The sociology of . . ." is a mystification "in that it proposes to apply, to the empirically abstracted features of historical social systems, categories derived from an ideology of society in general."[14] Marxism's attitude to such attempts is to stress the need for an historically specific theory, relating each aspect to the totality of a specific society and mode of production. Examination of law *presupposes* questions of State, ideology and the class struggle. Ignorance of this results in gross historical distortion, for example, in arguing that Joel Barnett's research[15] on the Rent Act 1957 provided little information about inter-class struggle Cain misses the far more decisive point that Barnett produced a mystification of that Act. In 297 pages he made not the slightest attempt to ground his "data" in a theory of rent, law or politics!

Cain demonstrated that in many of his major works Marx' writings on law were subservient to and encompassed by his theory of the State and politics in the capitalist mode of production. In fact much of his writing on law was contained in his correspondence, and the direction of this reveals the element of praxis in Marx the revolutionary. Here he was usually concerned to expose the weaknesses of the anarchists and the anarcho-syndicalists, in particular the "petty bourgeois" deviations of Michael Bakunin and the *Alliance de la Démocratie Socialiste*. The fundamental clash within the First International, which led to Bakunin's expulsion in 1872, was between different attitudes to revolutionary strategy and the post-revolutionary State. The anarchist solution was of course to be repaid with compound interest at Kronstadt in 1921. The centralists held that the dictatorship of the proletariat was a prerequisite for the consolidation of the *political* revolution; the anarchist argued that the immediate premise of a *social* revolution was the abolition of the State. In contemporary "communist" societies (State capitalist, or degenerate workers' State, depending on your allegiances) orthodox Marxism has held sway. This orthodoxy was itself the motive force behind struggles within the Communist Academy of State and Law of Pashukanis, Krylenko, Berman and others after 1925. Thus, the forgotten half of Marx' writings on law were intimately concerned with the political structure of the transitional phase, in essence a problem of praxis.

The decisive element missing from Cain's rendition is the location of revolutionary praxis and the class struggle. The centre of Marxist theory lies not in the academic justification of a system of knowledge but rather in the use of this scientific theory as a practical guide to action. It is only the most advanced theory that comprehends the existing modes of oppression and is capable of overthrowing these modes. A general description of a phenomenon utilising Marxist categories of knowledge becomes its explanation and therefore leads to a transformation of that phenomenon. When Hegel originally postulated that the world is Mind, he was expressing the interconnection between thought and its object, and affirming the ability of thought to master reality.[16] When Marx "stood Hegel on his head", or rather on his feet, he recognised that the development of his theory depended above all on conscious revolutionary action by the working class. The development of science is only made *real* through praxis. From this argument one wonders how appropriate Cain's guide will be to her public. Marxism lies in direct opposition to the method of bourgeois social science which posits an explanation confined within an ideology that aims at the perpetuation of existing phenomena.

NOTES

1.   Cain, "The Main Themes of Marx' and Engels' Sociology of Law," *British J. of Law and Society* 1: 136. Although Cain admits that her interpretation "leaves out all the dynamics and most of the theory" such a presentation, ignoring the rôle of the class struggle and the dialectical relationship between theory and practice, can only produce a distortion of Marx and the Marxist intent.

2.   N. Poulantzas, *Political Power and Social Classes*. London: Sheed and Ward, 1973.

3.   K. Marx, "Critique of Hegel's Philosophy of Right," in *Marx: Early Writings*. T.B. Bottomore and M. Rubel (eds.), London: Watts, 1963.

4.   K. Marx, "On the Jewish Question," in *Karl Marx, Early Texts*. D. Mc Lellan (ed.), Oxford: Blackwell, 1971.

5.   K. Marx, *The Economic and Philosophic Manuscripts of 1844*. New York: International Publishers, 1971.

6.   K. Marx. "The Eighteenth Brumaire of Louis Bonparte," in *Selected Works*. K. Marx and F. Engels, Moscow: Progress Publishers, 1969.

7.   K. Marx, *Capital*, vol. I. London: Lawrence and Wishart, 1970.

8.   K. Marx and F. Engels, "The Communist Manifesto" in *Selected Works, op. cit.* Marx's position towards the lumpenproletariat has been discussed by P.Q. Hirst, "Marx and Engels on Law, Crime and Morality," in *Critical Criminology.* I. Tylor, P. Walton and J. Young (eds.), London: Routledge and Kegan Paul, 1975, pp. 205-230. In relation to the attempts by radical criminologists and deviance theorists to construct Marxist theory of crime, Hirst argues: Crime and deviance vanish into the general theoretical concerns and the specific scientific object of Marxism. Crime and deviance are no more a scientific field for Marxism than education, the family or sport. The objects of marxist theory are specified by its own concepts: the mode of production, the class struggle, the state, ideology, etc.; *Ibid.,* p. 204. And law, it must be remembered, is only one of many elements in the State apparatus.

9.   K. Marx, *Pre-Capitalist Economic Formations*. E.J. Hobsbawn (ed.), London: Lawrence and Wishart, 1964.

10.   For example see "Engels to C. Cafiero in Barletta," and "Marx to F. Bolte in New York," in *Marx, Engels, Lenin on Anarchism and Anarcho-Syndicalism:* Moscow: Progress Publishers, 1972.

11.   K. Renner, *The Institutions of Private Law and their Social Function*. London: Routledge and Kegan Paul, 1949, p. 58.

12.   M. Weber, *The Protestant Ethic and the Spirit of Capitalism.* New York: Scribner, 1958.

13.   Editorial, *Brit. J. of Law and Society* 1: 1. Here we find "The aim of the *British Journal of Law and Society* is to follow the tradition of transcending disciplinary boundaries by taking as its focus the subject area of law in society". The phrase ". . . transcending disciplinary boundaries" could be read as an attack on compartmentalisation, but this would not be in keeping with the editorial policy responsible for articles so far selected for the *Journal.*

14.   M. Shaw, *Marxism Versus Sociology.* London: Pluto Press, 1974. See also H. Lefebvre, *The Sociology of Marx.* London: Allen Lane, 1968, pp. 22-24; "For quite a number of reasons, then, we shall not make a sociologist out of Marx . . . Marxian thought is simply too broad in scope to fit into the narrower categories of philosophy, political economy, history and sociology. Nor is it correct to refer to it as 'interdisciplinary'— a conception recently advanced (not without risk of confusion) to remedy the disadvantages of a latter-day division of labour in the social sciences."

15.   M.J. Barnett, *The Politics of Legislation.* London: Wiedenfield and Nicholson, 1969.

16.   G. Hegel, *Phenomenology of Mind.* J.B. Baillie (trans.), 2nd ed., London: 1931.

DATE DUE

The Library Store   #47-0106